Defending Mentally Disordered Persons

Kris Gledhill is a barrister who specialised in mental health and prison law and was a legal member of the Mental Health Review Tribunal. He is now a senior lecturer at the Auckland University Law School, New Zealand, with research interests in mental health law, prison law and comparative criminal and human rights law, and has recently been appointed as the inaugural Director of the New Zealand Centre for Human Rights Law, Policy and Practice. Kris is editor of the *Mental Health Law Reports* and the *Prison Law Reports* and author of books including *Mental Health Tribunals – essential cases* (Southside Legal Publishing, 2nd edition, 2009).

The purpose of the Legal Action Group is to promote equal access to justice for all members of society who are socially, economically or otherwise disadvantaged. To this end, it seeks to improve law and practice, the administration of justice and legal services.

Defending Mentally Disordered Persons

Kris Gledhill

LAG Legal Action Group
2012

This edition published in Great Britain 2012
by LAG Education and Service Trust Limited
242 Pentonville Road, London N1 9UN
www.lag.org.uk

British Library Cataloguing in Publication Data
a CIP catalogue record for this book is available from the British Library.

This book has been produced using Forest Stewardship Council (FSC) certified paper. The wood used to produce FSC certified products with a 'Mixed Sources' label comes from FSC certified well-managed forests, controlled sources and/or recycled material.

FSC
www.fsc.org
MIX
Paper from responsible sources
FSC® C020438

Print ISBN 978 1 903307 28 1
ebook ISBN 978 1 908407 05 4

Typeset by Regent Typesetting, London
Printed in Great Britain by Hobbs the Printers, Totton, Hampshire

Preface

The idea for this book came from Guy Vassall-Adams, and some years ago. I am grateful to Guy for developing his practice in a different area, which gave me the opportunity to step in. Thanks also to Esther Pilger at Legal Action Group (LAG) for managing to maintain a list of publications, including new and hence untested texts such as this one, in what must be a challenging commercial environment.

The established practitioner texts in criminal law all contain a basic account of the law relevant to people in the criminal justice system who have mental disorder; and there is a very good guide, *Advising Mentally Disordered Offenders, A Practical Guide*, by Carolyn Taylor and Julia Krish with Dr Frank Farnham, published by The Law Society (second edition, 2009). Whilst mental health law and criminal law are both central to the work of LAG, it was necessary to try to write a text that added to what was already available. My aim has been both to set out the law comprehensively but also to provide arguments for where the law could be developed further through the appellate process. I hope that provides some justification for the length of some of the text. I have tried to take into account cases and developments up to 1 March 2012.

As always, there are many people to thank. As to individuals, in addition to Guy and Esther, I want to thank in particular the copy editor, Jen Cowan, who raised many pointed questions and made many useful suggestions. Turning to collective thanks, my interest in mental health law was prompted and maintained by numerous colleagues, both in practice and in academia, who have managed to ensure that this is an area of law that has been vibrant during the period of almost twenty years that I have been involved in it. There are also a number of judges who have given the area due prominence. Collective thanks are owed to those groups.

I most want to thank my children, who have put up with a workaholic father without complaint, allowing me too often to be semi-engaged with family life as I have spent much of the last two decades with work constantly on my knee. Iffa, Ashaka, Kafele and Kiska, I love you all very much.

Kris Gledhill
Auckland

March 2012

Contents

PART II: PRE-COURT MATTERS

PART III: PROCEDURE AND EVIDENCE

Table of cases

R v Dietschmann [2001] EWCA Crim 2052, [2003] UKHL 10, [2003] 1 AC 1209, [2003] MHLR 333, HL	14.60, 14.62, 14.67, 14.68, 21.11
R v Dietschmann [2003] EWCA Crim 1257, [2003] All ER (D) 203 (Apr), CA	14.66–14.68
R v Dix (1982) 74 CrAppR 306	14.41, 14.48–14.52
R v Donovan (1981) 3 CrAppR(S) 192	16.47
R v Doonan [2005] EWCA Crim 1182, [2005] MHLR 210	18.169, 18.171
R v Dorking Justices ex p Harrington [1984] AC 743	9.198
R v Doughty (1986) 83 CrAppR 31 9	14.112
R v Dr Collins and Ashworth Hospital Authority ex p Brady [2000] MHLR 17, [2000] Lloyd's Rep Med 355	2.101
R v Drew [2003] UKHL 25, [2003] 1 WLR 1213, [2003] MHLR 282, HL, *Affirming* [2001] EWCA Crim 2861, [2002] MHLR 65, CA	16.19, 17.92–17.95, 18.180, 18.181, 18.191–18.194, 18.196, 18.199, 18.204, 18.211, 18.221, 18.222, 18.227
R v Dryden [1995] 4 All ER 987	14.129
R v Duffy [1949] 1 All ER 932n	14.108, 14.112, 14.113
R v Dunbar [1958]1 QB 1	14.80, 14.82
R v Dunn (1990) 91 CrAppR 237	11.21
R v Egan (1992) 95 CrAppR 278	14.65
R v Egan (Michael) [1998] 1 CrAppR 121, [1999] 3 WLR 1204	9.126–9.129, 9.134, 12.72
R v Ensor [2009] EWCA Crim 2519, [2010] MHLR 4	6.16, 9.64, 11.52
R v Erskine; R v Williams [2009] EWCA Crim 1425, [2009] MHLR 215, [2009] 2 CrAppR 29	21.26, 21.30, 21.31, 21.36, 21.38, 21.41
R v Everett [1988] Crim LR 826	11.15, 11.16
R v Fairley [2003] EWCA Crim 1625, [2003] MHLR 310	9.170
R v Fell [2000] 2 CrAppR 464	19.20
R v Felstead [1914] AC 534	12.111
R v Fenton (1975) 61 CrAppR 261	14.55–14.58, 14.60
R v Friend [1997] 1 WLR 1433	11.46, 11.49
R v G [2003] UKHL 50, [2004] 1 AC 1034	9.136, 9.137, 15.1
R v Galbraith (1981) 73 CrAppR 124, [1981] 2 All ER 1060, [1981] 1 WLR 1039	11.38, 11.40, 14.73
R v Galfetti [2002] EWCA Crim 1916, [2002] MHLR 418	18.27, 18.28, 18.250
R v Gardner (1993) 14 CrAppR(S) 364	19.20
R v Ghulam [2009] EWCA Crim 2285, [2010] 1 WLR 891, [2009] MHLR 325	9.85, 9.86, 9.88, 9.89, 9.235, 10.17

Table of statutes

Table of statutory instruments

Table of European legislation

Abbreviations

AC	Approved clinician
ACPO	Association of Chief Police Officers
AMHP	Approved mental health professional
ASBO	Anti-social behaviour order
ASW	Approved social worker
AWOL	Absent without leave
CAA 1968	Criminal Appeal Act 1968
CAA 1995	Criminal Appeal Act 1995
CAMHS	Child and adolescent mental health services
CDA 1998	Crime and Disorder Act 1998
CJA 1967	Criminal Justice Act 1967
CJA 1972	Criminal Justice Act 1972
CJA 1987	Criminal Justice Act 1987
CJA 1988	Criminal Justice Act 1988
CJA 2003	Criminal Justice Act 2003
CJCSA 2000	Criminal Justice and Court Services Act 2000
CJIA 2008	Criminal Justice and Immigration Act 2008
CJPOA 1994	Criminal Justice and Public Order Act 1994
CLA 1800	Criminal Lunatics Act 1800
CLAM	Criminal Legal Aid Manual
CQC	Care Quality Commission
CPA	Care Programme Approach
CP(I)A 1964	Criminal Procedure (Insanity) Act 1964
CPIA 1996	Criminal Procedure and Investigations Act 1996
CP(IUP)A 1991	Criminal Procedure (Insanity and Unfitness to Plead) Act 1991
CPR 2010	Criminal Procedure Rules 2010
CPR 2011	Criminal Procedure Rules 2011
CPS	Crown Prosecution Service
CRC	Convention on the Rights of the Child
CRPD	Convention on the Rights of Persons with Disabilities 2006
C(S)A 1997	Crime (Sentences) Act 1997
CTO	Community treatment order
CYPA 1969	Children and Young Persons Act 1969
DOLS	Deprivation of liberty safeguards
DPP	Director of Public Prosecutions

DSM-IV-TR	Diagnostic and Statistical Manual of the American Psychiatric Association (revised fourth edn)
DVCVA 2004	Domestic Violence, Crime and Victims Act 2004
DVLA	Driver and Vehicle Licensing Agency
ECHR	European Convention on Human Rights
ECT	Electro-convulsive therapy
ECtHR	European Court of Human Rights
HA 1957	Homicide Act 1957
HRA 1998	Human Rights Act 1998
ICCPR	International Covenant on Civil and Political Rights
ICD-10	International Classification of Diseases of the World Health Organization (tenth edn)
IMHA	Independent mental health advocate
IPCC	Independent Police Complaints Commission
MCA 1980	Magistrates' Courts Act 1980
MCA 2005	Mental Capacity Act 2005
MHA 1959	Mental Health Act 1959
MHA 1983	Mental Health Act 1983
MHA 2007	Mental Health Act 2007
MHRT	Mental Health Review Tribunal
OASys	Offender Assessment System
PACE	Police and Criminal Evidence Act 1984
PCCA 1973	Powers of Criminal Courts Act 1973
PCC(S)A 2000	Powers of Criminal Courts (Sentencing) Act 2000
PCMH	Plea and case management hearing
PH	Preliminary hearing
PND	Penalty notice for disorder
PSI	Prison Service Instruction
PSO	Prison Service Order
RC	Responsible clinician
RMO	Responsible medical officer
ROA 1974	Rehabilitation of Offenders Act 1974
SOA 2003	Sexual Offences Act 2003
SOAD	Second opinion appointed doctor
TLA 1883	Trial of Lunatics Act 1883
YJCEA 1999	Youth Justice and Criminal Evidence Act 1999
YOI	Young offender institution

PART I

Introductory matters

CHAPTER 1

Introduction to the legal framework

Overview

1.1 The main statutes regulating questions that arise in relation to defendants in the criminal justice system who have mental disorders are the Mental Health Act (MHA) 1983 and the Criminal Procedure (Insanity) Act (CP(I)A) 1964. The MHA 1983 contains various powers relating to pre-trial matters, such as the obtaining of medical reports or treatment, sentencing options, and the regulation of what happens to those sent into hospital, including their treatment and release. The CP(I)A 1964 regulates the procedure relevant to the question of fitness to stand trial in the Crown Court and also disposals for those found not guilty by reason of insanity there.

1.2 Another statute to note is the Trial of Lunatics Act 1883, though that only sets out the special verdict of not guilty by reason of insanity in the Crown Court. There are also provisions in various other statutes that may raise issues of relevance to those with mental disorder: for example, the Homicide Act 1957 and its definitions of 'diminished responsibility' and 'provocation' (the latter having now become 'loss of control'), the Criminal Justice and Public Order Act (CJPOA) 1994 and the question of adverse inferences from silence, special measures directions as to the procedure at the trial under the Youth Justice and Criminal Evidence Act 1999 and various parts of the sentencing provisions in the Powers of Criminal Courts (Sentencing) Act 2000 and the Criminal Justice Act 2003.

1.3 Also of relevance to a full understanding of the law is the Mental Capacity Act (MCA) 2005, which regulates actions taken in relation to those who do not have the capacity to decide for themselves; this is administered by the Court of Protection. The Tribunals, Courts and Enforcement Act 2007 is the primary statute in relation to the tribunal that controls the release of most people detained in England under the MHA 1983; for Wales, the relevant body is the Mental Health Review Tribunal for Wales, which is governed by the MHA 1983.

1.4 While much of the law relevant to defendants with mental disorder is now regulated by statute, the common law remains of relevance in a number of respects, for example in relation to the definition of what amounts to insanity as a defence, or the test of whether or not a defendant is able to participate in a trial.

1.5 Naturally, to the extent that the actions taken impact on the fundamental rights of the defendant, then the Human Rights Act (HRA) 1998 and the European Convention on Human Rights (ECHR) will also be relevant. So, issues might arise in relation to the ECHR article 2 duty to protect life; the need to avoid inhuman or degrading treatment by reason of article 3; the need to ensure that deprivation of liberty is not arbitrary and in breach of article 5; the fair trial provisions of article 6; and the protection of the autonomy rights in article 8.

The scheme of the Mental Health Act 1983

1.6 The MHA 1983 contains the following parts, various of which may be relevant to the criminal justice system:

- Part I defines mental disorder;
- Part II sets out the provisions relating to the compulsory admission to hospital of civil patients and placement under guardianship;
- Part III is concerned with patients in criminal proceedings or in prison;
- Parts IV and 4A regulate the question of treatment without consent;
- Part V deals with tribunals;
- Part VI deals with the interplay between the mental health laws in the various parts of the United Kingdom (and also the Channel Islands and Isle of Man);
- Part VII dealt with the management of the property and affairs of patients, but this has now been replaced by the MCA 2005, which has a much wider remit, covering both financial affairs and also personal welfare matters;
- Part VIII deals with various powers of local authorities, including in relation to after-care, and of the Secretary of State;
- Part IX sets out various criminal offences relating to the Act;
- Part X contains various miscellaneous and supplementary provisions, including general interpretation provisions.

1.7 Patients detained under the civil provisions of the MHA 1983 are called Part II patients and those detained under the criminal provisions are referred to as Part III patients. Parts I, IV and V are relevant to both Part II and Part III patients.

1.8 In addition to the supplementary secondary legislation that is to be expected, there is also a significant amount of 'soft law' arising in the mental health context. A Code of Practice offering guidance is issued by the Secretary of State for Health under MHA 1983 s118; a separate one is issued for Wales by the Welsh Ministers.[1] The English Code has to be laid before Parliament and either House may pass a resolution requiring it to be withdrawn to be amended: MHA 1983 s118(4). The Welsh Code is laid before the Welsh Assembly.

1.9 Given the importance of compliance with the requirements of legality, which includes the need to have a law in place to control certain situations, it has been determined that the Code should be followed unless there is good reason not to do so. This proposition arises from the decision of the House of Lords in *R (Munjaz) v Mersey Care NHS Trust*:[2] the issue arising in this case was whether a high secure hospital[3] could have a regime as to the placement of patients in seclusion that differed from the guidance set out in the Code of Practice. On the facts, the special nature of the detained population allowed a different approach, though there were dissenting views on this among the judicial committee. The general approach that the guidance in the Code of Practice should be followed in the absence of good reason was so that it could provide soft law for the purpose of phrases such as 'in accordance with the law' in parts of the ECHR, including the privacy right arising under article 8.

1.10 There are also significant additional elements of guidance as to practices that are or should be followed in relation to the exercises of discretions that arise under the MHA 1983. For example, prisoners may be transferred to hospital if they are in need of treatment: this arises under MHA 1983 s47 or s48, as discussed in chapters 20 and 8; the Secretary of State for Justice, who is responsible for the transfer, has issued guidance on how he or she will exercise the discretion.[4] This is a document that sets out policies and so may feature in a challenge to the actions taken under the discretion in a judicial review. In addition, there is more general guidance on the operation of the

1 The English Code is available at: www.dh.gov.uk/en/Publicationsandstatistics/Publications/PublicationsPolicyAndGuidance/DH_084597; the Welsh Code can be found at www.wales.nhs.uk/sites3/page.cfm?orgid=816&pid=33960. The National Assembly for Wales (Transfer of Functions) Order 1999 SI No 672 contains the basic transfer of functions to the Welsh government.

2 [2005] UKHL 58, [2006] 2 AC 148, [2005] MHLR 276.

3 See paras 1.20–1.27 below for the descriptions of levels of hospital security.

4 *Good practice procedure guide: the transfer and remission of adult prisoners under s47 and s48 of the Mental Health Act*, Department of Health, April 2011, available at www.dh.gov.uk/en/Publicationsandstatistics/Publications/PublicationsPolicyAndGuidance/DH_125767.

MHA 1983 in the form of the Reference Guide issued by the Secretary of State for Health.[5]

The civil scheme for detention and compulsion

1.11 At a number of points when questions arise in relation to defendants with mental disorder in the criminal courts, powers that are available under the civil provisions of the statute may be important. For example, as the main impact of a final order made in relation to a defendant sent to hospital by the criminal courts under a hospital order (which, as noted below, is imposed under MHA 1983 s37 if it is the most appropriate disposal) is effectively to place the defendant in the position of a patient detained under the civil provisions of the MHA 1983,[6] consideration may be given to seeking to divert someone from the criminal justice system into the civil hospital system without the need for a criminal trial. As another example, there may be methods of securing medical reports or pre-trial treatment by using civil powers rather than those that arise under the criminal powers in the statute.

1.12 The various areas of the civil regime are:

a) *The powers of detention under Part II of the MHA 1983:* While it is possible for placement in hospital to be on a voluntary basis (under MHA 1983 s131, leading to the status of an informal patient), there are also powers to detain for assessment and treatment under section 2 or for treatment under section 3;[7] there are also powers to detain an informal patient who is seeking to leave against medical advice (under section 5). The patient may be moved between hospitals under section 19: this may be necessary to reflect the developing needs of the patient. It should be noted, however, that many hospitals will have a significant number of units on different sites, but under the same management, and patients can be moved between these administratively, without the need to use section 19.

5 Last revised in September 2008, following changes to the MHA 1983 by the MHA 2007, which was accompanied by changes in the delegated legislation. Available at www.dh.gov.uk/en/Publicationsandstatistics/Publications/PublicationsPolicyAndGuidance/DH_088162.

6 This is subject to provisions in MHA 1983 Sch 1 which change various details but not the essence of the detention regime.

7 The power to detain for treatment is renewable under MHA 1983 s20, and could be indefinite.

b) *The powers of treatment:* This is separately regulated under Part IV of the MHA 1983, which sets out the circumstances in which it is possible to treat a detained person without his or her consent (and includes those detained under most of the Part III powers relating to criminal proceedings).

c) *The powers of treatment in the community:* This contains several elements, including the granting of leave to detained patients (under section 17), which leaves them with a status of 'liable to detention' and so still subject to the treatment without consent provisions of Part IV; the use of the community treatment orders (CTOs) that were introduced by the MHA 2007 and are regulated by MHA 1983 ss17A–17G, treatment under which is regulated by MHA 1983 Part 4A;[8] there is also guardianship under section 7, though that does not include any powers to compel treatment. In addition, those who have been detained under the treatment provisions are entitled to aftercare under MHA 1983 s117, though there is no duty to accept such treatment. There are also various other statutes relating to community care.

d) *The regulation of release:* This can be by the treating clinician or the hospital managers under MHA 1983 s23; in relation to civil patients, the nearest relative also has the power to direct release unless the patient is dangerous. The judicial body that reviews ongoing detention is the tribunal: in Wales, this is the Mental Health Review Tribunal; in England, it is a chamber of the First-tier Tribunal established under the Tribunal Service and now part of the Courts Service, which took over the functions of the Mental Health Review Tribunal for England.

1.13 This scheme is described in more detail in chapter 2.

8 This replaced a regime of after-care under supervision, under MHA 1983 ss25A–25J, as introduced by the Mental Health (Patients in the Community) Act 1995; the difference between what was in place and the community treatment order regime may be more a matter of perception than a question of a completely new set of powers being introduced. (See Kris Gledhill, 'Community treatment orders', *Journal of Mental Health Law*, 2007, pp149–169.)

The criminal provisions of the Mental Health Act 1983

1.14 The criminal regime under Part III of the MHA 1983, in outline, involves the following:

a) The power of the criminal courts to remand a person to hospital for the preparation of a medical report, which arises under section 35 of the MHA 1983.
b) A pre-trial or pre-sentence remand to hospital for treatment can be ordered, though only by the Crown Court, under section 36.
c) A sentence of an interim hospital order can be made under section 38 of the Act; this is not a final sentence, since it is made with the purpose of assessing whether a hospital order should be made.
d) A sentence of a hospital order can be made under section 37, and in the case of a magistrates' court can be made without a conviction. The Crown Court can make an order without a conviction in limited circumstances under section 51, and it is also an available sentence following a finding of not guilty by reason of insanity or a finding of unfitness to stand trial together with a finding that the defendant was responsible for the act charged. The latter situation arises under the CP(I)A1964 and the Criminal Procedure (Insanity and Unfitness to Plead) Act 1991.
e) The Crown Court can also add a restriction order to a hospital order, which places various restrictions on the regime applicable to the patient.
f) Those in custody – both pre-sentence and post-sentence – can be transferred to hospital if their mental health requires it, by transfers under sections 47 and 48, to which a restriction direction can be added.
g) It is also possible for the Crown Court to make an order that combines a prison sentence with a transfer to hospital, such that if the defendant no longer needs to be in hospital detention he or she will be placed in prison. This is the hospital and limitation direction of sections 45A and 45B.
h) Finally, the guardianship order that exists in the civil regime can also be imposed by the criminal courts under section 37.

1.15 In addition, there are various other police powers to note, which include powers of arrest or detention that arise in relation to those who are liable to detention, but also powers that exist in relation to people in the community who need to be assessed for detention. These arise under MHA 1983 ss135 and 136: the former allows entry to a private place under a warrant, the latter provides a power to detain if a person appearing to need immediate care and control on account of mental disorder is found in a public place.

1.16 These various provisions arising under the criminal regime are described in more detail in subsequent chapters.[9]

1.17 There are some significant overlaps between the Part II regime and the Part III regime. In particular:

i) By reason of section 40(5), the basic effect of a court making a hospital order under section 37 is that the patient is treated as if detained under section 3, and so the various aspects of that regime – such as transfer between hospitals, leave, placement on a CTO, the need to renew detention – apply, as do the provisions relating to discharge. There are some modifications, set out in Schedule 1 to the MHA 1983. The regime of treatment without consent also applies. If a restriction order is added by the Crown Court under section 41, there are more significant modifications (including that the CTO regime is disapplied, and there is no need to renew detention – that is, it continues until a positive decision is taken to discharge). Similarly, a guardianship order under section 37 has the same effect as a guardianship order made under the civil provisions, namely section 7. The impact of the making of the various orders made under Part III is considered in detail in subsequent chapters.

ii) Due to the nature of the overlap in terms of effect, the criteria for the imposition of various orders under Part III are often in similar terms to those that apply under Part II; accordingly, some of the core phrases used are the same.

1.18 It is also to be noted that the MHA 1983 Part II and Part III powers may sometimes be used together. In *R v North West London Mental Health NHS Trust ex p Stewart*,[10] there was a challenge to the use of a section 3 civil detention on a conditionally discharged restricted patient. The Court of Appeal upheld the view of the trial judge that the civil provisions of Part II could co-exist with the criminal provisions in Part III. To give an example, the detention of a patient under section 35 for the preparation of a medical report might be combined with a civil detention under section 2 or section 3 that might allow treatment.

9 The history of this structure can be traced back to the acceptance of recommendations made by the Butler Report, more properly the *Report of the Committee on Mentally Abnormal Offenders* Cmnd 6244, 1975.

10 [1998] QB 628.

Different types of hospital

1.19 Most of the provisions of the statute relate to detention in a 'hospital'. This is a word defined in MHA 1983 s145 as a health service hospital (under the National Health Service Act (NHSA) 2006 or the National Health Service (Wales) Act 2006), or local authority accommodation that is used as a health service hospital. However, MHA 1983 s34(2) provides that in relation to Part II (the civil provisions) any reference to a 'hospital' includes a reference to a 'registered establishment', which is defined in section 34(1) as an independent hospital registered under the Care Standards Act 2000 in which 'treatment or nursing (or both)' are provided for people under the MHA 1983. Section 55(5) indicates that section 34(2) is applicable for the purposes of Part III as well. Accordingly, the hospitals in which patients can be detained are National Health Service (NHS) or private hospitals. Quite why this definition could not be included in section 145, as opposed to being in sections 34 and 55, is not immediately apparent.

Security levels

1.20 There are different levels of security in psychiatric hospitals and units within any particular hospital. At the highest level are those hospitals that provide 'high security psychiatric services', which is defined in NHSA 2006 s4 as hospital accommodation and services for:

> persons who
> (a) are liable to be detained under the Mental Health Act 1983, and
> (b) in the opinion of the Secretary of State require treatment under conditions of high security on account of their dangerous, violent or criminal propensities.

There is a similar definition in the National Health Service (Wales) Act 2006, with the opinion being that of the Welsh Ministers. The statutory provisions note that these services are limited to people who meet the definition, but that the 'hospital premises' at which high security psychiatric services may be provided may be a hospital or a part of a hospital which is treated as a separate unit. This will allow for the development of services outside the three high secure hospitals: Ashworth, Broadmoor and Rampton. These hospitals were formerly known as special hospitals and were run as special health authorities, but each is now part of a wider mental health trust within the NHS.

1.21 It is to be noted that patients must be detained to be in a high secure setting, though this might be pursuant to a civil order: a voluntary patient cannot be in a high secure setting. There are some specific statutory provisions relevant to patients in high security hospitals, such as the power of the Secretary of State to make transfers of patients to and from such hospitals (see MHA 1983 s123, which is headed with the previous name 'special hospitals'), and additional restrictions on correspondence by reason of section 134.

1.22 The next level of security is medium security.[11] There are a large number of medium secure facilities in both the public and private mental health sector: each area will have a Regional Secure Unit with a specialist forensic team, but there are many other Medium Secure Units, either as free-standing hospitals or as specific units within a particular hospital. The importance of this latter point is that section 47 of the Crime (Sentences) Act 1997 allows the making of a hospital order to a specific unit rather than to the wider hospital.

1.23 Below medium security is the Low Secure Unit. The differences between the levels of security will be the type of security available in terms of fencing and locks before patients can access the outside of the unit.

1.24 Finally, there are open hospital settings, though it is to be noted that such hospitals may have locked wards as well as open ones.

1.25 It is to be noted that MHA 1983 s118(2A), which was added by MHA 2007 s8, requires the Secretary of State to include in the Code of Practice[12] a statement of the general principles that should inform the making of decisions under the MHA 1983, including ensuring that restrictions on liberty are minimised (see section 118(2B)(c)). One of the guiding principles set out in Part 1 of the Code is the 'least restriction principle', which states that:

> People taking action without a patient's consent must attempt to keep to a minimum the restrictions they impose on the patient's liberty, having regard to the purpose for which the restrictions are imposed.[13]

11 More guidance on these levels of security can be found on the Department of Health website at www.dh.gov.uk/en/Healthcare/Mentalhealth/Secureservices/index.htm.

12 See para 1.8 above.

13 The Welsh Code of Practice uses a different structure, including a set of principles under the rubric of 'the empowerment principles', one of which is the retaining of the independence of the patient wherever possible, and includes the use of the least restrictive option (paragraph 1.8). There are also the 'effectiveness and efficiency principles', which include compliance with the Welsh Assembly Government's strategies, which include the least restrictive option (paragraph 1.23).

1.26 This will no doubt provide support to a challenge being made to the level of security to which a patient is subject: although it is established that conditions of detention, including the level of security, do not engage the ECHR article 5 right to liberty,[14] the additional restrictions imposed on a patient by reason of an unnecessary level of security may amount to a breach of the rights guaranteed by ECHR article 8 or, in an extreme case, article 3.[15]

1.27 The question of security is not just a matter of the physical arrangements aimed at preventing absconding, since it may also be necessary to deal with patients whose behaviour is disturbed. This is also governed by the 'least restriction principle', but is subject to specific guidance in part 15 of the Code of Practice.[16] So paragraph 15.8 notes that: 'Interventions such as physical restraint, rapid tranquillisation, seclusion and observation should be used only where de-escalation alone proves insufficient, and should always be used in conjunction with further efforts at de-escalation.'[17]

Specialisations

1.28 In addition to being categorised by levels of security, hospitals and units within hospitals may have different specialities or a particular focus. As is outlined below, the generic phrase 'mental disorder' covers a wide variety of conditions, which may require different approaches. Conditions or the approach to treatment taken in one place may be incompatible with a particular patient's condition: for example, treating a patient with an eating disorder on a general admission ward that focuses on patients who have been admitted in a state of high distress may not be appropriate. The location of treatment may be of importance for courts in light of the introduction of the 'appropriate treatment' test, which is described in more detail in chapter 2.

1.29 In this connection, mental health services may be arranged according to the groups of patients they target. Some common examples are:

14 See *Ashingdane v UK* (1985) 7 EHRR 528, which related to the delay in transferring a patient from a high secure hospital to a low secure setting.

15 *R (Munjaz) v Mersey Care NHS Trust* [2005] UKHL 58, [2006] 2 AC 148, [2005] MHLR 276, at paras 27ff.

16 See also part 19 of the Welsh Code.

17 See also Code of Practice para 15.17, which states that: 'Interventions such as physical restraint, seclusion or rapid tranquillisation should be considered only if de-escalation and other strategies have failed to calm the patient.'

- child and adolescent mental health services (CAMHS), which are designed for children (ie those under 16) and young persons (aged 16 and 17);
- psycho-geriatric services or mental health services for older people;
- learning disability services; and
- general adult mental health services.

1.30 At a more specific level, there may be services that specialise in eating disorders, autistic spectrum disorders, and so on. For patients who are involved in the criminal justice system, the main focus will probably be forensic mental health services, though others may also be relevant.

Personnel and terminology

Personnel

1.31 Mental Health Act 1983 s11(2) provides that applications under Part II are addressed to the managers of the hospital, and section 6(2) provides that an application gives the managers authority to detain the patient; in relation to Part III patients, evidence has to be given on behalf of the managers that a bed is available within the relevant time scale. The hospital managers have a power of discharge under MHA 1983 s23, and exercise various other functions. So one key group of personnel are the *hospital managers*. The term is defined in MHA 1983 s145 as the relevant NHS body that operates the particular hospital (such as a Primary Care Trust, Foundation Trust or Local Health Board) or the person registered under the Care Standards Act 2000 in relation to an independent hospital. Various parts of the NHSA 2006 and the National Health Service (Wales) Act 2006 contain provisions as to how the various health service bodies carry out their functions, or provide for regulations to be made. What happens often depends on the nature of the function: so the obligation of the managers to check the propriety of forms relating to the admission of civil patients will usually be delegated to an employee of the body, often known as the Mental Health Act Administrator; whereas the power to determine the release of patients under section 23 will usually be delegated to a body of independent people, who may be referred to as 'associate managers' to stress that they are not employees of the relevant body. Guidance on this is given in chapter 30 of the Code of Practice in England, and chapter 11 of the Code of Practice for Wales.

1.32 The following are the main terms that describe the professional personnel who operate in the mental health system. Many of the terms are defined in the MHA 1983, and have changed as a result of the MHA 2007:

a) *Approved clinician (AC) and responsible clinician (RC):* The MHA 1983 used the term 'responsible medical officer' (often shortened to RMO) to designate the medical doctor who was in charge of the treatment of the patient; this is now the 'responsible clinician' or 'RC' (MHA 1983 s34, as substituted by MHA 2007 s9 to reflect the fact that the person in charge need not be a medical doctor (and in particular may be a psychologist, perhaps particularly in relation to personality disorders). All clinicians must be approved. The definition of 'approved clinician' in MHA 1983 s145 refers to someone approved by the Secretary of State or the Welsh Ministers for that role (and various directions are in place as to this process): an approved clinician who is a doctor is also approved for the purposes of MHA 1983 s12 in terms of giving medical recommendations for admission to hospital, which is also required for the criminal provisions by section 54. Reference may be seen to someone being 'section 12 approved'.[18]
b) *Approved mental health professional (AMHP):* The term used in the MHA 1983 as enacted was the 'Approved Social Worker', who carried out various functions under the Act, and in particular took the lead in terms of making applications for detention under the civil provisions. This was amended by the MHA 2007 to allow professions other than social workers to carry out the role – for example, community psychiatric nurses. The approval process is set out in MHA 1983 s114. Doctors may not be AMHPs.
c) *Attorney (or donee of a lasting power of attorney):* A person who is entitled to make decisions for a person who lacks capacity; regulated by the MCA 2005.
d) *Care co-ordinator:* The person in charge of co-ordinating the services to be provided to a patient under the Care Programme Approach.
e) *Care Quality Commission (CQC):* The body that has the function of monitoring the operation of the Mental Health Act, including various specific functions such as the appointment of second

18 A doctor can be approved for the purposes of MHA 1983 s12 without being an approved clinician: this may turn on whether they work in psychiatry and so need to be an AC or work in general practice, for example, and so may need to be involved in the process of detaining people but do not otherwise work in psychiatry.

opinion appointed doctors.[19] This role was previously held by Mental Health Act Commission, but it was taken over by the CQC under the Health and Social Care Act 2008. In Wales, the task is carried out by the Healthcare Inspectorate Wales.[20]

f) *Independent mental health advocate (IMHA):* See the description of 'advocacy' in the following paragraph.
g) *Nearest relative:* The relative assigned the role by statutory definition (in MHA 1983 s26) to be consulted in relation to admissions for treatment; also has the power to seek the discharge of a civil patient under section 23, subject to a barring order. They may be the subject of an application for displacement if they act unreasonably.
h) *Responsible clinician:* The approved clinician in charge of the treatment of a patient; see the discussion under 'approved clinician', above.
i) *Second opinion appointed doctor (SOAD):* The doctor appointed by the CQC (or the Healthcare Inspectorate Wales) to review medical treatment in various situations (as outlined in the discussion of 'treatment' below).
j) *Secretary of state:* In relation to various powers affecting civil patients, the Secretary of State for Health may be involved; in relation to restricted patients and in relation to transfers from prison, the Secretary of State for Justice acts as the relevant minister.
k) *Tribunal:* The judicial body involved in the regulation of the detention of patients. Formerly the Mental Health Review Tribunal, but now a chamber of the First-tier Tribunal in England or the Mental Health Review Tribunal for Wales. Appeals from these bodies go to the Upper Tribunal.

Terminology

1.33 In addition to the personnel of the mental health system, there are also a number of often-used terms that are terms of art within the system. These include:

- *Absent without leave (AWOL):* A patient who is liable to be detained who is away from hospital without permission; this includes patients who have absconded, but also patients who have been recalled and have not returned to the hospital. It also covers people

19 See www.cqc.org.uk and the various relevant links from its website.

20 See www.hiw.org.uk/page.cfm?orgId=477&pid=34629.

under guardianship who are away from their places of residence. (See chapter 3 on powers of arrest and detention.)

- *Absolute discharge:* The release of a restricted patient without any terms, such that the restriction order comes to an end.
- *Admission for assessment:* A short-term civil admission for the purposes of assessment (or assessment and treatment), under MHA 1983 s2 (outlined below). An emergency application may be made for admission for assessment, which is governed by section 4 of the Act and differs from a section 2 application in that it is supported by only one doctor as opposed to the two doctors needed for a section 2 application.
- *Admission for treatment:* Civil detention for treatment, initially for six months but renewable; governed by MHA 1983 ss3 and 20 (outlined below).
- *Advance decision (or advance directive):* This is a decision made under the MCA 2005 by a patient who has capacity to refuse treatment in the future when capacity is lacking. This is of limited effect in relation to patients liable to detention and treatment under the MHA 1983, the provisions of which take precedence. However, it may be relevant in relation to electro-convulsive therapy: see MHA 1983 s58A, and the discussion below of the treatment of mental disorder.
- *Advocacy:* Section 30 of the MHA 2007 added sections 130A–130D to the MHA 1983, requiring the establishment of independent mental health advocates to assist patients who are detained or subject to a CTO, or some patients who are not detained but are subject to certain treatments. Part 20 of the Code of Practice gives further details as to purpose of and arrangements for the IMHA process. (See Part 25 of the Welsh Code.)
- *After-care:* This refers to the arrangements that have to be made for people who have been detained and leave hospital. It arises under MHA 1983 s117, which provides a gateway to various community care services;[21] this is all supposed to be planned so as to allow a seamless package of care, pursuant to the Care Programme Approach (see below).

21 It is a free-standing duty of provision and so the charging regime that arises in relation to other community care provisions does not apply in relation to provision of aftercare under MHA 1983 s117: see *R v Manchester City Council ex p Stennett (and related actions)* [2002] UKHL 34, [2002] 2 AC 1127, (2002) 5 CCLR 500, [2002] MHLR 377.

- *Appropriate medical treatment:* This is a term of art discussed in chapter 2; its availability is a precondition to detention for treatment. 'Medical treatment' is also a term of art.
- *Barring order:* If the nearest relative seeks to discharge a civil patient and the responsible clinician believes that the patient will act in a manner that is dangerous to the patient or others, a barring order may be issued; this triggers rights to reviews by the hospital managers and the tribunal.
- *Capacity:* The ability to make a decision, which is presumed to exist in relation to adults and so has to be displaced. Under section 3 of the MCA 2005, it turns on the ability to understand, retain, use and weigh the information relevant to a decision, and to communicate the decision. The question of capacity may arise in relation to decisions as to treatment for mental disorder, though it is to be noted that if the patient is placed under the MHA 1983, the consent to treatment provisions of the MHA 1983 rather than the MCA 2005 govern such treatment. In relation to children, the language often used is competence: central to this is the 'Gillick competence' test, following the decision of the House of Lords in *Gillick v West Norfolk AHA*,[22] to the effect that children may make their own decisions on the basis of their ability to decide rather than on the basis of age.
- *Care Programme Approach (CPA):* The system of providing care for adults with ongoing needs, designed to ensure that there is a seamless provision of care. This was introduced by Department of Health guidance in 1991; it has been updated. Anyone with needs of any complexity should be dealt with under the CPA (or equivalents such as the Children's Assessment Framework or the Single Assessment Process for older adults), and a care co-ordinator will be assigned to the case.
- *Community care:* The arrangements for the provision of services to vulnerable people, made under various statutes, including the National Assistance Act 1948 and the National Health Service and Community Care Act 1990. This covers people who are vulnerable on account of mental disorder. There is also the phrase 'care in the community', which describes the movement away from the provision of care in institutional settings to the provision of care in small group homes or with individual carers; this particularly affected those with learning disabilities.

22 [1986] AC 112.

- *Community treatment order (or supervised community treatment):* Described in more detail below, this is an order allowing ongoing control over a patient who was formerly detained for treatment but then released into the community under a CTO. The detention order is merely suspended and can be reactivated. This does not apply in the case of a restricted patient, who can be released on a conditional discharge, which has a similar effect.
- *Conditional discharge:* The release of a restricted patient subject to the possibility of recall; various conditions can be imposed. (See chapters 18 and 20.)
- *Compulsory treatment:* The treatment that may be imposed under Part IV of the MHA 1983 patient in relation to those liable to be detained; Part 4A has separation provisions for those under a CTO. These arrangements may also be called the 'consent to treatment' provisions, that being the heading of Part IV (even though its main effect is to provide limitations on the relevance of the patient's consent).
- *Deprivation of liberty safeguards (DOLS):* The arrangements introduced by the MHA 2007, by way of amendments to the MCA 2005, to provide a system to regulate the position of people who lack the capacity to consent to the making of arrangements for themselves and who are in fact detained. Part of the regime deals with the question of whether patients should be detained under the MHA 1983 instead. This group of compliant incapacitated patients are sometimes referred to as those in the 'Bournewood gap', after the case that revealed the issue: see *R v Bournewood Community and Mental Health Trust ex p L.*[23] Its European Court of Human Rights (ECtHR) counterpart, which determined that the regime upheld in the domestic courts, namely the informal treatment of such patients in reliance on their best interests, was not adequate for the purposes of ECHR article 5: see *HL v UK.*[24]
- *Displacement of the nearest relative:* The process under MHA 1983 s29 of replacing the nearest relative of the patient, typically on the basis that there is an objection to the making of an application for admission for treatment that is unreasonable; the county court is the location for this process.
- *Guardianship:* Available under MHA 1983 ss7 and 37 to allow the placement of the individual under the control of a guardian; the central power arising is control over the place of residence.

23 [1999] 1 AC 458.

24 (2005) 40 EHRR 32, (2004) 7 CCLR 498, [2004] MHLR 236.

- *Holding powers:* If a patient is an informal patient (which is permissible under MHA 1983 s131) and decides to leave against advice to stay, a nurse may use holding powers granted under section 5(4) to detain the patient for up to six hours, and a doctor or approved clinician may furnish a report under section 5(2) that leads to the detention of the patient for up to 72 hours, in each case to allow the determination of the question of whether an application should be made to detain the patient under the provisions of MHA 1983 s2 or s3.
- *Hospital direction:* An order made under MHA 1983 s45A (described further in chapter 18); accompanied by a limitation direction (there being no option in this regard). The effect is that the patient is a restricted patient with an underlying prison sentence and so is detained in hospital, but if the basis for detention in hospital ceases, the patient will be transferred to prison to serve the sentence imposed.
- *Hospital order:* The criminal court's order that equates to the civil admission for treatment; may be combined with a restriction order. This is discussed in detail in chapter 18.
- *Informal status:* A voluntary decision to remain in hospital; should only be used in relation to a patient who has capacity, since otherwise the DOLS provisions (see above) might well apply. An informal patient who leaves against medical advice may be subject to the exercise of a holding power.
- *Interim hospital order:* A temporary hospital order designed to test whether a full hospital order should be made (discussed in chapter 18).
- *Leave of absence:* Permission to a patient who is liable to be detained to be absent from the unit in which he or she is liable to be detained; to be read with AWOL and a CTO (see above).
- *Medical treatment:* Widely defined interventions that have the purpose of dealing with mental disorder (discussed in chapter 2).
- *Place of safety:* A temporary holding place pending either assessment for admission to hospital (which will often be a police station) or pending a bed becoming available when an order has been made in criminal proceedings to place someone in hospital (in which case the place of safety will often be a prison). This is discussed further in relation to police powers and also in relation to court powers pre-trial and in relation to sentencing.
- *Recall:* The process of directing the return to hospital of a patient who is on leave, subject to a CTO or a restricted patient who has been conditionally discharged.

- *Restricted patient:* A patient who is detained under a hospital order to which a restriction order is added, or a prisoner transferred from prison with a restriction direction added, or a defendant sentenced to a hospital direction with a limitation direction. Restricted patients are subject to a different regime in relation to matters such as leave and transfer (see chapter 18).

1.34 Various powers may also be referred to by the statutory section that gives force to them. Mental health professionals may also refer to the set forms that are provided for their use under the Mental Health (Hospital, Guardianship and Treatment) (England) Regulations 2008,[25] or their Welsh equivalent.[26]

1.35 A full list of terms can be found in annex A to the Code of Practice or appendix 1 to the Code of Practice for Wales.

The definition of 'mental disorder'

The medical definition

1.36 While it is obviously beyond the scope of this book or the competence of the author to provide anything that amounts to an authoritative summary of psychiatric terms or conceptions, since this is an area of practice where there is a significant overlap between law and medicine, it is important to have some familiarity with medical terminology and practice.

1.37 The medical profession makes significant use of two manuals for the classification of the different mental disorders. One is the American Psychiatric Association's Diagnostic and Statistical Manual, which is currently in a revised fourth edition, abbreviated as DSM-IV-TR. There is also the World Health Organization's International Classification of Diseases, which is currently in its tenth version and is abbreviated as ICD-10.[27] This covers physical and mental disorders: chapter 5 relates to mental disorders.

1.38 The different classifications of mental disorder in ICD-10 are as follows. It is to be noted that a large number of behaviours have been 'medicalised' in the sense that they are given a label as a recognised medical condition. Naturally, the degree of the disorder might vary from barely discernible to acute:

25 SI 2008 No 1184.

26 Mental Health (Hospital, Guardianship, Community Treatment and Consent to Treatment) (Wales) Regulations 2008 SI No 2439.

27 Available at www.who.int/classifications/icd/en/.

a) *Organic, including symptomatic, mental disorders:* These are disorders that result from injuries or diseases that impact upon the brain and cause dysfunction. Dementia is an example, including Alzheimer's disease.
b) *Mental and behavioural disorders due to psychoactive substance use:* This includes a wide range of disorders of varying severity, including the consequences of acute intoxication (with alcohol or drugs) or withdrawal, dependence syndromes, amnesic syndromes as a consequence of substance abuse, and psychotic syndromes caused by such abuse.
c) *Schizophrenia, schizotypal and delusional disorders:* These are disorders with distortions of thinking and perception, which can include thought insertion and hallucinations, but might also include low mood and passivity. Schizophrenia is an example of a delusional disorder, though it is to be noted that it has several forms, including catatonic and paranoid, and various other delusional disorders have schizophrenia-like symptoms (which may be important in terms of the likelihood of recurrence and the prognosis for recovery).
d) *Mood [affective] disorders:* This covers disorders when people have a mood that is particularly low (depression) or elated (manic), usually accompanied by a change in the person's overall level of activity. In addition to clinical depressions, another common instance is bipolar affective disorder, which involves repeated disturbances in which the mood is disturbed either in an elevated or depressed form.
e) *Neurotic, stress-related and somatoform disorders:* This includes the various phobias (that is, anxieties in situations that are not dangerous, for example agoraphobia), obsessive-compulsive disorders, post-traumatic stress disorder and dissociative disorders (that is, loss of the normal integration between awareness and control of bodily functions). Somatoform disorders are those that involve beliefs that there are physical problems that are non-existent (so including hypochondriacal disorder).
f) *Behavioural syndromes associated with physiological disturbances and physical factors:* This covers disorders such as those linked with eating (anorexia and bulimia); sleep disorders not due to another mental or physical disorder and matters, such as sleepwalking; and sexual dysfunction that has no organic or disease-based cause, and also excessive sexual drive.
g) *Disorders of adult personality and behaviour:* This covers a variety of conditions and patterns of behaviour that are found to be clinically

significant in that they are persistent and represent the lifestyle of the individual and his or her method of interacting with others; in other words, they are enduring patterns of behaviour. They also require some form of extreme or significant deviation from the norm in society. As well as the various personality disorders, which are described below, this group includes various disorders of habit (such as pyromania) and disorders of gender identity, and also disorders of sexual preference, of which one example is paedophilia.

h) *Mental retardation:* This is the arrested or incomplete development of the mind, linked with impaired skills linked to the overall level of intelligence, including cognitive and social skills. It is more often now called mental impairment or learning disability, and can be of various levels of severity.
i) *Disorders of psychological development:* These are disorders linked to the delayed development of functions (language, visuo-spatial skills, motor co-ordination) that normally develop as a child matures. Autism is a pervasive developmental disorder involving various types of abnormal functioning and sometimes involving various phobias and tantrums, though there is a version of it – Asperger's syndrome – that may involve problems with unusual social interactions and repetitive behaviours but without the general retardation in language or cognitive abilities.
j) *Behavioural and emotional disorders with onset usually occurring in childhood and adolescence:* This group of disorders includes matters such as various forms of hyperactivity, or other forms of disturbed action or emotion (such as separation anxiety). There is also a group of disorders which are labelled as 'conduct disorder' and which involve persistent dissocial, aggressive or defiant conduct by children.
k) *Unspecified mental disorder:* That is, anything that cannot otherwise be classified.

1.39 It is to be noted that people may have more than one diagnosis: a term that is often seen in this context is 'co-morbidity' or 'dual diagnosis'. There may also be circumstances in which a particular mental disorder is made worse by the patient's use of alcohol or drugs. It may also be the case that symptoms might be common to more than one specific form of disorder – for example, a mood disorder may involve psychotic symptoms.

1.40 In the criminal justice sphere, it may be common to come across people with a personality disorder of some form, given that these may involve anti-social tendencies.[28] Among those listed in ICD-10 are:

a) *Paranoid personality disorder:* This includes recurrent and unjustified suspicions, misconstruing of the actions of others as hostile or negative, and an excessive level of self-importance.
b) *Schizoid personality disorder:* Withdrawal from social situations, with a preference for solitary activities and introspection, and with a limited capacity to express feelings and to experience pleasure.
c) *Dissocial personality disorder:* Disregard for social obligations and norms, and a gross lack of concern for the feelings of others. People with such a disorder may not respond to punishment, have a low tolerance to frustration, a limited ability to restrain aggression and a tendency to blame others or rationalise improper behaviour.
d) *Emotionally unstable personality disorder:* This involves a tendency to impulsive and unpredictable action without consideration of the consequences, which may lead to outbursts of emotion and aggressive or self-harming behaviour.
e) *Histrionic personality disorder:* This disorder is characterised by theatricality and egocentricity, and also a lack of consideration for others.
f) *Anankastic personality disorder:* This disorder, which may involve elements of obsessive-compulsive, is characterised by excessive caution, stubbornness and preoccupation with details.
g) *Anxious [avoidant] personality disorder:* This entails excessive insecurity and inferiority, and a tendency to avoid activities because of an exaggeration of the risks involved; it also involves a hypersensitivity to criticism and rejection.
h) *Dependent personality disorder:* This disorder involves a pervasive reliance on others and so an inability to make decisions, and a fear of being abandoned and inability to respond properly to the demands of daily life.

1.41 There are also instances of some mental illnesses being involved in situations of violence or anti-social behaviour, although it is important not to overstate this. Nevertheless, there have been surveys that revealed that a significant proportion of prisoners have a recognisable psychiatric condition: a 1998 survey put the figure at over 90 per cent

28 Services for people with personality disorder are described at www.dh.gov.uk/en/Healthcare/Mentalhealth/Personalitydisorder/index.htm.

when account was taken of substance dependency.[29] The Department of Health has indicated that: 'Between 5% and 13% of people living in the community, 40% and 50% of psychiatric in-patients and 50% and 78% of prisoners are diagnosable with a personality disorder'.[30]

The ECHR and the definition of 'mental disorder'

1.42 It does not follow from the fact that someone is within a medical classification of mental disorder that the person will be within the legal definition as set out in the MHA 1983 or any other relevant statute. It may also be necessary to consider the requirements of the ECHR, article 5(1) of which provides a right to liberty but allows it to be lost in various situations, including '(e) the lawful detention ... of persons of unsound mind'. The question of 'lawfulness' is discussed below. As to the meaning of 'unsound mind', this was considered in *Winterwerp v Netherlands*.[31] In essence, the court devolved this question to the medical profession. The court noted of the phrase 'unsound mind' at paragraph 37 of its judgment that:

> This term is not one that can be given a definitive interpretation: ... it is a term whose meaning is continually evolving as research in psychiatry progresses, an increasing flexibility in treatment is developing and society's attitude to mental illness changes, in particular so that a greater understanding of the problems of mental patients is becoming more wide-spread.

1.43 The court did provide some limited guidance both as to what was not permitted by the ECHR and what was required to meet the obligations it imposed. As to the former, it noted that it was obvious that the concept of 'unsound mind' would not be made out 'simply because his views or behaviour deviate from the norms prevailing in a particular society'.[32] What was required was 'a true mental

29 Singleton et al, *Psychiatric morbidity among prisoners in England and Wales*, HMSO, 1998; a summary is available at www.ons.gov.uk/ons/rel/psychiatric-morbidity/psychiatric-morbidity-among-prisoners/psychiatric-morbidity-among-prisoners--summary-report/index.html. At p23 of the summary, the authors comment on the fact that many prisoners had several disorders, noting that: 'Only one in ten or fewer showed no evidence of any of the five disorders considered in the survey (personality disorder, psychosis, neurosis, alcohol misuse and drug dependence) and no more than two out of ten in any sample group had only one disorder.'

30 See www.dh.gov.uk/en/Healthcare/Mentalhealth/Personalitydisorder/index.htm.

31 (1979) 2 EHRR 387.

32 (1979) 2 EHRR 387 para 37.

disorder', which in turn was something based on 'objective medical expertise'.[33] It can be seen that this effectively delegates the question of what amounts to mental disorder to the medical profession, since the question is not whether there is a mental disorder but whether there is an adequate medical opinion as to its existence.

1.44 This is no doubt inevitable, given that limitations on the expertise of judges or other fact-finders in a court setting, who cannot be expected to recognise mental disorder without appropriate expert evidence being given.[34] As to whether it is problematic to have this effective devolution to the profession, it is of course to be noted that the relevant clinicians can be expected to give their views based on the standards of their profession, which include the objective elements of the diagnostic manuals. Having said that, it is also to be noted that there are comments that recognise the relative lack of certainty in psychiatry. Baroness Hale noted, in *R (B) v Ashworth Hospital Authority*,[35] that:

> ... psychiatry is not an exact science. Diagnosis is not easy or clear cut. As this and many other cases show, a number of different diagnoses may be reached by the same or different clinicians over the years.

1.45 This may lead to debate as to whether or not it is appropriate for there to be a significant level of delegation. The case-law seems pretty clear as to the level of delegation that does occur. Of course, this delegation may be complicated by the possibility of professionals disagreeing, including on the question of whether a person is mentally disordered or not, in which case the court will be compelled to reach a decision; this is discussed further below.[36]

'Mental disorder' in the Mental Health Act 1983

The basic definition

1.46 For the purposes of the MHA 1983 there is a very wide basic definition of 'mental disorder' and so the medical definition is an almost complete fit with the legal definition; what appears in a diagnostic manual and so meets the *Winterwerp* test will be covered by the domestic statute. The legal definition of 'mental disorder' is set out in MHA 1983

33 (1979) 2 EHRR 387 para 39.

34 There might be an exception to this general point in the case of a court made up of specialist judges.

35 [2005] UKHL 20, [2005] 2 WLR 695, (2005) 8 CCLR 287, [2005] MHLR 47 para 35.

36 See para 1.65.

s1: this is the definition for both the civil provisions and the criminal sections of the Act. It has changed as a result of the MHA 2007.

1.47 The original definition of 'mental disorder' in MHA 1983 s1(2) was that it 'means mental illness, arrested or incomplete development of mind, psychopathic disorder and any other disorder or disability of mind'. The wider phrase 'any other disorder or disability of mind' was relevant for some parts of the Act; for example, for detention under section 2. However, four categories – namely mental illness, mental impairment, severe mental impairment and psychopathic disorder – were relevant for most purposes; at least one of these had to be present for the purposes of detention for treatment under section 3 of the Act or the imposition of a hospital order under section 37. On some occasions, it was the existence of mental illness or severe mental impairment that were relevant, such as the transfer of a remand prisoner to hospital under section 48, or psychopathic disorder, which had to be shown for a hospital direction to be made under section 45A. The relevance of these categories was removed by the MHA 2007, which amended the statute so that only the basic definition of mental disorder was relevant. Section 1(2) as amended now defines mental disorder as 'any disorder or disability of the mind'.

Exclusions

1.48 However, this basic definition is subject to two further provisions.

Dependence on drugs or alcohol

1.49 First, if the mental disorder is nothing more than dependence on drugs or alcohol, then it is not to be considered a disorder or disability of the mind: see MHA 1983 s1(3), as amended by the MHA 2007. Such dependence is considered a mental disorder for the purposes of the World Health Organization's International Classification of Diseases: see ICD-10, classifications F10–19. There are, as has been noted, mental disorders that can be caused by alcoholism or drug addiction, such as a drug-induced psychosis; these will be covered.

1.50 Previously, the exclusions were wider, and it was stated that a person was not to be considered as mentally disordered 'by reason only of promiscuity or other immoral conduct, sexual deviancy or dependence on alcohol or drugs': MHA 1983 s1(3) as originally enacted. The aim behind the change of language was to remove exclusions that were no longer necessary because it was said that they could no longer give rise to a diagnosis of mental disorder,[37] but which had

37 See MHA 2007 Explanatory Notes para 24.

been introduced previously because of past misuse of mental health legislation. This explained the removal of promiscuity and immoral conduct, which it was said had been included in the past to prevent the detention of unmarried mothers and homosexual people.[38]

1.51 The removal of the exclusion of sexual deviancy was designed to ensure that disorders of sexual preference that are recognised clinically as mental disorders are covered by the Act: 'paraphilias like fetishism or paedophilia' are given as examples in the Explanatory Notes to the MHA 2007.[39] This, naturally, means that advocates representing defendants convicted of sexual offences that may reveal the presence of a paraphilia should investigate whether it might be possible to secure a hospital order disposal (or some other sentence reflecting mental health treatment) if that is a better outcome for the client than the alternatives.

1.52 Given the breadth of the definition adopted in *Winterwerp* of what counts as being of 'unsound mind' for the purposes of ECHR article 5(1)(e), as noted above, this domestic definition should be compliant with this admittedly low test. One point is worth making: efforts made during the passage of the bill that became the MHA 2007 to exclude from the definition of mental disorder anything that reflected solely 'cultural, religious or political beliefs' were rejected by the government majority in the House of Commons.[40] In the light of the restriction set out in *Winterwerp* that mental disorder could not arise from having views or engaging in behaviour that differs from the norm,[41] it seems difficult to understand why express language to that effect was rejected: however, given the need for a ECHR-compliant meaning by reason of the interpretive obligation in section 3 of the HRA 1998, this will be the interpretation that is adopted.

Learning disability

1.53 The second qualification to the basic definition of mental disorder is that there are additional provisions if the mental disorder is a learning

38 See the proceedings of the Public Bill Committee, 24 April 2007 (afternoon sitting), cols 45–46. Available at www.publications.parliament.uk/pa/cm200607/cmpublic/cmpbment.htm.

39 MHA 2007 Explanatory Notes para 24.

40 It was added by the House of Lords: *Hansard*, HL Debates col 906ff, 19 February 2007 (available at www.parliament.uk/business/publications/hansard/lords/by-date/); but removed during the Committee Stage in the House of Commons, when the language that passed into law was substituted (as outlined above).

41 (1979) 2 EHRR 387 para 37.

disability. That is 'a state of arrested or incomplete development of the mind which includes a significant impairment of intelligence and social functioning'. It is provided that this is not a mental disorder for the purposes of various sections of the Act, including long-term admission under MHA 1983 s3 (civil) or s37 (criminal) unless it is 'associated with abnormally aggressive or seriously irresponsible conduct' on the part of the individual. This is the consequence of MHA 1983 s1(2A), (2B) and (4) as amended by the MHA 2007.[42]

1.54 Paragraph 34.4 of the Code of Practice, issued under MHA 1983 s118, gives some general guidance on these additional elements in the definition of learning disability:[43]

> *Arrested or incomplete development of mind:* An adult with arrested or incomplete development of mind is one who has experienced a significant impairment of the normal process of maturation of intellectual and social development that occurs during childhood and adolescence. By using these words in its definition of learning disability, the Act embraces the general understanding that features which qualify as a learning disability are present prior to adulthood. For the purposes of the Act, learning disability does not include people whose intellectual disorder derives from accident, injury or illness occurring after they completed normal maturation (although such conditions do fall within the definition of mental disorder in the Act).
>
> *Significant impairment of intelligence:* The judgement as to the presence of this particular characteristic must be made on the basis of reliable and careful assessment. It is not defined rigidly by the application of an arbitrary cut-off point such as an IQ of 70.
>
> *Significant impairment of social functioning:* Reliable and recent observations will be helpful in determining the nature and extent of social competence, preferably from a number of sources who have experience of interacting with the person in social situations, including social workers, nurses, speech and language and occupational therapists, and psychologists. Social functioning assessment tests can be a valuable tool in determining this aspect of learning disability.

1.55 The point is then made at paragraph 34.5 that the person as a whole should be assessed, which may mean that a person with an IQ somewhat higher than 70 may nevertheless be learning disabled if there is a severe impairment of his or her social functioning, and equally that

42 It is a mental disorder for the purposes of various short-term powers of detention, including admission for assessment and treatment under MHA 1983 s2.

43 See also Welsh Code para 34.9, though it is to be noted that it is in somewhat different terms.

someone with relatively good social functioning may be diagnosed with a learning disability on the basis of a low IQ.

1.56 The language of the definition has also been subject to judicial interpretation in relation to the predecessor term in the MHA 1983 as enacted, that is 'mental impairment'. The MHA 1983 had two categories of learning disability, namely mental impairment and severe mental impairment: the difference between the two was that the impairment was significant in the case of mental impairment and severe in the case of severe mental impairment, and so a matter of degree. The points that have arisen from the case-law are, first, the need for the impairment to relate to both intelligence and social functioning, not either of those elements. So, in *R v McDonagh*,[44] the Court of Appeal in Northern Ireland, considered the definition of severe mental impairment in article 3(1) of the Mental Health (Northern Ireland) Order 1986,[45] which was in similar terms to the definition of learning disability. The court quashed hospital orders that had been made on the basis of evidence that considered only the defendant's intelligence but did not assess his social functioning. A point was made that IQ tests might not change over time, but that training might lead to an improvement in social functioning. The court also commented that standard IQ testing is not the whole picture in relation to 'intelligence' either.[46]

1.57 In addition, the question of what amounts to 'seriously irresponsible' conduct has been considered and held to require a restrictive definition by the Court of Appeal in the case of *Re F*:[47] this involved a 17-year-old young woman who was assessed to have a mental age of between five and eight years; she had been removed from the parental home (along with her younger siblings), but wanted to return home, despite the poor quality of parenting and risks of sexual abuse. An effort was made to invoke the civil provisions of the MHA 1983 (via a guardianship order to control her residence), and so the question arose of whether she was mentally impaired on the basis that her

44 [2008] NICA 6, [2008] MHLR 219.

45 Which allows a hospital order to be made on the basis of mental illness or severe mental impairment: see articles 3 and 44 of the Order.

46 See in particular paragraph 37; the court relied in part on the judgment of the English Court of Appeal in *Megarry v Chief Adjudication Officer* (1999) 143 SJ LB 267, examining the phrase 'severe impairment of intelligence' for the purposes of a higher allowance for a particular welfare benefit, gave an example of a claimant with Down's syndrome who might have a low IQ but little social dysfunction.

47 *F (a child) (care order: sexual abuse)* [2000] 1 FLR 192, *Re TF (a child: guardianship)* [1999] MHLR 175.

wish to return home was 'seriously irresponsible'. The preference for a restrictive interpretation, which was not met on the facts, was based on the statutory history of the language but also the need to impose a restrictive definition over criteria that could be used for the purposes of detention.

1.58 The requirement that the disability be 'associated with' the relevant conduct was also part of the definition of mental impairment. It was held not to require causation. In *R (P) v Mental Health Review Tribunal and Rampton Hospital*,[48] Stanley Burnton J commented that counsel was correct to submit that 'the phrase "is associated with" denotes an association which may not be the result of causation'.

1.59 There is also the question of the temporal connection with the behaviour. In *P*, the judge had to consider this in relation to the definition of psychopathic disorder, which was another of the categories of mental disorder and was defined in MHA 1983 s1(2) as originally enacted as a disorder that 'results in abnormally aggressive or seriously irresponsible conduct on the part of the person concerned ...'. Stanley Burnton J decided that there was no need for a temporal connection: in other words, that the absence of recent such behaviour did not lead to the conclusion that there was no psychopathic disorder.[49] This was upheld by the Court of Appeal,[50] Pill LJ commenting at paragraphs 23–25 that the absence of recent conduct that was abnormally aggressive or seriously irresponsible could mean that the disorder no longer persisted but could also mean that it persisted but had not recently manifested itself.

1.60 In *Lewis v Gibson*,[51] the Court of Appeal applied this approach to the definition of what was at the time mental impairment, Thorpe LJ commenting that: 'To make a balanced assessment of the patient's present state some regard must be had to the past history and the future propensity. A conclusion based only on the recent past, which might represent a transient phase of quiescence, would be superficial'.[52]

48 [2001] EWHC Admin 876, [2002] MHLR 250 at para 26.

49 *R (P) v Mental Health Review Tribunal and Rampton Hospital* [2001] EWHC Admin 876, [2002] MHLR 250 at para 23.

50 [2002] EWCA Civ 697, [2002] MHLR 253.

51 [2005] EWCA Civ 587, [2005] MHLR 309.

52 [2005] EWCA Civ 587, [2005] MHLR 309 para 31. See Code of Practice paras 34.8 and 34.9, which include guidance as to the meaning of learning disability to the effect that the question should be the likelihood of recurrence of behaviour that has not recently occurred. Code of Practice for Wales para 34.10 refers to recent or persistent behaviour and so seems to be out of line with the judicial interpretation.

The extended coverage of personality disorder

1.61 As has been noted, the original definition of mental disorder included as a catch-all the reference to 'any ... disorder or disability of mind' that now forms the basic definition; but for longer-term detentions, it was necessary to find mental illness, psychopathic disorder, mental impairment or severe mental impairment. These categories are all still covered, since they fall within the wider definition, but it is important to recognise the impact of this wider coverage. A significant impact in the criminal setting is that the MHA 1983 now includes all forms of personality disorder, not only those that are severe enough to merit the description 'psychopathic disorder': in other words, a personality disorder that does not result in seriously irresponsible or abnormally aggressive behaviour or does not involve mental illness is now covered by the Mental Health Act whereas previously it was not. Reference can be made to the width of what is counted within ICD-10, at classifications F60–69, to amount to a personality disorder, under the general rubric of 'deeply ingrained and enduring behaviour patterns, manifesting as inflexible responses to a broad range of personal and social situations'.[53] These definitions are outlined above.

1.62 The importance of this is that Parliament has extended the range of what might be dealt with through the hospital system as opposed to the criminal justice system as a method of responding to allegedly criminal conduct. This might include such options as diversion from the criminal justice system, whether before a trial or at the sentencing stage.

1.63 The Code of Practice has a specific section setting out guidance on people with personality disorders.[54] It is noted, among other things, that '[g]enerally, people who have personality disorders present a complex range of mental health and other problems' and that 'a very small subgroup of people with personality disorders may be anti-social and dangerous; anti-social personality disorder is strongly associated with offending, and it is estimated that personality disorders have a high prevalence within offender populations'.[55]

1.64 The Code goes on to indicate that '[p]eople with personality disorders may present and behave in very different ways from those with other mental disorders'.[56] The aim of this and subsequent

53 See ICD-10, introductory comments to paras F60–69.

54 Chapter 35; there is no equivalent chapter in the Code of Practice for Wales.

55 Code of Practice para 35.2.

56 Code of Practice para 35.4.

commentary is to ensure that there is assessment by someone with a proper understanding of the diagnosis, which may apply with equal force in the criminal justice context. Given that features such as substance misuse and recurrent relationship difficulties are often found with personality disorders,[57] it may be a common feature of many defendants in the criminal justice system and so worthy of exploration in case there might be prospects of diagnosis and diversion.

Evidential issues and mental disorder

1.65 Given the centrality of expert opinion in the assessment of whether there is a mental disorder, a need might arise to resolve a difference of medical opinion as to whether a defendant has a mental disorder. This was what happened in *Kiernan v Harrow Crown Court*,[58] in which the Divisional Court dealt with a challenge to a decision by the Crown Court on a committal for sentence. Four psychiatrists had given evidence, two of whom felt that there was a mental illness requiring hospital treatment, and two of whom did not; the latter two were supported by a further doctor who gave a written report. The Divisional Court quashed the hospital order made by the Crown Court judge, finding that he had failed to give adequate reasons as to why he preferred the evidence in favour of the finding that there was a mental illness. This in turn meant that the Divisional Court heard evidence: it preferred the evidence of the doctors who found that there was no mental illness, and so the decision of the Crown Court was quashed as being contrary to the weight of the evidence and the matter was remitted for a proper sentence to be imposed. The point of principle arising from this case is that in situations that might arise in which there is a difference of evidence as to whether there is a mental disorder or not, the court must give adequate reasons for its conclusion as to the conclusion it reaches. The same principle no doubt applies to the other medical-evidence based criteria for the making of an order under the Mental Health Act, in relation to which there may be a difference of medical view.

57 Code of Practice para 35.2.

58 [2003] EWCA Crim 1052, [2005] MHLR 1. The matter was commenced as an appeal to the Court of Appeal; however, because of limitations in the jurisdiction of the Court of Appeal in relation to committals for sentence (Criminal Appeals Act 1968 s10 at that time not covering a hospital order), the court reconstituted itself as a judicial review court.

Other ECHR issues

The ECHR and lawfulness of detention

1.66 The presumptive right to liberty in ECHR article 5(1) may be taken away 'in accordance with a procedure prescribed by law' in several situations, including following conviction (subparagraph (a)) and '(e) the lawful detention ... of persons of unsound mind'. The importance of the presumption of liberty was made clear in *R (H) v Mental Health Review Tribunal, North and East London Region*,[59] in which the Court of Appeal granted a declaration that it was incompatible with the Convention presumption of liberty to require a patient to prove the reverse of the admission criteria to secure release under MHA 1983 s72: this led to a change in the statutory language, such that release follows unless the tribunal is satisfied as to the criteria for admission continuing to be met.[60]

1.67 The question of what amounts to 'unsound mind' has been discussed above. In addition to the presence of mental disorder, compliance with article 5(1) requires that the detention be 'lawful'. What amounts to lawfulness was also discussed in the *Winterwerp* case.[61] The ECtHR expressed the opinion at paragraph 39 of the judgment that:

> ... except in emergency cases, the individual concerned should not be deprived of his liberty unless he has been reliably shown to be of 'unsound mind'. The very nature of what has to be established before the competent national authority – that is, a true mental disorder – calls for objective medical expertise. Further, the mental disorder must be of a kind or degree warranting compulsory confinement. What is more, the validity of continued confinement depends upon the persistence of such a disorder ...

1.68 In other words, the question of detention involves not just the existence of mental disorder but the existence of a disorder such as to make detention a proper response; and because the nature, or at least the degree, of a mental disorder may be changeable, the existence of the criteria for detention must be shown to continue. This is aside from the question of the review process under article 5(4).

1.69 In this context, it is also a general principle arising under article 5 that a loss of liberty must be a proportionate response. This point was

59 [2001] EWCA Civ 415, [2002] QB 1, [2001] MHLR 48.

60 Mental Health Act 1983 (Remedial) Order 2001 SI No 3712.

61 (1979) 2 EHRR 387.

made in the case of *Litwa v Poland*,[62] which related to the detention of an alcoholic, which is also permitted under article 5(1)(e): the ECtHR laid out the following proposition:

> 78. The Court reiterates that a necessary element of the 'lawfulness' of the detention within the meaning of Art 5§1(e) is the absence of arbitrariness. The detention of an individual is such a serious measure that it is only justified where other, less severe measures have been considered and found to be insufficient to safeguard the individual or public interest which might require that the person concerned be detained. That means that it does not suffice that the deprivation of liberty is executed in conformity with national law but it must also be necessary in the circumstances.

1.70 On the facts, it had not been shown that it had been necessary to detain Mr Litwa in a sobering-up centre when he had been found drunk and allegedly abusive in a public place since the alternative option of taking him home did not appear to have been considered.

1.71 This covers what might be regarded as the substantive question of lawfulness. In addition, the adequacy of the procedural safeguards is relevant. Such provisions are necessary to ensure that there is detention in accordance with the law and to ensure that it meets the criteria on the merits. The importance of procedural safeguards was made clear in *HL v UK*.[63] In this case, a patient with severe learning problems was held in hospital without being formally detained because he was compliant: had he attempted to leave he would have been detained, but the issue never arose. As a result, he was accorded informal status in English law and, as he lacked capacity to make decisions relating to his treatment, decisions were taken by the clinical team in accordance with their assessment of his best interests. The House of Lords had held that this was lawful in English law, overturning the decision of the Court of Appeal to the effect that the MHA 1983 provided the complete code for any detention on account of mental disorder: see *R v Bournewood Community and Mental Health Trust ex p L*.[64]

1.72 The ECtHR found that there had been a breach of article 5(1) because, although it was clear that HL was suffering from a mental disorder and so was of 'unsound mind', the absence of adequate procedures before he was detained or to ensure that detention was warranted on an ongoing basis meant that the protection against

62 App No 26629/95, [2000] MHLR 226.

63 App No 45508/99, (2005) 40 EHRR 32, (2004) 7 CCLR 498, [2004] MHLR 236.

64 [1999] 1 AC 458.

arbitrary detention at the heart of article 5(1) could not be guaranteed. A contrast was drawn between the formalities involved in the detention of non-compliant patients under the MHA 1983 (such as the need for statutory criteria to be satisfied, requirements as to consultation, the time limits on detention before a renewal process had to be followed) and the reliance on a professional view that detention was needed in the case of compliant individuals without capacity. This decision led to the introduction of a detailed regime regulating the detention of the significant number of patients without capacity but otherwise compliant and so not placed under the MHA 1983. This regime is to be found in Schedules A1 and 1A to the MCA 2005, as inserted by the MHA 2007.

1.73 In addition to this substantive test and the procedural safeguards, a further point is that detention must be in a clinical environment to meet the requirement of lawfulness. This was established in *Ashingdane v UK*,[65] which concerned an alleged breach of article 5(1) on the basis that the patient was held in conditions of greater security than was necessary. In the course of dismissing the claim as not engaging article 5, it was said:

> 44. The Court would further accept that there must be some relationship between the ground of permitted deprivation of liberty relied on and the place and conditions of detention. In principle, the 'detention' of a person as a mental health patient will only be 'lawful' for the purposes of sub-paragraph (e) of paragraph 1 if effected in a hospital, clinic or other appropriate institution authorised for that purpose. However, subject to the foregoing, Art 5(1)(e) is not in principle concerned with suitable treatment or conditions ...

1.74 In this connection, see also *Aerts v Belgium*,[66] in which it was determined that the detention in a prison hospital wing of a man committed to hospital by the criminal courts after being found not responsible for his criminal actions breached article 5(1)(e) because of the need for an appropriate relationship between the place of detention and the basis upon which detention was ordered, which in relation to a person detained on the basis of mental disorder had to be a clinical setting. *Ashingdane* and *Aerts* also make it plain that even if the route into detention was an order made in criminal proceedings such that it is a detention that is within article 5(1)(a), the requirements of article 5(1)(e) are also applicable to the lawfulness of the detention.

65 (1985) 7 EHRR 528.
66 (2000) 29 EHRR 50.

Other aspects of the ECHR

1.75 ECHR article 5(4) provides a right for those detained 'to take proceedings by which the lawfulness of his detention shall be decided speedily by a court and his release ordered if the detention is not lawful'. This is a habeas corpus right. It has been interpreted to require that applications at regular intervals be allowed: see *De Wilde and others v Belgium*,[67] which related to vagrants (another group covered by article 5(1)(e)) and was applied to the mental health sphere in *X v UK*,[68] in which the ECtHR held:

> 52. ... By virtue of Art 5(4), a person of unsound mind compulsorily confined in a psychiatric institution for an indefinite or lengthy period is thus in principle entitled, at any rate where there is no automatic periodic review of a judicial character, to take proceedings at reasonable intervals before a court to put in issue the 'lawfulness' – within the meaning of the Convention ... – of his detention, whether that detention was ordered by a civil or criminal court or by some other authority.

1.76 Such a review must be of the merits of detention. In essence, since the *Winterwerp* criteria as to the lawfulness of detention make it plain that this rests on matters that may change over time, there is a need to reassess the existence of that lawfulness over time. In addition, the court that carries out the task of review for the purposes of article 5(4) must have power to order release. These two components must run together: so, in *X v UK*, the ECtHR found a breach of article 5(4) because the domestic law as it then stood, under the MHA 1959, was that the Mental Health Review Tribunal could only make recommendations to the Home Secretary as to the release of restricted patients (that is, those made subject to special restrictions on account of their perceived dangerousness, on which see chapter 18) and habeas corpus or judicial review proceedings involved only an examination of whether lawful procedures had been followed and would not examine whether detention was justified on the merits. So there was a court that could order release and another court that could consider the merits of detention, but no court that could both review the merits of detention and order release. The statute was changed to meet this objection: so MHA 1983 s73 allows the tribunal to direct the release of restricted patients.

67 (1979) 1 EHRR 373.
68 (1981) 4 EHRR 188.

1.77 The final right expressly mentioned in article 5(4) is that to a speedy decision. In *R (KB and others) v Mental Health Review Tribunal*,[69] the Administrative Court applied the principle that countries that sign up to the ECHR thereby guarantee that they will be able to comply by its requirements:[70] the consequence of this was that the judicial system had to be organised to allow speedy hearings and any problems caused by the lack of resources had to be addressed. On the facts, the problem was repeated adjournments or failures to hear cases on the date set, largely because of a shortage of medical members of the tribunal.

1.78 What amounts to speedy is a fact-specific test, so it will depend on the complexity of the case. But some indication of the potential rigours of what is required comes from *E v Norway*,[71] where a breach was found when eight weeks passed between application and court judgment. The sequence of events is worth noting: E was transferred from a hostel to a secure setting (amounting to detention) on 21 July 1988; he applied for a court hearing on 3 August 1988, but did not have one until 7 September 1988, the reasons for the delay being judicial holidays and then difficulties contacting lawyers, including his own; the judgment was given on 27 September 1988. The ECtHR held that this did not meet the requirements of speediness, noting that it was necessary to have practical arrangements in place to allow urgent matters to be dealt with during vacation periods.

1.79 The ECtHR has also held that there are various implicit requirements in article 5(4), in particular arising from the need to follow a judicial process. This requires, for example, proper safeguards against bias or the appearance of bias: see *DN v Switzerland*.[72] In this case, a breach was found because a psychiatrist member of the tribunal determining the lawfulness of detention had expressed a concluded opinion in advance of the hearing. The psychiatrist had been acting as a judge rapporteur, giving evidence to the tribunal as well as sitting as a member of it.

1.80 Another case with significant implications arising in this context is *Megyeri v Germany*,[73] in which the ECtHR found that, in order for the periodic review under article 5(4) to be effective, it might be necessary to have additional procedural safeguards: on the facts, the

69 [2002] EWHC 639 (Admin), [2003] MHLR 1.
70 See, for example, *Bezicheri v Italy* (1990) 12 EHRR 210.
71 (1990) 17 EHRR 30.
72 [2001] MHLR 117.
73 (1992) 15 EHRR 584.

importance of ensuring that a case relating to liberty was presented adequately meant that there should be a presumption in favour of appointing a lawyer even if the patient had not requested one.

1.81 Other aspects of the ECHR that might be relevant are articles 3 and 8. The former has been argued in relation to the conditions of detention and also the use of medication without the consent of the patient. The leading case from the ECtHR is *Herczegfalvy v Austria*,[74] in which the complaint was about the forcible administration of food to counter a hunger strike, of neuroleptic medication, and isolation and attachment with handcuffs to a security bed. The principle set out was in the following terms:

> 82. The Court considers that the position of inferiority and powerlessness which is typical of patients confined in psychiatric hospitals calls for increased vigilance in reviewing whether the Convention has been complied with. While it is for the medical authorities to decide, on the basis of the recognised rules of medical science, on the therapeutic methods to be used, if necessary by force, to preserve the physical and mental health of patients who are entirely incapable of deciding for themselves and for whom they are therefore responsible, such patients nevertheless remain under the protection of Article 3, whose requirements permit of no derogation. The established principles of medicine are admittedly in principle decisive in such cases; as a general rule, a measure which is a therapeutic necessity cannot be regarded as inhuman or degrading. The Court must nevertheless satisfy itself that the medical necessity has been convincingly shown to exist.

1.82 In other words, as is the case in relation to the definition of mental disorder, there is an effective delegation to the medical profession, subject to review by the courts that applies a requirement that the doctors can demonstrate that treatment is necessary and that this has been shown to the standard 'convincingly'. This led to a significant number of judicial review cases, following the acceptance that it was proper to have such challenges once the HRA 1998 was in place;[75] in *R (N) v Dr M and others*,[76] the Court of Appeal confirmed that it was also necessary for the reviewing court to be satisfied that the proposed treatment was in the best interests of the patient and also that the need for the treatment to be shown 'convincingly' to exist required more than evidence on the balance of probabilities.

74 (1992) 15 EHRR 437.

75 *R (Wilkinson) v Broadmoor Hospital and others* [2002] 1 WLR 419, [2001] MHLR 224.

76 [2003] 1 WLR 562, [2003] MHLR 157.

The question of the extent to which the issue of treatment is not just a question for the judicial review court but also relevant to the tribunal and also to any court ordering detention is discussed below in relation to the addition to the test for detention in the MHA 2007, namely that there be appropriate treatment available, is discussed in chapter 2.

1.83 In extreme cases, poor conditions of detention have been held to breach article 3: this arose from severe overcrowding in a prison hospital in the case of *Romanov v Russia*.[77] It may also arise from lack of adequate psychiatric treatment, as in *Kucheruk v Ukraine*[78] and *Keenan v UK*.[79] The latter involved a failure to provide adequate care to a prisoner with psychiatric problems, who committed suicide when his release date was put back as the result of a disciplinary adjudication.

1.84 As for article 8 and the right to respect for privacy and family-related matters, while this has been widely-defined to cover all aspects of the right to self determination and autonomy, the fact that proportionate interferences with those rights are permitted to support various societal aims means that a breach of article 8 will arise in limited circumstances. In essence, if the interference is justified for the purposes of article 5, it is difficult to see that it will not be proportionate for the purposes of article 8. But there may be some relevant situations: for example, holding a detainee far away from family when a suitable facility is closer might not be a breach of article 5 but might be a breach of article 8.[80]

77 [2006] MHLR 7.

78 [2008] MHLR 1.

79 [2001] Prison LR 180, (2001) 33 EHRR 913.

80 Examples of challenges that have failed include: the monitoring and recording of telephone calls by patients in a high secure hospital was upheld on the grounds of security in *R (N) v Ashworth Special Hospital Authority* [2001] MHLR 77; in *R (E) v Ashworth Hospital Authority* [2002] MHLR 150, restrictions on cross-dressing by a male patient in the same hospital were upheld on the basis of both therapeutic and security concerns; and in *R (RH) v Ashworth Hospital Authority* [2001] MHLR 241 the refusal to allow condoms to be issued because there was a no-sex policy was upheld, despite the dangers of infection with a sexually transmissible disease if the policy was breached.

CHAPTER 2

The civil scheme

continued

Introduction

2.1 This chapter provides an outline of the civil system of provision for the needs of those with mental disorder, both in the community and in hospital. The value of knowledge about this for the criminal practitioner is that it may be possible to secure positive outcomes in the criminal justice arena by making use of the civil regime.

The basic framework for intervention

Community care assessments and provision

2.2 The existence of a mental disorder is, obviously, a basis for an individual to seek medical assistance from the relevant parts of the National Health Service (NHS). But it may also give rise to obligations on health and local authorities to plan and provide assistance under the various elements of community care legislation:[1] in other words, pro-actively to co-ordinate and provide assistance rather than leaving it to the recipient to ask for help. As an example of community care provision, a duty to provide accommodation to people in need of assistance may arise under section 21 of the National Assistance Act (NAA) 1948 in relation to 'illness' or 'disability'. The legislative list of people for whom welfare arrangements may be made include those suffering from 'mental disorder of any description'.[2]

2.3 The basic duty of assessment in relation to such services arises under section 47 of the National Health Service and Community Care Act 1990, which provides that:

> (1) ... where it appears to a local authority that any person for whom they may provide or arrange for the provision of community care services may be in need of any such services, the authority –
> (a) shall carry out an assessment of his needs for those services; and
> (b) having regard to the results of that assessment, shall then decide whether his needs call for the provision by them of any such services.

2.4 If the patient has needs of any complexity, then the provision of services should be co-ordinated in a systematic fashion through the Care Programme Approach (CPA), introduced in a Department of Health

1 Full details on the law relating to community care can be found in Clements and Thompson, *Community care and the law*, 5th edn, LAG, 2011.

2 NAA 1948 s29(1).

circular to health and social services in 1990;[3] this was reviewed and updated guidance was published in March 2008, *Refocusing the Care Programme Approach*.[4] The CPA requires a systematic assessment, the formulation of a care plan and the assignment of a care co-ordinator to implement the plan, and a process of regular review of the care plan.

2.5 So, a criminal justice client who has problems relating to matters such as reliable accommodation and access to assistance and who is mentally disordered may well be within the scope of a community care obligation. An assessment of those needs under section 47 of the National Health Service and Community Care Act 1990 may lead to the provision of facilities that might be important for matters such as whether there is a fixed abode for the purposes of bail. This may also be relevant to putting together interventions that may work together with the arrangements under a community penalty to secure a full package to address a client's needs and the risks they pose, which may be relevant at the sentencing stage.

2.6 One element of community care that arises under the Mental Health Act (MHA) 1983 is the power of guardianship: this is put in place under section 7 of the Act, by the patient's nearest relative or an approved mental health professional (AMHP),[5] supported by two medical recommendations to the effect that the patient has a mental disorder of a nature or degree that warrants the use of guardianship and that it is necessary for the welfare of the patient or the protection of others. The powers available to the guardian are to control the residence of the person subject to guardianship, to require that access be given to a medical practitioner and also to require that the subject attend a nominated place for medical treatment, occupation, training or education (see MHA 1983 s8).

2.7 Two linked points are worth noting: in the first place, this regime can be put in place for the protection of others, and so it is clear that it can have a role to play in a situation where the criminal justice system may be involved. Second, the criminal courts can also impose a guardianship order as a sentence, under MHA 1983 s37; this may allow arguments about the value of diverting someone into the civil mental health system rather than making use of the criminal justice system to lead to the same disposal.[6]

3 HC(90)23/LASSL(90)11.

4 Available at www.dh.gov.uk/en/Publicationsandstatistics/Publications/PublicationsPolicyAndGuidance/DH_083647.

5 See chapter 1 for an explanation of these terms.

6 It is to be noted that the criminal courts cannot compel the making of a guardianship order: the making of such an order under section 37 requires

The framework for detention under the Mental Health Act 1983

2.8 If someone in need of treatment for mental disorder is not willing to be a voluntary patient under MHA 1983 s131, then consideration may be given to the use of the powers of detention that exist under the Act. The existence of mental disorder is a necessary precondition to such detention. As noted in chapter 1, article 5(1)(e) of the European Convention on Human Rights (ECHR) makes it necessary for the mental disorder to be of a nature or degree as to warrant detention. The MHA 1983 complies with this.

2.9 The essential structure of Part II of the MHA 1983, the civil powers of detention, is as follows:

- Admissions to hospital can be for assessment and treatment or for treatment, under sections 2 and 3 respectively; the former is a short-term detention of up to 28 days which cannot be renewed; the latter can be a longer-term detention, initially for up to six months, but renewable under section 20 if the criteria for admission continue to apply.
- Admission is pursuant to an application form which is invariably completed by an AMHP, though it can also be by the nearest relative of the patient, and which in either situation has to be supported by two medical reports.
- Patients can be transferred between different hospitals.
- Patients can be granted leave to be absent from hospital.
- Patients placed under section 3 of the MHA 1983 can be released into the community with ongoing obligations placed on them in the form of a community treatment order (CTO).

2.10 It is to be noted that there are no age limits for the use of the civil powers of detention; this is unlike guardianship, which is only available for those aged 16 or over, though other orders are available under the Children Act 1989. There is, however, a duty under MHA 1983 s131A to ensure that accommodation for those under 18 is suitable for the age of the patients. In practice, there may be a separate team involved, namely the child and adolescent mental health services (CAMHS). In this context, an issue to be considered is whether the better approach is to use the Children Act 1989, and in particular

the co-operation of the local authority that would invariably be responsible for putting a civil guardianship order in place. See *R (Buckowicki) v Northamptonshire County Council* [2007] EWHC 310 (Admin), [2007] MHLR 121.

an order under section 25 of that Act to place the child in secure accommodation: this has the advantage of ensuring that a court is involved in the decision-making process.

2.11 It is also worth noting that those aged 16 or 17 who have the relevant capacity are able to make their own decisions as to whether or not to be an informal patient under section 131.[7] In relation to those under 16, it may also be that they have capacity to make their own decisions: this depends on the 'Gillick competence' test, following the decision of the House of Lords in *Gillick v West Norfolk AHA*[8] that the law allows children to make their own decisions on the basis not of an age limit but of a test of competence. The corollary of this was that the ability of the parent or guardian to take the decision on behalf of the child was limited to circumstances in which the child was not capable of taking the decision on his or her own behalf. The effect of section 131 is that it will be presumed that a child of 16 or 17 can make their own decisions, but that can be displaced on the demonstration that they do not have the capacity; but in relation to children under 16, an assessment of their capacity will have to be made to determine whether they can make their own decisions. This is reflected in part 36 of the Code of Practice (and parts 16 and 33 of the Code of Practice for Wales).

2.12 The questions of treatment and release are regulated separately from the question of detention. In relation to treatment, Part IV of the MHA 1983 provides as follows:

- Particularly invasive treatments require the consent of the patient and the approval of a second doctor, known as the second opinion appointed doctor (SOAD) because their role is to provide the second opinion and they are appointed for that purpose by the Secretary of State (or the Welsh Ministers). This is carried out by the Care Quality Commission (CQC) in England (which took over the role of the former Mental Health Act Commission);[9] in Wales, the task is carried out by the Healthcare Inspectorate Wales.[10]

7 Many patients who need treatment for mental disorder in a hospital setting will do so on a voluntary basis and so will not need to have compulsion used; it is to be noted, however, that there are short-term holding powers under MHA 1983 s5 that allow a nurse to detain an informal patient for up to six hours and allow a doctor to detain for up to 72 hours to allow consideration of whether formal powers need to be invoked.

8 [1986] AC 112.

9 See www.cqc.org.uk/ and the various relevant links from its website.

10 See www.hiw.org.uk/page.cfm?orgId=477&pid=34629.

- Electro-convulsive therapy (ECT) requires the consent of a patient aged over 18 and the certification of the treating clinician or a second doctor that the patient has the capacity to consent; for children under 18, the test for ECT is whether they have consented but the certification of the capacity to consent must come from a SOAD.
- Medication for longer than three months requires either the consent of the patient (and a certificate from the treating clinician or a second doctor as to the capacity to consent) or approval from a SOAD.
- Any other treatment is lawful provided that it is authorised by the Responsible Clinician (RC), that is the clinician in charge of treatment.

2.13 There are additional provisions relating to emergency treatment, which can be given even if the conditions that otherwise apply are not met. This regime applies to patients who are liable to be detained, which includes those on leave under MHA 1983 s17. There is a separate regime for the treatment of those who are subject to compulsion in the form of the CTO, which is regulated by Part 4A of the MHA 1983, and in essence provides for urgent or emergency treatment, but otherwise there must be consent or an absence of capacity.

2.14 As for discharge, there are two separate regimes. There is an administrative release provision, set out in MHA 1983 s23, which can be directed by the RC or the hospital managers; the patient's nearest relative may also apply to exercise this administrative discharge, which takes effect after 72 hours unless the RC bars it by filing a report under section 25 to the effect that the patient would be likely to act in a manner dangerous to himself or others and so should remain detained. The second regime is the judicial regime, by application to the Tribunal (namely the Mental Health Review Tribunal for Wales or the First-tier Tribunal in England) for discharge under MHA 1983 s72 or s73, which in essence requires an order for release if it is not shown that the criteria for detention continue to apply. Rights to apply are provided by MHA 1983 ss66 and 69. There are also provisions whereby the hospital managers have to refer a case to a tribunal if the patient has not made an application for some time: see section 68 of the Act. In the case of a restricted patient, this duty is exercised by the Secretary of State for Justice under section 71.

Detention under Mental Health Act 1983 ss2 and 3

Mental Health Act 1983 s2

Criteria and procedure for imposition

2.15 The two main powers of detention that arise under MHA 1983 Part II are sections 2 and 3. Under the former:

> (2) An application for admission for assessment may be made in respect of a patient on the grounds that–
> (a) he is suffering from mental disorder of a nature or degree which warrants the detention of the patient in a hospital for assessment (or for assessment followed by medical treatment) for at least a limited period; and
> (b) he ought to be so detained in the interests of his own health or safety or with a view to the protection of other persons.

2.16 In terms of the procedures to be followed, by reason of section 11 of the Act, the application may be made by an AMHP or the nearest relative of the patient; and if it is made by an AMHP, the nearest relative must be informed either before or within a reasonable time (and so can consider the exercise of their powers of discharge under section 23). The AMHP is the mental health professional (other than a doctor) who is authorised by the local authority under section 114 to carry out functions under the Act. Previously, the role was carried out only by a social worker and the term used was Approved Social Worker: the changes were made by sections 18 and following of the MHA 2007, though it will remain common for the AMHP to be a social worker.

2.17 The role of nearest relative is assigned by MHA 1983 s26.[11] In essence, this gives precedence to relatives according to a statutory list of priority; however, if the patient 'ordinarily resides with or is cared for' by another relative, the latter takes priority.[12] It is also possible for the nearest relative to delegate his or her role to another: see regulation 24 of the Mental Health (Hospital, Guardianship and Treatment) (England) Regulations 2008[13] and regulation 33 of the Mental Health (Hospital, Guardianship, Community Treatment and Consent to Treatment) (Wales) Regulations 2008.[14]

11 A summary of the functions of the nearest relative was given in *R (M) v Secretary of State for Health* [2003] EWHC 1094 (Admin), [2003] MHLR 348.

12 See *Re D (mental patient: nearest relative)* [2000] MHLR 50 for guidance on what is meant by residing with or being cared for so as to get priority in the list.

13 SI 2008 No 1184.

14 SI 2008 No 2439.

2.18 MHA 1983 s2(3) provides that the application – whether made by the AMHP or the nearest relative – must be accompanied by two medical recommendations which certify that the criteria in section 2(2) are met.[15] Further regulation as to the medical recommendations is contained in section 12: the doctors involved must have examined the patient no more than five days apart, though they can carry out a joint examination, and at least one of the doctors must be certified as having expertise in psychiatry. The 'section 12 approved' tag is obtained by compliance with training and refresher courses carried out by NHS bodies, to whom the approval process is delegated. In addition, one of the doctors should have previous acquaintance with the patient if that is practicable.[16]

Length of detention

2.19 Once an application is made, by lodging it with the hospital named in the application form, it gives authority to detain so long as the detention commences within 14 days beginning on the date of the last of the medical recommendations: see MHA 1983 s6(1).[17] The detention may continue for up to 28 days, by reason of section 2(4); this 28-day period may be extended if efforts are being made to put a section 3 detention into place and the patient's nearest relative has objected to that (by reason of section 11(4), which is discussed below) and steps are being taken to replace the nearest relative on the grounds that his or her objection is unreasonable (which is done by an application to the county court under MHA 1983 s29).

Discharge

2.20 A section 2 patient can be discharged under section 23 by the RC, the hospital managers or the nearest relative (but the latter's application may be barred under section 25 if the patient is dangerous). An application may also be made to the tribunal by the patient, the right

15 An emergency application can be made under MHA 1983 s4 on the basis of one medical recommendation; the second medical recommendation must be obtained within 72 hours of the patient being admitted to hospital.

16 For an example of when it was not practicable, see *R (TTM (by his litigation friend TM)) v Hackney LBC and East London NHS Foundation Trust* [2011] EWCA Civ 4, in which the Court of Appeal upheld the decision of the High Court that a disagreement among doctors who knew TTM provided a good reason for concluding that two doctors who did not know the patient should be involved in the assessment; this involved giving the word 'practicable' a broad meaning.

17 If it is an MHA 1983 s4 emergency application, admission must be within 24 hours.

arising under section 66. The tribunal must discharge if the criteria for detention – that there is a mental disorder, that it is of a nature or degree which warrants detention in hospital for assessment (or assessment plus treatment) for at least a limited period, and that this ought to happen to protect the patient's health or safety or to protect others – do not still apply at the time it meets: see section 72(1)(a). Although the administrative discharge provisions under section 23 do not have any set criteria, the Code of Practice states that the 'essential yardstick' is whether the criteria for detention continue to apply: see paragraph 31.14 (and paragraph 27.14 of the Welsh Code is of similar effect).

Mental Health Act 1983 s3

Criteria in outline and procedure for imposition

2.21 As for detention under MHA 1983 s3, the procedural requirements are similar to those under section 2 with one significant alteration, namely that under section 11(4) of the 1983 Act there is a duty to consult the nearest relative in advance (subject to requirements of practicability) and the application cannot proceed if the nearest relative objects. At that point a decision may have to be taken to apply to the county court to seek to displace the nearest relative on the basis that the objection is unreasonable; this occurs under section 29.

2.22 The test on the merits under section 3 is in the following terms:

> (2) An application for admission for treatment may be made in respect of a patient on the grounds that–
> (a) he is suffering from mental disorder of a nature or degree which makes it appropriate for him to receive medical treatment in a hospital; and
> (b) [deleted by Mental Health Act 2007]
> (c) it is necessary for the health or safety of the patient or for the protection of other persons that he should receive such treatment and it cannot be provided unless he is detained under this section; and
> (d) appropriate medical treatment is available for him.
>
> ...
>
> (4) In this Act, references to appropriate medical treatment, in relation to a person suffering from mental disorder, are references to medical treatment which is appropriate in his case, taking into account the nature and degree of the mental disorder and all other circumstances of his case.[18]

18 Former MHA 1983 s3(2)(b) was repealed by the MHA 2007: it related to the requirement that mental impairment and psychopathic disorder be

Discharge

2.23 As is the case in relation to a patient detained under section 2, a section 3 patient can be discharged under section 23 by the RC, the hospital managers or the nearest relative (subject to the barring provisions of section 25). As noted above, these administrative discharge provisions are without a set test, but the Code of Practice indicates that the test is essentially whether the criteria for detention continue to apply. Paragraph 31.16 of the Code notes the criteria that apply under section 3 (and paragraph 27.15 of the Welsh Code is of similar effect, though it does not draw a distinction between section 2 or section 3 detention). Under paragraph 31.19 (and paragraph 27.17 in Wales), the Code notes that if there has been the barring of a nearest relative application to discharge, the managers should also consider whether the dangerousness criterion is made out.

2.24 An application may also be made to the tribunal by a patient detained under section 3, the right to apply arising under section 66. The tribunal must discharge if the criteria for detention – mental disorder of a nature or degree which makes liability to detention in hospital appropriate, detention being necessary for the health or safety of the patient or the protection of others, and the availability of appropriate treatment – do not still apply at the time it meets (by section 72(1)(b)). In addition, if the nearest relative has sought to effect a discharge under section 23 and this has been barred, the nearest relative may apply to the tribunal and it must discharge if it does not find that the barring criteria are made out, namely the likelihood of dangerous behaviour.

Renewals

2.25 Detention under MHA 1983 s3 lasts for six months in the first instance; thereafter, it can be renewed under section 20 for a further six months and then 12 months at a time if the criteria for detention continue to apply.[19] If it not renewed, the detention will lapse. There is only one right to apply to a tribunal during each period of detention

treatable. The reference to these categories of disorder and the treatability test, and the impact of their absence, are discussed below.

19 The application to renew must be made by the RC, who must interview the patient (MHA 1983 s20(3)) and consult with another person who has been 'professionally concerned' with the patient's medical treatment (section 20(5)); there must also be a written agreement from such a person but who is from a profession other than the RC that the criteria for detention are met (section 20(5A)). The person consulted will usually be the one who provides the written agreement.

(that is, the initial application and each renewal), but the exercise of the powers under section 23 may be considered more frequently.

Reviews of detention without application by the patient

2.26 A patient does not have to exercise his or her right to apply to a tribunal. However, to avoid the danger of patients being detained without independent review because the patient lacks the capacity to apply for release or fails to make an application when one ought to be made, the MHA 1983 imposes both administrative and judicial checks on detention that do not depend on an application by a patient or a nearest relative.

2.27 In relation to the administrative review, this should be a meaningful review of the merits of detention. This proposition arises from the following steps. In the first place, the application to detain for treatment under section 3 or to renew under section 20 has to be addressed to the hospital managers: section 6 provides that the section 3 application provides authority to the managers to detain and section 20(3) states that the application to renew shall be addressed to the managers.

2.28 In relation to the initial receipt of an application, the Mental Health (Hospital, Guardianship and Treatment) (England) Regulations 2008,[20] and their Welsh equivalent,[21] indicate that the relevant application form[22] has to be served on an officer of the managers who has been authorised to receive it. Part 13 of the English Code of Practice, and Part 10 of the Welsh Code, set out additional guidance on what should occur. So, paragraphs 13.7–13.11 of the English Code indicate that, among other things, someone of 'appropriate seniority' should be in charge of the overall process, it is necessary to have an officer always available (with access to a manager for advice), and the application forms should be scrutinised and any necessary rectifications carried out. Among the checks, it is stated that:

> Medical recommendations should also be scrutinised by someone with appropriate clinical expertise to check that the reasons given appear sufficient to support the conclusions stated in them.

2.29 Turning then to Part 30 of the English Code and Part 11 of the Welsh Code, there are reminders that the managers have to ensure that

20 SI 2008 No 1184.

21 Mental Health (Hospital, Guardianship, Community Treatment and Consent to Treatment) (Wales) Regulations 2008 SI No 2439.

22 See regulation 4 of and Schedule 1 to the respective Regulations.

people are in hospital only when that is justified. So paragraph 30.11 of the English Code notes that:

> It is the hospital managers' responsibility to ensure that the authority for detaining patients is valid and that any relevant admission documents are in order.

2.30 This makes it clear that there are two separate tasks, namely checking the admission documents but also confirming that the authority for detention is valid: the latter can make sense as an additional obligation only if it is necessary for the managers to look to the substance of the detention as well. This is what is supposed to happen on a renewal, as MHA 1983 s20(3) indicates that when the renewal report is provided to the managers, they shall inform the patient 'unless they discharge the patient' under section 23. In a pre-Human Rights Act (HRA) 1998 authority, *R v Managers of Warlingham Park Hospital ex p B*,[23] it was determined that this meant that the furnishing of the report provided the authority to detain. However, it has been determined that the managers retain a discretion to discharge: see *R v Riverside Mental Health Trust ex p Huzzey*.[24] This again only makes sense if there is an obligation on the managers not only to check whether the documentation stating that the detention should be renewed but also to consider the merits of detention.

2.31 The obligation of the managers to carry out a review is consistent with the approach endorsed as arising under ECHR article 5(1)(e). As has been discussed in chapter 1, the requirements of the lawfulness of detention on the basis of 'unsound mind' include objective medical expertise of the existence and persistence of a mental disorder of a kind or degree warranting confinement. But there is another part of the *Winterwerp* judgment to note:[25] at paragraph 39 of the judgment, it is noted that these matters have to be established 'before the competent national authority'. While this may be contrasted with the requirement of a court review that is necessary for the purposes of article 5(4), such that the detention process does not have to be carried out by a court, the phrase does suggest that the relevant professionals who have formed the view that the criteria for detention are made out are required to justify their views in front of an independent body. This can be satisfied if the managers carry out a proper review of the merits of detention when it is put in place or renewed. This will cover

23 (1994) 22 BMLR 1.
24 (1998) 43 BMLR 167.
25 (1979) 2 EHRR 387.

both patients who actively seek to challenge their detention but also those who do not make an application to the managers.

2.32 The second method by which a review is secured even if the patient does not request it also involves the managers. They are under a statutory duty to make sure that the ongoing detention of patients is referred to the tribunal if the patient does not make an application. This arises under MHA 1983 s68: this applies if the patient has been detained for six months (whether the detention started under section 2 or section 3) without making an application to a tribunal; or, if the patient is a section 3 patient whose detention has been renewed under section 20, three years has passed since the last review by a tribunal. This latter provision is subject to an exception in the case of patients under 18: in such a case, the time limit is 12 months.

2.33 Finally, it is possible for the Secretary of State for Health to refer the case of a Part II patient to the tribunal at any time: see MHA 1983 s67.

Comparison between Mental Health Act 1983 s3 and Part III

Criteria for detention

2.34 It has already been noted that MHA 1983 Part II and Part III can co-exist.[26] In addition, there is a significant overlap between the criteria for detention for treatment under section 3 and those that arise under Part III of the Act. The common requirements are the existence of mental disorder, that it be of a nature or degree that makes detention in hospital appropriate, and that there be appropriate treatment available.[27]

2.35 What is different is that a prerequisite for a section 3 order is that it be necessary for the protection of the patient or others that such treatment be given, which does not arise under Part III. Rather than this necessity test, section 36 (remand for treatment) requires the court to form the view that a remand to a hospital is preferable to a remand in custody; for section 37, the court has to be satisfied that it is the most suitable method of disposing of the case; an interim hospital order under section 38 requires the court to wish to investigate

26 See chapter 1 and the case of *R v North West London Mental Health NHS Trust ex p Stewart* [1998] QB 628.

27 MHA 1983 s35, which does not authorise admission for treatment, but is limited to preparation of a medical report, does not have these criteria; but a section 2 or 3 order may be put in place at the same time.

making a section 37 order; and an order under section 45A is predicated on a decision to reject the making of an order under section 37. For the Part III orders made by the Secretary of State, namely transfers under sections 47 and 48, the necessity test is replaced by the need to conclude that it is 'expedient in the public interest' to carry out the transfer. Whether this different language makes a difference in practice is discussed below: see para 2.68.

Procedural requirements

2.36 The procedural requirements under MHA 1983 Part III are also similar to those arising under Part II in that two doctors are required to give evidence to support the finding that the medical criteria are made out. While there are no specific time limits as between the date of the examination and the admission, as is the case in relation to civil admissions, that is because the court making the order must be satisfied as to the existence of the criteria on the merits at the time it makes the order and so there is no need for specific time limits to ensure that the evidence is up to date, and there are requirements that a bed be available within a set time, namely seven days under sections 35 and 36, and 28 days under sections 37, 38 and 45A.[28]

2.37 There are also time limits on the effect of an order made under Part III, as there are in relation to civil orders. Under sections 35 and 36, the limit is 12 weeks; under section 38, it is 12 weeks, but then renewable for 28 days at a time up to a maximum of 12 months. If the order is a hospital order under section 37, it takes effect as if a section 3 order had been put in place and so the detention last for six months unless a restriction order under section 41 is added (one of the effects of such an order being that the duration provisions do not apply).

2.38 However, there are two significant procedural differences as between those arising under the civil and criminal parts of the MHA 1983. In the first place, there is no need for any consultation with the nearest relative. In addition, the patient does not necessarily have the same access to a tribunal: this turns on the section in place. Those who remain under the direct jurisdiction of the criminal courts (that is, those under sections 35, 36 and 38) do not have access to a tribunal, but are able to raise their ongoing detention with the court. For

28 See also chapters 8 and 20 and the discussion of the transfer direction under MHA 1983 ss47 and 48: there is no specific time limit, but case-law has made clear that up-to-date evidence is required. Transfer directions under sections 47 and 48 are valid only for 14 days.

remand prisoners in hospital after being transferred under section 48, there is a right to apply to a tribunal immediately; and so they have rights similar to those detained under section 3.[29] The same is the case for serving prisoners transferred under section 47.

2.39 Those made subject to a hospital order under section 37 do not have access to a tribunal unless the order is renewed under section 20 after the initial six-month period (or, if a restriction order is in place, after six months have elapsed). Despite the latter restriction, the RC or the hospital managers may exercise their administrative powers of release under section 23 (in the case of a restricted patient, this is possible with the consent of the Secretary of State, by reason of section 41(3)(c), though the minister also has a power of discharge under section 42); in other words, there is an administrative power to discharge but the normal judicial body involved in the regulation of the detention of people with mental disorder is excluded for six months. Since there has to be some mechanism to determine whether the mental disorder requires detention in order to comply with ECHR article 5(1)(e), it would not be permissible to have no mechanism for release from detention. It is perhaps incongruous that this is not carried out by a judicial body, but the Convention need for a judicial review of detention arises under article 5(4), and the lack of access to a court for six months after a court-imposed detention order does not seem to breach the ECHR. The different treatment of those in hospital under sections 47 and 48 is because their placement in hospital is an administrative decision not a court decision.

Detention for treatment – the 'nature or degree', 'appropriate for detention' and 'medical treatment' criteria

2.40 As noted, aside from the absence of the necessity test, the main civil and criminal powers involving detention for treatment have a significant degree of overlap. In particular, the existence of a mental disorder, or rather of an adequate medical opinion as to its existence, is a prerequisite to the use of the powers. In addition, it must be of a nature or degree that makes detention for medical treatment appropriate. These elements must all be founded on the medical evidence. The next sections will consider the criteria on the merits in more detail.

29 MHA 1983 s69 provides this right.

2.41 The mental disorder must be 'of a nature or degree which makes it appropriate for him to be detained in hospital for medical treatment' to allow an order to be made under MHA 1983 s37; in section 3, this test is split into two components, namely that the mental disorder is 'of a nature or degree which makes it appropriate for him to receive medical treatment in a hospital' and 'it cannot be provided unless he is detained'. The language of these two tests involves several questions: What is meant by 'nature or degree'? What is the test of 'appropriateness' of detention? And what amounts to 'medical treatment'?

Medical treatment

2.42 Two statutory points are central to an understanding of what amounts to medical treatment. First, MHA 1983 s145(1) contains the following definition of what amounts to 'medical treatment': it 'includes nursing, psychological intervention and specialist mental health habilitation, rehabilitation and care'. This is supplemented by section 145(4), which provides that: 'Any reference in this Act to medical treatment, in relation to mental disorder, shall be construed as a reference to medical treatment the purpose of which is to alleviate, or prevent a worsening of, the disorder or one or more of its symptoms or manifestations.'

2.43 Both relevant parts of section 145 are the result of the MHA 2007. The original definition in section 145(1) of the 1983 Act was that medical treatment 'includes nursing, and also includes care, habilitation and rehabilitation under medical supervision'. The revised language[30] is probably not much of a change, in the sense that as the definition originally used was not exclusive, the additional features mentioned could have been interpreted in. The new language makes it clear that what is medical includes what comes from the field of psychology, not just psychiatry. Examples of what are covered, given by the Explanatory Notes to the MHA 2007, are 'cognitive therapy, behaviour therapy and counselling'.[31]

2.44 The further amendment was that section 145(4) was added.[32] The importance of this language becomes evident when one considers what was present in the unamended MHA 1983, which was that in relation to two of the categories of mental disorder – mental

30 Introduced by MHA 2007 s7(1).

31 MHA 2007 Explanatory Notes para 39.

32 Introduced by MHA 2007 s7(2).

impairment and psychopathic personality disorder – detention was only possible if the disorder met the requirement of 'treatability'. The language of sections 3 and 37 was that detention was possible only if the treatment for which the patient was to be detained 'was likely to alleviate or prevent a deterioration of his condition'. In other words, stopping things getting worse was sufficient. Case-law made it clear that the test was met by action that dealt with the symptoms or manifestations of the disorder without having an impact on the underlying disorder. So, in *B v Croydon Health Authority*,[33] the Court of Appeal considered the question of whether feeding via a naso-gastric tube of a woman whose psychopathic disorder included compulsive self-harming and who refused to eat amounted to 'medical treatment' for the consent to treatment provisions of MHA 1983 s63 and so could be imposed without consent. The court held that the language covered treatment given to alleviate the symptoms of the disorder as well as treatment designed to remedy its underlying cause. In *Reid v Secretary of State for Scotland*,[34] Lord Hope commented that, when considered in the context of disorders to which the treatability test applied, medical treatment clearly covered treatment aimed to alleviate or to prevent a deterioration of the mental disorder, but extended to 'treatment which alleviates or prevents a deterioration of the symptoms of the mental disorder, not the disorder itself which gives rise to them'.[35]

2.45 There were also judicial comments to the effect that consideration of treatability required a long-term approach. In *R v Canons Park Tribunal ex p A*,[36] Roch LJ noted that not only would the test be met by treatment that, while unlikely to alleviate the patient's condition, was likely to prevent a deterioration; but that immediate alleviation or prevention of a deterioration in the patient's condition was not needed, provided that such alleviation or stabilisation was likely to occur in due course, including from such longer-term improvements as increasing the patient's insight or motivation to cooperation with treatment. Indeed, it was possible for there to be an interim

33 [1995] Fam 133.

34 [1999] 2 AC 512.

35 [1999] 2 AC 512 p531. See also Lord Hutton at p551.

36 [1995] QB 60 at 81. The holding in this case – that treatability did not have to be considered by the tribunal considering release – was effectively overruled by *Reid*. (Roch LJ dissented, holding that it had to be considered, which was the conclusion in *Reid*.) Comments made in relation to treatability remained valid. See also *R (Wheldon) v Rampton Hospital Authority* [2001] EWHC Admin 134, [2001] MHLR 19 for an example of a long-term approach.

deterioration in the patient's condition (for example, as a result of anger at being detained).

2.46 However, there were limited instances of patients being released because they were found not to be treatable.[37] The MHA 2007 repealed the treatability test in order to prevent arguments about the efficacy of treatment and to remove as a ground of release from detention the refusal of a patient to co-operate with treatment.[38] The proposal initially made was merely to have the appropriate treatment test, which is discussed below, but the provision adding section 145(4) of the MHA 1983 was introduced at a late stage of the passage of the Mental Health Bill to ensure that there was some requirement for a therapeutic benefit from treatment.

2.47 The language of section 145(4) of the MHA 1983 is different from the treatability test: in the first place, it applies to all mental disorders (whereas previously the old test applied only to psychopathic disorder and mental impairment); and second, it relates to the aim behind treatment, not the effect of it – so the question is not the actual efficacy of the treatment, but the potential and purpose. However, it has to be read in conjunction with the need for appropriate treatment to be available: this may have reintroduced arguments about the efficacy of treatment and whether the lack of co-operation from the patient means that detention is not proper. This is discussed below, starting at para 2.73.

Nature or degree

2.48 The nature or degree of the disorder relates to separate qualities: the degree is its current severity, but the nature of the disorder involves looking at the duration and prognosis relevant to a disorder, and so will consider the question of the potential for changes in the degree. In the Code of Practice, it is noted at paragraph 4.3 of the English Code, and paragraph 2.20 of the Welsh Code, that:

> Nature refers to the particular mental disorder from which the patient is suffering, its chronicity, its prognosis, and the patient's previous response to receiving treatment for the disorder. Degree refers to the current manifestation of the patient's disorder.

37 See *Noel Ruddle v Secretary of State for Scotland* [1999] MHLR 159 for a reported case.

38 See *Fourth Report of the Joint Committee on Human Rights in Session 2006–2007* (HL Paper 40, HC 288) paras 17–20 considering the Mental Health Bill: the committee felt that this proposal did not present any human rights concerns.

2.49 Confirmation that the reference to 'nature or degree' in the statute is meant to be disjunctive rather than involving an assessment of both the nature and current degree was given in *R v Mental Health Review Tribunal ex p Smith.*[39] Popplewell J accepted that it was open to a tribunal on the facts to decline to release a patient whose condition appeared to be stable if the nature of the condition was such that it was a chronic condition and subject to relapse.[40] Other case-law has confirmed that it can be proper to uphold detention on the basis of the nature of the disorder if the likelihood is that there will be a relapse out of hospital in a relatively short time-scale (such that the degree of the disorder would then justify detention). In *R v MHRT ex p Moyle,*[41] Latham J noted that detention on the basis of the nature of the disorder was unlikely to be appropriate '[i]f the Tribunal are not satisfied that there is no probability of relapse in the near future'. Recently, in *CM v Derbyshire Healthcare NHS Foundation Trust and Secretary of State for Justice,*[42] the Upper Tribunal has determined that a tribunal erred in upholding detention on the basis of the nature of the disorder when its factual findings were that the patient would become chaotic in about six months, disengage from treatment and relapse after two months. Upper Tribunal Judge Levenson held that this did not meet the test for detention on the basis of the nature of the disorder because it did not involve a relapse in the near future.

2.50 The important point for the advocate to note is that it will be a matter of expert evidence as to whether the symptoms of mental disorder represent a single incident (such as a drug-induced psychotic state) or a chronic and relapsing nature. The latter may mean that a defendant who at present appears to be well may nevertheless have a mental disorder of a nature that justifies being in hospital.

Appropriateness of detention

2.51 The next issue is the appropriateness of detention. This is linked to the nature and degree of the disorder and involves investigation of whether the treatment programme is such that it is appropriately provided by hospital treatment. MHA 1983 s37 sets a test of whether this nature or degree of the disorder makes it 'appropriate for him

39 4 August 2008, (1999) 47 BMLR 104, [1999] COD 148.

40 However, he noted that it was possible for a mental disorder to be such that the nature and degree were much the same.

41 [1999] MHLR 195 at para 36.

42 [2011] UKUT 129 (AAC), [2011] MHLR 153.

to be detained in a hospital for medical treatment'; this is similar in sections 36, 45A, 47 and 48. In section 3, the phraseology is different: the question posed here is whether it is 'appropriate for him to receive medical treatment in a hospital [which] cannot be provided unless he is detained': see section 3(2)(a) and (c). The latter phrase appears as part of the necessity test (discussed below), namely that the treatment that is appropriate is necessary for the protection of the patient or others and cannot be provided unless there is detention. The language for the imposition of the Part III orders collapses these two elements – appropriateness of treatment and the provision of it in detention – into the one test, namely the appropriateness of detention in hospital for the treatment.

2.52 In the civil setting, the fact that the treatment cannot be provided unless the patient is detained is a reference to the patient not being willing to receive treatment as a voluntary patient. If the patient is willing to be a voluntary patient, then detention is not required.[43] In a criminal setting, the danger of having this criterion would be that a defendant who was willing to be in hospital could not receive a hospital order if the language to the effect that treatment 'cannot be provided unless he is detained' was part of the test. It should be noted that when a section 37 order is renewed, as is the case with a section 3 admission, the test under section 20 mirrors that under section 3, though referring to the need for the patient to continue to be detained.

2.53 Another part of the test is that treatment has to be in a hospital. At first sight, the language used suggests that the condition must be such that in-patient treatment is the only possible method of providing assistance. However, section 17 of the statute allows detained patients to be released on leave.[44] Such a patient remains 'liable to detention' and so is subject to the statutory provisions relating to treatment without consent. In the context of challenges brought by patients arguing that their detention could not be renewed because the amount of leave they were receiving meant that they were effectively out-patients, the courts have imposed a much lower test for the validity of detention. This lower test is first described, and then its potential value to a defendant in criminal proceedings is addressed.

43 Different considerations may apply if the patient does not have the capacity to consent: in such a case, a detention order should be put in place to ensure that safeguards are available if the remainder of the test for detention is made out. This follows from *HL v UK* (2005) 40 EHRR 32, (2004) 7 CCLR 498, [2004] MHLR 236: see chapter 1.

44 See para 2.98 below.

2.54 The starting point is *R v Hallstrom ex p W, R v Gardner ex p L*:[45] in this case, McCullough J determined that a patient could not be admitted under section 3 and immediately released on section 17 leave so as to be in the community but subject to the consent to treatment provisions; nor could detention be renewed under section 20 for that purpose.

2.55 In *B v Barking, Havering and Brentwood Community Healthcare NHS Trust*,[46] an attempt was made to extend this proposition to a patient who spent five days a week out of hospital but returned for monitoring and testing of whether she was avoiding illicit drugs. The Court of Appeal upheld the ruling of McCullough J in *W* and *L* to the extent that there was a requirement for some in-patient treatment. They did correct a further part of his ruling: his view that words in section 20(4)(c) that treatment could not be provided 'unless he continues to be detained' meant that a patient who was on leave could not have his or her section renewed was overturned. McCullough J had taken this literally; the Court of Appeal held that there was a statutory drafting error and that it must have been the intention of Parliament to have covered patients who were liable to be detained. One can see the force of the judge's view, given that there ought to be a careful reading of any statutory provision that relates to a deprivation of liberty: it is perhaps unusual for the Court of Appeal to have rewritten a statutory provision rather than pointing out the possible error and leaving it to Parliament to correct any such error.

2.56 In addition, the Court of Appeal considered the meaning of the phrase 'treatment in hospital' that appears in MHA 1983 s20(4)(a) and also s3. Lord Woolf MR noted that if the facts revealed a treatment programme involving some in-patient and some out-patient treatment, the statutory test was made out if the situation was that:

> ... for the treatment as a whole to be successful there will often need to be an inpatient element to the treatment which means it is in fact 'appropriate for him to receive medical treatment in a hospital' and 'that it cannot be provided unless he continues to be detained'.

2.57 Lord Justice Thorpe expressed the same conclusion, expressly rejecting the contention for a narrow construction of section 20: he noted the width of the definition of medical treatment, which included the use of leave under section 17, and commented that the use of five days leave per week did not prevent the conclusion that her 'home base' was the hospital and the period of time in hospital remained

45 [1986] QB 1090.
46 [1999] 1 FLR 106.

'an essential part of the treatment package', such that her status was a 'detained patient enjoying generous weekly leaves of absence to put her possible rehabilitation to the test'.

2.58 This approach was taken a step further in *R (DR) v Mersey Care NHS Trust*,[47] which involved a patient whose leave under section 17 allowed her to sleep at her own home every night and required her merely to attend hospital for an occupational therapy session on a Friday and a ward round on a Monday; she received medication at home, but the evidence was that she would only accept medication because the treatment order was in place, failing which her condition would deteriorate rapidly. Her challenge to the renewal of her treatment order under section 20, which was based on the argument that there was no adequate level of in-patient treatment, was rejected by the High Court. Mr Justice Wilson commented that the distinction between in-patient and out-patient treatment was one that was too subtle to represent the law, noting at paragraph 29 that 'When I eat at a restaurant, I eat in a restaurant' and that 'There is no magic in a bed' given that there was limited scope for treatment at night in any event. He concluded that, as the patient in the *B v Barking* case had been receiving some in-patient treatment, it was natural that the Court of Appeal had made reference to in-patient treatment. But the proper question was whether a 'significant component of the plan for the claimant was for treatment in hospital',[48] in which context he referred to the wide definition of what amounted to medical treatment and the value of leave as a component of the treatment plan in light of its role in preserving links with the community and also of building up the relationship with the clinical team. On the facts, Wilson J held that the day of occupational therapy and the monitoring by way of attendance at the ward round met the 'significant component' test he had set out.

2.59 In *R (CS) v Mental Health Review Tribunal*,[49] the patient was required to attend a ward round once every four weeks and had a weekly session with a psychologist but otherwise lived outside hospital. The attendance at the ward round did include what was termed motivational interviewing that was designed to assist her move to outpatient treatment; and it was also her choice to receive her medication, which was delivered by way of a depot injection because of poor compliance with oral medication, in hospital because she did not

47 [2002] EWHC 1810 (Admin), [2002] MHLR 386.

48 [2002] EWHC 1810 (Admin), [2002] MHLR 386 para 30.

49 [2004] EWHC 2958 (Admin), [2004] MHLR 355.

want to receive it at home. A challenge was made to the tribunal decision to uphold her detention, in which the tribunal had commented that her likely non-compliance with medication and deterioration in the absence of the element of compulsion. This was dismissed by the High Court on the basis that there was a sufficient element of treatment in hospital to meet the requirements of the statutory provisions. Pitchford J used the phrase that the control exercised by the treating psychiatrist was 'gossamer thin',[50] but it was not so insignificant as to fail to meet the test of being hospital treatment.

2.60 At one level, this extended interpretation of the ambit of the statute, used to defeat claims by patients, can be viewed as an unfortunate method of extending the remit of the compulsory powers under the MHA 1983. These cases all occurred at a time when the statute did not allow compulsory treatment of those who were not in-patients – the CTO regime that was introduced by the MHA 2007 and which is described below. The introduction of that regime has included a specific requirement that clinicians consider using the CTO rather than leave lasting more than seven days,[51] and so it may be that a patient in the position of the patients in these cases would be under a CTO. However, the relevant statutory language as to the appropriateness of treatment in hospital remains in place.

2.61 The further question arising is whether use can be made of this extended interpretation of what amounts to hospital treatment in other contexts. There are two practical scenarios that might arise. In the first case, advocates who form the view that a judge may be persuaded to impose a hospital order and that such an order would be a better outcome for a defendant should remember that a defendant's condition does not have to be such as to require the defendant to be locked in hospital. This is because the law as interpreted in these cases gives a potentially wide scope for what amounts to treatment in hospital and what amounts to detention or liability to detention in a hospital, given that leave is both a treatment and something that maintains the status of the patient as someone who is liable to detention and so can be maintained under a hospital order. In addition, the court may benefit from an explanation of the possibility that the patient may be placed on a CTO.

2.62 The second practical point that may arise is where the judge indicates that he or she is not minded to impose a sentence such as a community order with a condition of out-patient treatment but is

50 [2004] EWHC 2958 (Admin), [2004] MHLR 355 para 46.
51 MHA 1983 s17(2A) and (2B), as introduced by MHA 2007 s33.

minded to impose a hospital order. It may be that in such a case, an explanation of what might be called the 'long leash' interpretation of the statutory provisions as to detention will persuade the judge that the community sentence may be similar in practice and so should be used. The practical difference is that a patient who is on leave (or on a CTO) with an underlying hospital order may be returned to hospital; but a patient who is subject to a community order with a treatment direction is someone who may be placed under the civil provisions of the MHA 1983 if that should be necessary.

Detention for treatment – the 'necessity' criterion

2.63 In a civil setting, once it has been determined that the patient has a mental disorder and that the nature or degree of that disorder makes hospital treatment appropriate, the next part of the statutory test is whether the treatment is necessary for the protection of the patient and others and it cannot be provided other than in detention. So, MHA 1983 s3(2)(c) requires, as does section 20(4)(c), that 'it is necessary for the health or safety of the patient or for the protection of other persons that he should receive such treatment and it cannot be provided unless he is detained under this section'.[52] The reference to 'such treatment' is to the treatment in hospital that is appropriate in light of the nature or degree of the disorder; the fact that the treatment cannot be provided unless the patient is detained is a reference to the patient not being willing to receive treatment as a voluntary patient.

2.64 It is clear that it is necessary to consider separately the necessity test as well as the appropriateness test: the latter may be met without the former being met. For example, in *R v London South and South West Region Mental Health Review Tribunal ex p Moyle*,[53] in quashing a tribunal decision, Latham J noted at paragraph 40 that:

> ... the Tribunal failed to deal adequately with the question of whether or not it was necessary for the health or safety of the patient or for the protection of other persons that he should receive hospital treatment. The Tribunal was obliged to consider this as a discrete question. The test of 'necessity' is different from the test of 'appropriateness'.

52 The only difference in the language of MHA 1983 s20 is that 'is detained' is replaced by 'continues to be detained'.

53 [1999] MHLR 195.

2.65 However, he added that, while it should not be assumed to be the case, the same facts might be a proper basis for findings both in relation to the appropriateness and necessity of detention.

2.66 The test of necessity is clearly a higher test than one of desirability.[54] What is said in paragraph 4.4 of the English Code of Practice is that:

> ... consideration must be given to whether there are alternative means of providing the care and treatment which the patient requires. This includes consideration of whether there might be other effective forms of care or treatment which the patient would be willing to accept, and of whether guardianship would be appropriate instead.[55]

2.67 In relation to those features of the health or safety of the patient that might make detention necessary, at paragraph 4.6 the Code gives various examples of the factors that can be taken into account in relation to the patient's health or safety, including the question of the deterioration of the condition without treatment and the patient's own ability to manage their disorder. The protection of others – which can relate to one person (see *R v North West London Mental Health NHS Trust ex p S*[56]), and can also relate to psychological harm (see Code of Practice para 4.8) – involves weighing the nature of the risk to other people, the likelihood of harm and the severity of that harm (see Code of Practice para 4.7), which also notes the need to take into account various features, including that it may be difficult to differentiate risk of harm to the patient and to others, and the capacity of carers to manage the risks, and whether other methods are available.

2.68 The necessity part of this test does not appear in MHA 1983 s37 or any other parts of the criminal provisions for detention (though it does apply to the renewal of a section 37 order under section 20). Rather, the Part III orders include various tests: it has to be preferable to a remand in custody for a section 36 remand for treatment, the most suitable disposal for a section 37 hospital order, and the test for transfers under sections 47 and 48 is expediency in the public interest.[57] But if the civil necessity test is met, then detention in

54 So in *Reid v Secretary of State for Scotland* [1999] 2 AC 512, HL, Lord Clyde at 540 made the obvious point that: 'The standard here is one of necessity, not desirability.'

55 At paragraph 2.27, the Welsh Code notes the importance of looking for effective alternative ways of providing support or treatment.

56 (1996) 39 BMLR 105.

57 An interim hospital order under MHA 1983 s38 is predicated on the court wishing to investigate making a section 37 order, and so it must include a preliminary view that a hospital order might be the most suitable; and an order

hospital would seem to be preferable, the most suitable response and expedient. In that way, the language of the criminal sections is able to incorporate the civil detention test. The alternative, after all, will be a prison remand, where the consent to treatment provisions will not apply (and so treatment will be problematic in the absence of consent) and where the facilities and staff expertise are unlikely to match those available to a hospital.

2.69 In this context, it is worth noting that the Secretary of State has a duty of care to ensure that prisoners are transferred under MHA 1983 s47 (that is, a duty to make use of the statutory power); so once there are reasonable grounds to suspect that a prisoner may need treatment in a psychiatric hospital, the appropriate steps have to be taken to arrange this. These propositions arise from *R (D) v Home Secretary and National Assembly for Wales*,[58] which related to a failure to secure a transfer from a young offender institution: on the facts, Stanley Burnton J found that there was no breach of the common law duty he outlined. He noted the possibility of a claim for damages for a breach of ECHR article 8 or, in an extreme case, of article 3.

2.70 While it will not be possible to impose a private law duty on courts to make use of their MHA 1983 Part III powers, the reasoning of Stanley Burnton J would sound out a public law duty on courts to act to secure an appropriate hospital placement if provided with evidence to the effect that hospital treatment might be required. Similarly, the HRA 1998 would apply to a court decision, such that it would be illegal by reason of HRA 1998 s6 not to take a decision that was required by a Convention argument. (There is nothing in the language of any of the statutory powers that suggests a compulsion to breach Convention rights and so would provide a defence under HRA 1998 s6(2).)

2.71 It may also be suggested that the language of the MHA 1983 Part III tests allow a person to be placed in hospital when the civil necessity test is not met; this would be because the language of it being preferable, the most suitable response or expedient suggests a lesser test. There are reasons to be cautious about this: there might be options such as release on bail to consider in relation to pre-trial powers (in which case detention cannot be seen to be necessary); and in relation to a hospital order sentence or post-sentence transfers, the effect of a transfer is to leave the patient in the situation of a section 3 patient,

under section 45A is predicated on a decision to reject the making of an order under section 37, and so it is not the most suitable disposal in light of the need to include an underlying prison sentence.

58 [2004] EWHC 2857 (Admin), [2005] MHLR 17.

to whom the necessity test applies. Having noted these reasons to be cautious, it can of course be said that Parliament could have used the necessity test and has not done so, which suggests that another test must be in place.

2.72 As to the potential problem with a necessity test in the criminal context being construed so as to prevent a Part III order in relation to a consenting patient, an order would be both necessary and would meet the test set in the criminal provisions in order to overcome the fact that the consent of the patient to being in hospital would not be an adequate reason for them not meeting their obligation to be in prison. In other words, the making of the order would be necessary in light of the alternative.

Detention for treatment – the 'appropriate treatment' criterion

The statutory language

2.73 The need for it to be appropriate for there to be detention in hospital for treatment has been discussed above. The word 'appropriate' appears in a further part of the statutory test for detention: added to the MHA 1983 by MHA 2007 s4 is a provision that detention for treatment, whether under MHA 1983 s3 or s37, or the renewal provisions of section 20,[59] can only be imposed if appropriate treatment is available for the patient. In other words, even if the nature or degree of the mental disorder is such as to make detention for medical treatment in a hospital appropriate, and the necessity test is met (if applicable), the applicant for civil detention must indicate that 'appropriate medical treatment is available for him'. Similarly, the court can only impose a section 37 hospital order if it finds that there is such treatment.

2.74 The definition of 'appropriate medical treatment', even though it is relevant to various provisions, is not found in the general definition section of MHA 1983 s145, but is in the new section 3(4):[60]

59 It also appears in MHA 1983 s36, the Crown Court remand for treatment; the additional Crown Court powers under sections 45A and 51(6) discussed below; the Secretary of State's powers of transfer under sections 47 and 48; and the tribunal powers of discharge in section 72. Some of these changes are effected by MHA 2007 s4, some by s5.

60 Added by MHA 2007 s4(3).

> (4) In this Act, references to appropriate medical treatment, in relation to a person suffering from mental disorder, are references to medical treatment which is appropriate in his case, taking into account the nature and degree of the mental disorder and all other circumstances of his case.

Appropriateness of treatment in Mental Health Act 1983 Part IV

2.75 A parallel amendment to the MHA 1983 may throw light on the meaning of this 'appropriate treatment' test. One of the consequences of admission to hospital, which is discussed in more detail below, is that the question of treatment without consent is not regulated by the general common law, which applies in relation to physical conditions. Under this, the patient's consent is required (or there is an assault); and if the patient does not have the capacity to consent, treatment can be given if it is necessary and in the best interests of the patient.[61] If the patient is detained under the MHA 1983, treatment for mental disorder can be given on the direction of the treating clinician at the outset (subject to special rules for more invasive treatments); and if the treatment is medication, after three months the continuation of treatment depends on the patient's consent or, if the patient does not consent or is not capable of consenting, the approval of a second doctor: see MHA 1983 s58. This provision has been reworded by the MHA 2007, so that the second opinion appointed doctor, or SOAD, as he or she is known, assesses whether, despite the lack of consent or inability to consent, 'it is appropriate for the treatment to be given': MHA 1983 s58(3)(b).[62] Also added was MHA 1983 s64(3),[63] which reads:

> (3) For the purposes of this Part of this Act, it is appropriate for treatment to be given to a patient if the treatment is appropriate in his case, taking into account the nature and degree of the mental disorder from which he is suffering and all other circumstances of his case.

61 The starting point for this statement of approach is *Re F* [1990] 2 AC 1.

62 Added by MHA 2007 s6(2). Previously, the test applied by the SOAD was whether, despite the lack of consent by the patient or the inability of the patient to consent, it should be given when regard was had to the likelihood of the treatment alleviating or preventing a deterioration of the patient's condition: this is not so different from the obvious meaning of whether treatment is appropriate.

63 Added by MHA 2007 s6(3).

2.76 In short, the test to be applied by the doctor deciding whether a particular form of treatment should be given without consent is the same as the test to be applied in deciding whether a person should be detained in hospital for treatment. This did not used to be the case. MHA 1983 s58 as originally drafted required the SOAD to determine whether, having regard to the prospect of the treatment working, it should be given despite the lack of consent; and the test for the imposition or continuation of detention had no particular reference to the efficacy of treatment save in relation to the finding that psychopathic personality disorder or mental impairment was treatable.[64] Accordingly, under the previous language, responsibility for court review of questions of detention and treatment went to separate courts. In *R (B) v (1) Dr SS (2) Dr G (3) Secretary of State for the Health Department*,[65] one of the issues arising was the extent to which a Mental Health Review Tribunal (MHRT) could, in determining whether detention for treatment was appropriate, assess the treatment plan proposed for the patient. Lord Phillips CJ, giving the judgment of the Court of Appeal, noted at paragraph 65 that:

> Whilst the jurisdiction of MHRTs extends to the propriety of detention for treatment it does not extend to issues relating to the propriety of treatment pursuant to section 58.

2.77 He did go on to make the point that the tribunal was a specialist body equipped to deal with medical questions, unlike the Administrative Court, to which judicial reviews of the lawfulness of decisions under MHA 1983 s58 would come. In that circumstance, the Court of Appeal held that if the real question to be addressed was whether there was no need for treatment because the patient was not in fact mentally disordered,[66] such that the patient did not need to be in hospital, any judicial review challenge to the decision to authorise medication should be adjourned until a tribunal had considered whether the patient should be in hospital at all.[67]

2.78 There is still separate regulation in the statutory regime of detention for treatment and treatment imposed, but detention for treatment is only possible if appropriate treatment is available: this suggests that the previous dichotomy is open to question because

64 See the discussion at paras 2.44–2.47 above.

65 [2005] EWCA Civ 28, [2006] MHLR 131.

66 The same would apply to questions of treatability, or indeed whether the mental disorder was of the relevant nature or degree as to make detention appropriate.

67 [2005] EWCA Civ 28, [2006] MHLR 131 para 66.

the tribunal, as part of its role of ensuring that detention should only be continued if appropriate treatment is available,[68] has to look at the same test as the SOAD. The same would apply to whoever causes the detention in the first place, including the criminal court imposing a hospital order.

Appropriateness wider than clinical appropriateness

2.79 As to what is meant by 'appropriate', it is to be noted that the legislation does not use the phrase 'clinically appropriate', which it could have done if the only question was whether the medical profession would support the treatment. Even though such a narrow interpretation would still allow the court to inquire into questions of the likely efficacy of treatment, perhaps balancing any value against questions of unpleasant side effects or issues of whether less invasive treatment was available,[69] the wider, natural meaning of appropriateness allows further issues to be investigated. It is to be noted that this criterion for detention is a matter that is separate from the question of whether it is appropriate to detain: a positive answer to the latter cannot be an answer to the former, given that the court is required to address the question of availability of appropriate treatment in the place to which the patient will be sent under the hospital order.

2.80 Guidance is given on the operation of the Mental Health Act in the Code of Practice issued under MHA 1983 s118 by the Secretary of State.[70] In the 2008 Code issued after the amendments were introduced by the MHA 2007, the test of appropriateness of treatment was described as involving account being taken of both the nature and degree of the disorder and all the circumstances of the patient 'including cultural, ethnic and religious considerations'.[71] Accordingly:

> The appropriate medical treatment test requires a judgement about whether an appropriate package of treatment for mental disorder is available for the individual in question. Where the appropriate medical treatment test forms part of the criteria for detention, the medical

68 See MHA 1983 s72(1)(b)(iia).

69 This is not the text for an examination of the questions of the propriety of the biological model of psychiatry, pursuant to which much treatment involves medication designed to restore balances in the brain: suffice it to say, there are other schools of thought to the effect that our limited understanding of the brain prevents any conclusion that this theory is correct. See, for example, Joanna Moncrieff, *The myth of the chemical cure*, Palgrave Macmillan, 2008.

70 See chapter 1. A Welsh Code is issued by the Welsh Assembly.

71 Code of Practice para 6.8; the Welsh Code of Practice contains the same language at paragraph 4.7.

treatment in question is treatment for mental disorder in the hospital in which the patient is to be detained.[72]

2.81 So, the question of whether appropriate treatment is available must involve assessing whether the proposed treatment is actually provided at the hospital in which the person will be detained.[73] This may be important if the needs of the patient are for specialist intervention which is available only in certain hospitals. But a judgment must also be made about whether what is proposed is appropriate for the patient. The breadth of the questions that might have to be investigated is set out at paragraphs 6.10 and 6.11 of the English Code (paragraphs 4.9 and 4.10 of the Welsh Code):

> 6.10. The test requires a judgement about whether, when looked at in the round, appropriate medical treatment is available to the patient, given:
>
> - the nature and degree of the patient's mental disorder; and
> - all the other circumstances of the patient's case.
>
> In other words, both the clinical appropriateness of the treatment and its appropriateness more generally must be considered.
>
> 6.11. The other circumstances of a patient's case might include factors such as:
>
> - the patient's physical health – how this might impact on the effectiveness of the available medical treatment for the patient's mental disorder and the impact that the treatment might have in return;
> - any physical disabilities the patient has;
> - the patient's culture and ethnicity;
> - the patient's age;
> - the patient's gender, gender identity and sexual orientation;
> - the location of the available treatment;
> - the implications of the treatment for the patient's family and social relationships, including their role as a parent;
> - its implications for the patient's education or work; and
> - the consequences for the patient, and other people, if the patient does not receive the treatment available. (For mentally disordered offenders about to be sentenced for an offence, the consequence will sometimes be a prison sentence.)

2.82 Paragraph 6.10 makes express reference to the point that something that is clinically appropriate might not meet the statutory test when account is taken of all the other relevant features, of which those listed in paragraph 6.11 are examples. Some of these are features

72 Code of Practice para 6.9; Welsh Code para 4.8.

73 Code of Practice para 6.13 provides that: 'Medical treatment must actually be available to the patient. It is not sufficient that appropriate treatment could theoretically be provided.' See Welsh Code para 4.12.

that are more clinical in their nature, such as the impact of physical health on the treatment for mental health, but others clearly allow wider questions to be raised about the proportionality of detention. So, it may be found that treatment is not appropriate because it is too disruptive to family relationships or deprives the defendant of the chances of education and work. This also allows the judgment about whether someone should be detained to be informed by matters such as the impact of the stigma of being 'sectioned' and the loss of autonomy this entails.

Appropriateness and the co-operation of the patient

2.83 Another question that might arise is whether the treatment is appropriate in the light of the attitude of the defendant towards the treatment (or a part of the package). This might be of real importance if the treatment programme is a psychological therapy of the sort that requires a patient's co-operation and participation. The English Code of Practice makes the point that the defendant's willingness to engage can be relevant but not determinative: a clinically suitable treatment that will only be provided on the basis of engagement 'can potentially remain appropriate and available'.[74] The language of this 'potentially' meeting the appropriate treatment test suggests that there may be circumstances in which the lack of any willingness to engage would mean that the appropriate treatment test is not in fact met. In particular, paragraph 6.17 of the English Code, and paragraph 4.16 of the Welsh Code, note that: 'Simply detaining someone – even in a hospital – does not constitute medical treatment.'

2.84 Chapter 35 of the English Code of Practice gives further guidance on questions of particular relevance to people with a personality disorder. It notes that, while there must be a clinical judgment made about the individual circumstances of the patient, there are various themes relevant. In the first place, it is noted that there is generally a need for 'relatively intense and long term, structured and coherent' treatment approaches,[75] which patients may not engage in for some time for reasons of lack of motivation;[76] but that securing engagement is important because '[s]ustainable long-term change is more likely to be achieved with the voluntary engagement of the patient'.[77] It is

74 Code of Practice para 6.19; Welsh Code para 4.17.
75 Code of Practice para 35.10.
76 Code of Practice para 35.11.
77 Code of Practice para 35.10.

noted that the usual treatment process is psycho-social,[78] reflecting the fact that personality disorders are formed as a result of psychological deficits caused by problems in a person's social development. However, it is also noted that even if the patient is not engaged in such a programme, he or she may require other treatments, including nurse and specialist care, to manage the risks posed, which may count as appropriate medical treatment.[79]

2.85 The long-term nature of the process may mean that treatment will have to continue in a community setting. Paragraph 35.13 of the Code notes that the methods of securing such a continuation of treatment may involve the use of guardianship (which arises under MHA 1983 s7), a CTO (under section 17A), or a conditional discharge in the case of a restricted patient (which may be imposed by a tribunal under section 73 or by the Secretary of State under section 42). As for the criteria for determining whether it is safe to deliver treatment in the community, it is suggested that account be taken of various factors, including the nature of the treatment process and the level of support it requires.[80]

2.86 As has been noted at para 2.46 above, one the reasons behind the removal of the treatability test in relation to psychopathic disorder and its replacement by the appropriate treatment test was that it would stop arguments about the efficacy of treatment if the patient refused to cooperate. However, in the light of the need for treatment to have the purpose of working and for appropriate treatment to be available, it is not entirely clear that the legislation has achieved its aims. In particular, there have been challenges to decisions to uphold detention by patients who have argued that their lack of co-operation meant that they were merely being detained because there was no prospect of them ever cooperating with treatment. This argument failed on the facts in one case, where it had been found that there was more than containment, though the Upper Tribunal judge accepted the proposition that mere containment was not the function of the hospital system: see *MD v Nottinghamshire Health Care NHS Trust*.[81]

2.87 In a subsequent case, the same judge, Upper Tribunal Judge Jacobs, noted the importance of the tribunal giving an individualised assessment of the treatment available for a personality-disordered patient and the patient's willingness to engage or resistance to

78 Code of Practice para 35.12.

79 Code of Practice para 35.11.

80 Code of Practice para 35.14.

81 [2010] UKUT 59 (AAC), [2010] MHLR 93.

engagement. In *DL-H v Devon Partnership NHS Trust and Secretary of State for Justice*,[82] the challenge was to the adequacy of the reasons of the tribunal, which had noted that treatment was available with which it hoped the patient would begin to engage. This was held not to be sufficient because it was necessary for a tribunal to assess the treatment available for the particular personality-disordered patient and his or her willingness or resistance to participate in treatment. The questions that had to be addressed were the treatment that was available, the benefit it might have for the patient and whether the patient was truly resistant to engagement. The problem on the facts, which led to the decision being quashed and remitted for re-hearing, was that there was evidence of the patient's level of hostility to nursing staff being such that they did not seek to engage with him: the result of this was that it might be the case that there was no prospect of him engaging and so the tribunal had not given adequate reasons as to why there was something that amounted to appropriate treatment.

Limitations on the breadth of the appropriateness question

2.88 Having noted the breadth of what can be considered under the question of the appropriate treatment test, it is to be noted that the decision-maker does not have to form a view as to what the treatment package should be in order to secure the best outcome for the patient. This is the point made in the Code of Practice:[83]

> Treatment need not be *the most appropriate* medical treatment that could ideally be made available. Nor does it need to address *every* aspect of the person's disorder. But the treatment available at any time must be *an appropriate response to the patient's condition and situation*. (Emphasis added.)

2.89 In other words, something that amounts to a suitable response will meet the test even if there might be arguments to the effect that there is a better treatment or a better package of treatment. One question that might arise in this context is that of the proper diagnosis of the patient, since although there are often situations in psychiatry when a particular medication represents a suitable response to a variety of conditions, there might well be more contentious circumstances in

82 [2010] UKUT 102 (AAC), [2010] MHLR 162.

83 Code of Practice para 6.12; Welsh Code para 4.11.

which there is a consensus that a patient has some form of mental disorder but where the particular form of disorder has to be determined in order to make a proper judgement as to what is the appropriate treatment.

2.90 An additional limitation on the impact of the appropriate treatment requirement relates to the time period that has to be considered by the decision-maker: the current position of the patient has to be considered, not what is likely to happen in the future. (That is a task that will fall to those involved in justifying detention on an ongoing basis.) This point is made in the Code of Practice, which states that:

> People called on to make a judgement about whether the appropriate medical treatment test is met do not have to be satisfied that appropriate treatment will be available for the whole course of the patient's detention ... What is appropriate may change over time, as the patient's condition changes or clinicians obtain a greater understanding of the patient's case. But they must satisfy themselves that appropriate medical treatment is available for the time being, given the patient's condition and circumstances as they are currently understood.[84]

Appropriateness and proportionality of detention

2.91 As a matter of ECHR case-law, the proportionality of detention is central to its lawfulness: see, for example, *Litwa v Poland*[85] and *HL v UK*.[86] It has been commented that the test for detention set out in the MHA 1983 provides a regime that ensures that detention is permitted only when it is proportionate, and so there is no need for separate consideration of this issue of proportionality: see *R (CS) v Mental Health Review Tribunal*,[87] in which Pitchford J noted that '[a]rticle 5 protects against arbitrary detention: it does not incorporate any additional requirement of proportionality'.[88] This was because the statutory test did not allow for arbitrary detention.[89] Whether or not this was correct (it being noted that *Litwa* is not cited in *CS*),

84 Code of Practice para 6.20; Welsh Code para 4.18.

85 App No 26629/95, [2000] MHLR 226, (2001) 33 EHRR 1267.

86 App No 45508/99, (2005) 40 EHRR 32, [2004] MHLR 236.

87 [2004] EWHC 2958 (Admin), [2004] MHLR 355 at paras 51–52. See also *DL-H v Devon Partnership NHS Trust and Secretary of State for Justice* [2010] UKUT 102 (AAC), [2010] MHLR 162 at para 27.

88 [2004] EWHC 2958 (Admin), [2004] MHLR 355 para 51.

89 [2004] EWHC 2958 (Admin), [2004] MHLR 355 para 52. That in turn meant that there was no need for a tribunal, which has an overriding discretion as to discharge as well as a duty to discharge if the criteria for detention were not made out, to conduct a proportionality review after considering the statutory test.

the inclusion of the 'appropriate treatment' test means that issues relevant to the question of whether detention for treatment is a proportionate response is clearly now part of the statutory regime by virtue of the factors that can be taken into account under the appropriate treatment test by the relevant decision-makers when deciding whether to impose or continue detention.

Detention for treatment – the place of discretion

2.92 Does it follow from the existence of the criteria for detention that it will be put in place? The statutory regime contains an element of discretion. This arises in relation to a section 37 hospital order by reason of the need for the court to find that the disposal be the most suitable outcome in the case. In relation to a section 2 or 3 application, the statutory language indicates that an application to detain *may* be made if the criteria are made out. Neither section provides that the application must be made if the criteria are made out. MHA 1983 s13, which is headed 'Duty of approved mental health professionals to make applications for admission or guardianship', provides a duty to assess if the local social services authority 'have reason to think that an application for admission to hospital or a guardianship application may need to be made' in relation to a person. In addition, if the assessment leads the AMHP to form the view that the application ought to be made and that it is 'necessary or proper' for the application to be made by the AMHP as opposed to it being made by the nearest relative, then there is a duty to make the application. In such a case, there will have to be a choice made as to which application to make. But there remains a discretion arising from the question of whether an application 'ought' to proceed, given that the statute could have been phrased as a duty to make an application on a finding that the criteria for detention were made out.

2.93 There may also be a question of whether a common law duty of negligence is in play if a patient is found to pose a risk to self or to others; alternatively, there may be arguments under the HRA 1998 in the light of obligations that might arise to protect the life of the patient or others. In *Savage v South Essex Partnership NHS Foundation Trust*,[90] the House of Lords held that ECHR article 2 imposes an 'operational' obligation on health authorities and staff if they know or ought to know that a particular patient presents a 'real

90 [2008] UKHL 74, [2009] 1 AC 681, (2009) 12 CCLR 125, [2009] MHLR 41.

and immediate' risk of suicide to take such steps as are reasonable to prevent the suicide. The House of Lords applied *Osman v UK*[91] and *Keenan v UK*[92] in reaching this conclusion: the former related to a risk posed by an individual to others, the latter was a self-harm situation, and so this principle will cover the situations applicable to an assessment carried out by an AMHP. When the trial judge came to apply this test to the facts, he noted that comments in the House of Lords indicated that this was a higher test than a negligence standard, but he found the higher test to be met.[93] It is worth commenting that the cause of action in play in *Savage* was of breach of the HRA 1998 and ECHR article 2 (the right to life) because the claim was brought by the daughter of the deceased rather than her husband: the daughter had no dependency and was not the next of kin able to represent the estate of her mother and so could not phrase the claim in common law negligence. But the latter cause of action would be available to an appropriate claimant.[94]

2.94 *Savage* related to a patient who was detained in hospital: in *Rabone and Rabone v Pennine Care NHS Trust*,[95] it was determined by the Supreme Court that the same approach applied to a voluntary patient if the risk posed was the same. There may be some limitations on common law negligence claims, as shown in the case of *Clunis v Camden and Islington HA*,[96] where the Court of Appeal held that the public law duty to provide after-care under MHA 1983 s117 was not something for which the relevant psychiatrist owed a common law duty of care such that he or she could be sued for damage caused by the non-provision of after-care. The court left open the question of whether there was a duty of care in relation to certifying fitness to be detained.[97]

91 [2000] Inquest LR 101.

92 [2001] Inquest LR 8, [2001] Prison LR 180.

93 [2010] EWHC 865 (QB), [2010] MHLR 311. He found that the deceased had not been supervised with adequate frequency.

94 On the facts, that would have been the husband of the deceased, who did not wish to take action. See, as an example, *Dunn v South Tyneside Health Care NHS Trust* [2003] EWCA Civ 878, [2004] MHLR 74, which related to a patient who absconded, attempted suicide and suffered brain damage as a result. Her claim was phrased in negligence, though it was unsuccessful on the facts.

95 [2012] UKSC 2, (2012) 15 CCLR 13.

96 [1998] QB 978.

97 [1998] QB 978 p993B. See also *Palmer v Tees Health Authority* [1999] MHLR 106, in which it was held that there was no duty of care to a third party affected by a patient who was not detained when arguably he should have been to contain the danger he posed.

2.95 One particular situation in which the question of the discretion might arise is if the patient has recently been released from detention by a tribunal, given that the relevant professionals involved in placing a patient under an admission order might well disagree with the decision of the tribunal. This was the factual scenario in *R (Von Brandenburg) v (1) East London and the City Mental Health NHS Trust and (2) Snazell.*[98] The House of Lords had to consider the propriety of the proposition established in *R v Managers of South Western Hospital ex p M,*[99] that the professionals had to exercise their own judgment and so could not be bound by the decision of the tribunal. The House of Lords determined that the rule of law meant that effect had to be given to court decisions, such that it would not be lawful for an application to detain to be made in the face of a tribunal decision to discharge unless the view was formed that there was information not known to the tribunal that might have caused it to reach a different decision. Such material could be a change in the patient's condition, the reneging on a promise to co-operate (for example, declining to take medication, which was the factual situation in the case, so leading to a relapse), or the discovery of fresh information relevant to the patient's condition that was not in front of the tribunal (for example, a recent attempt at suicide that had not come to light before the hearing). Lord Bingham, speaking for the House, made clear that these were just examples, and that there could be other situations in which the professionals could detain a recently-released patient;[100] moreover, the duty could only arise if the social worker making the application[101] knew about the tribunal decision, there being no duty of enquiry.[102]

The consequences of being admitted to hospital

Detention

2.96 A duly completed application for admission provides authority to detain: see MHA 1983 s6(1) in relation to civil applications; there

98 [2003] UKHL 58, [2004] 2 AC 280, [2004] MHLR 44.

99 [1993] QB 683.

100 [2003] UKHL 58, [2004] 2 AC 280, [2004] MHLR 44 para 10.

101 The law at the time required an approved social worker to make the application rather than an AMHP, who will usually be a social worker but need not be. This was a change introduced by the MHA 2007.

102 [2003] UKHL 58, [2004] 2 AC 280, [2004] MHLR 44 para 11.

is a consequent right to convey to the hospital named in the application form. Similarly, there are rights to convey and detain that are described in the relevant chapters relating to the powers arising under the criminal powers of the Act. The detention is carried out by the managers of the relevant hospital: MHA 1983 s6(2).[103] They are able to rely on an application which 'appears to be duly made': MHA 1983 s6(3). If the form is not in fact duly made, the High Court may grant habeas corpus to secure the release of the patient – for example, if the form asserts that there has been the consultation with the nearest relative mandated by MHA 1983 s11(4), but there has not been such consultation.[104]

2.97 The authority to detain is in the hospital named on the application form. It is now common for a single hospital to comprise different wards or units, which may be on different sites. It is also possible that the needs of the patient may change over time – whether for reasons of needing a different level of security, specialist treatment, or to be closer to family, or many other legitimate reasons – such that he or she would better be placed in a different hospital. Transfers between different hospitals are possible under MHA 1983 s19 and regulations made thereunder; if the patient has been sent to hospital under a hospital order together with a restriction order,[105] transfer requires the consent of the Secretary of State (whose decisions are taken by the Mental Health Unit of the Ministry of Justice).[106] Transfers may also be made as between a state of detention and being under guardianship.

2.98 Detained patients may be granted leave to be absent from hospital by the clinician in charge of treatment, the responsible clinician (RC). The power to grant this arises under MHA 1983 s17: leave may be subject to conditions, and may be for a specific period or may

103 See chapter 1 for a discussion of who the managers are.

104 See *Re S-C* [1996] QB 599, and *In re M* [1999] MHLR 154: the latter led to a claim for damages, the Court of Appeal holding that while the hospital managers could not be sued in the light of MHA 1983 s6(3), the local authority as the employer of the AMHP who made the application that was not duly completed could be sued for causing what was an improper detention, which might sound in the common law tort of false imprisonment or a breach of the HRA 1998 and ECHR article 5: see *R (TTM) v LB Hackney* [2011] EWCA Civ 4, [2011] MHLR 171. The Court of Appeal in the latter case also held that the requirement in MHA 1983 s139 for proof of negligence before an action could be brought in relation to the use of powers under the MHA 1983 was to be interpreted to cover action that led to detention that was not in accordance with the law.

105 See chapter 18.

106 MHA 1983 s41(3)(c).

indefinite.[107] The same power exists in relation to a patient who has been sent to hospital by the criminal courts under a hospital order. If the patient has been made subject to a restriction order as well, leave requires the consent of the Secretary of State. Leave may be revoked by the RC if it appears to be 'necessary so to do in the interests of the patient's health or safety or for the protection of other persons'. If the patient is a restricted patient, leave may also be revoked by the Secretary of State: see MHA 1983 s41(3)(c). Section 41(4) indicates that the power of recall may be exercised by the Secretary of State at any time. Patients on leave remain 'liable to detention', which is important for issues such as treatment without consent, discussed below. Those who do not return to hospital once leave has come to an end or has been revoked may be arrested under section 18: this is discussed in chapter 3.

Treatment without consent

2.99 The separate fundamental right to autonomy is engaged in relation to questions of treatment: the standard principle is that people are able to make their own decisions as to treatment, including the right to chose not to accept professional advice. This does not apply if the patient is without the capacity to make a decision, in which case the general common law rule was that decisions could be taken on the basis of the best interests of the patient; this is now regulated by the Mental Capacity Act (MCA) 2005, under section 3 of which a lack of capacity is defined as an inability:

(a) to understand the information relevant to the decision,
(b) to retain that information,
(c) to use or weigh that information as part of the process of making the decision, or
(d) to communicate his decision (whether by talking, using sign language or any other means).

The best interests principle is codified in MCA 2005 s4. There is also the provision made in sections 24 and following for advance decisions to refuse treatment, namely a decision made when the person has capacity as to what should happen after he or she has lost capacity.

2.100 However, MCA 2005 s28 provides that treatment decisions in relation to mental disorder that are regulated by the MHA 1983 remain governed by that Act. The MHA 1983 introduced a separate regime

107 MHA 1983 s17(2).

for the imposition of treatment without consent: under the predecessor statute, the MHA 1959, there was no such provision and so the question of forcing treatment was a matter for implication. Part IV of the MHA 1983 provides as follows:

a) Under section 63, treatment[108] by or under the direction of the RC can be given without the consent of the patient. But
b) Medication cannot be given for more than three months without consent or the approval of a second doctor (by reason of section 58).
c) Electro-convulsive therapy requires consent or, if the patient cannot consent, a second doctor has approved it (by reason of section 58A); but an advance directive can be made to indicate a refusal to accept ECT, or a decision can be made by the substitute decision-making process under the MCA 2005 not to consent to ECT.
d) Particularly invasive treatments – psychosurgery and the use of hormone implants to reduce the male sex drive – require consent and a second medical opinion and support from two non-medical reviewers (see section 57 and the Mental Health (Hospital, Guardianship and Treatment (England) Regulations 2008).[109]
e) These exceptions to the general right to treat set out in section 63 are all in turn subject to the emergency treatment provisions of section 62, which allows urgent treatment that is immediately necessary to save the patient's life, prevent a serious deterioration of the patient's condition, alleviate serious suffering or prevent violent or dangerous behaviour.

2.101 The role of the second doctor is clearly important: that doctor is appointed for the purpose, and is known as the second opinion appointed doctor or SOAD. However, the statute does not exclude the involvement of the courts. The decisions made in relation to treatment are public law decisions and so are amenable to challenge by way of judicial review. Initially this was on the standard judicial review test of irrationality, which was hard to meet: see *R v Dr Collins and Ashworth Hospital Authority ex p Brady*.[110] However, once the HRA

108 'Medical treatment' is widely defined in MHA 1983 s145 to include nursing, psychological treatments and rehabilitative work.

109 SI 2008 No 1184. Psychosurgery is listed as a particularly invasive treatment in MHA 1983 s57; the hormone treatment is added by the Regulations, made under section 57(1)(b); other treatments can be added by the Code of Practice issued under section 118. The equivalent regulation for Wales is contained in SI 2008 No 2439, made by the National Assembly for Wales.

110 [2000] MHLR 17, [2000] Lloyd's Rep Med 355.

1998 came into force, it became accepted that it was necessary for the court review to investigate not just the rationality of the decision but also whether it affected any fundamental rights and so whether it was legal. The first case to make this point was *R (Wilkinson) v The RMO, Broadmoor Hospital and others*,[111] in which a restricted patient in a high secure hospital objected to anti-psychotic medication, which was approved by a SOAD. He resisted the efforts to administer it, and was physically restrained on his bed to be injected, during which he suffered an angina attack. He commenced judicial review proceedings after obtaining an opinion from another psychiatrist that the medication was not necessary because he did not have a psychotic illness. The Court of Appeal, in ruling that the doctors involved in the decision-making would have to attend to give evidence during the judicial review proceedings, determined that various fundamental rights were engaged on the facts: his ECHR article 2 right to life (because of the risk of a fatal heart attack from resisting treatment); his article 3 right not to be subject to torture or inhuman or degrading treatment (arising from the process of the forced medication and, in light of the evidence he had obtained, the fact that it might not be justified); his article 8 right to privacy (which would be breached by the violation of his fundamental right to autonomy and bodily inviolability); and his article 6 right to a fair trial in relation to these rights. *Brady* was no longer to be followed.

2.102 In subsequent cases that have challenged the legality of the administration of medication to detained patients, despite the existence of the SOAD approval, it is fair to say that none of them has led to a decision taken under the MHA 1983 being overturned.[112] Indeed, there was something of a roll-back from the position in *Wilkinson* in that it was established that the process in front of the judicial review court need not involve oral evidence if the matter could be determined on

111 [2001] EWCA Civ 1545, [2002] 1 WLR 419, [2001] MHLR 224.

112 In *R (N) v M and others* [2003] 1 WLR 562, [2003] MHLR 157, the Court of Appeal gave further guidance, in upholding a High Court decision to grant doctors the right to impose medication (reported at [2003] MHLR 138) after a trial of the issue. See also *R (PS) v (1) Dr G (RMO) (2) Dr W (SOAD)* [2004] MHLR 1; *R (B) v (1) Dr Haddock (2) Dr Rigby (3) Dr Wood* [2005] MHLR 317 (High Court) and [2006] MHLR 306 (CA); *R (B) v (1) Dr SS (2) Dr AC (3) Secretary of State for the Health Department* [2005] MHLR 96; *R (B) v (1) Dr SS (2) Dr G (3) Secretary of State for the Health Department* [2005] MHLR 347 (High Court), [2006] 1 WLR 810, [2006] MHLR 131 (CA); *R (Taylor) v (1) Dr Haydn-Smith (2) Dr Gallimore* [2005] MHLR 327. For a Scottish example, see *Petition of WM* [2002] MHLR 367.

the basis of the papers;[113] it was also held that the existence of a contrary medical view did not prevent it being shown convincingly that the contested treatment was medically necessary, the standard necessary to avoid a breach of article 3,[114] and that a judge could properly give additional weight to the views of the treating clinician in the light of his or her level of involvement with the patient.[115] The only suggestion of an advance from *Wilkinson* in terms of protection of the autonomy rights of the patient was the finding at first instance in *R (N) v M and others*[116] that the need for a lawful process to be followed to meet the requirements of ECHR article 8 incorporated the best interests test applicable to decisions taken on behalf of people without capacity.

2.103 The fact that detention and treatment questions were separate was reflected in the fact that these arguments about treatment were in judicial review decisions before the High Court rather than in decisions about the propriety of detention taken by the Mental Health Review Tribunal. In *R (B) v (1) Dr SS (2) Dr G (3) Secretary of State for the Health Department*,[117] one of the issues arising was the extent to which a MHRT could, in determining whether detention for treatment was appropriate, assess the treatment plan proposed for the patient. Lord Phillips CJ, giving the judgment of the Court of Appeal, noted that:

> Whilst the jurisdiction of MHRTs extends to the propriety of detention for treatment it does not extend to issues relating to the propriety of treatment pursuant to section 58.[118]

2.104 He did go on to make the point that the tribunal was a specialist body equipped to deal with medical questions, unlike the High Court. This would mean that if the real question arising was whether there was no need for treatment because the patient did not need to be in hospital, any judicial review challenge to the decision to authorise medication should be adjourned until a tribunal had considered whether the patient should be in hospital at all.[119]

113 See *R (N) v M and others* [2003] 1 WLR 562, [2003] MHLR 157, *R (B) v (1) Dr Haddock (2) Dr Rigby (3) Dr Wood* and *R (Taylor) v (1) Dr Haydn-Smith (2) Dr Gallimore* [2005] MHLR 327.

114 *Herczegfalvy v Austria* (1992) 15 EHRR 437.

115 *R (N) v M and others* [2003] 1 WLR 562, [2003] MHLR 157.

116 *R (N) v M and others* [2003] MHLR 138: this was endorsed on appeal.

117 [2005] EWCA Civ 28, [2006] MHLR 131.

118 [2005] EWCA Civ 28, [2006] MHLR 131 para 65.

119 [2005] EWCA Civ 28, [2006] MHLR 131 para 66.

2.105 As has been discussed above under the appropriate treatment test, the statutory regime now provides that the availability of appropriate treatment is both part of the test for detention and the test that the SOAD must apply, which leads to the prospect of argument that the tribunal is now much better placed, and perhaps under a duty, to involve itself in an inquiry into what the treatment plan for the patient is and whether that meets the test of being appropriate.

Release on a community treatment order

2.106 The MHA 2007 added the regime of the CTO to the MHA 1983, in the form of sections 17A–17G. This allows a patient who has been detained under MHA 1983 s3 or s37 to be released, but subject to continuing supervision and with the power of the RC to recall the patient. The underlying detention is merely suspended. In many regards, a patient on a CTO is in the same position as a patient on section 17 leave, though he or she is not classified as 'liable to be detained' and so there are separate provisions regulating treatment without consent, to be found in part 4A of the MHA 1983: these effectively require consent, a lack of capacity, or an emergency.[120] However, the context of consent is the prospect of recall. The recall power may be exercised if the view is formed by the RC that treatment is required in hospital and in the absence of recall to hospital for that treatment there would be a risk of harm to the health or safety of the patient or other persons.[121] There is also a power of recall if the patient declines to attend for an assessment as to whether the criteria for the CTO to be renewed apply or whether the authority to provide treatment should continue.[122] While in the community, the patient is liable to recall; once recalled, the patient is liable to be detained.

2.107 A restricted patient, namely one detained under MHA 1983 s37 together with a restriction order under section 41, may not be placed on a CTO. However, he or she may be released from detention by the tribunal (under section 73) or the Secretary of State (under section 42): the discharge may be absolute or conditional, the latter meaning that the patient is liable to recall to hospital, this power being exercisable by the Secretary of State (under section 42(3)). As with a CTO patient, once the recall has been ordered, the patient becomes liable to detention. This means that there are powers of arrest, discussed in chapter 3.

120 See MHA 1983 ss64C (adults) and 64E (children under 16).

121 See MHA 1983 s17E(1).

122 See MHA 1983 s17E(2).

Release

2.108 The regime as to release engages both ECHR article 5(1)(e) and (4). In the first place, the *Winterwerp* criteria discussed in chapter 1 mean that detention is only lawful if the mental disorder continues to require detention: this implies a review process. In addition, the habeas corpus requirement of article 5(4) involves the right to have a court review of the lawfulness of detention and the prospect of the court ordering release.

2.109 The statutory regime includes administrative release provisions, set out in MHA 1983 s23. The RC or the hospital managers may discharge if the criteria for detention are not made out (and indeed are duty bound to do so in order to comply with article 5(1)(e): Part 31 of the Code of Practice, and Part 27 of the Welsh Code, contain guidance on the frequency and practice of managers' reviews). In addition, the patient's nearest relative may also apply to exercise this administrative discharge, which takes effect after 72 hours unless the treating clinician bars it by filing a report under section 25 to the effect that the patient would be likely to act in a manner dangerous to himself or herself or others and so should remain detained. In such a case, the managers should review the detention and apply the more stringent criterion.

2.110 This administrative process does not comply with article 5(4). However, there is also a judicial regime, by application to the tribunal (namely the Mental Health Review Tribunal for Wales or the First-tier Tribunal in England) for discharge under MHA 1983 s72 or s73, which in essence requires an order for release if it is not shown that the criteria for detention continue to apply.[123] Rights to apply are

123 The tribunal also has a discretion as to discharge in any case, which can arise only if the criteria for detention are in fact made out (since otherwise the duty to discharge would be applicable). There is no such discretion if the patient is a restricted patient: in such a case, MHA 1983 s73 applies, which does not include any discretion to discharge. Prior to being amended by the MHA 2007, section 72(2) of the MHA 1983 required that, in considering the discretion, the tribunal take into account the likelihood of medical treatment alleviating or preventing a deterioration of the patient's condition and, if the patient suffered from mental illness or severe mental impairment, the likelihood of the patient being able to obtain care or prevent exploitation if discharged. (Failure to address the former of these issues was a reason for quashing a discretionary discharge in *R (East London and the City Mental Health NHS Trust) v Mental Health Review Tribunal* [2005] EWHC 2329 (Admin), [2006] MHLR 1.) As section 72(2) has been deleted, the power of discharge is now expressed as an untrammelled discretion; but since detention will only follow if there is a conclusion that the patient has a condition that makes detention appropriate and necessary and that appropriate treatment is available, it seems unlikely that

provided by sections 66 (for civil patients) and section 69 (for criminal patients). There are also provisions whereby the hospital managers have to refer a case to a tribunal if the patient has not made an application for some time: see section 68. In the case of a restricted patient, this duty is exercised by the Secretary of State for Justice under section 71.

2.111 Patients on a CTO remain liable to recall to detention, and also have a right to challenge the propriety of the continuation of their status on a CTO. If they are recalled to hospital and their CTO is revoked, so returning to the status of a detained patient, this must be referred to a tribunal. Similarly, conditionally discharged restricted patients may apply under MHA 1983 s75 for the discharge to be made absolute; and if such a patient is recalled to detention, the case must be referred to a tribunal.

Aftercare

2.112 Patients who have been detained under MHA 1983 s3, and also under various criminal provisions – sections 37, 45A, 47 or 48 – are entitled to aftercare on being released from hospital for so long as they need it: this is both medical care and community care. This arises under MHA 1983 s117, and it has been determined that this is a free-standing duty for which the charging provisions of other community care legislation do not apply: see *R v Manchester City Council ex p Stennett*.[124]

The interplay between the civil and criminal provisions

2.113 Two things should be noted. First, a patient can be subject to both Parts II and III of the MHA 1983. This was established in the case of *R v North West London Mental Health NHS Trust ex p Stewart*.[125] This related to the use of civil powers to detain a conditionally discharged restricted patient: his argument that recall under the conditional discharge was the only power available was rejected. But the holding

it will be proper to grant a discretionary discharge in other than a very unusual situation. However, Parliament had the opportunity to remove the discretion and did not do so, and so it must be possible to use it in some situation.

124 [2002] UKHL 34, [2002] 2 AC 1127, [2002] MHLR 377. The case is reported under various names as it involved various applicants and local authorities.

125 [1998] QB 628.

as to the provisions in the different parts being open to use at the same time may have practical implications: see, for example, the discussion in chapter 7 as to the power to use the civil powers when a patient is remanded to hospital for the preparation of a report rather than for treatment.

2.114 In addition, there is the provision in MHA 1983 s22. This has the consequence that the longer-term civil powers, detention under section 3 or a guardianship under section 7, will cease to operate if the patient is detained in prison for six months or more (whether on remand or as a sentenced prisoner). A CTO will also come to an end, because it relies on the underlying section 3 order remaining in place.

PART II

Pre-court matters

CHAPTER 3

Powers of arrest under the Mental Health Act 1983

Introduction

3.1 The powers of arrest that can be exercised by the police or by private citizens in relation to suspected offending or breaches of the peace and so on – which are beyond the scope of this work – will invariably involve an element of discretion. As a result, while these powers of arrest apply if the subject of the arrest is mentally-disordered or appears to be so disordered, the presence or apparent presence of mental disorder may be relevant in two obvious ways.

3.2 First, if the power of arrest turns on the fact that or a reasonable suspicion that an offence has been committed or is about to be committed – as, for example, in relation to the general powers of arrest for constables set out in section 24 of the Police and Criminal Evidence Act 1984 (PACE) or the lesser powers of non-police officers in section 24A – the mental disorder may be relevant to whether or not the arrestee is within the statutory provisions.

3.3 Second, if the circumstances are such that there is an alternative to these general powers of arrest, for example because the circumstances are such that there is a power of arrest that arises under the Mental Health Act (MHA) 1983, that may affect the propriety of using one of the general powers of arrest. For example, PACE contains a specific restriction on the general power of arrest in section 24: under section 24(4) and (5), the power of summary arrest requires reasonable grounds to believe that one of several reasons makes arrest necessary. These include, in section 24(5)(c), necessity arising from the need to protect the person or others from physical injury. But if that aim can be achieved by making use of another power of arrest, it may be a basis for argument that the section 24 criteria do not apply – though it must be noted that the decision-maker will have a significant discretionary area of judgment in finding reasonable grounds for the belief.

3.4 It is also possible that the only relevant power is one arising under the MHA 1983. These are described in two parts. First, there are those that apply to people who are already subject to orders under the Act and who have absconded. Second, there are circumstances in which the police may assist the relevant professionals to assess someone who may meet the criteria for detention, or in which the police may form the view that a person should be detained in order to be assessed by those professionals.

Patients subject to orders under the Mental Health Act 1983

3.5 There are various powers to detain patients who have been made subject to an order of detention under the MHA 1983, some described as powers of arrest, some described as powers to take into custody, and others described as powers to retake.

Patients involved in criminal proceedings

3.6 Powers described as arrest powers exist in the following sections of the MHA 1983:

a) Under section 35(10), which arises if a person who has been remanded to a hospital for a medical report – before or after conviction – absconds from that hospital, or while being conveyed to or from that hospital. The power of arrest is to take the person before the remanding court 'as soon as practicable' (for the court to decide whether to terminate the remand and deal with the prisoner in any other way open to it – which might well be to order the production of a medical report in custody, or perhaps in a hospital with a higher level of security).
b) Section 36(8) provides that the power under section 35(10) applies in relation to a defendant who has been remanded to a hospital by the Crown Court for treatment.
c) Section 38(7) makes similar provision in relation to a defendant who has been placed in hospital under an interim hospital order (or while being conveyed to or from such a hospital). Again, once detained, the person is to be taken to court as soon as practicable and the court may decide what to do.

3.7 In relation to each of these powers, the patient may be held in a place of safety pending the patient's admission to hospital. Before the person has arrived at the hospital, he or she may be held in a place of safety: the somewhat convoluted powers that apply in this scenario are described below.

Patients detained under the civil powers or final orders of the criminal courts

3.8 Patients who have been detained under the civil powers set out in sections 2 or 3 of the MHA 1983 or under a final hospital order made under section 37 may be allowed to be outside hospital in various situations, the first of which is the granting of leave: this may be granted by the responsible clinician (RC) under section 17. If a hospital order patient has also been made subject to a restriction order under section 41, then the granting of leave requires the consent of the Secretary of State (whose decisions are taken by the Mental Health Unit of the Ministry of Justice).[1] In the case of a patient who is in hospital by reason of a transfer from prison under sections 47 or 48, that is treated as a section 37 order; if a restriction direction is added under section 49, the patient is treated as if a restriction order has been made and so the consent of the Secretary of State will be required for any leave.

3.9 A patient who has been granted leave remains liable to detention under whichever section is applicable. Leave may be revoked by the RC under section 17(4) if it appears to be 'necessary so to do in the interests of the patient's health or safety or for the protection of other persons'. If the patient is a restricted patient, leave may also be revoked by the Secretary of State: see section MHA 1983 s41(3)(c). Section 41(3)(d) indicates that the power of recall may be exercised by the Secretary of State at any time. Since the power of the Secretary of State is to exercise the power set in section 17 to recall a patient, the grounds for revocation that govern the RC should also apply to the Secretary of State. Since the patient will be returned to detention on the basis of his or her mental disorder, the basis for the necessity to detain should be a matter arising out of the patient's mental disorder. So, for example, if a patient on leave has committed a criminal offence that has no connection with his or her mental disorder, the power of recall should not be invoked.

3.10 The MHA 2007 added the regime of the community treatment order (CTO) to the MHA 1983, in the form of sections 17A–17G. A patient who has been detained under section 3 or section 37 of the MHA 1983 can be released subject to conditions and continuing supervision: the underlying detention is merely suspended, and the patient can be recalled if the RC forms the view that treatment in hospital is required to counter a risk of harm to the health or safety of the patient or other persons (see section 17E(1)). There is also a power of recall if the patient declines to attend for an assessment as to whether the criteria for the CTO to be renewed apply or whether the authority to provide treatment should continue (section 17E(2)). While in the community, the patient is liable to recall; once recalled, the patient is

1 MHA 1983 s41(3)(c).

liable to be detained, and section 17E(6) notes that the notice of recall is sufficient authority for the hospital managers to detain.

3.11 The CTO regime does not apply to a restricted patient, namely one detained under MHA 1983 s37 together with a restriction order under section 41. But such a patient may be released from detention by the tribunal (under section 73) or the Secretary of State (under section 42): if the RC or hospital managers wish to exercise their power of discharge under section 23, the consent of the Secretary of State is required (or the relevant support can be expressed to a tribunal). The discharge may be absolute or conditional, the latter meaning that the patient is liable to recall to hospital on the direction of the Secretary of State (under section 42(3)). As with a CTO patient, once the recall has been ordered, the patient becomes liable to detention.

3.12 The mechanism that exists for ensuring that patients who should be in hospital, whether because they should not have left in the first place or because they have been recalled from leave under section 17, is in section 18. It provides a power to take into custody in such a case: section 18(1) provides such a power in relation to someone who absconds, fails to return at the end of a time of leave, is recalled or is absent from a place where he or she is required to reside under a grant of leave. This power is exercisable by a police officer, hospital staff or anyone authorised by the hospital managers, or by an approved mental health professional (AMHP). Patients taken into custody may be returned to the hospital or place they are required to reside. However, under section 18(4), the power to take into custody is valid only for six months from the date of absconding or the end of the period for which detention was authorised.[2] In the case of shorter term detentions – namely those under MHA 1983 s2, which is for 28 days, or sections 4 and 5, which are for 72 hours at most – the time limit for taking the patient into custody expires when the liability to detention under the statute ceases: see section 18(5).

3.13 There is a similar power exercisable by the same people to take into custody a recalled CTO patient: this power was added as section 18(2A) of the MHA 1983 by the MHA 2007.[3] This is also subject to section 18(4), that is the power can only be exercised during six months from the date of absence without leave or the end of the order, whichever is later. Similarly, in the case of restricted patients, once the Secretary of State has issued the warrant of recall, the patient

2 MHA 1983 ss21, 21A and 21B set out regulations for what is to happen to patients who have been taken into custody after being absent without leave.

3 See MHA 2007 Sch 3 para 3, which is put into effect by MHA 2007 s32(4).

is treated as if absent without leave and so liable to be detained under section 18: see section 42(4)(b). Since most restriction orders are of unlimited duration, the recall will not expire.[4]

3.14 The warrant of recall relating to a restricted patient may authorise detention in a hospital other than the one from which the patient was released when discharged, and so the power to detain rests with the hospital named (see MHA 1983 s42(3) and (4)(a)), in which case the patient is treated as absent from that hospital and so can be returned there. Similarly, a CTO patient may be recalled to a different hospital from that in which he or she was detained or which is responsible for the patient's treatment (a transfer being possible under section 19A): see section 17E(3). In such a case, the power of conveyance after the patient has been taken into custody is to the named hospital.

3.15 The Code of Practice issued under section 118 of the MHA 1983 indicates that there is a more general power to take a patient to a different hospital than the one in which he or she will be detained. Paragraph 22.5 of the English Code and paragraph 29.7 of the Welsh Code suggest that the hospital to which the patient is taken may detain the patient pending the making of arrangements to return the patient provided that they have a written authorisation (which may be in faxed form).

3.16 Police officers may be involved in the arrest of patients who are classified as being unlawfully at large: the statutory power is to take into 'custody' and 'return' to the relevant hospital. Does this allow the patient to be held in a police station? In most cases, it will be possible to take the patient straight to the relevant hospital; but there might be scenarios involving patients who are far distant from the relevant hospital. In such a situation, it may be that there is a need for transportation to be arranged by the relevant hospital, given that police transportation may not be suitable or the patient may be in need of being escorted by nursing staff. The statutory language is far from clear as to whether taking a patient to a police station is lawful. On the one hand, there are two elements to the power, one being to take into custody and the other being to return to the relevant hospital. It may be argued that any appropriate location can be used for holding the patient in custody pending the arrangement of the return. On the other hand, it could be argued that there is in fact only one power, namely to return the patient, having taken them into custody

4 A restriction order must now be of unlimited duration: language allowing it to be for a time specified by the court was removed by the MHA 2007. There may be a small number of patients subject to time limited restriction orders for whom section 18(4) means that the power to take into custody might expire.

(ie taking control of the patient)[5] for that purpose; that the absence of any language relating to the use of a police station as a place of safety tells against such a power being available; and that the provisions of the Code of Practice suggesting that a patient can be taken to any hospital gives a better solution to the scenario when the patient may need a holding place until his or her return can be arranged.

Absconding from places of safety

3.17 Those who are made subject to orders under MHA 1983 s35, s36 or s38 may be remanded to a 'place of safety' while they are awaiting the place in the relevant hospital: this will normally be a prison, and so any escape from there would bring with it the powers of arrest that apply to those in prison. Section 137 of the Act provides that anyone who is in a place of safety (or who is being conveyed to any place or kept in custody) is in legal custody; and section 138 provides a power to retake such a person by the person who had custody of the defendant, by a constable or by an AMHP. In relation to civil patients, section 6 provides that an application to detain under sections 2 or 3 provides authority to 'take and convey' the person to the hospital set out in the application form. The language of section 137(1) relating to patients being in legal custody while being conveyed is relevant to this situation.[6]

3.18 Section 138 then provides that people who are in legal custody by virtue of section 137 can be retaken if they escape. This may be done by any person who had the patient in custody immediately before the escape, or by any constable or AMHP: section 138(1)(a). Further, by reason of section 138(1)(b), a patient who is liable to be detained under the civil provisions of the Act or subject to guardianship or a CTO may be retaken by a person who has the authority to act under section 18 in relation to a patient absent without leave. Section 138(4) indicates that 'so far as it relates to' an escape from a hospital, it also covers escape during transfers between hospital (under section 19) or while being taken to hospital under section 37 or its equivalent (for example, section 51(6), or a transfer under section 47) or the place of safety pending such an admission. But it achieves this by referring to an application under Part III of the Act, the criminal provisions,

5 See MHA 1983 s137, which provides that a person is in legal custody during conveyance: this supports the view that the reference to 'custody' covers the physical control over the body of the person.

6 Also covered is the power arising under MHA 1983 s42(6), which is a general power to allow a restricted patient to be taken to any place 'in the interests of justice or for the purposes of any public inquiry'.

and then excluding the admissions under sections 35, 36 and 38: this is presumably because these sections all have specific arrest powers attached to them, as detailed above.

3.19 Section 138(2) provides a time limitation on the use of section 138(1)(b) – presumably as extended by section 138(4) – to the time limits applicable under section 18 'unless he is subject to a restriction order under Part III of this Act'. This can cover a hospital order patient if a section 41 order is made, or its equivalent under section 51(6), or a transferee from prison under sections 47 and 48 if a restriction direction under section 49 is added and remains in effect. The time limit under section 138(4) may be extended if the patient is taken into custody in the last week of the underlying authority to detain: by reason of section 138(6), the provisions of section 21 apply, which have the effect of allowing detention for a week from the date of capture if the authority to detain would otherwise runs out during that week.

3.20 There is room for argument as to whether sections 137 and 138 apply to those who are in hospital. It has been held that the provisions of section 137 and the consequent power to retake under section 138 do not apply in relation to people detained in hospital as opposed to being detained while being conveyed there: see *R v Broadmoor Special Hospital Authority and another, ex p S and other*.[7] At first sight this seems a sensible reading of the statutory language. Mr Justice Potts was concerned with the question of the lawfulness of the searching regime at Broadmoor Hospital, one of the three high secure hospitals in England, and one of the arguments raised to justify the power of random searching was that MHA 1983 s137(2) authorised it through the language that confers on the person who takes the patient into custody 'all the powers of ... a constable' and so incorporates the power of searching arising under PACE. The judge rejected the premise to this argument, which is that the power of detention under section 137 covers patients in hospital: his chain of reasoning included noting that the lawfulness of detention under the various detention provisions of the 1983 Act is conferred by those sections and so there was no need to place any reliance on section 137; and the provisions of section 18 allowed the detention of absconding patients, and so 'the detention "in hospital" under Part II of the Act is a different concept to detention by virtue of section 137'.

3.21 The judge's conclusion as to section 137 was that: 'The section is concerned with the detention and conveyance of patients to hospital and is limited to that. It is not apt to cover the regime in hospital

7 15 October 1997, *Times*, 5 November 1997.

once a patient has been conveyed there'. Although the case went on appeal, there was no contention on appeal as to any express statutory power of search and so the argument based on section 137 was not taken any further.[8]

3.22 There is, however, a further statutory provision to note, namely MHA 1983 s40(6), which provides that where a hospital order patient has been admitted to hospital and is absent without leave, and a warrant has been issued under section 72 of the Criminal Justice Act (CJA) 1967, then if the patient is arrested on that warrant outside the UK, Channel Islands and the Isle of Man, the patient is treated as having been taken into custody under MHA 1983 s18 as soon as he or she is arrested. The aim behind this section is to cover the situation of patients who abscond and go abroad: it has the effect of stopping the potential for the time limits under section 18(4) running out while the patient is in custody on arrest but before being returned. CJA 1967 s72 creates a power for a magistrates' court to issue warrants in various situations, including:

(a) an offender unlawfully at large from a prison ... after being convicted of an offence; or
(b) a convicted mental patient liable to be retaken under section 18, 38(7) or 138 of the Mental Health Act 1983 ...

The interplay to note is that between the language in section 40(6) as to people having been admitted to hospital and section 138 (one of the circumstances in which a warrant may be issued under section 72): this suggests that section 138 must be applicable to people who have been admitted to hospital, which in turn would mean that section 137 was not to be limited to those being conveyed, since section 138 rests on section 137. This interpretation also provides a ready basis for authorising the use of force in all circumstances in which a patient is taken into custody, since section 137(2) provides that any person, including a police officer, who has authority under the Act to take a person into custody or convey or detain them has the 'powers, authorities, protection and privileges which a constable has' – which will include the power to use reasonable force.

3.23 The argument against this interpretation is that the creation of powers of arrest and detention should be construed narrowly and so if Parliament has not used adequate language and is seeking to make use of general language (that is, that in sections 137 and 138) to cover all forms of custody in order to provide a catch-all power that

8 See *R v Broadmoor Special Hospital Authority and another ex p S, H and D*, 5 February 2008.

is akin to an arrest power, that is not an interpretation that should be permitted. This may be the tenor of Potts J's conclusion in the *Broadmoor* case, that section 137 covered only conveyance and so should not be construed to cover all detention powers because it grants other powers as well. However, he found that there was a power of search, which was implicit in the power to detain and treat, and so had no express statutory basis at all.

3.24 To return to the case involving an arrest pursuant to the CJA 1967 s72 warrant, it authorises the person to be produced before the court that issued the warrant for the purposes of confirming identity and that the preconditions for the issuance of the warrant in fact apply; the court can then direct that the person be returned to prison or, if a convicted mental health patient, to be held in custody or a place of safety pending admission to hospital: CJA 1967 s72(2).

3.25 If the scenario does not involve a CJA 1967 s72 warrant, the question may arise as to where the person in custody can lawfully be taken. As in relation to those who are absent without leave from hospital, there is no reference to being empowered to take the person to a place of safety; indeed, the statutory language of 'retaking' the person suggests that nothing is permissible beyond returning the person to the status the person was in before absconding. Accordingly, it may be that the only lawful approach is to take the person detained directly to the location to which the person was being conveyed at the time of absconding, or back to the place of safety from which the person absconded. This would mean that it would be unlawful to take the person anywhere else. The argument against this narrow conclusion is that it may present practical problems, particularly if the patient is a significant distance away from the relevant location.

Guardianship patients

3.26 It is also the case that if a patient is subject to guardianship under MHA 1983 s7, which can also be imposed by a criminal court under section 37, the order may include a condition as to residence: see section 8(1)(a). A patient who is absent from his or her residence without the permission of the guardian may also be taken into custody by a constable, an officer of the local social services authority or anyone authorised in writing by the guardian or the social services authority.[9] The purpose of this is to return the person to the place of

9 See also guidance given in part 22 of the English Code of Practice and part 29 of the Welsh Code. The relevant paragraphs relating to guardianship,

residence: section 18(3). If the place of residence is not one with any security and the patient cannot be persuaded by staff to stay, this may lead to action being taken under section 19 to transfer the patient from guardianship to an admission to hospital.

3.27 Section 138 is also relevant in this context: it refers to people who are in legal custody under section 137 and who were 'subject to guardianship' (section 138(1)(b)). This presumably means that someone who is being returned to his or her place of residence who escapes while being conveyed can be retaken by virtue of section 138.

Policies as to absconding patients

3.28 The MHA 1983 indicates that various professionals can be involved in the retaking of patients who have absconded: the police are only one such group. But there may be circumstances which make it more or less preferable for the police to be involved. The Code of Practice suggests[10] that policies should be in place for how to deal with situations of patients going missing, whether from hospitals or places of residence under guardianship, or while under a CTO. It is said that these policies should be agreed with the police and any other relevant agencies, such as the ambulance service. The areas to be covered include the immediate action to be taken, including who should be informed (nearest relatives, people who might know where the patient is, people who might be at risk and so on) and whether there should be a search and of what. It is suggested that the police should not be involved as a matter of course, but rather should be involved if the patient is particularly vulnerable, is dangerous, is a restricted patient or it is otherwise desirable in light of the patient's history.

3.29 The language of the relevant paragraphs of the Code refers only to detained patients and those on a CTO: but the context of the chapter is patients who are absent without leave, and so it should be taken to include all patients who are liable to immediate detention, which includes those on leave who have been recalled and conditionally discharged patients who are in the community but have been recalled. In the latter case, the Mental Health Unit at the Ministry of Justice will be involved as well, as it issues the warrant of recall.

paragraphs 22.6 and 29.9 respectively, do not mention the power of the police to make use of the power in MHA 1983 s18 in relation to guardianship patients, though it is mentioned in relation to other powers.

10 Code of Practice paras 22.10 and following; Welsh Code paras 29.10 and following.

Warrant to enter premises

3.30 The various powers to take someone into custody arguably do not by themselves authorise entering into premises. However, there are two routes to securing access to premises. If a patient who is liable to be taken into custody is reasonably thought to be in particular premises, and admission has been refused or it is reasonably suspected that it will be refused, a warrant may be issued on the application of a police officer or any other person authorised to take the patient into custody to allow a police officer to enter the premises, using force if necessary, and remove the patient: this arises under section 135(2).[11] In the execution of the warrant, the police officer may be accompanied by a person who is authorised under the Act to take or retake a patient: in paragraph 10.6 of the English Code of Practice, it is suggested that this is a good idea, as it may allow the person to be taken straight to where they are supposed to be. (It is also no doubt a good idea in Wales as well, although the Code of Practice for Wales does not refer to warrants under section 135(2), as opposed to those arising under section 135(1), discussed below.)

3.31 There is also a power of entry that arises under PACE s17(1)(d). This allows the police to enter and search any premises if they are aiming to recapture a person who is unlawfully at large and being pursued. The House of Lords held in *D'Souza v Director of Public Prosecutions*[12] that a patient who is absent without leave and liable to be retaken is 'unlawfully at large' within the meaning of PACE s17(1)(d). However, it also held that the pursuit has to be almost contemporaneous with the entry into the premises for the power to arise – that is, a pursuit or chase, however short in time or distance.

Patients not subject to orders under the Mental Health Act 1983

3.32 Police officers have two significant powers in relation to people who are not subject to detention under the MHA 1983 but who perhaps should be. These are in sections 135 and 136: the former relates to the obtaining of a warrant for the police to enter premises with mental health professionals to allow an assessment of someone who may

11 This expressly applies also to patients who are liable to be detained under the Scottish mental health legislation.

12 [1992] 1 WLR 1073.

require detention under the Act; the latter is the power of the police to detain someone who appears to be mentally disordered and require detention accordingly. Accordingly, section 135 will apply when the relevant mental health authorities know someone who may need detention but they cannot obtain access; section 136 will apply when the police happen across someone.

3.33 There are some features of the two powers that overlap, namely the length of detention is up to 72 hours and is in a 'place of safety'. The distinct elements of the powers are described first, and then there is discussion of the common features, particularly what amounts to a place of safety and the use of police stations for that role.

Mental Health Act 1983 s136

3.34 Section 136(1) allows a police constable[13] to take a person to a 'place of safety' if the following conditions are met:

i) the person is found 'in a place to which the public have access';
ii) the person appears 'to be suffering from mental disorder';
iii) the person appears to be in 'immediate need of care or control'; and
iv) the constable thinks it is necessary to take action 'in the interests of that person or for the protection of other persons'.

3.35 The purpose of this action, which can lead to detention for up to 72 hours, is to allow the person to be examined by a doctor and assessment by an AMHP with a view to determining whether it is necessary to take further action to detain the patient under the MHA 1983 or make such other arrangements as are necessary: section 136(2). The question of what can happen during this 72-hour period, which applies also to the second power arising, that under section 135, is discussed below.

'Place to which the public have access'

3.36 As to what is a place to which the public have access, the English Code of Practice suggests in paragraph 10.12 that this can be 'by payment or otherwise' and so will include stadia, cinemas and so on. The equivalent paragraph in the Welsh Code, paragraph 7.6, does not include this reference to payment or otherwise, but it is no doubt

13 Note that this is a reference to someone who holds the office of constable, which is every member of a police force, including all special constables: see Police Act 1996 s29.

implicit in the statutory concept of a place to which the public have access. Had it been meant to limit the power to places to which there is free access, appropriate language could have been used.

3.37 Aside from the question of whether access has to be free, there is also a question of whether the place has to be open to the public at the time the power of arrest is used. For example, would it include a public house that had been hired out for a private party? In such a case, the question would be whether it being open to a group of people, namely those invited, is sufficient to bring it within the section. On the one hand, it is a power of detention and as such should attract a narrow construction; on the other hand, it might be thought that it is a power designed for positive purposes, namely assistance for mental disorder or the protection of the public, which may support a wider construction.

3.38 Would it also cover a place that is sometimes open, at a time when it is closed – for example a shop that has closed for the night? The statutory language could easily have been phrased so that is was 'at the material time' a public place. Similar arguments to those noted above might be deployed to support a narrow or wider construction, though in such situations, there might well be alternative powers of arrest in any event.

3.39 One particular example might be whether the power covers a house garden or a common area in a block of flats. There is a general principle of the civil law of trespass that anyone can enter a private plot of land for the purposes of approaching the front door to attempt to communicate with the householder, unless this implied licence is revoked by signs or devices such as locked gates: see, for example, *Robson v Hallett*.[14] Does the power to enter under an implied licence mean that the location is a public place? In *R v Roberts*,[15] which involved a charge of having a bladed article in a public place, contrary to CJA 1988 s139,[16] it was held that a front garden was not made a public place because lawful visitors might enter. Similarly in *Williams v Director of Public Prosecutions*,[17] it was held that a block of flats to which access was controlled by security systems and intercoms was not a public place. In contrast, a balcony in a block of flats that did not have barriers or signs saying that only residents could go

14 [1967] 2 QB 939.

15 [2003] EWCA Crim 2753, [2004] 1 CrAppR 16.

16 There are numerous references in other statutes to events that occur in a public place. See para 3.40.

17 (1992) 95 CrAppR 415.

there is a public place: see *Knox v Anderton*.[18] In *Harriot v Director of Public Prosecutions*,[19] in quashing a conviction under CJA 1988 s139 in relation to an incident outside the front door of a bail hostel, the Divisional Court noted that *Knox v Anderton* involved a location that the landlord of the flats, the local authority, knew was being used as a public thoroughfare. It held that the open area between the hostel and the road, which was akin to a front garden, was not a place to which the public have access. Mr Justice Mitting, in a concurring judgment, noted the following point of principle at paragraph 16. He did not accept the prosecution submission that 'the phrase "to which the public has access" is synonymous with "from which the public is not excluded"'. Rather, the correct approach was that:

> A private garden, clearly delimited as such, is not a place to which the public have access merely because public access is not physically obstructed by a fence, wall or gate, or legally prohibited by a notice or by any combination of them. It remains a private not a public place unless evidence is led which proves that members of the public do in fact have access to it by going onto it in their capacity as members of the public. In the absence of such evidence, a private garden, whether of a single dwelling house, a block of flats or a hostel, is not a place to which the public have access.

3.40 There are numerous references in other statutes to events that occur in a public place. For example, section 19 of the Firearms Act 1968 makes it an offence to carry a firearm in a public place, and section 57 of that Act defines a public place as including 'any highway and any other premises or place to which at the material time the public have or are permitted to have access, whether on payment or otherwise': this is in similar terms to the definition used in section 139 of the CJA 1988.

Removal to a public place

3.41 An issue that might arise when another power of arrest has been used in a private place is whether the arrestee can be removed to a public place and then detained under MHA 1983 s136. In *Seal v Chief Constable of South Wales Police*,[20] though the main question was whether civil proceedings for false imprisonment were a nullity because they did not have permission under section 139(2) of the

18 (1983) 76 CrAppR 156; see also *Carter v Metropolitan Police Commissioner* [1975] 1 WLR 507.

19 [2005] EWHC 965 (Admin).

20 [2007] UKHL 31, [2007] 1 WLR 1910, [2007] MHLR 282.

Mental Health Act 1983,[21] the underlying facts were that Mr Seal had been arrested under section 136 after having been arrested inside his mother's house for causing a breach of the peace: the use of section 136 occurred after he was taken outside his mother's house pursuant to the breach of the peace arrest. The House was split on the procedural point arising, the majority finding that the proceedings relating to the use of section 136 were a nullity (which was a problem because the limitation period had expired by the time the point was raised and so leave could not be sought); Lord Woolf and Lady Hale dissented.

3.42 Lady Hale also engaged with the underlying merits of the claim, noting that the police invoked MHA 1983 s136 after they had removed Mr Seal from a private place, and commenting at paragraph 60 that this was problematic for them because:

> If he was 'removed' under s136 of the Mental Health Act from his mother's home, he cannot have been 'found in a place to which the public have access'. If he was arrested in her home for a breach of the peace, and then 'removed' under s136 after they had taken him outside, can it be said that they 'found' him there? (To say otherwise would deprive s136 of much of its usefulness when an arrested person is later discovered to have a mental disorder.)

3.43 These comments are necessarily obiter, and the issue was not discussed by the other Lords. Some limited support for Lady Hale's position comes from the subsequent case of *Cumberbatch v Crown Prosecution Service*,[22] in which the question was whether a defendant was properly convicted of assaulting a police officer in the execution of her duty, contrary to section 89 of the Police Act 1996, when the police officer was one of a group of officers who had purported to detain Ms Cumberbatch's father under MHA 1983 s136 in his home. The alleged assault occurred out in the public street. The Divisional Court held that the question of whether the police officer was acting lawfully in the public place was tied up with the lawfulness of the original arrest in the private place, and it quashed the conviction on the basis that there had been a failure to address the question of the lawfulness of the original arrest in the court below. Although there was no argument in the case about what section 136 requires, and so the court proceeded on an assumption that this argument was

21 MHA 1983 s139(1) provides that liability arising out of a breach of powers arising under the MHA 1983 requires negligence or bad faith; section 139(2) requires that the leave of the High Court be obtained to commence civil proceedings.

22 [2009] EWHC 3353 (Admin), [2010] MHLR 9.

correct, the lack of an argument to the effect that the arrest was lawful and so the officer was acting in the execution of her duty only makes sense if the prosecution decided that they could not argue to the contrary.

3.44 In another High Court decision, *McMillan v Crown Prosecution Service*,[23] a person was convicted of being drunk and disorderly in a public place; but she was in the public place because a police officer had helped her there from a private garden, where she had been acting in a disorderly fashion. When she was disorderly again, the arrest occurred. However, the factual finding was that the action in helping the defendant into the public place was a reasonable action to take;[24] in particular, the officer was trying to stop the disorder by negotiating an end to it by removing the woman from the address (which was her daughter's address) to encourage her to go home, and was concerned that her drunken state would mean that it was dangerous for her to walk down steps unaided.[25] It was only when the attempt to prevent the disorder failed because the defendant continued to be disorderly in the public place she had now reached that the arrest occurred. These very different facts should not undermine the point made by Lady Hale that if the person is only in the public place because of the action of the police that is unlawful, then it is wrong to conclude that the precursor to the use of MHA 1983 s136, namely that the person is *found* in a public place, is made out.

3.45 It should be noted that the possibly unlawful removal of people into a public place so that the MHA 1983 s136 power can be used may be a significant problem in practice. There is evidence that a large proportion of the use of section 136 is in relation to people who are outside their homes, and that there may be instances of arrest powers that are exercisable in private places being used to get people into public places in order that they can then be detained under section 136. The Mental Health Act Commission, which operated as a statutory watchdog under the MHA 1983 but which has now been merged into the Care Quality Commission (CQC), has expressed these concerns. So in its Twelfth Biennial Report, covering 2005–

23 [2008] EWHC (Admin) 1457.

24 And that it was an alternative to making an arrest for an offence under Public Order Act 1986 s5 (causing harassment, alarm or distress) or for causing a breach of the peace: see Public Order Act 1986 s40(6), which preserves common law powers to deal with breaches of the peace; and PACE s17(6), which preserves the common law power of arrest.

25 See [2008] EWHC (Admin) 1457 paras 11–13.

2007 and called *Risk, rights, recovery*[26] it stated at paragraph 4.63, having mentioned the facts in *Seal*:

> ... we have heard of several other instances where s136 has been used to detain a person who has been asked or made to step outside of their home (or another private property) by police. Indeed, at a meeting with one London-based social services authority in this period, we noted that its audit showed that 30% of s136 arrests were recorded as having been made at or just outside the detainee's home. Police officers were 'inviting' people out of their homes, or arresting them for a breach of the peace and 'de-arresting' them once outside to then invoke s136 powers. We suggested that this was at the very least a misuse of the powers given under the Act, and that the social services and police authorities should jointly explore alternative means of managing persons about whom the police have concerns that would not undermine the protections offered by the Act. We suggested, for example, that the police could be given a dedicated telephone number to contact ASWs and trigger an assessment under the Act.

The other criteria under Mental Health Act 1983 s136

3.46 In addition to the requirement that the person is in a public place, the constable must form a view that the person is apparently mentally disordered to such an extent that there is an immediate need for care and control and that this is necessary for the interests of the person or the protection of others. The power is not phrased as one that requires reasonable grounds for believing that these criteria are met: this may be contrasted to the powers of arrest in PACE s24, which involve reasonable grounds as to the belief that an arrest is necessary for one of the reasons given in the section. The absence of such language in MHA 1983 s136 is a pointer to an entirely subjective standard. However, the language of necessity and the immediacy of the need for care and control set a reasonably high test pointing to something of an emergency situation. This is necessary to comply with the requirements of *Winterwerp v Netherlands*[27] that there be objective medical evidence of mental disorder except in cases of emergency.

26 Available at www.archive.cqc.org.uk/findareport.cfm, which under the heading Publications from previous commissions links through to the National Archives website and the relevant reports. This concern was repeated in its Thirteenth Biennial Report, *Coercion and consent*, covering the period 2007–2009, at paras 2.138–2.139. The reference to an 'ASW' is to an approved social worker, whose function has now been taken over by an AMHP.

27 (1979) 2 EHRR 387; see chapter 1.

Mental Health Act 1983 s135(1) warrant

3.47 The second police power of detention of a person who might be mentally disordered is that of assisting an AMHP who is taking action under a section 135(1) warrant to search for and remove a patient who may need to be assessed from a private place.[28] The warrant is issued to the police officer, who is to be accompanied by an AMHP and doctor when it is executed.

Application

3.48 The application for a warrant is to be made by an AMHP on information on oath, and must set out the following criteria:

> ... that there is reasonable cause to suspect that a person believed to be suffering from mental disorder–
> (a) has been, or is being, ill-treated, neglected or kept otherwise than under proper control ... or
> (b) being unable to care for himself, is living alone in any such place.

3.49 The statutory language creates the unusual situation that if there is more than one person believed to be unwell and unable to look after themselves or each other, the issue of a warrant may be problematical: the conditions of paragraph (b) would not be met, and the conditions of paragraph (a) might not be met if there is no ill-treatment, or no relationship imposing a duty of care that might be neglected, or no situation involving the risk of harm to others.

3.50 There is no need for the patient to be named in the warrant: section 135(5). Accordingly, the warrant can be sought in relation to an unknown occupant. A question might arise as to whether the application should be inter partes (with service of notice of application on the occupant or, if the patient and any other occupant is known, on named parties). Given that the application relates to a civil right as to trespass to property (which could also sound in the European Convention on Human Rights (ECHR) article 8 right to autonomy) and a civil right as to liberty, it is arguable that it should engage ECHR article 6 and hence arguments as to whether fairness requires an inter partes procedure. Domestic law, however, seems to prevent that possibility.

28 This is separate from the power of the magistrates' court to issue a warrant under MHA 1983 s135(2) in relation to a patient who is liable to be taken into custody or retaken after escape, as outlined above. Such patients are already liable to be detained under the Act.

3.51 In *Ward v Commissioner of Police for the Metropolis*,[29] which is discussed below, it was suggested[30] that the procedural requirements that arise under sections 15 and 16 of PACE apply to a warrant under section 135. PACE s15 indicates that the various safeguards apply to 'the issue to constables under any enactment ... of warrants to enter and search premises', which seems apt to cover MHA 1983 s135 as any power of entry is necessarily accompanied by a power to search for the patient in the premises. One of the relevant procedural provisions is that the application for a warrant 'shall be made ex parte': PACE s15(3). There are two potential statutory interpretation arguments to note. The first is that section 15(3) relates to 'such a warrant', and it is not entirely clear whether this relates to a warrant issued to a constable (which is what is referred to in section 15(1)) or a warrant applied for by a constable (which is the focus of section 15(2)). The argument that it is the latter – and so would not cover a warrant under MHA 1983 s135(1)[31] – is supported by the fact that section 15(4), which relates to the giving of evidence on the application by the police officer who makes the application. The point that follows from this is that it is open to argument that section 15(3) does not apply to an application for a warrant sought by a person other than a police officer and so there is no requirement that the application be ex parte.

3.52 The second argument is that, even if the reference in PACE s15(3) to 'such a warrant' refers back to any warrant issued to a police officer, even if sought by someone else, the phrase 'shall be made ex parte' could be read as subject to an implied conditions that it is to be made ex parte unless the requirements of ECHR article 6 reveal the need for an inter partes hearing. This technique is possible under the interpretive obligation set out in section 3 of the Human Rights Act 1998; a similar condition was read into language to the effect that an application to set a tariff (ie the punitive part of a life sentence) in relation to a mandatory life sentence 'is to be determined by a single judge of the High Court without an oral hearing' by the Divisional Court in *R (Hammond) v Home Secretary*.[32]

29 [2005] UKHL 32, [2006] 1 AC 23, [2005] MHLR 128.

30 [2005] UKHL 32, [2006] 1 AC 23, [2005] MHLR 128 at paras 26 and 27.

31 Contrast a warrant under MHA 1983 s135(2), discussed above, which may be sought by a constable.

32 [2004] EWHC 2753 (Admin), [2005] 2 Prison LR 218. This issue was not argued when the case went to the House of Lords on appeal: [2005] UKHL 69, [2006] 1 Prison LR 1.

Discretion as to issue

3.53 The language of MHA 1983 s135(1) does not replicate the provision of section 135(2) that admission has been refused or it is apprehended that it will be. However, the issue of a warrant is discretionary, and a relevant feature in the exercise of the discretion may be whether the power under MHA 1983 s115 is applicable and has been used without success. This provision allows an AMHP to enter any premises in which a mentally disordered patient is living if there are reasonable grounds to believe that the patient is not under proper care. It is expressed in the statute that this power cannot be used in relation to a hospital; while it may be thought that it is designed to cover places such as hostels or other places of specialist accommodation, the word 'premises' could cover any private house. The fact that the section refers to mentally disordered patients rather than using language such as that appearing in section 135, namely persons believed to be mentally disordered, may mean that it is limited to premises which are known to contain someone who has been diagnosed as mentally disordered. However, it is to be noted that the definition of a 'patient' in MHA 1983 s145 includes a person who appears to be suffering from mental disorder. There is no clear difference between someone who appears to be mentally disordered and someone who is believed to be so disordered. Accordingly, whilet there is no complete overlap between the section 115 power and the circumstances in which a warrant may be sought under section 135, the former is a power that might be adequate in many situations, particularly as a police officer might be able to accompany the social worker if, for example, it was thought that there might be a risk of a breach of the peace or of violence.

Conditions in warrant

3.54 The warrant under MHA 1983 s135(1), if sought and issued, authorises a constable to enter the premises specified, to use force to effect the entry if that is required, and to remove the patient 'if thought fit' to a 'place of safety' for up to 72 hours. The purpose of the warrant is to allow arrangements to be made for the patient, which might include the making of an application under the civil provisions of the MHA 1983. There are procedural requirements as to the execution of the warrant by the police: under section 135(4), an AMHP must accompany the officer, as must a doctor (though there is no requirement in the statute that it be a psychiatrist). This is no doubt to ensure that there is expert assistance and also to provide an indication to the police as to whether the reasonable grounds on the basis of which the warrant was sought are well-founded. If there are two doctors in attendance, one of whom is a psychiatrist, it might well be possible to complete all the necessary formalities for the making of an order under MHA 1983 s3 or s4 rather than having to rely on the place of safety power; if only one doctor is present, it might be possible to make an order under section 4.[33]

3.55 Whether conditions beyond those expressly required by the statute can be imposed was considered by the House of Lords in *Ward v Commissioner of Police for the Metropolis.*[34] The magistrates issuing the warrant had specified that a named psychiatrist and GP be present, but it had been executed with a different psychiatrist present and no GP; Mrs Ward had been taken to a hospital as a place of safety, held overnight and then released on the basis that her condition did not require detention. She sought damages for false imprisonment on the basis of an argument that the execution of the warrant was defective in the light of the non-compliance with the conditions. The Court of Appeal had determined that it had been open to the magistrates to impose the conditions as a method of protecting the patient against the draconian power contained in section 135, and that the arrest and detention was accordingly unlawful.[35]

3.56 The House of Lords reached a contrary conclusion and so allowed the appeal, holding that the inclusion of the specific names was superfluous; that meant that the absence of those people at the execution of the warrant did not affect the lawfulness of the action taken. It is worth noting that the appeal proceeded without Mrs Ward being represented, in contrast to the position in the Court of Appeal, albeit that the House of Lords had an appearance from an amicus curiae. It is also worth noting that, as was pointed out by Lord Rodger in paragraph 7 of his short concurring opinion, there was nothing in the evidence to suggest that the magistrate involved had actually specified the names in the warrant for the purpose of protecting the interests of the patient: rather, it just seems that they were added because it was believed that this was the required approach. Accordingly, the legal argument occurred in a context other than one in which there was a positive conclusion as to the value of imposing conditions, perhaps as a prerequisite to the granting of the warrant.

33 See chapter 2.

34 [2005] UKHL 32, [2006] 1 AC 23, [2005] MHLR 128.

35 [2003] EWCA Civ 1152, [2003] MHLR 389.

3.57 The leading judgment was that of Lady Hale and the base point of her analysis was a paternalistic approach: that is, rather than starting with the need to offer protection against unnecessary interference with the right to liberty, she emphasised the importance of being able to ensure that people in need were placed under compulsion. So, she commented that the main purpose of MHA 1983 s135(1) is to enable access to be gained to someone who is potentially very vulnerable and in need of care, and so there was no reason to cut down the width of the powers or potentially delay the execution of the warrant and the making of the necessary arrangements.[36] The need for protection of the patient's civil liberties was recognised, but it was said that this could be achieved by having any appropriate professional present, and did not have to be one who was familiar with the patient.[37] To this was added grounds for construction of the statutory language based on the legislative drafting history, which had progressively relaxed the requirement for names to be included in the warrant: so in section 15(2) of the Mental Deficiency Act 1913, which allowed similar warrants in relation to people with a mental deficiency, the warrant had to name the police officer and doctor involved in the execution of the warrant.[38] Further, it was noted that Parliament could have easily included appropriate language to confer the power to specify named professionals but had not done so.[39] Adopting the approach that incidental powers can be added that are necessary for the operation of a statutory power,[40] there was no necessity of allowing the power to specify the identity of those who should be present when the warrant was executed.

3.58 While this interpretation must clearly be accepted to be the law, it is worth commenting that there are fairly obvious arguments that can be put the other way. First, as a starting point for the implication of additional powers aside from those expressly mentioned, there is a principle that public bodies, including courts, can exercise such additional powers as are not inconsistent with their express powers: for example, in *R (Roberts) v Parole Board*,[41] the House of Lords held that the Parole Board could introduce a special advocate regime (with the consequent decision to keep relevant evidence away from

36 [2005] UKHL 32, [2006] 1 AC 23, [2005] MHLR 128 para 24.
37 [2005] UKHL 32, [2006] 1 AC 23, [2005] MHLR 128 para 25.
38 [2005] UKHL 32, [2006] 1 AC 23, [2005] MHLR 128 para 21.
39 [2005] UKHL 32, [2006] 1 AC 23, [2005] MHLR 128 para 22.
40 [2005] UKHL 32, [2006] 1 AC 23, [2005] MHLR 128 para 23.
41 [2005] UKHL 45, [2005] 2 AC 728, [2005] 2 Prison LR 262.

the prisoner and his representatives) because that would allow it to deal fairly with the issues: this was a matter of a residual discretion. This is a much wider test than the necessity test applied by Baroness Hale.

3.59 Second, as to the importance of ensuring that patients who need care can get it quickly, allowing the magistrate to specify names is not inconsistent with that aim: in the first place, it would be a question on the individual case as to whether the power was exercised at all, and in the second place, in any urgent situation that arose, those executing the warrant would have a defence to any action brought in tort that their action was justified by necessity.[42] As for the point that the civil rights of the patient are protected by having any professional present, while that might be true in many situations, there might just be situations in which the patient was known to services, had a better relationship with certain named professionals, and would benefit from having those professionals present; or it might be that the particular circumstances of the patient was such that someone with particular expertise would be able to make a speedy decision as to whether there was any need to take further action. What the decision of the House of Lords does is exclude this possibility of the addition of sensible conditions in order to protect the patient.

Other procedural matters

3.60 It is clear that the language of the statute does not require that the AMHP who attends with the constable be the one who applied for the warrant; that is no doubt sensible in that the warrant may be sought by someone other than the AMHP who is best acquainted with the patient, and indeed the application may be made in relation to someone who has not had any contact with local mental health services before, such that there is no reason to prefer any AMHP in any relevant role.

3.61 As noted above, it was suggested by Baroness Hale in *Ward*[43] that PACE ss15 and 16 apply. This sets out a number of procedural safeguards, including such matters as a time limit from the grant of the warrant to its execution, and the insistence on copies and records being kept. It is worth noting in relation to the limit on the execution of the warrant that this is significant because of the importance of having up to date information for the taking of action on the basis of someone's mental health. The time limit in PACE s16(3) was initially

42 See *Re F* [1990] 2 AC 1.

43 [2005] UKHL 32, [2006] 1 AC 23, [2005] MHLR 128 at paras 26 and 27.

one month, but has now been extended to three months, under amendments introduced by the Serious Organised Crime and Police Act 2005. The need to avoid arbitrariness in detention on the basis of mental disorder requires evidence that the disorder persists, since the severity of a disorder may change over time: see the discussion in chapter 1. While the execution of a warrant does not necessarily lead to detention, the engagement of other fundamental rights, including those arising under ECHR article 8, supports the need for up-to-date evidence before it is appropriate to execute the warrant. The absence of any specific power in section 135 to add a lesser time limit than the statutory one in PACE s16 emphasises the difficulty caused by the *Ward* decision: a magistrate who thinks it would be a good idea to make sure that the warrant cannot be executed other than while the evidence is valid may not be able to impose a time limit on the warrant unless he or she concludes that that is not just desirable (the test rejected in *Ward*) but necessary.

Use of Mental Health Act 1983 s135

3.62 Statistics as to the use of use of section 135 in situations in which it led to detention in a hospital as places of safety show that in 1998–99, there were 239 such detentions, and the figure for 2008–09 was 264; however, these two figures are lower than in the period 2003–07, when the numbers were between 300 and 400, and much lower than the figure for 2007–08, which was 503. In 2009–10 and 2010–11, the numbers were, respectively, 262 and 288.[44]

Guidance in the Code of Practice

3.63 The Codes of Practice for both England and Wales contain significant guidance on the use of the powers under MHA 1983 ss135 and 136, and the interplay between mental health services and the police, which may arise in the context of a situation of actual or potential disorder, and in the case of a section 136 detention in particular may arise when police attend the scene of what has been reported to be a suspected crime but involves a person who is better described as someone in need of assessment under the mental health system

44 See Appendix 2 Table 5 in *In-patients formally detained in hospitals under the Mental Health Act 1983 and patients subject to supervised community treatment: 1998–99 to 2008–09*, October 2009 and the update for 2009/10 and 2010/11, October 2010 and October 2011 respectively, available at www.ic.nhs.uk/statistics-and-data-collections/mental-health/mental-health-act.

rather the action under the criminal justice system. In other words, this interplay may be a method by which people can be diverted away from the criminal justice system at the time of their first involvement with the police.

3.64 So part 10 of the English Code of Practice and part 7 of the Welsh Code make various suggestions. These are set out in chronological fashion. Dealing first with section 135 and the application for a warrant, it is suggested (in paragraph 10.7 of the English Code and paragraph 7.3 of the Welsh Code) that local authorities should ensure that there is guidance available to AMHPs on how and when to apply for a warrant. Interestingly, neither Code makes reference to the power available under MHA 1983 s115, the use of which might mean that it is unnecessary to obtain a warrant. Both Codes suggest that the guidance issued to AMHPs should cover what information should be in the application made to the magistrate,[45] and the Welsh Code makes specific reference suggesting that the information should include the alternatives to a warrant that have been considered (which would have been the obvious place to mention section 115) and information on the identified place of safety to which the patient will be taken; paragraph 10.11 of the English Code suggests that there should be advance planning of the appropriate place of safety, and so this is information that can no doubt be included in the application for the warrant. The English Code also outlines the need for information on out-of-hours applications for warrants.

3.65 In relation to the execution of the warrant, paragraph 10.3 of the English Code suggests that it is 'helpful' if the doctor who must accompany the police officer executing the warrant under section 135 is approved for the purposes of MHA 1983 s12 (which will often mean that the doctor is practising as a psychiatrist on a full-time basis, though not necessarily so), whereas paragraph 7.4 of the Welsh Code makes the suggestion that it should be the patient's responsible clinician. The latter will make sense if the patient is known to services and currently has an assigned RC. It is established that the Code is a matter of soft law, namely that it should be followed unless there is good reason not to: *R (Munjaz) v Mersey Care NHS Trust*.[46] So, while magistrates cannot impose such conditions as the attendance of the RC, in the light of *Ward*, it is a feature of the soft law set out in the Code.

3.66 Paragraph 10.9 of the English Code notes that the mental health authorities involved should ensure that ambulance or other transport

45 Code of Practice paras 10.7 and 10.8; Welsh Code para 7.3.

46 [2005] UKHL 58, [2006] 2 AC 148, [2005] MHLR 276.

is available. Part 11 of the Code sets out detailed guidance on the need for protocols to be established as to the use of ambulance services for a range of possible needs in relation to the transportation of patients with mental disorder, who may present different issues because of the ability to convey on the basis of a legal power rather than consent. Paragraph 11.11 notes the particular importance of not leaving AMHPs to negotiate arrangements on an ad hoc basis. Part 9 of the Welsh Code contains equivalent guidance on matters of conveyance.

Place of safety

What can be a place of safety?

3.67 Once the warrant has been executed under MHA 1983 s135 or the person detained under section 136, the power of detention arising is to take the patient to a place of safety. This is defined in section 135(6) as:

> ... residential accommodation provided by a local social services authority under Part III of the National Assistance Act 1948, a hospital as defined by this Act, a police station, an independent hospital or care home for mentally disordered persons or any other suitable place the occupier of which is willing temporarily to receive the patient.

The MHA 2007 added subsections (3A) and (3B) to MHA 1983 s135,[47] and subsections (3) and (4) to section 136,[48] which provide that patients may be moved between places of safety by a police officer, AMHP or person authorised by either the officer or AMHP (for example, ambulance personnel or a psychiatric nurse), provided only that the length of detention in the various places of safety does not exceed the maximum of 72 hours authorised by these sections.

3.68 There is also significant guidance in the Mental Health Act Code of Practice on what should be used as a place of safety: in particular, while the statute includes a wide variety of places within the definition of a place of safety, including a police station, it is fairly obvious that a police station is less than satisfactory in that role, and certainly not as sensible as a hospital setting. This is also reflected in a 2008 Home Office Circular, *Police stations as places of safety*,[49] which notes that a police station is to be used only in exceptional circumstances,

47 MHA 2007 s44(2).

48 MHA 2007 s44(3).

49 Home Office Circular 7/2008, May 2008. Available at www.homeoffice.gov.uk/about-us/corporate-publications-strategy/home-office-circulars/circulars-2008/007-2008/.

inter alia because it creates the impression that the patient is a criminal, and should not even be considered the second best option; this Circular also alerts police to the fact that the MHA 2007 allows people to be moved between places of safety, so that a patient held in a police station can be moved on from there.

3.69 Despite this, it is apparent that it remains the most usual location to which a person is taken on arrest. This emerges from the Independent Police Complaints Commission's (IPCC's) research paper *Police custody as a 'place of safety': examining the use of section 136 of the Mental Health Act 1983.*[50] In this, it was noted[51] that despite comments in 1997 from the Royal College of Psychiatrists that police stations were poorly designed to deal with people with mental disorders and police staff not trained to deal with the problems that might be caused by mentally unwell people, and 2006 guidance from the Association of Chief Police Officers (ACPO) to the effect that police cells were not equipped to deal with people with mental disorder and might in fact exacerbate their problems,[52] nevertheless the view still seemed to be that the police station was a first resort rather than a last resort. Part of the reason for this was identified as the unsuitability of hospital accident and emergency departments for those detained under section 136, or even the lack of appropriate facilities in psychiatric units. The particular unsuitability of the police station was made apparent by the fact that approximately half of people who commit suicide in police custody have mental health problems (though not all of those would have been detained under section 136).

3.70 The IPCC research paper revealed some interesting findings. In summary, in 2005–2006, there were some 11,500 detained in police stations in England and Wales under section 136, as opposed to 5,900 people detained in hospital for assessment under place of safety provisions.[53] Moreover, there were significant variations in different

50 M Docking, K Grace, and T Bucke, Independent Police Complaints Commission research and statistics series: Paper 11, September 2008. Available at www.ipcc.gov.uk/en/Pages/mh_polcustody.aspx.

51 *Police custody as a 'place of safety': examining the use of section 136 of the Mental Health Act 1983* at p3.

52 Citing Royal College of Psychiatrists, *Standards of places of safety under section 136 of the Mental Health Act 1983*, Council Report CR61, April 1997; and *Guidance on the safer detention and handling of person in police custody*, produced on behalf of ACPO and the Home Office by the National Centre for Policing Excellence, 2006.

53 *Police custody as a 'place of safety': examining the use of section 136 of the Mental Health Act 1983* p10; the hospital figure might include those detained under MHA 1983 s135 as well as s136.

parts of the country, with rates of section 136 detention per 10,000 of the population ranging from 1 in one police area to 277 in another, with an average across the county of 57.[54] There were also variations based on the ethnic origin of the person, and while the majority of detainees were white, the rates as a proportion of the population indicated that black people were significantly more likely to be held under section 136 (3.3 per 10,000, as opposed to 1.8 per 10,000 for white people and 1.6 per 10,000 for Asian people).[55] The research sought to explain some of the findings; for example, it was suggested that higher rates of use of section 136 might result from the presence of major airports or suicide spots, or from a local approach of arresting someone for an underlying offence or an alleged breach of the peace rather than using section 136. It was concluded that: 'The availability of alternatives to police custody appeared to be the biggest factor in reducing its use as a place of safety'.[56] A number of recommendations were made designed to reduce the incidence of police stations being used as places of safety.

3.71 The calls made in the IPCC research paper are consistent with the guidance in the Code of Practice. Paragraphs 10.20 and following of the English Code indicate that policies should be developed between the local police, health and ambulance services that identify the place or places to be used for people detained under sections 135 and 136, in which the approach is that '[a] police station should be used as a place of safety only on an exceptional basis' and indeed should not be the automatic second choice if the first choice is not available.[57] As to what should govern the choice, the approach is that it should be a place where mental health services are provided, unless there is an urgent physical healthcare need. It is noted, however, that the test of exceptional circumstances for the use of a police station may be met if 'the person's behaviour would pose an unmanageably high risk to other patients, staff or users of a healthcare setting'.[58] It is also suggested that, if a patient is taken to a police station, arrangements should be in place to ensure a prompt transfer to a more suitable

54 *Police custody as a 'place of safety': examining the use of section 136 of the Mental Health Act 1983* p10 and table on page 11; Cheshire was the lowest, Sussex the highest.

55 *Police custody as a 'place of safety': examining the use of section 136 of the Mental Health Act 1983* pp12–14, including a table on page 13.

56 *Police custody as a 'place of safety': examining the use of section 136 of the Mental Health Act 1983* p38.

57 Code of Practice paras 10.21–10.22.

58 Code of Practice para 10.21.

place of safety or the carrying out of the necessary assessment of the patient. The Welsh Code is in similar terms, at paragraphs 7.17 and following.

3.72 Paragraph 10.17 of the English Code of Practice notes the importance of including within the policy provisions that deal with various related topics, including the commissioning and provision of secure places of safety in healthcare settings, so as to avoid the need to use police stations; and matters of conveyance, which start with the proposition that ambulance transport is better than police transport unless it is extremely urgent or there is a risk of violence. The Welsh Code contains similar provisions in paragraphs 7.11 and following.

3.73 If the place of safety is a police station, then various provisions of PACE relating to detention in a police station apply: see chapter 4.

Statistics as to places of safety

3.74 There are specific duties to make records in relation to patients detained under place of safety provision – see paragraphs 10.40 and following of the English Code of Practice and paragraphs 7.43 and following of the Welsh Code. There is evidence that these records may be stored by the Criminal Records Bureau, despite there being nothing that is criminal in the nature of the arrest: the former Mental Health Act Commission criticised this approach in its Twelfth Biennial Report for the period 2005–2007.[59]

3.75 Statistics on the use of hospital facilities to detain patients under MHA 1983 s136 suggest that there has been success in transferring patients to places of safety in hospitals: so in 1998–1999, there were 2,827 admissions under section 136, which rose steadily to become 8,495 admissions in 2008–2009 and 14,111 in 2010–11.[60] While this might also reflect an increased use of section 136, it would be surprising if there had been a three-fold increase in the use of the section 136 power in the decade and no change in the proportion of those taken to hospital under the power.

3.76 There is another potentially important set of statistics, which is that many more of the patients admitted to hospital under section 136 are re-graded to informal patients rather than to patients who are placed under detention. So the figures for 1988–1989 were that 1,894 patients became informal, 648 were placed under section 2 and 308 placed under section 3; in 2008–2009, the figures were 6,236, 1,325

59 *Risks, rights, recovery* para 2.147.

60 See note 44 above for sources.

and 426 respectively.[61] The latter figure represents 78 per cent being made informal and 22 per cent being placed under detention.[62] If this represents a trend, it suggests that a smaller percentage of those admitted under section 136 are being made formal patients.

3.77 The importance of the guidance, research and statistics is that if a legal representative is called in to deal with someone who is being held in a place of safety in a police station, it may assist in the construction of an argument that the client should be moved from the station quickly.

Absconding

3.78 If someone absconds from a place of safety to which he or she has been taken under MHA 1983 s135 or s136, there is a power to retake that person: see MHA 1983 ss137 and 138. This power can be exercised by a constable or an AMHP or whoever had custody of the patient. However, this power lasts only for 72 hours from the time of escape: see section 138(3).

Release

3.79 The purpose of the detention in a place of safety under MHA 1983 s135(1) or s136 is for the making of arrangements for the further care of the person. This is phrased slightly differently in the different sections. In section 135(1), the purpose of the action is expressed as being 'with a view to the making of application ... under Part II of the Act, or of other arrangements for his treatment or care'; under section 136, it is for the purpose of an examination by a doctor and an interview by an AMHP and of making any necessary arrangements. If an application under Part II is not possible – for example, because the criteria for detention are not thought to be made out – does sectiion 135 allow detention while other arrangements are made? This turns on whether the view is taken that the language allows alternative steps to be taken, perhaps in a sequential order: that would, however, be a surprising conclusion, namely that detention is permissible even though the arrangements being put in place are not for detention. The language of section 136, allowing the assessment process and the making of the necessary arrangements is also less

61 See *In-patients formally detained in hospitals under the Mental Health Act 1983 and patients subject to supervised community treatment: 1998–99 to 2008–09* Appendix 2 table 6a.

62 In 2010–11, the figures were 10,753, 1,948 and 428 respectively, which is similar. See note 44 above for sources. 2010–2011 Appendix 2 table 60.

than clear: does this only cover the making of arrangements if they involve further detention under part II of the Act? Again, it would be surprising for a statute to allow detention for the purposes of setting up a non-custodial arrangement.

3.80 Paragraph 10.31 of the English Code of Practice indicates that the authority to detain under sections 135(1) or 136 ends as soon as it has been decided that an application under Part II will not be made: this also means that if a doctor concludes that the criteria for detention are not made out, the patient must be released even if the AMHP has not yet arrived. Paragraph 7.10 of the Welsh Code is to similar effect, though it only refers to section 136.

Searching

3.81 Section 26 of PACE, as part of the aim of consolidating powers of arrest, abolished various powers of arrest save those mentioned in Schedule 2 to the Act: this preserves some powers set out in the MHA 1983, namely those mentioned in sections 18, 35(10), 36(8), 38(7), 136(1) and 138. The inclusion of the power in section 136 as a preserved power in turn means that the power to search upon arrest under PACE s32 applies.[63] This provides that:

> (1) A constable may search an arrested person, in any case where the person to be searched has been arrested at a place other than a police station, if the constable has reasonable grounds for believing that the arrested person may present a danger to himself or others.

3.82 There is also a power to search for concealed items that might be used to escape from custody, though there are limitations on what the officer may require the person to take off in public – it cannot go beyond an outer coat, jacket or gloves. If reasonable force is required, it may be used: PACE s117. If the patient is taken to a police station, then a search may be authorised by the custody officer under PACE s54 (to which PACE s117 applies), and the searching officer may seize items that may be used to cause injury; and an intimate search may be authorised by an inspector under section 55 if there

63 See Code of Practice for Wales para 7.23, which specifically refers to section 32; the English Code of Practice is less clear, though it states at paragraph 10.45 that a person is 'deemed to be "arrested"' and so can be searched as if arrested for an offence. The Mental Health Act Commission has recorded that there have been instances of failures to search, with the result that patients in hospitals have been found to have knives: *Coercion and consent: thirteenth biennial report 2007–2009*, CQC, 2009, para 2.136.

are reasonable grounds to believe that is necessary to find a concealed item that might cause physical injury (or a Class A drug).[64]

3.83 If the patient is taken to a hospital, then there is probably also a power of search. In *R v Broadmoor Special Hospital Authority and another, ex p S and other*,[65] the High Court and then the Court of Appeal indicated that this was implicit in the power to detain and treat. However, the context was whether the power existed in a high secure hospital setting, namely that in which the most dangerous patients were detained. A finding that a power to search was a self-evident and pressing need in order that the hospital could provide a safe environment in that context will not necessarily apply in other mental health contexts. However, the MHA 1983 s136 context involves an emergency scenario, such that a power to search may also be self-evident and pressing. In *R (Anderson) v HM Coroner for Inner North Greater London*,[66] which related to an inquest into the death of a patient taken to a hospital as a place of safety, Collins J determined that the need to keep the detainee safe until he or she could be seen by a doctor meant that reasonable force could be used. It is a limited step from this to suggest that searching is permissible. The criteria for section 135, however, do not have the same element of urgency and so it may be open to argument as to whether the power of search exists. It would, perhaps, be unfortunate if there was a differential scenario that encouraged the use of the police station as a place of safety because it allowed searching.

64 See Code of Practice para 10.45; the Welsh Code notes in paragraph 7.23 that the arrestee status allows the custody sergeant to 'identify' the items the person has, which perhaps understates the position.

65 15 October 1997, *Times*, 5 November 1997 (High Court), 5 February 2008 (Court of Appeal).

66 [2004] EWHC 2729 (Admin), [2004] Inquest LR 155.

CHAPTER 4

Treatment in the police station

Introduction

4.1 The Police and Criminal Evidence Act 1984 (PACE) sets out a framework for detention in a police station: in charge of this is the custody officer, the police officer who has the special role of regulating the treatment of people in police custody.[1] Those in detention have various rights. Section 39 of PACE places a general duty on the custody officer to ensure that there is treatment in accordance with these rights.

4.2 While PACE is designed to provide a comprehensive regime for all questions arising in relation to people detained in police custody as suspects, it has already been noted in chapter 3 that police stations are used, albeit often inappropriately, as places of safety for people detained under sections 135 and 136 of the Mental Health Act (MHA) 1983. So this statute has to be read together with PACE in relation to those detainees.

4.3 Under section 66 of PACE, the Secretary of State is required to issue Codes of Practice relating to the exercise of various statutory powers, including the detention, treatment, questioning and identification of persons by police officers.[2] The Codes include notes for guidance, which do not set out additional duties, but may be of relevance in the proper understanding of the Code. The Codes may be updated following appropriate consultation: PACE s67. The status of the Codes and their value is set by PACE s67(10) and (11), the former providing that the failure to abide by a provision in the Code is not 'of itself' a matter that can lead to civil or criminal liability; but section 67(11) provides that the Code is admissible in evidence, and 'shall be taken into account' by a court if it is relevant to any question before it.

4.4 An obvious such question in relation to criminal proceedings is whether any evidence is admissible. This is regulated by PACE and is described further in chapter 11. In short, section 76 of PACE prohibits the use of confessions obtained in circumstances where it might be unreliable as a result of anything said or done: mental disorder may be relevant to this. In addition, there is specific provision made in the statute for confessions by persons who are 'mentally handicapped': under section 77, there is a special need for caution before

1 PACE s36 requires the appointment of custody officers at police stations designated under section 35 for the detention of suspects. PACE s39 sets the basic duty of the custody officer to ensure that there is compliance with PACE and the Codes of Practice.

2 The Codes are available at www.homeoffice.gov.uk/police/powers/pace-codes/.

convicting if the case against such a person rests 'wholly or substantially' on a confession. The definition of mental handicap in section 77(3) is 'a state of arrested or incomplete development of mind which includes significant impairment of intelligence and social functioning' and is similar to the definition of learning disability used in the MHA 1983 as amended. In addition, PACE s78 allows the exclusion of evidence if 'having regard to all the circumstances, including the circumstances in which the evidence was obtained, the admission of the evidence would have such an adverse effect on the fairness of the proceedings that the court ought not to admit it'. Factors relevant to the question of fairness may include whether there was compliance with the duties arising under PACE and the Codes of Practice in relation to mentally disordered defendants.

4.5 The most relevant of the Codes is Code C, which relates to the detention, treatment and questioning of persons by police officers. Annex E to Code C sets out a useful summary of the relevant provisions relating to people who are mentally disordered or otherwise vulnerable on account of a mental health condition. Paragraph 1.10 of Code C makes clear that it applies to arrestees and those who are detained in a police station under the place of safety provisions of MHA 1983 ss135 and 136.[3] Aside from the provisions relating to the reviews of detention of suspects, set out in part 15 of Code C (and discussed below in relation to mentally disordered suspects), the other provisions of Code C should apply to those detained under the provisions of the MHA 1983. The reason why part 15 will not apply is that is that the detention of those in a place of safety is covered by the MHA 1983 and different duties to secure speedy assessment and removal from the police station.

The importance of assessment

4.6 In the light of the provisions outlined above, including the potential consequences in relation to evidence, it is clearly important for police officers, and particularly the custody sergeant, to identify who is mentally disordered. There is another relevant reason. In *Reeves v Commissioner of Police for the Metropolis*,[4] the House of Lords accepted that

3 Code C para 1.12 sets out an exclusion, namely an arrest under MHA 1983 s136(2) in relation to someone whose detention arises under the Scottish mental health legislation, in which case the person's rights are as arise under Scottish law.

4 [2000] 1 AC 360.

those detained in police stations were more at risk of self-harm: this fact combined with the total control exercised over detainees meant that, unusually, it was appropriate to impose a duty of care on the detaining body to prevent a person self-harming. This applies even if the detainee is not mentally-disordered: if there is mental disorder as well, it is well-known that the risks of self-harming behaviour are significant.[5] This knowledge informs the need to ensure that care is taken of people with mental disorder who, contrary to the policy of trying to avoid the use of police stations, end up there.

4.7 The starting point is the question of who is covered by any provisions relating to people with mental disorder. While it may be obvious that this test is met if a person has been detained under MHA 1983 s135 or s136, it will also happen that a person who has been arrested on suspicion of an offence or for a breach of the peace may be mentally disordered. This will not necessarily be obvious to the arresting officer (or, indeed, even to a psychiatrist until after the benefit of a lengthy assessment of the sort that cannot occur in a police station).

4.8 A precautionary principle applies. Paragraph 1.4 of Code C provides that any suspicion formed by a police officer that a person may be mentally disordered or otherwise vulnerable should lead to the application of the relevant safeguards, as should the police officer being told in good faith that that is the situation. This will continue unless there is clear evidence to dispel the suspicion, such as might be provided by an expert medical opinion. Note for guidance 1G reiterates the need for a custody sergeant to assume that the relevant provisions apply in cases of doubt, and also indicates that a mentally vulnerable person is one whose mental state or mental capacity is such that they 'may not understand the significance of what is said, of questions or of their replies'. The note then gives the definition of 'mental disorder' that applied under the MHA 1983 before it was amended by the MHA 2007. Since the last version of Code C came into effect on 31 January 2008, it is perhaps surprising that there was no reference to the updated definition that had been enacted by then, though not yet brought into force. In any event, the wider definition should now be the default understanding.

5 See, for example, T Bucke, R Teers, S Menin, J Payne-James and M Starke, *Near misses in police custody: a collaborative study with forensic medical examiners in London* , Independent Police Complaints Commission (IPCC) Research and Statistics Series: Paper 10, 2008 (available at www.ipcc.gov.uk/Documents/ipcc_near_miss_report.pdf), in which it was found that over 40 per cent of incidents in police stations that did or could have resulted in serious self-harm involved people with mental disorder, including a form of personality disorder.

4.9 The custody officer is under an obligation to make an assessment of a detainee arriving at a police station. Part 3 of Code C sets out the initial action that must be taken, and is split into the 'normal procedure' and the procedure for special groups, one of which is those who are mentally disordered or otherwise mentally vulnerable. One part of the normal procedure involves making an assessment of whether the suspect is someone who requires an appropriate adult (see paragraph 3.5(c)(iv)), which, as is described below, is the key safeguard for a person who is mentally disordered or vulnerable. That will trigger the need for the special safeguards.

4.10 Paragraph 3.5(c)(iii) notes the need to assess whether someone might need immediate medical assistance: and under paragraph 9.5, clinical attention must be secured as soon as reasonably practicable.[6] The point of principle to note here is that those who are involved in the criminal justice process have the same rights as anyone else to psychiatric assessment and treatment.[7] Another statute that might be relevant in this context is the Mental Capacity Act (MCA) 2005: sections 5 and 6 of this Act allow restraint and treatment of a person who lacks capacity in a manner that represents a necessary and proportionate response to prevent harm to the patient.

4.11 Paragraphs 3.6 and following note the need for risk assessments and steps to deal with risks identified, such as additional monitoring; paragraph 3.10 notes that risk assessment is an ongoing process. Home Office Circular 32 of 2000, which deals particularly with the need to ensure that information as to risks travels with a detainee who is moving, provides additional guidance on features that are relevant to a process of risk assessment.[8]

4.12 Naturally, a custody officer may not have the necessary skills to make a proper assessment of whether there is mental disorder or vulnerability: even if it is something that seems to be apparent, the value of expert assistance is clear. Paragraph 3.6 provides that a risk assessment has to be carried out in relation to the prospects of self-harm or danger posed to others, which may arise from features such

6 Code C para 9.6 notes that this is not meant to delay any action designed to secure an assessment if the detainee is in the station by reason of section 136; that should apply to MHA 1983 s135 detention as well.

7 See paragraph 33.2 of the Code of Practice issued under MHA 1983 s118. This notes the need to consider admission to hospital if the person appears in need of treatment.

8 *Detainee risk assessment and revised Prisoner Escort Request (PER) form*, Home Office Circular 32/2000, August 2000. Available at http://webarchive.nationalarchives.gov.uk/+/http://www.homeoffice.gov.uk/docs/hoc3200.html.

as mental disorder or vulnerability. In doing that, the custody officer may have to consult with an appropriate 'health care professional'. The phrase is defined in note for guidance 9A as 'a clinically qualified person working within the scope of practice as determined by their relevant professional body'. It is then added that the appropriateness of the use of the particular professional turns on the duties they are called on to carry out. It may be that the responsible thing for any particular professional is to suggest that there be a more suitably qualified person carry out a more specialist assessment.[9]

Detention

4.13 If a person is arrested for an offence, PACE sets out the full code for detention, as section 34(1) provides that no detention is permissible other than in accordance with the Act. Part IV of PACE regulates the length of detention of suspects. The starting point is that the defendant should be charged if there is sufficient evidence, or released whether on bail or not, unless the custody officer 'has reasonable grounds for believing that his detention without being charged is necessary to secure or preserve evidence relating to an offence for which he is under arrest or to obtain such evidence by questioning him' (section 37(2)). The question of charging is dealt with in more detail in chapter 5, and may involve consideration of whether any mental disorder makes it appropriate to charge as it may affect whether there is adequate evidence or whether it is in the public interest to charge as opposed to diverting the defendant away from the criminal justice system.

4.14 If the opinion under section 37(2) is formed and detention is authorised, section 40 requires reviews of detention after six hours and then at nine-hour intervals by an inspector; if the defendant has been charged but detained rather than being released on bail, reviews have to be carried out as well, but by the custody officer. The aim of the review is to determine whether the conditions for detention still apply. Mental disorder may be relevant: for example, if the suspect has difficulties in being interviewed, this will be a relevant feature to take into account in determining whether it is proper to continue to authorise detention.

9 See, for example, Code C Annex G para 5, in which it is suggested that a health care professional might have to be asked whether a more specialist opinion be sought as to fitness to be interviewed.

4.15 The basic limit for police detention without charge is 24 hours: PACE s41. This may be extended by a superintendent for 12 hours and then by a court for a further 36 hours, under, respectively, PACE ss42 and 43. In each situation, the offence must be indictable, the detention must be necessary to secure evidence or obtain it by questioning, and the investigation must be proceeding diligently and expeditiously. The court warrant can be extended under section 44 to a maximum detention period of 96 hours. Features relating to the mental health of the suspect may be relevant at this stage, and again a question that might be relevant is whether or not it is better to make appropriate arrangements to deal with any mental disorder and return to the investigation subsequently, particularly in relation to the obtaining of evidence by questioning. So it is specifically noted at paragraph 15.2A of PACE Code C that, while the decision to detain a mentally disordered suspect for more than 24 hours will turn on the circumstances, account should be taken of the person's vulnerability and any alternatives that exist to police custody.

4.16 One particular part of the review process merits mention: PACE s40(12)–(14) provide that the reviewing officer shall allow the detainee (or the solicitor representing the detainee) the chance to make representations as to whether he or she should continue to be detained, but this may be refused in relation to representations by the detainee if the officer considers that 'he is unfit to make such representations by reason of his condition or behaviour'. In *Megyeri v Germany*[10] the European Court of Human Rights (ECtHR) found that, in the context of a review of ongoing detention under a court order that a person be confined in hospital, the need for the periodic review under article 5(4) of the European Convention on Human Rights (ECHR) to be effective might require additional procedural safeguards in the case of a person who was mentally disordered. On the facts, the importance of ensuring that a case relating to liberty was presented adequately meant that there should be a presumption in favour of appointing a lawyer even if the patient had not requested one. Albeit that detention in a police station will involve a shorter period, the underlying point of principle behind *Megyeri* is of equal application: namely, that there has to be compensation for the lesser abilities of some people with mental disorder to represent themselves. Accordingly, the provisions allowing the reviewing officer not to invite representations from a person who in unable to make them as a result of mental disorder

10 (1992) 15 EHRR 584.

do not mean that a lesser protection should result: rather, the officer should consider the need to take alternative steps that allow proper representations to be made. The appropriate adult may be involved in making representations as to whether or not detention should be continued: that is permitted in paragraph 15.3 of Code C, but not required. But the effect of the reasoning behind *Megyeri* is that more may be required, including perhaps ensuring that a lawyer is able to make representations to ensure that there is equivalent treatment. Paragraph 15.3A, it is to be noted, indicates that the officer considering the question may allow representations to be made by 'other people having an interest in the detainee's welfare'.

4.17 Reviews of detention may be carried out by telephone or video-conferencing facilities: PACE ss40A and 45A. Paragraph 15.3C of Code C notes that the factors the reviewing officer must take into account in deciding whether to undertake this review by one of these methods include any mental vulnerability of the detainee. A personal review may have particular benefits in this situation, for example by allowing a more considered review of any entries in the custody record.

4.18 One particular situation in which a review is carried out is when a decision is made as to whether detention can be extended to 36 hours if the criteria of PACE s42 apply. Paragraph 15(2) of Code C notes that this might apply to a mentally vulnerable person, but regard should be had to features such as the special vulnerability of the detainee and any alternatives to police custody.

4.19 PACE s34 also provides language that is suitable to all forms of detention, including those that do not relate to suspicion of having committed an offence. Section 34(2) requires the custody officer to release immediately a person once the grounds for detention have ceased to apply. In relation to a suspect, this would be when there is enough evidence to charge or, if not, no basis for detaining further to obtain more evidence. It would also apply to detention under sections 135 or 136 of the MHA 1983 if, contrary to policy, a police station is used as a place of safety. The purpose of detention under those provisions is to allow arrangements to be made for the further care of the arrestee: but that will only be if the necessary examination to assess any need for the use of formal powers under the Act demonstrates the need for further detention. So, for example, paragraph 10.31 of the English Code of Practice issued under the MHA 1983 indicates that the authority to detain under MHA 1983 s135(1) or s136 ends as soon as it has been decided that an application under Part II will not be made.[11] In addition, as a result of the MHA 2007, it is permissible to move a patient who is being held in a police station as a place of safety to a more therapeutic environment within the 72-hour period. These matters are discussed in chapter 3; the important point for any legal representative who attends a police station in relation to someone being held there as a place of safety is that the clear policy is that people should not be held under place of safety provisions in police cells and, as there is a power to move the person from the police station to a more suitable location even before he or she has been assessed, consideration should always be given to the exercise of that power.

Rights in detention

Introduction

4.20 Other rights guaranteed under PACE apply to all detainees, including those who are mentally disordered and whether they have been detained under MHA 1983 s135 or s136 or a criminal arrest power. They include:

a) the right only to be searched in the manner set out in PACE ss54 and 55;
b) the right to have someone informed of detention, guaranteed in section 56; this may be delayed in certain cases in relation to someone arrested of an indictable offence, which will not apply in the case of a person detained under the MHA 1983;
c) the right to legal advice under section 58.

4.21 The process of ensuring that these rights are accorded is systematised in Code C to the Codes of Practice under PACE. Paragraph 3.1 provides that a person who is arrested must be told of their continuing rights to have someone informed, to consult privately with a solicitor (including through the free scheme of police station advice), and also to consult the Codes of Practice. A written notice setting out these matters, and also their other rights in custody, must also be supplied, by reason of paragraph 3.2.

4.22 As is noted above, the principle established in *Megyeri* suggests the importance of providing additional safeguards in relation to

11 Paragraph 7.10 of the Welsh Code is to similar effect, though it only refers to MHA 1983 s136.

people who are mentally disordered in order to make sure that the rights guaranteed are effective in practice. So, for example, the rights to have someone informed about detention, or to have legal advice, are expressed as being rights that turn on the detainee making the request. This connotes that the detainee has the capacity to make the decision as to whether or not someone should be contacted or legal advice obtained: accordingly, since liberty is involved, there may be an argument arising under article 5 of the ECHR that if the person does not have the relevant capacity on account of mental disorder, it is necessary to ensure that someone is contacted. At the same time, it should not be assumed that the presence of mental disorder means that a person does not have the capacity to make his or her own decisions as to the exercise of these rights. Given that police officers are not experts on questions of capacity, it would seem sensible to ensure that the police forensic medical examiner is asked to assess the capacity of a person who has not made any request as to the exercise of these rights. This approach is reflected in the provisions in PACE Code of Practice C as to the appointment of an 'appropriate adult'.

4.23 As noted above, assessment of whether a detainee is mentally disordered is a key process to be followed at the outset. Once a person in detention has been found to be or is deemed to mentally disordered or vulnerable, Code C provides guidance on two separate areas of concern. The first of these is the conditions in which the detainee is kept and any advice that the custody officer must obtain as to how best to deal with such persons. The second is the steps that ought to be taken to regulate the interaction between the police and the suspect in light of the fact that part of the purpose behind the suspect being in custody may be to obtain evidence that might be relevant to the criminal justice process. The former concern will be of relevance to all detainees; the latter will be of concern in relation to detainees who have been arrested under police powers to arrest in relation to a criminal offence rather than people who have been detained on a place of safety basis, though it is not inconceivable that a detention that was put in place on MHA 1983 s136 grounds will lead to a prosecution. For example, if an assessment is carried out on a section 136 that leads to the conclusion that the arresting officer's suspicion of mental health problems is ill-founded, that may lead to the conclusion that behaviour that the officer thought was not criminal because of mental health problems in fact could be classified as criminal and perhaps legitimately the subject of criminal proceedings.

Appropriate adult

4.24 The 'appropriate adult' is a key figure, particularly in relation to interaction with the police investigating an offence. The definition of the 'appropriate adult' is contained in paragraph 1.7(b) of Code C.[12] It can be a relative, guardian or carer, someone experienced in dealing with mentally disordered or mentally vulnerable people, or some other responsible adult: in relation to the latter two categories, the role cannot be fulfilled by a police officer or police employee. Note for guidance 1.D suggests that someone with experience or training in the care of people who are mentally disordered or vulnerable may be preferable to a relative who has no qualifications, but it adds that the wishes of the detainee in this regard should be respected if practicable. Note for guidance 1F also notes that an adult who is acting as a solicitor or an independent custody visitor cannot be an appropriate adult as well. There are also problems if the person selected might be a witness or victim, or might be a suspect: Note for guidance 1B prevents such a person being an appropriate adult even if he or she is a parent.

4.25 The appropriate adult should be informed about the place and grounds of detention and asked to attend the station. The purpose of this attendance is to ensure that the detainee is assisted in relation to the exercise of the rights accorded under PACE and the Codes of Practice. So, if the nearest relative had not been with the detainee on reception into the police station, the steps taken in terms of seeking to make sure that the detainee is aware of his or her rights have to be repeated: Code C para 3.17. The appropriate adult must be called in even if a doctor indicates that a mentally vulnerable person is fit for interview.[13]

4.26 Given the importance of the role of the appropriate adult, the Code confers a right to see the appropriate adult in private (in paragraph 3.18); however, as is recorded in note for guidance 1E, an appropriate adult is not covered by legal professional privilege. The custody officer should also make sure that the role of the appropriate adult in terms of providing advice and assistance is outlined to the person carrying out the role.

4.27 Before dealing with the specifics of the involvement of the appropriate adult, it is worth considering the propriety of the role. At first sight, it is in accordance with the general principles arising from

12 There is a separate definition in Code C para 1.7(a) in relation to juveniles, who are also to be provided with an appropriate adult.

13 See *R v Aspinall* (1999) *Times* 4 February, [1999] MHLR 12.

cases such as *Megyeri*, discussed above, namely that someone should be involved to assist those who are less-well equipped to help themselves. However, there is a caveat. It has been decided in relation to obligations to consult the nearest relative of the patient who is being detained under MHA 1983 s3 (on which see chapter 2) that if the patient wishes to preserve his or her privacy, including the fact that there is a suspicion of mental disorder, then it might be necessary not to consult. This would be achieved by construing the requirement in MHA 1983 s11(4) that consultation be carried out on the basis of practicability as not applying. This was decided in *R (E) v Bristol City Council*,[14] though the factual matrix involved a situation in which there was evidence that it might be positively harmful to E's mental health if her nearest relative was consulted and the nearest relative would not be able to offer anything to the process required by consultation in light of her estrangement from her sister.

4.28 On the basis of this, it is suggested that the rights of a person with mental disorder to keep that private and to make their own decisions are involved, such that article 8 of the ECHR is engaged. However, the question always arising will be whether any breach of the right to respect for privacy is lawful and proportionate and so justified in terms of article 8(2). The lawfulness is provided by the provisions of PACE and the Code of Practice, which amount to a legal code in the same way as the Code of Practice issued under MHA 1983 s118. (See *R (Munjaz) v Mersey Care NHS Trust*,[15] which establishes that this 'soft law' is adequate for the purposes of article 8.) On the facts of *E*, there was no proportionality, but that will be fact-specific. It may be open to suggestion that the importance of what might happen in a police station, and the needs of the criminal justice system to ensure that any evidence is not subsequently challenged on the basis of a contention that the person was not in fact capable of protecting his or her own interests, are factors that justify the requirement to contact an appropriate adult if the person appears to be mentally disordered and even if they may retain the capacity to take their own decisions.

4.29 Aside from the question of whether to involve an appropriate adult, there is the separate question of the proper person to carry out that role, in relation to which similar arguments can be made. It has been established, for example, that a defendant's choice as to who should be the appropriate adult should be respected: *Director*

14 [2005] EWHC 74 (Admin), [2005] MHLR 83.

15 [2005] UKHL 58, [2006] 2 AC 148, [2005] MHLR 276.

of Public Prosecutions v Blake,[16] in which an estranged parent with whom the suspect had no empathy and who was called in against the protestations of the suspect, was not an appropriate adult (leading to the exclusion of a confession).

Conditions of detention

4.30 Turning then to the specifics and the question of the conditions of detention, paragraph 8.2 of Code C requires that cell conditions are suitable. It is noted that particular care is required in relation to the use of restraints that might be called for in light of the behaviour of a detainee. This reflects the importance of placing detainees who have mental health difficulties in a setting that is able to deal with their needs. As has been noted, 'place of safety' detainees should be held in a police station as a matter of last resort only. As police station detention still happens, paragraph 3.16 of the Code emphasises the need for those detained under MHA 1983 s136 to be assessed as soon as possible by the relevant professionals and either moved to the place where their care can be administered or discharged if the assessment reveals that the person cannot be held under the MHA 1983.

4.31 As there will be situations in which a detainee in a police station has specific needs for clinical treatment, Code C para 9.5 imposes a duty on the custody officer to secure treatment as soon as reasonably practicable for someone who appears to be suffering from mental disorder. This cannot depend on a request being made, nor on whether the detainee appears to have had recent clinical attention; if the need remains, it must be met: Code C para 9.5A. If the defendant is in the police station as a place of safety pending an assessment, the fact that some clinical assessment can be carried out in a police station cannot, however, be used as a reason to justify a delay in making a transfer to hospital if the detainee has been placed under MHA 1983 s136. Rather, this duty to secure a clinical examination in the police station is a supplemental safeguard pursuant to which the custody officer can obtain a check on the condition of a detainee pending the arrival of suitable professionals to carry out the assessment under section 136. This is the suggestion contained in paragraph 9.6 of Code C, in which it is emphasised that this should be considered in particular if there is likely to be any significant delay in the formal assessment process.

16 [1989] 1 WLR 432.

4.32 As mentioned at the outset, the risk of self-harm by people in custody was recognised in *Commissioner of Police for the Metropolis v Reeves*,[17] which on the facts led to a decision that it was fair to impose a duty of care to prevent self-harm in a custodial setting. This risk and the need to respond to it is one of the reasons behind the requirements in PACE ss54 and 55 that detainees be searched and anything that might cause self-harm taken away. This may mean that a more cautious approach is taken to those who appear to be vulnerable in terms of what is removed from them.

4.33 However, the vulnerability of the person may mean that the fact of carrying out the search, and particularly if it is a strip search or an intimate search, may itself be problematic. Accordingly, Annex A to Code C, which regulates the conduct of intimate and strip searches, provides at paragraphs 5 and 11 that an intimate or strip search of a mentally disordered or otherwise mentally vulnerable person requires the presence of an appropriate adult. A strip search can only be carried out by an officer of the same gender as the detainee, and the appropriate adult must be of the same gender unless the detainee has made a specific request for an appropriate adult of the opposite gender: Code C Annex A para 11(d). Similar provision is made in paragraph 5 in relation to intimate searches. However, the strip search may proceed without an appropriate adult in a case of urgency. In relation to an intimate search, there is no provision for it to take place in the absence of the appropriate adult, whereas a juvenile may request that the appropriate adult not be present and the appropriate adult may agree to that; it is difficult to see why a person who is mentally disordered or otherwise vulnerable should not have a similar right, particularly as the appropriate adult may be a stranger to them, albeit a stranger with training relevant to their role.

4.34 The vulnerability of detainees is also an explanation for the need set out in paragraph 9.3 of Code C to the effect that detainees should be checked at least hourly: this allows for the possibility that more frequent checks may be necessary. Note for guidance 9B suggests that 'mentally vulnerable' detainees should be visited more frequently where possible: this should probably be understood to apply to mentally disordered detainees as well, who may face additional vulnerabilities so as to require additional monitoring.

17 [2000] 1 AC 360.

4.35 It is to be noted that paragraph 9.13 of Code C also requires the health care professionals involved in attending to the clinical needs of the detainee be asked about the fitness of the detainee for further detention or for interview, and whether any safeguards should be put in place. If any clinical finding is relevant to the ongoing well-being of the detainee, that should be recorded in the custody record; other clinical findings can be recorded there, and if not there should be a note of where they are recorded.

4.36 The need to inform an appropriate adult of the grounds for detention and the place of detention of a mentally disordered person can be viewed as a protective process, given that incommunicado detention may itself be problematic. Part 5 of Code C deals specifically with the right not to be held incommunicado, which extends to a right to receive visits at the discretion of the custody officer: see Code C para 5.4. The involvement of the appropriate adult being a supplemental right accorded to those with mental disorder or vulnerability, it would seem open to argument that the fact that an appropriate adult is involved is not a factor that is relevant to whether or not other visits should be allowed.

Legal advice

4.37 One of the specific rights mentioned is that to have legal advice. The decision as to whether to seek such advice is then subject to a dual request, since either the detainee or the appropriate adult can ask for it: Code C para 3.19. Note for guidance E1 to Annex E provides a reminder that the purpose of the right to legal advice is to protect the interests of the person, and that there is no reason to delay access to legal advice if an appropriate adult is due to attend. It is also noted that the appropriate adult cannot undermine the lawyer–client privilege and the privacy that requires,[18] such that the detainee should always be allowed to have a private consultation with a solicitor in the absence of the approved adult if that is the request of the detainee.

18 On which see Code C, note for guidance 6J, which notes that: 'This right to consult or communicate in private is fundamental. If the requirement for privacy is compromised because what is said or written by the detainee or solicitor for the purpose of giving and receiving legal advice is overheard, listened to, or read by others without the informed consent of the detainee, the right will effectively have been denied.'

Cautioning and interviewing

4.38 What is said to police officers, both during informal exchanges and in the course of a formal interview, may provide evidence that will later be used in court. Concerns about the accuracy of comments attributed to detainees has led to the requirement for contemporaneous recording of interviews, invariably by way of audio tapes (though, strictly, that is only required for indictable offences): PACE Code E deals with this.[19] Any comment made outside an interview that might be relevant must be recorded and the suspect must be given the opportunity to verify the record: Code C para 11.13. It would seem proper that the appropriate adult be present when this is done.

4.39 The significance of interviewing is reflected in another procedural protection that is required, the giving of cautions. Code C para 10.12 provides that a caution must be repeated in the presence of an appropriate adult. One of the occasions on which a caution is required is on arrest: see Code C paras 10.4 and 10.5. At this stage, the arrestee is to be warned that: 'You do not have to say anything. But it may harm your defence if you do not mention when questioned something which you later rely on in court. Anything you do say may be given in evidence.' Naturally, if the arresting officer was not aware of the circumstances on the basis of which subsequently it is established that an appropriate adult is required, the caution will have to be repeated: it should follow that any statement made pursuant to the initial caution will be considered as made without compliance with Code C, and so may found an argument for exclusion under PACE ss76–78.

4.40 A caution is also required at the start of an interview with the police: paragraph 10.1 of Code C phrases the duty as arising 'before any questions about an offence, or further questions if the answers provide the grounds for suspicion, are put to them if either the suspect's answers or silence, (ie failure or refusal to answer or answer satisfactorily) may be given in evidence to a court in a prosecution'.[20] Paragraph 10.8 adds the requirement to provide a reminder about the caution whenever there has been a break in questioning, which may involve repeating the caution in full. The requirement that this caution be given in the presence of the appropriate adult, arising from

19 Breaches of the contemporaneous recording requirement might found a reason for excluding the evidence under PACE s78: see *Keenan* [1990] 2 QB 54.

20 See also Code C para 11.1A, which states that: 'An interview is the questioning of a person regarding their involvement or suspected involvement in a criminal offence or offences which, under *paragraph 10.1*, must be carried out under caution' (emphasis in original).

paragraph 10.12, is a minor part of the role of the appropriate adult in interviews. In the first place, paragraph 11.15 provides a prohibition on the interview of a mentally disordered or vulnerable defendant (or the provision of a written statement under caution) in the absence of an appropriate adult, save in limited circumstances. Those are, first, that paragraph 11.1 prevents any interview other than at the police station (for example, an interview at the place of arrest) unless the delay in taking the arrestee to the police station would be likely to lead to serious consequences in the form of interference with evidence, harm to other people, serious loss of or damage to property, hindering the recovery of property involved in the crime or the alerting those not yet arrested.

4.41 It may also be possible to have an urgent interview at a police station without an appropriate adult if the provisions of Code C para 11.18 apply, namely that if delay will have the same consequences as are set out in paragraph 11.1 and it is found by an officer of at least superintendent rank that the interview would not cause significant harm to the mental state of the suspect. However, such an interview must be for limited purposes, namely obtaining information to avert the unfortunate consequences that justify the urgent interview.

4.42 An important consideration in this context is the fitness of the interviewee to be interviewed. By reason of Code C para 12.3, the custody officer must assess whether the suspect is fit to be interviewed. This is a matter of general application, and can be affected by the physical and mental state of the suspect, and also the impact that the interview might have on that state. It is specifically provided that an interview that will cause significant harm to the physical or mental state of the suspect will not be allowed. In addition to the involvement of the appropriate adult, paragraph 12.3 indicates also that there shall be consultation with the investigating officer and also appropriate health care professionals. Annex G to Code C provides guidance. The key question is the risk that the interview may pose to the physical or mental health of the detainee or the risk that statements made might be found unreliable (which would be a ground for them being excluded in any court proceedings). The assessment process is to be informed by the features listed at paragraph 3 of Annex G, namely:

(a) how the detainee's physical or mental state might affect their ability to understand the nature and purpose of the interview, to comprehend what is being asked and to appreciate the significance of any answers given and make rational decisions about whether they want to say anything;

(b) the extent to which the detainee's replies may be affected by their physical or mental condition rather than representing a rational and accurate explanation of their involvement in the offence;
(c) how the nature of the interview, which could include particularly probing questions, might affect the detainee.

4.43 It is noted that this is a question that must be addressed in relation to the particular defendant and the impact of the disorder in his or her case, since the important question is not whether a suspect has a mental disorder but whether that disorder impacts on the fitness of the suspect to be interviewed. So, paragraph 4 of Annex G notes that health care professionals who are asked to assess a suspect should concentrate on the 'functional ability' displayed, and that 'it is possible for a person with severe mental illness to be fit for interview'.

4.44 It is important to note that the custody officer remains the decision-maker in relation to the relevant questions arising, namely whether the interview should proceed and with what safeguards. Paragraph 8 of Annex G makes this clear. This in turn means that the advice to be sought from the relevant health professional has to be in a form to allow the custody officer to make a decision. Paragraph 7 indicates that the health care professional should advise the custody officer of the particular risks involved, and record this in the custody record; and paragraph 6 notes that the advice given should be as to the whether the condition of the patient is likely to improve, will require treatment, or be amenable to treatment, and how long any improvement will take.

4.45 It is also noted in Annex G to Code C that advice should be sought from these professionals on whether the presence of an appropriate adult will mean that an interview is able to proceed, and also on the question of whether the time taken in an interview might mean that a reassessment is required after a certain time: paragraph 5. The corollary of the latter suggestion is that it might be that a suspect is fit for a short interview but might not be fit for a longer interview. As is discussed in chapters 9 and 10 in relation to the conduct of a trial, it is possible that participation in the criminal justice process may be rendered fair by making modifications that take into account the needs of the person with mental disorder. That is true of activities in the police station as well.

4.46 It may be that the particular health care professional who gives advice is compelled to suggest that a more specialist opinion be sought – for example, a police surgeon who is a general practitioner rather than an MHA 1983 s12 approved psychiatrist may not be as well placed to assess the fitness of a suspect to be interviewed than such a psychiatrist. This is also suggested in Code C, Annex G para 5.

4.47 If an interview can proceed, which will invariably be with an appropriate adult present, the role that he or she carries out is to offer advice, observe the propriety of the interview and facilitate communication: in short, it is not a passive role, and the officer or officers conducting the interview have to make sure that the appropriate adult is informed of his or her role. This is set out in Code C para 11.17. Further information about the reason for special concern is provided in note for guidance 11C, which sets out that, while mentally disordered or vulnerable persons can provide reliable evidence, they may also provide information that is unreliable, misleading or self-incriminating without doing so knowingly. It adds that this risk of unreliability makes it important that corroboration be sought of admissions made.

4.48 In note for guidance E3, attached to Annex E2 to Code C, it is noted that this problem of the risk of unreliability is a danger which the presence of the appropriate adult is designed to remedy, and so the use of the power under paragraph 11.18 should be limited to 'exceptional cases', which are when 'it is necessary to avert an immediate risk of serious harm'. The notes for guidance are not part of the Code for the purposes of being taken into account in determining the admissibility of evidence, but note E3 is a matter of the logic of putting two parts of the Code together, since the risk of unreliability of statements made in the absence of an appropriate adult suggests that it can only be in limited circumstances that it can be sensible to have such an interview if any answers have limited value for any purpose.

4.49 It is to be noted that the custody officer is not limited to the question of having an appropriate adult present. Paragraph 8 of Annex G notes that the required safeguards of the Code might be supplemented and gives the example of having an appropriate health care professional present during the interview to carry out the function of monitoring the impart of the interview on the condition of the suspect.

Identification parades

4.50 The purpose of detention in a police station as a suspect is to make a decision as to whether or not to charge: see PACE s37. Questioning is an important part of the process, since it may lead to additional evidence (or dispel suspicions). Another important process may be an identification parade. The conduct of these is governed by Code D: this contains notes that consent from a mentally vulnerable person requires the presence of the appropriate adult for it to be valid (paragraph 2.12) and that a suspect shall be given notice of the special arrangements for a mentally vulnerable person before an identification parade takes place (paragraph 3.17(viii)). This implies the need for appropriate caution and the active involvement of the appropriate adult in much the same way as would occur in an interview, namely advising and checking the propriety of what is happening.

Summary of provisions relating to mentally disordered detainees

4.51 Annex E of Code C provides a useful summary:

a) there is the precautionary principle of treating a person as mentally disordered or vulnerable if there is any suspicion or information provided to that effect (see Code C para 1.4);
b) who can be an 'appropriate adult' is defined (see Code C para 1.7(b) and note 1D);
c) the appropriate adult must be informed of the grounds for and place of detention and asked to attend the police station if not already there; when the grounds are given to the detainee, that must be done in the presence of the appropriate adult or repeated when the appropriate adult attends (see Code C paras 3.15–3.17);
d) the appropriate adult can decide that legal advice is required (see Code C para 3.19 and note E1); if the detainee seeks legal advice before the appropriate adult arrives, that should be respected, and the detainee has a right to consult with a solicitor without the appropriate adult (see note E1);
e) clinical attention must be secured as soon as reasonably practicable, and this must not delay any assessment called for by reason of MHA 1983 s136 (see Code C paras 9.5 and 9.6);
f) the section 136 assessment must be carried out as soon as possible; detention in the police station must cease once the arrangements have been made for their care or it is decided that they are not mentally disordered (see Code C para 3.16);
g) any caution must be in the presence of an appropriate adult or repeated once he or she is present (see Code C para 10.12);

h) interviews or the signing of a written statement must not occur in the absence of an appropriate adult unless urgent and must cease once the risk has been remedied (see Code C paras 11.1, 11.15 and 11.18–11.20);
i) appropriate adults are to be informed of their role in interviews is to advise, check on the fairness of the process and facilitate communication (see Code C para 11.17);
j) if an appropriate adult is available, he or she must be allowed to make representations about the continuation of detention at a review (see Code C para 15.3);
k) charging must take place in the presence of the appropriate adult, who is to be given the written notice (see Code C paras 16.1–16.4A);
l) intimate or strip searches must be in the presence of the appropriate adult unless it is urgent or there is a risk of serious harm; the appropriate adult must be of the same sex unless the detainee specifically requests otherwise (see Code C Annex A paras 5 and 11(c));
m) caution must be used before using a restraint (see Code C para 8.2).

4.52 Although not mentioned in Annex E, there are also hints of special processes in relation to identification parades: see Code D paras 2.12 and 3.17.

4.53 The decision as to whether to charge is discussed in chapter 5. If a charge is laid, or other relevant action taken, the suspect will be informed, and this is to be done in the presence of the appropriate adult. A written notice of any charge is to be given to the appropriate adult.

CHAPTER 5

The decision to prosecute – diversion

Diversion from the criminal justice system – introduction

5.1 One of the reasons why an arresting officer may choose to use section 136 of the Mental Health Act (MHA) 1983 instead of a power of arrest on suspicion of the commission of an offence is a view that the mental health system should be used to deal with the situation rather than the criminal justice system.

5.2 It may also become apparent during the course of the detention of a person arrested under a criminal arrest power that the person is mentally disordered and that consideration should be given to diversion away from the criminal justice system. This may happen in two very distinct situations: one may be that the presence of mental disorder means that it is unlikely that there will be a successful prosecution, for example because of difficulties in proving a relevant mens rea. Second, it may also be that even though there is clear evidence of an offence, a question-mark arises as to whether it is in the public interest to prosecute.

5.3 Given statistics on the number of serving prisoners with mental health problems, it may be suggested that the policy as to diversion is not being used very well.[1] The response, of course, would be that the figures would be different if there were no policy in place.

5.4 There are various possibilities that arise under the rubric of diversion. These include simply taking no further action from the point of view of a criminal charge; this may perhaps be done in conjunction with arrangements to have the relevant professionals carry out an assessment with a view to admission under the MHA 1983 (or perhaps the planning of community care services).[2] There is a more formal process available, namely that of a caution or conditional caution; it might also be possible to consider some step such as arranging for an anti-social behaviour order to be sought.

5.5 In this context, it is to be noted that quick decisions may not always be possible, and so suspects may be bailed to return to a police station while discussion is had as to whether to divert, which may involve matters such as considering evidence, including evidence relevant to the mental disorder of the suspect (in relation to which

1 A 1998 survey found that over 90 per cent of prisoners had a recognisable psychiatric condition (including drug or alcohol addiction): Singleton et al, *Psychiatric morbidity among prisoners in England and Wales*, HMSO, 1998.

2 See chapter 2.

lawyers can be proactive in obtaining relevant reports), or the views of victims of crime.

The test for a criminal prosecution

Code for Crown Prosecutors

5.6 The approach to decisions as to whether or not to prosecute is set out in the Code for Crown Prosecutors, issued under section 10 of the Prosecution of Offences Act 1985 by the Director of Public Prosecutions (DPP). The 2010 version of the Code[3] sets out in paragraph 4.1 that what is called the Full Code Test for a prosecution involves assessing, first, the evidential sufficiency that an offence has been committed and, second, whether there are public interest factors against a prosecution. These two stages are the evidential stage and the public interest stage. In relation to serious matters where there are reasonable grounds to believe that further evidence is expected within a reasonable time and there are substantial grounds to object to bail, a Threshold Test may be applied under part 5 of the Code in order to inform a decision to charge and object to bail, but the Full Code Test must be applied once the further evidence has become available.

The evidential stage

5.7 The evidential stage of the Full Code Test is described further at paragraph 4.5 of the Code, and involves satisfaction 'that there is sufficient evidence to provide a realistic prospect of conviction against each suspect on each charge'. If this test is not met, there is no justification for a prosecution. In reaching this necessary conclusion for a prosecution, account is to be taken of what the defence case may be. Also relevant are issues relating to the admissibility and reliability of the evidence: this is set out at paragraph 4.7. In relation to the admissibility of evidence, obvious questions might relate to whether there was compliance with the Police and Criminal Evidence Act 1984 (PACE) and Code C of the PACE Codes of Practice, as described in chapter 4. Even if it is admissible, the reliability of the evidence may impact on whether there is a realistic prospect of conviction; this may involve assessing matters that might be affected by questions of mental disorder, such as the reliability of any confession made in

3 The Code is available at www.cps.gov.uk/publications/prosecution/index.html.

light of the level of understanding of the suspect, or the credibility of any witnesses.[4]

The public interest stage

5.8 The involvement of a public interest test for prosecutions pre-dates the establishment of the Crown Prosecution Service (CPS) under the Prosecution of Offences Act 1985 and the issuing of the Code for Crown Prosecutors. It was set out in a parliamentary statement by the Attorney-General on 29 January 1951, which was confirmatory of an existing practice. He stated that:

> It has never been the rule in this country – I hope it never will be – that suspected criminal offences must automatically be the subject of prosecution because the rule was that a prosecution would occur wherever it appears that the offence or the circumstances of its commission is or are of such a character that a prosecution in respect thereof is required in the public interest.[5]

5.9 The phraseology of the current test suggests that evidential sufficiency will normally lead to a prosecution, since paragraph 4.12 notes that a prosecution is usually to follow 'unless the prosecutor is sure that there are public interest factors tending against prosecution which outweigh those tending in favour'. There is also the question of an out-of-court disposal, namely a conditional caution, which is described below.

Aggravating features and mental disorder

5.10 It is also noted at paragraph 4.12 that the public interest in favour of a prosecution is more likely to be met if the offence is more serious or the offender has committed previous offences. Paragraph 4.16 gives more details of common factors in favour of a prosecution. Questions of mental disorder may be of obvious relevance to some of these factors. So, factors a) and b) refer to whether 'a conviction is likely to result in a significant sentence' and a court order that exceeds what is available under a conditional caution. If the accused is a person with significant mental health needs, then account can no doubt be taken of the prospect that the end of the process will be a non-punitive order made under section 37 of the MHA 1983 or a community sentence with a mental health treatment requirement. These are discussed in detail in chapters 18 and 19. The point to be

4 These are discussed in chapters 4 and 11.

5 *Hansard* HC Debates vol 483, 29 January 1951; and see Code for Crown Prosecutors para 4.10.

made at this stage is that similar outcomes might well be available through the civil powers of the MHA 1983, such that nothing more is available via the criminal justice system in terms of securing the treatment of the accused.

5.11 On the other hand, if the offending is more serious or suggestive of future danger such that a sentence of a hospital order combined with a restriction order might be made, a disposal that cannot be obtained except through the criminal justice system, this may favour proceeding with a charge and a trial. Having said that, it is to be noted that patients detained under the civil powers of the MHA 1983 may be placed in such level of security as the risk they are assessed to pose requires: so it is not necessary to proceed through the criminal justice system to secure a particular level of hospital security.[6]

5.12 Similarly, paragraph 4.16 factor s) in favour of a prosecution refers to 'grounds for believing that the offence is likely to be continued or repeated'. If the reason behind the offending is untreated mental disorder, then the civil mental health system may be just as successful as securing the avoidance of further offending as the criminal justice system. In this connection, however, it should be noted that one form of mental disorder is personality disorder, an extreme form of which might be marked by an enduring pattern of committing offences. It may be argued that part of the treatment process entails seeking to persuade the defendant to take responsibility for his or her actions. This was the situation in *R (Wheldon) v Rampton Hospital Authority*:[7] a patient was prosecuted for assaults committed in a high secure hospital, and at the sentencing hearing the treating psychiatrist had recommended a custodial sentence on the basis that accepting responsibility for his actions was a precondition to the patient being treatable.[8] In other words, there may be instances in which the clinical team supports a period in custody, effectively seeking to make use of it as a therapeutic tool in that it encourages subsequent engagement in therapy.

6 See chapter 1 for a discussion of the different levels of security in psychiatric hospitals.

7 [2001] EWHC Admin 134, [2001] MHLR 19.

8 The challenge made in the case was to the hospital accepting the patient back at the end of the short prison sentence imposed, but the application was dismissed on the basis that it was open to the psychiatrist to find the criteria for detention made out on assessing the patient at the end of the prison sentence. This was under the previous treatability requirement for psychopathic disorder, which has been modified since the case: see chapter 2.

5.13 Other features that are listed as being supportive of a prosecution are the victim being a public servant, which might include a mental health professional: see factor d).[9] The value of this may be said to be linked to both seeking to secure responsibility on the part of the offender, but also to either deterrence of the offender from repeating such conduct or general deterrence in relation to other offenders. It may be thought that deterrence should not be taken into account in relation to an accused who has a mental disorder such that a hospital order or other mental health disposal is likely because, as is noted in chapter 16, the principles of sentencing under the Criminal Justice Act (CJA) 2003 – which allow a deterrent sentence to be imposed – are excluded if a hospital order is made and it is accepted that the hospital order is a treatment disposal rather than one raising the traditional aims of sentencing. However, as in the case of *Wheldon*, it is possible that the criminal justice system might be used as a tool to reinforce the need for a particular offender to take responsibility for his or her actions or to provide an indication of what will happen if there is criminal misbehaviour involving a mental health professional as a victim. Nevertheless, this can only be proper if the factual situation is that the defendant's condition is such that the acceptance of responsibility or deterrence from further misbehaviour might be an outcome that can be secured by the use of the criminal justice system.

5.14 Another aggravating feature that is recorded as making a prosecution more likely to be in the public interest is the presence of a motivation based on bigotry of some form: this is factor h). The point to be made in this connection is that apparent bigotry may be a manifestation of a delusional system; if that is the case, then the value of a prosecution on account of that factor must be questioned.

5.15 A final factor to be mentioned is factor r), which notes the value of a prosecution having 'a significant positive impact on maintaining community confidence'. It is suggested that this is a feature that should be read as if the community confidence were suitably-informed, since there can be no proper role for ill-informed factors. In this connection, as has already been noted, the civil mental health

9 In July 2008, a memorandum of understanding was agreed between the CPS and the National Health Service (NHS) as to the use of prosecutions to safeguard NHS staff: *Memorandum of understanding between the NHS Counter Fraud and Security Management Service and the Crown Prosecution Service.* It notes, among other things, that one in six members of staff working in mental health and learning disability services was assaulted in the year 2006–2007. The memorandum is available at www.cps.gov.uk/publications/agencies/mounhs.html.

system is designed to offer protection to the public and can do so without the need for what might be characterised as a show trial.

Mitigating features and mental disorder

5.16 Public interest factors that make a prosecution less likely are set out at paragraph 4.17 of the Code, and include some that are of obvious relevance if a defendant has a mental disorder. However, the existence of mental disorder in relation to a victim or witness may also be a factor that has to be taken into account. Of most direct relevance are factors g) and j). The former relates to the possible difficulties that might be caused to the physical or mental health of a victim; the latter refers to the fact that:

> j) the suspect is, or was at the time of the offence, suffering from significant mental or physical ill health, unless the offence is serious or there is a real possibility that it may be repeated. Prosecutors apply Home Office guidelines about how to deal with mentally disordered offenders and must balance a suspect's mental or physical ill health with the need to safeguard the public or those providing care services to such persons[.]

5.17 As to the other features in favour of not prosecuting, mental disorder may be relevant to some of those. For example, factor a) looks at whether the court is likely to impose a nominal penalty: given that the aim of a hospital order involves stepping outside the realm of punishment, this is a relevant consideration. Factor c), while not directly relevant, since it refers to regulatory proceedings and civil penalties that address the seriousness of the offending, makes the point of asking whether there is anything more that a criminal prosecution can achieve: this approach is no doubt similar to the question of what else would result compared to the use of the civil provisions of the MHA 1983, which are able to provide protection to the public.

5.18 Factor d) allows the prosecution to take into account whether the offence was the result of a mistake or misunderstanding; this may include a mistake arising from a misperception caused by a mental disorder. It should be noted that this might not arise solely in the case of a delusional disorder – for example, a feature of a personality disorder might be that a person takes an unusual view of events, such that their reactions are to some extend conditioned by a disorder that suggests the need for treatment rather than punishment via the criminal justice system.

5.19 A final matter that might be relevant is that factor f) allows questions of delay to be taken into account, at least in relation to a less serious offence. The potential for mental disorder to be relevant here is that if a suspect with mental disorder is admitted to hospital before the criminal justice proceedings become active, and a significant time elapses before the suspect is properly able to be charged, the staleness of the process might be a reason against proceeding.

Other guidelines

5.20 The Home Office guidelines to which reference is made in paragraph 4.17 of the Code for Crown Prosecutors include the indication in Home Office Circular 66/90 of September 1990 that: 'It is government policy that, wherever possible, mentally disordered persons should receive care and treatment from the health and social services'.[10] More specifically, even if there is evidence that justifies a prosecution, the public interest may lead to a different conclusion. The starting point for the assessment of this public interest is that: 'It is desirable that alternatives to prosecution, such as cautioning by the police, and/or admission to hospital, if the person's mental condition requires hospital treatment, or support in the community, should be considered first before deciding that prosecution is necessary'.[11]

5.21 In putting this policy into effect, it is noted that the police should consider issuing a caution, and, if the criteria for a caution are not met, should consider the need for any action, given the alternatives of a civil admission or even the provision of informal support.[12] The Circular notes that this requires effective co-ordination with the relevant community services.[13] This is spelled out in more detail in Home Office Circular 12/95, which among other things gives examples of local good practice as a manner of encouraging the development of the necessary inter-agency co-operation to ensure that diversion is put into effect.

10 Home Office Circular 66/90 para 2. Part of the reason for this, noted at paragraph 3, was that provisions for mentally disordered offenders in the prison system was such that courts should be encouraged to send those in need directly to NHS facilities.

11 Home Office Circular 66/90 para 2. It has been commented that there has been a change in attitude away from diversion by reason of the emphasis on risk management and control rather than care and treatment: see P Barlett and R Sandland, *Mental health law: policy and practice,* 3rd edn, Oxford University Press, 2007, p199. However, in the 2009 *Bradley Report: Lord Bradley's review of people with mental health problems or learning disabilities in the criminal justice system* (available at www.dh.gov.uk/en/Publicationsandstatistics/Publications/PublicationsPolicyAndGuidance/DH_098694) and government responses to that report, the policy of diversion has been reaffirmed, at least in theory.

12 Home Office Circular 66/90 para 4.iii.

13 Home Office Circular 66/90 paras 2, 4.iii.

5.22 The CPS also has guidance on these matters, which is meant to reflect the above central government policy as to diversion.[14] Among other things, this notes that information about alleged offenders who have mental disorder might come from various sources, including the police, but also from relatives, friends and custody staff; and that the Crown Prosecutor provided with such information may have reason to cause further investigations to be carried out, or to take steps such as securing that any court appearance is at a court which has arrangements in place for the assessment of defendants. It also specifically notes the need to consider the potential impact of mental disorder on the formulation of mens rea by the offender, or the reliability of any apparent confession, as well as any public interest factors to which the existence of mental disorder gives rise.

5.23 The CPS general guidance on mentally disordered offenders also has specific guidance as to the public interest factors that should be considered in determining whether a prosecution is needed. This involves asking whether action has been taken under Part II of the MHA 1983, it being noted that 'A prosecution is less likely to be needed if the offender is already receiving treatment that the court is likely to order on conviction'; naturally, this does not exclude a prosecution. Although it is also noted that a prosecution would be improper for the purpose of securing treatment for mental disorder, the factors that should be taken into account include the probable impact of a prosecution on the offender's health, the potential impact of treatment on offending behaviour but also the possible impact of a prosecution on such behaviour.

Cautioning, warning and reprimanding

5.24 A conclusion that the Full Code Test under the Code for Crown Prosecutors is met does not necessarily mean that there will be a prosecution, because there is also provision for out-of-court disposals, including a caution or a conditional caution, or in the case of youths the use of the warning and reprimanding system. Indeed, these are given prominence in the second core document used by the CPS in addition to the Code for Crown Prosecutors, namely its Core Quality Standards.[15] Standard 3 notes the value of out-of-court

14 Available at www.cps.gov.uk/legal/l_to_o/mentally_disordered_offenders/.

15 Available at www.cps.gov.uk/publications/core_quality_standards/index.html.

disposals because of their scope for securing speedy reparation for victims and action against offenders.

Simple cautions – adults

5.25 The practice of cautioning is set out in Home Office Guidance, the latest version of which is Home Office Circular 16/2008.[16] It notes that a caution is available for all offences, including indictable-only offences, though the latter should lead to a caution only after there has been consultation with the CPS. See also parts 10 and 23 of the DPP's Guidance on Charging,[17] Decisions as to simple cautions in indictable-only cases must be referred to Crown Prosecutors.[18]

5.26 The fact that there can be cautions in indictable-only cases may be inconsistent with the basic proposition that the process is designed for 'low-level offending' (as noted in paragraph 3 of Home Office Circular 16/2008). However, from the point of view of someone representing a defendant with mental health issues who has been charged with an indictable-only offence, it should first be noted that it is clearly accepted that such offences can be dealt with by way of a caution: although Home Office Circular 16/2008 notes in paragraph 3 that only in exceptional circumstances should it be a method of dealing with anything other than low-level crime, it makes it clear at paragraph 11 that it is possible if the CPS so decide.

5.27 It should also be noted that the assessment of whether offending is 'low-level' could quite properly be taken to refer to an assessment of the level of culpability of an offender: this might mean that it can be said that where mental disorder provides a proper basis for saying that responsibility is diminished significantly or for mitigation of the sentence, then a more serious offence can properly be classified as

16 Available at http://webarchive.nationalarchives.gov.uk/+/http://www.homeoffice.gov.uk/about-us/publications/home-office-circulars/circulars-2008/016-2008/.

17 Fourth edition, January 2011, which will be introduced among police areas gradually. This is available at www.cps.gov.uk/publications/directors_guidance/dpp_guidance_4.html.

18 In the memorandum of understanding agreed between the CPS and the NHS as to the use of prosecutions to safeguard NHS staff, it is recorded at part 8 that cautions will not be administered without obtaining the views of the victim. This is available at www.cps.gov.uk/publications/agencies/mounhs.html. This is a stronger statement than generally applicable: paragraph 20 of Home Office Circular 16/2008 refers to the views of the victim being obtained where appropriate.

being 'low-level' in comparison to the same offence committed by an offender without any mental disorder.

5.28 The criteria for the use of a simple caution, which are described in part 9 of Home Office Circular 16/2008, are:

i) the person to be cautioned is aged 18 or older;[19]
ii) there is a realistic prospect of conviction;
iii) a caution is in the public interest;
iv) a caution is appropriate in the light of the offence and the offending history; and
v) there is a clear and reliable admission.

The final factor may be the matter that is problematic if there are question marks over the reliability of any confession in light of the mental disorder; it is also recorded at paragraph 25 of Home Office Circular 16/2008 that the offender must give informed consent to the administration of the caution. However, it is noted in the CPS guidance on mentally disordered offenders[20] that it should not be assumed that a person with a mental disorder is ineligible: it is suggested that suitable steps be taken, perhaps with assistance from a suitable member of a psychiatric liaison team or some other appropriate professional, to ensure that the defendant understands what is happening and can give informed consent.

5.29 The consequences of a caution are that it is recorded as offending behaviour, may influence decisions by the police of the defendant comes to their notice again, may be cited in court proceedings, will feature if police records are used for vetting purposes and may have to be declared for matters such as visas. It will also mean, in relation to a caution for a sexual offence, that the offender has to register on the sex offender register for two years: see sections 80 and 82 of the Sexual Offences Act 2003. In the light of the significant consequences that may flow, there have been instances of cautions being set aside in judicial review proceedings because of the lack of informed consent, starting with *R v Commissioner of the Metropolitan Police ex p Thompson*.[21]

5.30 If an offender cannot be cautioned, for example because of doubts about the reliability of a confession in the light of mental disorder, that does not necessarily mean that the matter will have to proceed.

19 Reprimands or warnings, or conditional cautions are available for youths: see below.

20 Available at www.cps.gov.uk/legal/l_to_o/mentally_disordered_offenders/.

21 [1997] 1 WLR 1519.

If the public interest criteria for a caution are present, but there is no reliable confession or informed consent to the caution because of mental disorder, the question to be addressed is whether the appropriate course is to take no further action, which could be combined with an informal warning as to future conduct.

Reprimands and warnings

5.31 In the case of those aged under 18, the formal caution is not possible because there is a statutory alternative: this is set out in sections 65 and 66 of the Crime and Disorder Act (CDA) 1998. A reprimand is possible if there is a realistic prospect of a conviction, an admission, and the public interest supports a reprimand rather than a prosecution; it is not possible if there has been a previous conviction, and if there has been a previous reprimand, the next step should be a warning. It is also possible to start at a warning if the offence is more serious. A warning should only be given once, unless any further offence is more than two years after the previous warning and is not sufficiently serious to justify a charge. The features that might be relevant to the use of a caution in the case of an adult will invariably support the use of a reprimand or warning as appropriate in the case of a youth with mental health problems; and if there are doubts as to the ability of the youth to make the necessary admission, that can be used to support the view that no further action should be taken and the civil mental health system called into play (or action taken under the Children Act 1989).

Conditional cautions

5.32 Section 22 of the CJA 2003 provides a statutory basis for a conditional caution to be given by police officers or a prosecutor if the criteria set out in section 23 of the Act are met. These include that there is sufficient evidence of the offence and that it has been admitted (not necessarily during the course of the investigation, though it must be admitted before the caution is issued). Conditions can be imposed, including ones relevant to the rehabilitation of the offender (see section 22(3)(a)), and the consequence of failure to abide by the conditions can be that a prosecution is instituted.

5.33 The prosecutor must form the view that a conditional caution is proper: in other words, it is not a decision for the police, even though the police may be involved in administering the caution.[22] In reaching this decision that the conditional caution is proper, a Code of Practice offering guidance is issued by the Secretary of State for Justice and laid before Parliament: see CJA 2003 s25. The current version of this Code of Practice, the sixth edition, was brought into effect in January 2010.[23] Part 4 of the Code notes that public interest factors may be taken into account, but there is nothing specifically mentioned relating to mental disorder. There is also an indication that accepting guilt and being willing to accept conditions may support a caution, which may cause problems if an offender with mental disorder has difficulties in this regard or might have a defence based on the disorder. Part 5 of the Code gives guidance on the types of conditions that might be imposed, which may be for rehabilitative purposes, which will include situations where mental disorder has been implicated in the offending for some reason:[24] paragraph 5.3 of the Code notes that a 'problem-solving approach' should be applied to the conditions, aiming to change behaviour. Part 6 of the Code, however, suggests that conditions should be capable of completion within a fairly short time period, and with a maximum of 16 weeks if the offence is summary-only. This is to allow time for prosecution if conditions are not met, but it may present difficulties in the case of mental health problems that are of a chronic nature and require a longer time-frame.

5.34 There is specific guidance on the application of conditional cautions to offenders with mental disorder. In the document, *Diverting offenders with mental health problems and/or learning disabilities within the National Conditional Cautioning Framework*,[25] it is noted that a conditional caution is a serious matter, forming part of a criminal record, and should not be used where a simple caution or information action would be preferable.[26] There are also examples given of

22 PACE ss37(7) and (7B) and 37B are relevant in this regard: they relate to the power of the custody officer to detain or release on bail while advice is sought as to charging or the use of an alternative such as a conditional caution.

23 The Code is available at www.cps.gov.uk/legal/a_to_c/cautioning_and_diversion/.

24 Code para 5.11 notes the possibility of underlying problems implicated in the offending.

25 CPS, 2010. Available at www.cps.gov.uk/legal/d_to_g/diverting_offenders_with_mental_health_problems_and_or_learning_disabilities_within_the_national_/.

26 *Diverting offenders with mental health problems and/or learning disabilities within the National Conditional Cautioning Framework* para 5.

local schemes that are relevant to dealing with mental health problems: part of the aim of the document is to encourage those areas of the country that do not have appropriate provisions in place to develop them.[27]

5.35 There was no provision for conditional cautions for youths in the original legislation, but section 48 of and Schedule 9 to the Criminal Justice and Immigration Act 2008 have inserted sections 66A–66H into the CDA 1998 to allow for youth conditional cautions. This is due to be introduced gradually.

Anti-social behaviour orders

5.36 Another alternative to prosecution that might be considered is the putting into place of an anti-social behaviour order (ASBO).[28] These can be sought both after a conviction and without the need for such a conviction: see CDA 1998 ss1 and 1C.[29] Anti-social behaviour is action that is likely to cause harassment, alarm or distress to those outside a person's family; it can lead to an application being made to the local magistrates' court for an order prohibiting conduct specified in the order for at least two years. The test for including prohibitions in an ASBO is that it is necessary to protect the public from anti-social behaviour to include such conditions. A breach of the order is a criminal offence carrying up to five years' imprisonment.

5.37 The question of the propriety of an ASBO being issued against an individual with a mental disorder was considered in *Cooke v Director of Public Prosecutions*,[30] which involved someone with a personality disorder (and possibly an autistic spectrum disorder) who had been convicted of a minor public order offence based on aggressive begging in a town centre. The ASBO conditions included not to beg or engage in various other acts. The Divisional Court upheld the ASBO on the basis that Mr Cooke was capable of complying with it and so it did not criminalise his mental disorder. However, Dyson LJ noted at paragraph 10 that if the factual scenario was that 'by reason of mental incapacity an offender is incapable of complying with an order, then

27 *Diverting offenders with mental health problems and/or learning disabilities within the National Conditional Cautioning Framework* para 13.

28 For a full account of the law relating to ASBOs, see M Sikand, *ASBOs: a practitioner's guide to defending anti-social behaviour orders*, LAG, 2006.

29 The initial provisions have been supplemented, including by the Anti-social Behaviour Act 2003.

30 [2008] EWHC 2703 (Admin), [2008] MHLR 348.

an order is incapable of protecting the public and cannot therefore be said to be necessary to protect the public'. But he added at paragraph 13 that the mere fact that someone had a personality disorder and so was liable to disobey an ASBO was not a sufficient reason not to make an order.

5.38 It has also been noted by the Court of Appeal that it is possible to combine an ASBO with an order such as a hospital order, but that such a course might be considered artificial: see *R v Chaudhury*.[31]

Penalty notices for disorder

5.39 A further alternative to commencing a criminal prosecution is the use of the penalty notice for disorder (PND) regime contained in Part 1 of the Criminal Justice and Police Act 2001, which allows on-the-spot fines to be issued by officers in uniform in the street or by authorised officers in police stations for various low level offences. Guidance issued by the Secretary of State for the exercise of this power notes that the PND regime is not appropriate for those who cannot understand the process by reason of mental disorder.[32]

Charging and post-charging actions

5.40 If diversion, whether formal or not, is not appropriate, an offender with mental disorder may be prosecuted. In the police station, this will usually involve being charged. Paragraph 16.1 of Code C of the PACE Codes of Practice indicates that the question of charging turns on a reasonable belief that there is sufficient evidence of a realistic prospect of conviction. Naturally, the presence of mental disorder may be relevant to the offence charged, perhaps particularly in relation to the mens rea. In this context, it is worth noting that it may be proper for the custody officer to defer the question of charging to the CPS.[33]

31 [2011] EWCA Crim 936, [2011] MHLR 157 at paras 17 and 18.

32 The guidance is issued under Criminal Justice and Police Act 2001 s6; it can be found in the Police Operational Guidance issued by the Home Office in March 2005, paragraph 7.3. The Guidance is available at www.homeoffice.gov.uk/publications/police/operational-policing/penalty-notices-guidance/.

33 This is contained in PACE ss37(7), 37A and 37B: the detainee may be held in custody or released pending this outcome. See also PACE Code of Practice, Code C para 16(1A) and (1B). See www.cps.gov.uk/publications/directors_guidance/dpp_guidance_4.html for the guidance issued which is effective from January 2011.

5.41 It is also provided in paragraph 16.1 that: 'If the detainee is … mentally disordered or otherwise mentally vulnerable, any resulting action shall be taken in the presence of the appropriate adult if they are present at the time'.

5.42 The steps to be taken after charge are, first, the giving of a caution, including the warning as to adverse inferences from silence (the form being 'You do not have to say anything. But it may harm your defence if you do not mention now something which you later rely on in court. Anything you do say may be given in evidence'. If the circumstances are such that adverse inferences cannot be drawn – which are described in Annex C and cover a situation where a defendant has asked for legal advice but it has not been provided prior to charge – an alternative caution is proper, namely that: 'You do not have to say anything, but anything you do say may be given in evidence'.

5.43 The second step is the giving of a written notice of charge, containing details of the offence: see Code C para 16.3, which also states expressly that the notice should be given to an appropriate adult when the detainee is mentally disordered or otherwise mentally vulnerable.

5.44 The third step depends on whether an officer wishes to show the detainee a written statement or interview with another person about the offence, which is done together with a caution about anything said being given in evidence and a reminder that nothing need to be said and that the detainee has a right to legal advice; this is set out in Code C para 16.4, and paragraph 16.4a indicates that a copy has to be given to the appropriate adult if the suspect is mentally disordered or vulnerable.

5.45 The final point is that, while post-charge interviewing is generally prohibited, it may be allowed in limited circumstances, namely to minimise harm or loss to another or others, to clear up an ambiguity, or to allow a detainee the chance to comment on new information if that is in the interests of justice. Any such interview should be accompanied by a caution that nothing need be said but that anything said may be given in evidence, and that there is a right to legal advice.

5.46 Paragraph 16.6 notes the need to carry out these steps in the presence of the appropriate adult if he or she is at the station, or to repeat them once he or she arrives: however, this is subject to the question of whether the detainee is still present. This is because it is noted in Code C, Note for Guidance 16C that there is no power under PACE to delay the taking of steps that are provided for in Code C paras 16.2–16.5 in order to await the arrival of the appropriate adult.[34]

5.47 This may produce an invidious position of taking steps that may be important in the context of subsequent proceedings and for which the role of the nearest relative is very important, such that arguments might be presented to exclude any evidence that is incriminatory. But it is equally important to detain only when there are lawful grounds to do so, and the lack of a statutory power to wait until the appropriate adult arrives can be taken as a decision by the legislature that it is not proportionate to detain in that situation. This in turn means that custody officers must take steps to co-ordinate with the appropriate adult to ensure attendance at the time when a decision on charge is likely to be made.

5.48 Note for Guidance 16C also records that decisions on bail cannot be deferred or bail refused because the appropriate adult is not yet present. Once an offender has been charged, PACE s38 requires the custody officer to make a decision about whether or not to release the person or detain them for the next available court sitting. The power to detain depends on the presence of a ground for withholding bail,[35] such as the need to ensure attendance at court, prevent further offending or injury to a person or damage to property. PACE s47(1A) allows the custody sergeant to impose conditions, though some conditions are available to courts only, including attending for a medical report: see Bail Act 1976 s3A(2).[36]

5.49 In making the decision as to bail and as to any conditions, it is to be noted that paragraph 33.2 of the English Code of Practice issued under MHA 1983 s118 indicates that:

> 33.2 People who are subject to criminal proceedings have the same rights to psychiatric assessment and treatment as anyone else. Any person who is in police or prison custody or before the courts charged

34 Code C Annex E para 11 (the summary of matters relating to those with mental disorder) is in stronger terms, suggesting that the charge can only be in the presence of the appropriate adult; but this must reflect the inadequacy of the summary.

35 PACE s38(2A) requires the custody sergeant have regard to the same factors as arise under the Bail Act 1976.

36 An application may be made to the custody officer (or another one at the same station) to vary the conditions (though that may lead to more onerous conditions): see Bail Act 1976 s3A(4)). The magistrates' court may also vary the conditions on application: see Magistrates' Courts Act 1980 s43B(1) and (2).

with a criminal offence and who is in need of medical treatment for mental disorder should be considered for admission to hospital.[37]

5.50 For example, if the defendant meets the criteria for detention under the civil provisions of the MHA 1983, the custody sergeant may be able to release on bail so as to allow detention under those provisions. In an extreme situation, a failure to allow that to happen may amount to treatment that breaches article 3 of the European Convention on Human Rights; the Codes of Practice note that mentally disordered people may be at significant risk of self-harm in police stations.[38]

5.51 This is subject to the caveat that section 25 of the Criminal Justice and Public Order Act (CJPOA) 1994 indicates that those with a previous conviction for homicide or rape or various other serious sexual offences who are charged with such an offence a second time can be granted bail only in exceptional circumstances: if a defendant is in need of care for mental disorder, this might be argued to provide an exceptional circumstance. It is worth noting that a finding of not guilty by reason of insanity or of being unfit to stand trial but having committed the act count as convictions for this statute: see CJPOA 1994 s25(5).[39]

37 There are equivalent provisions in paragraph 32.2 of the Welsh Code of Practice.

38 This is a feature that has justified the imposition of a duty of care to prevent suicide irrespective of a diagnosis of mental disorder: see *Metropolitan Police Commissioner v Reeves* [2000] 1 AC 360.

39 There is also a power in PACE s37(8A) and (8B) to detain for the purpose of testing for the presence of a class A drug if PACE ss63B and 63C apply.

PART III

Procedure and evidence

CHAPTER 6

Bail and other preliminary and procedural matters

Introduction

6.1 If a defendant with mental health problems is charged and either bailed to appear in court or held in custody and produced to court, a number of issues might arise in relation to which mental health issues may be relevant. These include the question of legal aid funding and release on bail. The question of whether there are good reasons for a prosecution to continue, which has been discussed in chapter 5, is something that involves a duty of continuous review – so new information coming to light as to a defendant's mental disorder and developments such as the use of the civil powers of detention may have to be assessed in order to determine whether the evidential sufficiency test or the public interest test continue to be met. If it ceases to be met, proceedings can be discontinued: whether one of the formal methods of diversion are used will depend on the circumstances and whether any necessary preconditions are met.

Securing information about a defendant's mental health

6.2 A court may need additional information about the mental health of a defendant. There are various powers to remand a defendant to a hospital for the preparation of a report or for treatment, though only the Crown Court can do the latter: these powers of remand to hospital are discussed in chapter 7. In addition, a number of courts have schemes working in conjunction with local health service to make clinical staff available at court on a regular timetable: the option of remanding a defendant to an appropriate day might be available, and in the larger urban areas it might be appropriate to transfer a case to a court that has such a scheme.[1]

6.3 If there is no established court assessment scheme operating, it is to be noted that Mental Health Act (MHA) 1983 ss39 and 39A contain

1 In some jurisdictions, specialist mental health courts have developed, which have an expertise in dealing with mental health-related issues that arise at trial or in relation to sentencing. An experiment with such a court in England was recently carried out, at Stratford and Brighton magistrates' courts, and produced positive results: see *Mental Health Court pilot: feasibility of an impact evaluation*, Ministry of Justice Research Summary 7/10, available at www.justice.gov.uk/publications/research-and-analysis/moj/mhc-process-feasibility-evaluation.htm.

duties on local hospital and social service authorities to provide information to courts that are minded to impose sentences of hospital orders (final or interim) or guardianship on the services available in the local area. In relation to those under 18, hospital authorities also have a duty as to the provision of information about facilities if the court is considering making a remand to hospital for a report or for treatment.

6.4 The Code of Practice issued under MHA 1983 s118 suggests that a named person should be appointed to carry out the liaison role to which these duties apply: see English Code paras 33.6 and 33.7 and Welsh Code paras 32.20 and 32.22. It is to be noted in relation to adult defendants, the language of the Codes does not limit this to final disposals: and the nominated person would have the skill to provide information relevant not just to final disposals but also to methods to secure assistance with court procedures from the outset.

6.5 To be remembered in this context is the option to remand on bail with a condition or conditions designed to secure medical treatment or the preparation of a necessary medical report;[2] indeed, this may be more appropriate if the court has in mind some form of community-based disposal. There is also the option to remand on bail with such limited restrictions as allow the defendant to be a patient under the civil provisions of the MHA 1983, which are outlined in chapter 2, namely the short-term detention for assessment and treatment under MHA 1983 s2 or the longer-term detention for treatment under section 3. If a patient is placed under the civil provisions, the responsible clinician (RC) can grant leave under section 17 for the purposes of attendance at court: this can include the patient being brought by staff from the hospital, since leave can involve a direction that the patient remain in the custody of staff, under section 17(3). It is also possible that a patient might be able to attend court without an escort if granted leave (and it may also be that a patient effectively resides outside hospital under MHA 1983 s17 or on a community treatment order under section 17A, in which case he or she will be in a position to attend court). The interplay between the Bail Act (BA) 1976 and questions of mental disorder is discussed further below.

2 Bail Act 1976 s3(6)(d).

Securing funding

6.6 This is not the appropriate place to describe the public funding system in detail. Broadly speaking, the grant of funding turns on the interests of justice (and whether that requires legal representation if the client does not wish to pay for it privately) and the means of the defendant. The interests of justice test will turn on various features, particularly the seriousness of the offence and any complexities that might arise. The presence of mental disorder may have a significant impact on this, which is recognised in the Criminal Legal Aid Manual.[3]

6.7 There are two additional procedural matters that should be noted. First, one of the reasons for giving priority to the processing of an application for legal aid is that the defendant has mental health problems: see part 4.2 of the Manual at page 40. In addition, the normal requirement that an application for legal aid be signed by the defendant may be waived if there are difficulties caused by the defendant's mental health, though this will involve decision-making by the National Courts Team: see part 4.4.5 and part 4.4.6 at pages 53–54.[4]

6.8 In the latter section, it is noted that an applicant for legal aid who lacks capacity as defined in the Mental Capacity Act (MCA) 2005 may secure representation on the basis of a form signed by someone who has been formally appointed under the MCA 2005 as an attorney or deputy, but also by someone who is the 'nearest relative or guardian', a 'Litigation friend' or 'Any other person who is acting in the applicant's best interest and who has sufficient knowledge of the applicant's financial affairs to be able to sign the declaration on the applicant's behalf'. The provision of information as to finances is viewed as a pre-condition of the third party's ability to sign; it is expressly stated that anyone involved in or associated with the solicitor's firm that will obtain the representation order cannot perform the role.

6.9 The term 'nearest relative' is to be found in MHA 1983 s26 and it describes the person who has to be consulted before a patient is

3 Available at www.legalservices.gov.uk/docs/cds_main/criminal_legal_aid_manual_feb_2012.pdf.

4 It is noted at page 54 that solicitors may be asked to provide information to verify that the defendant cannot sign, including the defendant's living circumstances and whether he or she has been detained under the MHA 1983, and how any disorder manifests itself in terms of affecting the ability of the defendant to provide instructions.

detained under section 3 of the Act and who can apply for the patient's discharge under section 23.[5] The nearest relative is defined by giving priority to relatives according to a list, but then by allowing a relative with whom the patient resides or who cares for the patient to take priority on account of that. A 'guardian' is also someone appointed to that role under MHA 1983 s7. And a 'litigation friend' is also a term of art, arising under rules of court in the civil setting and meaning someone who acts in litigation where a person is incapable of controlling their affairs by reason of mental disorder. While the Manual does not indicate that it has these particular provisions in mind, it is perhaps to be understood that the drafter was aware that they were terms with a specific meaning in the mental health context. There is also the final general term covering anyone who has the relevant information and can act in the best interests of the defendant.

6.10 Part 4.4.6 of the Manual also notes that some such defendants will not be able to give instructions, and then suggests that most of them will not proceed through the criminal system: that sounds like a sensible proposition, since a defendant who does not have capacity to understand that the signature required is for legal representation is unlikely to have the capacity to participate in the criminal process.

Taking and giving instructions

6.11 A fundamental starting point, of course, is that a lawyer must act on instructions. If a client is mentally disordered, this may present some ethical difficulties. In the context of mental health tribunal proceedings, which are concerned usually with the release of patients under MHA 1983 ss72–75, the Law Society has issued guidance on representation,[6] in which a distinction is drawn between clients with and without capacity to litigate. It is noted that there is in the civil context a test of litigation capacity, namely being able to understand the issues on which consent or a decision is likely, with legal and other relevant advice.[7] The guidance suggests that the threshold is not high and that people with serious mental disorder may be able to provide instructions. If, however, the client is without capacity,

5 See chapter 2 for more information on the civil provisions of the MHA 1983.

6 *Representation before mental health tribunals*, May 2011. Available at www.lawsociety.org.uk/productsandservices/practicenotes/mentalhealthtribunal/3386.article.

7 The authority for this is *Masterman-Lister v Brutton and Co* [2003] 1 WLR 1511, [2003] MHLR 166.

a solicitor can act only if instructed by someone able to act for the client, such as a deputy appointed under the MCA 2005 or the holder of a power of attorney. Naturally, a solicitor is not in a position to assess capacity, and expert advice must be sought.

6.12 This guidance may be helpful in part in a criminal setting by analogy. However, the more important question is of fitness to stand trial or to participate in the trial process, which is discussed in chapters 9 and 10. A defendant who is not fit to stand trial may nevertheless be able to give instructions on matters such as whether they wish to have an application made for bail and which conditions of bail are acceptable, and whether they are able and willing to comply with investigations into their mental state of the sort that might be important in the conduct of proceedings.

6.13 It is worth outlining at this stage the sorts of matters on which expert evidence might be useful:

a) The current mental state of the defendant might be relevant to fitness to participate and the appropriate disposal (whether a disposal under the MHA 1983 or a sentence based on the dangerousness of the offender); whether, if the defendant can participate, it would be improper to allow adverse inferences to be drawn; whether the defendant should be on bail to better facilitate treatment or remanded to hospital rather than in custody, and also the question of discontinuance on public interest grounds.
b) The mental state of the defendant at the time of any interaction with the police may be relevant to questions such as the admissibility of any apparent confession or whether there should be an adverse inference from failing to comment in the police station.
c) The mental state of the defendant at the time of the incident may be relevant to whether there is a basis for raising an insanity defence, of suggesting that any mens rea was not formed, and it may go to partial defences to homicide (diminished responsibility, infanticide or loss of control or provocation), and perhaps also to whether such general defences as duress or self-defence are made out, and whether an honest but mistaken belief clouded the defendant's judgment and actions.

6.14 The question of discontinuance has been mentioned already; all the other questions will be addressed in subsequent chapters. In terms of the question of who to approach, there may be various factors. A client who is well-known to mental health services may have an RC who knows the client in detail; at the same time, that clinician may be a general psychiatrist rather than one versed in the interface between the criminal justice system and mental health. Forensic clinicians, whether psychiatrists or psychologists, may be much more familiar with what is required for a criminal court.

6.15 In terms of the choice between a psychiatrist and psychologist, the former are medical doctors and there are various occasions when a medical report is necessary. However, in relation to various questions such as the intelligence and social functioning ability of a defendant with a learning disability or an autistic spectrum disorder, it may be that tests of the sort that psychologists are most familiar with will be useful. There may, of course, be situations when both a psychiatrist and psychologist can provide relevant information.

6.16 To be noted is the duty applicable to expert witnesses by reason of the Criminal Procedure Rules (CPR) 2011,[8] Part 33 of which sets out the specific duties of the expert both in relation to the structure of the report and processes such as meetings between experts. A single joint expert report may be ordered by the court, but it is to be noted that in many situations, such as findings of unfitness to stand trial or the making of a hospital order, it is necessary for two experts to give evidence. There are also duties set out as to the service of reports; failures to comply with this duty may raise an issue as to whether a party is not meeting the general obligation to assist the overriding objecting in rule 1 of the CPR 2011 because failures as to timely service may cause problems in relation to case management: see, for example, *R v Ensor*,[9] in which the Court of Appeal upheld a decision not to admit expert evidence relating to whether an adverse inference direction should be given in relation to the defendant's failure to give evidence, which was based on the late service of the relevant report.

The interplay between mental disorder and the Bail Act 1976

Grounds for withholding bail

6.17 Section 4 of the BA 1976 provides a presumptive right to bail, subject to a limited number of circumstances in which there is a statutory presumption against bail being granted. Under section 25 of the Criminal Justice and Public Order Act (CJPOA) 1994, those with a previous conviction for homicide or rape or various other serious

8 SI No 1709.

9 [2009] EWCA Crim 2519, [2010] MHLR 4.

sexual offences who are charged with such an offence a second time can be granted bail only in exceptional circumstances: if a defendant is in need of care for mental disorder, this might be argued to provide an exceptional circumstance. It is worth noting that a finding of not guilty by reason of insanity or of being unfit to stand trial but having committed the act count as convictions for this statute: see CJPOA 1994 s25(5).[10] A second exception arises by way of BA 1976 Sch 1 para 2A, under which the presumption in favour of bail does not apply to someone who is alleged to have committed a further indictable or either way offence while on bail.

6.18 The presumption in favour of bail that applies in most circumstances means that the prosecution have to put forward good reasons why bail should not be granted, which are set out in Schedule 1 to the BA 1976. If the offence can be punished with imprisonment, Schedule 1 Part I para 2(1) provides a power to decline to grant bail if there are 'substantial grounds for believing' that the defendant would abscond, commit a further offence or obstruct justice, including by interfering with witnesses.[11] This applies as much to a defendant with mental disorder as it does to a defendant without mental disorder, and it may be that arguments can be put forward that rely on mental disorder for assessing these grounds. Care should no doubt be taken to ensure that any arguments have a proper basis and do not rely on prejudicial assumptions as to the impact of mental disorder.

6.19 As with the preparation of necessary medical reports, it is also possible that arrangements under the civil provisions of the MHA 1983 will provide a basis for answering such grounds, or even that the sort of monitoring that can be arranged through community care arrangements (to which a person in need of such assistance is entitled) will provide management for any risky behaviours. See chapter 2 for an outline of the community care framework and of the basis for intervention under the MHA 1983. Such arrangements may also provide a reason for granting bail to someone who has been charged with a further offence while on bail (when the presumption in favour of bail is disapplied): the use of the civil powers might provide adequate satisfaction that the risks of further offending are contained. The same line of argument can apply in relation to defendants arrested for breaching bail conditions: see Schedule 1 para 6. It may also be

10 There is also a power in Police and Criminal Evidence Act 1984 (PACE) s37(8A) and (8B) to detain for the purpose of testing for the presence of a class A drug if PACE ss63B and 63C apply.

11 See BA 1976 Sch 1 Part II in relation to non-imprisonable offences, which includes the absconding and own welfare grounds discussed below.

that a defendant whose bail position is affected by the provisions of Schedule 1 para 6A, relating to having tested positive for class A drugs, can be positively assisted by the intervention of civil mental health services, since it is common that mental disorder may be affected by drug abuse and that mental health services will have access to additional services designed to deal with the problems of drug abuse.

6.20 An additional ground for withholding bail is provided under Schedule 1 para 3, namely: 'if the court is satisfied that the defendant should be kept in custody for his own protection or, if he is a child or young person, for his own welfare'. Again, the obvious point arising is that the need to protect the defendant may well be secured best by the use of the civil powers that arise under the MHA 1983. In this connection, it is worth noting that the policy that governs the situation of those with mental disorder in the criminal justice system should not have their access to treatment delayed.[12] This may mean that a court should allow release (perhaps with suitable conditions) to allow access to treatment or care: while prison facilities may be able to provide care, it may well be rudimentary compared to what is provided by the hospital sector.

Conditions on bail

6.21 The existence of a ground for withholding bail does not necessarily mean that there is to be a remand into custody, since it may be possible that suitable conditions on release will meet the relevant concerns. Bail Act (BA) 1976 s3(6) specifically provides the power to impose conditions such as are necessary to secure surrender to custody, no further offending or obstruction of justice; section 3(6)(ca) provides a power to impose conditions for the protection of the defendant and section 3(6)(d) refers to the defendant making himself or herself available for inquiries or reports.

6.22 Again, there might be an interplay between health services and the court. To give a simple example: if a defendant is of no fixed abode, which might support grounds to believe that absconding is more likely, but the reason the defendant has no fixed abode is that he or she has mental health problems that have led to homelessness, the involvement of mental health services – whether community care services or a hospital place at the outset, which might lead

12 See, for example, the provisions of Part 33 of the Code of Practice under the MHA 1983, discussed in chapter 5; and paragraph 4 of the guidance in Home Office Circular 66/90.

to community-based provision once stability is achieved – might be to the benefit of all. So the use of a bail hostel, which might often be the response to the position of a defendant of no fixed abode, might be a step that should be followed only if a defendant cannot be placed in a therapeutic setting. (Indeed, it may be that bail hostels are not willing to accept defendants with mental health problems.) See also BA 1976 s3(6C)–(6F) and following in relation to the need to make arrangements for reports on people who have tested positive for class A drugs: this might be possible via mental health services.

6.23 There may also be circumstances in which conditions are imposed to deal with issues that might arise in the course of the trial. One such is the requirement imposed by virtue of BA 1976 s3(6A) that a person accused of murder who is placed on bail must be required to co-operate with the preparation of psychiatric reports unless such reports have been obtained. It is suggested that as the involvement of a doctor may have implications for rights arising under article 8 of the European Convention on Human Rights, a defendant should be allowed an element of choice in relation to such a report: there may be proper reasons to require a report to assist the court to ensure that it is fully informed as to issues that might arise, but since a medical examination will involve a review of matters protected by confidentiality, the question of the proportionality of the intervention may be affected by whether or not the defendant is allowed an element of choice.

6.24 As to typical conditions that might be applied, there may be conditions as to residence, co-operation with reports, co-operation with community mental health teams, and perhaps even conditions as to residence in a hospital setting. However, it should be noted that conditions such as the latter may prove problematic if, for example, the defendant's mental state changes and he has to move to a different hospital. It may also be objected that such a condition secures what the MHA 1983 only allows by way of a formal remand to hospital under sections 35 and 36 of that Act.

Breach of bail

6.25 Finally, it is worth commenting that the offence of breaching the duty to attend court, which is an incident of bail, provides a defence of reasonable cause. The involvement of mental health issues may be relevant to whether that exists, particularly if a defendant has been placed under the civil powers from the community and does not attend court: the clinical team may not necessarily be aware of the court appearance or might advise that a defendant is not fit to attend court.

Case management

6.26 The era of active case management, now governed by the CPR 2011 and including the duty of the parties set out in rule 1.2 to assist the court to secure the overriding objective of dealing with cases justly, may be affected by mental disorder-related questions. This applies both in the magistrates' court and in the Crown Court. For example, as is discussed in chapters 10 and 13, issues relating to fitness to trial and insanity in the magistrates' court may involve the need to adjourn to seek appropriate evidence: in *R (Singh) v Stratford Magistrates' Court*,[13] the Divisional Court suggested that the potential for adjourned hearings is such that cases involving these issues should, where possible, be put in front of a district judge so that continuity can be achieved.[14]

6.27 In the Crown Court, there is the regime of preparatory hearings for complex, serious or lengthy cases, or serious fraud cases: see Criminal Justice Act 1987 s7 and Criminal Procedure and Investigations Act 1996 s29, as supplemented by Part 15 of the CPR 2011. It is always possible that the reasons for complexity include matters relating to mental disorder: as an example, see *R v B, W, S, H and W*,[15] in which two of the ten defendants in a sexual abuse trial were found to be unfit to stand trial and an issue arising was whether the further proceedings involving defendants who were unfit should be tried at the same time as the trials of the other defendants (on which see chapter 9).

6.28 The more normal procedural hearing in the Crown Court is the preliminary hearing (PH) or the plea and case management hearing (PCMH): reference should be made to paragraph IV.41 of the Consolidated Practice Direction.[16] One of the grounds for a PH rather than a PCMH is where there are 'case management issues which call for' a PH: it may be argued that the involvement of mentally vulnerable defendants, the prospect of having to explore such issues as fitness to stand trial or participate, the need to secure that defendants are placed in a suitably therapeutic environment, or indeed the other issues that arise under the rubric of mentally disorder and its impact on the trial process, are such that active case management is

13 [2007] EWHC 1582 (Admin), [2007] MHLR 274.

14 [2007] EWHC 1582 (Admin), [2007] MHLR 274 para 42.

15 [2008] EWCA Crim 1997, [2008] MHLR 320.

16 Available at www.justice.gov.uk/guidance/courts/procedure-rules/criminal/pd_consolidated.

particularly warranted. However, it is to be noted that box 9 of the current PCMH questionnaire (labelled as revised July 2011) includes a requirement to indicate details of any issues of fitness to stand trial: and the guidance note to the form indicates the need to set a timetable for the expert evidence in the case. See also parts 12 in relation to expert evidence generally, 18 and 19 in relation to any special measures for vulnerable defendants, 22 in relation to any questions of admissibility of interviews, 30 in relation to any other issues of law and 34 in relation to any other special arrangements.

6.29 It is also worth noting that paragraph IV.36 requires advance notice and sets out requirements for applications to stay Crown Court proceedings for abuse of process: see chapter 9 relating to ability to participate, which includes both the formal fitness to stand trial process and the wider question of the ability of the defendant to participate, which may lead to an abuse of process argument.

6.30 Some of these procedural matters merit more detailed consideration, which is provided in the following chapters.

Attendance of the defendant

6.31 As is discussed in relation to fitness to participate, the defendant is generally required to be present. However, it is also clear that a trial may proceed in the absence of the defendant. The authority that establishes the principles on this question is *R v Jones*,[17] in which it was confirmed that there was a discretion to proceed in the absence of the defendant. As to the factors relevant to the exercise of the discretion,[18] it was noted that caution is the watchword and that 'a defendant afflicted by involuntary illness or incapacity will have much stronger grounds for resisting the continuance of the trial than one who has voluntarily chosen to abscond'.[19] The emphasis in the case is on the situation of someone who voluntarily and consciously waives the right to appear at their trial by absconding, which will not be the description to be applied to someone who is not able to attend by reason of mental disorder. It may therefore be a very unusual situation in which it is proper to proceed when a defendant is not able to exercise his or her right to attend by reason of mental disorder.

17 [2002] UKHL 5, [2003] 1 AC 1.

18 Noted at [2002] UKHL 5, [2003] 1 AC 1 para 11 to be different from the position in Scotland.

19 [2002] UKHL 5, [2003] 1 AC 1 per Lord Bingham at para 6.

However, it is also to be noted that not all mental disorders deprive people of capacity, and so it is also possible that a defendant who needs to be in hospital on account of mental disorder has the same ability to consent to the trial continuing in his or her absence as if the defendant were indisposed by reason of a physical illness.

CHAPTER 7

Remand prisoners and transfer to hospital – court powers

Remand for a report under Mental Health Act 1983 s35

Reasons for a report

7.1 There are several obvious reasons why it might be necessary to obtain a psychiatric report. For example, in relation to the trial stage, there may be the questions of whether there is an insanity defence, or whether the defendant is fit to stand trial; there may also be questions such as the admissibility of evidence or whether a defendant should be subject to an adverse inference direction in the light of mental disorder.

7.2 Reports will also be relevant at the sentencing stage. In the first place, the making of a hospital order or a guardianship order under section 37 of the Mental Health Act (MHA) 1983 has as a precondition that there are two medical reports that attest to the medical criteria under the Act being met. The second reason why a medical report might be necessary at the sentencing stage arises from section 157(1) of the Criminal Justice Act (CJA) 2003, which requires the court to obtain a medical report before passing a custodial sentence if 'the offender is or appears to be mentally disordered'. This does not arise in relation to a sentence fixed by law, and the court can disapply the requirement if it forms the view that it is unnecessary.[1] Although this can be an oral report, it may often be that a written report is more practical (and that will often be the only possibility unless the court has some form of duty psychiatrist arrangement).

Criteria

7.3 If there are reasons why a medical report cannot be obtained with the defendant on bail, MHA 1983 s35 provides the court with a power to remand an accused to hospital for a report on his or her mental condition. A precondition to the use of this power is that it is not practicable to obtain it with the defendant on bail: this does not necessarily mean that the defendant is not co-operating, as it may be that the lack of practicability arises from the fact that the defendant is not on bail and cannot properly be admitted to bail. Section 35 may of particular value in such a situation, as the preparation of an accurate medical report might be more likely as a result of a placement in hospital rather than a placement in a prison setting (for example, because

1 CJA 2003 s157(2).

the doctor preparing the report will have the benefit of more contact and/or more assessment by clinically-trained or experienced staff). Accordingly, it is an option that defence advocates should bear in mind rather than relying on the preparation of a report on a defendant remanded into custody.

7.4 The 'accused' for the purposes of this power depends on whether the matter is in front of the Crown Court or the magistrates. It is defined in section 35(2) as someone awaiting trial or someone who 'has not yet been sentenced or otherwise dealt with for the offence on which he has been arraigned' in the Crown Court.[2] In relation to the magistrates' court, the section 35 power applies in two situations:

a) In relation to people who have been convicted of an offence carrying imprisonment or found to have committed the act or omission charged of such an offence. In the latter situation, the magistrates are able to impose a hospital order or a guardianship order without recording a conviction.[3]
b) If the person consents to such a remand.

This latter situation does not seem on its face to be limited to a situation after a finding of guilt or that the act or omission was committed or caused;[4] however, it is suggested that it must involve a capacitated consent.[5]

7.5 The test on the merits for the making of an order under section 35 is two-fold: first, the evidence from the doctor must leave the court satisfied that there is reason to suspect that the defendant is mentally

2 But note that the power cannot be exercised if the sentence is fixed by law: see MHA 1983 s35(3). This excludes the power in relation to a defendant convicted of murder (but not prior to the trial).

3 See MHA 1983 s37(3), which allows the summary court to deal with the issue of insanity and unfitness to stand trial, or simply to proceed without recording a conviction.

4 In *R v Calder Magistrates' Court ex p Grant*, 11 May 1998 (CO/655/98), Richards J expressed a preliminary view that the magistrates seemed to be in error in considering that section 35 could only be used when the court was moving towards a disposal of a case.

5 A patient can be placed in a psychiatric hospital as a voluntary patient under MHA 1983 s131 or under the compulsory powers; the effect of *HL v UK* [2004] MHLR 236, (2005) 40 EHRR 32, (2004) 7 CCLR 498 is that patients without capacity who are compliant and placed in hospital under the common law doctrine of necessity are given inadequate protection for the purposes of article 5 of the European Convention on Human Rights (ECHR). The detention of such patients is now regulated by the Deprivation of Liberty Safeguards in Mental Capacity Act (MCA) 2005 ss4A and 4B and Schs A1 and 1A, as inserted by the MHA 2007. It would be incongruous if section 35 authorised what amounts to detention on the basis of consent without capacity.

disordered; and second, as already noted, the court must also find that a remand on bail for the provision of a report would be 'impracticable'.[6] This should ensure that the use of the power of detention is proportionate;[7] it clearly requires that consideration first be given to the use of bail.

Procedural prerequisites

7.6 There are a number of procedural matters to note. MHA 1983 s35(3) requires a medical report from a 'registered medical practitioner' before the remand under section 35 is put into place. Section 54(1) provides that this doctor must be one who is approved by the Secretary of State under MHA 1983 s12 as having special experience in psychiatry.[8]

7.7 The other procedural requirement, set out in section 35(4), is that the court must be satisfied that a bed is available within seven days: this can be based on evidence from the approved clinician who will prepare the report or from the managers of the hospital.

7.8 The availability of a bed is an essential prerequisite to detention, and so is to be viewed as mandatory rather than merely directory. Accordingly, in *R (Bitcon) v (1) West Allerdale Magistrates' Court (2) Eden Valley Primary Care Trust*,[9] the High Court held that the magistrates had been correct to find that they could not exercise the power under section 35 on the basis of evidence that a particular unit had a space for the defendant but could offer it only if funding

6 MHA 1983 s35(3)(b).

7 Which is necessary to comply with ECHR article 5(1): see *Litwa v Poland* [2000] MHLR 226, App No 26629/95.

8 A hospital order or guardianship order cannot be imposed under MHA 1983 s37 unless at least one medical report is from a doctor approved under MHA 1983 s12. The need for the involvement of a section 12 approved doctor also arises under CJA 2003 s157, as the report under that section must be provided by such a doctor: see section 157(6). Any such report must provide information of the sort that the court has to take into account under section 157(3), namely the condition and the likely effect of a custodial sentence on the condition and the treatment for it, which requires expertise from a psychiatrist. It is worth commenting that information might also be provided in the pre-sentence report, which is required under CJA 2003 s156: it may be that the information in this report – which could include second-hand information provided following discussion with mental health professionals – might be sufficient to allow the court to form the view that there is no need to obtain a full psychiatric report; it might also reveal that a full medical report should be sought.

9 [2003] EWHC 2460 (Admin), [2003] MHLR 399.

was made available, which the relevant funding authority declined to provide on the basis of its assessment that the placement was inappropriate for the defendant.[10] (The consequence of this was that the defendant was placed in prison.)

7.9 In the period between the remand date and the availability of the hospital place, the defendant may be detained in a 'place of safety', which will often be a prison, though it could also be a hospital willing to receive the patient on a temporary basis.[11]

Renewals

7.10 The remand under MHA 1983 s35 may be for up to 28 days at a time, with a maximum of 12 weeks in total:[12] any renewals must be based on evidence from the person due to provide the report at the end of the process that a further period is necessary to complete the report.[13] As a result of changes introduced by the MHA 2007, this person must be an 'approved clinician'. This can include someone who is not a doctor (and in particular the changes were introduced to allow psychologists and others to take charge of the treatment of patients). Whether the report should be from a doctor will depend on the purpose for which the report is designed. In some cases, such as a report for the purposes of a hospital order, since it is likely that the report will come from the MHA 1983 s12 approved doctor whose

10 The judicial review proceedings also challenged the refusal to provide funding: Collins J held that it was not unreasonable on the facts, given that the primary care trust involved had not had the chance to make any representations to the court as to whether or not the MHA 1983 s35 power should be used. He left open the question of whether it would be lawful for a funding authority to refuse to provide funding if its representations were rejected by a court after a proper hearing: see paragraphs 22 and 23. It is to be noted that is has been held that a local authority can decline to agree to a guardianship order that a court wished to impose: see *R (Buckowicki) v Northamptonshire County Council* [2007] EWHC 307 (Admin), [2007] MHLR 121. That being so, is it different to frustrate a court decision under section3?

11 See MHA 1983 s55(1) for the definition of 'place of safety', which also includes a police station. In relation to children, the relevant definition is in Children and Young Persons Act 1933 s107, and it includes local authority homes or other locations the courts finds suitable, in addition to police stations and hospitals. (The definition of 'place of safety' is different from that applicable to people taken into police custody under MHA 1983 ss135 and 136, which includes local authority residential accommodation and any other suitable place.)

12 MHA 1983 s35(7).

13 MHA 1983 s35(5).

report is necessary, it is almost inevitable that such a person will be the approved clinician. In other situations, the approved clinician might not be a doctor – which may lead to a situation where the court has a report on the basis of which detention is renewed that is not from a doctor. So an initial remand requires evidence from a doctor, but renewals of the remand (and ongoing loss of liberty) can be based on evidence from clinicians who are not doctors. It is possible that that might be challenged as not complying with the requirements of the ECHR, though this will turn on whether the need for 'objective medical expertise' as set out in the case of *Winterwerp v Netherlands*[14] can be met by a psychologist.

7.11 The renewals do not require a represented defendant to be brought to court.[15] Patients who are detained under section 35 do not have any right of access to a tribunal, which under Part V of the MHA 1983 has the power to discharge a patient from hospital.[16] However, a defendant has the right to contest any further remand and may obtain his or her own evidence from a doctor or an approved clinician in order to seek an order that the remand be terminated at any time.[17] This right of access to the criminal court is no doubt the reason for the lack of access to a tribunal. However, it is suggested that if the clinical team in the hospital setting forms the view that the requirements for detention in hospital are no longer met, they should make arrangements with the court for the matter to be returned there so as to avoid a breach of article 5(1)(e) of the ECHR (which requires that the grounds for detention continue).

7.12 Time spent in custody under section 35 should be taken into account in reducing any custodial sentence imposed: this follows from CJA 2003 ss240 and 242. The former requires the court imposing a sentence to reduce it by the period for which the offender has been remanded in custody; the latter includes detention under section 35 as within the definition of a remand in custody.

14 (1979) 2 EHRR 387; see chapter 1.

15 MHA 1983 s35(6).

16 The right to apply to a tribunal is set out in MHA 1983 s66 (for civil patients) and s69 (for criminal patients); but patients under section 35 (or section 36, which is discussed below, or the interim hospital order under section 38) are not mentioned.

17 MHA 1983 s35(7) and (8).

Effect of an order

Detention

7.13 The legal effect of an order under MHA 1983 s35 is as follows. First, in relation to detention, section 35(9) gives authority to a constable or any person directed by the court to convey the defendant from court to hospital within the time period specified in the court order (which has to be within seven days) and then gives authority to the hospital to detain. Section 35(10) allows the arrest of a patient who absconds from a hospital or during conveyance. The patient can be returned to court, which may set aside the remand and use some other power. Section 35(10) does not, it should be noted, apply to abscondees from places of safety; however, section 137 provides that anyone who is in a place of safety is in legal custody, and section 138 provides a power for such a patient to be 'retaken' by the person who had custody of the defendant, by a constable or by an approved mental health professional (AMHP).[18]

7.14 If there is no bed immediately available and a place of safety is used, the directions for detention there will provide the necessary authority for conveyance and detention in the place of safety and further conveyance to the hospital once the bed is available: the authority as to conveyance is 'to the hospital specified'[19] and so can be from the place of safety or directly the court. Naturally, care must be taken to ensure that anyone who carries out the conveying of the defendant is a constable or has a specific authorisation from the court.[20]

7.15 However, a problem might arise if the hospital cannot admit the patient within the period specified. Section 35(9)(b) provides that the hospital managers 'shall admit ... and thereafter detain' the patient: such mandatory language suggests that the managers do not have an

18 See the discussion in chapter 3 about powers of arrest in relation to places of safety.

19 MHA 1983 s35(9).

20 If there is conveyance without authority, any action that might be brought by a patient seeking any remedy in tort, such as a claim of false imprisonment on the basis that the action of conveying was outside the lawful authority, would have to demonstrate that the action was taken in bad faith or negligently: see MHA 1983 s139, which provides a defence to civil action even in circumstances of a want of jurisdiction whenever the defendant was purporting to act under the Act unless those additional criteria are met. However, in *R (TTM (by his litigation friend TM)) v Hackney LBC and East London NHS Foundation Trust* [2011] EWCA Civ 4, [2011] MHLR 171, the Court of Appeal found that section 139 could be read down by reason of section 3 of the Human Rights Act 1998 to cover any situation in which the relevant official acted in a manner contrary to the provisions of the MHA 1983.

option to refuse. Such an interpretation is supported by the fact that an order under section 35 can only be made if the hospital indicates that arrangements have been made. But the practical realities of life are such that a hospital may find itself in a situation where the bed offered has disappeared because of an emergency situation; or that the condition of the defendant has deteriorated (whether in the place of safety, or after admission) so as to make it no longer appropriate for the hospital to offer a place. The only option in that case is to return the matter to court immediately.

7.16 Another possible lacuna in the statute is that there is no provision for transfer between different places of safety, such as might be necessary if there is a change in the condition of the patient; it is to be noted that this is in contrast to the place of safety provisions of MHA 1983 ss135 and 136, which were amended by the MHA 2007 to allow transfers between places of safety. It might be suggested that court could include in its directions under section 35(4) as to the use of a place of safety allow transfer to any other suitable location as the needs of the defendant might require; however, this is not consistent with the statutory language that requires the court to give directions relating to 'a place of safety' rather that referring to 'a place or places of safety'.[21]

Treatment

7.17 The detention of a patient in hospital deals with his or her right to liberty; there is the separate fundamental right to autonomy, which is engaged in relation to questions of treatment. This is a common law principle (at least in relation to people with capacity); in terms of the ECHR, it is reflected in article 8, the right to respect for privacy interests. The MHA 1983 introduced a separate regime for the imposition of treatment without consent; but section 35 is not covered by this: see section 56(3). However, urgent treatment that is immediately necessary to save the patient's life, prevent a serious deterioration of the patient's condition, alleviate serious suffering or prevent violent or dangerous behaviour is governed by MHA 1983 s62, which applies to any patient by reason of section 56(1). The term 'patient' is defined in MHA 1983 s145 as a person who is or appeared to be mentally disordered, and so includes someone detained under section 35. If the patient is without capacity, it may also be possible for treatment to be given under the provisions of the MCA 2005.

21 MHA 1983 s135(3A) and (3B) and s136(3) and (4).

7.18 However, a patient can be subject to both Parts II and III of the MHA 1983: this was established in the case of *R v North West London Mental Health NHS Trust ex p Stewart.*[22] Accordingly, a section 35 patient can be placed under sections 2 or 3 of the MHA 1983 and will then be subject to the treatment without consent provisions as a result of that status. In this regard, paragraphs 33.29 and 33.30 of the English Code of Practice issued under section 118 of the MHA 1983 suggest that the clinical team should ensure that the matter is referred back to court or use made of the Part II powers. Paragraph 32.31 of the Welsh Code is of similar effect.

Leave and transfer

7.19 If a defendant has been placed under a hospital order, he or she may be granted leave under MHA 1983 s17 or transferred under section 19. This does not apply under section 35,[23] as the terms of a remand under section 35 require that the patient be detained in accordance with the requirements of the section.[24] However, in the *Reference Guide to the Mental Health Act,*[25] issued by Department of Health (2008), it is said at paragraph 3.20 that leave of absence is not permissible 'without the express agreement of the remanding court'. Accordingly, if this may be a necessary part of the assessment or treatment process (since how a patient copes with leave may be important in terms of assessing the disorder or as part of the treatment regime, which includes rehabilitation), a request should be made at the time of remand. The same paragraph of the Reference Guide states that transfer between hospital requires a new remand to the different hospital: this is consistent with the power being to remand to 'a hospital' rather than to 'such hospital or hospitals as may be specified' (or similar language). This may be of reduced importance in the era of hospital trusts that manage several units, since transfer between different units managed by the same trust is an administrative matter that does not involve the use of section 19 powers.

22 [1998] QB 628.

23 In this regard, the same regime applies under MHA 1983 s36, which is discussed below, and section 38, an interim hospital order, discussed in chapter 18.

24 The same applies in relation to MHA 1983 s36; and section 40(3) requires detention in accordance with the terms of section 38.

25 Available at www.dh.gov.uk/en/Publicationsandstatistics/Publications/PublicationsPolicyAndGuidance/DH_088162.

Use of the power

7.20 A matter of potential concern is the limited use of the power arising under section 35: statistics from the NHS Health and Social Care Information Centre in October 2009[26] show that the power is rarely used. The number of such remands in England into both National Health Service (NHS) and private hospitals has dropped from 261 in 1998–99 to just 119 in the 2008–09 period.[27] Unfortunately, in the absence of figures for the number of remands on bail, and whether they have risen accordingly, it cannot be said definitively that the section 35 power is being forgotten by courts. However, it seems likely that many of the medical reports are prepared on prisoners who are remanded into custody rather than to hospital: in the 2008–09 period, there were a total of 957 hospital orders made (either with or without a restriction order), and so it seems overwhelmingly likely a large number of people for whom a remand under section 35 might have been appropriate were not so remanded.

Remand for treatment under Mental Health Act 1983 s36

Criteria

7.21 The other remand power arising under the MHA 1983, section 36, is headed 'Remand of accused person to hospital for treatment': section 36(2) extends the definition of accused to a person 'who at any time before sentence is in custody in the course of a trial', and so it also applies post-trial and pre-sentence. However, this power is available only to the Crown Court and in relation to an offence punishable by imprisonment.[28] It is available specifically as an alternative to a remand into custody: section 36(1). In relation to someone who is in custody pending an appearance in the magistrates' court but needs

26 Available at www.ic.nhs.uk/statistics-and-data-collections/mental-health/mental-health-act.

27 Appendix 2 to the Report. In 2010–11, the number was down to 85: see tables 2a and 2b in appendix 1 to the report of October 2011 covering 2010–11.

28 It does not apply in relation to anyone charged with an offence for which the sentence is fixed by law, ie murder: note that this exclusion applies both before and after conviction. This means that anyone standing trial for murder who needs medical treatment for a psychiatric condition must either be released on bail or, on the more likely scenario of being remanded in custody, transferred by the Secretary of State under MHA 1983 s48, which is discussed in chapter 8.

treatment for mental disorder, there are two routes: one is to rely on the power of the Secretary of State to transfer a remand prisoner to hospital, discussed in chapter 8; but there is also the option of the defendant being released on bail so that the civil powers of detention can be used.

7.22 The test on the merits is that the Crown Court is satisfied of the defendant that:

(a) he is suffering from mental disorder of a nature or degree which makes it appropriate for him to be detained in a hospital for medical treatment; and
(b) appropriate medical treatment is available for him.[29]

7.23 This is as amended by the MHA 2007, which introduced the 'appropriate treatment' requirement,[30] amended the definition of what amounts to medical treatment[31] and allowed the power to be used in relation to all forms of mental disorder: previously, the power could only be exercised in relation to mental illness or severe mental impairment, but these categories have been removed and replaced by the single concept of mental disorder.[32] The question of the 'nature or degree which makes it appropriate for him to be detained in a hospital for medical treatment' was in the MHA 1983 as enacted.

7.24 These criteria are discussed in detail in chapters 1 and 2. In essence:

- A 'mental disorder' is any disorder or disability of mind, though if it is a learning disability it is also necessary that it be associated with abnormally aggressive or seriously irresponsible conduct. The only exclusion from the definition of mental disorder is addiction to alcohol or drugs. The new definition is deliberately wider.
- 'Medical treatment' is widely defined, extends to nursing and psychological intervention, can cover dealing with the symptoms or consequences of the disorder without necessarily dealing with the underlying disorder, and, while it need not have any guarantee of being effective must at least have the purpose of assisting.
- The degree of a disorder is its current severity, and the nature of a disorder is its duration and prognosis, and particularly its tendency to relapse. Detention can be justified on the basis of nature even if the current degree is not severe.

29 MHA 1983 s36(1).

30 It applies to all powers to detain for treatment: see MHA 1983 ss3, 37, 45A, 47 and 49; it does not apply in relation to section 2, which is designed for assessment.

31 MHA 1983 s145(1) and (4).

32 MHA 1983 s1.

- The appropriateness of detention turns on the question of whether the treatment should be provided at a hospital. In a civil context, this may raise questions of whether the treatment can be provided as an out-patient or as an informal patient, but in a criminal context involving remand prisoners the alternative is treatment in a prison context.
- The appropriate treatment criterion means that there must be treatment that is appropriate in the light of both clinical and non-clinical factors.

7.25 The appropriateness of detention in hospital is worth further consideration. Several paragraphs of the Code of Practice issued under section 118 of the MHA 1983 are of particular relevance. Paragraphs 33.2 and 33.3 note that those involved in criminal proceedings have the same rights to assessment and treatment by psychiatric services, and so admission to hospital, given that speedy specialist intervention might be of benefit both to them and to the prospect of the trial proceeding with dispatch.[33] In addition, paragraphs 33.31 and 33.32 note the importance of arrangements to be made by prison healthcare staff and NHS commissioners to ensure that any needs for in-patient treatment are identified and acted upon within the same time-frame as would apply to the admission of a patient from the community; and even if there is consent to treatment in the prison, an assessment should be made of whether the environment contributes to the disorder.[34]

Procedural requirements

7.26 The findings must be based on reports from two doctors;[35] by reason of MHA 1983 s54(1), at least one of these doctors must be an approved psychiatrist under MHA 1983 s12. Otherwise, the procedural provisions of MHA 1983 s36 mirror those in section 35 in terms of the need for evidence that there is a bed within seven days,[36] with a power to direction detention in a place of safety in the interim. The arguments noted above in relation to the potential lacunae under section 35 are equally applicable.

33 See also Welsh Code para 32.2; paragraph 32.3 contains the reminder that a prison health care centre does not count as a hospital for the purposes of the treatment provisions of the MHA 1983.

34 Welsh Code paras 32.23–32.25 are to similar effect.

35 MHA 1983 s36(1).

36 MHA 1983 s36(3).

Renewals

7.27 The maximum duration of each remand is 28 days and the overall maximum is 12 weeks;[37] the test for renewal is whether it is 'warranted' (which must look back to the substantive test for detention for treatment, namely the nature or degree of the disorder and the availability of appropriate treatment) and the supporting evidence comes from the 'responsible clinician'. This term refers to the approved clinician in charge of the patient's case,[38] and so need not be a doctor (and so the questions that arise under section 35 in relation to compliance with the ECHR apply here, with the supplemental point that the further remand can be based on one report whereas two are required for the initial remand). The renewal can take place in the absence of a represented patient.[39]

7.28 Time spent in custody under section 36 should be taken into account in reducing any custodial sentence imposed at the end of the criminal process: this follows from CJA 2003 ss240 and 242. The former requires the court imposing a sentence to reduce it by the period for which the offender has been remanded in custody; the latter includes detention under section 36 as within the definition of a remand in custody.

Effect of order

7.29 The legal effect of the making of orders under MHA 1983 s36 is that the powers of conveyance and detention, and of arrest of abscondees, that arise under section 35(9) and (10) apply to remands under section 36 as well. Such patients do have access to the criminal court to argue against the renewal of their detention or seek its termination; and they are entitled to obtain their own expert evidence in this regard.[40] However, as is the case with section 35 patients, it is suggested that if the clinical team in the hospital setting forms the view that the requirements for detention in hospital are no longer met, they should make arrangements with the court for the matter to be returned there so as to avoid a breach of article 5(1)(e) of the ECHR (which requires that the grounds for detention continue).

7.30 Section 36 patients are in a similar position to section 35 patients in relation to leave under section 17 and transfer under section 19:

37 MHA 1983 s36(4) and (6).
38 MHA 1983 s55(1).
39 MHA 1983 s36(5).
40 MHA 1983 s36(6) and (7).

the terms of a remand under section 36 require that the patient be detained in accordance with the terms of the section. As in noted above, the Department of Health *Reference Guide to the Mental Health Act* suggests that leave of absence may be permitted by the court, and so it should be sought at the time of the remand if leave might be a part of the treatment process; the Guide also suggests that transfers between hospitals are not permitted and so a fresh order by a court will be necessary (though transfers between different units within a hospital will be possible, which might include different sites).

7.31 In terms of treatment without consent, the position of those detained under section 36 is different from that of those detained under section 35, which no doubt explains the requirement for a second medical report for a section 36 remand. A patient detained under section 36 is subject to the whole of the treatment without consent regime, thus:

i) under section 63, treatment[41] by or under the direction of the clinician in charge of treatment can be given without the consent of the patient, but
ii) medication cannot be given for more than three months without consent or the approval of a second doctor (by reason of section 58),
iii) electro-convulsive therapy requires consent or, if the patient cannot consent, the approval of a second doctor (by reason of section 58A), and
iv) particularly invasive treatments – psychosurgery and the use of hormone implants to reduce the male sex drive – require consent and a second medical opinion and support from two non-medical reviewers (see section 57 and the Mental Health (Hospital, Guardianship and Treatment) (England) Regulations 2008).[42]

These exceptions are all in turn subject to the emergency treatment provisions of section 62.

7.32 It is worth noting that MHA 1983 s56(3) expressly exempts from the definition of 'liable to be detained' a patient who is detained in a place of safety under MHA 1983 s37 or s45A: there is no similar

41 'Medical treatment' is widely defined in MHA 1983 s145 to include nursing, psychological treatments and rehabilitative work.

42 SI 2008 No 1184. Psychosurgery is listed as a particularly invasive treatment in MHA 1983 s57; the hormone treatment is added by the Regulations, made under section 57(1)(b); other treatments can be added by the Code of Practice issued under section 118 of the MHA 1983. The equivalent regulation for Wales is contained in SI 2008 No 2439, made by the National Assembly for Wales.

language in relation to a person detained in place of safety pending admission to a hospital under section 36, though such a person would be within the definition of 'patient' under section 145, namely a person suffering or appearing to suffer from mental disorder and is arguably liable to be detained in light of the making of the court order. Since the place of safety under section 36 may well be a prison or some other place where treatment without consent is not appropriate, there is no good reason why the place of safety detention pending admission under section 36 should not be treated in the same way as a section 37 place of safety.

Use

7.33 It has been noted that the use of MHA 1983 s35 powers has declined in recent years: in relation to section 36, while there has been no decline, it must be a matter of concern that it has remained at a low level for the last decade. The statistics provided by the NHS Health and Social Care Information Centre[43] show, in the report of October 2009, that there have not been more than 23 remands under section 36 in any year in previous 10 years. There were 19 such remands in the year 2008–09. In the same year, there were 345 transfers under MHA 1983 s48: even though section 48 covers civil and immigration detainees as well as remand prisoners, it is a figure that suggests a significant number of remand prisoners had a need to be in hospital but that the Crown Court was willing to allow that to be achieved administratively rather than through the court power to control the appropriate remand of a defendant before the court. This is all the more problematic because the criteria under section 48, as discussed in chapter 8, include that there is an urgent need for treatment.

43 Available at www.ic.nhs.uk/statistics-and-data-collections/mental-health/mental-health-act. In 2009–10, the total rose to 30, but in 2010–11, it fell to 16: see tables 2a and 2b to appendix 1 to the report of October 2011 giving updated figures.

CHAPTER 8

Transfer of remand prisoners under Mental Health Act 1983 s48 by the Secretary of State

Introduction

8.1 If a court does not take steps to allow the transfer to hospital of a prisoner who needs treatment for mental disorder, or if there is no power for the court to act (as, for example, in the case of someone on trial for murder or someone who is in the custody of the magistrates' court, such that Mental Health Act (MHA) 1983 s36 does not apply), another possible route into hospital is the warrant of transfer by the order of the Secretary of State under MHA 1983 s48.

Test for transfer

Prisoners covered

8.2 Four groups of prisoners are covered by the power of transfer under MHA 1983 s48:

a) remand prisoners in the jurisdiction of the Crown Court;
b) those remanded into prison by the magistrates' court;
c) civil prisoners; and
d) immigration prisoners.

As to the latter two groups, civil prisoners are defined in section 48(2)(c) as prisoners committed to prison for a limited term but who are not treated as convicted prisoners for the purposes of MHA 1983 s47 (which relates to the transfer of serving prisoners and is discussed in chapter 20). The final group covered by section 48 are those detained under the Immigration Act 1971 or the Nationality, Immigration and Asylum Act 2002.

8.3 The two types of remand prisoner are described in section 48(2) as:

> (a) persons detained in a prison or remand centre, not being persons serving a sentence of imprisonment or persons falling within the following paragraphs of this subsection;[1]
> (b) persons remanded in custody by a magistrates' court[.]

The reason for the distinction between these two groups of prisoners is that there is a different process applicable by which the transfer may be brought to an end, which is discussed below.

1 The other 'following paragraphs' are those that describe civil and immigration detainees.

Criteria for transfer

8.4 The criteria for a transfer, set out in MHA 1983 s48(1), are that the Secretary of State is satisfied that:

(a) that person is suffering from mental disorder of a nature or degree which makes it appropriate for him to be detained in a hospital for medical treatment; and
(b) he is in urgent need of medical treatment; and
(c) appropriate medical treatment is available for him[.]

In addition, the Secretary of State has to be satisfied that the transfer is expedient in the light of the public interest and the circumstances of the case: this arises from the fact that the power of transfer is that applicable under section 47, which includes the expediency test.

8.5 This is as amended by the MHA 2007, which introduced the 'appropriate treatment' requirement,[2] amended the definition of what amounts to 'medical treatment',[3] and allowed the power to be used in relation to all forms of mental disorder: previously, the power could only be exercised in relation to mental illness or severe mental impairment, but these categories have been removed and replaced by the single concept of mental disorder.[4] The question of the 'nature or degree which makes it appropriate for him to be detained in a hospital for medical treatment' and the need for urgent treatment were in the MHA 1983 as enacted.

8.6 Aside from the urgency requirement, these criteria are discussed in detail in chapters 1 and 2 and summarised at paras 7.2 and 7.25.

8.7 As to the criterion that there be urgent need for treatment, it is difficult to understand the reason for this. If the statute created a comprehensive system whereby courts could ensure that there were transfers for treatment, such that there was no real need for action by the Secretary of State except in an urgent case, it would be understandable. But there is no such comprehensive structure. MHA 1983 s36, which contains a court power of transfer from custody, covers only those in the custody of the Crown Court (and then not those charged with murder). Civil prisoners are detained where the Secretary of State directs, though there may be instances – such as that under section 48 of the Family Law Act 1996 – where a remand may be into hospital for the preparation of reports, but not for treatment;

2 It applies to all powers to detain for treatment: see MHA 1983 ss3, 37, 45A, 47 and 49; it does not apply in relation to section 2, which is designed for assessment.

3 MHA 1983 s145(1) and (4).

4 MHA 1983 s1.

immigration detainees may apply for bail,[5] but the place of their detention is for the executive. Accordingly, MHA 1983 s48 is the only mechanism for transfer for treatment in many situations it covers.

8.8 However, it may be that the interpretation given to 'urgent' does not add significantly to the appropriateness test. In the Department of Health publication *Procedure for the transfer of prisoners to and from hospital under sections 47 and 48 of the Mental Health Act (1983)*[6] it was noted that '"urgent" is defined as "if the doctor would have recommended in-patient care for that person were they seen at an out-patient clinic in the community"'.[7] This is a test that would obviously be met if it was felt to be appropriate to detain a patient in hospital, such that an urgency requirement does not add anything.

8.9 It is to be noted that there is no power under section 48 (or indeed under section 47 in relation to serving prisoners) to transfer for the purpose of assessment of whether there is any need for a transfer for treatment. However, section 22(2) of the Prison Act 1952 provides that:

> The Secretary of State may –
>
> ...
>
> (b) if he is satisfied that a person so detained requires medical investigation or observation or medical or surgical treatment of any description, direct him to be taken to a hospital or other suitable place for the purpose of the investigation, observation or treatment;
>
> and where any person is directed under this subsection to be taken to any place he shall, unless the Secretary of State otherwise directs, be kept in custody while being so taken, while at that place, and while being taken back to the prison in which he is required in accordance with law to be detained.

8.10 This language on its face covers the investigation of psychiatric treatment, though it is suggested that the reference to treatment, given that it contains no provision for treatment without consent, must

5 See part 4 of the Asylum and Immigration Tribunal (Procedure) Rules 2005 SI No 230.

6 Version 4, October 2007, available at www.dh.gov.uk/en/Publicationsandstatistics/Publications/PublicationsPolicyAndGuidance/DH_081260. However, it should be noted that this document has been superseded by the current document, *Good Practice Procedure Guide: The transfer and remission of adult prisoners under s47 and s48 of the Mental Health Act*, April 2011, which does not contain any such definition; this is available at www.dh.gov.uk/en/Publicationsandstatistics/Publications/PublicationsPolicyAndGuidance/DH_125767.

7 *Procedure for the transfer of prisoners to and from hospital under sections 47 and 48 of the Mental Health Act (1983)*, version 4, 2007, page 8.

be treatment with the consent of the patient (subject to the Mental Capacity Act).

Procedural requirements

8.11 The procedural requirements for a transfer under MHA 1983 s48 are that there must be two medical reports,[8] and by reason of section 54(1) of the Act, at least one of these must come from someone who is approved under section 12 of the MHA 1983 as having expertise in psychiatry. A hospital must be specified, and the patient must be received into that hospital before the end of 14 days commencing on the date the transfer order is made.[9]

Effect of transfer

8.12 The effect of a transfer is that the prisoner is treated as though a hospital order had been made in his or her case: this arises from MHA 1983 s47(3), which is applied to section 48 transfers as a result of section 48(3). This in turn means that section 40 of the Act is applicable, which provides authority to detain;[10] in addition, the prisoner becomes a patient liable to be detained under the Act and so is covered by the consent to treatment provisions of Part IV of the Act.

Restriction direction

8.13 MHA 1983 s49 is also relevant. This provides a power to make the transferred prisoner subject to a restriction direction, which has the effect of placing the patient in the same position as if a restriction order had been made under section 41 of the Act. If the patient is a remand prisoner, that is under section 48(2)(a) or (b), the transfer direction has to be accompanied by a restriction direction.[11] One of

8 MHA 1983 s48(1), which reads in the requirements of section 47(1) as to the need for two medical reports.

9 MHA 1983 s47(2), as read over by reason of section 48(3).

10 MHA 1983 s40(1)(b); the provisions of section 40(1)(a), relating to the power to convey to the hospital and admit within 28 days, is otiose.

11 The statistics provided by the NHS Health and Social Care Information Centre, *In-patients formally detained in hospitals under the Mental Health Act 1983 and patients subject to supervised community treatment: 1998–99 to 2008–09*, October 2009 (available at www.ic.nhs.uk/statistics-and-data-collections/mental-health/mental-health-act), indicate that the vast majority of section 48 transfers are with a restriction direction: so there were 405 section 48 transfers with a restriction direction in 1998–1999 and 30 without, 384 with in 2007–2008 and

the main effects of this is that certain powers that exist in relation to hospital order patients, including leave and transfer, can be exercised only with the consent of the Secretary of State. The policy is that leave will only be granted for medical treatment or to attend court, unless there are exceptional circumstances.[12]

Bringing the transfer to an end[13]

8.14 The circumstances in which the MHA 1983 s48 transfer comes to an end depend on the status of the prisoner before transfer.

Crown Court detainees

8.15 Those covered by MHA 1983 s48(2)(a), namely Crown Court remand prisoners, are subject to the further provisions of section 51 of the Act. There are three circumstances in which the section 48 transfer direction may come to an end. The first is if the underlying case is disposed of: section 51(2), including by the making of a hospital order. It is to be noted that a hospital order can be made without convicting a defendant if the accused has been transferred to hospital under section 48, the criteria for a hospital order are made out, the papers indicate that the making of an order is proper and it is 'impractical or inappropriate' to bring the detainee before the court.[14]

8.16 One question that might arise is whether a finding that a defendant is not fit to stand trial (and any consequent order made if the defendant is found to have committed the act charged) amounts to a 'disposal' of the case. It clearly does if the defendant is found not guilty; but if a positive finding is made, it remains possible for the defendant to be remitted for trial in some circumstances, and so the case may be considered to be alive. However, it is noted that the language used in section 51(2) is 'disposed of' rather than 'finally

17 without; in 2008–2009, there were 341 transfers with a restriction direction and only 4 without (Appendix 2). The report for 2010–11 shows 403 transfers with restrictions and 10 without: tables 2a and 2b in appendix 1.

12 See Appendix 6 to the *Good Practice Procedure Guide: The transfer and remission of adult prisoners under s47 and s48 of the Mental Health Act, April 2011, available at* www.dh.gov.uk/en/Publicationsandstatistics/Publications/PublicationsPolicyAndGuidance/DH_125767.

13 For civil and immigration detainees, see MHA 1983 s53 for transfer back; the test is as for remand prisoners, but it can only happen if a restriction direction is added, which is discretionary in the case of such prisoners.

14 This is discussed further in chapter 9; see *R (Kenneally) v Snaresbrook Crown Court* [2001] EWHC Admin 968, [2002] MHLR 53 for guidance on the need to construe the impracticability test strictly.

disposed of'. As such any order made as a result of the fitness to stand trial process should count, since the case will disappear from the court's lists and will not reappear unless and until there is an order of remittal.

8.17 The second route for the transfer to come to an end is if, before the case is disposed of, the Secretary of State is informed that there is no longer a need for treatment in hospital or that no effective treatment can be given at that particular hospital. A warrant may be issued to remit the patient back to any place of detention under the court-ordered remand: section 51(3). If the concern is what is available for the patient at the particular hospital, it might be possible for a fresh transfer from prison to another hospital to be put in place, and no doubt it should be possible to co-ordinate these so that the patient can be sent to the further hospital directly.

8.18 The Secretary of State can be satisfied of this need to remove the patient from a hospital when informed as to the substantive test by the responsible clinician (RC – that is, the clinician in charge of the patient's treatment),[15] any other approved clinician (that is, a person approved for the purposes of the Act),[16] or a tribunal.

8.19 The right of a patient to apply to a tribunal is conferred by section 69(2), and arises as soon as the transfer has been put into effect. This applies to the patient even if a restriction direction is imposed: although the special restrictions arising under section 41 include the non-applicability of sections 66 and 69(1) (see section 41(3)(b)), this does not exclude section 69(2) and so it must apply.

8.20 The substantive test for the remission of the patient, it should be noted, does not refer to the appropriate treatment test: when that test was added to various parts of the MHA 1983 by the MHA 2007, it was not added to this subsection. However, there is the effective treatment test, which was already there in section 51(3): this seems to raise the prospect of a situation that there is treatment that is not working for the patient adequately to meet the test of effectiveness, despite being appropriate; and no doubt there will also be treatments that are effective but not appropriate, given that the question of appropriateness involves wider questions than just the clinical efficacy of a particular treatment. It may be unfortunate that the test for admission and remission is not the same.

8.21 This mismatch, namely that appropriate treatment is part of the test for a transfer to hospital but not part of the test for a transfer

15 See MHA 1983 s55(1).

16 See MHA 1983 ss145 and 12(2).

from hospital, is particularly obvious when the advice to the Secretary of State comes from a tribunal. The patient will be restricted, as a restriction direction has to be imposed in the case of remand prisoners, and so the tribunal will meet under section 74. This refers back to the test in section 73, which in turn refers back to section 72(1)(b), including the appropriate treatment test.

8.22 The power under section 74 is to make a recommendation to the Secretary of State with two elements to it: the first is to explain whether it would have granted a discharge had section 73 applied (which is obligatory if there is no appropriate treatment), and the second is to make a recommendation as to whether or not the patient should remain in hospital if not discharged (in other words, that the patient should stay in hospital rather than being returned to prison). The Secretary of State has 90 days to respond to any such recommendation, which may be to allow discharge; if no response is given, then the managers of the hospital have to arrange a return to prison. This could also be the trigger for the Secretary of State to make a decision pursuant to section 51(3): but the test applied by the tribunal under section 74 is not the 'effective treatment' test set out in section 51(3), and so it will be necessary for the tribunal to bear in mind the need to apply this additional test.

8.23 The third method by which a section 48 transfer may come to an end is on a direction from the trial court, which has power under section 51(4) to direct that the patient be remitted to prison or released on bail if satisfied that there is no longer a need for treatment or if no effective treatment can be given. However, this can only happen on the basis of evidence from the RC. If the evidence is from other psychiatrists to the effect that hospital detention is no longer proper, the Crown Court would be limited to releasing on bail so as to bring the custodial order to an end.

Magistrates' court detainees

8.24 Where the MHA 1983 s48 order is made in relation to a person is remanded in custody by a magistrates' court, the provisions of section 52 govern the circumstances in which the order comes to an end. Under section 52(5), the magistrates have the same power as the Crown Court to bring the transfer to an end, namely if satisfied on the evidence of the responsible clinician that there is no longer a need for treatment or no effective treatment can be given: it is to be noted that the power of the Secretary of State that exists under section 51 to remit the defendant from hospital is not replicated in section 52.

8.25 The transfer to hospital also finishes if the underlying remand in custody comes to an end, as will happen if the defendant is sentenced, acquitted, or released on bail. This follows from the provisions of section 52(2). If the underlying remand by the magistrates is extended, the section 48 transfer continues (section 52(3)); and if the period of remand comes to an end because the person is sent in custody to the Crown Court, the transfer direction does not end in that situation (section 52(2)).

Use

8.26 Government statistics confirm that the use of MHA 1983 s48 remained relatively static during the period 1998–99 to 2008–09: there were around 350 transfers per year together with a restriction direction (which would include remand prisoners).[17]

17 NHS Health and Social Care Information Centre, *In-patients formally detained in hospitals under the Mental Health Act 1983 and patients subject to supervised community treatment: 1998–99 to 2008–09*, October 2009, available at www.ic.nhs.uk/statistics-and-data-collections/mental-health/mental-health-act. It rose to over 400 in 2010–11: see updated report from October 2011, tables 2a and 2b in appendix 1.

CHAPTER 9

Inability to participate – Crown Court

continued

Introduction

9.1 Since 1800, statutes have regulated the question of whether someone was fit to stand trial in light of mental disorder. However, the statutory question of fitness to be tried does not encompass the whole story: there is a wider question of capacity to participate in a trial process both as a matter of the common law and in order to comply with article 6 (right to a fair trial) of the European Convention on Human Rights (ECHR). There may be situations in which a defendant cannot properly be tried despite meeting the fit to stand trial test; put another way, the statutory question of fitness to stand trial may best be viewed as a sub-category of the wider question of the ability to participate to the extent required by article 6.

9.2 This chapter will consider the issue in the context of the Crown Court; as a different statutory regime applies in relation to summary trials, there is a separate chapter that deals with the magistrates' court. This chapter covers the right to participate in a criminal trial as a matter of the common law and under the ECHR; it then covers the statutory regime relating to fitness to stand trial before discussing the provisions that have developed recently in relating to modifying the criminal process to secure participation. Broadly speaking, there are two scenarios. In the more serious situations, there is an inability to participate which means that no trial is possible. In the less serious scenario, participation is possible if the process is modified. There is a continuum of scenarios, and it is likely that there is a grey area where the dividing line may be difficult to discern with clarity.[1]

9.3 Finally, there is a limited process whereby a Crown Court can make a hospital order without the defendant even attending court, which arises under section 51 of the Mental Health Act (MHA) 1983 and which is outlined.

1 In *R v Diamond* [2008] EWCA Crim 923, [2008] MHLR 124 at paras 46–49, Thomas LJ noted the evidence of one of the psychiatrists was that he had come across several instances of defendants who were fit to stand trial but might not be capable of giving reliable instructions on whether to raise the question of diminished responsibility, so suggesting that there was a gap between fitness to stand trial and fitness to make rational decisions, which might result in them being convicted of a more serious offence than was deserved. The issue was not discussed in detail in the light of the evidential position in the case; the judge noted that the role of defence counsel was the follow the instructions of the defendant who was found fit to trial.

The right to participate as an element of fair trial

The common law position

9.4 It is a long-standing feature of the English criminal trial process that a defendant has to be able to participate in it. This is a central reason why the defendant must usually be present. So, in *R v Lee Kun*,[2] Lord Reading CJ stated:

> There must be very exceptional circumstances to justify proceeding with the trial in the absence of the accused. The reason why the accused should be present at the trial is that he may hear the case made against him and have the opportunity ... of answering it. The presence of the accused means not only that he must be physically in attendance, but also that he must be capable of understanding the nature of the proceedings.

9.5 The Chief Justice noted that if the inability to comprehend arose from communication problems or an inability to speak English, then an interpreter was required; this applied unless the court was satisfied that the defendant was aware of the evidence against him or her (and even then, any variations from the expected evidence had to be translated). On the facts, which involved a defendant who did not speak English, depositions from the committal proceedings had been translated into his language, and the failure to translate the trial proceedings did not result in a miscarriage of justice.

9.6 It has subsequently been confirmed that the failure to ensure that there is adequate translation means that the trial is a nullity: see *R v Iqbal Begum*,[3] where a plea of guilty to murder was set aside because it emerged that the interpreter had not been able to speak the language of the defendant, who was originally from rural Pakistan. The Court of Appeal found that the defendant had not fully understood the implications of the charge and the possible defences, and so it could not be sure that the guilty plea entered was proper; as such the trial was a nullity.

9.7 Another case involving interpreters was *Kunnath v The State*.[4] An Indian national who was convicted in Mauritius of importing heroin had indicated during the trial that he had not understood the evidence given. Although there had been an interpreter, he had only

2 [1916] 1 KB 337, at 341. See also *R v Smellie* (1919) 14 CrAppR 128: a trial judge could remove a defendant from the dock but not out of the hearing of a witness who might be intimidated by the presence of the defendant.

3 (1991) 93 CrAppR 96.

4 [1993] 1 WLR 1315.

translated when directed to do so by the judge: as the judge had not directed that the prosecution evidence be translated, the interpreter had not done so. It was not a case where the defendant knew what the evidence against him was. The Privy Council held that the failure of the judge to ensure that the defendant had understood the evidence, or to order a retrial when it became apparent that something had gone wrong with the translation, meant that there had not been a fair trial. It commented that the presence of the defendant at a trial was required:

> ... not simply that there should be corporeal presence but that the defendant, by reason of his presence, should be able to understand the proceedings and decide what witnesses he wishes to call, whether or not to give evidence and if so, upon what matters relevant to the case against him.[5]

9.8 The conviction was quashed: the committee disagreed with the Mauritian Court of Criminal Appeal's view that there had been no miscarriage of justice.

The position under the ECHR

9.9 Expressed in terms of the ECHR, the basic right to a fair trial in relation to any criminal trial is set out in article 6(1) and a number of specific rights are set out in article 6(3). Article 6(1) provides that:

> In the determination of ... any criminal charge against him, everyone is entitled to a fair and public hearing within a reasonable time by an independent and impartial tribunal established by law.

The presumption of innocence is contained in article 6(2), and various minimum standards for criminal trials are set out in section 6(3), including:

> (a) to be informed promptly, in a language which he understands and in detail, of the nature and cause of the accusation against him;
> (b) to have adequate time and facilities for the preparation of his defence;
> (c) to defend himself in person or through legal assistance of his own choosing or, if he has not sufficient means to pay for legal assistance, to be given it free when the interests of justice so require;
> (d) to examine or have examined witnesses against him and to obtain the attendance and examination of witnesses on his behalf under the same conditions as witnesses against him;
> (e) to have the free assistance of an interpreter if he cannot understand or speak the language used in court.

5 [1993] 1 WLR 1315 at 1319.

Interpreters

9.10 The common law position relating to interpreters is matched by the express right to an interpreter set out in ECHR article 6(3)(e). The failure of the judge to ensure that there was translation was the basis for a finding of a breach of article 6 in *Cuscani v UK*:[6] the applicant had admitted a significant VAT and tax fraud on legal advice, though there had not been an interpreter present and his command of English was limited; although an interpreter was ordered for a hearing set to determine the quantum of the fraud, none attended, but the hearing proceeded in any event, at the end of which he was sentenced to four years' imprisonment. The European Court of Human Rights (ECtHR) found that, while defence counsel had not raised an objection, it was a failure of the trial judge, who was the custodian of the requirements of fairness, 'to reassure himself that the absence of an interpreter at the hearing ... would not prejudice the applicant's full involvement in a matter of crucial importance for him'.[7]

The more general right to participate under the ECHR

9.11 In addition to the right to an interpreter, the express rights mentioned in article 6(3) include the right to defend oneself in person (article 6(3)(c)) and to examine witnesses (article 6(3)(d)). Prima facie, this entails participation by the defendant. An argument the other way is that, since the right to defend oneself if phrased as an alternative to the right to choose legal representation, the granting of the latter excludes the need to secure the former. The same line of argument applies in relation to examining witnesses, since there is the alternative of the right to having witnesses examined: so the defendant does not have to be able to participate if adequately represented.

9.12 In this regard, it could be suggested that there is a difference: the fact that the right to an interpreter in article 6(3)(e) applies if the person cannot 'understand or speak' the language of the court only makes sense if there is a right to participate in the process. So, the language of the ECHR indicates that a right to participate is at least implicit.

9.13 The question of whether participation was required was considered by the ECtHR in *Stanford v UK*.[8] This involved a man convicted

6 (2003) 36 EHRR 2.

7 (2003) 36 EHRR 2 at para 38.

8 App No 16757/90, judgment adopted on 24 January 1994; (1994) Series A/282-A p11.

of serious sexual offences who alleged that he could not hear the evidence of the victim clearly. This was the result of the design of the court and the arrangements made to allow the victim to give evidence; because of her soft voice, she could be heard by the judge, jury and lawyers, but it was difficult for Mr Stanford to hear her from the dock. His solicitor confirmed in a statement made to the Solicitors' Complaints Bureau (to whom Mr Stanford had complained after his trial) that it was known that Mr Stanford had hearing difficulties, but also noted that he had provided full instructions on the victim's statement and stated that the view was taken by his legal team that he did not need to hear her give evidence; there was also a tactical decision taken that it would appear intimidating to place Mr Stanford in proximity to the victim.

9.14 Mr Stanford's application for leave to appeal to the Court of Appeal had been dismissed even though the court accepted that he had had difficulties hearing the key evidence against him. The ECtHR, to which he then applied, noted that English law as to the need for defendants to attend trial was to ensure that they could hear the evidence and be able to answer it.[9] It also recorded that the parties had not disputed that:

> Article 6, read as a whole, guarantees the right of an accused to participate effectively in a criminal trial. In general this includes, inter alia, not only his right to be present, but also to hear and follow the proceedings. Such rights are implicit in the very notion of an adversarial procedure and can also be derived from the guarantees contained in sub-paragraphs (c), (d) and (e) of paragraph 3 of Article 6, – 'to defend himself in person', 'to examine or have examined witnesses', and 'to have the free assistance of an interpreter if he cannot understand or speak the language used in court'.[10]

9.15 The ECtHR therefore discounted the prospect of a narrower understanding of article 6(3)(c) and (d). However, on the facts it found that there was no breach of article 6 because the lack of a complaint in the course of the trial meant that no decision had been made by a state official that the trial should proceed without Mr Stanford being able to hear; and he had not disagreed with the tactical decision taken by

9 Citing *R v Lee Kun* [1916] 1 KB 337 (noted above) and *R v Smellie* (1919) 14 CrAppR 128.

10 App No 16757/90, judgment adopted on 24 January 1994; (1994) Series A/282-A p11 para 26. See also *Ektabani v Sweden* (1988) 13 EHRR 504, in which the failure of the Swedish Court of Appeal to hold an oral hearing on a review of a conviction, when it had power to review the facts and the law, breached the 'right to be heard in person' (paragraph 33).

competent counsel not to position him so that he could hear. It is worth commenting that the position in *Cuscani* was similar in that there had been no complaint by counsel and so no judicial decision: on those facts, the ECtHR was of the view that the judge had a duty to ensure that the defendant could understand. By analogy, it should have been the judge's obligation to ensure that Mr Stanford could hear, irrespective of the lack of an application by counsel. However, if Mr Stanford was fully engaged in a tactical decision that left him unable to hear, the facts could be distinguished on the basis of a waiver of the right to participate.

Participation and mental disorder or vulnerability

9.16 The endorsement of the proposition that it was necessary to secure participation by the defendant in *Stanford* allowed arguments in subsequent cases involving mental vulnerability, arising both from immaturity and also specific concerns as to a recognisable disorder. The first was the decision of the Grand Chamber of the ECtHR in *T and V v UK*.[11] This involved two ten-year-old boys who killed a two-year-old boy, were charged with murder and stood trial in the Crown Court[12] when they were aged 11. Despite their age, the only changes to the normal trial procedure were an early end to the court day (to match the end of the school day) and a ten-minute break every hour;[13] they had also seen the courtroom in advance, had been given an explanation of the process, and were placed in a raised dock so that they could see proceedings. T and V were convicted of murder, sentenced to an indeterminate sentence of detention during Her Majesty's Pleasure and their identities were revealed.[14]

11 (2000) 30 EHRR 121, [1999] Prison LR 189.

12 Magistrates' Courts Act 1980 s24 required a trial on indictment when a child was charged with homicide. There was a discretion to commit to the Crown Court if the offence was sufficiently serious that it might require a sentence beyond the powers of the summary courts.

13 (2000) 30 EHRR 121, [1999] Prison LR 189 para 9. It was also noted that the defendants had been taken to the court room in advance, and alerted to the processes by way of the pack of books and games given to child witnesses; they were allowed to spend time with their parents and social workers during breaks, and the judge had indicated to the social workers who sat in the dock with them that he would adjourn if they reported signs of stress or tiredness on the part of the defendants, which happened only once. There was a significant media interest in the trial, and a hostile crowd gathered outside the court to meet the defendants, and occasionally attempted to attack the vehicles in which they travelled.

14 An order had been made at the start of the trial under Children and Young Persons Act 1933 s39 to prohibit publication of any identifying details or

9.17 A number of issues were raised in the ECtHR proceedings, including whether article 6 had been breached because of the defendants' inability to participate: this argument was based on their age and also their respective mental states. As to the latter, there was expert evidence that V was immature and showed post-traumatic effects of his actions, extreme distress and guilt, and had fears of the terrible retribution he expected from the trial, as a result of which he had difficulty in thinking or talking about the events in question and so had not revealed a full account.[15]

9.18 The expert evidence relating to T was that, while he was of at least average intelligence, he showed signs of post-traumatic stress disorder in that he was preoccupied with the events of the offence, and was affected by a high level of anxiety and poor eating and sleeping patterns: these features limited his ability to instruct his lawyers, testify adequately in his defence and understand the procedures fully (though not to the extent that he was unfit to stand trial for the purposes of the Criminal Procedure (Insanity) Act 1964, as amended).[16] There was also evidence to demonstrate that the boys knew the difference between right and wrong.[17]

9.19 An application to stay the criminal trial had been made, but only on the basis that adverse publicity made a fair trial impossible; it had been rejected.[18] There is no mention of any application based on the two boys' inability to participate. This was despite the recent ruling of the Privy Council in *Kunnath v The State*,[19] which is discussed above.

photographs; this was lifted after conviction to allow them to be named, which led to the publication of photographs and other details, as a result of which the trial judge granted an injunction to cover the publication of information relating to their whereabouts.

15 *T v UK* para 11. There was also prosecution expert evidence that, although he knew the difference between right and wrong, he had 'cried inconsolably and shown signs of distress' whenever he was asked about the events in question and 'was not able to talk about the events in issue in any useful way': paragraph 12.

16 *T v UK* para 11.

17 *V v UK* para 12; *T v UK* para 11. At the time, it was presumed that children aged less than 14 did not know that a crime was wrong and so this had to be proved by the prosecution: this – the doli incapax rule – was abolished by Crime and Disorder Act 1998 s34 (as interpreted by the House of Lords in *R v JTB* [2010] UKHL 20).

18 *V v UK* para 10.

19 [1993] 1 WLR 1315.

9.20 There was also evidence before the ECtHR as to the impact of the domestic trial proceedings, particularly on V,[20] who had not been able to pay attention during them; there was less relevant expert evidence relating to T,[21] though his own evidence to the ECtHR had been that he had shut out the trial process as he felt intimidated. There was also material as to the systematic problems of using the adult court process for children, namely that delays compromised access to the therapy that was necessary for a child who had committed a serious act.

9.21 The ECtHR held that, although it was not impermissible to try such young children,[22] account had to be taken of their vulnerability (in terms of their level of maturity and intellectual and emotional capacities); arrangements had be made to promote their ability to participate, and on the facts to reduce the level of intimidation arising from the intense media and public interest in the case. Also relevant was the expert evidence as to mental health matters that showed that V was unlikely to have been able to give informed instructions and T had a limited ability.

9.22 The government relied on the competence of counsel and the modified trial process. The conclusion of the ECtHR was that the limited steps taken in the domestic proceedings had been inadequate; it noted that one particular modification – a raised dock that had been used to allow them to see proceedings – had in fact left them exposed to a heightened level of scrutiny and discomfort. The court rejected the government's argument resting on the availability of competent counsel, distinguishing *Stanford v UK* on the basis that Mr Stanford could consult with his lawyers during the proceedings and during breaks, whereas the problems faced by V and T were such that they would not be able to co-operate with or provide instructions to their lawyers.[23]

20 *V v UK* paras 17–19.

21 *T v UK* paras 16–17.

22 Children and Young Persons Act 1933 s50 as amended by Children and Young Persons Act 1963 s16(1) sets the age of criminal responsibility in England and Wales at ten years: the court noted at paragraph 50 of *V v UK* that the relevant age was seven in Cyprus, Ireland, Switzerland and Liechtenstein; eight in Scotland; 13 in France; 14 in Germany, Austria, Italy and many Eastern European countries; 15 in the Scandinavian countries; 16 in Portugal, Poland and Andorra; and 18 in Spain, Belgium and Luxembourg. It was also noted that in a report of 1995, the UN Committee on the Rights of the Child, which exists under the UN Convention on the Rights of the Child 1989, had recommended that the UK raise the age of criminal responsibility (see *V v UK* para 47).

23 *V v UK* para 90, *T v UK* para 87. Judge Baka dissented on this point, finding that a public trial could be necessary even though children were on trial, that the stress of facing a serious charge could affect the ability to participate of an

9.23 The government had also noted that a public trial had been necessary in relation to grave charges in order to maintain confidence in the administration of justice. As to the value of public trials, the ECtHR noted that:

> ... where appropriate in view of the age and other characteristics of the child and the circumstances surrounding the criminal proceedings, this general interest could be satisfied by a modified procedure providing for selected attendance rights and judicious reporting.[24]

9.24 When these features were added to the expert evidence about the ability of the applicants to participate, and particularly V, the involvement of skilled lawyers had not been adequate to comply with the requirements of article 6.[25]

9.25 It is worth commenting that, just as Mr Stanford's application under the ECHR had failed in large part because his counsel had not raised in the domestic proceedings the points considered by the ECtHR, that was also the position in *T and V*, since it had been open to their counsel to have argued that the trial should not proceed because they could not participate. This was the common law position, or at least was clearly arguable as such by analogy to *Kunnath* and earlier cases. In addition, much of the evidence adduced before the ECtHR as to the boys' inability to participate, particularly in the case of V, could have been obtained during the trial, as could the more general evidence as to the unsuitability of the adult Crown Court process for dealing with young children, which would have been relevant to an application to stay on that ground. The fact that the trial could only take place in the Crown Court because the charge was of homicide did not mean that the trial *had* to take place: the abuse of process

adult also (albeit that it would be more problematic for a child), but that the measures taken on the facts to assist the applicants had been adequate; it was commented that any inability of the applicants to participate 'was not because his case was tried publicly by an adult court but rather because his position objectively was not significantly different from that of accused persons who are lacking legal knowledge, suffering mental disease or of low intelligence, such that they can be said to be subjects of the criminal process rather than active participants in it. In this situation, fairness of a criminal trial cannot mean much more than ensuring that the child is defended adequately by highly trained professional counsel and that the necessary facilities for the defence are fully provided – as they were in the present case. In terms of fairness of criminal proceedings, it is rather illusory to expect that a child of this age could give any legally relevant instruction to his or her lawyer in order to facilitate his or her defence.'

24 *V v UK* para 87.

25 A minority opinion was that the process amounted to a breach of ECHR article 3 as well.

jurisdiction remained, and indeed was invoked, albeit unsuccessfully, in relation to adverse publicity.

9.26 Further, since some procedural modifications were made to the normal course of the trial in terms of the length of the court day and the number of breaks, it seems patent that there could have been more modifications to the formality of the process to reduce the alienation of the defendants (such as an absence of wigs and gowns, the use of a more suitable court room and so on), as they were within the powers of the trial court. There is no indication that further modifications were sought by those representing V and T but rejected by the trial judge.

9.27 However, a government contention that domestic remedies had not been exhausted because the points being taken in the European proceedings had not been raised in the domestic proceedings, such that the application was inadmissible, was rejected. V and T had replied that their inability to participate was not of such as level as to allow them to demonstrate that they were unfit to plead (and in any event would only have prolonged the case as the prosecuting authorities would have sought to postpone the case until they were fit to stand trial).[26] The ECtHR held that the domestic law rulings that non-participation from language difficulties meant that a trial was unfair and could not proceed did not indicate that there was a remedy for non-participation for reasons connected to mental disorder and immaturity. It noted that no example was cited of such problems falling short of the fitness to plead test that had led to a stay in proceedings. Accordingly, the finding was that the government had not met its burden of proof in relation to the availability of an effective remedy.[27] Of course, had an application to stay on the basis of inability to participate been made in the domestic trial, that might well have demonstrated that there was such a remedy.

9.28 There was a concurring opinion from Lord Reed, the ad hoc UK judge sitting on the ECtHR for the case.[28] He drew a distinction between the legitimacy of having a trial and the process to be followed in the trial. He accepted that a trial could be held for children whose level of maturity was such that criminal responsibility could be ascribed to them, but held that it did not have to mirror the process

26 *V v UK* para 55.

27 *V v UK* paras 59–61.

28 The full-time UK judge, Sir Nicolas Bratza, had been a member of the former European Commission on Human Rights, which at the relevant time had considered cases at the admissibility stage, and so was excluded from participating in the court process.

applied to adults 'if a child is too immature for such procedure to provide him with a fair trial'. The same approach, noted Lord Reed, arose in relation to the sentencing regime, which might be different to that applicable to adults 'if their immaturity has the consequence that they were less culpable or that reformative measures are more likely to be effective'.

9.29 He also commented that while it was recorded on the face of article 6(1) that the normal rules as to public trials could be modified when juveniles were involved:

> There is on the other hand nothing in Article 6 to indicate that there can be any derogation, in cases involving children, from the principle that the trial process should provide for the effective participation of the accused, who must be able to follow the proceedings and to give instructions where necessary to his lawyer.

9.30 Lord Reed's conclusion was that the securing of effective participation by children might require modifications of the process that took into account the maturity and intellectual and emotional capacity of the child, and that not enough had been done on the facts.

9.31 The ECtHR considered the need for participation again in the case of *SC v UK*.[29] He was aged 11 when, with an older boy, he was involved in an attempt to snatch the bag of an elderly lady, who fell and fractured her arm. The charge of attempted robbery was committed to the Crown Court for trial on the basis that it might be appropriate to impose a sentence beyond the powers of the youth court. The expert evidence was that SC had learning difficulties that put his powers of reasoning and communication at the level of a younger child: but the experts could not say, at least not confidently, that he met the statutory test for being unfit to stand trial. An application to stay the proceedings on the basis that it was an abuse to proceed in the light of SC's limited abilities was rejected by the trial judge, who – having described SC as 'streetwise' – noted that wigs and gowns would not be worn, he would not be in the dock, and frequent breaks would be taken.[30] SC was convicted and sentenced to two-and-a-half years' detention; leave to appeal was refused.[31] He then applied to the ECtHR.

29 (2005) 40 EHRR 10, App No 60958/00, judgment of 15 June 2004.

30 These were consistent with the Practice Direction that is discussed below, even though the trial took place before it had been issued: this made it clear that more could have been done in V and T's trial.

31 *SC v UK* para 31: the ECtHR records that the Court of Appeal felt that the judge had borne in mind the decision in *T and V v UK*.

9.32 The government emphasised that the trial, which lasted a day and was concerned only with the question of whether SC had been subject to duress by the older boy, had not involved the intense scrutiny that had arisen in the trial of T and V and had been marked by more relaxed procedures; it also pointed out that there was no specific evidence of the sort available in *V and T* to the effect that SC had not been able to follow the trial. As to the latter point, there was nothing beyond a statement from the social worker who had sat with SC in the Crown Court, in which the view was expressed that, despite the social worker's efforts to explain, SC 'did not comprehend the situation he was in'.[32]

9.33 The ECtHR gave a more detailed account than had been set out in *V and T v UK* of what was meant by effective participation, stating that it:

> ... presupposes that the accused has a broad understanding of the nature of the trial process and of what is at stake for him or her, including the significance of any penalty which may be imposed. It means that he or she, if necessary with the assistance of, for example, an interpreter, lawyer, social worker or friend, should be able to understand the general thrust of what is said in court. The defendant should be able to follow what is said by the prosecution witnesses and, if represented, to explain to his own lawyers his version of events, point out any statements with which he disagrees and make them aware of any facts which should be put forward in his defence ...[33]

9.34 Applying this to the facts, the ECtHR concluded that the evidence of SC's limited intellectual ability and the view of the social worker who sat with him meant that effective participation had not been secured.[34] It was able to give a greater degree of specificity as to what its ruling meant. A state could seek the conviction of a defendant with a restricted ability to participate, but a specialist tribunal should be involved that could adapt its procedures to take account of the defendant's difficulties.[35]

9.35 In relation to a young defendant, the obvious choice of specialist venue is the youth court. For adults with mental disorder, there is not that option – though it is commonplace in some other common

32 *SC v UK* para 17. It had been used in the application to the Court of Appeal for permission to appeal the conviction.

33 *SC v UK* para 29.

34 *SC v UK* para 34.

35 *SC v UK* para 35. It is worth noting that Judges Pellonpaa and Bratza dissented, finding that the evidence as to SC's abilities did not show that, in light of the arrangements made, he had not been able to participate.

law jurisdictions to have special mental health courts designed to deal with persons with mental disorder who are somehow engaged in the criminal justice system.[36] There may, however, be methods by which advocates can seek to avoid a trial, meaning that an alternative approach has to be adopted. The abuse of process jurisdiction is central to this.[37]

Other relevant international standards as to participation

9.36 In his judgment in *V and T*, Lord Reed also suggested that the ECtHR's conclusion as to the requirements under the ECHR was consonant with other standards in international law, in particular the Convention on the Rights of the Child (CRC)[38] and the International Covenant on Civil and Political Rights (ICCPR).[39] The latter is in many respects a worldwide version of the ECHR: both indicate in

36 For basic information, see the Bradley Report: *Lord Bradley's review of people with mental health problems or learning disabilities in the criminal justice system*, Department of Health, April 2009 (available at www.dh.gov.uk/en/Publicationsandstatistics/Publications/PublicationsPolicyAndGuidance/DH_098694), p70. Pilot mental health courts were established in Brighton and Stratford. The results were positive; and they were successful in identifying needs that would have been unmet otherwise: see Ministry of Justice Research Summary 7/10, September 2010, available at www.justice.gov.uk/publications/docs/mhc-feasibility-study-imapct-evaluation.pdf and Research Series 18/10, September 2010, available at www.justice.gov.uk/publications/docs/mhc-process-evaluation.pdf.

37 For a detailed account of the abuse of process jurisdiction, see Colin Wells, *Abuse of process*, 2nd edn, Jordans, 2011.

38 Adopted by the General Assembly of the United Nations in November 1989, resolution 44/25 of 20 November 1989; text available at www2.ohchr.org/english/law/crc.htm. The UK signed it on 19 April 1990 and ratified it on 16 December 1990.

39 Adopted and opened for signature, ratification and accession by General Assembly resolution 2200A (XXI) of 16 December 1966; the text is available the Website of the United Nations High Commissioner for Human Rights at hwww2.ohchr.org/english/law/, which contains link to the Covenant; another source is http://treaties.un.org/Pages/CTCs.aspx, the page containing the 'Certified True Copies of Multilateral Treaties Deposited with the Secretary-General', chapter 4 of which is the section relating to human rights matters. The UK signed it on 16 September 1968 and ratified it on 20 May 1976. The UK has neither signed nor ratified the First Optional Protocol to the ICCPR, which allows individual complaints to be taken to the UN Human Rights Committee; the rationale for this is that the ECtHR provides an appropriate forum, but i) various other signatories to the ECHR allow access to the UN Human Rights Committee and ii) some of the rights set out in the ICCPR are not set out in the ECHR.

their preambles that they seek to give effect to the Universal Declaration of Human Rights,[40] and they set out a roughly similar list of rights. However, in a number of respects the ICCPR contains supplemental language, and in relation to the right to a fair trial, article 14(4) provides that: 'In the case of juvenile persons, the procedure shall be such as will take account of their age and the desirability of promoting their rehabilitation.'

9.37 The CRC seeks to ensure the application of the rights set out in other conventions to children. CRC article 40 sets out the rights of children in criminal proceedings, including the need for special procedures (so article 40(2)(vii) refers to a right to privacy, which may apply in relation to criminal proceedings, article 40(3) encourages the use of diversion, and article 40(4) sets out the need to have additional rehabilitative options for the disposal of a case involving a child). This approach is consistent with a theme running through human rights jurisprudence to the effect that ensuring equality of respect may require that more be done to assist people who have specific disadvantages.

9.38 For example, those who are detained on account of mental disorder have a right to a regular review of their detention under ECHR article 5(4). This provision does not contain the specific rights set out in article 6, but it has been determined that the right to a review by a court calls for a court-like procedure, which may require that account be taken of any special needs of the person in detention. So, in *Megyeri v Germany*[41] the question was whether the failure to ensure that a patient had a lawyer during reviews of his detention breached article 5(4): the context was that he had not asked for a lawyer (and so his autonomous choice not to have a lawyer had been respected). The ECtHR noted that:

> The judicial proceedings referred to in Article 5(4) need not always be attended by the same guarantees as those required under Article 6(1) for civil or criminal litigation. None the less, it is essential that the person concerned should have access to a court and the opportunity to be heard either in person or, where necessary, through some form of representation. Special procedural safeguards may prove called for in order to protect the interests of persons who, on account of their mental disabilities, are not fully capable of acting for themselves ...[42]

40 UN General Assembly Resolution 217(III) of 10 December 1948; the text is available at www.un.org/en/documents/udhr/.

41 (1993) 15 EHRR 584.

42 (1993) 15 EHRR 584 para 22.

9.39 In the circumstances of a review of detention, this meant that there should be legal representation in the absence of special circumstances. The underlying principle is that the vulnerabilities of a participant have to be taken into account, as was the holding in *V and T v UK*.

9.40 A development in international human rights law that is worth noting in this context is the UN Convention on the Rights of Persons with Disabilities 2006 (CRPD),[43] which follows the model of the CRC in providing a reminder that all groups in society have human rights and that supplemental or modified rights that take account of the special circumstances of a particular group might be required. So the CRPD sets a general obligation in article 4 that states should 'ensure and promote the full realization of all human rights and fundamental freedoms for all persons with disabilities without discrimination of any kind on the basis of disability'. To understand the import of this, it is necessary to understand what amounts to 'discrimination on the basis of disability'; this is defined in CRPD article 2:

> 'Discrimination on the basis of disability' means any distinction, exclusion or restriction on the basis of disability which has the purpose *or effect* of impairing or nullifying the recognition, enjoyment or exercise, on an equal basis with others, of all human rights and fundamental freedoms in the political, economic, social, cultural, civil or any other field. It includes all forms of discrimination, including denial of reasonable accommodation. [Emphasis added.]

9.41 The final phrase is a term of art that is also defined in article 2 in the following terms:

> 'Reasonable accommodation' means necessary and appropriate modification and adjustments not imposing a disproportionate or undue burden, where needed in a particular case, to ensure to persons with disabilities the enjoyment or exercise on an equal basis with others of all human rights and fundamental freedoms.

9.42 In short, the need to ensure equality of treatment means that appropriate adjustments have to be made to procedures to overcome the impact of any disability, by whatever are the necessary legislative, administrative and other steps to modify existing laws and practices

43 Adopted by the UN General Assembly on 13 December 2006, during the 61st session of the UN; General Assembly resolution A/RES/61/106. It was opened for signature on 30 March 2007, in accordance with article 42: the UK signed it on that date and ratified it on 8 June 2009; it entered into force on the 20th ratification, which occurred as of 3 May 2008. The text can be found through the same links as mentioned in note 39 above in relation to the ICCPR.

that amount to discrimination (article 4)[44] so as to guarantee the 'equal protection and equal benefit of the law' (article 5). In the context of the right to a fair trial, CRPD article 13 notes the need to ensure effective access to justice on the same terms for persons with disabilities; this requires, inter alia, 'the provision of procedural and age-appropriate accommodations, in order to facilitate their effective role as direct and indirect participants, including as witnesses, in all legal proceedings'. As discrimination is often a reflection of the attitudes of others, article 13 also entails 'appropriate training for those working in the field of administration of justice, including police and prison staff'.

Fitness to stand trial – the statutory regime

Introduction

9.43 When enacted, section 4 of the Criminal Procedure (Insanity) Act (CP(I)A) 1964 stated that it dealt with the question of 'unfitness to plead'. Following amendments introduced by the Criminal Procedure (Insanity and Unfitness to Plead) Act (CP(IUP)A) 1991, the heading is now 'Finding of unfitness to plead'. However, as both the original and the amended section actually address whether a trial can occur, the issue raised is not merely fitness to enter a plea of guilty or not guilty but fitness to plead in the sense of the ability to take part in the process of pleading that describes a trial. The substantive question raised in section 4(1) (both as originally enacted and under the amended Act) is whether there is a 'disability such that apart from this Act it would constitute a bar to his being tried'. In addition, subsections (2), (3), (4) and (5) all make reference to 'the question of fitness to be tried'.

9.44 The rest of the section, together with section 4A, which was introduced by the CP(IUP)A 1991, deals with procedural matters; section 5 of the CP(I)A 1964, together with provisions of the CP(IUP)A 1991 that were not inserted into the CP(I)A 1964, deal with the question of disposal.

9.45 So the three broad issues are the substantive test for fitness to stand trial; the procedures involved in making such a finding; and the consequences.

44 Part of this is the obligation of awareness-raising under CRPD article 8.

What is meant by fitness to stand trial?

Criminal Lunatics Act 1800

9.46 The starting point for determining the substantive test remains the 19th century authority *R v Pritchard*.[45] He was charged with bestiality, shown by medical evidence to be deaf and unable to speak, but able to read and write: the indictment was given to him to read and he indicated that he was not guilty. However, there was also evidence that he was of limited intellectual capacity.[46] Alderson B instructed the jury as to the test to apply in the following terms:

> There are three points to be enquired into: – first, whether the prisoner is mute of malice or not; secondly, whether he can plead to the indictment or not; thirdly, whether he is of sufficient intellect to comprehend the course of the proceedings in the trial so as to make a proper defence – to know that he might challenge any of you to whom he may object – and to comprehend the details of the evidence, which in a case of this nature must constitute a minute investigation. Upon this issue, therefore, if you think that there is no certain mode of communicating the details of the trial to the prisoner, so that he can clearly understand them, and be able properly to make his defence to the charge; you ought to find that he is not of sane mind. It is not enough, that he may have a general capacity of communicating on ordinary matters.

9.47 The jury found that Mr Pritchard was not fit to stand trial. At that time, the statutory test to be applied – under the Criminal Lunatics Act (CLA) 1800 – was whether a defendant was 'insane ... so that such person cannot be tried', and the impact of a finding of unfitness to stand trial was that a person was detained during His or Her Majesty's Pleasure (ie indefinitely).[47] It was confirmed in subsequent case-law that being 'insane' for the purposes of the statutory test included those who had no mental disorder but were unable to hear or speak: see *R v The Governor of HMP Stafford ex p Emery*.[48] In

45 (1836) 7 C&P 303, 173 ER 135. For an account of what was in place prior to then, see *Ex p Emery* (below) and Grubin, 'What Constitutes Fitness to Plead?' [1993] Crim LR 748–758.

46 The phraseology of the original report (at p304) is that: 'It was ... sworn by several witnesses that the prisoner was nearly an idiot, and had no proper understanding; and that though he might be able to be made to comprehend some matters, yet he could not understand the proceedings on the trial.'

47 CLA 1800 s2. However harsh that might seem, it is to be noted that the charge faced by Mr Pritchard was a capital felony, and so a trial might have had a worse outcome for him.

48 [1909] 2 KB 81.

this case, Lord Alverstone CJ noted that common law authority had allowed a trial to proceed if a defendant was found 'mute by the visitation of God' and who could not read either; he expressed the view that the extended meaning given to the statutory test of insanity was reasonable, being preferable both to putting on trial (and punishing if convicted) a person who had such fundamental difficulties of communication and also preferable to a finding of not guilty.

9.48 The question of what was meant by inadequate comprehension, the part of the test of more obvious relevance to defendants with some forms of mental disorder, was reviewed by a five-judge Court of Criminal Appeal in *R v Podola*,[49] which also considered the CLA 1800. The court rejected the argument that a defendant who had no memory of the events charged on account of hysterical amnesia was unfit to stand trial. The court applied *Pritchard* and confirmed that the question was the ability of the defendant to follow the trial process, not whether the defendant had a full recollection of events and could provide full instructions on that basis.

Criminal Procedure (Insanity) Act 1964

9.49 As noted above, the test now applicable under section 4(1) of the CP(I)A 1964 is whether there is a 'disability such that apart from this Act it would constitute a bar to his being tried'. In *R v Robertson*,[50] the Court of Appeal confirmed that the introduction of the CP(I)A 1964 did not change the substantive test. The judge had directed the jury to assess whether on the evidence – which was that he was mentally-ill with paranoia – the defendant could 'apprehend the course of the proceedings at his trial so as to make a proper defence, to challenge a juror to whom he may wish to object, and to understand the details of the evidence'. He was found unfit and ordered to be admitted to hospital.[51] On appeal, it was suggested that the judge had fallen into error because of the reference to a 'proper defence' (which had been a theme of questioning of the experts). The court quashed the finding because of the danger that the jury had been misled into thinking that the question was whether the defendant was incapable of acting in his best interests. However, the court also endorsed that the test was as set out in *Pritchard*. This was even though the CP(I)A 1964

49 [1960] 1 QB 325, (1959) 43 CrAppR 220.

50 [1968] 1 WLR 1767.

51 At the time a finding of unfitness meant that the defendant was automatically detained; this was amended in 1991, as is discussed below.

repealed the CLA 1800 which was considered in *Pritchard*[52] and so the question for the Court of Appeal was whether a 'disability such that apart from this Act it would constitute a bar to his being tried' meant the same as 'insane'.[53]

9.50 More recently, in *R v John M*,[54] the Court of Appeal had to consider a contention that short-term memory problems meant that a defendant was not fit to stand trial. At the time, the question was determined by a jury, which had considered conflicting evidence and found him fit to stand trial; he was subsequently convicted of the offences charged. The trial judge granted a certificate that the matter was fit for consideration by the Court of Appeal on the question of what the fitness to stand trial test was. The Court of Appeal again endorsed the *Pritchard* test and the judge's summary of it, namely that the test was met if the defendant was capable of:

> (1) understanding the charges; (2) deciding whether to plead guilty or not; (3) exercising his right to challenge jurors; (4) instructing solicitors and counsel; (5) following the course of the proceedings; and (6) giving evidence in his own defence.[55]

9.51 The court also endorsed the trial judge's further explanations of what was meant by these criteria, such as that being able to instruct lawyers meant being able to understand the questions asked by his legal team and being able to convey answers to those questions, even if they were implausible or unreliable: it was the jury's task to determine the question of their accuracy.[56] Similarly, being able to follow the course of the proceedings entailed being able to understand what was said in court and comment on it, even if the comment was neither valid nor helpful.[57]

52 CLA 1800 s8(5)(a). (This repeal language has also been repealed by the Statute Law (Repeals) Act 1974, no doubt because an alternative process was in place.)

53 See also *R v Berry* (1978) 66 CrAppR 156, in which the Court of Appeal endorsed the view in *Robertson* that *Pritchard* set out the substantive test.

54 [2003] EWCA Crim 3452, [2004] MHLR 86.

55 [2003] EWCA Crim 3452, [2004] MHLR 86 para 20. It will be noted that 'fitness to plead' is only the second of these competencies. It is also to be noted that this is an updated and extended version of what is actually mentioned in *Pritchard* – see para 9.46 above – in which the judge referred to being able to 'plead to the indictment or not' and to 'comprehend the course of the ... trial so as to make a proper defence', which was split into being able to challenge jurors, follow the details of the evidence, and make a defence.

56 [2003] EWCA Crim 3452, [2004] MHLR 86 para 21. The same test was applied to being able to give evidence: paragraph 24.

57 [2003] EWCA Crim 3452, [2004] MHLR 86 para 22–23.

9.52 This approach was confirmed in *R v Moyle*,[58] in which the defendant had been assessed as fit to stand trial at the time of the trial, but subsequently found to have concealed the extent of his illness and also to have included trial participants in his delusional system. Doctors then expressed the view that he had been unfit to stand trial, but the Court of Appeal held that his delusions had not meant that he had been unable to follow the trial or provide instructions.

Concerns about the Pritchard *test*

9.53 It is surprising that there has not been more argument about whether the *Pritchard* test remains applicable, given that it was developed in relation to a very different statutory test. The current case-law indicates that an assessment of whether there is a 'disability' that would bar a trial is the same as asking whether a defendant was 'insane' and so could not be tried.

9.54 In addition, the failure to take into account the reliability of the defendant's account or capacity to give instructions on tactical decisions is problematic. It is no doubt possible that someone with a mental disorder can fully participate in a trial; and it is also the case that some instructions from people without a mental disorder are implausible, as the Court of Appeal in *John M* indicated. But surely it makes a difference if the implausibility of the instructions and the account given arises from a mental disorder which causes the defendant to have a skewed perception of the evidence or of the importance of decisions made in the course of the trial: for example, if the defendant has a mental illness and gives instructions that are implausible objectively speaking but make sense within the delusional system, that defendant is not participating in the process. An analogy is the test for capacity in the Mental Capacity Act (MCA) 2005, which requires an ability to understand, retain and weigh information in order to make a decision, and to communicate the decision. In *R v C*,[59] the House of Lords held that an irrational fear arising from a mental disorder might mean that someone had no capacity to consent to sexual touching for the purposes of section 30 of the Sexual Offences Act 2003 because any decision did not represent their autonomous choice as it would be affected by the mental disorder. It was also noted that the correct approach was the ability of the person to make the relevant decision, namely whether to consent to sexual touching with the particular person in the particular

58 [2008] EWCA Crim 3059, [2009] MHLR 91.

59 [2009] UKHL 42, [2009] 1 WLR 1786, [2009] MHLR 189.

circumstances, rather than the ability of the person to consent to sexual touching as a general matter. If this approach is applied to fitness to stand trial, the question would be whether the defendant's instructions amounted to proper choices in relation to the specific facts alleged in the trial: if mental disorder meant that there were no proper choices being made, it seems difficult to see that this amounts to participation in the trial.

9.55 In this connection, it should be noted that the jurisprudence on fitness to stand trial was all developed at the time when the consequence of being found unfit to stand trial was compulsory detention. This would understandably mean that arguments would be raised by counsel representing defendants to suggest that a high standard should be applied before such a finding was made.[60] However, there might be good reason to revisit this in the light of the fact that:

i) the finding of unfitness now leads to a further process, not automatic detention; and
ii) a proper understanding of the question of fairness as now illuminated by the ECHR emphasises the need for participation by a defendant.

9.56 A final concern that should be noted about the test is the extent to which it can be considered to have been supplanted by the MCA 2005, which has been mentioned briefly above. This provides a statutory test for determining whether people lack capacity, namely an inability to make a decision 'because of an impairment of, or a disturbance in the functioning of, the mind or brain': MCA 2005 s2(1). The test for this is set out in section 3, which refers to an inability to understand relevant information, retain, use or weigh or retain the information, or communicate it. Section 4 of the MCA 2005 then requires that decisions be taken in accordance with the best interests of the person. The question arising is whether or not this statute, which is of general application but has been excluded from various areas, should be held to apply in relation to the *Pritchard* test.

The procedure for determining fitness to stand trial

9.57 The CP(I)A 1964, both as enacted and as amended by the CP(IUP)A 1991, required that a jury determine the issue of unfitness to stand trial. The jury would be a separate one considering just the question of unfitness if it was raised and determined on arraignment; but if

60 *Robertson*, discussed above, was such a case.

the question was determined after that stage, it was a matter for the judge to determine whether to empanel a separate jury or make use of the one already considering the trial. However, unfitness is now a question for the trial judge: CP(I)A 1964 s4(5) as amended by section 22 of the Domestic Violence, Crime and Victims Act (DVCVA) 2004.[61] Other procedural questions that arise are who can raise the question, how is it raised, when it should be raised and, once raised, when it should be determined, the burden of proof and the nature of the evidence required.

Who can raise the issue?

9.58 As to the question of who can raise the issue, section 4(1) of the CP(I)A 1964 regulates the process whenever the question of fitness to stand trial is raised 'at the instance of the defence or otherwise': so the issue can be brought forward by the defence, the prosecution or the court. This was the position before the CP(I)A 1964: see *R v Beynon*.[62]

How is the issue raised and when should it be raised?

9.59 In *R v McCarthy*,[63] it was determined that the issue is not raised merely by an inquiry as to the possibility that a defendant might be unfit to stand trial. The defendant in this case had represented himself at trial on charges of sending offensive messages through the postal system, in the form of postcards to the Hampstead Magistrates' Court, which led to a custodial sentence of 12 months. This was apparently actuated by paranoid beliefs. Neither the defence nor the prosecution raised the issue of fitness to stand trial. Medical reports confirmed that Mr McCarthy was deaf, unable to speak for all practical purposes, and delusional; they also indicated that he was fit to stand trial if the evidence was written down for him and he was questioned and could answer in writing. The judge had asked one of the doctors to confirm his view as to fitness to stand trial: on appeal

61 It was CP(I)A 1964 s4(4) as originally enacted, which became section 4(5) as a result of the substitution of language by the CP(IUP)A 1991. The DVCVA 2004 made a number of changes to the process, which are described below. It also substituted equivalent changes in the courts-martial process: see DVCVA 2004 s26 and Sch 3, making changes to the Army Act 1955, the Air Force Act 1955 and the Naval Discipline Act 1957, and also the Courts-Martial Appeal Act 1968.

62 [1957] 2 QB 111, in which the issue was raised by the prosecution.

63 [1967] 1 QB 68.

it was submitted that this meant that the question of fitness to stand trial had been raised and so a decision had to be made on it (even if postponed), which in turn meant that the conviction was improper.

9.60 This appeal point was no doubt legitimately raised as a method of seeking to overturn what might be viewed as a harsh conviction and sentence, but the Court of Appeal dismissed it. Lord Parker CJ noted that the question of fitness to stand trial is not triggered by a doubt arising as to the defendant's ability but only when the parties or the judge decide that the issue arises. Unfortunately, the court gives no further guidance on what is required beyond clarifying that it requires more than a doubt on the issue. So does it require some evidence, or that there is a case to answer on the point, or some other standard such as that the party has reasonable grounds to believe that they can meet their burden of proof on the issue (which may be different according to who raises it)?

9.61 In *R v Borkan*,[64] the defendant clearly had mental health problems but two medical reports had been prepared in which assessments were set out that he was fit to stand trial. On the day fixed for the trial, he pleaded guilty after the judge refused to adjourn for the preparation of a further report on fitness to stand trial and was sentenced to imprisonment. He was subsequently transferred to hospital under MHA 1983 s47. The Court of Appeal, in dismissing an appeal against conviction, held that the medical evidence in front of the court to the effect that he was fit to stand trial meant that there was no issue to the contrary to determine. However, Kennedy LJ did comment at paragraph 12 of the judgment that there might be a situation in which 'the behaviour of a defendant, as observed by the judge and the lawyers in court, is such as to call for medical assistance in relation to the question of whether he or she is fit to plead and to stand trial'. That would call for an adjournment for medical evidence: but that was not the case on the facts.

9.62 This suggests that as there has to be medical evidence on which to found a finding of unfitness, which is discussed below, the absence of such evidence means that the issue does not arise unless there is something in the behaviour of the client that makes it obvious to the lawyers that there is an issue. It would be unfortunate, however, to take this approach too far: it is to be noted that there was medical evidence in *Borkan* to the effect that the issue had been addressed in appropriate reports and he was competent to stand trial, and so it could well be proper to say that in the absence of extreme behaviour

64 [2004] EWCA Crim 1642, [2004] MHLR 216.

to suggest that something had changed since the last medical report, there was no proper basis for the matter being investigated further. The reason not to take the comments in *Borkan* beyond their facts is that they may suggest that a defendant has to be acting in a floridly unwell manner before lawyers can be said to have a valid reason to raise unfitness. Mental disorder can be much more subtle than that in its interaction with the ability of the defendant to participate in the trial process.

9.63 Other points that should be noted in this context are that, first, the prosecution obligations under the 'minister of justice' approach to draw to the attention of the court and the defence any material in their possession that might be relevant to the issue; this may have been obtained, for example, if there was any question raised as to whether or not the defendant should be diverted from the criminal justice system rather than prosecuted, one of the relevant features in that context being information as to mental disorder, including informal information that might justify further investigation.

9.64 The second point to be noted is that the general duty arising under Part 1 of the Criminal Procedure Rules 2011[65] to assist the court in securing the overriding objective of dealing with cases justly means that issues on which medical evidence might be required should be raised as soon as practicable in order to allow the case management powers of the court to be used: see *R v Ensor*,[66] which related to medical evidence as to whether a defendant could not give evidence and so should not face an adverse inference direction, in which it was ruled that the late notice of the relevant evidence justified it not being admitted. Although a court could not properly ignore late evidence that a defendant is not fit to stand trial, since proceeding with a trial that is fundamentally flawed cannot be right, any failure to notify in advance that fitness might be an issue that could lead to a costs order.

9.65 The need for evidence may also have implications for other procedural matters, such as the custody time limits. This arose in *R (Alexander) v Isleworth Crown Court*,[67] in which the prosecution response to a defence report supporting fitness to stand trial was that it would require its own medical evidence. A date was set for a hearing on the question of fitness, but the prosecution evidence was delayed as the expert instructed had become ill: as the date fixed for the new hearing

65 SI No 1709.

66 [2009] EWCA Crim 2519, [2010] MHLR 4.

67 [2009] EWHC 85 (Admin), [2009] MHLR 136.

was beyond the custody time limits, it was necessary for them to be extended if the defendant was to remain in custody. On the facts, the judge found that there was good cause and that the prosecution had acted with due diligence, the test under the Prosecution of Offences Act 1985. In upholding this, the Divisional Court noted that there was no obligation on the prosecution to secure their own evidence until the defence had provided the necessary two reports in favour of the defendant being unfit.

9.66 As to when the issue should be raised, it seems self-evident that if there is a proper basis for suggesting that a defendant is not fit to stand trial, including because he or she cannot provide proper instructions, then the matter must be raised by whoever has the relevant basis for raising the issue as soon as that suspicion is harboured.

When should the issue be determined?

9.67 Once it has been raised, a decision has to be made as to whether or not the court needs to determine the issue. At first sight, it would seem obvious that an issue that has been raised that may reflect on whether a defendant can properly be tried must be dealt with as soon as it has been raised before the court. It seems to have been the case that under the CLA 1800 the issue had to be dealt with as a preliminary issue if raised at arraignment: *R v Beynon*,[68] in which it was also noted that if the issue arose during the trial the judge had then to determine it and, if the defendant was not fit, had to stop the trial.

9.68 The CP(I)A 1964 also has that as a starting point. CP(I)A 1964 s4(4) notes that the 'question shall be determined as soon as it arises'.[69] This was implicit in the concept of a disability that amounts to a bar to a trial occurring, namely that it had to be determined whether the case could proceed. However, this is subject to subsections (2) and (3), which provide, respectively, that the question may be postponed until the opening of the defence case and shall not be determined if the jury has already acquitted the defendant.[70] The judge's decision

68 [1957] 2 QB 111. In *R v Webb* [1969] 2 QB 278, Sachs LJ noted at 282 that: 'Before the passing of the Act of 1964, the issue of fitness to plead had of necessity to be disposed of before arraignment'. However, in *R v Roberts* [1954] 2 QB 329, Devlin J held that a jury could be sworn to consider both the fitness to stand trial of the defendant and whether there was a case to answer. This was not followed in *Beynon*, but, as is noted below, was the procedure put in place by the CP(I)A 1964.

69 In the CP(I)A 1964 as originally enacted, it was in section 4(3).

70 These two sections were combined in CP(I)A 1964 s4(2) as originally drafted. The changes were introduced by the CP(IUP)A 1991.

on postponement requires satisfaction that 'it is expedient to do so and in the interests of the accused', as provided by section 4(2). The purpose behind the discretion is to allow the judge to assess whether there is a case to answer, on the basis that an acquittal of a weak prosecution case will be in the best interests of the defendant. The guidance as to this comes from two cases that were decided before the reforms introduced by the CP(IUP)A 1991, namely at a time when the effect of a finding of unfitness led to the detention of the defendant during Her Majesty's pleasure.

9.69 In *R v Webb*,[71] the issue of fitness to stand trial was raised by the prosecution before arraignment, relying on evidence that the 26-year-old defendant operated at the level of a seven-year-old. A defence application to postpone consideration of the issue, on the basis that it was felt that the evidence on the indecent assault charge for which Mr Webb was being tried was weak, was rejected. The defendant was found unfit to stand trial and ordered to be detained. The finding was quashed by the Court of Appeal. Sachs LJ, giving the judgment of the court, noted that 'one of the main objects' of the changes introduced by the CP(I)A 1964 was to allow the defendant to avoid the 'much dreaded' order of detention during Her Majesty's pleasure 'where the defence was in a position to demolish the prosecution case by cross-examination or upon some point of law before the time came for the defence to be opened'. This was achieved by allowing consideration of the question to be postponed.[72] This power, being a general discretion, had to be exercised in a judicial manner, in other words by taking into account relevant factors. Those were identified as the nature of the disability and the chance of challenging the prosecution case: the relevance of the former is mentioned expressly in the language of section 4(2),[73] and the latter arises from the purpose behind the introduction of the discretion to postpone.

9.70 Sachs LJ commented that it was clear that 'if there are reasonable chances of the prosecution case being successfully challenged so that the defence may not be called upon, then clearly it is as a rule in the interests of the accused that trial of the issue be postponed until after arraignment'.[74] The reference to this being 'as a rule' means, of course, that it must turn on the particular facts. However, it is worth noting that this approach is not limited to being the general rule

71 [1969] 2 QB 278.

72 [1969] 2 QB 278 at 282.

73 Both as originally enacted and as substituted by the CP(IUP)A 1991.

74 [1969] 2 QB 278 at 282.

when the case seems weak on the papers: Sachs LJ went on to say that in relation to 'lesser chances' of showing that there was no case to answer 'if there are sufficient chances to warrant such a challenge the issue should be postponed until after that challenge has been made'.

9.71 As to the question of the 'nature of the disability', the court seems to have taken into account[75] both Mr Webb's ability to comprehend (noting that he had been able to carry out low-skilled employment) and also the lack of any suggestion that his condition was one that merited the hospital disposal that would follow on the finding.[76]

9.72 *Webb* was upheld in *R v Burles*,[77] in which Lord Parker CJ set out the procedure as follows:

> ... a trial judge must ... first consider the apparent strength or weakness of the prosecution case as disclosed on the depositions or statements as the case may be. He should then go on to consider the nature and degree of the suggested disability, something which will be disclosed in the medical reports before the judge; then, having paid attention to those two matters, he must ask himself: what is expedient and in the prisoner's interest? Approaching the matter on that basis one can envisage cases to which there can really only be one answer: thus the prosecution case may appear so strong and the suggested condition of the prisoner so disabling that postponement of the trial at issue would be wholly inexpedient. Again, the prosecution case may be so thin that whatever the degree of disablement it clearly would be expedient to postpone the trial. Between these two extremes it falls to the judge to weigh up the various considerations, and as a matter of discretion to order that the issue be either tried forthwith or postponed.[78]

9.73 Applying that to the facts of *Burles*, which involved a manslaughter charge in relation to which the prosecution conceded that there was no case to answer in light of the medical evidence as to the defendant's very limited intellectual abilities – such that, on arraignment, the prosecution would have had to offer no evidence and allow a not guilty verdict to be entered – the Court of Appeal held that the certainty of an acquittal meant that it was clearly expedient and in the interests of the defendant, irrespective of the nature of his disability, to postpone consideration of the issue of fitness to be tried. The court accepted that there might be situations in which the defendant might not be able to give any coherent instructions, but its holding suggests that this could be outweighed if the case was particularly weak.

75 [1969] 2 QB 278 at 282–283.

76 CP(I)A 1964 s5 as enacted; see below.

77 [1970] 2 QB 191.

78 [1970] 2 QB 191 at 196.

9.74 In so holding, the court found that the trial judge's view that the question of postponement only applied to people who were sane but had communication difficulties and so could follow proceedings with appropriate translation was wrong.[79] However, one must have some sympathy for the trial judge's position, since one of the competencies tested is ability to understand the plea, and an inability in relation to that means that the person is not fit to stand trial: it seems reasonable to conclude that the statute did not permit a sham, namely one premised on the false view that the defendant could understand the process adequately. However, if the statute is read as a pragmatic compromise (which is an obvious connotation of the test being phrased as expediency and the potentially paternalistic reference to the 'interests' of the defendant), the outcome of the Court of Appeal's approach has obvious sense. The same pragmatism would support taking a contrary approach to postponement if the prosecution evidence appears strong and the medical evidence suggests strongly that the defendant cannot participate at any level.

9.75 Having said all that, it should be noted that *Webb* and *Burles* were decided when the CP(I)A 1964 provided that the consequence of a finding of unfitness to stand trial was that the trial ended and detention in hospital had to be ordered. The amendments introduced by the CP(IUP)A 1991 mean that the consequence of a finding of unfitness to stand trial is that the court must determine, first, whether the actus reus was committed and, if so, can then make a range of orders depending on the condition of the defendant. As a consequence of these changes, it is suggested that the court should be less likely to postpone consideration of unfitness to stand trial because it must in any event determine whether it is shown that the actus reus was caused (not just to the case to answer standard), and the interests of the defendant in terms of disposal are now better protected. The only real advantage from the prospect of the defendant of postponing the question of fitness to stand trial until after the end of the prosecution case is if the basis for a submission of no case to answer might arise out of a mens rea issue, which is not a part of the trial of the facts under the CP(IUP)A 1991's procedure.

9.76 If the defendant's condition changes after the defence case has started (or the basis for a finding of unfitness does not become apparent until after that time), there can be no question of postponement. Clearly, the issue can be raised, since the question of fitness to follow the trial and give instructions is something that must be assessed

79 [1970] 2 QB 191 at 196.

on an ongoing basis through to the end of the trial. But there is no power to postpone the determination of the issue once the defence case has opened.

Evidential matters in determining unfitness to stand trial

9.77 The determination of unfitness to stand trial is one that requires at least two doctors to give evidence, which can be written or oral, and at least one of those doctors must be approved for the purposes of MHA 1983 s12 as an expert in psychiatry: this arises from section 4(6) of the CP(I)A 1964. It states that the finding cannot be made 'except on the written or oral evidence of two or more registered medical practitioners, at least one of whom is duly approved'; the latter term is further defined in section 8(2) of the CP(I)A 1964 and refers across to the MHA 1983.

9.78 It is worth noting the implication of this for the question of what is meant by the substantive test of unfitness to stand trial. As is noted above, this has been held to refer to those who have communication difficulties that do not reflect any question of mental disorder, that being the *Pritchard* test that has been continued under the CP(I)A 1964, and yet the procedural prerequisite for demonstrating unfitness includes a psychiatrist. Such a doctor may have no basis for opining on questions of deafness, ability to speak (save that he or she may be able to determine whether it is a catatonic muteness caused by a mental disorder), or the ability of the defendant to make use of aids to communication that might allow him or her to follow the trial or meet the other aspects of the test. This statutory provision suggests that the substantive test should be confined to those whose inability to participate is the result of mental disorder: this argument is supported by the disposals available, discussed below, which are linked to mental disorder.

9.79 To return to the medical evidence required, it must support the view that the defendant is not fit to stand trial. This emerges from *R v Borkan*,[80] which has been mentioned above. An appeal against conviction was raised on the ground that the judge should have engaged in the process of determining fitness to stand trial on the request of the defence. Although counsel had concerns about the defendant's ability to stand trial, a report obtained pre-trial from a psychiatrist contained the view that Mr Borkan was fit to stand trial. The trial commenced but was aborted in order to allow a further report on fitness to stand trial to be obtained: the second psychiatrist also

80 [2004] EWCA Crim 1642, [2004] MHLR 216.

found him fit to stand trial, though noting that he had personality problems. When an application to adjourn the trial again failed, Mr Borkan admitted two of the three counts on the indictment and was sentenced to imprisonment (and subsequently transferred to hospital under MHA 1983 s47).[81]

9.80 The Court of Appeal dismissed the appeal on the basis that the jury (this being a case from before the changes introduced by the DVCVA 2004) could only find a defendant unfit to stand trial if there was medical evidence to that effect; as there was medical evidence to the contrary effect, it was held that the judge had been right not to swear a jury to consider the issue. Kennedy LJ noted that:

> ... it would seem to follow from the wording of the statute, and [counsel for the Appellant] accepts this, that a jury can only find a defendant unfit to plead or stand trial if there is medical evidence to that effect. In the present case the medical evidence was all one way and it was to the opposite effect.[82]

9.81 It is suggested that this should not be taken to mean that the doctors must reach the conclusion that in their view the defendant meets the legal test: rather, it must be that they provide evidence that, when considered by the court, leads to the conclusion that the legal test is met. Expert evidence is generally admissible when it contains matters likely to be outside the knowledge of the judge or jury;[83] and, although it is permissible to have an expert give an opinion on the question that has to be determined by the court – usually referred to as evidence on 'the ultimate issue' – it remains a matter for the court to make the final decision.[84] On that basis, evidence of psychiatric diagnoses and of the impact of a condition on an individual are beyond the capability of the judge or jury, which is why expert evidence is necessary; and although the psychiatrist can express a view on fitness to stand trial, the question cannot be delegated to the expert and must remain a matter for the court. As fitness to be tried is a legal construct, not a medical question, the determination turns on whether the court finds that the expert evidence demonstrates that the legal test is met.

9.82 Accordingly, the comments of Kennedy LJ should not be understood to mean that there must be a conclusion in the psychiatric reports that the defendant is unfit to stand trial: that would mean

81 See chapter 20.

82 Paragraph 11.

83 *R v Turner* [1975] QB 834.

84 *R v Stockwell* (1993) 97 CrAppR 260.

that the determination of unfitness to stand trial requires a dual key decision by the two doctors involved and then the court, which is not right.[85] Having said that, it is to be noted that a further authority supports the view that there must be two reports in favour of unfitness: in *R (Alexander) v Isleworth Crown Court*,[86] the prosecution indicated that it would obtain its own evidence but did instruct its own expert until two defence reports had been served. When the prosecution expert fell ill, a hearing had to be delayed until after the custody time limits had expired, such that an application was made for them to be extended. The Divisional Court upheld a finding that the prosecution had acted with due diligence, noting that it was not obliged to obtain evidence until the defence had provided the necessary two reports in favour of the defendant being unfit. The same arguments as set out above can be raised against this view.

9.83 It is certainly the case that any lawyer reviewing the medical evidence must assess whether any conclusions expressed on the ultimate issue are based on an accurate view of the law. It was noted in *R v Murray*[87] – in which a view was formed pre-trial that a defendant was fit to stand trial but the Court of Appeal accepted subsequent evidence to the contrary – that the medical and legal concepts do not always sit together well. Accordingly, it is best for a lawyer to check carefully that the medical views on legal topics are based on a correct understanding of the law.

9.84 It is also plain that the court can reject a view formed by the medical witnesses to the effect that the defendant is unfit to stand trial: this emerges from a statement of principle by Scott Baker LJ in *R v Miller and Miller*,[88] where at paragraph 17 he noted that: 'Although his decision will be informed by the medical evidence, the decision, in the judgment of this Court, is that of the judge and not that of the doctors or any of them'. On the facts, the medical evidence was to the effect that Mr Miller was mentally impaired and would have difficulties in following the trial and providing ongoing evidence, rather

85 At paragraphs 6 and 7, Kennedy LJ notes that the psychiatrists reached conclusions as to the test not being met, and sets out that at least one of them made reference to some of the competencies involved in reaching the conclusions, the reasoning process to those conclusions is not met. See also the discussion of similar language in the context of the insanity verdict, at paras 12.91–12.93 belwo, which provides further support for this contrary proposition.

86 [2009] EWHC 85 (Admin), [2009] MHLR 136.

87 [2008] EWCA Crim 1792, [2008] MHLR 191 at para 6.

88 [2006] EWCA Crim 2391.

than that he could not do so,[89] and the appeal court noted that no instance was given of him having been unable to follow proceedings. The judge's ruling that Mr Miller had been fit to stand trial was upheld. It was noted that the judge had to keep any ruling as to fitness to follow the proceedings under review.[90]

9.85 The trial judge in *Miller and Miller* had commented that the judge was, by reason of experience, suitably placed to determine the fairness of proceeding against a defendant:[91] this was not specifically upheld by the Court of Appeal, but it was the basis for a subsequent decision that the judge is able to reject a contention as to unfitness to stand trial by reliance on his or her own view as to the abilities of the defendant. In *R v Ghulam*,[92] the Court of Appeal considered an appeal based on a judicial refusal to consider the question of fitness to stand trial when raised during the summing-up: the application was supported by medical evidence, but the judge indicated that his assessment of the manner in which the defendant had appeared during the trial meant that he was satisfied that the trial should continue. The Court of Appeal dismissed an appeal, holding that a determination of fitness does not require supporting medical reports and can be based on the judge's observations.

9.86 In many ways, the facts in *Ghulam* were ill-equipped for the point of law argued. It seems that the trial had not been conducted with the provisions of the CP(I)A 1964 at the forefront. So, although the trial had been long-delayed, an application to adjourn was made at the outset on the basis of a short letter from a trainee psychiatrist which indicated that a full report would be forthcoming but stated that the defendant 'was not able to stand trial at present' because it would cause a deterioration in his mental and physical health (ie, not addressing the statutory test). By the time the full report was available, in which the doctor expressly referred to *Pritchard* and the relevant competencies and set out his view that the defendant understood the charge and could enter a plea, but that he could not challenge jurors or follow the evidence or give evidence, the trial was near its end: and

89 See [2006] EWCA Crim 2391 paras 16 and 18.

90 See [2006] EWCA Crim 2391 para 21: 'The judge, having given a ruling in favour of the prosecution was, in the judgment of this Court, under an obligation to keep that ruling under review during the course of the trial in case anything transpired that might suggest to him his earlier ruling had been erroneous.' And paragraph 25: 'In the result, it is our view that the proof of the pudding in this case was in the eating.'

91 See [2006] EWCA Crim 2391 para 18.

92 [2009] EWCA Crim 2285, [2010] 1 WLR 891, [2009] MHLR 325.

Mr Ghulam had given instructions as to the challenging of a juror. The judge declined the application made, which was to discharge the jury rather than have a finding of unfitness to plead made, and did so on the basis of his view that the medical evidence was wrong in the light of the defendant's ability during the trial to follow it and give evidence.

9.87 The Court of Appeal dismissed the appeal against this ruling, noting that the initial letter did not properly raise the question of fitness to stand trial, that there could not be a finding of unfitness without at least two medical reports and so the more detailed report was not sufficient by itself, and that in any event it was permissible for the judge to make a finding that a defendant was fit without two medical reports and on the basis of his or her own observations of the ability of the defendant to deal with the trial process. It was also noted that the judge had never in fact been directed to the relevant statutory provisions.

9.88 The court was no doubt correct that the need for a finding of unfitness, being one that leads to the fact-finding procedure and possible disposal without consideration of mens rea questions, as described below, should require evidence of a sort that is not required for the contrary conclusion, which allows the criminal trial to continue.[93] However, the judgment should not be taken as an indication that a judge is competent to step outside his or her area of expertise and to make what are in effect medical judgments about the capacities of a defendant. It may be possible, for example, for a defendant to appear rational on the surface and able to follow proceedings or to give evidence that is internally consistent but still to be suffering from a mental disorder that undermines his or her ability to weigh the evidence being given or give an account that reflects competency to stand trial. Having said that, it must also be right to say that a doctor's assessment made outside the courtroom and in advance of the trial will be weaker than an assessment made as to how the defendant in fact coped with a trial (given that concerns expressed in advance might turn out to be not fulfilled in practice). A second point about this judgment is the role of the defendant's apparent ability to challenge a juror: that could not by itself mean that a defendant is competent in all other areas relevant to the substantive test, and unfitness in any one area is sufficient to meet the test.

93 [2009] EWCA Crim 2285, [2010] 1 WLR 891, [2009] MHLR 325 para 18.

Burden and standard of proof

9.89 The burden of proof falls on the party who raises the issue and the standard of proof follows the usual criminal approach, namely on the balance of probabilities if raised by the defence: see *Podola.*[94] Although this was decided under the CLA 1800, there is no suggestion that the CP(I)A 1964 changed this approach. It was not expressly stated by the Court of Criminal Appeal in *Podola* that if the burden was on the prosecution it required proof beyond a reasonable doubt, but this was confirmed to be the case in *Robertson*, albeit on a concession from the prosecution.[95] It has not been resolved what is the burden of proof if the judge raises the issue: naturally, if the judge makes his or her concerns known and either of the parties wishes to take the judicial invitation to raise the issue, the burden and standard of proof applicable to that party will govern: but if neither party wishes to raise the question but the judge finds it necessary to do so, it seems likely that the onus applicable to the prosecution will apply in light of the potential consequence of taking away the defendant's right to a trial on the issue of his or her guilt, which has featured in cases such as *Ghulam* as an indicator of the need for good reasons to find unfitness.

9.90 Naturally, if one party raises the issue, the other side may wish to contest the question. Another question may be the impact of steps that can be taken to assist participation. These have come up in the context of the common law test, and are described below, and include modifications to the trial process and such steps as appointing intermediaries: but they will be of relevance to the statutory question as well.

If unfitness is found: the fact-finding exercise

9.91 If it is found that a defendant is fit to stand trial, the trial proceeds. A finding of unfitness under the CLA 1800 led to the end of the trial and a statutorily-mandated order of detention during Her Majesty's pleasure; section 5 of the CP(I)A 1964 as originally enacted required an order of admission to hospital on a finding of unfitness. However, that was amended by the CP(IUP)A 1991, which by section 2 inserted section 4A into the CP(I)A 1964 to require that there be a process of

94 [1960] 1 QB 325 at 350–351.
95 *R v Robertson* [1968] 1 WLR 1767 at 1773.

determining whether the actus reus had been committed.[96] That has raised significant questions, particularly in relation to the application of the fair trial requirements of article 6 of the ECHR.

The fact-finding exercise

9.92 The CP(I)A 1964 as enacted provided by section 4(5) that: 'Where ... it is determined that the accused is under a disability, the trial shall not proceed or further proceed'. In the statute as revised by the CP(IUP)A 1991, it is now stated in section 4A(2) that the trial does not proceed, but the subsection goes on to state that:

> ... it shall be determined by a jury –
> (a) on the evidence (if any) already given in the trial; and
> (b) on such evidence as may be adduced or further adduced by the prosecution, or adduced by a person appointed by the court under this section to put the case for the defence,
>
> whether they are satisfied, as respects the count or each of the counts on which the accused was to be or was being tried, that he did the act or made the omission charged against him as the offence.

9.93 This is the trial of the facts in relation to the offence alleged. The changes introduced by section 22 of the DVCVA 2004 to remove the role of the jury in deciding the question of fitness to stand trial, described above, did not extend to removing the role of jury in making the finding as to whether the act or omission charged is made out. However, the DVCVA 2004 did change some relevant language consequent on the removal of the jury from the deciding the question of fitness to stand trial: under CP(I)A 1964 s4A(5) as originally inserted, the fact-finding was carried out by a different jury than that which determined fitness to stand trial if the issue had been raised on arraignment, but by the same jury as was sworn in relation to

96 In *R v M, K and H* [2001] EWCA Crim 2024, [2001] MHLR 177, [2002] 1 WLR 824, discussed below, it was noted at paragraph 34 that: 'It was passed as a result of the case of Valerie Hodgson, who had confessed to the murder of her father, had been found unfit to plead and, without any investigation of the facts in any hearing, had been committed to prison, and subsequently, to a secure hospital. It was later found that she had not committed the act of murder'. It was a recommendation of the Report of the Committee on Mentally Abnormal Offenders, Cmnd 6244, October 1975 (the Butler Committee): chapter 10 of this report noted the unsatisfactory nature of the existing arrangements and proposed a 'trial of the facts' solution for when the defendant was found to be under a disability. The automatic detention on a finding of unfitness does not necessarily breach ECHR article 5: see *R (Juncal) v Home Secretary and others* [2008] EWCA Civ 869, [2008] MHLR 193, which related to a detention that commenced in Northern Ireland on the basis of a finding of unfitness alone.

the trial if the question arose part-way through the trial. Now that the jury has been removed from the question of determining fitness to stand trial, section 4A(5) has been amended by the DVCVA 2004 to indicate that if the question is raised after arraignment, the jury to which reference is made in subsection (2) is that conducting the trial.[97]

9.94 Before turning to the questions to which this process has given rise, and because the questions arising and the answers given are in part illuminated by the rest of the process, this will be described in brief first (and discussed in further detail below). Once the determination has been made that the defendant is unfit to stand trial, a jury is sworn or, if already sworn in the trial process, commences its new role. The jury makes its determination on the evidence already called and on further evidence called by the prosecution and by the person appointed to conduct the defence case: this terminology makes it clear that there is a different role to that of defence counsel following instructions. If the jury find that the act or omission relevant to the count (or any one of them if more than one) was done by the accused, then a finding to that effect is made (CP(I)A 1964 s4A(3)); but if the jury are 'not so satisfied', they return a 'verdict of acquittal' (CP(I)A 1964 s4A(4)). If there is a finding on the facts against the accused, then the court proceeds under CP(I)A 1964 s5, which as substituted by the CP(IUP)A 1991 and then further substituted by the DVCVA 2004, provides that the court may impose a hospital order under the MHA 1983 (perhaps with a restriction order under section 41 of the MHA 1983), a supervision order or an absolute discharge. It is to be noted that various other statutes may be applicable: for example, registration as a sex offender under section 80 of the Sexual Offences Act 2003 is required following a finding of the commission of the actus reus of a relevant offence.

9.95 Another preliminary point to note is that, as the finding of unfitness brings an end to the criminal trial, it also brings to an end the instructions of the defence advocate. Section 4A(2) of the CP(I)A 1964 requires the trial court to appoint a person to put the case for the defence. The Court of Appeal has indicated that this person might not be the same person as had represented the defendant before the finding of unfitness. In *R v Norman*,[98] at paragraph 34(iii), the Court of Appeal noted that:

97 See paras 9.162–9.116 below for discussion of what happens if there are co-defendants to the person who is unfit to stand trial.

98 [2008] EWCA Crim 1810, [2008] MHLR 206.

> ... it is the court's duty ... carefully to consider who is the best person to be appointed by the court to put the case for the defence. ... The duty under s4A(2) is a duty personal to the court which must consider afresh the person who is to be appointed; it should not necessarily be the same person who has represented the defendant to date, as it is the responsibility of the court to be satisfied that the person appointed is the right person for this difficult task. As is evident from Prof MacKay's paper to which we have referred, there are relatively few cases where the trial of the issue as to whether the defendant did the act are contested and are therefore outside the experience of most. The responsibility placed on the person so appointed is quite different to the responsibility placed on an advocate where he or she can take instructions from a client. The special position of the person so appointed is underlined by the fact that the person is remunerated not through the Criminal Defence Service, but out of central funds. Given the responsibility that the Act places on the court, it would not be unusual if the judge needed a little time to consider who was the best person to be so appointed.[99]

9.96 The approach of the person appointed will usually be by way of testing the prosecution evidence. It is to be noted that if the trial of the facts does not commence until part-way through the trial, it may consider the evidence already adduced: this may make it difficult for anyone new to represent the defence position and is a factor to support the appointment of the same advocate who had already acted. In this connection, it is to be noted that even though instructions cannot be given by the defendant, the approach set out in the MCA 2005 in relation to decisions taken on behalf of someone who does not have capacity, which is the duty set out in section 4 of the Act to act in the person's best interests. But this includes, in section 4(6), the need to consider 'so far as is reasonably ascertainable' the person's wishes and feelings, and in section 4(7) the need to take account if appropriate and practicable of the views of carers and those interested in the welfare of the person. So it may be appropriate for the advocate appointed to engage in a proper process of consultation to determine the extent to which his or her actions should be guided by the principles in the MCA 2005, which are designed on the whole to ensure

99 The research to which reference is made is RD Mackay, B Mitchell and L Howe 'A continued upturn in unfitness to plead – more disability in relation to the trial under the 1991 Act' [2007] Crim LR 530. This is part of a series of research papers on the issue: see also RD Mackay 'The decline of disability in relation to the trial' [1991] Crim LR 87, RD Mackay, *Mental condition defences in the criminal law*, Clarendon Press, 1995, pp 221–224, and RD Mackay and G Kearns 'An upturn in unfitness to plead? disability in relation to the trial under the 1991 Act' [2000] Crim LR 532.

that a person without capacity is allowed to participate in the process that affects him or her.

Is the trial of the facts a criminal trial?

9.97 The obvious reason for defence counsel – or, in the language of CP(I)A 1964 s4A(2), the person putting the case for the defence – wishing to raise such a challenge is that a criminal trial cannot proceed if the defendant is unable to participate because that would amount to a breach of ECHR article 6(3). The interpretive obligation under section 3 of the Human Rights Act (HRA) 1998 would then come into play and the apparently mandatory language of section 4A(2) that it 'shall be determined by a jury' whether the accused committed the act or omission could not doubt be read as subject to an implied condition that 'provided it was possible to have a fair trial that complied with article 6 ECHR, it shall be determined by a jury' whether the act or omission was committed by the accused.[100] Since the finding of unfitness to stand trial would prevent any possibility of compliance with article 6, the process would have to end, presumably under the abuse of process jurisdiction of the court. However, it has been held that the trial of the facts is not a criminal trial; this case-law will be described first before the question is raised of whether the civil provisions of article 6 apply.

9.98 The criminal charge provisions of ECHR article 6 were raised in the Court of Appeal in the case of *R v M, K and H*.[101] K was a psychiatrist charged with four counts of rape and 15 counts of indecent assault of patients over a 20-year period. He was found unfit to stand trial in the light of an organic brain disease and opiate medication taken to counter the effects of surgery for colon cancer. An argument that making use of CP(I)A 1964 s4A was an abuse of process because it breached article 6 was dismissed by the trial judge. At the end of the section 4A process, the only finding against K was that he had committed one of the indecent assaults: he was acquitted of some

100 The argument as to this is based on the conclusion of the Divisional Court in *R (Hammond) v Home Secretary* [2004] EWHC 2753 (Admin), [2005] 2 Prison LR 218, in which the process of High Court judges setting tariffs for existing mandatory lifers under language stating that the decision was to be made 'without an oral hearing' was held to be subject to an implied condition that an oral hearing could be held if necessary to comply with article 6; this conclusion was not appealed when the matter when to the House of Lords ([2005] UKHL 69, [2006] 1 Prison LR 1), though some members of the House were clear to make the point that they did not endorse this holding, at least not with the benefit of full argument.

101 [2001] EWCA Crim 2024, [2001] MHLR 177, [2002] 1 WLR 824.

matters, and the jury could not agree on others, which were ordered to lie on the file. He was granted an absolute discharge.

9.99 H was a juvenile found unfit to stand trial in relation to two counts of indecent assault; a similar abuse of process argument was rejected, and the section 4A process led to findings that he had committed the acts; he was absolutely discharged.[102] M was also charged with historic sex offences, involving his children, and found unfit to stand trial: his claim that further proceedings would breach article 6 was rejected in a preliminary ruling that was declared to be a ruling at a preparatory hearing within the meaning of Criminal Procedure and Investigations Act (CPIA) 1996 s29.

9.100 Their appeals were joined as they raised similar points, centred on the question of whether the section 4A process was criminal in its nature for the purposes of article 6. K and H both argued that the section 4A procedure that had been followed against them was criminal in its nature, relying on matters such as the name of the statute, the fact that a finding could result in stigma and a loss of liberty, and also the fact that a finding was treated in the same way as a conviction for statutes such as the Rehabilitation of Offenders Act (ROA) 1974:[103] this was the precursor to the argument that article 6 was breached, because the accused was not able to participate and was deprived of equality of arms (arising from the provisions of article 6(3)(d), the right to witnesses on the same terms as those applicable to the prosecution). Reliance was also placed on the presumption of innocence in article 6(2): it was suggested that it was breached in the light of the inability of the accused to give evidence. A point was also taken for K that the purpose of section 4A was the protection of the public by providing for a psychiatric disposal, and should be used only in circumstances in which the defendant presented a risk.

9.101 The prosecution answer to this last argument was to point out that the availability of an absolute discharge meant that the statute was not limited to public protection. The other arguments taken by the prosecution were that the section 4A procedure was mandatory (and so ousted any common law abuse of process jurisdiction), did

102 Not mentioned in the Court of Appeal, he was also required to register under the Sex Offender Register: see paragraph 1 of the opinion of Lord Bingham in the House of Lords, discussed below.

103 ROA 1974 s1(4) states that: 'references to a conviction, however expressed, include references ... (b) to any finding (other than a finding linked with a finding of insanity) in any criminal proceedings ... that a person has committed an offence or done the act or made the omission charged'. It is to be noted that the finding that a person committed the act but is not guilty by reason of insanity is excluded.

not involve the determination of a criminal charge for the purposes of article 6, and that if the matter was criminal the procedures set out in the statute were fair. It was also argued that the ruling in M's case did not amount to a ruling in a criminal matter, and so could not be a preparatory hearing for the purposes of the CPIA 1996.

9.102 The Court of Appeal answered the main question in favour of the prosecution, finding that the section 4A process was not a criminal trial but that, if it was, it met the requirements of article 6. The court determined that the fact that there could be no conviction or order amounting to a penalty prevented the process being a criminal matter.[104] The court noted at paragraph 21 that of the potential disposals, the admission order (which was subsequently replaced by the hospital order by the DVCVA 2004, but in any event took effect as if it was a hospital order[105]), the guardianship or supervision and treatment order,[106] and the absolute discharge, the first three were concerned with care and treatment. The court commented that the 'absolute discharge' had different criteria from those governing its imposition following a conviction: so, section 5(4) of the CP(IUP)A 1991 indicated that the references in section 1A(1) of the Powers of Criminal Courts Act (PCCA) 1973[107] to conviction and it being 'inexpedient to inflict punishment' took effect as if they referred to the finding that the act or omission was caused and to the absolute discharge being the most suitable order. This meant that the order 'does not imply either conviction or that punishment is inexpedient', but that the act was done by the accused and an absolute discharge was most suitable.

104 Paragraphs 19–21 and 23–24; the absence of a penalty or punitive aim was described as 'a decisive factor' at paragraph 24. The court relied on the case of *R (McCann) v Manchester Crown Court* (CA) [2001] 1 WLR 1084 and its discussion of the leading European Court of Human Rights jurisprudence, notably *Engel v Netherlands* (1976) 1 EHRR 647: *McCann* related to anti-social behaviour orders, and the holding that they were not criminal was subsequently upheld by the House of Lords, [2003] 1 AC 787. Other cases reaching a similar conclusion are *B v Chief Constable of Avon and Somerset Constabulary* [2001] 1 WLR 340, relating to sex offender orders, and *Gough v Chief Constable of Derbyshire* [2002] QB 1213, relating to football banning orders.

105 CP(IUP)A 1991 Sch1 para 1(3).

106 The court spoke about the two orders, since a guardianship order is not available for someone of H's age.

107 The court should have referred to section 12 of the Powers of Criminal Courts (Sentencing) Act (PCC(S)A) 2000, which had replaced the provisions of the PCCA 1973; PCC(S)A 2000 s165(1) and Sch 9 para 133 made the relevant changes to the CP(IUP)A 1991.

9.103 The court continued with its reasoning: the finding of facts that might amount to a criminal offence was insufficient to make the procedure criminal in its nature, since that was the feature in various civil and disciplinary proceedings.[108] Nor did the potential loss of liberty amount to a problem in this regard, since that could only affect someone of unsound mind within the meaning of ECHR article 5(1)(e) (which meant that the protections of article 5(4) were those applicable).[109]

9.104 For the second part of the holding, which rested on the assumption that ECHR article 6 did apply, whether in relation to the determination of a criminal charge or of civil rights or obligations, was that it was not necessarily breached if a defendant could not enjoy the rights guaranteed. The court said at paragraph 31 that the argument that a trial would breach article 6 if the defendant could not participate 'confuse[s] the rights assured by article 6 with the enjoyment of those rights. The State can only assure rights to its citizens: it cannot ensure that all its citizens are able, in practice, to use those rights'. Accordingly, on this legalistic distinction, it was held that a trial could still be fair if efforts were made to minimise any disadvantages caused by mental disability and any limitation on the rights was no greater than required and supported a suitable objective. In this connection, the court noted that the ECtHR had not suggested that the defendants in the case of *V and T v UK* (discussed above) could not be tried if appropriate arrangements had been made.[110] The court held that the CP(I)A 1964 as amended by the CP(IUP)A 1991 balanced the public interest in ascertaining whether the acts of a criminal offence had been committed, and identifying and dealing appropriately with those responsible, against the interests of the accused and did so in a manner that was fair.[111]

9.105 Dealing with the ancillary points, the court found that the abuse of process jurisdiction was not ousted by the CP(I)A 1964, but that the basis for any abuse application could not arise from the mental

108 [2001] EWCA Crim 2024, [2001] MHLR 177, [2002] 1 WLR 824 para 26. In relation to disciplinary proceedings, these have subsequently been found to be criminal if the penalty is not shown by the state to be not appreciably detrimental, which loss of liberty for punitive purposes will be: see *Ezeh and Connors v UK* (2004) 39 EHRR 1, [2004] Prison LR 95. However, given the involvement of punitive aims that are not present in CP(I)A 1964 s4A proceedings, this development in the case-law does not affect the central reasoning of the court.

109 [2001] EWCA Crim 2024, [2001] MHLR 177, [2002] 1 WLR 824 para 22.

110 [2001] EWCA Crim 2024, [2001] MHLR 177, [2002] 1 WLR 824 paras 32–33.

111 [2001] EWCA Crim 2024, [2001] MHLR 177, [2002] 1 WLR 824 para 34.

disability of the accused, since that would avoid the whole point of CP(I)A 1964 ss4 and 4A.[112] In addition to the holding that the matter was not criminal, the court also noted that M's case did not involve the sort of complexity or length that would allow the interlocutory appeal process of the CPIA 1996, and the ruling was on whether there was an abuse of process, which was not a point of law of the sort covered by the appeal mechanism.[113]

9.106 The appeal of H and applications for leave in K and M were dismissed. The case of H was appealed further to the House of Lords, the Court of Appeal having certified that there was a point of law of general public importance and the House granting leave to appeal. In *R v H*[114] the House of Lords upheld the view of the Court of Appeal that the section 4A process was not a criminal trial. The question certified was whether there was a determination of a criminal charge for the purposes of article 6(1), a breach of the presumption of innocence in article 6(2), given that the finding that the person 'did the act' did not look at the mens rea, or a breach of the need for equality of arms under article 6(3)(d).[115]

9.107 The essence of the argument put for H was as it had been in the Court of Appeal: namely, that as a matter of substance, there was the determination of a criminal charge.[116] The indecent assault charges involved, it was noted, required only proof of non-accidental touching in circumstances of indecency, and so the finding that the 'act' was committed was the same, and certainly carried the same stigma, and the ROA 1974 and Sex Offenders Act 1997 applied in the same way.[117] It was also noted than an acquittal could follow.

9.108 The prosecution, joined by the Home Secretary as an interested party, accepted that articles 6(2) and (3) could not be satisfied by the section 4A process: but they contended that any loss of liberty was done in a manner that complied with article 5 or article 6(1) in

112 Accordingly, it must rest on matters such as oppressive behaviour by state agencies, loss of vital records or an assurance of non-prosecution. See [2001] EWCA Crim 2024, [2001] MHLR 177, [2002] 1 WLR 824 paras 35–37.

113 [2001] EWCA Crim 2024, [2001] MHLR 177, [2002] 1 WLR 824 para 17.

114 [2003] UKHL 1, [2003] 1 WLR 411, [2003] MHLR 209.

115 [2003] UKHL 1, [2003] 1 WLR 411, [2003] MHLR 209: Lord Bingham at para 1 sets out the question in full.

116 [2003] UKHL 1, [2003] 1 WLR 411, [2003] MHLR 209 para 12.

117 See now section 80 of the Sexual Offences Act 2003, which, for the purposes of the sex offender registration and notification provisions, includes a finding that the act was done under CP(I)A 1964 s4A (and also a finding of not guilty by reason of insanity) as well as a conviction for an offence as the trigger.

relation to the determination of civil rights.[118] It is important to note that counsel for H accepted that there was no breach of article 5 or article 6(1) in its application to civil matters,[119] and so the only matter that fell for determination by the House was whether or not the section 4A procedure was criminal.

9.109 In dismissing the appeal, the House of Lords adopted as authoritative the guidance in *Engel v Netherlands*,[120] and so looked to the classification in domestic law, the nature of the offence and the severity of the penalty risked or imposed. At paragraph 16 of his opinion, Lord Bingham said that the section 4A procedure was clearly not criminal from the point of view of the domestic classification as the statute provided that the trial ended, the jury had no power to convict and took a different oath,[121] there was no question of punishment if the decision of the jury was that the act had been committed (given the orders that were available, including the absolute discharge and its criteria that, as noted above, did not involve considering whether punishment was expedient or otherwise). As to the applicability of the notification requirements relating to sex offenders if the actus reus involved a sexual offence, it was held that they were designed to protect the public rather than to punish the accused against whom the finding was made. The applicability of the ROA 1974 was explained as being to allow those subject to findings under the section 4A procedure to benefit from the rehabilitation provisions.

9.110 Turning to the nature of the offence, Lord Bingham noted at paragraph 18 that the procedure followed lacked the 'essential features of criminal process'. For this comment, he relied on his own speech as Lord Chief Justice in the Divisional Court case of *Customs and Excise Commissioners v City of London Magistrates' Court*,[122] where he said:

> It is in my judgment the general understanding that criminal proceedings involve a formal accusation made on behalf of the state or by a private prosecutor that a defendant has committed a breach of the criminal law, and the state or the private prosecutor has instituted

118 [2003] UKHL 1, [2003] 1 WLR 411, [2003] MHLR 209 para 13.

119 [2003] UKHL 1, [2003] 1 WLR 411, [2003] MHLR 209 para 14.

120 (1976) 1 EHRR 647; see paragraph 15 (referring to paragraph 82 of *Engel*).

121 [2003] UKHL 1, [2003] 1 WLR 411, [2003] MHLR 209 at para 5, Lord Bingham noted: 'There appears to be no prescribed form of oath for this jury, but under the practice followed at the Central Criminal Court (and perhaps elsewhere) the jurors swear or affirm that they "will faithfully try whether the defendant did the act charged against him and ... will give a true verdict according to the evidence".'

122 [2000] 1 WLR 2020; the quoted comment is at page 2025.

proceedings which may culminate in the conviction and condemnation of the defendant.

9.111 His reasons for this conclusion were again that there could be no conviction or punishment. As to the third *Engel* criterion, it was noted that counsel for H had accepted that none of the orders were punitive: for Lord Bingham, this was a telling feature, since the essence of criminal law was the imposition of a penalty to proscribe conduct and provide a deterrent.[123] He then expressly endorsed the reasoning of the Court of Appeal.

9.112 The view that the process is not criminal has also been endorsed by the ECtHR, in an admissibility decision, *Antoine v UK*.[124] Reliance had been placed on articles 6(1), (2) and (3)(d), but the court, having noted the decision of the House of Lords in *R v H*, commented that the absence of the threat of conviction meant that it was not criminal. In the underlying domestic trial, a hospital order had been made (and indeed was mandatory as it was found that the actus reus of murder had been committed), but the court was satisfied that this demonstrated a purpose of determining whether Mr Antoine needed to be detained as dangerous.

9.113 While it must be accepted that the section 4A procedure is not a criminal trial, it is worth pointing to arguments the other way that do not seem to have been addressed in the case-law and which might therefore lead to the issue being revisited at some stage. First, the acceptance that an order for detention in hospital (or even the use of a guardianship or supervision and treatment order) is in no way punitive is not quite as clear as the connotations of hospitalisation might as first sight suggest. The obvious point to make is that a hospital order is available after a conviction as well and, while that is not imposed for the purposes of punishment, it cannot be suggested that it turns the entire process into something that is not criminal in nature; equally, the orders are open to the court following a finding that the defendant was not guilty by reason of insanity (see chapter 12), and that is clearly a criminal process.[125] In short, the House of

123 [2003] UKHL 1, [2003] 1 WLR 411, [2003] MHLR 209 para 20.

124 App No 62960/00, [2003] MHLR 292. This is the follow-on from *R v Antoine*, which is discussed below.

125 A point of statutory interpretation favouring a viewpoint that there is a clear distinction between a finding of not guilty by reason of insanity and a finding under CP(I)A 1964 s4A is that Bail Act 1976 s2 defines 'conviction' to include a finding of not guilty by reason of insanity but does not mention a finding of committing the act under CP(I)A 1964 s4A. However, it does include a finding of committing the act for the purposes of section 11 of the PCC(S)A

Lords concentrated on the outcome of the process and the absence of a penalty when, had it done so in the context of the range of situations that can lead to a non-penal outcome but are clearly criminal, it ought to have concluded that the outcome is only one factor.

9.114 As to whether there is a penalty risked, it is to be noted that the order for admission to hospital, if it is combined with a restriction order – which is risked for the purposes of the third *Engel* criterion – is a detention that is indeterminate in nature, which makes it difficult to argue that it is not of an appreciably detrimental effect (even if it is not the purpose of the sentence to cause a detriment). Furthermore, hospital units for forensic patients often involve significant levels of security and restrictions that do not differ to any great extent from being in prison. The response to this argument will be that the third *Engel* criterion is expressed as referring to an action taken as punishment: the counter point to this is that a concentration on the purpose of a measure to the exclusion of its impact is too narrow. After all, a judge in a standard criminal trial could form the view that he or she wishes to impose a community order with a condition of attendance at a rehabilitative programme for the purpose of benefitting the defendant. That purpose would not prevent it being a penalty in the light of its impact on the defendant's autonomy rights.

9.115 There are various additional points that suggest the need to qualify Lord Bingham's conclusion that the section 4A process is clearly not criminal in domestic law. Aside from the point made in the Court of Appeal as to the name of the CP(I)A 1964 suggesting that it dealt with a process the legislature believed was criminal, there is the argument arising from the fact that the criminal burdens and standards of proof apply and the fact that appeals can be taken to the Court of Appeal Criminal Division (discussed below), which is at least incongruous in relation to something that is not criminal in domestic law. Indeed, an argument to the effect that an order made under the CP(I)A 1964 was not criminal and so could be appealed to the Civil Division of the Court of Appeal in judicial review proceedings was rejected by the Court. In *R (South West Yorkshire Mental*

2000, which applies only to the magistrates' court (where the CP(I)A 1964 is not relevant). In contrast, in Criminal Justice and Public Order Act (CJPOA) 1994 s25, which provides that those with a previous conviction for homicide or rape or various other serious sexual offences who are charged with such an offence a second time can be granted bail only in exceptional circumstances, a finding of not guilty by reason of insanity or of being unfit to stand trial but having committed the act count as convictions for this statute: see CJPOA 1994 s25(5).

Health NHS Trust) v Bradford Crown Court,[126] Mr A had been found to have committed the actus reus of murder and the statute provided that he had to be made subject to an admission order as a result. (See CP(I)A 1964 s5(3), discussed below.) The statute at the time provided that it was for the Home Secretary to specify the hospital, but the judge purported to direct admission to a particular hospital, and no timely order was made by the Home Secretary. When this error (and others in the process) came to light, an application was made by the hospital to quash the Crown Court order so that it could be remitted and remade in its proper form; A argued that this should not be permitted to occur, with the aim of ensuring that any detention in hospital had to be under the civil provisions (which had been put in place to ensure that he was detained somehow). The High Court found that the civil detention had been of no effect, but that the order of the Crown Court purporting to direct A's detention was valid until set aside and so Mr A's detention was lawful: the Crown Court order was, however, based on an error of law and so was quashed and remitted to be made properly. There was a point as to whether the decision of the Crown Court judge was on a matter 'relating to trial on indictment' and so outside the scope of judicial review by reason of section 29(3) of the Senior Courts Act 1981,[127] but it was accepted that there was authority to the effect that it was.

9.116 Mr A wished to take the matter further, but section 18(1) of the Senior Courts Act 1981 provides that the Court of Appeal has no jurisdiction in relation to High Court judgments 'in any criminal cause or matter'. The appeal route on a criminal matter was to the House of Lords, but this was only possible if the point of law was certified as a matter of general public importance[128] and the High Court had declined to do this. The Court of Appeal[129] held that it had no jurisdiction as it was a 'criminal cause or matter' despite the ruling in *R v H* that it was not a criminal trial. Pill LJ concluded that:

> Where proceedings are initiated in the Crown Court following an allegation of a breach of the criminal law, it appears to me that an overall view of the proceeding is appropriate ...
>
> The Crown Court orders under consideration did not cease to be orders in 'a criminal cause or matter' because, upon the verdicts entered, the statute empowered the court to make a custodial order

126 [2003] EWHC 640 (Admin), [2004] MHLR 137.

127 The 'Supreme Court Act 1981' until the name was changed by the Constitutional Reform Act 2005.

128 Administration of Justice Act 1960 s1.

129 [2003] EWCA Civ 1857, [2004] 1 WLR 1664, [2004] MHLR 142.

in the absence of a conviction. The orders were in no way collateral to the criminal proceeding which had been initiated by the making of the criminal charge. They provided a method of giving effect, in circumstances in which a conviction is not appropriate, to what had plainly been initiated as a criminal proceeding. [130]

9.117 It has also been determined that somebody found to have committed the actus reus only and ordered to be detained under a hospital order by reason of section 37(3) of the MHA 1983 – which, as the next chapter discusses, is the process for dealing with unfit defendants in the magistrates' court – is nevertheless an 'offender'. This arose in determining whether magistrates could exercise the power under section 142 of the Magistrates' Courts Act 1980 to reopen and vary the order made in relation to an offender. In *R v Thames Magistrates' Court ex p Ramadan*,[131] the Divisional Court held that the description included a person found to have committed the act. This allowed the court to overcome the practical problem of a hospital order that should not have been made because it had not been clarified that a bed was available. Although 'offender' has a criminal connotation, it would no doubt be argued that this is a case that involves a pragmatic approach being taken to solve a problem that should not have arisen.

9.118 Perhaps worthy of more weight, reference can also be made the evidential scheme applicable. In *R v M (KJ)*,[132] one of the questions raised on the appeal was whether the trial judge had been correct to admit into evidence in the fact-finding process a statement of a witness who claimed he was too fearful to give oral evidence: this turned on section 23 of the Criminal Justice Act (CJA) 1988, which provided for the admission of such evidence subject to a discretion to exclude under section 26 on the basis of unfairness to the accused. The argument as to whether the judge was correct in the exercise of his discretion was carried out in terms of the requirements of ECHR article 6(3)(d), and the Court of Appeal expressly found at paragraph 62 of its judgment that there had been a breach of article 6 despite the fact that it was considering a section 4A procedure to which article 6 is not supposed to be applicable.

9.119 The question of whether the proceedings were criminal for the purposes of the applicability of the hearsay evidence rules does not

130 [2003] EWHC 640 (Admin), [2004] MHLR 137 paras 33 and 34.

131 [1999] 1 CrAppR 386.

132 [2003] EWCA Crim 357, [2003] 2 CrAppR 21, 322.

seem to have been the subject of argument in that case. In *R v Chal*,[133] the Court of Appeal (Criminal Division) had to consider whether the provisions of the CJA 2003 that replaced those in the CJA 1988 to provide for the admissibility of hearsay evidence if it is in the interests of justice[134] or in certain specified situations, including situations where a witness is not available,[135] apply to the section 4A procedure: Mr Chal argued that the judge had been wrong to allow in an eyewitness statement from a man who could not be traced. The Court of Appeal had to consider the definition of 'criminal proceedings' in CJA 2003 s134, namely 'criminal proceedings in relation to which the strict rules of evidence apply'.

9.120 The court noted that it had two choices, namely confining admissibility to proceedings which could culminate in a finding of guilt or the imposition of a penalty, or 'more generally so as to include all proceedings within the compass or framework of criminal proceedings, including ancillary proceedings which cannot of themselves involve conviction or punishment, in so far as the strict rules of evidence are applicable to them'.[136] It chose the latter approach, suggesting that it was plain that the hearsay provisions were intended by Parliament to cover section 4A proceedings, or that there was such an overlap between the process and a criminal trial that the same rules should be adopted.[137] The court noted that the criminal standard of proof applied, the jury deliberated as did a jury in a criminal trial, and the task of finding that the act or omission charged was carried out must require the same process as applicable to a trial in which that was a matter the jury had to be satisfied about. It noted that it could be impractical to have any other result because if the section 4A process was commenced part-way through the trial the jury was obliged to consider the evidence already adduced before it.[138]

9.121 The net effect of this case-law is that the section 4A process is not a criminal trial for the purposes of ECHR article 6, but it is a criminal proceeding for the purposes of the rules of evidence and is a criminal cause or matter for the purposes of domestic appeal proceedings.[139] The reasoning of *Chal* is instructive: it noted that there is

133 [2007] EWCA Crim 2647, [2007] MHLR 313.
134 CJA 2003 s114.
135 CJA 2003 s116.
136 [2007] EWCA Crim 2647, [2007] MHLR 313 paras 20 and 21.
137 [2007] EWCA Crim 2647, [2007] MHLR 313 para 33.
138 [2007] EWCA Crim 2647, [2007] MHLR 313 paras 24–27.
139 See also *R (Ferris) v Director of Public Prosecutions* [2004] EWHC 1221 (Admin), in which it was noted that the proceedings had hallmarks of both civil and

a narrow approach, such as was adopted in *R v H*, or a more holistic approach. Since the normal approach to human rights matters is not narrow and legalistic interpretations, but broad and generous,[140] the approach set out in *R v H* appears, when set against the other case-law, to fall into the trap of being overly limited.

9.122 It is to be noted that Lord Bingham clearly had policy considerations in mind. He stated at paragraph 18 of his opinion that:

> It would be highly anomalous if s4A, introduced by amendment for the protection of those unable through mental unfitness to defend themselves at trial, were itself to be held incompatible with the Convention. It is very much in the interest of such persons that the basic facts relied on against them (shorn of issues concerning intent) should be formally and publicly investigated in open court with counsel appointed to represent the interests of the person accused so far as possible in the circumstances. The position of accused persons would certainly not be improved if s4A were abrogated.

9.123 This, however, does not answer the point put on behalf of H that if he was unable to participate in the process, but his condition had been such as to require detention in a hospital setting, the civil procedures of the MHA 1983 could be used. It is far from obvious that sitting through a court process in which a defendant cannot participate can be 'very much' in their interest. This is particularly so when account is taken of the extent of the inquiry that is possible under the section 4A procedure, which is discussed next: in particular, if the accused committed the act but did so in circumstances where mens rea was absent and so an acquittal is merited, this is not something that is possible. A finding that the accused committed the acts in that situation is of limited benefit to the accused.

criminal proceedings. On the facts, the defendant had been found to have committed the actus reus of murder in 2000, but was in 2003 remitted for trial (see below), but again found unfit to stand trial. The question then arose as to what should happen in the further section 4A procedure, the prosecution submitting that the jury should be informed that a previous jury had found the facts in a manner that was binding upon them. The Divisional Court held that principles of issue estoppel applicable to civil proceedings did not apply to the section 4A process, which could be seen as sharing some of the characteristics of a criminal trial for the purpose of the issue estoppel point.

140 See *Minister of Home Affairs v Fisher* [1980] AC 319 at 328, per Lord Wilberforce.

What has to be proved in the fact-finding process? The guidance in Antoine

9.124 The question for the jury under CP(I)A 1964 s4A(2) and (3) is whether they are 'satisfied' that the accused 'did the act or made the omission charged against him as the offence'. At first sight, this seems to refer to the actus reus of the offence rather than the mens rea – but the distinction between these two components of an offence is not always easy.

9.125 This issue was considered by the House of Lords in *R v Antoine*.[141] The allegation was of murder by Mr Antoine and a co-defendant. The latter was convicted of manslaughter on the basis of diminished responsibility under section 2 of the Homicide Act 1957, on showing that he had an 'abnormality of mind' that 'substantially impaired his mental responsibility for his acts and omissions'.[142] But Mr Antoine was found to have committed the act of murder and had not been allowed to raise the question of diminished responsibility. The House considered two questions, one wider than the other. The point of law of general public importance certified by the Court of Appeal was whether an accused could rely on section 2 of the Homicide Act 1957 in the fact-finding process. The parties asked the House to consider a wider question, namely whether the jury had to be 'satisfied of more than the actus reus of the offence? Must the jury be satisfied of mens rea?'[143]

9.126 The reason for the narrower and wider questions was that the trial judge had ruled against the defence submission that they could seek to demonstrate diminished responsibility (on the basis that the statutory language precluded it), but, following *R v Egan (Michael)*,[144] had ruled that the prosecution had to prove both the actus reus of murder and the appropriate mens rea, failing which the defendant was entitled to be acquitted.[145] The jury found that Mr Antoine had committed the act (including the mens rea element), and so the judge imposed the mandatory order of admission to hospital with a restriction order. The Court of Appeal in *Egan* was considering the appeal of an accused alleged to have snatched a bag: on the question of the approach to take to the section 4A procedure, Ognall J stated that the

141 [2001] 1 AC 340, [2000] MHLR 28.

142 This language has now been amended by Coroners and Justice Act 2009 s52: the question of diminished responsibility is discussed further in chapter 14.

143 [2001] 1 AC 340, [2000] MHLR 28 paras 12 and 13.

144 [1998] 1 CrAppR 121.

145 [1998] 1 CrAppR 121.

court was 'satisfied, and indeed both counsel agree, that although the words "the act" are used in the relevant legislation, the phrase means neither more nor less than proof of all the necessary ingredients of what otherwise would be an offence, in this case theft';[146] accordingly, dishonesty and an intention permanently to deprive had to be shown. The wider question raised in *Antoine* was designed to test whether *Egan* was correct.

9.127 The Court of Appeal in *Antoine*[147] had suggested that *Egan* was wrong in the light of a different approach taken to an analogous situation if the question was whether someone was not guilty by reason of insanity. In *Attorney General's Reference No 3 of 1998*,[148] the Court of Appeal had decided that when the defendant was not guilty by reason of insanity, which meant that the court had to address the question under the Trial of Lunatics Act 1883 of whether the defendant 'did the act or made the omission charged', the prosecution had only to prove the actus reus of the crime, namely whether the defendant 'has caused a certain event or that responsibility is to be attributed to him for the existence of a certain state of affairs, which is forbidden by criminal law'.[149] It was said expressly that mens rea did not have to be proved and the defendant's state of mind was irrelevant on the statutory test (save for the question of whether he was insane). The court was considering a reference following an acquittal because the trial judge had considered himself bound by *Egan* and had directed an acquittal because the defendant's insanity had prevented him forming the mens rea required for the offences of aggravated burglary and affray. It held that *Egan* was not binding when the issue was insanity, but also commented that it appeared to have been decided per incuriam, since the language used in the CP(I)A 1964 matched that in the Trial of Lunatics Act 1883 and the case-law surrounding the 1883 Act and the statutory framework clearly suggested that the statutory language excluded consideration of mens rea matters.

9.128 Accordingly, the Court of Appeal in *Antoine* had significant dicta to the effect that *Egan* was wrongly decided. Although, given that Mr Antoine had been found to have committed the actus reus with the relevant mens rea, that question was not strictly in front of it, it endorsed the comments in *Attorney General's Reference No 3 of 1998*

146 [1998] 1 CrAppR 121 at 124–125.

147 [1999] 3 WLR 1204.

148 [1999] 2 CrAppR 214, [2000] QB 401.

149 The court adopted as correct this view of the authors of Smith and Hogan, *Criminal law*, 8th edn, p28.

as to *Egan*, noting that the language used in the CP(I)A 1964 was not apt to include mens rea questions. On the question properly in front of the Court of Appeal, namely whether diminished responsibility could be raised, it held that the trial judge had been correct in his ruling. In so ruling, the court used reasoning that was in part inconsistent with *Egan*: so Lord Bingham CJ for the court stated that section 2 of the Homicide Act 1957 applied only where the defendant was shown to have committed the actus reus of murder with the mens rea, which could not apply under CP(I)A 1964 s4A, given that it only considered the act and not all the ingredients of murder. This only makes sense if *Egan* is wrong. The Court of Appeal also stated that a conviction does not follow under the section 4A process, which is the point at which the diminished responsibility provisions apply. It was also noted that if the jury made a finding as to diminished responsibility, it would not be possible for there to be a remittal for trial on the charge of murder if fitness was regained, which was an additional reason not to allow the jury making a decision under section 4A to consider the issue.

9.129 In the House of Lords, the ratio of the Court of Appeal was upheld, namely that diminished responsibility could not be raised during section 4A proceedings, and its questioning of *Egan* was also found warranted. The reasoning as to the narrower, certified question rested on two points. In the first place, it was said that any conclusion by a jury acting under section 4A that a defendant charged with murder had a diminished responsibility would require it to acquit, which could not have been intended by the drafter of the statute. This conclusion, at paragraph 17 of the opinion of Lord Hutton, is unfortunately stated without any reasoning. It may be that what he had in mind was that the lesser included offence provisions of section 6(2) of the Criminal Law Act 1967 only refer to findings of guilt of various lesser alternatives, which is not possible under the section 4A procedure. However, this does not exclude the common law provisions as to lesser-included offences, which are not abrogated by the statutory provisions.[150] In any event, a count of manslaughter could be added to the indictment, as is often done when there is a doubt as to whether the jury can determine a lesser included offence.

9.130 Lord Hutton's next point was to agree with the Court of Appeal that there is no liability to conviction for murder and so the jury cannot apply the provisions of section 2 of the Homicide Act 1957. This merits some closer consideration. The structure of section 2

150 See *R v Saunders* [1988] AC 148.

of the 1957 Act as it then stood involves three relevant subsections: subsection (3) provides that the impact of the section is that there is liability to be convicted of manslaughter rather than murder; subsection (2) provides that the defence has the burden of proof that there is no liability to conviction for murder; and subsection (1) sets the substantive test, namely that there shall be no conviction for murder if the accused's abnormality of mind means that his or her responsibility is substantially diminished.

9.131 There is an alternative construction available of this statutory language to that adopted by Lord Hutton: the key provision is section 2(2) of the Homicide Act 1957, which provides that: 'On a charge of murder, it shall be for the defence to prove that the person charged is by virtue of this section not liable to be convicted of murder'. The key requirement is that there is a charge of murder: that still applies even if the CP(I)A 1964 s4A process is being followed. Section 2(3) provides that the effect of the proof of diminished responsibility is that there is liability to be convicted of manslaughter rather than murder: in other words, the jury rules out murder, and indicates that the issue for determination is manslaughter; this is wholly consistent with the language of section 2(1) that the defendant 'shall not be convicted of murder'. Given that the jury sitting under section 4A is entitled to acquit, there is nothing inconsistent between the provisions of that and the Homicide Act 1957, since it is acquitting of murder.

9.132 This suggests that the reasoning of Lord Hutton is too narrow: he interprets 'liable to conviction of murder' as meaning that the jury has reached the conclusion that the accused should be convicted of murder and then, and only then, considers the question of diminished responsibility. The alternative construction works on the premise that if there is a charge of murder and hence liability to conviction of that if the elements are made out, the jury can rule out the prospect of considering whether there is murder by considering the question of diminished responsibility at an earlier stage of its deliberations.

9.133 The final part of Lord Hutton's reasoning was to adopt the view of the Court of Appeal that there was a significant problem if the accused could not be remitted to stand trial for murder if the section 4A jury had reached a conclusion that there was diminished responsibility. Why this is a problem is not, however, explained: there would have been a jury finding to the effect that the accused was not guilty of murder.

9.134 Of course, despite these arguments to the contrary, the ruling of the House of Lords represents the law and so the former language of diminished responsibility does not arise under the section 4A procedure: consideration of whether the new language of diminished responsibility is deferred until after consideration of the wider question considered by the House of Lords in *Antoine*, namely the applicability of questions of mens rea. The central conclusion in this regard was that *Egan* was wrong because section 4A mentioned the act not the offence, and so drew a distinction between the actus reus component (which had to be considered) and the mens rea component (which did not). So, in the words of Lord Hutton, with whom all the other judges agreed, section 4A struck the balance between the accused who was unfit to stand trial and in fact was innocent and the accused who had:[151]

> ... committed an injurious act which would constitute a crime if done with the requisite mens rea ... [T]he section strikes this balance by distinguishing between a person who has not carried out the actus reus of the crime charged against him and a person who has carried out an act (or made an omission) which would constitute a crime if done (or made an omission) with the requisite mens rea.

9.135 This distinction, however, is not always clear, because the lawfulness of the act may turn on what was perceived by the defendant: in other words, irrespective of questions of mens rea, the mind of the defendant may be relevant to whether the act is a guilty act. So, section 3 of the Criminal Law Act 1967 makes lawful the use of force that is reasonable in preventing crime or effecting a lawful arrest: but this is a test that depends on subjective factors and so what was in the mind of the defendant. In summarising what this requires, Lord Morris in *Palmer v R*[152] stated that:

> If there has been an attack so that defence is reasonably necessary, it will be recognised that a person defending himself cannot weigh to a nicety the exact measure of his defensive action. If the jury thought that in a moment of unexpected anguish a person attacked had only done what he honestly and instinctively thought necessary, that would be the most potent evidence that only reasonable defensive action had been taken.

9.136 In other words, the apparently objective nature of reasonable force is conditioned by the subjective perceptions of the defendant. There is a more general principle that mistaken views of the facts may provide a defence, in the sense that the criminality or otherwise of the defendant's actions are to be judged according to his or her view of the facts

151 [2001] 1 AC 340 at 375–376, [2000] MHLR 28 para 53.
152 [1971] AC 814.

rather than the facts as objectively ascertained. So, for example, in *R v Morgan*,[153] the House of Lords held that a mistaken belief that a women was consenting to sexual intercourse provided a defence to a charge of rape; this was applied in various further situations, including self-defence (see *Beckford v R*)[154] and gross indecency with children (see *B v Director of Public Prosecutions*,[155] in which it was held that the prosecution had to disprove the existence of an honest belief that a child was 14 or over for the purposes of the offence of inciting a child under 14 to commit an offence of gross indecency). Similarly, in *R v G*,[156] the House confirmed that the concept of recklessness involved not an assessment of whether there was the unreasonable running of an objectively-established risk, but whether the defendant perceived the risk and took it when it was unreasonable. Lord Bingham explained his conclusion by noting that:

> ... it is not clearly blameworthy to do something involving a risk of injury to another if (for reasons other than self-induced intoxication ...) one genuinely does not perceive the risk. Such a person may fairly be accused of stupidity or lack of imagination, but neither of those failings should expose him to conviction of serious crime or the risk of punishment.[157]

9.137 Lord Hutton had to recognise that such arguments, or even the simple assertion that it was all an accident and so not criminal at all (eg, picking up the wrong coat by mistake) 'almost invariably involve some consideration of the mental state of the defendant'. He set out the following rule:[158]

> If there is objective evidence which raises the issue of mistake or accident or self-defence, then the jury should not find that the defendant did the 'act' unless it is satisfied beyond reasonable doubt on all the evidence that the prosecution has negatived that defence. ... But what the defence cannot do, in the absence of a witness whose evidence raises the defence, is to suggest that the defendant may have acted under a mistake, or by accident, or in self-defence, and to submit that the jury should acquit unless the prosecution satisfies them that there is no reasonable possibility that that suggestion is correct. I consider that the same approach is to be taken if defence counsel wishes to advance the defence that the defendant, in law, did not do the 'act'

153 [1976] AC 182.
154 [1988] AC 130.
155 [2000] 2 AC 428.
156 [2003] UKHL 50, [2004] 1 AC 1034.
157 [2003] UKHL 50, [2004] 1 AC 1034 para 32.
158 [2001] 1 AC 340 at 376–377, [2000] MHLR 28 para 57.

because his action was involuntary, as when a man kicks out and strikes another in the course of an uncontrollable fit brought about by a medical condition. In such a case there would have to be evidence that the defendant suffered from the condition.

9.138 This is very much of a rough and ready compromise. For example, if the only evidence of a mistake is from the accused, who by definition cannot participate, then the matter cannot be raised. In addition, it is to be noted that if the objectively-ascertainable misperceptions arose from insanity, that is also ruled out on the basis that it goes to mens rea, which is not part of the question of whether the act was committed or the omission was made. (Lord Hutton expressly commented that the decision in *Attorney-General's Reference (No 3 of 1998)* was correct.) But when one adds the comments noted above that objective evidence of involuntariness can be adduced, what is the status of involuntariness that is classified as insanity because it arises from an internal cause?[159]

Case-law subsequent to Antoine

9.139 Expressly left open by Lord Hutton in *Antoine* was the question of whether provocation could be raised.[160] It was decided by the Court of Appeal in *R v Grant*[161] that it could not be raised because it 'inevitably requires examination of the defendant's state of mind, in determining whether there has been a sudden and temporary loss of self-control and whether that loss of self-control was caused by the conduct of the deceased'.[162] The argument to the contrary is fairly clear, namely that the question of provocation entails consideration of whether the action taken was in response to provocative language or conduct, which is essentially a question of causation rather than mens rea, albeit that it is linked to a defendant's motivation. However, just as *Antoine* raises the idea that various issues such as mistake or self-defence which involve looking into the mind of the defendant can be raised on the basis of objective evidence, the obvious question is why provocation cannot be raised on that basis as well.

159 The suggestion made by RD Mackay and G Kearns in 'An upturn in unfitness to plead? Disability in relation to the trial under the 1991 Act' [2000] Crim LR 532 at 544 is that if insanity is excluded, that means that the question of insane involuntariness cannot be raised in front of the jury, and so the jury would have no option but to acquit.

160 Lord Hutton reserved his opinion on this issue: [2001] 1 AC 340 at 377, [2000] MHLR 28 para 59.

161 [2001] EWCA Crim 2611, [2002] QB 1030, [2002] MHLR 41.

162 [2001] EWCA Crim 2611, [2002] QB 1030, [2002] MHLR 41 para 44.

9.140 Also left open in *Antoine* was the question of secondary participation in a murder.[163] This can be a complex question that turns on the scope of the joint enterprise. So in *R v Mitchell*,[164] the Court of Appeal summarised the law in the following terms at paragraph 22:

> ... where two persons embark on a joint enterprise, each is liable for what is done in pursuit of that joint enterprise, unless one goes beyond the scope of what was agreed. It therefore necessary to decide what was agreed ... Often there is little distinction between tacit agreement and foresight of the probable commission of an act.

9.141 This approach was applied in the CP(I)A 1964 s4A context in *R v M (KJ)*,[165] in which one of several co-defendants charged with a joint enterprise murder by stabbing had too limited an intellectual capacity and was too suggestible to be able to follow the trial process or give evidence. The Court of Appeal confirmed that in directing the jury on the question of their approach to finding whether the accused had committed the act of murder, the judge had to inform them that they had to be satisfied that he had the relevant knowledge, which was a matter for them to infer from the evidence available. Lord Justice Potter, giving the judgment of the court, noted at paragraph 46:

> Thus, whereas the *actus reus* of the principal offender is doing the very act which causes the death, that of a secondary party is the act of participation in the joint venture/common purpose and, under section 4A(2), that is the matter upon which the jury must concentrate in order to determine whether or not the secondary party is to be regarded as having done the act of murder alleged against him. To that end, the jury must decide as a matter of fact (a) whether there was a common purpose, (b) what it was, (c) whether the act of the actual perpetrator went beyond the common purpose by being radically different from any act which the defendant realised might be done in the course of the attack. Put thus, for the jury to determine whether or not the defendant has done the act of murder for the purposes of section 4A(2) involves in part an investigation of his state of knowledge. Equally, however, the three elements which require to be decided are, in the absence of evidence from the defendant, susceptible of determination upon an objective basis by inference from the facts presented in the evidence and it is upon that basis that they must be dealt with under the section.

9.142 The court then upheld as correct the direction of the judge that the question was whether the jury was satisfied that the accused was the

163 [2001] 1 AC 340 at 377, [2000] MHLR 28 para 60..

164 [2008] EWCA Crim 2552, [2009] 1 CrAppR 31.

165 [2003] EWCA Crim 357, [2003] 2 CrAppR 21, 322.

stabber or took part in what he knew was an attack with a knife.[166] But, following *Antoine*, this had to be determined 'as a matter of inference from the independent evidence of witnesses and not from the evidence of the defendant or the suggestions of counsel'.[167] The implication of this is that it is fair to consider the question of the knowledge of the accused without any way of being able to hear from him and assess his credibility because he cannot take part in any process. This seems difficult to reconcile with any concept of justice.

9.143 At best, it might be possible to have evidence of whether an allegation that a defendant was unlikely to have acted in a particular way. For an example of this, see *R v Norman*:[168] the allegation was of child abduction from refusing to allow a child to leave; the evidence included an allegation that Mr Norman had told the child's mother in a telephone call that he would not let the child out of his flat. Mr Norman had Huntington's Disease, a degenerative disease of the central nervous system which brought on progressive mental impairment. On appeal, it was suggested that evidence should be admitted from an expert in the disease to the effect that Mr Norman's condition meant that he would not have acted in a confrontational manner because he would have been compliant with all suggestions made to him rather than making spontaneous arguments to the contrary. The Court of Appeal did not have to answer this question because it considered that the finding that Mr Norman committed the act was unsafe on other grounds: but it was commented that the argument for the admissibility of this evidence was a 'cogent submission'. In other words, when a defendant is not able to give evidence because he is unfit to stand trial, it may be possible to introduce expert evidence to the effect that suggestions as to the defendant's conduct or words are inconsistent with his disorder. It is suggested that this remains an unsatisfactory distance from anything that amounts to a fair process.

9.144 One further case should be mentioned, as it reveals the difficulty in applying the distinction between actus reus and mens rea: the charge in *R (Young) v Central Criminal Court*[169] was dishonestly concealing material facts contrary to section 47(1) of the Financial Services Act 1986. Under this, it was criminal to make a statement, promise or forecast known to be misleading, false or deceptive or to dishonestly conceal material facts, if done with the intention of inducing or being

166 [2003] EWCA Crim 357, [2003] 2 CrAppR 21, 322 para 47.

167 [2003] EWCA Crim 357, [2003] 2 CrAppR 21, 322 para 42.

168 [2008] EWCA Crim 1810, [2008] MHLR 206.

169 [2002] 2 CrAppR 12, 178.

reckless as to whether it would induce entering into an investment agreement. The allegation was that the defendant was an investment advisor to an investment fund, that the fund was advised to invest in certain bonds, and that he did not reveal that he had an interest in one of the bonds and was planning to make arrangements to ensure that the value of his bond was enhanced.

9.145 The trial judge had ruled that the section 4A procedure would have to involve an investigation into the fact of whether the accused had this purpose when he offered his advice: in other words, the jury was asked to consider what was in the mind of the defendant in terms of his intended future conduct at the time that he concealed the material facts, even though they could not be asked to consider whether he intended thereby to induce the contract to be entered into or was reckless as to whether it would induce it or even whether he was dishonest. The judge purported to grant leave to appeal from a preliminary hearing, but on the basis that the section 4A procedure had been ruled outside the scope of being a criminal proceeding for the purpose of preparatory hearings and appeals to the Court of Appeal (see *R v M, K and H*,[170] discussed above), the matter proceeded as a judicial review application by the accused.

9.146 The challenge was to the effect that a concealed fact could not be something in the defendant's head (ie, his plans as regards the bonds); but the Divisional Court upheld the ruling of the trial judge, Rose LJ setting out his conclusion that it was a matter of statutory construction as to whether a matter of intention by a defendant was a matter of fact and so part of the actus reus, and that the statute in play was one which made it a fact. The result was that:

> ... it is appropriate for the jury charged with the inquiry under section 4A of the 1964 Act to consider the intentions of the defendant, not, of course, in relation to dishonesty, and not in relation to the purpose of making the representations, but his intention in respect of one of the facts represented, according to the particulars of the offence, to those said to be the victims of his activity.[171]

9.147 A question which then arises is whether this approach is of wider application, such that actus reus states that imply a mental element can only be met if the jury is able to infer it (which they will have

170 [2001] EWCA Crim 2024, [2001] MHLR 177, [2002] 1 WLR 824.

171 [2002] 2 CrAppR 12, 178 para 35. It is to be noted that had the defence submission been correct, the section 4A inquiry would have inquired into less; it is not readily apparent how this could have benefitted the defendant, but there must have been a tactical consideration within the context of the criminal litigation and any surrounding civil or disciplinary proceedings.

to do without the benefit of any participation from the defendant). The obvious example is that offences of possession of drugs for the purposes of the Misuse of Drugs Act 1971 imply knowledge: see the discussion by the House of Lords in *Warner v Metropolitan Police Commissioner*.[172]

9.148 It can be seen, therefore, that the question of what has to be proved in the section 4A process, ie what amounts to the relevant act or omission, is a far from easy question to answer. In particular, any suggestion that it involves a clear line as between elements of the mind of the defendant and the acts of the defendant is an attempt to impose a rationalisation that does not properly reflect the complexities in play. For this reason, it may be that the views expressed by the ECtHR in *Antoine v UK*[173] cannot be the final word on the topic of the non-applicability of the criminal provisions of article 6 to the section 4A procedure. In that case, the ECtHR had favoured the government view that the proceedings under section 4A were not criminal because there was no jeopardy of a criminal conviction or penalty (and so should be viewed as having to comply with article 5 rather than article 6). The court noted that:

> ... no conviction was possible. The Court considers that these proceedings did not therefore concern the determination of a criminal charge. ... While it is true that the section 4A hearing has strong similarities with procedures at a criminal trial, the Court notes that the proceedings were principally concerned with the *actus reus*, namely whether the applicant had carried out an act or made an omission which would have constituted a crime if done or made with the requisite *mens rea*. ... The Court is satisfied therefore that the essential purpose of the proceedings was to consider whether the applicant had committed an act the dangerousness of which would require a hospital order in the interests of the protection of the public.[174]

9.149 But the court does not mention that it was addressed on the features of domestic law in which the section 4A process is considered as criminal (for the purposes of rules of evidence and appeal) or the extent of the overlap between the concepts of actus reus and the mens rea. The ECtHR, it is noted, does not have a strict concept of precedent and has reviewed its decisions when it has reached a different understanding of what domestic law involves: see, for example, the case of *Stafford v UK*,[175] in which it took a different approach to its

172 [1969] 2 AC 256.

173 App No 62960/00, [2003] MHLR 292.

174 [2003] MHLR 292 paras 35–37.

175 App No 46295/99, (2002) 35 EHRR 1121, [2002] Prison LR 181.

established jurisprudence in whether article 5(4) applied to the post-tariff detention of mandatory lifers.

9.150 In addition to the prospect of the revisiting of the question, two further questions need to be addressed: the first is whether the domestic law as developed in *R v Antoine* might be different now that the test for diminished responsibility has been amended; the same question arises in relation to *Grant* and the new test for provocation. The second question is whether, even if article 6 in its criminal aspect does not apply, the question not raised in *Antoine v UK*, namely the civil aspect of article 6, means that the current approach under section 4A meets the requirements of that part of article 6.

9.151 The language of section 2 of the Homicide Act 1957 has been amended by the Coroners and Justice Act 2009. Section 52 of that Act substitutes new language for section 2(1) of the Homicide Act 1957.[176] Diminished responsibility now arises from a recognised medical condition that substantially impairs the accused's ability to understand the nature of his conduct, form a rational judgment or exercise self-control. These factors, and in particular the latter feature, seem to be akin more to the question of the voluntariness of conduct, namely a part of the doing of the act or the making of the omission rather than being features of the mens rea. Having said that, it remains the case that the language of the defence provides that the defendant is not to be convicted of murder, and so the essential reasoning behind *Antoine*, namely that the trial could not get to consider the question of murder because it would not look into mens rea questions, is still applicable.

9.152 The same can be said for the replacement for provocation:[177] section 56 of the Coroners and Justice Act 2009 abolishes the common law and/or statutory partial defence of provocation,[178] and sections 54 and 55 introduce a partial defence of 'loss of control'. This is made out in relation to a murder charge if there was a loss of self-control from a qualifying trigger and a person of the age and sex of the defendant and sharing all of the defendant's circumstances but

176 This is in effect from 4 October 2010, by reason of the Coroners and Justice Act 2009 (Commencement No 4, Transitional and Saving Provisions) Order 2010 SI No 816 para 5.

177 The relevant provisions are brought into force by the Coroners and Justice Act 2009 (Commencement No 4, Transitional and Saving Provisions) Order 2010 paras 5 and 6.

178 Homicide Act 1957 s3 was the governing statutory provision, which is commonly thought to have both clarified but also amended the common law test; it is valid as a defence only to murder, and then only reduces the offence to manslaughter.

with a 'normal degree of tolerance and self-restraint' would have lost control. The relevant qualifying triggers are a fear of serious violence from the victim or grave circumstances that caused the defendant to have a justifiable sense of being seriously wronged.

9.153 This inevitably involves looking at the state of mind of the defendant, and so the essential reasoning in *Grant* remains applicable. Equally, the contrary argument, namely that it can be raised on objective evidence without any need to examine the mens rea of the defendant, remains applicable under this new language.

9.154 An issue that might arise is, what approach would be taken if the circumstances of the murder could have been prosecuted as infanticide under the Infanticide Act 1938? This is discussed in chapter 14; in essence it involves the killing by a woman of her own child under the age of 12 months in circumstances where her mind is disturbed. It can be returned as a verdict when the charge is murder and, as it involves a different actus reus, it is suggested that it would be open as a finding of fact during a section 4A process.

The civil provisions of ECHR article 6

9.155 Applying *R v H*[179] to the summary trial process in *Crown Prosecution Service v P*,[180] a topic discussed in more detail in the next chapter, Smith LJ commented that:

> It is clear since *R v H* that the fact that a child cannot take an effective part in the fact-finding process does not infringe his Article 6 rights. That process is part of the protective jurisdiction contemplated by the MHA 1983 and the child's Article 6 rights are not even engaged.[181]

9.156 This comment goes too far unless it is restricted to the criminal aspects of article 6, which is what was in play in *R v H* in the House of Lords. The case proceeded on the basis that *if* the civil aspect of article 6 applied, it was satisfied.[182] It is clear from ECtHR case-law that the right to liberty is a civil right and so if it is lost, then article 6 does apply.[183] Moreover, it is established that there must be participation

179 [2003] UKHL 1, [2003] MHLR 209.

180 [2007] EWHC 946 (Admin), [2007] MHLR 262.

181 [2007] EWHC 946 (Admin), [2007] MHLR 262 at para 55.

182 [2003] UKHL 1, [2003] 1 WLR 411, [2003] MHLR 209 para 13: the argument of the prosecution was that any loss of liberty was justified by reason of ECHR article 5(1)(e). The appellant's case was limited to the criminal aspects of article 6: paragraph 14.

183 See *Aerts v Belgium* (1998) 29 EHRR 50 para 59; in *R (PD) v West Midlands and North Mental Health Review Tribunal* [2003] EWHC 2469 (Admin), [2004] MHLR 25, [2004] EWCA Civ 311, [2004] MHLR 174, the question arising

in any such process. So, in *Shtukaturov v Russia*,[184] the factual context was a court decision to the effect that the applicant should be deprived of his capacity. The ECtHR gave the following guidance: first, while it has invariably dealt with questions of the detention of psychiatric patients under article 5 rather than article 6:

> ... the Court has consistently held that the 'procedural' guarantees under Article 5§§1 and 4 are broadly similar to those under Article 6§1 of the Convention ...[185]

9.157 Second, while the requirements of article 6 could be modified 'in order to secure the good administration of justice, protection of the health of the person concerned, etc', the margin of appreciation allowed to the member states in this regard was limited by the overarching principle that 'such measures should not affect the very essence of the applicant's right to a fair trial as guaranteed by Article 6'.[186] On the facts, a breach of article 6 was found because Mr Shtukaturov had not been able to participate in the court proceedings as to the loss of his capacity, in which he was both an interested party and the subject of the proceedings:

> His participation was therefore necessary not only to enable him to present his own case, but also to allow the judge to form his personal opinion about the applicant's mental capacity ... The Court concludes that the decision of the judge to decide the case on the basis of documentary evidence, without seeing or hearing the applicant, was unreasonable and in breach of the principle of adversarial proceedings enshrined in Article 6§1...[187]

9.158 The context of this holding was the reminder that in cases relating to the loss of liberty, it had been found that 'a person of unsound mind must be allowed to be heard either in person or, where necessary, through some form of representation', and the conclusion that the loss of personal autonomy arising from a declaration as to the lack of capacity is just as important.[188] What is important to note is that this language replicates the provisions of article 6(3)(c) on which, together with the right to challenge witnesses and the right to an

was whether the medical member of the tribunal appeared biased, and the Administrative Court and then the Court of Appeal discussed this in the context of article 6 applying to the detention of a patient.

184 [2008] MHLR 238.

185 [2008] MHLR 238 para 66.

186 [2008] MHLR 238 para 68.

187 [2008] MHLR 238 paras 72–73.

188 [2008] MHLR 238 para 71.

interpreter, the *Stanford* decision as to the right to participate was based. It seems unarguable that those other rights would not be held to apply as well.

9.159 Accordingly, when the court in domestic proceedings is engaged in finding the facts, it cannot be said that article 6 is not engaged because, if the end result may be a loss of liberty, the civil aspects of article 6 are applicable, as they are if aspects of autonomy are lost, as happened in *Shtukaturov*. It has to be noted that the factual context in that case was somewhat extreme: he had lost his capacity without being informed of the proceedings that led to the decision and the relevant medical report on him, which included an interview, had been compiled without him being informed of its purpose; and when he found out what had happened and sought to appeal, his guardian placed him in hospital and the hospital refused to allow him to see his lawyers in private. However, the language used by the ECtHR suggests that a wider degree of participation in an adversarial process is necessary to secure compliance with article 6.

9.160 It may be possible to modify procedures, provided that the very essence of the right to a fair trial is retained. The Court of Appeal in *R v M, K and H*[189] suggested that efforts to minimise any disadvantage faced by a defendant with mental disorder who is nevertheless fit to stand trial can lead to a trial that is fair: see paragraph 31 of the judgment. If the defendant's mental disorder is such that he or she is unfit to stand trial, the court held that that process in the CP(I)A 1964 complied with the requirements of fairness, balancing the public interest in ascertaining whether acts have been committed and identifying and dealing with the people who have committed those acts and the interests of those persons: see paragraph 34. However, as has been developed above, the question of whether someone committed an act that is criminal, such that it is appropriate for society to detain them for protective reasons, may involve an assessment that can only be carried out with the participation of the person because their evidence is central to determining whether the act was committed. The inability of the defendant to participate in this may make the process fundamentally unfair and so in breach of article 6 in its civil context, given that liberty may be lost. The abuse of process jurisdiction might be engaged as the way to prevent any further steps in the court process.

9.161 The existence of the civil detention provisions of the MHA 1983 is relevant in this context: any concerns about the risk posed by the

189 [2001] EWCA Crim 2024, [2001] MHLR 177, [2002] 1 WLR 824.

defendant can be met by those provisions if it is not possible to complete the section 4A process. At the same time, it could well be said that an assessment of the risk posed – which would be relevant for the civil detention provisions as well – would turn on the determination of whether or not he or she was involved in the act (and whether it arose in circumstances in which what was going on in the mind of the proposed patient was relevant to the level of risk): so those civil provisions will not necessarily solve all difficulties. However, it is suggested that on the whole the civil detention provisions are preferable to a determination under section 4A in which the defendant cannot participate because they do not involve the recording of a formal finding and the various consequences that flow from that, which are discussed below.

Fact-finding and criminal trial – co-defendants

9.162 One discrete issue is what should happen when one of several co-defendants is unfit to stand trial. This occurred in *R v B, W, S, H and W*,[190] in which two of the ten defendants in a sexual abuse trial were found to be unfit. The judge directed that there be a separate trial for the eight fit defendants and that the outcome of that trial would determine whether there should be a fact-finding exercise for the two unfit defendants, one of whom was allegedly at the centre of the allegations. The prosecution challenged this ruling, which was made at a preparatory hearing and so subject to an appeal under section 35 of the CPIA 1996. The Court of Appeal considered the interplay between the provisions of the CP(I)A 1964 and the Juries Act 1974. The relevant provision of the CP(I)A 1964, as amended when the fact-finding process was introduced in 1991, was section 4A(5), which indicated that a fresh jury should be sworn if the finding of unfitness was made on arraignment by the jury sworn to determine fitness, but that the trial jury should determine it if the finding of unfitness arose subsequent to arraignment. When the determination of unfitness was made into a judge-only question by the DVCVA 2004, section 4A(5) was amended to provide that: 'Where the question of disability was determined after arraignment of the accused, the determination under subs(2) is to be made by the jury by whom he was being tried'.

9.163 However, another relevant provision is that in section 11(4) of the Juries Act 1974, which provides that a jury 'shall try only one issue'. Section 11(5)(b) had provided an exception to this if the judge

190 [2008] EWCA Crim 1997, [2008] MHLR 320.

directed that the trial jury determine the issue of fitness to plead: but this was removed by the DVCVA 2004. The Court of Appeal held that there was no prohibition on a single jury determining the guilt of fit defendants and the commission of the actus reus by unfit defendants: indeed, it was noted that if the finding of unfitness had occurred during the trial, the finding of the facts would have to be made by the same jury, and the court noted that the stage at which the finding of unfitness should not make a difference.

9.164 That still made it necessary to explain the provision in section 11 of the Juries Act 1974 that limits a jury to the determination of only one 'issue'. The court held that this limits the jury to one indictment, however many counts and/or co-defendants are charged in it: and as the determination of whether the act was committed is a lesser included matter within each count, there is no need for express language to allow the jury to consider it. The language of the former section 11(5)(b) of the Juries Act 1974 had been necessary because the question of fitness to stand trial is an additional issue to that contained in the questions the jurors have to decide when they are empanelled to try the indictment.

9.165 That meant that the judge had a discretion as to whether there should be a single jury: that had to be exercised judicially on the facts, taking into account the interests of the defendants, the witnesses and the public. The Court of Appeal was of the view that the central role played by one of the unfit defendants meant that the trial of the facts in his case should be determined at the same time as the guilt or otherwise of the defendants who were fit to stand trial: this was because of the absence of any prejudice to the co-defendants by having the jury determine only the actus reus as against him in the counts he faced, his interest in the matter being determined speedily, the value of witnesses having to give evidence once only, and the public interest in simultaneous rather than successive proceedings where that was possible. However, the other unfit defendant was alleged to have played only a minor role and so separate consideration of his involvement was appropriate.

9.166 The case was to return to the Court of Appeal after B was found to have committed the acts and dealt with by way of a hospital order with restriction order: see *R v MB*.[191] When the case had been tried after the initial visit to the Court of Appeal, it transpired that a co-defendant, B's wife, was running a 'cut-throat' defence of duress by B (which was contrary to how she had answered police questioning):

191 [2010] EWCA Crim 1684, [2011] MHLR 163.

this involved allegations demonstrating bad character on the part of B, which he was unable to answer due to his inability to participate. That in turn meant that it was unfair for the trial of the facts in relation to B to occur at the same time as the trial of the guilt of his co-defendant. The trial judge, however, had felt that the first ruling from the Court of Appeal precluded him from allowing the case to be severed. On the further appeal to the Court of Appeal by MB, the Court held that the trial judge should not have felt constrained from making a ruling on severance in light of the new facts and should have severed the case. This emphasises that the trial of the facts must be a fair process.

Disposals

9.167 The CP(I)A 1964 s5 as enacted provided that there was only one consequence on a finding that the offender was under a disability so as to be unfit to stand trial (or not guilty by reason of insanity), which was admission to such hospital as the Secretary of State directed (which had to occur within two months).[192] The CP(I)A 1964 Sch 1 provided that the admission took effect as a hospital order with a restriction order without limit of time under sections 60 and 65 of the MHA 1959 (which became sections 37 and 41 of the MHA 1983: see chapter 18). The previous form of disposal was an order of 'strict custody until His (Her) Majesty's pleasure shall be known': section 2 of the CLA 1800. This took effect as committal to a psychiatric hospital until the Home Secretary ordered release.

9.168 A replacement section 5 was inserted into the CP(I)A 1964 by CP(IUP)A 1991 s3 to provide that a finding of unfitness to stand trial and that the defendant had done the act or made the omission charged could lead to one of four orders. These were:

i) an order for admission to such hospital as might be specified by the Secretary of State;
ii) a guardianship order within the meaning of the MHA 1983;
iii) a supervision and treatment order; or
iv) an absolute discharge. More detail on the admission order and the supervision and treatment order was provided in CP(IUP)A 1991 Schs 1 and 2.

192 CP(I)A 1964 Sch 1 para 1; the court could direct admission to a place of safety in the interim (under Sch 1 para 2).

9.169 The regime was again amended by DVCVA 2004 s24.[193] This replaced CP(I)A 1964 s5 to provide that the orders available were:

i) a hospital order (with or without a restriction order), which had the same effect as if made under the MHA 1983;
ii) a supervision order; or
iii) an absolute discharge.

Also added was section 5A, which made provisions to allow sections 35, 36 and 38 of the MHA 1983 (namely remand to hospital for a report or treatment or the making of an interim order) to cover a defendant who had been found unfit but to have done the act or made the omission. Finally, Schedule 1A was added to the CP(I)A 1964 to make further provision as to supervision orders.[194]

Hospital order/admission order

9.170 A number of issues have arisen in relation to the use of the hospital order disposal. One that previously arose, when the order was an admission order, but should no longer arise, related to the complexity of having an order that was not a hospital order but which took effect as if it was a hospital order under MHA 1983 s37, as CP(IUP)A 1991 Sch 1 provided, and CP(IUP)A 1991 Sch 1 para 2(1)(b) also allowed the sentencing court to give a direction that had the effect of imposing the equivalent of a restriction order under MHA 1983 s41. This was a hospital order in all but name, but the selection of the hospital had to be carried out by the Secretary of State rather than by the court making the order. Errors did occasionally occur, with courts purporting to impose hospital orders or the Secretary of State not perfecting the order. This caused some complications in terms of how to remedy the error. In *R v Fairley*,[195] a hospital order had been made where an admission order should have been made, but the Court of Appeal had no jurisdiction to correct the matter as section 9 of the Criminal Appeal Act (CAA) 1968 provided only for appeals against sentences imposed following a conviction; and, though there was a statutory right to appeal against the findings of unfitness and the commission of the act, in section 15 of the CAA 1968, there was

193 Brought into force on 31 March 2005: see Domestic Violence, Crime and Victims Act 2004 (Commencement No 1) Order 2005 SI No 579.

194 CP(I)A 1964 Sch 2 as inserted by the CP(IUP)A 1991 was repealed: see DVCVA 2004 s58(2) and Sch 11. It was also repealed expressly by DVCVA 2004 s24(5), as was Schedule 1.

195 [2003] EWCA Crim 1625, [2003] MHLR 310.

no appeal against the disposal.[196] The court reconstituted itself as a judicial review court and treated the appeal as an application for judicial review, and quashed the orders made. This gap has been filled: CAA 1968 ss16A and 16B, as added by DVCVA 2004 s25,[197] allow appeals to the Court of Appeal against the imposition of a hospital order or a supervision order under CP(I)A 1964 s5.[198] Such an appeal requires the leave of the Court of Appeal or a certificate of fitness to appeal from the trial judge. It is expressly provided that an appeal taken against an interim hospital order made under CP(I)A 1964 s5A does not prevent the trial court taking the steps it finds appropriate in relation to the renewal of such an order or the imposition of an order on the completion of the interim order (CAA 1968 s16B(2)); the Court of Appeal may also impose an interim hospital order and pass the matter back to the trial court (CAA 1968 s16B(3)). Not surprisingly, there is no appeal against an absolute discharge.

9.171 Another question arose from the fact that the power to make an admission order was not limited to the situation in which the criteria set out in MHA 1983 ss37 and 41 as to the making of a hospital order or a restriction order also applied. This arose in two contexts, namely the circumstances in which hospitalisation was necessary in the discretion of the court; but also in relation to what should happen if the underlying charge was murder, because CP(I)A 1964 s5(3) provided

196 The jurisdictional point had been decided in *R v Mohammed Latif* [2002] EWCA Crim 2115 and [2002] EWHC 1916 (Admin), [2003] MHLR 65: this involved a challenge to the propriety of the making of an admission order rather than the making of supervision and treatment order after a finding of unfitness to stand trial but to have done the act alleged, but the Court of Appeal noted that it had no jurisdiction to consider such an appeal; it reconstituted itself as a judicial review court, and dismissed the challenge.

197 Brought into force on 31 March 2005: see Domestic Violence, Crime and Victims Act 2004 (Commencement No 1) Order 2005 SI No 579.

198 Although a failure to follow correct procedures arguably meant that detention breached ECHR article 5(1) (see *Nakach v Netherlands* [2006] MHLR 22, which related to the failure to compile a record of a hearing of an appeal against the extension of a detention order, as required by domestic law), it was held that such errors were technicalities that did not affect the lawfulness of the detention. On this, see *R (A) v Harrow Crown Court* [2003] EWHC 2020 (Admin), [2003] MHLR 393, in which it was held that an erroneously made hospital order under which the defendant was detained for around seven months before it was corrected amounted to an irregular order of the Crown Court that was nevertheless effective in law until set aside (applying *R v Cain* [1985] AC 46) and so detention was lawful. (It was noted that there had been medical evidence to justify detention and so it was not arbitrary for the purposes of article 5.) See also *R (SW Yorkshire Mental Health NHS Trust) v Bradford Crown Court* [2003] EWHC 640 (Admin), [2004] MHLR 137.

that if the underlying offence carried a sentence fixed by law (that is, murder), then the admission order was the only sentence, and it had to be combined with a restriction order by reason of CP(IUP)A 1991 Sch 1 para 2(2).

9.172 As to the latter situation, in *R v Grant*[199] the defendant had been found unfit to be tried in the light of her mental impairment but to have committed the act of killing her partner. The mandatory sentence of an admission order with a restriction order was made even though some medical evidence suggested that a guardianship order or an admission order without a restriction order would have been appropriate.[200] One argument was whether the issue of provocation could be raised: as noted above, it was decided that it could not. The court sat as the Court of Appeal for that purpose; it became a Divisional Court in relation to a case stated appeal, raising the question of whether the mandatory disposal breached ECHR articles 5 or 6.[201] Mr Justice Richards for the court concluded that as the process was not criminal, article 6 did not apply, and so the question was whether article 5 was breached by the requirement that Ms Grant be admitted to hospital. On this point, the Secretary of State argued that there was no arbitrariness because it was within the power of Parliament to require admission in light of the nature of the underlying act provided that an immediate application to the Mental Health Review Tribunal could be made (by reason of MHA 1983 s69(2)(a)).

9.173 The court accepted that the right to make an immediate application to a tribunal meant that there was compliance with the requirements of article 5(4).[202] But it left open the question of whether there was necessarily compliance with article 5(1). While the statutory scheme was one that was open to Parliament,[203] given that the mandatory order of admission would only follow a decision by the prosecution to charge murder rather than manslaughter, and then consideration of fitness to stand trial and whether the defendant committed the actus reus, it was potentially problematic that the court did not consider whether the expert evidence meant that a hospital order was warranted since that might mean that a judge had to impose detention when it was not needed and so was, at least arguably, arbitrary. However, on the facts, the court concluded that the medical evidence

199 [2001] EWCA Crim 2611, [2002] QB 1030, [2002] MHLR 41.
200 [2001] EWCA Crim 2611, [2002] QB 1030, [2002] MHLR 41 para 30.
201 [2001] EWCA Crim 2611, [2002] QB 1030, [2002] MHLR 41 para 8.
202 [2001] EWCA Crim 2611, [2002] QB 1030, [2002] MHLR 41 para 51.
203 [2001] EWCA Crim 2611, [2002] QB 1030, [2002] MHLR 41 paras 51–54.

justified detention and so it was not necessary to reach a final decision on the potential point of dispute.

9.174 The question of whether the criteria under the MHA 198 applied was considered in *Narey v HM Customs*,[204] which involved charges of importing class A drugs. The challenge on a case stated appeal was to the judge's decision to impose a restriction order as well as make an admission order. The Divisional Court rejected the argument that the criteria contained in the MHA 1983 were to be read across to the sentences introduced by the CP(IUP)A 1991: this was said to arise from the fact that the court would have heard evidence in relation to the existence of mental disorder in the process of deciding whether the defendant was fit to stand trial. However, the court also held that the restriction order had to be justified, and was not on the facts.

9.175 The reasoning of the court has to be placed in context to be understood. Steel J commented[205] that the absence of any express indication in CP(IUP)A 1991 Sch 1 that the restriction order criteria as set out in MHA 1983 s41 had to be satisfied in the context of a finding made in relation to a defendant found not fit to stand trial meant that: 'It follows ... that ... section 5 of the 1964 Act and Schedule 1 to the 1991 Act does not contain any express requirement for psychiatric evidence that the defendant constituted a risk of serious harm to the public'.[206] At first sight, this seems to be a somewhat flimsy basis for drawing a distinction between action taken under MHA 1983 s41 and CP(IUP)A 1991 Sch 1, particularly as the regime to which the defendant is subjected is that arising under the MHA 1983: this is a feature that ought to carry with it at least the implication that the relevant criteria for imposition are the same.[207] However, it is suggested that the comments of the judge once put into context mean no more than that there is a procedural difference, namely that there is no requirement of a doctor to be called to give evidence as to the risk. In other words, in the language quoted, the point being made is that there is no need for psychiatric evidence supporting the view that the restriction order criteria are made out. This reading arises

204 [2005] EWHC 784 (Admin), [2005] MHLR 194.

205 [2005] EWHC 784 (Admin), [2005] MHLR 194 paras 13–16.

206 [2005] EWHC 784 (Admin), [2005] MHLR 194 para 16.

207 In paragraphs 5 and 6 of *Jones v Isleworth Crown Court* [2005] EWHC 662 (Admin), [2005] MHLR 95, Moses J quoted the terms of the power in the schedule allowing a restriction order to be made and commented that it referred the court back to the provisions of MHA 1983 s41. The point arising in *Narey* was not raised in the case, but it is to be noted that Moses J read the CP(IUP)A 1991 as reading in the requirements of the MHA 1983.

from two points: first, the judge was dealing with a submission to the effect that the restriction order was wrong because no psychiatric evidence of the risk to the public had been adduced;[208] second, the court rephrased the case that had been stated to it and provided answers as following:

1) Is there a statutory requirement to hear oral evidence from a psychiatrist implied into CP(IUP)A 1991 Sch 1 para 2(1)(b) via the application, mutatis mutandis, of MHA 1983 s41(2)? Answer: No.
2) Is it necessary to demonstrate a risk of serious harm from which the court believes the public need protection? Answer: Yes.
3) Whether the offence of being knowingly concerned in the importation of illegal drugs is capable of constituting serious harm to the public? Answer: Yes.
4) Whether there was sufficient evidence upon which an order, analogous to a restriction order, under CP(IUP)A 1991 Sch 1 para 2(1)(b) might properly be made? Answer: No.

9.176 The answer to question 1 suggests that Steel J was concerned more with the procedural issue of whether the judge was required to call evidence (as must happen before a restriction order can be made under the MHA 1983); answers 2 and 4 emphasise the need to have proper evidence, and it had been noted at paragraph 17 of the judgment that:

> The only possible justification for restriction without limit of time must be one that the appellant (or his equivalent) poses a risk of serious harm to the public. For this purpose it is almost inevitable that the court will benefit from the assistance of medical evidence.

9.177 Further changes to the statutory regime were made by the DVCVA 2004: this substituted a further version of section 5 of the CP(I)A 1964, which now provides that the options available on a finding of unfitness to plead but to have committed the act or a special verdict being entered are a hospital order under MHA 1983 s37, which can be combined with a restriction order if the criteria under section 41 are met, or a supervision order or an absolute discharge. The option of a guardianship order has been removed. As to the making of an order when the underlying charge is murder, section 5(3) provides that:

208 [2005] EWHC 784 (Admin), [2005] MHLR 194 para 12: part (a) of the four-step submission being made.

(3) Where –
   (a) the offence to which the special verdict or the findings relate is an offence the sentence for which is fixed by law, and
   (b) the court have power to make a hospital order,
   the court shall make a hospital order with a restriction order (whether or not they would have power to make a restriction order apart from this subsection).

9.178 In other words, the statute still requires a restriction order in the case of a finding in relation to a murder charge but only if the court has the power to make a hospital order. This deals with the problem identified in *Grant* of a situation in which the medical evidence does not support an admission to hospital. As to whether a mandatory restriction order is problematic, the government argument will no doubt be that, as it argued in *Grant*, it is open to Parliament to provide that this should be the reaction to the involvement of the defendant in the actus reus of such a serious offence. However, given that the court has the discretion as to whether or not to make a hospital order as opposed to a supervision order, it seems strange to require a restriction order rather than leaving it to the court. It might be that a court would take the view that the hospital order was not the most appropriate disposal because it had to be combined with a restriction order; moreover, given that the process of determining whether the act was committed does not allow for full consideration of questions of provocation (or, as it has become, loss of control) and the like, such that the finding could cover a wide range of situations which might have very different implications in terms of future risk, it is difficult to argue that the finding in relation to a murder charge necessarily suggests a level of risk that merits a restriction order.

9.179 The DVCVA 2004 s24 adds section 5A to the CP(I)A 1964: this provides for modifications to section 37 of the criteria in the MHA 1983 to make it suitable for the section 5 setting (for example, reading references to convictions as including the making of findings in the unfitness to stand trial process). In addition, the provisions of MHA 1983 ss35, 36 and 38 as to remands for reports or treatment and the making of an interim hospital order, which exist to allow a court to be informed as to whether a hospital order should be made, apply by reason of section 5A(2). In addition, MHA 1983 s39, which allows the court to order the provision of information as to hospital facilities, will be applicable: its precondition is that the court is minded to make a hospital order, which clearly covers such an order made under the CP(I)A 1964 as it has been amended.

9.180 All this indicates that the substantive criteria from the MHA 1983 are equally applicable to a hospital order made under the CP(I)A 1964. As to the point raised in *Narey* about the procedural requirements from the MHA 1983 being read across, namely the calling of oral psychiatric evidence as to risk, it remains the case that there is nothing in the amended CP(I)A 1964 that expressly states that a doctor has to give oral evidence or limits the making of an order to a finding of a risk of serious harm from further offending. However, it is arguable that it is implicit in relation to any charge other than murder. This is because the language of section 5(3) as to the making of a restriction order if the underlying charge is of murder 'whether or not they would have power to make a restriction order apart from this subsection' suggest that there must be a power to make a restriction order in scenarios other than such a charge: but section 5(2) creates a general discretion to impose 'a hospital order (with or without a restriction order)', which in turn must mean that the existence of the criteria that create the power to impose a restriction order must be found elsewhere than in the CP(I)A 1964. And the only place is in MHA 1983 s41, which sets both substantive and procedural criteria for the imposition of a restriction order.

9.181 Consequently, the regime for making a hospital disposal under the CP(I)A 1964 is now more aligned to that applicable under the MHA 1983: the decision is entirely one for the court and the Secretary of State no longer has any role in deciding the hospital to which a defendant should be admitted (though if a restriction order is added, the Secretary of State's powers in respect of granting leave and discharge are applicable, as they are if the order is imposed following a conviction).

9.182 One consequential change was made in relation to access to a tribunal: under MHA 1983 s69(2), a patient who was 'treated as subject to a hospital order' in various situations, including by reason of an order under CP(I)A 1964 s5, was entitled to a tribunal hearing in the first six months of detention; in contrast, a hospital order patient could not apply until after six months, no doubt on the basis that there had been judicial consideration of whether hospitalisation was required at the sentencing hearing. Now that this judicial consideration is given in relation to a hospital under the CP(I)A 1964, because the hospital order criteria apply in full, MHA 1983 s69(2) was amended to remove the right to make an application when the order was made under the CP(I)A 1964 (and treated as a hospital order by reference to the CP(IUP)A 1991): see DVCVA 2004 Sch 10 para 19.

9.183 The other powers of disposal mentioned in the revised CP(I)A 1964 s5 are specific to the CP(I)A 1964 and CP(IUP)A 1991, and so are considered further here.

The supervision order

9.184 As a result of the DVCVA 2004, the supervision order replaces the supervision and treatment order introduced by the CP(IUP)A 1991. The detailed provisions relevant to the original order were contained in CP(IUP)A 1991 Sch 2: this was repealed twice, both by the general repeal provisions set out in DVCVA 2004 s58 and Sch 11 that cover various provisions and also specifically by section 24(5) of the Act. However, DVCVA 2004 s24(2) and Sch 2 add a new Schedule 1A to the CP(I)A 1964 to regulate the new order. In the light of the fact noted above that the making of an order compelling admission to hospital is no longer necessary if the underlying charge is of murder, the supervision order can be used in relation to any situation.

9.185 The supervision order places the supervised person under the supervision of a social worker or probation officer for up to two years: CP(I)A 1964 Sch 1A para 1(1). It can only be made if it is in all the circumstances 'the most suitable means of dealing with the accused', that the supervising officer is willing to act and that arrangements have been made for the treatment specified in the order: CP(I)A 1964 Sch 1A para 2. The reference to it being the most suitable method of dealing with the accused, rather than including a reference to the underlying offence, no doubt reflects the fact that the absence of responsibility means that the focus should be on the offender: however, this does not exclude such matters as the protection of the public if it is felt that the accused presents an ongoing risk. The supervising officer must be in the area in which the defendant will reside: CP(I)A 1964 Sch 1A para 3.

9.186 As for the arrangements for treatment, the court may add a requirement as to out-patient treatment 'with a view to the improvement of his mental condition' (CP(I)A 1964 Sch 1A para 4(1)) and/or treatment for a physical condition if it is likely to cause risk to the patient and can be treated (CP(I)A 1964 Sch 1A para 5(1) and (2)). Medical evidence is required in both situations (which can be written or oral); two doctors must give evidence, and one must be 'duly registered' in relation to any psychiatric treatment (though not if it is treatment only for a physical condition). The phrase 'duly registered' is no doubt meant to cover being duly approved for the purposes of

MHA 1983 s12. The psychiatric condition must be assessed as not requiring the making of a hospital order.

9.187 The regime as introduced under the CP(IUP)A 1991 was limited to treatment for a mental disorder, but, by virtue of CP(IUP)A 1991 Sch 2 para 4, a treatment requirement was obligatory and could include treatment as an in-patient in a hospital or nursing home. It is possible under CP(I)A 1964 Sch 1A to add a requirement as to residence (paragraph 8), but in the light of the revocation of the power to require residence in a treatment setting and the fact that the residence requirement existed in the original provisions, it is suggested that the residence power cannot include a treatment setting. There is nothing, however, to prevent a defendant agreeing to residence in a treatment setting, including perhaps a hostel setting attached to a hospital. Indeed, CP(I)A 1964 Sch 1A para 6 makes express mention of the power of the doctor providing treatment under paragraphs 4 or 5 to make alternative arrangements for treatment, including as a resident patient, but only with the consent of the person being supervised.

9.188 There are also provisions for the amendment or revocation of the supervision order (and these must be explained to the defendant, as well as the impact of any treatment requirements: CP(I)A 1964 Sch 1A para 3(2)).[209] Amendments are possible in relation to matters such as changes of residence: CP(I)A 1964 Sch 1A para 3(5) requires the defendant to keep in touch with the supervising officer and notify any change of address; paragraph 10 allows the magistrates' court to move the supervision to another area if the defendant has moved or is planning to move to that area; any of the requirements in the supervision order that can only be met in the original area have to be cancelled or substituted with other requirements that can be met.

9.189 In addition, the magistrates' court may revoke the supervision order if to do so would be 'in the interests of the health or welfare of the supervised person' or it would be 'inappropriate for the order to continue' in light of changed circumstances: see CP(I)A 1964 Sch 1A para 9. Requirements set out in the order can be amended under paragraphs 11 and 12: this includes cancelling requirements (if, for example, there is medical evidence that different treatment is required, or that the defendant is no longer susceptible to treatment) or adding new ones, and the treatment period can be extended (though not beyond the two-year maximum period).

209 A copy of the order has to be given to the defendant: CP(I)A 1964 Sch 1A para 3(3).

An order for absolute discharge

9.190 If the defendant does not require any form of medical treatment or supervision, the only disposal available is an order for absolute discharge. CP(I)A 1964 s5A(6), as introduced by DVCVA 2004 s24(1), makes amendments to the law regulating an absolute discharge contained in PCC(S)A 2000 s12 to ensure that the order can be made on a finding under CP(I)A 1964 s4A as well as on a conviction. Further, the normal criterion for an absolute discharge, namely that punishment is inexpedient, is replaced by the criterion of it being the most suitable disposal: this is no doubt because in the absence of a conviction, no question of punishment can arise. Of course, the order will be the most suitable if neither a hospital order nor a supervision order are appropriate. This might arise if, for example, the defendant has been placed under the civil provisions of the MHA 1983.

Ancillary orders

9.191 Although there is no guilty verdict in the CP(I)A 1964 s4A procedure, it is to be noted that it is treated in the same way as a conviction for various of the ancillary orders designed to provide public protection (as is a finding of not guilty by reason of insanity). So, the 'notification and orders' provisions set out in Part 2 of the Sexual Offences Act 2003 apply:

a) The sex offender registration and notification provisions apply to a finding of having committed the act as much as to a conviction: see section 80. Under section 97 of the Act, the police may apply to the local magistrates' court for a notification order to be made in relation to an offender who has not been caught by the provisions of sections 80 and following because the event occurred outside the UK; this covers a person found to have committed the act, by reason of section 97(2) of the Act.
b) Sexual offences prevention orders to protect the public from 'serious sexual harm' from the defendant can be made by a sentencing court in relation to people 'under a disability' who have done the act of certain sexual offences and also numerous other offences which might have a sexual motive: see section 104(3)(b) and Schedules 3 and 5. A sexual offences prevention order may also be made following an application by the police to the local magistrates' court under section 104(5), in which case it applies to a 'qualifying offender', who is defined in section 106(5)–(7) to include someone found to have committed the act; this includes

findings made before the 2003 Act came into effect by reason of section 106(4).

c) Foreign travel orders can be made to protection children from harm from 'sex tourism' under sections 114 and following of the statute; a 'qualifying offender' for the purposes of these provisions includes a person found to have committed the act by reason of section 116.

9.192 There is also a regime of 'risk of sexual harm orders' that can be made by the magistrates' court on the application of the police in relation to a person who has engaged in sexual activity (widely-defined) in the presence of children if children need to be protected: see sections 123 and following. This would include action in relation to which the defendant cannot be tried, though the comments made in chapter 5 in relation to anti-social behaviour orders and the value of making them if a person cannot comply by reason of mental disorder would apply in this context.

9.193 In addition, the provisions for making a violent offender order under sections 98 and following of the Criminal Justice and Immigration Act (CJIA) 2008 provide that a 'qualifying offender' includes someone found to have committed the act of one of the violent offences covered by the statute and sent to hospital or placed under a supervision order (see CJIA 2008 s99(2) and (3)).

Appeals

9.194 The Court of Appeal Criminal Division has various relevant powers arising under the CAA 1968. Its general power to hear appeals against convictions cannot apply in relation to findings of unfitness combined with a finding that the act was committed, given that this is not a conviction. It might be, however, that there was a conviction and the ground of appeal is that there should have been a finding that the defendant was not fit to stand trial: there might then be two alternative follow-ons, either that he or she did not commit the act and should be acquitted or that he or she committed the act and should be dealt with accordingly.

9.195 If the contention was that the defendant was unfit to stand trial and did not commit the act, such that the proper verdict was acquittal, the court would be able to quash the guilty verdict.[210] Its power to substitute a finding of unfitness to stand trial but that the act was committed arises under section 6(1) of the CAA 1968, provided that

210 *R v Podola* [1960] 1 QB 325 at 348.

it has the relevant medical evidence. It may then impose such sentences as could have been imposed under CP(I)A 1964 s5 or s5A (ie hospital order, supervision order or absolute discharge; the powers of remanding the defendant for reports or treatment or the making of an interim hospital order also apply): sections 6(2) and following, as substituted by DVCVA 2004 s24(3). The other provisions relating to the sentence in the Crown Court are mirrored in relation to the Court of Appeal: so CP(I)A 1964 s5A is applied, meaning that the Court of Appeal may remand for reports or treatment under MHA 1983 ss35 and 36 or make an interim hospital order under section 38. However, in relation to the latter, the matter is then remitted to the Crown Court for it to make any decisions as to the renewal of the order and the final disposal: see CAA 1968 s6(5) as substituted.

9.196 It is possible that appeals in this context will arise out of time on the basis of medical evidence coming to light that indicates that a defendant must have been unfit to stand trial. For example, in *R v Johnson*,[211] a 1976 conviction for murder was set aside in 2002 on the basis that an assessment at the time of the trial that Mr Johnson was not mentally ill was shown to be wrong. In another example, there had been detailed consideration of the question of fitness at the time of the trial. *R v Murray*[212] involved a January 2004 guilty plea to murder, the defendant declining to admit that her responsibility was diminished (even though that would have been accepted by the prosecution, leading to a manslaughter conviction). In July 2008, the Court of Appeal accepted the updated evidence that the decision to plead guilty was affected by mental abnormality that meant she had been unfit to stand trial.[213]

9.197 Appeals are also possible against a finding of unfitness to plead (a contention which, it is worth recalling, might be raised by the

211 [2002] EWCA Crim 1900, [2002] MHLR 308.

212 [2008] EWCA Crim 1792, [2008] MHLR 191.

213 See also *R v Grant* [2008] EWCA Crim 1870, [2008] MHLR 203, which relied on medical evidence obtained shortly after a trial. In *R v Walton (aka Wright)* [2010] EWCA Crim 2255, [2010] MHLR 335, the defendant was serving a custodial sentence for various offences but was then found not fit to stand trial in relation to another matter; the evidence meant that he would have been similarly affected at the time of the other offences, and so findings that he was unfit but committed the acts were substituted. In *R v Shulman* [2010] EWCA Crim 1034, [2010] MHLR 172, there had been concerns about Mr Shulman's fitness to stand trial but he had not co-operated with the preparation of reports, denying that he was ill: after he was convicted and sentenced to imprisonment, his mental health difficulties became apparent and the evidence prepared indicated that he had been unfit to stand trial. The Court of Appeal quashed the convictions and substituted findings that he had committed the acts.

prosecution and judge and argued against by the defence) and/or a finding that the act or omission was committed (which the defendant may deny even if he or she accepts the finding of unfitness). The right to appeal against either or both of these findings at the behest of the defendant is given by section 15 of the CAA 1968 if leave is granted by the Court of Appeal or the trial judge certifies that the case is fit for appeal, which are the same conditions as apply to any other appeal from the Crown Court.

9.198 The question for the Court of Appeal is set out in CAA 1968 s16: it is to test whether the finding is safe or not. The appeal will be dismissed if the finding or findings are safe, and the appeal will be allowed if the finding is unsafe. It is to be noted that if the court sets aside a finding of unfitness, it may order a retrial: see CAA 1968 s16(3). But if it only sets aside the finding that the act was committed, it must direct a verdict of acquittal: see CAA 1968 s16(4). In other words, there is no power to order a retrial in this scenario.[214] This will also mean that no remittal for trial is possible if the defendant becomes fit to stand trial: see *R v MB*,[215] in which the Court of Appeal confirmed that if the defendant had sought to appeal against the finding that he or she committed the acts – which on the facts of the case was on the basis that the process was conducted unfairly – and had been granted leave to appeal, the appeal was to be determined even if the defendant had recovered and had been remitted for trial (on which see below). This was because the remittal for trial did not extinguish the powers of the Court of Appeal or the right of the defendant to have a determination on the question on which leave to appeal had been granted. On the facts, the finding had to be quashed, leading to a verdict of acquittal and no prospect of a retrial.

9.199 A further scenario to note is that in relation to a finding of not guilty by reason of insanity, it is possible for the Court of Appeal to substitute a finding that the defendant was under a disability and

214 In *R v Norman* [2008] EWCA Crim 1810, [2008] MHLR 206, the Court of Appeal suggested that this gap be filled in order to secure the public interest. It is possible in an extreme situation, where there has been no lawful trial or verdict at all, that the writ of venire de novo will be issued to order a new trial: that might happen if, for example, the judge purported to make a finding rather than empanelling a jury. For an example of a case going so badly wrong, see *R v O'Donnell* [1996] 1 CrAppR 286, in which a finding of unfitness to stand trial was followed by a conviction and a hospital order (at a time when the proper disposal was an admission order): as this was an invalid conviction, a venire de novo was issued. The writ cannot issue following an acquittal, however: *R v Dorking Justices ex p Harrington* [1984] AC 743.

215 [2010] EWCA Crim 1684, [2011] MHLR 163.

committed the act if there is supporting medical evidence to this effect from two doctors, one of whom is duly approved as a psychiatrist. This arises under section 14 of the CAA 1968, which also includes a requirement to impose a sentence of the sort the Crown Court could. (As the sentencing regime for those found not guilty by reason of insanity is the same, this may involve the continuation of the existing disposal.)

9.200 A gap existed in the regime under the CAA 1968 if the appeal was against the order made to dispose of the case on the basis of the finding of unfitness. Given that the CP(I)A 1964 as it was enacted contained a mandatory disposal, it is no surprise that there would be no appeal provision in the CAA 1968 as enacted. However, when the trial court was given jurisdiction to find whether the act was committed and, if so, to choose the appropriate sentence in the 1991 statutory amendments, it might have been expected that there would be an amendment to the CAA 1968. However, there was not: while there was a wide definition of 'sentence' in CAA 1968 s50 as 'any order made by a court when dealing with an offender', the reference to an offender was not appropriate to cover someone who was found to have committed the act.[216] In any event the sentence appeal provisions under section 9 of the Act required a conviction. The remedy that had to be sought was judicial review: see *R v Mohammed Latif*.[217]

9.201 This gap in the jurisdiction of the Court of Appeal has been filled by the addition of sections 16A and 16B of the CAA 1968 by DVCVA 2004 s25. The combined effect of these sections is that appeals can be taken against the imposition of a hospital order or a supervision order made under CP(I)A 1964 s5. Such an appeal requires the leave of the Court of Appeal or a certificate of fitness to appeal from the trial judge. It is expressly provided that an appeal taken against an interim hospital order made under CP(I)A 1964 s5A does not prevent the trial court taking the steps it finds appropriate in relation to the renewal of such an order or the imposition of an order on the completion of the interim order (CAA 1968 s16B(2)); the Court of Appeal may also impose an interim hospital order and pass the matter back

216 See *R v H* [2003] UKHL 1, [2003] 1 WLR 411, [2003] MHLR 209 at para 8.

217 [2002] EWCA Crim 2115 and [2002] EWHC 1916 (Admin): this involved a challenge to the propriety of the making of an admission order rather than the making of supervision and treatment order after a finding of unfitness to stand trial but to have done the act alleged, but the Court of Appeal noted that it had no jurisdiction to consider such an appeal; it reconstituted itself as a judicial review court, and dismissed the challenge.

to the trial court (CAA 1968 s16B(3)). Not surprisingly, there is no appeal against an absolute discharge.

9.202 Prosecution appeals should also be mentioned. In relation to acquittals, it is possible for the prosecution to refer a point of law involved in an acquittal on indictment to the Court of Appeal under section 36 of the CJA 1972. On its face, applying that to this context, the reference to an acquittal suggests that a prosecution appeal is possible only if there was a finding of unfitness and that the defendant did not commit the actus reus, since that is the only circumstance in which there was an acquittal.[218] Accordingly, there would be no appeal possible if there was a ruling as to unfitness and a finding was then made that the act was committed. A question might then arise as to whether or not the prosecution could bring a challenge by way of judicial review: the issue here is the exclusion of judicial review over 'matters relating to trial on indictment' (as a result of section 29(3) of the Senior Courts Act 1981). It has been determined that the orders made in the process of determining whether the act was committed are outside this language because the trial on indictment stops as soon as the finding of unfitness is made: see *R v Mohammed Latif*.[219] But that reasoning rests on the proposition that the finding of unfitness is a matter relating to trial on indictment and so is within the exclusion of judicial review. This is subject to one caveat: if a judge has acted wholly outside his or her jurisdiction, the exclusion under Senior Courts Act 1981 s29(3) does not apply: see *R v Maidstone Crown Court ex p LB Harrow*,[220] in which a supervision order under the CP(I)A 1964 was quashed on the basis that the judge made it after purporting to find a defendant not guilty by reason of insanity without empanelling a jury and so acting wholly outside his jurisdiction under the indictment.

9.203 In relation to sentences, the prosecution has the power under section 36 of the CJA 1988 to refer an 'unduly lenient' sentence to the Court of Appeal. What amounts to a sentence and the process of sentencing is defined in section 35 of the CJA 1988 to include whatever counts as a sentence for the purposes of the CAA 1968 except an interim hospital order: this could encompass the making of a hospital order. However, the idea of an order that has been imposed for protective purposes being 'unduly lenient' – which has connotations

218 See, for example, *Attorney-General's Reference (No 3 of 1998)* [1999] 2 CrAppR 214.

219 [2002] EWCA Crim 2115 and [2002] EWHC 1916 (Admin), [2003] MHLR 65.

220 [1999] MHLR 84.

of not being adequately punitive – does not seem apposite to cover the making of an order under CP(I)A 1964 s5. However, as noted above, such a sentence is not made pursuant to a trial on indictment and so the prosecution would be able to take a challenge by way of judicial review.

Regaining fitness to stand trial

General

9.204 One of the central principles in relation to detention on the basis of mental disorder is that account must be taken of the possibility that the criteria for detention will cease to be met if a mental disorder improves (including as a result of treatment). Naturally, the same applies in relation to a person who has been found unfit to stand trial: it is possible that changes in the level of disability may mean that a defendant becomes fit to stand trial. The CP(IUP)A 1991 provided in Schedule 1 for the Secretary of State to remit the person for trial if he or she was 'satisfied that that person can properly be tried'; this decision required consultation with the responsible medical officer. However, it could only be made if the trial court had ordered that a restriction order be made together with an admission order and the restriction order had not been lifted by the Secretary of State under section 42 of the MHA 1983. Schedule 1 of CP(IUP)A 1991 was repealed by DVCVA 2004 s24(5), but by section 24(1) it also inserted section 5A(4) into the CP(I)A 1964, which is to the same effect. So if a hospital order and restriction order is made and is still in effect,[221] the Secretary of State 'if satisfied, after consultation with the treating psychiatrist, that the person can properly be tried may remit the person for trial, either to the court of trial or to a prison'. The statute also provides that the hospital and restriction order cease to have effect once the detainee arrives at the place to which he or she has been remitted.

9.205 It is somewhat incongruous that the court having made a finding of unfitness, the executive makes the decision that it no longer applies, as opposed to bringing the matter back to court if there are reasons to believe that the patient has become fit to stand trial. However, that is a common feature of mental health law, and occurs as well with the power of the Secretary of State to lift a restriction order. Of course, if there is a remittal but the defendant wishes to argue that

221 It might not be if, for example, the finding was quashed on appeal: see *R v MB* [2010] EWCA Crim 1684, [2011] MHLR 163, discussed above at para 9.198.

he or she remains unfit to stand trial, the court will be able to engage in determining the question again.

9.206 It is also to be noted that there is no obligation to make a remittal order. Accordingly, there is a discretion. It would seem appropriate that the criteria that determine whether or not there should be a prosecution in the first place, as opposed to diversion into the mental health system or simply the taking of no further action, would be relevant here. This is provided for in the Code for Crown Prosecutors and is discussed in chapter 5. In short, there will first have to be a decision as to whether or not there is a realistic prospect of conviction: this may have been affected by the passage of time because of the loss of witnesses or of exhibits relevant to proving guilt, or because of arguments that might be available that it is problematic to hold a trial. If this evidential test is met, it will be necessary to consider whether there are public interest reasons against prosecution: again, the passage of time, during which time the defendant will have been in hospital and receiving treatment, may mean that there are stronger reasons not to have a trial.[222]

9.207 If the defendant has not been made a restricted patient, while the statutory remittal power does not apply, it may be argued that the prosecution is able to bring a further prosecution for the same matter. In favour of this, it is to be noted that the plea in bar of autrefois convict would not apply because there had been no determination of guilt (though autrefois acquit would apply if there had been a finding that the defendant did not commit the act or omission of the offence).[223] The argument that there is no power to bring a prosecution again is that CP(I)A 1964 s4A(2) states that 'the trial shall not proceed or further proceed' if a finding of unfitness is made, which is language that is sufficient to cover any future trial; furthermore, the existence of the remittal power makes sense if this interpretation is adopted, since if it was otherwise possible to prosecute the defendant again there would be no need for the remittal power.

222 The Crown Prosecution Service (CPS) guidance on mentally disordered offenders (available at www.cps.gov.uk/legal/l_to_o/mentally_disordered_offenders/) notes that the CPS is consulted about resuming a prosecution and that the principles set out in the Code for Crown Prosecutors and the CPS Core Quality Standards apply.

223 See *Connelly v Director of Public Prosecutions* [1964] AC 1254 for guidance on the plea.

Regaining fitness before the trial of the facts or disposal

9.208 It is possible that there will be a gap between the finding of unfitness to stand trial and the hearing about whether the defendant committed the acts, particularly now that the former is a decision by the judge alone and so can be listed for determination as a preliminary matter. What should happen if the defendant regains fitness before the determination of the facts was raised in *R v Omara*:[224] after the finding of unfitness had been made, the trial judge had allowed an adjournment so that it could be determined whether medication could lead the regaining of fitness. (The obvious question, of course, is why this was not done before the finding of unfitness.) When Mr Omara regained fitness, and a transfer to hospital under MHA 1983 s48 was brought to an end, it was then agreed by counsel and the trial court that there was no method by which the finding of unfitness could be set aside. The finding of the facts was then carried out and Mr Omara was found to have committed the act of murder. This being before the amendments introduced by the DVCVA 2004, he was made subject to an admission order with a restriction order because that was the obligatory order under CP(IUP)A 1991 Sch 1 para 5. After six months, he was remitted for trial. In the meantime, he had commenced an appeal out of time against, among other things, the view taken that there had to be a determination of the facts. The Court of Appeal declined to grant the relevant extension of time, and so did not move to the merits of the point. But it was commented that it was at least arguable that CP(I)A 1964 s4A(2) should be read as requiring the jury to move to the determination of the facts provided that the defendant remained unfit.[225]

9.209 However, in *R v Hasani*,[226] where there had been findings of unfitness and that the act had been committed, the defendant regained fitness before disposal. He argued that, in the light of that, the only proper order was an absolute discharge, given that the other orders were to deal someone who required a mental health disposal. The judge, however, directed that he be rearraigned, noting that an absolute discharge was not the most suitable disposal in the light of the fact that the underlying offences included serious assaults. This was challenged in judicial review proceedings: without giving an

224 [2004] EWCA Crim 431.

225 [2004] EWCA Crim 431 paras 19–23; the court declined to rule on the merits because, irrespective of its ruling, the remittal for trial meant that there would be a full trial on the underlying charge.

226 [2005] EWHC 3016 (Admin), [2006] MHLR 79.

indication as to how this decision was not a matter relating to trial on indictment and so outside the judicial review jurisdiction of the High Court by reason of section 29(3) of the Senior Courts Act 1981, the court quashed the order of the judge. But it did so on the basis that the proper course was for him to follow a second procedure under section 4 of the CP(I)A 1964, namely the fitness of trial process: and that if there was a finding of fitness, the finding that the act was committed fell and there was no need to proceed to make an order under the CP(I)A 1964. The construction rules it applied were that a statute should be construed to lead to a sensible outcome and there was nothing in section 4 that indicated it could only be used once.

Being found unfit again on remittal

9.210 If the defendant is remitted for trial, it is possible that the defendant will again be found unfit to stand trial (whether because the Secretary of State erred in concluding that there should be a remittal or because the defendant's condition has deteriorated since remittal). A question that might arise in that context is whether there has to be a second finding of the facts. This arose in *R (Ferris) v Director of Public Prosecutions*.[227] The prosecution submitted that the finding of the first jury remained valid or that, if a second jury should be empanelled, it should be directed that the previous jury had made findings that were binding on it and so conditioned its verdict. The court found that the language of section 4A was mandatory and so a further fact-finding process was required; and that the reference to the jury determining the matter on the evidence already adduced before the finding of unfitness and any further evidence precluded this being done on the basis of the jury simply being told that a previous jury had made such a finding, so that no issue estoppel principles applied.

Participation in the trial process

9.211 As explained in the first part of this chapter, the core requirement for fairness is the ability of the defendant to participate to a proper extent. In *R (TP) v West London Youth Court*,[228] the context was a summary trial involving a youth of low intellectual capacity, but Scott Baker LJ at paragraph 7 of his judgment noted the requirements of

227 [2004] EWHC 1221 (Admin).
228 [2005] EWHC 2583 (Admin), [2006] MHLR 40.

fairness in language that seems apt to cover to Crown Court setting as well:

> ... the minimum requirements for a fair trial for the claimant were:
> i) he had to understand what he is said to have done wrong;
> ii) the court had to be satisfied that the claimant when he had done wrong by act or omission had the means of knowing that was wrong;
> iii) he had to understand what, if any, defences were available to him;
> iv) he had to have a reasonable opportunity to make relevant representations if he wished;
> v) he had to have the opportunity to consider what representations he wished to make once he had understood the issues involved.

9.212 Even though the first part of this summary may be said to be specific to the youth court and the doli incapax question that arises there, or at most is relevant in the Crown Court only when a youth defendant has been committed for trial because the offence is particularly serious, an adult defendant whose mental health is such that he or she does not know what is wrong is perhaps a candidate for removal from the criminal justice system on the basis that it cannot carry out its function if a defendant's capacities do not include the ability to know what is wrong.

9.213 At the same time, there is a competing interest, which Scott Baker LJ also noted at paragraph 18, namely the 'fundamental public interest in cases and defendants being tried'. What was identified in *V and T v UK*, as discussed at the outset of this chapter, was a gap between the formal test for fitness to stand trial in English law and the need to ensure effective participation. An implication arising from the facts of the case was that the evidence that T and V, and particularly V, required therapy to overcome the enormity of what they had done meant that a criminal trial was not an appropriate course of action: or that the importance of attributing criminal guilt in their case overlooked the need to ensure that justice is to be secured, of which a fair trial process is a component part. However, an alternative viewpoint was simply that more had to be done to secure the fairness of the process.

9.214 In the circumstances, three options presented themselves. First, the situation could have been left as it was during the trial of T and V, meaning that there would have to be a number of situations in which trials were stayed because defendants who were not unfit within the statutory regime could not participate in a manner that met the requirements of fairness. While the facts of *V and T v UK* were somewhat extreme, the example of *SC v UK*[229] indicated that the principle could apply in less serious cases.

9.215 Second, one option for reform would have been to extend the remit of the statutory fitness to stand trial regime, namely to allow fact-finding without an attribution of guilt on the back of a wider understanding of what amounted to unfitness. The third option, and the second option for reform, was to take steps to assist participation and hence reduce the prospects of stays being granted.

9.216 The latter option was the one taken. This was perhaps not surprising in the light of the apparent attraction in current times of ascribing criminal responsibility. But it could also be argued that, at least in relation to adult defendants, assisting participation is consistent with the anti-discrimination provisions of human rights law, namely the need to make reasonable amendments to processes to allow those with any form of disability to participate on equal terms.[230] This is also consistent with provisions of the MCA 2005 that are designed to ensure that people are only classified as being without capacity if efforts to assist have been unsuccessful. So, section 1(3) states that 'A person is not to be treated as unable to make a decision unless all practicable steps to help him to do so have been taken without success'.[231]

The response to *V and T v UK* – practice directions

9.217 The immediate response to the decision in *V and T v UK* was that a Practice Direction was issued, but only to cover trials of young persons in the Crown Court, the particular focus of that case: Practice Direction (Crown Court: Young Defendants) of 16 February 2000.[232] It required that account be taken of the 'age, maturity and development (intellectual and emotional) of the young defendant on trial

229 (2005) 40 EHRR 10, App No 60958/00, judgment of 15 June 2004.

230 In relation to children, there is more of an emphasis in the Convention on the Rights of the Child on taking steps that emphasise their differences.

231 And even if there is a lack of capacity, the need to act in the person's best interests includes the requirement in MCA 2005 s4(4) that the decision-maker 'must, so far as reasonably practicable, permit and encourage the person to participate, or to improve his ability to participate, as fully as possible in any act done for him and any decision affecting him'.

232 [2000] 1 WLR 659. At paragraph 17, it was noted that regard should be had to its terms in relation to appeal hearings and committals for sentence involved young defendants. This did not deal with the process for defendants whose vulnerability was not just on account of their age (which had not been the sole concern raised in relation to T and V).

and all other circumstances of the case',[233] with a view to adapting the trial process to avoid intimidation, humiliation or distress and ensure that '[a]ll possible steps ... be taken to assist the young defendant to understand and participate in the proceedings'.[234] Specifically, attempts should be made to have all participants at the same level in the courtroom, the defendant should normally be able to sit with family or those providing support, procedures should be explained, the trial timetable should reflect the difficulties of concentration for long periods (and so have regular and frequent breaks), wigs and gowns should not be worn unless there was good reason, police and uniformed security staff should not be present, and a proper balance should be drawn in relation to those who might want to attend the trial in the public or press galleries (in addition to the practice of making reporting restrictions as to the identification of young defendants).[235]

9.218 This became paragraph IV.39 of the Consolidated Practice Direction of 8 July 2002.[236] Eventually – by the Fifteenth Amendment to the Consolidated Practice Direction – the need to consider defendants who were vulnerable by reason of mental disorder was added. See now paragraph III.30 of the revised Consolidated Practice Direction:[237] this is in the part of the Direction that applies to both the Crown Court and the magistrates' court, relates to trials, appeals and sentencing hearings and covers all vulnerable defendants.

9.219 A 'vulnerable defendant' is defined by paragraph III.30.1 as children and young persons under 18 and adults who are mentally disordered within the meaning of the MHA 1983 or who have 'any other significant impairment of intelligence and social function'. The second part of this language, which is taken from that used in section 33A of the Youth Justice and Criminal Evidence Act (YJCEA)

233 Practice Direction (Crown Court: Young Defendants) para 2.

234 Practice Direction (Crown Court: Young Defendants) para 3. It was also noted at paragraph 4 that a young person indicted with an adult defendant should ordinarily be tried on his own unless 'a joint trial would be in the interests of justice and would not be unduly prejudicial to the welfare of the young defendant'.

235 Practice Direction (Crown Court: Young Defendants) paras 9–15. Also suggested was the step that had been taken in T and V of ensuring that the defendants visited the courtroom in advance (paragraph 6); in relation to high profile trials, the need for the police to provide appropriate security to avoid harassment was noted (paragraph 7).

236 Practice Direction (Criminal Proceedings: Consolidation) [2002] 1 WLR 2870.

237 Available at www.justice.gov.uk/courts/procedure-rules/criminal/pd_consolidated.

1999,[238] is arguably unnecessary: the definition of mental disorder in MHA 1983 s1 is 'any disorder or disability of the mind'.[239] This revised section 1 refers also to 'learning disability' as a form of mental disorder, which is defined as 'a state of arrested or incomplete development of the mind which includes significant impairment or intelligence and social functioning'.[240] This is, however, within the more general definition. However, even if part of the language used in the practice direction is unnecessary, it takes nothing away from the definition of mental disorder in the MHA 1983 and makes it clear that those with a learning disability are included. It prevents any argument to the effect that it has to be an impairment of the sort that would lead to formal action being taken under the MHA 1983 (even though this additional requirement is found not in the definitional section of what is a mental disorder but in the sections that define when formal action can be taken).

9.220 The steps required to provide for vulnerable defendants are in similar terms to those that previously applied only to young defendants. So, by paragraph 30.III.2, account has to be taken of the 'age, maturity and development (intellectual, social and emotional) of the defendant concerned and all other circumstances of the case' with a view to securing the overriding principle set out in paragraph 30.III.3, namely to ensure that a vulnerable defendant can 'understand and participate in' the trial or sentencing proceedings, which may require the modification of the normal trial process. The specifics are as before and outlined at para 9.217.[241]

238 Inserted by Police and Justice Act 2006 s47 of the providing for the use of live link evidence by vulnerable defendants, described below.

239 This is language as amended by the MHA 2007; the original definition in the MHA 1983 was 'mental illness, arrested or incomplete development of mind, psychopathic disorder and any other disorder or disability of mind', and the final clause made it as wide as the new definition.

240 Learning disability is only covered by certain of the provisions of the MHA 1983 if it is associated with abnormally aggressive or seriously irresponsible behaviour: see section 2A; however, this does not take it outside the general definition of mental disorder.

241 Consolidated Practice Direction paras III.30.9–17. Also suggested is that defendants visit the courtroom in advance (paragraph III.30.6) and, in high profile trials, police security to avoid harassment (paragraph III.30.7). The suggestion previously made that young defendants should be tried alone when jointly indicted with an adult is applied: the language now is that there should be a separate trial unless the court forms the 'opinion that a joint trial would be in accordance with Part 1 of the Criminal Procedure Rules 2011 (the overriding objective) and in the interests of justice' (paragraph III.30.4).

9.221 Useful guidance on the application of this in practice is found in the *TP* case, already mentioned.[242] The defendant there had a low intellectual capacity. The Divisional Court agreed that a trial could proceed. It relied on a structural feature, namely that the proceedings were in the youth court, a specialised court staffed by trained judges and where advocates had the necessary expertise.[243] This can be applied in the Crown Court as well in that judges may have special training, though there are problems in the court exercising control over advocates in the absence of a provision such as that in the fact-finding process under the formal fitness to stand trial process that requires the court to appoint the advocate for the fact-finding process.[244]

9.222 In addition, there were a number of specific steps that could be taken to assist with participation. Scott Baker LJ commented at paragraph 26 that the expert evidence in the case was to the effect that various steps could be taken, including:

i) keeping the claimant's level of cognitive functioning in mind;
ii) using concise and simple language;
iii) having regular breaks;
iv) taking additional time to explain court proceedings;
v) being proactive in ensuring the claimant has access to support;
vi) explaining and ensuring the claimant understands the ingredients of the charge;
vii) explaining the possible outcomes and sentences;
viii) ensuring that cross-examination is carefully controlled so that questions are short and clear and frustration is minimised.

Live-link evidence

9.223 Also contained in the practice direction, at paragraph III.30.13, is the reminder of the possibility of a direction to allow a vulnerable defendant to give evidence by live link under YJCEA 1999 s33A: a 'live link' is defined in section 33B of the Act as an arrangement whereby the accused can be away from the courtroom but see what is going on there and can be seen from the courtroom by the judge, jury if in the Crown Court, legal representatives, and any co-accused and interpreters. The use of live links for defendants was added to the YJCEA 1999 by section 47 of the Police and Justice Act 2006, the original provisions having been applicable only to witnesses but not

242 [2005] EWHC 2583 (Admin), [2006] MHLR 40.

243 [2005] EWHC 2583 (Admin), [2006] MHLR 40 para 25.

244 See para 9.95 above.

including defendants who were also witnesses.[245] It covers those who are vulnerable on account of age or mental disorder. For those under 18, the preconditions for the use of the live link are that 'his ability to participate effectively in the proceedings as a witness giving oral evidence in court is compromised by his level of intellectual ability or social functioning' and the use of the link would enable more effective participation. For those aged 18 or over, the test used has been adopted into the practice direction noted above, and requires a mental disorder or a significant impairment of intelligence and social function: if that means that he or she cannot participate effectively and the live link would enable more effective participation, then an appropriate direction can be given to allow the use of the link as the exclusive method by which the accused gives evidence. The application for a live link must come from the accused, but any party may seek to have it set aside in the interests of justice and the court may set it aside on its own motion. See rules 29.14–29.17 of the Criminal Procedure Rules 2011 for details on the process to be followed in seeking or varying a direction in relation to this matter.

9.224 It is to be noted that there are more extensive statutory provisions for witnesses who are vulnerable. The grounds for being classified as vulnerable, defined in YJCEA 1999 s16, include those whose evidence is likely to be diminished in quality by reason of mental disorder as defined in the MHA 1983, or a significant impairment of intelligence and social functioning. The special measures available for such witnesses, set out in sections 23–30, are the use of screens to prevent the accused seeing the witness (and vice versa), the use of the live link, the giving of evidence in private, the removal of wigs or gowns by the advocate and judge, the use of video-recorded evidence in chief, the use of intermediaries and devices to aid the communication of questions and answers to and by a witness.

9.225 A question that might arise is whether the absence of a statute that extends the special measures other than the live-link to a defendant means that these other measures are not available. The answer is a qualified 'no': in other words, the YJCEA 1999 may not be the only source of the power to modify the process, because the common law and the HRA 1998 might also be of assistance; but it may not be possible to provide for all the special measures in the absence of an express statutory regime. This is apparent from case-law to the effect

245 Indeed it was prohibited in their case by YJCEA 1999 s16; this was found not to breach ECHR article 6 in *R v Camberwell Green Youth Court ex p D and G* [2005] UKHL 4, [2005] 1 WLR 393.

that intermediaries can be made available to a criminal defendant despite the absence of that special measure being extended by statutory language.

Intermediaries

9.226 In *R v SH*,[246] the Court of Appeal was concerned with an appeal by a defendant due to stand trial for sexual offences who sought to use a pre-recorded interview for his evidence in chief and to have an intermediary when he was being cross-examined. The application was based on evidence as to his low IQ and consequent inability to follow the thread of questions or his answers (though not to the extent that he was not fit to stand trial). At a pre-trial hearing, the judge allowed the use of an intermediary in the form of a supporter. SH sought to appeal the refusal to allow the use of a video-recording. The Court of Appeal concluded that it had no power to hear the appeal because it was outside the statutory provisions as to interlocutory appeals in the CPIA 1996. However, it did endorse the proposition that the Crown Court had an inherent power, as part of its duty to ensure a fair trial, to allow an intermediary.[247] Also supported was the view that the judge could allow a detailed defence statement to be read or for a defendant with difficulties such as those demonstrated by SH to be allowed to refer to a document such as a defence statement.

9.227 However, the Court of Appeal was not prepared to endorse the use of a video-tape of evidence in chief because this gave rise to too many issues: such as who would record the evidence, how would it be done, and could a defendant re-record interviews until one was produced that was thought to be acceptable?[248]

9.228 In *C v Sevenoaks Youth Court*,[249] it was held that the need to be 'proactive in ensuring the claimant has access to support'[250] extends to ensuring that a defendant has an intermediary to assist both at trial and prior to trial. The facts of the case involved a 12-year-old boy due to stand trial in the youth court on charges of assault with intent to rob and theft. His complex mental health issues included hyperactivity (which was not adequately controlled by medication), low comprehension suggestive of a learning disability, a personality disorder and

246 [2003] EWCA Crim 1208.

247 [2003] EWCA Crim 1208 paras 25 and 26; the court suggested that it was no different from the use of an interpreter.

248 [2003] EWCA Crim 1208 paras 23 and 24.

249 [2009] EWHC 3088 (Admin), [2009] MHLR 329.

250 [2005] EWHC 2583 (Admin), [2006] MHLR 40 para 26, noted above.

possibly Asperger's Syndrome. A clinical psychologist who assessed him concluded that he did understand what he was charged with and the nature of his plea, and could give an account of events, but that he could not concentrate during a trial, nor listen to the evidence, nor instruct his solicitor about which parts of the evidence he did or did not accept. Perhaps surprisingly, the view formed was that C was fit to stand trial, but only if an intermediary was appointed to explain the evidence to C during the trial and interpret questions for him and his answers.

9.229 A second expert, a neuro-psychiatrist, confirmed that C's problems limited his ability to assimilate information or form coherent conclusions in a way that was required in court. Various suggestions were made by this expert as to assistance that could be provided, which were understood by the High Court to incorporate the use of intermediaries. It appears that no point was taken before the magistrates to the effect that C's capacity was so limited that he was unfit to stand trial;[251] rather, the issue raised was whether the court could appoint an intermediary to allow C properly to understand the evidence, give instructions, prepare for and follow the trial, and if necessary to give evidence on his own behalf. The magistrates' court had appointed one but then decided that it had no power to do so: it did this by noting that the special measures regime applicable to vulnerable witnesses under the YJCEA 1999, which includes under section 29 the power to allow a witness to give evidence through an intermediary, could not apply to defendants, as section 16(1) of the Act excluded it. As a result, it had revoked the appointment, which was the decision challenged.

9.230 The High Court determined that the lack of a statutory power to appoint an intermediary was not problematic, since the power was implicit in the magistrates' court's power to regulate its procedure to allow a defendant to participate; indeed, which was properly a duty in the light of the overriding objective under the Criminal Procedure Rules of dealing with criminal cases justly, which included recognising the rights of a defendant under ECHR article 6. The High Court made it plain that this duty extended not just to the conduct of the

251 Openshaw J summarised his evidence as follows: '"In terms of the current circumstances, the court has my recommendation of C lacking the pre-requisite capacity for effective participation in trial proceedings". But he does not say in terms that C is unfit to plead or unfit to be tried, nor, as I understand it, is that contended on his behalf' ([2009] EWHC 3088 (Admin), [2009] MHLR 329 paras 8 and 9).

trial but also covered the preparation for the trial.[252] The intermediary had to be someone with whom the defendant would have to develop a suitable rapport.[253]

9.231 So it is possible that other special measures of the sort that apply by reason of statute to witnesses may apply to defendants also. However, that may not extend to all such measures. In *R v Camberwell Green Youth Court ex p D and G*,[254] Baroness Hale, while noting the flexibility of the inherent powers of the court to control its procedure, suggested that it was 'clearly inappropriate' to apply some parts of the statutory scheme to a defendant because too many issues would arise. She endorsed the caution expressed in *R v SH*[255] about the difficulties of allowing a defendant to give evidence-in-chief by a video tape, since it would require regulation of such questions as who would record the evidence, how would it be done, and could a defendant re-record interviews until one was produced that was thought to be acceptable?[256] But if this is raised sufficiently in advance, why would it not be possible for appropriate directions to be given as to the process to be followed? The Court of Appeal in SH agreed than an intermediary was possible;[257] and that the judge could allow a detailed defence statement to be read or for a defendant with difficulties such as those demonstrated by SH to be allowed to refer to a document such as a defence statement.

Abuse of process

9.232 There remains the possibility that despite all these steps that can be taken to enhance the prospect of participation, they will turn out not to be effective. So, in the *TP* case,[258] having outlined the steps that could be taken, Scott Baker LJ confirmed that there was a jurisdiction to stay a trial: but this would be in exceptional circumstances

252 [2009] EWHC 3088 (Admin), [2009] MHLR 329 para 17.

253 Also raised was the question of the payment of the intermediary: at the time, it was done on a voluntary basis by the Ministry of Justice, but the court noted that in the absence of such payments, it might be proper for the Legal Services Commission to make payments under Access to Justice Act 1999 s14(2)(g) (ie its catch-all power 'to do anything else which it considers appropriate for funding representation').

254 [2005] UKHL 4, [2005] 1 WLR 393: see Baroness Hale at para 58.

255 [2003] EWCA Crim 1208.

256 [2005] UKHL 4, [2005] 1 WLR 393 paras 23 and 24.

257 [2005] UKHL 4, [2005] 1 WLR 393 paras 25 and 26; the court suggested that it was no different from the use of an interpreter.

258 [2005] EWHC 2583 (Admin), [2006] MHLR 40.

and only if efforts made to assist had been found wanting. As noted already, this reflected the public interest in having a trial, such that the starting point was to seek to deal with any difficulties in participation. But he added:

> ... the judge who is hearing the trial has a continuing jurisdiction to stay proceedings for abuse of process. Thus, if it becomes apparent during the course of the hearing that the claimant is unable effectively to participate, the judge can stay the proceedings at that point.[259]

9.233 It is suggested that this comment has to be read together with the point he also made as to the minimum requirements for a fair trial quoted at para 9.211 above, which Scott Baker LJ commented meant that the defendant:

> ... had therefore to be able to give proper instructions and to participate by way of providing answers to questions and suggesting questions to his lawyers in the circumstances of the trial as they arose.

9.234 The ongoing duty to secure a fair trial and the elements of what it involves means that the assessment of the ability to provide instructions cannot be assessed merely against prosecution written disclosure. Given the possibility of deviation from witness statements and supplemental oral evidence, the defendant needs to be able to follow the oral evidence as well. Although this was in a summary trial context, the Crown Court has such a jurisdiction as well.

9.235 In terms of the timing of the assessment of whether the defendant can participate, the High Court gave further guidance in *Crown Prosecution Service v P*.[260] This was again in the context of summary proceedings before a youth court. A decision by a District Judge to stay a trial at the outset on the basis that P was unable to participate effectively in the trial, even with appropriate assistance, was set aside on the basis that the question of a stay should rarely be determined before evidence on the charge had been called. Giving the leading judgment, Smith LJ noted that the medical evidence that would be available at the outset had to be considered together with the real evidence of the court's assessment of how the defendant was able to participate, which would take into account any special modifications to the process.[261]

259 [2005] EWHC 2583 (Admin), [2006] MHLR 40 para 18. It was also accepted to exist in *Crown Prosecution Service v P* [2007] EWHC 946 (Admin), [2007] MHLR 262.

260 [2007] EWHC 946 (Admin), [2007] MHLR 262.

261 [2007] EWHC 946 (Admin), [2007] MHLR 262 paras 51–55. See also *R v Ghulam* [2009] EWCA Crim 2285, [2009] MHLR 325: the Court of Appeal held

9.236 There is, however, an obvious argument against this approach: it involves proceeding with the trial without making a decision on the ability of the defendant to participate and in the context of evidence that he or she cannot participate. But there is a question-mark as to the jurisdiction to do that: by analogy, if there was evidence that a defendant needed an interpreter and the court suggested that it would proceed and assess at the end of the prosecution case whether the defendant had understood enough of the process, that would not be permissible because of the need to be satisfied that the defendant could participate from the outset. The same can be said in relation to an inability to participate on grounds of mental disorder. In contrast to the provisions of CP(I)A 1964 s4(2), which expressly authorises a court to proceed to the end of the prosecution case despite evidence of a disability that would otherwise bar a trial process, there is no equivalent statutory power in the context of an inability to participate that is not covered by the formal fitness to stand trial process. Consequently, while it is clear that the ongoing jurisdiction to consider whether there is an abuse of process in case things turn out to be worse than is thought at the outset of the trial, it is less than clear that there is an equivalent jurisdiction to see if things are better than they seem at the outset.

9.237 Aside from the question of whether there is any jurisdiction to defer considering the issue, the rationales put forward for delaying the determination of the issue of participation have clear responses to them.[262] The first point was the need to assess the real evidence of the court's assessment of the defendant, which might lead to it forming an opinion different to that of the medical professionals. To the extent that this amounts to a reminder that the decision remains one for the court and so cannot be devolved to experts, it is unproblematic; however, to the extent that it indicates that the 'common sense' of the court is worth more weight than the expert view, it is problematic because of the danger of the court proceeding with no solid basis. In any event, unless and until the defendant gives evidence, any view formed will be based on the reactions of the defendant sitting in the court during the evidence: it must be open to question whether this

that a judge who decided that a defendant was fit to stand trial had been able to rely on his own observations of the defendant during the course of the trial and so reject a medical report to the effect that the defendant was not fit to stand trial.

262 Some of the reasoning of Smith LJ is specific to the context of the summary trial and is considered in chapter 10. The parts of her reasoning that would translate to a Crown Court setting are reviewed here.

will give the court any real ability to make an assessment that could counter the view of the experts. A related point in the reasoning of Smith LJ was that the assessment had to be made in light of the impact of any special arrangements put in place: but the expert evidence could take this into account.

9.238 In summary, the abuse of process jurisdiction remains to prevent a trial proceeding if the defendant does not meet the formal unfitness to stand trial test but cannot participate. However, the ability of the court to be flexible in adapting its procedure means that there will be limited circumstances in which the defendant cannot participate. There is case-law that suggests that the determination of whether the trial should be stayed should be deferred to allow an assessment of how the defendant copes in practice: but there are arguments to the contrary that were not addressed in that case-law and which suggest that the issue should be determined at the outset.

9.239 The important practical points are that the jurisdiction to stay proceedings if a defendant cannot properly participate is a matter that should be kept under constant review. Further, it is a matter on which appropriate expert evidence is admissible: in *SC v UK*, the ECtHR was impressed by evidence from a social worker to the effect that SC did not understand what was happening, and so it may be that the expert evidence can come from any suitable professional with the necessary expertise. Other factors will be relevant, including matters such as the reactions of the defendant to police questioning on arrest and interview, and when questioned by the court; another feature may be the adequacy of the defendant's instructions for the purposes of cross-examination, though it is to be noted that this is a question that might require careful consideration as to whether legal professional privilege is involved, and it should also be remembered that the case-law from the ECtHR has emphasised the need of the defendant to be able to follow proceedings on an ongoing basis, not just to provide instructions on the witness statements.

Hospital order without conviction

9.240 As is discussed in chapter 10, the formal fitness to stand trial process does not apply in the magistrates' court: but the summary courts do have a power under MHA 1983 s37(3) to make a hospital order without recording a conviction. The Crown Court has a limited version of this power in MHA 1983 s51(5), which applies only if a defendant has been remanded in custody by a court, transferred to hospital by the Secretary of State under MHA 1983 s48, and it is 'impractical or inappropriate' to bring the detainee before the court. Section 51(5) and (6) together allow the court to make a hospital order under section 37 and a restriction order under section 41 (if the risk posed by the defendant requires it) if it is 'proper to make such an order' in the light of the committal documentation.

9.241 In *R (Kenneally) v Snaresbrook Crown Court*,[263] a three-judge Divisional Court held that, while the orders made were not punitive, the power to deprive someone of his or her liberty had to be construed restrictively, and so it could only be 'inappropriate' to bring someone before a court at all if a high degree of disability was present, though it did not have to amount to it being impossible to produce the defendant.[264] If the defendant can be brought to court (or if the preconditions of section 51(5) are not met), the question of fitness to stand trial or ability to participate may have to be answered.

9.242 Although the defendant in that situation will be in hospital at the time, it is necessary for the court to be satisfied that the medical criteria for admission to hospital continue to be met, namely that detention in hospital for medical treatment is appropriate in the light of the nature or degree of the mental disorder, and that appropriate medical treatment is available. This evidence must come from two doctors, one of whom is approved for the purposes of section 12 (by reason of section 54).

263 [2001] EWHC Admin 968, [2002] MHLR 53.

264 [2001] EWHC Admin 968, [2002] MHLR 53 para 32. On the facts, the defendant had been brought to the court building and so the test was not met.

CHAPTER 10

Inability to participate – summary trial

10.1 The outline of the right to participate in chapter 9 applies to all criminal trials; and the provisions in the Consolidated Practice Direction[1] relating to the need to take steps to secure participation by someone who is unable properly to participate without modifications also applies to both trials on indictment and those in the adult and youth summary courts. However, there is a different statutory regime for summary trials, since the Criminal Procedure (Insanity) Act (CP(I)A) 1964 does not apply, and different issues might arise under the Practice Direction: so the summary process is considered separately. This chapter sets out the relevant provisions that allow the court to assist participation in a trial and also provide jurisdiction to make findings that do not amount to a criminal conviction.

Introduction – the statutory provisions as to fact-finding

10.2 The CP(I)A 1964 refers to jury trials, and so on its face appears only to cover the Crown Court. However, there are circumstances in which a summary court can proceed without determining guilt. Magistrates are able to make an order under section 37 of the Mental Health Act (MHA) 1983 – a hospital order, which has no age limit, or a guardianship order, which can be made on someone aged 16 or over – without entering a conviction. This is a more extensive power than that applicable to the Crown Court under MHA 1983 s51, which covers only a defendant who has been transferred to hospital under section 48 of the Act and who is not fit even to be brought to court. MHA 1983 s37(3) provides that:

> Where a person is charged before a magistrates' court with any act or omission as an offence and the court would have power, on convicting him of that offence, to make an order under subsection (1) above in his case, then, if the court is satisfied that the accused did the act or made the omission charged, the court may, if it thinks fit, make such an order without convicting him.[2]

10.3 Initially, this power could be exercised in relation only to those who were classified as having a mental illness or a severe mental impairment; the precursor was section 60(2) of the MHA 1959, which

1 www.justice.gov.uk/courts/procedure-rules/criminal/pd_consolidated.

2 Before this section was amended by the MHA 2007, the power could only be exercised in relation to those whose mental disorder was 'mental illness or severe mental impairment'.

allowed the magistrates to proceed without a conviction in relation to those diagnosed with a mental illness or 'severe subnormality'. The amendment so that the reference is to mental disorder came as part of the changes introduced by the MHA 2007, discussed in chapter 2.

10.4 The power in the MHA 1983 is to be read in conjunction with section 11 of the Powers of Criminal Courts (Sentencing) Act (PCC(S)A) 2000, which provides that:

> (1) If on the trial by a magistrates' court of an offence punishable on summary conviction with imprisonment, the court –
> (a) is satisfied the accused did the act or made the omission charged, but
> (b) is of the opinion that an inquiry ought to be made into his physical or mental condition before the method of dealing with him is determined,
>
> the court shall adjourn the case to enable a medical examination and report to be made, and shall remand him.

Coverage

Initial case-law

10.5 Although the power in MHA 1983 s37(3) and its precursor in the MHA 1959 has been around for some considerable time, there was little jurisprudence on it until recently. The first case appears to be *R v Lincoln (Kesteven) Justices ex p O'Connor*,[3] which concerned the MHA 1959. This involved a defendant who was also a voluntary patient in a hospital who was being prosecuted for an assault occasioning actual bodily harm on a member of staff at the hospital: but he was viewed as without capacity to give instructions, and in particular was unable to consent to the either-way offence being tried summarily, and the magistrates took the view that it was necessary to commit the case for trial. The Divisional Court held that this was a situation in which the power to make a hospital order without a conviction was appropriate; aside from commenting that it would be proper to use this 'unusual power' only in a 'very rare' case, there was little indication as to when it should be used. It was also suggested that it would usually require the consent of the defendant's representatives – there was no mention of the question of whether there was any need for a defendant to

3 [1983] 1 WLR 335.

be fit to participate in a criminal process, which Mr O'Connor clearly was not.

10.6 In a further case, *R v Ramsgate Justices ex p Kazmarek*,[4] it was confirmed that the power could be used even if the question of fitness only arose after a defendant had elected trial by jury on an either-way offence. The Divisional Court, however, gives no indication of the grounds for its use, and Mann J expressly reserved the question of whether it could be used in relation to an indictable-only offence. It was confirmed that there was no such power in *R v Cheltenham Magistrates' Court ex p Thompson*,[5] on the basis that section 37(3) is limited to situations in which a defendant could be convicted in the magistrates court and so excluded indictable-only offences.

10.7 In the case of an indictable-only offence, it is sent to the Crown Court under sections 51 and 52 of the Crime and Disorder Act (CDA) 1998 without any consideration of the sufficiency of the evidence. It is to be noted that there is express provision in MHA 1983 s52(7) which allows the defendant to be sent to the Crown Court even if not present, so long as he or she is represented and the court has medical evidence that the accused is 'unfit to take part in the proceedings'. It is also provided in MHA 1983 s52(2) that if there has been a transfer direction issued under section 48 (on which see chapter 8), this will not expire if the accused is sent to the Crown Court for trial in custody.

Fitness to stand trial

10.8 It has now been established that the regime in MHA 1983 s37(3) and PCC(S)A 2000 s11 governs the question of fitness to plead in the magistrates' court. In *R (P) v Barking Magistrates' Court*,[6] the magistrates had purported to follow a process analogous to that applicable in the Crown Court (on the application of the defence and without objection from the prosecution or the court clerk) and had found the defendant, who had a low IQ, fit to stand trial. In a judicial review challenge to this, the High Court identified an error of law in the failure to recognise that PCC(S)A 2000 s11(1) and MHA 1983 s37(3):

4 (1985) 80 CrAppR 366.

5 (1996) 160 JP 207; (1996) 32 BMLR 69.

6 [2002] EWHC 734 (Admin), [2002] MHLR 304. It has also been adopted as a possible solution if a defendant in a summary trial might also be acquitted on the ground of insanity at the time of the trial: see *R (Singh) v Stratford Magistrates' Court* [2007] EWHC 1582 (Admin), [2007] MHLR 274.

> ... provide a complete statutory framework for a determination by the magistrates' court of all the issues that arise in cases of defendants who are or may be mentally ill or suffering from severe mental impairment in the context of offences that are triable summarily only.[7]

10.9 It was also noted that the powers given to the summary courts 'are considerably less strict and more flexible than the common law rules governing the issue of fitness to plead in the Crown Court'.[8]

10.10 Both at the time of the judgment in *P* and now, the idea that these statutes provide a complete framework is problematic. As noted, the provisions of MHA 1983 s37(3) originally applied only to mental illness or severe mental impairment: this was so when *P* was decided. This means that it did not cover a mental impairment that was not severe, or a psychopathic personality disorder, or any other form of mental disorder that could not be classed as a mental illness or severe mental impairment but might mean that a defendant could not follow a trial or provide instructions in a way that satisfied the requirement of being able to participate. Now that section 37(3) has been amended by the MHA 2007 to cover all instances of mental disorder, this concern has gone.

10.11 However, there remains a significant gap, namely that it might not be proper to make a hospital order or a guardianship order. In particular:

i) the power arises only in relation to imprisonable offences, and
ii) relatively strict criteria on the merits have to be met.

These are discussed in detail in chapters 2 and 18: in short, section 37(2) requires that the mental disorder be of a nature or degree that makes detention in hospital for medical treatment appropriate or to warrants reception into guardianship, in the case of a hospital order that appropriate treatment be available, and in either case that it be the most suitable method of disposing of the case. Accordingly, if the defendant has a mental disorder but it is not such as to require detention in hospital or guardianship, or the other parts of the test on the merits are not met, then no order can be made. It is to be noted that there is no power to make an interim hospital order under MHA 1983 s38 (which requires a conviction), but that medical reports can be obtained under section 35: see *Bartram v Southend Magistrates' Court*.[9]

7 [2002] EWHC 734 (Admin), [2002] MHLR 304 per Wright J at para 10.

8 [2002] EWHC 734 (Admin), [2002] MHLR 304 per Wright J at para 10.

9 [2004] EWHC 2691 (Admin), [2004] MHLR 319. If the defendant needs treatment and is unwilling to accept it voluntarily, the civil provisions of the MHA 1983 are available: see the discussion in chapter 7.

10.12 Similarly, there may be problems with the procedural requirements. A guardianship order can only be made in relation to those aged 16 or over and so is not available in the youth court. Both require supporting medical evidence; a hospital order also requires evidence that a bed is available;[10] and a guardianship order is invariably to a local authority and requires it to form a view that it is appropriate (in relation to which it does not have to follow the view of the court).[11]

10.13 The questions that arise in this context include:

i) what is the test to be applied that means a court should proceed to consider the making of an order under section 37(3) without a conviction;
ii) is this only possible if there is the prospect of such an order;
iii) when should the question be determined; and
iv) what happens to the underlying criminal charge?

These questions are discussed in the following sections, starting with a case in which it was suggested that the court can engage in the fact-finding mission even if no order is in prospect and should rarely stay proceedings without making a finding as to the facts and should invariably proceed at least to the end of the prosecution case.

Fact-finding not leading to disposal – youth court

The case-law

10.14 The case suggesting that it does not matter that the court might not make an order under the MHA 1983 arose in the context of a youth court trial. *Crown Prosecution Service v P*[12] involved a decision to stay the trial on charges of assault and attempted theft of a motor vehicle of a 13-year old defendant who had a low IQ and Attention Deficit Hyperactivity Disorder (ADHD). In June 2005, P had been found unfit to stand trial in the Crown Court (the charges there including a serious allegation, false imprisonment): the experts agreed that his poor concentration meant that following evidence in order to give instructions, giving evidence and taking advice from his lawyers

10 MHA 1983 s37(4).

11 See *R (Buckowicki) v Northamptonshire County Council* [2007] EWHC 310 (Admin), [2007] MHLR 121.

12 [2007] EWHC 946 (Admin), [2007] MHLR 262.

was beyond his abilities, such that he was not fit to stand trial.[13] One report, from a child and adolescent psychiatrist, included the view that a hospital order under the MHA 1983 was not warranted.

10.15 The same reports were adduced in the youth court, and a supplemental report confirmed that there had been no improvement in P's situation. The District Judge stayed the youth court trial on the basis that P was unable to participate effectively in the trial, even with appropriate assistance.[14] An issue that had been raised was whether a decision should be made at the outset of the trial or at a later stage, and he concluded that it should be determined at the outset but did not give reasons.[15] A case stated appeal was taken, raising inter alia the question of when fitness to stand trial or ability to participate was to be determined and whether it had been proper to stay the proceedings on the facts.

10.16 The prosecution argued that, as a hospital order could only be made if it was determined that the actus reus had been committed, the trial should proceed that far unless it was an exceptional case.[16] That would require three steps to be taken if the question of fitness to participate was raised:

i) consideration of the medical evidence provided at the outset;
ii) hearing the prosecution case to determine whether there was a case to answer; if so,
iii) determining whether there was effective participation, the answer to which would lead to the continuation of the matter as a trial or as a finding of whether the defendant committed the actus reus.

P's advocate accepted this proposal, but emphasised the possibility of cases that should be stayed at the outset, and argued that the facts revealed such a case because the evidence of inability to participate was very clear.[17]

13 The Crown Court judge had apparently stayed the proceedings rather than swearing a jury to determine whether P had committed the actus reus of the offences charged (in accordance with CP(I)A 1964 ss4, 4A and 5).

14 The District Judge referred to *R (P) v Barking Youth Court* (as to the existence of the fitness to stand trial process in the summary court), *SC v UK* (2005) 40 EHRR 10, App No 60958/00 and *R (TP) v West London Youth Court* [2005] EWHC 2583 (Admin), [2006] MHLR 40 (as to participation in a trial, and the jurisdiction to stay proceedings in the absence of an ability to participate).

15 [2007] EWHC 946 (Admin), [2007] MHLR 262 para 18.

16 [2007] EWHC 946 (Admin), [2007] MHLR 262 paras 27–29.

17 [2007] EWHC 946 (Admin), [2007] MHLR 262 paras 30 and 58. Smith LJ did accept at paragraph 58 that 'if the child is so severely impaired that he clearly cannot participate in the trial and if it is clear that there would be no point in

10.17 The High Court accepted much of the prosecution position. It confirmed that a trial could be stayed as an abuse of the process if the defendant did not have the capacity to participate, but held that this should rarely be determined at the outset, ie before evidence on the charge had been called. It also indicated that a finding of inability to participate should invariably be followed by the making of factual findings. Lady Justice Smith, giving the leading judgment, noted several rationales for the proposition that it would rarely be proper to stay proceedings before evidence had been heard. The first was that the medical evidence available at the outset could only be part of the material relevant to the decision on the ability to participate: real evidence in the form of the court's assessment of the ability of the defendant to participate might lead to it forming an opinion different to that of the medical professionals.[18] A related point was that the assessment had to be made in the light of the impact of any special arrangements put in place, which a pre-trial expert report could not assess. An additional reason for deferring the decision was that the court might want to consider whether there might be no case to answer and so an acquittal should follow.[19] As the District Judge had not followed this approach, the decision was declared to be wrong in law.[20]

finding the facts with a view to making an order under the MHA 1983, there would seem to be little purpose in proceeding'.

18 [2007] EWHC 946 (Admin), [2007] MHLR 262 paras 51–55. See by analogy *R v Ghulam* [2009] EWCA Crim 2285, [2009] MHLR 325: the Court of Appeal held that a judge who decided that a defendant was fit to stand trial had been able to rely on his own observations of the defendant during the course of the trial and so reject a medical report to the effect that the defendant was not fit to stand trial.

19 Smith LJ also felt that it was also necessary for the court to consider whether the child knew the difference between right and wrong, as her tentative (and obiter) view was that the doli incapax rule had not been abolished by section 34 of the CDA 1998, but rather changed from a presumption to a matter that had to be raised by the defence (ie an evidential burden, which would then require the prosecution to prove to the usual criminal standard that the child knew that the conduct was wrong): see [2007] EWHC 946 (Admin), [2007] MHLR 262 paras 37–47. The relevance of this was the prospect that proceedings should continue despite the inability of the child to participate because of a possible acquittal on the grounds of doli incapax, which might often be demonstrated by the same reports as were relevant to the issue of the ability of the child to participate: see paragraph 58. Gross J, the other judge on the court, accepted that the issue needed to be resolved, but did not think it right to express an obiter view: see paragraph 64. The House of Lords has since confirmed that the defence has been abolished: see *R v JTB* [2009] UKHL 20. That leaves, however, the question of the court determining whether there is a case to answer.

20 [2007] EWHC 946 (Admin), [2007] MHLR 262 para 59. It was not set aside on the facts, given the passage of time.

Arguments against delaying consideration

10.18 The suggestion that the magistrates might proceed to the stage of determining whether there is a case to answer may at first sight seem pragmatic. But it is worth assessing the different parts of this reasoning critically, given that there was little argument in front of the court. First, there is the question of whether it is possible to proceed when the defendant cannot participate or to turn a blind eye to this possibility. The point to note in this context is that the statutory language that gives such a power to the Crown Court is clear, but it is not reflected in the statutes applicable to the magistrates' court.

10.19 In the context of the formal fitness to stand trial process in the Crown Court, CP(I)A 1964 s4(1) refers to disabilities that are bars to a defendant being put on trial, in other words, to the carrying out of the trial process. But it then gives an express statutory power, in the form of section 4(2) of the 1964 Act, to allow the court to postpone the question until the opening of the defence case if it is expedient and in the interests of the accused. Two things would seem to follow from this. First, the statutory power to delay making the assessment of fitness to participate until the start of the defence case allows for the possibility of proceedings in which the defendant will be shown in due course to have been unable to participate (ie once that assessment is made). Second, in the absence of the power to postpone, the determination should be carried out as soon as the issue is raised, given that what is in issue is whether there is a bar to the trial proceeding.

10.20 The consequence of this would seem to be that unless there is a power to delay making the determination in the magistrates' court, the existence of a potential bar to being tried should be investigated as soon as the issue is raised. The statutory powers as to the making of an order without a conviction (MHA 1983 s37(3)) and before the method of dealing with the defendant is decided upon (PCC(S)A 2000 s11) do not contain an express power to delay. The latter is headed as a remand power; and the former is headed as a power to order admission to hospital. Neither the purposes of the powers to make an order without a conviction nor the language used seem apposite to allow the magistrates to avoid the normal consequence of a bar to a trial, namely that it not be allowed to proceed despite the possibility that the defendant might not be able to participate.

10.21 That is not to say that the court cannot revisit the issue if it is not persuaded at the outset that it cannot continue: but there is good reason to argue that a court that is persuaded that the defendant cannot participate, as was the position of the District Judge in *Crown Prosecution Service v P*, has no jurisdiction to proceed with what at that stage will be a criminal trial on the basis of a prospect that the defendant will be shown to be fit to participate. That would mean that the court is limited to proceeding with what cannot lead to a conviction and so is not a criminal trial, namely the question of whether the act was committed.

10.22 Even if there is jurisdiction to proceed without making a finding of fitness to participate, which the court in *Crown Prosecution Service v P* can be taken to have answered in the affirmative, there is the question of whether the rationales put forward by the court for delaying the determination of the issue of participation carry the weight they were given. The first was the need to take into account the real evidence of the trial court's assessment of the defendant, which might lead to it forming an opinion different to that of the medical professionals. To the extent that this amounts to a reminder that the decision remains one for the court and so cannot be devolved to experts, it is unproblematic; however, if it amounts to a view that the 'common sense' of the court is worth more weight than the expert view, it is problematic because of the danger of misunderstanding the capabilities of the defendant. In addition, given that the suggestion from Smith LJ was that the court should defer until the end of the prosecution case, it is a view that will be based on the reactions of the defendant sitting in the court during the evidence, not while giving evidence or doing something when the focus of the court will be on him or her. It must be open to question whether this will give the court any real ability to make an assessment that could counter the view of the experts.

10.23 A related point in the reasoning of Smith LJ was that the assessment had to be made in the light of the impact of any special arrangements put in place: the point made was that a pre-trial expert report could not assess this. There are two obvious responses to that: first, experts might well be or could be made aware of the special arrangements and include a view on those in their reports; second, the experts could be called to give oral evidence to the court, which could indicate how it planned to approach the case and ask the experts for their view on whether that would accommodate the needs of the defendant.

10.24 The third point was that the court might want to consider whether there was a case to answer, which might allow the defendant to be acquitted. But there is no reason why this cannot be done during the assessment of the facts – ie, there is nothing arising from the statutory power to impose a hospital order or guardianship order without a conviction that prevents the court from finding no case to answer and so acquitting the defendant while it is considering the question of whether the defendant committed the act or omission charged.

10.25 Accordingly, reviewing the arguments that were not canvassed in the *Crown Prosecution Service v P* case, there are good grounds to query whether there is any power to proceed without determining that the defendant is able to participate and also to suggest that, if there is a power to proceed in the situation, the reasons given for deferring the assessment until the end of the prosecution case are not particularly compelling. The contrary conclusion would not mean that a court is not able to proceed to consider the case: it is just that it will have to indicate at the outset that it has ceased to consider criminal guilt and so will be considering only whether the act has been committed.

Arguments against proceeding when no order to be made

10.26 The next part of the holding of the High Court in *Crown Prosecution Service v P* was that if a finding was made that the defendant could not participate and so the criminal trial should go no further, consideration should be given in most cases to determining whether the defendant had committed the act or omission charged.[21] This would apply if there was a possibility of a hospital order.[22] However, it was also noted that the fact-finding process might have other benefits, principally alerting the authorities to the possible need for care proceedings,[23] and perhaps simplifying such proceedings, even though findings made by the youth court would not be binding in that context. Accordingly, Smith LJ's conclusion was that: 'proceedings should be stayed as an abuse of process before fact-finding only if no useful purpose at all could be served by finding the facts'.[24]

21 This was not on the basis that PCC(S)A 2000 s11(1) and MHA 1983 s37(3) provided the complete framework, which was part of the holding in *R (P) v Barking Magistrates' Court*: Smith LJ commented that these provisions 'do not provide the solution to all the problems which may confront a youth court before which a young person of doubtful capacity appears' (paragraph 16). Her Ladyship noted at paragraph 48 that there were issues of doli incapax, fitness to stand trial and fitness to participate. The first point has been discussed in note 19 above; whether fitness to stand trial and fitness to participate are two questions is discussed below.

22 [2007] EWHC 946 (Admin), [2007] MHLR 262 paras 56–57.

23 It is recorded in the judgment that care proceedings were commenced: [2007] EWHC 946 (Admin), [2007] MHLR 262 para 22.

24 [2007] EWHC 946 (Admin), [2007] MHLR 262 para 56.

10.27 The suggestion, in other words, is that a trial court has the jurisdiction to make factual findings not in order to determine the propriety of a disposal within its express powers, but to assist a more general process of securing the welfare of the defendant. The reasoning of the court rests on the purpose of the youth justice system, as set out in the CDA 1998, namely the prevention of offending by children and young people.[25] Smith LJ noted that the framework was designed to provide for steps short of criminal proceedings if possible: as such proceedings would occur only when alternative steps were not appropriate, the obligation imposed on anyone who laid an information to commence criminal proceedings against a child to inform the local authority – as set in section 5 of the Children and Young Persons Act (CYPA) 1969[26] – provided the opportunity to consider diversion from the criminal justice system for children who had problems that might be dealt with by way of a care or supervision order under the Children Act 1989.[27] She then added that the facts relevant to the issue of diversion included the capacity of the defendant to participate in the trial.[28]

10.28 There can be little complaint as to these basic propositions, namely the importance of seeking alternatives to the criminal justice system and the need for the prosecution to consider questions of fitness to participate. However, it is difficult to see how they lead to the conclusion that a criminal court should, on finding that the defendant cannot participate in a trial, proceed to make factual findings unless there is a prospect of it making a disposal within its powers at the end of that process. An informal finding of facts to encourage care proceedings is not an obvious function of a criminal court, does not seem readily to arise from the need to encourage diversion (which by definition has not occurred), and is not necessary to secure the objective of ensuring that appropriate care proceedings are instituted as the local authority can take the necessary steps to involve the family

25 [2007] EWHC 946 (Admin), [2007] MHLR 262 paras 31 and 32, citing CDA 1998 ss37–39 (which put duties on local authorities to secure that aim, including by setting up youth offending teams).

26 [2007] EWHC 946 (Admin), [2007] MHLR 262 para 34.

27 [2007] EWHC 946 (Admin), [2007] MHLR 262 para 35. The most obvious purpose of the notification is to allow the local authority to carry out its duty under CYPA 1969 s9 of providing pre-sentence and other reports to the court.

28 [2007] EWHC 946 (Admin), [2007] MHLR 262 para 36. Or, on Her Ladyship's tentative view, the question of doli incapax. See chapter 5 for further guidance on the question of diversion.

courts if the alleged conduct demonstrates the grounds for a care or supervision order.[29]

Fact-finding in the adult magistrates' court

10.29 Despite the existence contrary arguments, *Crown Prosecution Service v P* sets out the law. A question arising is whether conclusions relating to the youth court context apply also to the adult magistrates' court. The statutory powers in MHA 1983 s37 and PCC(S)A 2000 s11 are applicable, as are the questions of whether there is jurisdiction or good reason to proceed to determine whether the act has been committed before assessing fitness to participate. While the view that the court should find the facts unless there are good reasons not to seems to arise in large part from the statutory regime that governs the youth justice system, there are some analogous provisions in an adult context. The mental health authorities have a range of actions available to them short of detention in hospital – for example, the provision of community care services such as accommodation under section 21 of the National Assistance Act 1948, described in chapter 2. The need for such provision may be more acute if the person has committed the act of a crime.

10.30 Accordingly, if there is value in youth courts engaging in problem-solving actions which fall unless the general rubric of therapeutic jurisprudence, it could be suggested that there is similar value in the adult court so acting. Of course, the fact that an adult court is unlikely to see such action as a legitimate use of its time and to find that it has no power to render a narrative verdict may suggest that a youth court has no such power in the absence of language that expressly gives it such a function. That in turn means that the courts are empowered only to consider whether the needs of the defendant require a formal order under the MHA 1983; otherwise, a conclusion that a defendant cannot participate should lead to a stay.

10.31 Two cases that seem consistent with this approach are *R (Singh) v Stratford Magistrates' Court*[30] and *R (Blouet) v Bath and Wansdyke Magistrates' Court.*[31] The former involved the question of insanity and

29 Children Act 1989 s31: a likelihood of harm to the child from unreasonable parenting or the child being out of control.

30 [2007] EWHC 1582 (Admin), [2007] MHLR 274.

31 [2009] EWCH 759 (Admin), [2009] MHLR 71.

is discussed in more detail in chapter 13; for present purposes, the important point is that at paragraph 35, Hughes LJ noted that:

> ... in all cases where an order under s37(3) is a possibility, the court should first determine the fact-finding exercise ... If the court is not satisfied that the act/omission was done/made, an unqualified acquittal must follow, whatever the anxieties may be about the accused's state of health.

10.32 This supports the point noted above that an acquittal can follow in the fact-finding process and limits the fact-finding process to one where there might be an order at the end of it. In the context of a potential insanity defence, Hughes LJ went on to note at paragraph 40 that having a trial on that issue was the only thing that could happen if the criteria for MHA 1983 s37 were not made out.

10.33 In *Blouet*, there were conflicting medical reports as to whether the defendant could participate, but the one that said he could stand trial was older and had been prepared without an interview. When the case was adjourned for trial, this was challenged on the basis that it should have been adjourned for a fact-finding hearing. The Divisional Court indicated that the proper process was to obtain up-to-date medical evidence and to proceed under MHA 1983 s37(3) if there was a prospect of an order being made. This again is consistent with the view that the proper approach to the fact-finding process is to follow it if there is a prospect that the power to make an order without a conviction might result.

Test for participation

10.34 Another question that arises in this context is what is the test to apply as to when the power to consider making an order without a conviction arises. In other words, is the precondition only that an order might be made, which might include situations in which a defendant is able to stand trial (because an order under section 37 might be made on conviction as well)? That would be inconsistent with the right to have a determination of guilt or innocence if a fair trial is possible, and so there must also be a reason to deprive someone of that right.

10.35 In the Crown Court, it seems clear that there are two questions: the first is that arising under *Pritchard* in relation to the statutory question of fitness to stand trial; the second is that of fitness to participate. In the magistrates' court, given the non-applicability of the CP(I)A 1964, that should leave the question of fitness to participate by reason of the common law and the article 6 of the European Convention on Human Rights (ECHR) obligations to ensure that there is a fair trial. However, in *Crown Prosecution Service v P*, Smith LJ noted at paragraph 48 that the youth court had to consider two or perhaps three issues of capacity, namely 'fitness to plead, ability to take part in a trial and possibly doli incapax'. She then commented that the former was the *Pritchard* test, which was not a prerequisite to being doli incapax. She then noted that the test for ability to participate[32] was not the same at the *Pritchard* test: and that one of the elements for this was having a sufficient understanding of the difference between right and wrong, and so might incorporate the doli incapax test.

10.36 There are two points to note about this. First, the authorities on which Smith LJ relied were cases arising in the context of youths, in relation to the which the need to understand the difference between right and wrong has been a central part of the proof of guilt for some time (although now removed by section 34 of the CDA 1998). Second, it may be that the particular concern of Smith LJ in making these comments was the overlap between fitness to participate and the additional question of doli incapax (her view being that the defence had not been removed). As such, it may be that she was not meaning to suggest that magistrates should consider both the *Pritchard* test and the wider fitness to participate test.

10.37 Certainly, other authorities proceed on the basis that the only question that arises in the context of a summary trial is that of fitness to participate. For example, in *R (TP) v West London Youth Court*,[33] the Divisional Court referred only to the question of the need to be able to participate effectively in the trial; similarly, in *R (Wotton) v Central Devon Magistrates' Court*,[34] which involved an elderly man with deteriorating cognitive functions, the High Court referred to the test of fitness to participate in the trial.

10.38 As is discussed in chapter 9, the common law has a long-standing rule that a defendant must be able to participate in the trial. But the case of *V and T v UK*[35] indicates that in relation to problems caused by mental disorder, it was thought that the statutory question of fitness to stand trial was the only relevant test. This involved a case

32 For which Her Ladyship cited *SC v UK* (2005) 40 EHRR 10, App No 60958/00 and *R (TP) v West London Youth Court* [2005] EWHC 2583 (Admin), [2006] MHLR 40.

33 [2005] EWHC 2583 (Admin), [2006] MHLR 40.

34 [2003] EWHC 146 Admin.

35 (2000) 30 EHRR 121, [1999] Prison LR 189.

arising in the Crown Court context: no application had been made to stay proceedings on the basis of the inability of the defendants to participate and they did not contend that they met the statutory test. However, a government contention that domestic remedies had not been exhausted because counsel for V and T had not raised a point about their inability to participate was dismissed because the government had not been able to point to a case in which proceedings had been stayed on those grounds if the formal fitness to stand trial was not met.[36]

10.39 There had been limited cases involving this issue in the summary context. It is to be noted that in one of these, *R v Lincoln Justices ex p O'Connor*,[37] the High Court held that magistrates could make a hospital order without a finding of guilt even if the defendant was unable to consent to summary trial because he or she lacked capacity; but part of the reasoning was that it was preferable to requiring a committal for trial to the Crown Court where the formal fitness for trial process would be carried out. In other words, there was no hint that there was any other process in the Crown Court and the use of MHA 1983 s37(3) power (which at the relevant time arose under MHA 1959 s60(2)) was seen as an alternative to this.

10.40 The ruling of the European Court of Human Rights (ECtHR) in *V and T v UK* made it clear that it was necessary to have a wider test, namely fitness to participate in the trial process. A summary of what is involved was given in *R (TP) v West London Youth Court*,[38] in which Scott Baker LJ noted of a youth court trial that:

> ... the minimum requirements for a fair trial for the claimant were:
> i) he had to understand what he is said to have done wrong;
> ii) the court had to be satisfied that the claimant when he had done wrong by act or omission had the means of knowing that was wrong;
> iii) he had to understand what, if any, defences were available to him;
> iv) he had to have a reasonable opportunity to make relevant representations if he wished;
> v) he had to have the opportunity to consider what representations he wished to make once he had understood the issues involved.

36 *V v UK* (2000) 30 EHRR 121, [1999] Prison LR 189 paras 59–61.
37 [1983] 1 WLR 335.
38 [2005] EWHC 2583 (Admin), [2006] MHLR 40 at para 7.

10.41 He added that this meant that the defendant:

> ... had therefore to be able to give proper instructions and to participate by way of providing answers to questions and suggesting questions to his lawyers in the circumstances of the trial as they arose.

10.42 Naturally, this involves an ongoing assessment, and so the assessment of the ability to provide instructions cannot be assessed against prosecution written disclosure; the possibility of deviation from witness statements and supplemental oral evidence means that the defendant needs to be able to follow the oral evidence as well. As has been noted above, the case-law suggests that the issue should not be determined until the end of the prosecution case, though there are arguments that point the other way.

Assisting participation – the practice directions

10.43 The response to the ruling in *V and T v UK* – which effectively identified a gap in the application of the common law – was something that could be accommodated through the common law, and so a practice direction was issued. This initially covered young persons in the Crown Court but has gradually been extended and the current iteration of the practice direction regime, in the form of paragraph III.30 of the Consolidated Practice Direction, covers all vulnerable defendants, whether in summary trial or trial on indictment. The discussion of these matters in paras 9.217–9.236, including the potential to raise an abuse of process argument, is also applicable to the summary process: indeed, most of the case-law arises from that context.

Fairness in the fact-finding process

10.44 If a court is in the mode of determining whether the defendant committed the act or omission rather than guilt of the offence, it seems clear that the case-law arising under the fitness to stand trial process and discussed in chapter 9 to the effect that this is not a criminal trial will apply with equal force. This in turn means that the provisions of ECHR article 6(3) do not apply. Purporting to follow *R v H*[39] in the summary trial process in *Crown Prosecution Service v P*,[40] Smith LJ commented that:

39 [2003] UKHL 1, [2003] MHLR 209.

40 [2007] EWHC 946 (Admin), [2007] MHLR 262.

> It is clear since *R v H* that the fact that a child cannot take an effective part in the fact-finding process does not infringe his Article 6 rights. That process is part of the protective jurisdiction contemplated by the MHA 1983 and the child's Article 6 rights are not even engaged.[41]

10.45 This comment goes too far unless it is restricted to the criminal aspects of article 6, which is what was in play in *R v H* in the House of Lords. The case proceeded on the basis that *if* the civil aspect of article 6 applied, it was satisfied.[42] It is clear from ECtHR case-law that the right to liberty is a civil right and so if it is lost, then article 6 does apply.[43] Moreover, it is established that there must be participation in any such process. This is addressed in detail in chapter 9, at paras 9.115–9.161, relying on *Shtukaturov v Russia,*[44] which related to removal of capacity, and established case-law to the effect that anything leading to a loss of liberty for the purposes of ECHR article 5(4) requires broadly the same protection as applies under article 6.

10.46 What must also be remembered in this context is that the question of whether the act was committed may often turn on evidence from the defendant. As is discussed in chapter 9, it has been determined that questions of mens rea are not relevant: this rests on *R v Antoine*[45] and cases that followed it. But it was recognised in *Antoine* that there might be instances in which what the defendant perceived would be very relevant to whether the act was a criminal one: for example, an accident or the use of self-defence based on a mistake of fact. It was noted in *Antoine* that:

> If there is objective evidence which raises the issue of mistake or accident or self-defence, then the jury should not find that the defendant did the 'act' unless it is satisfied beyond reasonable doubt on all the evidence that the prosecution has negatived that defence ... I consider that the same approach is to be taken if defence counsel wishes to advance the defence that the defendant, in law, did not do the 'act'

41 [2007] EWHC 946 (Admin), [2007] MHLR 262 at para 55.

42 [2007] EWHC 946 (Admin), [2007] MHLR 262 para 13: the argument of the prosecution was that any loss of liberty was justified by reason of ECHR article 5(1)(e). The appellant's case was limited to the criminal aspects of article 6: paragraph 14.

43 See *Aerts v Belgium* (1998) 29 EHRR 50 para 59; in *R (PD) v West Midlands and North Mental Health Review Tribunal* [2003] EWHC 2469 (Admin), [2004] MHLR 25, [2004] EWCA Civ 311, [2004] MHLR 174, the question arising was whether the medical member of the tribunal appeared biased, and the Administrative Court and then the Court of Appeal discussed this in the context of article 6 applying to the detention of a patient.

44 [2008] MHLR 238.

45 [2001] 1 AC 340, [2000] MHLR 28.

because his action was involuntary, as when a man kicks out and strikes another in the course of an uncontrollable fit brought about by a medical condition. In such a case there would have to be evidence that the defendant suffered from the condition.[46]

10.47 This concession does not cover all the situations in which it cannot be fair to find facts if a defendant cannot participate. For example, many criminal scenarios may turn on a simple conflict of evidence and whether the defendant or prosecution witness or witnesses are telling the truth: if the credibility of the defendant is central, the inability of the defendant to participate in the fact-finding process may render it unfair.

Resuming the trial process or varying the decision

10.48 In the Crown Court setting, there is a limited process for remittal for trial if someone has been found unfit to stand trial under the statutory process. If the trial has been stayed as an abuse of process because the defendant is unable at that particular time to participate, there may be different considerations. In short, while a normal abuse of process application will be based on a factual scenario that means that it can never be fair to hold a trial (such as delay or egregious conduct by prosecuting authorities, which will not improve), it may be that this does not apply in the case of an alleged offender who cannot go through a full trial because of what may be a temporary inability to participate.

10.49 At the same time, if the end result is that a hospital order is made without a conviction, and the defendant becomes able to participate, the value and hence the public interest of reviving the prosecution in a summary context must be open to question. So the possibility of resuming the trial process may be a matter of theoretical interest.

10.50 It may be different, however, if the case has been fixed for consideration of whether a defendant committed the act but the court forms the view that in fact there is no limitation on the defendant being able to participate in a trial. What is apparent from the caselaw is that there must be adequate notice given of the fact that the court will be conducting a trial rather than just an assessment as to whether to make an order under MHA 1983 s37(3). In *R (Varma) v Redbridge Magistrates' Court*,[47] a summary conviction was quashed

46 [2001] 1 AC 340, [2000] MHLR 28 per Lord Hutton at paras 57–58.
47 [2009] EWHC 836 (Admin), [2009] MHLR 173.

when magistrates had decided to proceed to a trial when a matter had been set down for a finding of the facts because of evidence that the defendant was not fit to stand trial. Directions had been given for updated medical evidence to be obtained prior to the hearing, and that further evidence was to the effect that the defendant was fit to stand trial. However, no effective notice had been given by the prosecution that it would apply to have a full trial; and the magistrates had failed to deal with the fact that there were conflicting medical views and that a court needed to determine which one was correct. The conviction therefore occurred in the context of a question mark over fitness to participate. What is interesting, however, is the remedy that was granted in the case, namely that the matter should be remitted for the section 37(3) process to be followed. That should not be the case if the defendant is not unable to participate, and so the proper course should be to assess the defendant's ability at the outset: this is another reason why, as has been argued above, the court should make a determination of fitness to participate at the outset and then, depending on the outcome of that, move ahead with a trial or, if appropriate, a process limited to finding whether the act was committed with a view to a disposal under the MHA 1983.

10.51 Another potential scenario is for a change in the condition of the defendant such that a hospital order is no longer appropriate. In *Bartram v Southend Magistrates' Court,*[48] a man was found to have committed the act and an interim hospital order was erroneously made (as that is limited to a conviction): the reports at the end of that process, however, indicated that a hospital order was not needed. In that situation, the magistrates' court ordered that the criminal trial resume. This was challenged successfully on the basis that the court should have considered a guardianship order as well.

10.52 A further scenario is that a hospital order has been made but cannot be put into practice: this was the position in *R v Thames Magistrates' Court ex p Ramadan,*[49] where the hospital specified should not have been because there was no bed available: one of the procedural prerequisites for the making of a hospital order is evidence that a bed is available and the court had erred in not ensuring that this precondition was met. The Divisional Court held that the magistrates could exercise the power under section 142 of the Magistrates' Courts Act 1980 to reopen and vary the order, which involved reading the reference in section 142 to an 'offender' to include someone ordered to

48 [2004] EWHC 2691 (Admin), [2004] MHLR 319.

49 [1999] 1 CrAppR 386.

be detained under MHA 1983 s37(3). The focus of the court was on whether section 142 applied. What passed unremarked was that Mr Ramadan was, on the variation of the section 37(3) order, remanded into custody for trial.

10.53 In *Bartram*, it was suggested that reopening the matter would also be proper in the case of a change in the mental disorder such that no section 37 order could be made, or on his recovery it was apparent from instructions that he had a good defence and might be acquitted.[50] This rests on a wide discretion to reopen the issue if that would be in the interests of justice.

10.54 One issue remaining from *Ramadan* is the remand into custody for trial. It is difficult to see the full picture as to why this happened. The indication in the report is that the hospital declined to accept Mr Ramadan without a restriction order attached: but the power of the magistrates to commit for the Crown Court to impose a restriction order, contained in MHA 1983 s43, arises only if there has been a conviction.[51] However, if the defendant cannot participate, there can be no conviction.

10.55 This may reveal a gap in the available options: while there is a power in relation to indictable-only offences to send a defendant to the Crown Court if he is not fit to appear at the magistrates' court but is represented, it is not the same in relation to either-way offences. Until committal proceedings are abolished, if and when relevant parts of the Criminal Justice Act 2003 to that effect come into force, they seem to require active participation from the accused or consent for proceedings in his or her absence. The mode of trial provisions of sections 19 and following of the Magistrates' Courts Act 1980 involve the court, if finding the case more suitable for summary trial, putting the defendant to an election involving whether he or she consents to summary trial. If the matter is to be committed to the Crown Court, Magistrates' Courts Act 1980 s4(4) refers to evidence in front of examining justices in the absence of an ill accused who is represented, but only if there is consent. These requirements for consent imply capacity, which may well be absent if the defendant is not fit to participate. See also Magistrates' Courts Act 1980 s11(2A), which prevents proceedings in the absence of the accused in a summary trial if there is an acceptable reason for a failure to attend, which

50 See [2004] EWHC 2691 (Admin), [2004] MHLR 319 para 19.

51 In *R v Horseferry Road Magistrates' Court ex p K* [1997] QB 23, it was noted that there can be no use of MHA 1983 s43 if there has been a finding of not guilty by reason of insanity, which was said to be a lacuna in the regime.

would be provided by mental disorder keeping the defendant away from court.

10.56 This gap may be understandable, of course: namely, if the matter is indictable only, all procedural matters, including fitness to stand trial, should be for the Crown Court: but in the case of lesser offences, there is always the option of dealing with the matter under MHA 1983 s37(3), which is clearly available in the case of an either-way offence and even after the defendant has elected trial in the Crown Court (as in *Kazmarek*, discussed above). That does, however, leave the gap noted above that a finding under MHA 1983 s37(3) in relation to an either way offence prevents a committal under MHA 1983 s43 for a restriction order.

CHAPTER 11

Evidence and mental disorder

Introduction

11.1 There are three distinct areas of evidence in relation to which mental disorder may be relevant. First is the admission into evidence of statements made by a person that are inculpatory, namely confessions: this is regulated by sections 76 and 78 of the Police and Criminal Evidence Act 1984 (PACE).[1] The second area is the failure to make a statement, whether as part of the response to the investigation of an allegation or as part of the trial process: the historic right to silence was removed by the Criminal Justice and Public Order Act (CJPOA) 1994, but questions of mental disorder may be relevant to whether it is possible to draw an adverse inference from silence. The third area is the weight to be attached to any evidence that is admitted; there is also provision in PACE relevant to this, namely section 77, but also relevant is the general duty of the judge to consider whether there is a case to answer.

The admissibility of evidence

The statutory framework

11.2 As is described in chapter 4, PACE sets out a framework for detention in a police station and treatment there, and by section 39 places a duty on the custody officer to ensure that there is treatment in accordance with the rights set out in PACE and also the Codes of Practice issued under section 66 of PACE.[2] The most relevant of the Codes is Code C, Annex E of which sets out a useful summary of the relevant provisions relating to the treatment of people who are mentally disordered or otherwise vulnerable on account of a mental health condition.

11.3 The Codes can be taken into account in relation to any question before a court, by reason of PACE s67(11), which will include the admissibility of evidence. Two sections of PACE are of particular relevance, namely the duty to exclude confessions in certain circumstances under section 76 and the power to exclude any evidence on the basis of unfairness in section 78.

11.4 PACE s76 requires the exclusion of a confession obtained in circumstances where it might be unreliable as a result of anything said

1 The common law still exists but it is unlikely to add anything to the questions raised in PACE ss76 and 78.

2 Available at www.homeoffice.gov.uk/police/powers/pace-codes/.

or done or where it has been obtained by oppression. The relevant language is as follows:

> (2) If, in any proceedings where the prosecution proposes to give in evidence a confession made by an accused person, it is represented to the court that the confession was or may have been obtained –
> (a) by oppression of the person who made it; or
> (b) in consequence of anything said or done which was likely, in the circumstances existing at the time, to render unreliable any confession which might be made by him in consequence thereof,
>
> the court shall not allow the confession to be given in evidence against him except in so far as the prosecution proves to the court beyond reasonable doubt that the confession (notwithstanding that it may be true) was not obtained as aforesaid.

11.5 In other words, an allegation that a confession might have been obtained in the precluded circumstances imposes on the prosecution an obligation to disprove the allegation to the criminal standard. This can be done by either proving that the precluded circumstances did not apply or that they did not have the causative effect alleged. A 'confession' is defined in PACE s82 as a statement in words or otherwise that is wholly or partly adverse; and 'oppression' is defined in section 76(8) to include anything that would breach article 3 of the European Convention on Human Rights (ECHR), the prohibition on torture or inhuman or degrading treatment, and any use of or threat of violence.

11.6 The reason for the duty on the court to exclude in this circumstance is the importance of ensuring that there is nothing to be gained from action that amounts to oppression or renders any statement made unreliable.[3] It is to be noted that this duty of exclusion arises even if the confession turns out to be true: the question is whether the accused was likely to say anything in light of the circumstances, such that it might well be unreliable, or that oppression was used.

11.7 This duty to exclude is to be read in conjunction with the power to exclude unfair evidence that arises under PACE s78. This provides:

> (1) In any proceedings the court may refuse to allow evidence on which the prosecution proposes to rely to be given if it appears to the court that, having regard to all the circumstances, including

3 See *R v Mushtaq* [2005] UKHL 25, [2005] 1 WLR 1513. This case also confirmed that the judge makes an initial analysis on a voir dire, which may lead to the evidence not being put in front of the jury; but that the jury must also consider the question if the judge ruled the evidence admissible because the question is ultimately one of fact and so for the jury.

the circumstances in which the evidence was obtained, the admission of the evidence would have such an adverse effect on the fairness of the proceedings that the court ought not to admit it.[4]

11.8 The grounds for exclusion may often be argued in tandem for various reasons. While section 78 includes all evidence not merely confession evidence, the concern of a defence lawyer under the heading of fairness will be evidence that implicates his or her client and so includes confession evidence. Section 76 will be used if the basis for the challenge is oppression or something that raises concerns about reliability; and section 78 will cover the unfairness of admitting evidence, which may also be made out by conduct that is oppressive or produces an unreliable confession. However, it may not need to go so far as to meet the section 76 test to be within section 78. Further, if the evidence does not come from the defendant, section 78 will be the provision on which to concentrate.

The interplay with mental disorder

11.9 The first issue is the question of what is meant by oppression. The test includes conduct that breaches ECHR article 3. Whether conduct amounts to torture or is inhuman or degrading treatment requires ill-treatment that attains a minimum level of severity. But the assessment of whether the necessary level of severity is met depends on all the circumstances of the case, such as the duration of the treatment, its physical and mental effects and, in some cases, the sex, age and state of health of the victim: see, among many authorities that make this point, *Keenan v UK*.[5] This case involved a breach of article 3 from the failure to prevent a man with mental health difficulties from killing himself in prison. The features that were of particular importance in the court's decision were the lack of appropriate medical notes that indicated that proper care had been taken and the failure

4 PACE s78(2) provides that: 'Nothing in this section shall prejudice any rule of law requiring a court to exclude evidence.' This makes clear that any duty to exclude under PACE s76 is not tempered by a secondary question of fairness. See also PACE s82(3), which indicates that: 'Nothing in this Part of this Act shall prejudice any power of a court to exclude evidence (whether by preventing questions from being put or otherwise) at its discretion.' Having said that, there may be limited grounds for arguing that any of the common law rules as to evidence did more than seeking to secure fairness in the trial process, which is now covered by PACE s78.

5 [2001] Prison LR 180, (2001) 33 EHRR 913.

to call in an appropriately qualified doctor to provide input into Mr Keenan's treatment needs.[6]

11.10 This gives an indication of the importance of having psychiatric expertise involved. It could also be argued that the importance of the various safeguards set out in the Codes of Practice for those who are mentally vulnerable is an indication of the seriousness of failing to look after the interests of those with mental disorder. It has been noted in relation to forced treatment that the position of powerlessness of patients requires that courts take special care in reviewing the conduct of the authorities: see *Herczegfalvy v Austria*.[7] Although this was a very different context, there are a number of points of analogy: it covers someone who is in detention and in relation to whom important decisions are taken by another person in circumstances where a duty to take care is imposed by law (whether the common law duty to protect from self-harm or, if the person is without capacity, the duty to act in accordance with the person's best interests under the Mental Capacity Act 2005). Accordingly, there are proper bases to construct an argument that significant failures to abide by the protective regime of the Code of Practice is something that might meet the test of being degrading or even inhuman and so requiring exclusion.

11.11 For an example of a case supporting the view that mental vulnerability is relevant to whether conduct is oppressive, see *R v Paris, Abdullahi and Miller*.[8] In this case, police officers had harangued a suspect in repeated interviews and eventually he made admissions. The Court of Appeal held that the judge should have excluded the relevant interview because of the conduct of the police (which inexplicably had not been brought to the attention of the judge because he had not been directed to the relevant parts of the interviews): in so ruling, Lord Taylor CJ noted that the tenor and length of the interviews mean that they were 'oppressive and confessions obtained in consequence of them would have been unreliable, even with a suspect of normal mental capacity', before noting that the relevant suspect, Mr Miller, was on the borderline of learning disabled.[9] The implication is clearly that mental vulnerability may be part of the assessment of whether there has been conduct that is oppressive.

6 See [2001] Prison LR 180, (2001) 33 EHRR 913 paras 113–114.

7 (1991) 15 EHRR 437.

8 (1993) 97 CrAppR 99.

9 (1993) 97 CrAppR 99 p105.

11.12 The second ground of exclusion under PACE s76(2) does not require conduct that meets that high standard for being oppressive: any conduct that means a confession is likely to be unreliable also produces a duty to exclude. As noted above, this duty of exclusion arises even if the confession turns out to be true: the question is whether the accused was likely to say anything in the light of the circumstances, such that it might well be unreliable. This is also something that allows account to be taken of the various obligations imposed under PACE and the Codes of Practice: even if the breaches do not amount to oppression, they might meet mean that the alternative part of the exclusion test is met.

11.13 An example of this in practice is the case of *R v Cox*,[10] in which a defendant with a mental impairment (his IQ of 58 putting him well into the lowest percentile) signed notes of interview that were read back to him as he could not read them in which he admitted involvement in two burglaries. The interview had been conducted without an appropriate adult present. However, the trial judge admitted the interviews into evidence because Mr Cox admitted one of the burglaries again in court, and so the judge formed the view that the confessions were likely to be true. In holding that this was an error of law, the Court of Appeal commented that the truth of the confession was not the point: rather it was whether it was likely to be reliable, to which the answer was no because it had been given without the protective mechanism of the appropriate adult being present during the interview. A similar mistake in a similar factual circumstance was made by the trial judge and corrected by the Court of Appeal in *R v Kenny*.[11]

11.14 Another example is *R v Moss*.[12] This involved a defendant who was described in the report as being on the borderline of mental handicap, though no details are given of this. By the time he made confessions to sexual offending with children, he had been in custody for nine days, had been denied access to a solicitor until after he had made admissions in the fifth of nine interviews, but then was allowed only to see a solicitor who had to withdraw because of a conflict of interest, as he represented a co-defendant, and then an articled clerk. Lord Justice Taylor for the Court of Appeal noted that: 'These cases are very much a matter of impression', before confirming that the unanimous impression of the court was that the circumstances were

10 [1991] Crim LR 276.
11 [1994] Crim LR 284.
12 (1990) 91 CrAppR 37.

such that the evidence should not have been allowed into the trial. Unfortunately, it is not clear whether this was on the basis of section 76 or section 78, which underlines the importance of arguing them both in the alternative.[13]

11.15 Other examples of findings that confessions should have been excluded can be found in *R v Everett*[14] and *R v Silcott and others*.[15] In the former, in which the defendant was said to have had a mental age of eight, the Court of Appeal noted that, while the police officers had not been aware of this, the question was what was objectively the case: on the actual facts, the need for an appropriate adult was clear. In the latter case, one of the suspects had obvious learning difficulties but had been denied access to legal advice.

11.16 One thing that follows from *Everett* is that the issue for the court is not whether police officers deliberately failed to carry out their duties. While the precautionary principle in the Codes of Practice means that special care is needed whenever there is a suspicion of mental vulnerability, the statutory language rests on whether the combination of the circumstances and the vulnerability leads to unreliability, not whether there was knowledge of the vulnerability.

11.17 This also applies in the context of PACE s78, as was found in *R v Aspinall*,[16] in which a break-down in communications meant that the interviewing officer was not aware that Mr Aspinall was mentally ill and so should not have been interviewed without an appropriate adult (even though the custody sergeant was aware of that). The interview also proceeded without a solicitor: he had asked for a solicitor but consented to being interviewed without one because he had by then been in detention for over 12 hours. However, his apparent lucidity meant that his mental illness was not apparent and the interview proceeded. The application to exclude the interview relied on section 78 only, the argument being that Mr Aspinall might have given answers designed to secure his early release in the light of his passive nature caused by his personality and mental disorder (that being supported by medical evidence). The Court of Appeal held that the decision of the trial judge to admit the evidence was flawed because it involved the same errors as had been made by the interviewing officer, namely relying on the apparent ability of the defendant to

13 See also *R v Gill*, discussed below: the propositions set out in para 11.19 were, the court noted, the same whether section 76 or 78 was applied.

14 [1988] Crim LR 826.

15 (1991) *Times* 9 December.

16 [1999] MHLR 12, [1999] 2 CrAppR 115.

deal with the situation. The Court of Appeal noted that the significance of the safeguards must be given proper weight, and concluded that the interview should have been excluded as unfair.

11.18 It should be noted, however, that the absence of an appropriate adult, or any other failure to comply with PACE or the Code, will not always mean that evidence should be excluded by reason of PACE s76 or s78. In *R v Gill and others*,[17] the Court of Appeal noted at paragraph 68 that the following propositions applied under section 76:

> (1) When an application is made under section 76 the court does not consider the reliability of the confession which has been made, but a hypothetical question. The court must decide whether, in the circumstances prevailing at the time, there is a likelihood any confession made at that time would be unreliable.
> (2) The words 'anything said or done' are wide enough to include an omission, for example, to interview a suspect without the presence of an appropriate adult, in circumstances where the Code of Conduct requires one to be present.
> (3) It may, in some cases, be material to consider whether a breach of the Code has occurred, but where, as in this case, it was not known to the police at the time, that the intelligence quotient of the applicant placed him in a category which entitled him to the presence of an appropriate adult, it is the consequences of the loss of the protection which the Code intended him to have, not whether there has been a breach, which is relevant.
> (4) The relevant question is whether, having regard to the purpose for which an appropriate adult is required, the absence on this occasion of the protection which such presence would have provided is likely to have rendered any confession made at that time unreliable. In short, would the presence of an appropriate adult have made any difference?

11.19 It was then noted by the court that while the defendant should have had an appropriate adult, the question to be addressed was what was lost by that absence, and on the facts it was held that the judge had been entitled to conclude that nothing different would have happened. That was very much a conclusion on the facts, but the statement of principle at paragraph 72 of the judgment is worth noting:

> It does not follow that the absence of an appropriate adult, in circumstances where one should have been present, will automatically give rise to the exclusion of a confession. Each case must be considered upon its own facts.

(On the facts, it was noted that the same result would apply when PACE s78 was being considered.)

17 [2004] EWCA Crim 3245.

11.20 The statement of principle in *Gill* must be true: but it must equally be true that the extensive range of protections in place for mentally vulnerable suspects means that the starting point is real concern about the reliability of any statement made – hence the obligation of the prosecution to prove to the criminal standard that the admission should not be excluded.[18]

11.21 In addition to the role of the appropriate adult in seeking to protect suspects who are vulnerable, the role of the solicitor may include a duty to intervene if there is misconduct by the police that might lead to a section 76 exclusion application being made in due course. This was part of the decision in *R v Paris, Abdullahi and Miller*,[19] in which there had been a solicitor present during the hectoring of the suspect. The Court of Appeal commented on the importance of the solicitor taking action to intervene if the conduct of the police was inappropriate.[20] This raises the important tactical question of whether it is better to allow the police to engage in conduct that is likely to result in any confession being found inadmissible, given that pointing out to police the error of their ways may lead to a change of tack in which a suspect will then make an admissible confession. In *R v Dunn*,[21] however, the Court of Appeal noted that a judge had been entitled to admit evidence obtained in breach of Code C when a solicitor's representative had been present. Although it is to be noted that the breaches were only as to the failure to record a conversation or allow the defendant to sign a note of it, not features relevant to the need to protect the defendant on account of mental disorder, the presence of a lawyer is a relevant factor as to fairness, which perhaps suggests that intervention is the better approach.

11.22 One potential approach is for a solicitor to intervene and then advise a client to make no further comment in the light of the inappropriate behaviour of the police to date, which has created the danger of unreliable statements by the client. That would give good grounds for arguing that there should be no adverse inference from being silent (on which see below). In this context, it will also be important for police station representatives to have some idea of the research on issues of the reliability of statements that might be made

18 Another example of admissions being admitted in relation to a defendant who had been entitled to an appropriate adult is *R v Law-Thompson* [1997] Crim LR 674, which involved a defendant who had Asperger's syndrome; however, there was a solicitor present in the interview and independent evidence of guilt.

19 (1993) 97 CrAppR 99.

20 (1993) 97 CrAppR 99 p110.

21 (1990) 91 CrAppR 237.

by people who are mentally vulnerable. This research has featured in several cases and knowledge of it may form the basis for advice as to whether or not a suspect should participate in an interview.

The importance of expert evidence

11.23 The significant research as to the reliability of admissions and the circumstances in which an unreliable admission may be made indicates that it does not necessarily involve police misconduct. See, for example, *R v Ward*,[22] in which one of the features on which the Court of Appeal relied in quashing the conviction was evidence that a confession to a terrorist bombing was the consequence of mental disorder. Unfortunately, expert evidence to the effect that the confession was likely to be unreliable was not obtained until after the conviction, even though the defendant had reneged on her confessions by then: the defence approach at trial had been that Ms Ward was clearly a fantasist, but the outcome of the trial and the appeal suggests that this should be reinforced by evidence.[23]

11.24 In *R v Blackburn*,[24] the Court of Appeal, considering a reference from the Criminal Cases Review Commission, was concerned with the question of the admissibility of a confession to attempted murder and attempted buggery. The admission was made initially some three hours after an interview began, and then continued for some time thereafter. The police contended that a written statement was then provided by the accused, who was aged 15 at the time of the interview, was detained in an approved school secure unit and had the house warden present but no solicitor. There was expert evidence of two forms: one was linguistic evidence to the effect that the written statement could not have been entirely the work of the defendant, which cast doubt on the police account of how the statement was produced.

11.25 The other expert evidence was from a psychologist and dealt with the circumstances in which a person vulnerable on account of their age might become compliant and say what they thought was required to please the interrogator. The prosecution had objected to the latter evidence on the basis that it was not something on which the jury

22 [1993] 1 WLR 619, (1993) 96 CrAppR 1.

23 Being fair to the trial team, it should be noted that there was also significant forensic evidence against the defendant which was consistent with her confession: but it was undermined by material the prosecution did not disclose at the time.

24 [2005] EWCA Crim 1349, [2005] 2 CrAppR 440.

needed assistance, but the Court of Appeal ruled that it was likely to be something outside the experience of the jury and so should be admitted.[25] This evidence, together with the circumstances of the admission, satisfied the Court of Appeal that any admission would have been unreliable and so should have been excluded. This case emphasises the importance of investigating whether there is research evidence on the question of the reliability of admissions in light of vulnerability, whether arising from youth or from a form of mental disorder.

11.26 In this respect, see also *R v O'Brien*,[26] in which the Court of Appeal held that expert evidence was admissible in relation not only to recognised mental illness but also any abnormality that might have the potential to make a confession unreliable. The court was keen to place some limit on this, however, and indicated that:

> First, the abnormal disorder must not only be of the type which might render a confession or evidence unreliable, there must also be a very significant deviation from the norm shown. ... Second, there should be a history pre-dating the making of the admissions or the giving of evidence which is not based solely on a history given by the subject, which points to or explains the abnormality or abnormalities.[27]

11.27 The court records that the need for limitations was accepted by all counsel in the case. However, it should be noted that there are questions as to the two limitations imposed. In relation to the first one, if the disorder may be linked with unreliable confessions, why does it have to be a severe version of the disorder: that should go to whether there is unreliability on the facts not the admissibility of evidence if it relates to something on which the jury need expert assistance. As to the second point, while additional corroborative evidence may be of relevance, the question of whether an expert has successfully made a finding based only on an interview or interviews with the defendant is again a matter that goes to weight rather than admissibility (though in practice any expert will seek corroboration to be clear as to the validity of the account from the accused).

25 [2005] EWCA Crim 1349, [2005] 2 CrAppR 440 para 28.

26 [2000] Crim LR 676, transcript of 25 January 2000.

27 [2000] Crim LR 676, transcript of 25 January 2000, page 38.

Warnings to the jury and finding no case to answer

11.28 In addition to the question of the admissibility of evidence, PACE s77 notes the special need for caution before convicting if the case against someone who is 'mentally handicapped' rests 'wholly or substantially' on a confession by him or her and an 'independent person' was not present at the time of the confession. Section 77(1) requires that the judge warn the jury of this special need for caution. In a summary trial, the court has to warn itself of this need: section 77(2); similarly, in the limited circumstances in which a trial on indictment can proceed without a jury, the court has to so direct itself, under section 77(2A). If such a defendant enters a guilty plea, there may also be a duty on the court to assure itself that these provisions have been met, though, naturally, the presence of a legal representative may allow the court to assume that the availability of a line of defence based on section 77 has been canvassed.

11.29 The trial judges in *Cox* and *Moss*, discussed above, had given juries directions in accordance with section 77: but the appeal decisions were to the effect that section 76 was not satisfied. However, the approaches of the judges illustrate the fact that there is an interplay between the sections, namely that if the evidence meets the test for admissibility but there has been a breach of the obligation to have an independent person present, there still may be a reason to doubt the veracity of the admission made if it is without significant corroboration.

11.30 The application of section 77 gives rise to a number of questions:

i) what is a confession,
ii) what is a mental handicap for the purposes of the section,
iii) who is an independent person and
iv) when does the state of the state of the prosecution case require the caution?

11.31 A 'confession' is as defined in PACE s82 as any statement adverse to the suspect. The definition of mental handicap in section 77(3) is 'a state of arrested or incomplete development of mind which includes significant impairment of intelligence and social functioning' and is similar to the definition of learning disability used in the Mental Health Act (MHA) 1983 as amended (which in turn means that it is narrower than the states that amount to mental disorder). It has been noted that it is important for a judge to make a proper finding, based on medical evidence, as to whether a defendant meets the definition of mental handicap: in *R v Ham*,[28] an appeal was allowed when a judge relied on evidence from the interviewing officer and inferences from a police surgeon, and his view that the defendant appeared to be streetwise and confident in interview.

11.32 It is to be noted that the fact that the section uses the phrase 'independent person' rather than 'appropriate adult'. There is limited assistance in the statute as the definition in that section 77(3) excludes police officers or employees from the definition. Guidance on who counts as an independent person can be found in the case of *R v Bailey*,[29] in which it was noted that the independence has to be from the person to whom the confession is made:[30] that meant that confessions made to a friend would be within section 77. The court also suggested the purpose of the requirement:

> The independent person is required because the mentally handicapped person may have difficulty in recalling accurately what he or she said, and independent evidence as to the emotional and mental state of the mentally handicapped person may be desirable. Further, an independent person may, if the mentally handicapped person is or becomes obviously unfit to speak, give sensible advice to the mentally handicapped person.[31]

11.33 This suggests that, as is the case with an appropriate adult, the independent person has to be someone with the ability to provide empathy and advice. However, the use of the different terminology does have one effect: the prohibition on a solicitor being an appropriate adult[32] does not mean that he or she cannot be an independent person.[33]

11.34 As to the state of the prosecution case that requires the warning, namely one that is 'wholly or substantially' reliant on the confession, it has been suggested in *R v Campbell*[34] that this can be rephrased as 'whether the case for the Crown is substantially less strong without the confession made in the absence of the appropriate adult'.[35] This is perhaps a much wider phrase that is implicit in the statute. The test was not met on the facts of the case, because there was identification evidence.

28 (1997) 36 BMLR 169.

29 [1995] 2 CrAppR 262.

30 [1995] 2 CrAppR 262 p282.

31 [1995] 2 CrAppR 262 p282.

32 Code C Guidance Note 1F; it is implicit in the fact that the appropriate adult has roles such as determining whether to seek a solicitor.

33 See *R v Lewis (Martin)* [1996] Crim LR 260.

34 [1995] 1 CrAppR 522.

35 [1995] 1 CrAppR 522 p535.

11.35 It was also suggested in *Campbell* that the judge should give an explanation of why the warning is given, though without any specific form of words being mandatory save the statutory phrase 'special need for caution'. The need for an explanation was found to be implicit in the fact that the judge must explain that the need for this arises from the mental handicap and the absence of the independent person. The Court of Appeal commented:

> What then should the judge do? It seems to us that he should explain why a confession from a mentally handicapped person may be unreliable. This is best done by reference to the former guidance note at 13(b) of Code C (now Code C, Annex E, guidance note E3). This note indicates that persons who are mentally disordered or mentally handicapped may, without wishing to do so, provide information which is unreliable, misleading or self-incriminating. The explanation should be tailored to the particular evidence in the case, for example if there is evidence that the accused is particularly suggestible, prone to acquiesce, comply, or give in to pressure. The judge should go on to explain that the function of the appropriate adult is designed to minimise the risk of the accused giving unreliable information by seeing that the interview is conducted properly and fairly and facilitating, if need be, communication between the police and suspect.[36]

11.36 However, it has also been held that if the judge gives the jury appropriate reminders about the importance of taking into account a defendant's intellectual difficulties, this may substitute for giving a formal warning under PACE s77: see *R v Qayyum*.[37] However, it is to be noted that the reason for the defect in the case seems to have been that no one involved in the trial raised it, and so the focus of the Court of Appeal was whether the defect made a difference rather than on whether the section does not impose an obligation. It clearly does impose a duty to explain, particularly as that includes a reason to explain why the warning is given: so *Qayyum* does not diminish this duty, rather it makes the point that an error may not be fatal to the

36 See also *Bailey* [1995] 2 CrAppR 262 at p283: 'Third, the judge should explain why a confession from a mentally handicapped person may be unreliable, tailoring that explanation to the evidence in the particular case and bearing in mind the words of paragraph C: E3 of Annex E of Code C of the Codes of Practice for the Detention, Treatment, and Questioning of Persons by Police Officers. Finally, the judge should explain that the function of the appropriate adult is designed to minimise the risk of the accused giving unreliable information by seeing that the interview is conducted properly and fairly and perhaps assisting in the communication between the confessor and the person receiving the confession.'

37 [2006] EWCA Crim 1127, [2007] Crim LR 160.

safety of the conviction. Indeed, in *R v Lamont*,[38] the Court of Appeal quashed a conviction because of a failure to give a section 77 warning, which was said to be an essential part of a fair summing-up.

11.37 One final point on the content of the explanation arises from *Bailey*. It will often be the case that the defendant has reneged on the confession by the time of the trial: indeed, the whole process under section 77 is predicated on the danger of false confessions and so it is to be expected that there will be situations in which the confession is withdrawn. Part of the reason for quashing the conviction was that the judge had not given the section 77 warning but also had not included an adequate reminder as to what was the appellant's case as to the confession and why it was not accurate and truthful.[39]

11.38 The need for caution in such a situation may also mean that a judge has to intervene to take the case from the jury. There is a general duty to do that in accordance with the case of *Galbraith*.[40] The basic proposition is that if there is no evidence on which a properly directed jury could convict, then the case should be withdrawn from the jury at the end of the prosecution case (or the magistrates should direct an acquittal). The relevant case is *R v Mackenzie*:[41] the appellant here – who had been convicted of two manslaughters on the basis of diminished responsibility and also two counts of aggravated arson – had confessed to numerous homicides. The prosecution did not accept the truth of the majority of these confessions but their case on the two manslaughters of which he was convicted rested entirely on his confessions. Mr Mackenzie had an IQ in the range of 73–76 and so was categorised as having a mental handicap; he also had a personality disorder that made him seek attention and had spent some time in custody on the charges because his inability to distinguish between fact and fiction meant that he was unfit to stand trial. In quashing the manslaughter convictions, the Court of Appeal noted that *Galbraith* meant that a judge should withdraw the case where:

> (1) the prosecution case depended wholly upon confessions; (2) the defendant suffered from a significant degree of mental handicap; and (3) the confessions were unconvincing to a point where a jury properly directed could not convict upon them.[42]

38 [1989] Crim LR 813.

39 [1995] 2 CrAppR 262 at p275.

40 (1981) 73 CrAppR 124.

41 Fully reported as *R v Mackenzie* (1993) 96 CrAppR 98; also reported as *R v McKenzie (Practice Note)* [1993] 1 WLR 453.

42 (1993) 96 CrAppR 98 per Lord Taylor CJ at p108.

11.39 The court went on to give examples of what might amount to an unconvincing confession, noting that the test would be met if it lacks 'the incriminating details to be expected of a guilty and willing confessor' or is 'inconsistent with other evidence' or just that it is 'otherwise inherently improbable'. On the facts, the prosecution argued that the confessions that were found believable by the prosecution and accepted by the jury were reliable because they revealed that Mr Mackenzie had knowledge of the killings that could only have been acquired by the killer. But the court found that there was no significant special knowledge that could not have been obtained by the defendant from the police or from reports as to events, and there were errors and striking omissions in the confessions which together with the false confessions to other killings meant that the convictions were unsafe. However, the arson convictions were upheld because there was independent evidence relating to them (and pleas of guilty in relation to a second indictment involving sexual offending were not challenged).

11.40 It seems that Mr Mackenzie met the definition of mental handicap, though he also had a personality disorder. Given that the principle in *Galbraith* is of general application, there is no reason why it should be limited to situations of mental handicap: if, for example, the case turns on confessions made in the sort of circumstances found in *Mackenzie* by a person with an attention-seeking element to a personality disorder but who is not mentally handicapped within the meaning given in section 77, it would seem equally unsafe to leave that the jury.

Adverse inferences

11.41 The right to silence is a historical tradition but has largely been removed in England and Wales by Part III of the CJPOA 1994, which includes in sections 34–39 regulation on the circumstances in which inferences can be drawn from silence (though the inference cannot be the sole basis for a decision to find a case to answer or to convict: see CJPOA 1994 s38(3)). Of course, strictly speaking, there remains a right to silence in the sense that no compulsion to speak arises:[43]

43 Contrast the situation in *Saunders v UK* (1997) 23 EHRR 313, where a failure to provide information to government inspectors was enforceable by contempt proceedings.

but it is no longer a free choice, because the exercise of the right may have consequences, and so it is now a conditional right.

11.42 In short, section 34 provides that if a defendant fails to mention in interview or on being charged a fact that is relied on in his or her defence at the trial, the court may draw 'such inferences ... as appear proper' if the fact was one that the accused 'could reasonably have been expected to mention', this assessment to be made 'in the circumstances existing at the time'. The question of reasonableness allows account to be taken of mental disorder. In the important case of *R v Argent*,[44] Lord Bingham CJ noted that:

> The courts should not construe the expression 'in the circumstances' restrictively: matters such as time of day, the defendant's age, experience, mental capacity, state of health, sobriety, tiredness, knowledge, personality and legal advice are all part of the relevant circumstances; and those are only examples of things which may be relevant. When reference is made to 'the accused' attention is directed not to some hypothetical, reasonable accused of ordinary phlegm and fortitude but to the actual accused with such qualities, apprehensions, knowledge and advice as he is shown to have had at the time.[45]

11.43 Accordingly, mental disorder and vulnerability – which after all is a central feature that calls for special treatment in the police station – is going to be relevant in two ways. It is a relevant circumstance that the accused has mental disorder; and the question is not what a reasonable person would do but a question of whether a person with the characteristics of the defendant would reveal the relevant fact, and those characteristics can include the consequences of mental disorder. See also *R v Howell*,[46] in which the Court of Appeal noted at paragraph 24 that:

> The kind of circumstance which may most likely justify silence will be such matters as the suspect's condition (ill-health, in particular mental disability; confusion; intoxication; shock, and so forth – of course we are not laying down an authoritative list), or his inability genuinely to recollect events without reference to documents which are not to hand, or communication with other persons who may be able to assist his recollection. There must always be soundly based objective reasons for silence, sufficiently cogent and telling to weigh in the balance against the clear public interest in an account being given by the suspect to the police.

11.44 When a police station representative forms a view that a mentally vulnerable defendant is not in a position to provide a reliable account,

44 [1997] 2 CrAppR 27.

45 [1997] 2 CrAppR 27 p33.

46 [2003] EWCA Crim 1, [2005] 1 CrAppR 1.

that might be a good reason to advise that no comments should be provided.

11.45 There are also requirements to account for objects, substances, marks or presence in a place by reason of CJPOA 1994 ss36 and 37, failing which inferences can be drawn. The argument based on mental disorder for not drawing an inference under these sections is different from that applicable under section 34 as there is no question of whether the failure was reasonable: the inference can only be drawn if the suspect is given an explanation of the consequences of the failure, and it is possible that a defendant's mental disorder may be such that he or she cannot understand the warning given.

11.46 The right to remain silent in a trial is also removed by the CJPOA 1994, section 35 of which provides that the failure to give evidence at trial is a matter from which adverse inferences can be drawn. However, section 35(1) excludes this possibility if 'the physical or mental condition of the accused makes it undesirable for him to give evidence'. The case-law on this has suggested that it may be unusual for the test to be met. In *R v Friend*,[47] the defendant was aged 15 but assessed as having a mental age of less than ten and so meeting the definition of a mental handicap: but the trial judge ruled that the undesirability test was not met and so an adverse inference was proper, relying on the fact that the court could accommodate any difficulties he might face. The Court of Appeal upheld this ruling, and took as its starting point that the question would arise only in rare cases because the unfitness to plead test would cover the majority of cases of mental disorder.[48] There is no basis given for this view, but the court followed up with the legitimate point that a defendant who was fit to stand trial would be able to follow proceedings.[49] The court did not seek to define what was meant by it being undesirable for the defendant to give evidence, but gave the following examples: 'A physical condition might include a risk of an epileptic attack; a mental condition, latent schizophrenia where the experience of giving evidence might trigger a florid state'.[50]

11.47 In *R (Director of Public Prosecutions) v Kavanagh*,[51] Stanley Burnton J set out the general proposition that the adverse inference will only be proper if there is strength in the prosecution case that requires

47 [1997] 1 WLR 1433.
48 [1997] 1 WLR 1433 at 1440.
49 [1997] 1 WLR 1433 at 1441.
50 [1997] 1 WLR 1433 at 1442.
51 [2005] EWHC 820 (Admin), [2006] Crim LR 370.

an answer (which will allow the legitimate inference that the failure to provide that must mean that there is no realistic answer available).[52] He also considered the effect of section 35(1), noting first that it was not engaged merely because the defendant had a mental health condition, since it had to be that it had to be one that made giving evidence undesirable; and second that many difficulties went to the weight of the evidence not the desirability or otherwise of silence.[53] There was also a requirement, he noted at paragraph 17, for proper evidence of the mental condition that made it undesirable to give evidence: this would not be made out by a comment from a legal representative or, on the facts, the mother of the defendant that he had been suffering from depression that required medication (which related to the past and so could not provide much assistance).

11.48 The approach in *Kavanagh* was endorsed by the Court of Appeal in *R v Tabbakh*.[54] This involved a charge of preparing for terrorist attacks, to which the defence was that fireworks were being made. The defendant had post-traumatic stress disorder and a history of self-harming behaviour, all of which was properly validated by expert evidence. There were three risks which the defence argued made it undesirable for him to give evidence such that no adverse inference direction should be given: the first was that he might not be able to keep control of himself in the witness box as a result of the disorder; the second was of incomplete recall of evidence; and the third was that the stress of giving evidence might result in an increased risk of self-harm. However, the judge ruled that any concerns in relation to the defendant's performance in the witness box could be taken into account by the jury; and as to the risk of self-harm, he accepted that there was such a risk but held that it was not of the most serious kind and that it had to be balanced against the importance of hearing from the defendant on the facts of the case (ie in contrast to a case in which the defendant could not add much). The overall conclusion was that it was not undesirable for Mr Tabbakh to give evidence. The Court of Appeal accepted the approach in *Kavanagh* that CJPOA 1994 s35 introduced a wide question for the judge, which could not be satisfied by mere difficulty: rather it had to rise to the level of making it undesirable.

52 [2005] EWHC 820 (Admin), [2006] Crim LR 370 para 19. This proposition arises from *R v Cowan* [1996] QB 373, in which a submission that an adverse inference should only be possible in exceptional circumstances was rejected as contrary to the plain language of the section.

53 [2005] EWHC 820 (Admin), [2006] Crim LR 370 para 18.

54 [2009] EWCA Crim 464.

11.49 It is open to question as to how far this can go. One reading of *Tabbakh* is that there is a balance to be drawn, weighing the risk of self-harm against the value of the evidence that might be given. This might suggest that significant risk of serious self-harm could be justified if the account by the defendant could be of crucial importance. However, a point must arise at which the risk of self-harm would amount to conduct that might be classified as inhuman and degrading and so prohibited by ECHR article 3. Indeed, the example given in *Friend* of causing a floridly psychotic episode would seem to meet this test, which suggests that it has set the bar too high.

11.50 The simple fact is that the question in the statute is whether it is undesirable for the accused to give evidence, which must be a much lower test than a consequence that would breach article 3. Indeed, the approach of the trial judge in *Tabbakh* is almost one that suggests the key question is whether evidence from the defendant is desirable whereas the question more naturally arising from the language of CJPOA 1994 s35 is whether the process of giving evidence would have an undesirable effect on the mental disorder of the accused (or it would present an unedifying spectacle in the court room). While the indication in the case-law that it is proper for the court to take into account the steps that can be taken to assist the defendant, it seems open to argument that the courts have indicated a test much higher than undesirability.

11.51 It is to be noted that the adverse inference directions cannot be applicable if the question before the court arises under the fitness to stand trial process of determining whether the act was committed, because the guilt of the defendant is not in issue in those proceedings and so the adverse inference provisions of the CJPOA 1994 do not apply.

11.52 A final point to note is that the fact that an application may be made should be raised, and supporting evidence supplied, in a manner that complies with the duty arising under Part 1 of the Criminal Procedure Rules 2011[55] to assist the court in securing the overriding objective of dealing with cases justly. Such evidence may require case management steps to be taken. In *R v Ensor*,[56] which related to medical evidence as to why a defendant could not give evidence and so should not face an adverse inference direction, late notice of the relevant evidence was held to justify a refusal to admit it.

55 SI No 1709.

56 [2009] EWCA Crim 2519, [2010] MHLR 4.

Witnesses and mental disorder

11.53 The focus of this text is mentally disordered accused, but it is to be noted that there is a comprehensive regime of special measures set out in the Youth Justice and Criminal Evidence Act (YJCEA) 1999 for vulnerable witnesses. The grounds for being classified as vulnerable, set out in section 16 of the YJCEA 1999, include those whose evidence is likely to be diminished in quality by reason of mental disorder as defined in the MHA 1983, or a significant impairment of intelligence and social functioning. The special measures available for such witnesses, set out in sections 23–30, are the use of screens to prevent the accused seeing the witness (and vice versa), the use of the live link, the giving of evidence in private, the removal of wigs or gowns by the advocate and judge, the use of video-recorded evidence in chief, the use of intermediaries and devices to aid the communication of questions and answers to and by a witness.

11.54 In addition, as has been described in relation to defendants who are unable to participate, steps can be taken at common law to modify normal procedures to take into account the effect of mental disorder. This relates to the question of the fairness of a trial, and so courts must accommodate the needs of a witness – whether appearing for the prosecution or the defence – in order to ensure that the trial is fair for the parties.

11.55 The interests of witnesses may also be reflected in relation to disclosure. An example of this in the context of mental disorder is *R (TB) v Stafford Crown Court.*[57] The complainant in relation to allegations of a sexual nature had been in receipt of psychiatric treatment; the defendant sought an order that her medical records be disclosed, which the judge ordered in part. However, the process of determining whether there should be disclosure had not involved TB in any meaningful way. The High Court on a judicial review application held that the confidential nature of the medical records meant that they were protected by ECHR article 8 and so there was a need for a lawful procedure to determine whether disclosure was proportionate; it noted that this interest belonged to the patient rather than the hospital which was asked to make disclosure, which might not have the same position as the witness. Further, the obligation to deal with cases justly, set in the Criminal Procedure Rules, together with the obligation of the court as a public body to secure ECHR rights, meant that the court was required to follow a process reflecting the

57 [2006] EWHC 1645, [2007] MHLR 115.

interests of the witness. The Criminal Procedure Rules at the time, the 2005 Rules,[58] made no express provision to allow the witness to make representations, but as it was not prohibited the High Court held that the lower court should improvise. Rule 28(5) of the 2010 Rules contains express provision for service of the relevant summons to produce a confidential document (or give evidence about confidential information) to be served on the person whose confidentiality is affected.

11.56 Public law and anti-discrimination or equality law may also be in play in relation to the treatment of witnesses, including victims. In particular, while it may be possible for a prosecutor to form a view that a witness who has a mental disorder is less credible, there must be a proper basis for the opinion. This is made plain by the case of *R (FB) v Director of Public Prosecutions*.[59] FB, who had a history of psychotic illness, was the victim of a serious assault; he identified his assailant (whom he knew), but the defendant indicated to the police that FB had left the scene and was attacked by someone unknown. A medical report on FB's mental condition was obtained by the prosecution, and the conclusion expressed was his illness *might* affect his perception and recollection of events so as to make his account unreliable, but it was not suggested either that he was incapable of giving reliable evidence or that there could be any suggestion that the identification of the defendant might have involved delusions. When the prosecution offered no evidence on the day of the trial on the basis that they could not say that FB was a reliable witness, the decision was challenged by judicial review: the High Court granted a declaration that the decision was irrational because either the medical report had been misread as suggesting that FB was incapable of being a reliable witness, or the decision-making process involved unfounded stereotyping that mental illness made him not credible.

11.57 The High Court also found that the action of the prosecution amounted to a failure to offer protection to someone who had been ill-treated, which would lead to FB feeling abandoned and not protected by the law, and so breached ECHR article 3 and justified an award of damages of £8,000. There was also a challenge based on the Disability Discrimination Act 1995 as amended. Section 21B of the Act made it unlawful for a public authority to discriminate against a disabled person in carrying out its functions: but decisions in relation

58 SI 2005 No 384.

59 [2009] EWHC 106 (Admin), [2009] MHLR 61, [2009] 1 CrAppR 38.

to bringing or not bringing or ending criminal prosecutions were exempted from this duty (by reason of section 21C(4)) in order to allow for situations in which a prosecutor formed the view that a disabled person was less reliable as a result of his or her disability.[60] However, there was also a general duty imposed on public bodies by section 49A of the 1995 Act to have due regard to the need to promote equality, which might involve taking addition steps to assist a person with disabilities, and which would include equality of protection by the criminal law. Toulson LJ noted:[61]

> 62. I can see that the general duty may have significance at the investigative stage and when considering how a witness may be assisted to give evidence to the court (which might in some cases include the use of special measures under Part II of the Youth Justice and Criminal Evidence Act 1999). If, for example, a witness suffers from a disorder which would make their speech unintelligible to a jury, it may nevertheless be possible with suitable expert assistance for that impediment to be overcome. That may in turn have a bearing on the application of the evidential test under the Code. But when it comes to assessing the substantive merits of the evidence which the prosecution is able to place before the court, measured against the likely defence or defences, it is difficult to see what scope section 49A has or should have to affect the decision. If the substantive quality of the evidence is such as to pass the merits test, the prosecution should go ahead (subject to the public interest test). If not, there should not be a prosecution. In other words, in that situation section 49A adds nothing to the ordinary position under public law principles.

11.58 His final conclusion was that the failure to continue with the prosecution indicated that there was also a breach of section 49A, but that there was no real benefit arising from this analysis in light of the conclusion on the public law irrationality challenge that had succeeded. What is important to note is that, whether arising under general public law principles of being found in disability discrimination law – and note that the Equality Act 2010, which restates and in some

60 Toulson LJ indicated at paragraph 58 that the rationale for section 21C was obvious: 'The consequence of applying s21B to decisions not to prosecute could be that if the prosecutor reasonably considered that a complainant's evidence was unreliable, as a result of a disability, a decision not to prosecute in such circumstances might amount to unlawful discrimination'. This is actually less than obvious: it would be differential treatment, but it would not be unlawful if it was justified. It is perhaps unfortunate that section 21C was enacted so as to provide exemptions as opposed to having suitable language providing for justification for differential treatment if it had an objective basis.

61 *R (FB) v Director of Public Prosecutions* [2009] EWHC 106 (Admin) para 62.

ways extends the Disability Discrimination Act 1995, is gradually being brought into effect – there are principles arising outside the usual sources for the criminal law that may affect how witnesses with mental disability are treated.

PART IV

Substantive criminal law and mental disorder

CHAPTER 12

Mental disorder amounting to insanity at the time of the offence – Crown Court

continued

Introduction

12.1 The traditional approach to criminal responsibility is based on the motif of choice: so in *R v Kennedy*,[1] the House of Lords commented at paragraph 14:

> The criminal law generally assumes the existence of free will. ... generally speaking, informed adults of sound mind are treated as autonomous beings able to make their own decisions how they will act ...

12.2 The corollary of this is that where defendants are not exercising choice, it may not be appropriate to categorise them as criminal. An extreme version of this is the idea of automatism, namely when someone is acting in an involuntary fashion and not exercising a choice. It may also be that the choice is limited to only one realistic course of action, which is what happens in a situation of duress or necessity; self-defence may also be seen as an example of this, as the choice that is exercised is one that is a justified choice (provided that it meets the requirements of self-defence in terms of the reasonableness of the action).

12.3 In addition to having control over the act or omission that constitutes the crime, another central principle is that there must be some sort of moral fault in the form of a guilty mind (though crimes of strict liability are a significant part of the criminal regime).

12.4 It is clear that issues of mental disorder may impact upon these questions of liability. It is possible that a mental disorder may control a defendant's actions to the extent that he or she is not acting voluntarily, or acting without a mens rea (or without a mens rea that represents a free choice). It is also possible that a mental disorder plays a part but does not control the actions of the offender; in other words, it may have a disinhibiting effect which diminishes responsibility and so culpability. It is also obviously possible that a person who happens to be mentally disordered may make a choice to commit a crime and may do so after forming the appropriate mens rea.

12.5 One of the central issues that arises in the context of mental disorder and its impact on criminal responsibility is the insanity defence (discussion of which includes the interface with the circumstances in which a person is considered to be an automaton for reasons of mental disorder). In homicide cases alone, the presence of a mental

1 [2008] 1 AC 269. The context there was whether a person who provided drugs to someone who then took the drugs and died was responsible for the death: the House of Lords determined that the free choice of the drug taker meant that the drug supplier was not responsible for the death.

disorder may lead to a verdict of guilty of manslaughter rather than murder if there is a mental disorder that reduces responsibility; infanticide involves a diminished mens rea and also special actus reus circumstances. There may also be an impact on the other partial defence in a homicide context, namely provocation (or loss of control). In non-homicide cases, if the mental disorder does not allow a verdict of not guilty on the basis of insanity, it may be relevant to the formation of mens rea; but it may also be relevant to whether a defence such as self-defence or duress arises. Otherwise, the defendant will be guilty but any reduced culpability from mental disorder will be reflected in sentence.

12.6 This chapter considers the insanity verdict in the Crown Court, in which the common law regime has been replaced in part by statute; the next chapter considers the position in the magistrates' court, where there is no specific statutory regime that deals with the question of insanity, though a regime applicable to mentally-disordered defendants in general may be relevant. The diminished responsibility and infanticide provisions and the other circumstances in which mental disorder may have an impact on responsibility are discussed subsequently. The impact of mental disorder on sentence is covered in the next part of the book.

The history of the special verdict

12.7 The starting point for an understanding of the substantive test for the insanity defence is *M'Naghten's Case*,[2] which is discussed in the next section. But it is also important to realise that the insanity provisions are an unusual defence in that, in the Crown Court, they do not lead to an acquittal, but rather to a special verdict of not guilty by reason of insanity (which was for some considerable time a verdict of guilty but insane). This is a long-standing statutory modification of the perceived inadequacies of the common law.

12.8 The response to the acquittal of James Hadfield on a charge of attempting to assassinate the King[3] was the introduction of the Criminal Lunatics Act (CLA) 1800, under which a finding of insanity led to automatic detention for an indefinite period of time. This may have been in part to clarify the situation or make regular the approach that had been adopted in Hadfield's case: in *R v Horseferry*

2 (1843) 10 Clarke & Finnelly 200, 8 ER 718.
3 (1800) 27 How St Tr 765.

Road Magistrates' Court ex p K,[4] the Divisional Court recorded that: 'The defendant was acquitted but nevertheless confined. There was doubt as to the lawfulness of that detention and accordingly Parliament enacted the Criminal Lunatics Act 1800'. The long title of the Act set its purpose, namely 'an Act for the safe Custody of Insane Persons charged with Offences'. The preamble added that 'it may be dangerous to permit' individuals acquitted of serious offences by reason of insanity 'to go at large'. The method adopted was to require the jury to return, rather than a verdict of acquittal, a specific finding of insanity at the time of the commission of the offence: CLA 1800 s1. The consequence, also set out in section 1, was that the court was required to order that the defendant 'be kept in strict custody, in such place and in such manner as to the court shall seem fit, until His Majesty's pleasure shall be known'.

12.9 The CLA 1800 applied to 'treason, murder or felony'; the Insane Prisoners Act 1840 extended the special verdict to misdemeanours. Section 3 of this Act noted the expediency of the same approach and so extended the special verdict and the strict custody consequence to jury verdicts in relation to misdemeanours as well.

12.10 An important change was made by the Trial of Lunatics Act (TLA) 1883, which applies to all indictments and 'informations':[5] the reference to insanity at the time of committing the offence was changed to a reference to the person charged being insane at the time of doing the act or making the omission charged. The current language of TLA 1883 s2(1) is as follows:

> Where in any indictment or information any act or omission is charged against any person as an offence, and it is given in evidence on the trial of such person for that offence that he was insane, so as not to be responsible, according to law, for his actions at the time when the act was done or omission made, then, if it appears to the jury before whom such person is tried that he did the act or made the omission charged, but was insane as aforesaid at the time when he did or made the same, the jury shall return a special verdict that the accused is not guilty by reason of insanity.

12.11 The reference to 'the act' being done (or the omission being made) seems to have been intended to make clear that the concern was with

4 [1997] QB 23.

5 In *R v Horseferry Road Magistrates' Court ex p K* [1997] QB 23 the Divisional Court held that this language was not suited to cover trials in the magistrates' court; and that the reference to an 'information' is to the process that used to exist of laying an information in the High Court to commence a criminal prosecution on indictment. See chapter 13.

the actus reus only, not the mens rea as well; the latter is implicit in the reference to the offence, and may cause confusion in suggesting that the verdict requires that the offender have the mens rea for the offence as well, which may frustrate the purpose behind the special verdict process. Also changed by the TLA 1883 was that the special verdict became 'guilty but insane'; section 1 of the Criminal Procedure (Insanity) Act (CP(I)A) 1964 changed the terminology to 'not guilty by reason of insanity'.

12.12 It is to be noted that the statutory language requires a jury verdict. Accordingly, a judge cannot accept a plea of not guilty by reason of insanity,[6] since the jury must decide the matter. This applies even if the prosecution and defence agree that the only proper verdict is one of insanity. In such a case, the judge can no doubt give directions as to the only proper verdict.[7]

12.13 The verdict of the jury is based on the absence of responsibility for the act or omission. Its effect was initially a duty on the court to detain the defendant for public protection reasons. Since 1991, the courts have a limited choice as to disposal, which is discussed below. However, it is worth noting that the verdict is also treated as a conviction for various purposes. For example, the protective orders arising under the Sexual Offences Act (SOA) 2003 can be issued on the basis of a finding of not guilty by reason of insanity; equally, the violent offender order provisions of the Criminal Justice and Immigration Act 2008 apply to people found not guilty by reason of insanity, though depending on the order made.[8] It is worth noting, however, that the Rehabilitation of Offenders Act (ROA) 1974 does not apply,[9] presumably meaning that a finding is felt to be an acquittal for those purposes.

6 *R v Maidstone Crown Court ex p LB Harrow* [2000] QB 719, [1999] MHLR 84.

7 See *R v Kemp* [1957] 1 QB 399, discussed below, in which it is recorded that the judge made a ruling of law that the only proper defence was one of insanity and the verdict was returned by the jury without them retiring. In *R v Sullivan* [1984] AC 156, also discussed below, Lord Diplock stated at page 171 that if the evidence was very strong, such that a properly directed jury should accept it, 'It would be the duty of the judge to direct the jury that if they did accept that evidence the law required them to bring in a special verdict and none other'.

8 This is discussed further below.

9 ROA 1974 s1(4) states that: 'references to a conviction, however expressed, include references ... (b) to any finding (*other than a finding linked with a finding of insanity*) in any criminal proceedings ... that a person has committed an offence or done the act or made the omission charged' (emphasis added).

The test for insanity – the M'Naghten rules

12.14 The TLA 1883 notes that it governs the situation when the defendant is found to be 'insane, so as not to be responsible, according to law, for his actions'.[10] As such, it leaves it to the common law to determine the test for what amounts to insanity.

M'Naghten's Case

12.15 The judicial formulation as to the substantive test applicable looks first to *M'Naghten's Case* and what have become known as the M'Naghten rules. The traditionally accepted factual scenario is that the accused mistakenly assassinated the Private Secretary to the Prime Minister in the belief that he was attacking the latter, and at a time when he was deluded. Shortly before, there had been another acquittal on grounds of insanity in a high profile case, namely the treason trial of *R v Oxford*,[11] which related to an attempted assassination of Queen Victoria. In the light of concerns about these acquittals, the House of Lords asked the judges of the common law a series of questions as to what the law governing insanity was. *M'Naghten's Case* was not an appeal nor a judgment following an adversarial hearing. Despite this, it has become established as the common law test for insanity.

The questions and answers in M'Naghten's Case

12.16 The questions and answers given by Lord Chief Justice Tyndal are as follows:

1) 'What is the law respecting alleged crimes committed by persons afflicted with insane delusion in respect of one or more particular subjects or persons: as, for instance, where at the time of the commission of the alleged crime the accused knew he was acting contrary to law, but did the act complained of with a view, under the influence of insane delusion, of redressing or revenging some supposed grievance or injury, or of producing some supposed public benefit?'

   Answer: '... assuming that your Lordships' inquiries are confined to those persons who, labour under such partial delusions only, and are not in other respects insane, we are of opinion that, notwithstanding the party accused did the act complained of with

10 TLA 1883 s2.

11 (1840) 4 State Trials (New Series) 498.

a view, under the influence of insane delusion, of redressing or revenging some supposed grievance or injury, or of producing some public benefit, he is nevertheless punishable according to the nature of the crime committed, if he knew at the time of committing such crime that he was acting contrary to law; by which expression we understand your Lordships to mean the law of the land.'

2) 'What are the proper questions to be submitted to the jury, where a person alleged to be afflicted with insane delusion respecting one or more particular subjects or persons, is charged with the commission of a crime (murder, for example), and insanity is set up as a defence?'

3) 'In what terms ought the question to be left to the jury as to the prisoner's state of mind at the time when the act was committed?'

   Answer: '... the jurors ought to be told in all cases that every man is to be presumed to be sane, and to possess a sufficient degree of reason to be responsible for his crimes, until the contrary be proved to their satisfaction; and that to establish a defence on the ground of insanity, it must be clearly proved that, at the time of the committing of the act, the party accused was labouring under such a defect of reason, from disease of the mind, as not to know the nature and quality of the act he was doing; or, if he did know it, that he did not know he was doing what was wrong. The mode of putting the latter part of the question to the jury on these occasions has generally been, whether the accused at the time of doing the act knew the difference between, right and wrong: which mode, though rarely; if ever, leading to any mistake with the jury, is not, as we conceive, so accurate when put generally and in the abstract, as when put with reference to the party's knowledge of right and wrong in respect to the very act with which he is charged. If the question were to be put as to the knowledge of the accused solely and exclusively with reference to the law of the land, it might tend to confound the jury, by inducing them to believe that an actual knowledge of the law of the land was essential in order to lead to a conviction; whereas the law is administered upon the principle that every one must be taken conclusively to know it, without proof that he does know it. If the accused was conscious that the act was one which he ought not to do, and if that act was at the same time contrary to the law of the land, he is punishable; and the usual course therefore has been to leave the question to the jury, whether the party accused had a sufficient degree of reason to know that he was doing an act that was wrong: and this course we think is correct, accompanied with such observations and explanations as the circumstances of each particular case may require.'

4) 'If a person under an insane delusion as to existing facts, commits an offence in consequence thereof, is he thereby excused?'

   Answer: '... the answer must of course depend on the nature of the delusion: but, making the same assumption as we did before, namely, that he labours under such partial delusion only, and is not in other respects insane, we think he must be considered in the same situation as to responsibility as if the facts with respect to which the delusion exists were real. For example, if under the influence of his delusion he supposes another man to be in the act of attempting to take away his life, and he kills that man, as he supposes, in self-defence, he would be exempt from punishment. If his delusion was that the deceased had inflicted a serious injury to his character and fortune, and he killed him in revenge for such supposed injury, he would be liable to punishment.'

5) 'Can a medical man conversant with the disease of insanity, who never saw the prisoner previously to the trial, but who was present during the whole trial and the examination of all the witnesses, be asked his opinion as to the state of the prisoner's mind at the time of the commission of the alleged crime, or his opinion whether the prisoner was conscious at the time of doing the act that he was acting contrary to. law, or whether he was labouring under any and what delusion at the time?'

   Answer: '... the medical man, under the circumstances supposed, cannot in strictness be asked his opinion in the terms above stated, because each of those questions involves the determination of the truth of the facts deposed to, which it is for the jury to decide, and the questions are not mere questions upon a matter of science, in which case such evidence is admissible. But where the facts are admitted or not disputed, and the question becomes substantially one of science only, it may be convenient to allow the question to be put in that general form, though the same cannot be insisted on as a matter of right.'

Continuing validity

12.17 Although the medical understanding of mental disorder has changed significantly in the period since early Victorian times, the continuing validity of the M'Naghten rules has been confirmed. In

Bratty v Attorney-General for Northern Ireland,[12] which concerned the distinction between automatism that leads to a verdict of not guilty and circumstances that lead to a special verdict, the language of the judgment of the House of Lords follows the terminology of the M'Naghten rules. And in *R v Sullivan*,[13] Lord Diplock recorded that 'The M'Naghten Rules have been used as a comprehensive definition for this purpose by the courts for the last 140 years'. He added that the language of the rules was not particularly apt in its application to the factual situation before the House, which was the impact of epilepsy: but the rules were then applied to those facts.

12.18 In the more recent case of *R v Johnson*,[14] Latham LJ for the Court of Appeal commented at paragraph 14 that:

> It is to be remembered that the whole basis of what are described as the M'Naghten Rules in the answers given by the judges to a series of questions from the House of Lords which they dealt with without, it would appear, any argument by counsel. It has always been recognised that the M'Naghten Rules, accordingly, are rules which have to be approached with some caution ...

and went on at paragraph 24 to indicate that:

> There is room for reconsideration of rules and, in particular, rules which have their genesis in the early years of the 19th century. But it does not seem to us that that debate is a debate which can properly take place before us at this level in this case.[15]

12.19 The court then encouraged counsel to invite it to certify a point of law of general public importance, the precursor of an appeal to the House of Lords. The House, however, refused permission to appeal on 7 November 2007.[16] Accordingly, until there is that further review, which would now have to be by the Supreme Court, the M'Naghten Rules will be the starting point. The most important part of the

12 [1963] AC 386.

13 [1984] AC 156.

14 [2007] EWCA Crim 1978, [2007] MHLR 310.

15 The courts of Jersey have rejected the use of the M'Naghten rules as inconsistent with modern medical knowledge: see *Attorney-General v Prior* [2001] JLR 146. Other common law jurisdictions may have wider provisions – as, for example, the law of St Lucia, as discussed in *Phillip and John v R* [2007] UKPC 31, [2009] MHLR 352, in which the M'Naghten rules are supplemented by a test that the defendant acted under a delusion that meant he or she was unfit for punishment. The Privy Council noted that the M'Naghten test had been criticised almost from the time it was passed.

16 See House of Lords Journal 241 (session 2007–08), pp10–12 at p12, Judicial Business (available at www.publications.parliament.uk/pa/ld200708/ldjournal/241/002.htm#1).

answers is that given in response to questions two and three, but the others are worth noting.

Issues that arise in applying the substantive test

12.20 The application of the substantive test in the answer to the second and third questions means that the special verdict will be returned if the jury is satisfied as to various matters, namely:

1) the presumption of sanity has been displaced;
2) the inquiry is into the state of mind of the defendant at the time the relevant act was committed or omission was made;
3) there has to be a disease of the mind;
4) this disease has to cause a defect of reason so as to cause either:
   a) a lack of knowledge of the nature and quality of the act; or
   b) a lack of knowledge that the act was wrong.

The third and fourth parts of the test, and the main issues to which that has given rise, are discussed first.

The need for a disease of the mind: sane and insane automatism

Voluntariness

12.21 The requirement that there be a 'disease of the mind' has resulted in significant case-law. This phrase may have reflected the understanding of the judges at the time of *M'Naghten's Case* as to what psychiatry involved. The modern view that psychiatric illness is rooted in biological imbalances in or damage to areas of the brain was not understood to any great extent in early Victorian times.[17] Of course, the phrase represents a legal concept and so developments in medical understanding have to be adapted to that concept.

12.22 In order to understand the case-law, it is necessary to consider the question of voluntariness and automatism. Rarely a live issue in practice, responsibility for criminality rests on the assumption that a

17 See, generally, Edward Shorter, *A history of psychiatry*, Wiley, 1997. Shorter describes the current era as the Second Biological Psychiatry; what he calls the First Biological Psychiatry – 'nineteenth century alienists attempted to enlist the neurosciences' to provide a scientific basis for psychiatry – is described as coming to a dead end with the theory that mental illness was inherited and degenerated over generations, which fed the eugenics movements of the late 1800s and early 1900: see chapter 3 of the book.

defendant acts voluntarily, making a choice that merits punishment. So reflex actions or instances where a defendant is not in control of his or her actions do not give rise to criminal liability: see *Hill v Baxter*.[18] In this case stated appeal relating to driving through a stop sign that led to charges of dangerous driving and failing to obey a traffic sign, Lord Goddard CJ noted that there was no question of mens rea because the offences were strict liability. That did not mean that a defendant who was involved in the relevant act would always be convicted, because an acquittal could follow if the driver was not in control of his or her actions:

> ... there may be cases where the circumstances are such that the accused could not really be said to be driving at all. Suppose he had a stroke or an epileptic fit, both instances of what may properly be called acts of God; he might well be in the driver's seat even with his hands on the wheel, but in such a state of unconsciousness that he could not be said to be driving. A blow from a stone or an attack by a swarm of bees I think introduces some conception akin to novus actus interveniens.[19]

12.23 He added that 'a defence of automatism is, in effect, saying that the accused did not know or appreciate the nature and quality of his actions it is getting very near a defence of insanity'. Comments about the distinction between examples of lack of voluntariness that amount to automatism and those that amount to insanity were made in a concurring judgment by Devlin J, who noted policy reasons for treating insane automatism differently:

> For the purposes of the criminal law there are two categories of mental irresponsibility, one where the disorder is due to disease and the other where it is not. The distinction is not an arbitrary one. If disease is not the cause, if there is some temporary loss of consciousness arising accidentally, it is reasonable to hope that it will not be repeated and that it is safe to let an acquitted man go entirely free. But if disease is present, the same thing may happen again, and therefore, since 1800, the law has provided that persons acquitted on this ground should be subject to restraint.[20]

12.24 Voluntariness is presumed, and so the defendant has to lay a proper evidential foundation. This was emphasised by the Court of Appeal in *Attorney-General's Reference (No 2 of 1992)*,[21] which followed an acquittal on charges of causing death by reckless driving on the

18 [1958] 1 QB 277.
19 [1958] 1 QB 277 p283.
20 [1958] 1 QB 277 pp285–286.
21 [1994] QB 91.

basis of evidence that a driver had entered an automaton state as a result of the repetitive visual stimuli experienced during motorway driving (a condition described as 'driving without awareness' by the psychologist). The judge had ruled that the prosecution had to disprove to the criminal standard that this affected his driving, and the defendant was acquitted. However, the Court of Appeal held that the evidence could not establish automatism because the condition described amounted to one in which the defendant retained the ability to stay in lane and from which he could be aroused by a suitable stimulus: as such, it was a case of reduced control rather than no control, the latter, ie a complete loss of voluntary control, being necessary for automatism.[22] Once an evidential basis is made out, however, the prosecution has to prove voluntariness to the criminal standard.

Diseases of the brain and 'disease of the mind'

12.25 The Court of Appeal having reflected on the possibility of automatism in *Hill v Baxter*, in the almost contemporaneous case of *R v Kemp*,[23] Devlin J gave a further relevant ruling as a trial judge. The accused was charged with causing grievous bodily harm to his wife inflicted during a temporary lapse of consciousness caused by a physical condition, arteriosclerosis or hardening of the arteries. The question was whether this was a disease of the mind so as to give rise to a question of insanity. The position of Mr Kemp was that there was a defect of reason (and so something was wrong with his mind) and that he did not know the nature and quality of the act he was doing; this further part of the insanity test is discussed below. But he also argued that the defect did not arise from a disease of the mind and so his lack of voluntariness and hence responsibility should lead to an acquittal.[24] The medical evidence was that the early stages of arteriosclerosis, such as affected Mr Kemp, could cause temporary problems of automatism: in due course it would lead to a degeneration of the brain cells and cause ongoing psychiatric problems that would amount to a disease of the brain and so a disease of the mind, but that stage had not been reached.

22 See also *R v Isitt* (1978) 67 CrAppR 44, in which it was determined that a hysterical fugue did not amount to automatism because the defendant remained aware that he was driving (the charge being dangerous driving) even if he was not aware that there were legal or moral limitations on the manner of his driving.

23 [1957] 1 QB 399.

24 [1957] 1 QB 399 pp404–405.

12.26 In his ruling that the medical evidence was of insanity, Devlin J noted that medical and legal definitions might differ. He accepted the medical distinction between diseases of the mind that were caused by physical conditions and those that were regarded as not involving any physical cause (which he noted included schizophrenia and 'many of those diseases which are handled by psychiatrists').[25] But he added that 'The distinction between the two categories is quite irrelevant for the purposes of the law, which is not concerned with the origin of the disease or the cause of it but simply with the mental condition which has brought about the act'. The absence of any physical degeneration as would mean that there was a disease of the brain did not mean that the legal test for insanity was not met. The judge noted that: 'The law is not concerned with the brain but with the mind, in the sense that "mind" is ordinarily used, the mental faculties of reason, memory and understanding'.[26] He added that limiting the inquiry in court to the question of whether the brain was affected would cause considerable problems, since a finding of insanity could not be established if there was no evidence of any impact on the brain; and it would also undermine any question of question of temporary insanity, which the M'Naghten rules did not do.

12.27 The true purpose of the 'disease of the mind' requirement, decided Devlin J, was to limit the situations in which a defect of reason led to a finding of insanity: it would not apply to 'defects of reason caused simply by brutish stupidity without rational power' or an 'untrained mind'.[27] But as hardening of the arteries could affect the mind so as to cause a defect of reasoning, it was covered by the insanity provisions.

12.28 This approach was endorsed by the House of Lords in *Bratty v Attorney-General for Northern Ireland*.[28] The defendant's account was that he killed his victim during an epileptic seizure: he sought to raise three lines of defence to the charge of murder, namely automatism; lack of intent because his impaired mental condition meant that he could not form the intent; or insanity. The first defence would have led to an acquittal, the second to a conviction of manslaughter and the third a verdict of guilty but insane (that being the special verdict at the time). The trial judge's ruling that only the third line of defence

25 [1957] 1 QB 399 pp406–407.
26 [1957] 1 QB 399 p407.
27 [1957] 1 QB 399 p408.
28 [1963] AC 386.

could be raised on the evidence was upheld by the Court of Criminal Appeal in Northern Ireland and the House of Lords.

12.29 The House noted that there were two types of automatism, sane and insane, both of which had to have an evidential foundation; and the only evidential foundation on the facts was based on epilepsy, which gave rise to a defect of reason from a disease of the mind, and so the judge had been right to limit the jury to consideration of insanity or guilt of murder.[29] Viscount Kilmuir LC noted that a jury might find that a defendant did not know what he was doing without there being a disease of the mind, such as in the case of someone who had suffered a blow to the head or was a sleepwalker: but that would require evidence.[30] The ratio of the case rests on the question of the adequacy of evidential foundations of a line of defence, although there is also a recognition of a distinction between automatism and insanity.

12.30 Lord Denning added his own (albeit obiter) comments as to the approach to be adopted (though no other member of the House expressed agreement with him). In particular, he pointed to a public-safety need to categorise any involuntariness arising from a disease of the mind as insanity because an acquittal:

> ... would mean that he would be let at large to do it again. The only proper verdict is one which ensures that the person who suffers from the disease is kept secure in a hospital so as not to be a danger to himself or others. That is, a verdict of guilty but insane.[31]

He added:

> It seems to me that any mental disorder which has manifested itself in violence and is prone to recur is a disease of the mind. At any rate it is the sort of disease for which a person should be detained in hospital rather than be given an unqualified acquittal.[32]

Temporary conditions that do not amount to insanity

12.31 Subsequently, a further gloss was added to cover the question of a temporary condition, which confirms the possibility of automatism that is not insane. An epileptic seizure is a temporary situation, albeit one that might be liable to recur. So it is possible to have a situation of temporary insanity. But there might also be temporary conditions

29 Mr Bratty was convicted of murder.

30 [1963] AC 386 pp403–404.

31 [1963] AC 386 p410.

32 [1963] AC 386 p412.

that do not amount to insanity. In *R v Quick and Paddison,*[33] Mr Quick was charged with assault. His defence relied on a hypoglycaemic coma from the administration of insulin without adequate food (and also, it is recorded, a whisky and quarter of a bottle of rum): the evidence of the effect of hypoglycaemia – an excess of insulin in the bloodstream such that the sugar in the bloodstream cannot cope with it – was that it could give rise to a mental impairment causing uncontrollable aggression. The judge had ruled that this could give rise only to a verdict of not guilty by reason of insanity (as the verdict had by then become) and not a claim of automatism. This ruling caused Mr Quick to plead guilty to avoid the then mandatory sentence of detention during Her Majesty's Pleasure. He had been admitted to hospital on many occasions as a result of hypoglycaemia, even though he was a nurse and presumably aware of the need to maintain his sugar levels.[34]

12.32 However, was it a disease of the mind? The Court of Appeal recorded that Lord Denning's test in *Bratty*, namely a mental disorder manifesting itself in violence and prone to recur, was met. But, noted Lawton LJ, this caused problems:

> The difficulty arises as soon as the question is asked whether he should be detained in a mental hospital. No mental hospital would admit a diabetic merely because he had a low blood sugar reaction; and common sense is affronted by the prospect of a diabetic being sent to such a hospital, when in most cases the disordered mental condition can be rectified quickly by pushing a lump of sugar or a teaspoonful of glucose into the patient's mouth.[35]

12.33 Equally, the reference in *Kemp* to the law having no concern with how a defect of reason came about could not be accepted without more, as it would mean that a state of automatism from a kick to the head or while coming round from anaesthesia,[36] an outcome that had to be avoided as it 'would be regarded with incredulity outside a court'.[37] The solution was to adopt the reasoning of the New Zealand Court of Appeal in *R v Cottle,*[38] namely that not all malfunctioning of the mind arose from a disease of the mind. Accordingly, it was held that:

33 [1973] QB 910.
34 [1973] QB 910 pp915–916.
35 [1973] QB 910 p918.
36 [1973] QB 910 p918.
37 [1973] QB 910 p919.
38 [1958] NZLR 999.

> ... the fundamental concept is of a malfunctioning of the mind caused by disease. A malfunctioning of the mind of transitory effect caused by the application to the body of some external factor such as violence, drugs, including anaesthetics, alcohol and hypnotic influences cannot fairly be said to be due to disease. ... difficult border line cases are likely to arise. When they do, the test suggested by the New Zealand Court of Appeal in *R v Cottle* ... is likely to give the correct result, viz, can this mental condition be fairly regarded as amounting to or producing a defect of reason from disease of the mind?[39]

12.34 There was a caveat, however, which might mean that liability would not be avoided despite automatism: self-induced incapacity would not fit the test, nor would incapacity that could have been reasonably foreseen. The examples given were taking alcohol against medical advice when taking prescribed drugs or failing to have regular meals while taking insulin. The Court of Appeal quashed the verdict of guilty entered on the basis of Mr Quick's plea since it followed the judge's erroneous ruling of law; this was on the basis that he had been entitled to a jury verdict on whether he remained responsible. The case does not stand for the proposition that a hypoglaecemic coma amounts to a defence: rather, it stands for the proposition that the line of defence is not insanity but is automatism, but its success will turn on whether the defendant was aware that hypoglaecemia was developing and whether he or she should have taken the antidote, namely having a lump of sugar. As Lawton LJ concluded, Mr Quick 'might have had difficulty in answering these questions in a manner which would have relieved him of responsibility for his acts', but it was not clear that the jury would have convicted and so the verdict could not stand.[40]

Confirmation of the test

12.35 It can be seen that there are two policy aims in play: the need for public protection from the risk of repetition of dangerous behaviour which requires some form of protective disposal; and the need to avoid a conclusion that someone is insane as a matter of law when that would affront common sense. The effect of the co-existence of these two policies was confirmed by the House of Lords in *R v Sullivan*,[41] which related to a defendant who, while coming out of an

39 [1973] QB 910 p922.

40 [1973] QB 910 p923. A point of law of general public importance was certified; the House of Lords refused permission to appeal.

41 [1984] AC 156.

epileptic seizure, attacked an elderly neighbour who had been seeking to help him. The trial judge ruled that the only verdict the jury could return was not guilty by reason of insanity, and so a plea of guilty was entered. The ruling was upheld by the Court of Appeal (presided over by Lawton LJ, who had presided in *Quick*) on the basis that the special verdict was required 'whenever there is evidence of a total lack of understanding and memory due to a morbid inherent condition of the brain. Epilepsy brings about such total lack of understanding and memory ...'.[42]

12.36 This approach was followed in the House of Lords. As epilepsy had featured in *Bratty*, where it was concluded that insanity was the only defence, the defence position in *Sullivan* was that *Bratty* had been a case about the need to have proper evidence to support a defence. It was suggested that the evidence in Mr Sullivan's case demonstrated that the assault occurred during an epileptic episode, whereas it was more speculative in relation to Mr Bratty. A contrast was also drawn between the acceptance in *Bratty* that epilepsy was a disease of the mind, whereas the medical evidence in *Sullivan* was that no doctor would consider an episode of epilepsy, with its short-term electrical discharges into the brain, to be a disease of the mind: that would require a prolonged period of impact, usually more than a day.[43] Lord Diplock confirmed that the ratio of *Bratty* was that as the jury had, by convicting him of murder, rejected the argument of insanity and there was no evidence of automatism from any other cause and so nothing to be put to the jury.[44] He also upheld the approach in *Kemp* that the issue was one of the application of the medical evidence to the legal concepts:

> The nomenclature adopted by the medical profession may change from time to time ... but the meaning of the expression 'disease of the mind', as a cause of a 'defect of reason' remains unchanged for the purposes of the application of the M'Naghten Rules. I agree with what was said by Devlin J in *Kemp* that 'mind' in the M'Naghten Rules is used in the ordinary sense of mental faculties of reason, memory and understanding. If the effect of a disease is to impair these faculties so severely as to have either of the consequences referred to in the latter part of the rules, it matters not whether the aetiology is organic, as in epilepsy, or functional, or whether the impairment itself is permanent or is transient and intermittent, provided that it subsisted at the time of the commission of the act.[45]

42 [1984] AC 156 p164.
43 [1984] AC 156 pp169 and 172.
44 [1984] AC 156 p171.
45 [1984] AC 156 p172.

12.37 The policy reasons behind this were outlined in terms reminiscent of the language of Lord Denning in *Bratty*:

> The purpose of the legislation relating to the defence of insanity, ever since its origin in 1800, has been to protect society against the recurrence of dangerous conduct. The duration of a temporary suspension of the mental faculties of reason, memory and understanding ... cannot on any rational ground be relevant to the application by the courts of the M'Naghten Rules.[46]

12.38 Rather, it was said that the form of 'disease of mind' would be relevant to the actions taken by the Executive once the mandatory sentence was imposed (the effect of the finding at the time being detention in a psychiatric hospital). While amendments in 1991 made the appropriate disposal a matter for the court, the principle remains that the concept of insanity is widely defined for public policy reasons and covers not what the medical profession would consider to be a disease of the brain but what for the purposes of legal responsibility is any condition that has an impact on the mind's reasoning and control.

12.39 Lord Diplock also made clear that he accepted the limiting feature outlined in *Quick*, namely that a not guilty verdict could be returned on the basis of automatism of the non-insane type if there is a 'temporary impairment ... [that] results from some external physical factor such as a blow on the head causing concussion or the administration of an anaesthetic for therapeutic purposes'.[47] In other words, the way to avoid a finding of insanity is to find some external factor that might affect the functioning of the mind temporarily. Given that external factors can be implicated in the development of mental disorders, for example blows to the head causing brain damage that in turn causes the development of a mental disorder, or a drug- or alcohol-induced psychotic condition, there may be questions of what counts as 'temporary'.

Application of the approach adopted

12.40 This approach of giving a wide definition to disease of the mind while at the same time looking to see whether there is an external cause to avoid the need to raise insanity is clearly well-entrenched and so will only be amended if Parliament steps in. A number of other examples have been decided in cases before the Court of Appeal.

46 [1984] AC 156 p172.
47 [1984] AC 156 p172.

12.41 So, *R v Hennessy*[48] involved charges of driving while disqualified and taking a conveyance: they occurred during a hyperglycaemic episode caused by the failure of the defendant to take insulin or eat for several days despite having insulin-dependent diabetes. However, there was an additional feature, the impact of depression and troubles within his marriage; the medical evidence suggested that this could cause raised blood sugar that could lead to an impairment of awareness.[49] The Court of Appeal held that 'stress, anxiety and depression can no doubt be the result of external factors, but they are not ... in themselves separately or together capable in law of causing or contributing to a state of automatism'.[50] Rather than the conduct being caused by external, physical factors, there was a state of mind that was prone to recur.[51] The trial judge's view that there was a disease of the mind caused by diabetes was held to be correct.

12.42 Subsequently, in *R v Burgess*[52] a ruling in a trial for wounding with intent during an episode of sleepwalking that led to a finding of not guilty by reason of insanity was upheld. There was evidence that the defendant was infatuated with his victim. The Court of Appeal agreed that any defect of reason on the facts was due to some internal factor rather than having any external cause: the only potential external cause was the 'possible disappointment or frustration caused by unrequited love', but that was 'not to be equated with something such as concussion'.[53] It is worth noting that the Court of Appeal focussed on the mechanism of the medical condition and the internal/external dichotomy. As to the policy-based reasoning, namely the need to have some form of restraint for an illness that might recur, Lord Lane CJ noted that 'if there is a danger of recurrence that may be an added

48 [1989] 1 WLR 287.
49 [1989] 1 WLR 287 p290.
50 [1989] 1 WLR 287 p294.
51 [1989] 1 WLR 287 p294.
52 [1991] 2 QB 92.
53 [1991] 2 QB 92 p98. The court commented favourably on the holding of the Canadian Supreme Court in *R v Rabey* [1980] 2 SCR 513 that a dissociative state cause by the disappointment of finding that a fellow student did not think much of him could not be equated to an external psychological blow causing automatism but must reflect an internal failure and so be a disease of the mind. However, it is to be noted that sleepwalking is not necessarily a reflection of a disease of the mind: the Supreme Court of Canada in the case of *Stone* (1992) 95 DLR (4th) 27 noted the difficulty of assessing whether there was an internal cause or a recurring danger; see also RD Mackay and BJ Mitchell 'Sleepwalking, automatism and insanity' [2006] Crim LR 901; RD Mackay and M Reuber 'Epilepsy and the defence of insanity' [2007] Crim LR 782.

reason for categorising the condition as a disease of the mind'.[54] But he added: 'On the other hand, the absence of the danger of recurrence is not a reason for saying that it cannot be a disease of the mind'.[55] That would be a matter for the judge to decide by applying the evidence as to the operation of the relevant condition to the legal test. In upholding the judge's ruling, it was noted that he 'was right to conclude that this was an abnormality or disorder, albeit transitory, due to an internal factor, whether functional or organic, which had manifested itself in violence. It was a disorder or abnormality which might recur, though the possibility of it recurring in the form of serious violence was unlikely'.[56]

12.43 It remains possible that external stresses can cause non-insane automatism: in the first instance decision of *R v T*,[57] it was held that post traumatic stress arising from being a victim of a rape three days earlier was capable of being the sort of external emotional shock that could produce a dissociative state that would prevent criminal liability without amounting to insanity. However, this case, which has limited precedent value as it was a Crown Court decision, is difficult to understand: since post traumatic stress seems to be a recognised psychiatric illness that is unlikely to be temporary in its effect, it seems to fit on the side of insanity by reason of the internal/external distinction of principle and also the danger of repetition. However, it might be that the evidence on the facts was of a short-lived stress that would not amount to the recognised psychiatric condition.

Self-induced automatism

12.44 One of the issues in *Quick* was the non-availability of automatism if it was self-induced, such as arising from intoxication, or was a state of automatism that could have been avoided. In relation to intoxication, the general approach set out in *Director of Public Prosecutions v Majewski*[58] is to the effect that voluntary intoxication provides a mens rea in relation to crimes of basic intent but may mean that it is not possible to prove the mens rea of crimes of specific intent (ie those with a further purpose beyond the formation of the basic mens rea of

54 [1991] 2 QB 92 p99.
55 [1991] 2 QB 92 p99.
56 [1991] 2 QB 92 p101.
57 [1990] Crim LR 256.
58 [1977] AC 443.

intent or recklessness). *Majewski* involved alcohol; the same principle had been applied to the taking of illegal drugs in *R v Lipman*.[59]

12.45 The application of this approach to insanity caused by intoxication has involved much by way of implication rather than direct reasoning. Initially, in *Director of Public Prosecutions v Beard*,[60] Lord Birkenhead LC summarised earlier authorities as confirming that excessive intoxication could produce a situation in which a person was insane, albeit that it would be a temporary insanity. But *Quick* noted the approach in *Lipman* as support for the proposition that self-induced incapacity would not provide an excuse. When endorsing *Quick* and the possibility of temporary conditions that did not amount to insanity, Lord Diplock in *Sullivan* excluded a condition that was 'self-induced by consuming drink or drugs'.[61]

12.46 As to the question of whether the automatism could have been avoided, this was considered further in *R v Bailey*,[62] in which the defendant hit a man with an iron bar after taking insulin without adequate food and so developed hypoglaecemia. He was convicted of wounding with intent. The prosecution contended that failing to take food to avoid hypoglaecemia should be treated in a similar fashion to the approach adopted to self-induced intoxication. The Court of Appeal was not willing to go so far: it reasoned that while it was common knowledge that there was a risk of dangerous behaviour from alcohol or illicit drugs, that was not so in relation to the taking of insulin without food, even on the part of those with diabetes.[63] The approach to be adopted was whether the prosecution was able to prove that the defendant was aware of the risks in the situation so as to meet the test of recklessness, but without the benefit of the approach in relation to alcohol or illegal drugs (in effect the conclusive presumption of recklessness). On the facts, however, the Court of Appeal determined that Mr Bailey had not laid a proper evidential foundation for an argument of automatism and so the conviction was proper.

59 [1970] 1 QB 152: death caused during hallucinations induced by LSD amounted to manslaughter.

60 [1920] AC 479 at 500.

61 [1984] AC 156 at 172.

62 [1983] 1 WLR 760.

63 [1983] 1 WLR 760 at 764–765. See also the approach taken to intoxication other than by alcohol or an illegal drug, when the jury has to be informed that the question is whether the defendant had a knowledge of the risks that equated to the mens rea: for example, *R v Hardie* [1985] 1 WLR 64, relating to an offence of aggravated arson (ie reckless as to the endangerment of life) after taking prescription drug, in which the Court of Appeal held that the self-induced intoxication of a legal drug was not irrelevant.

Mixed causes

12.47 Another issue is the approach to adopt when there is more than one potential cause for automatism: it may be that one or more causes is a disease of the mind and that one or more is not. This arose shortly after the *Quick* decision in *R v Burns*.[64] The defendant was charged with an indecent assault, which involved him placing his penis in the mouth of the victim. His account was that he could not remember what had happened; during the day, he had taken pills for a stomach upset that contained morphine and in the evening he had drunk alcohol. He was an alcoholic and suffered from a form of amnesia, both of which were diseases of the mind in light of brain damage. The medical expert called suggested that Mr Burns had been acting as an automaton, but he was convicted. The Court of Appeal found that there were two causes for concern in the directions of the judge: in the first place, he had not made clear that in relation to automatism that was not insane, the defence obligation was to raise adequate evidence and the prosecution then had to prove voluntariness;[65] and he had not given an adequate direction on the effect of matters that did not give rise to questions of insanity when combined with the factors that were relevant to diseases of the mind. The Court of Appeal explained that this was an error because of the possible conjunction of factors:

> ... there was evidence that the appellant's unawareness resulted not simply from his disease of alcoholism and the brain damage caused by it nor from alcohol added to that disease, but from alcohol and the drug Mandrax added to that disease, and there was no evidence that the appellant knew that one or two pints of beer, or that Mandrax, would induce unconsciousness or amnesia in the peculiar sense in which the doctor used that term. Nowhere does the judge tell the jury that, if they thought other factors than disease of the mind might be a cause of his unawareness, they should consider automatism even if they rejected insanity, or that, if they thought one or more of those factors might not be known to the appellant to be likely to produce unawareness, they should acquit him altogether.[66]

12.48 In short, if there are features on the evidence that may give rise to an insanity verdict or to a not guilty verdict on the basis of automatism, care has to be taken to ensure that the two options are left to the jury (which has to be done in a manner that takes into account the

64 (1974) 58 CrAppR 364.
65 (1974) 58 CrAppR 364 p374.
66 (1974) 58 CrAppR 364 p374.

different burdens of proof). In relation to the question of automatism, it may be that the pre-existing disease of the mind is affected by alcohol and drugs in circumstances in which the defendant was not aware of the impact and so was not blameworthy.

12.49 See also in this context the case of *R v Roach*,[67] which involved a charge of wounding with intent. One line of defence was automatism; Mr Roach claimed to have no memory of the incident, which involved an attack on a supervisor at work with whom he did not get on. Two psychiatrists gave evidence for the defence: one considered that difficulties in his childhood had caused a personality disorder (though there might also have been some brain damage from a playground fall), and that conflicts he had had with his partner and his co-worker in conjunction with fatigue led to an incident of automatism that he described as insane automatism;[68] the second defence psychiatrist formulated a similar view, though he noted that there were impairments as a result of mixing prescription drugs (a mood stabiliser and an anti-depressant) and alcohol as well as fatigue.[69] The prosecution expert believed that there was no evidence of automatism.[70]

12.50 On the basis of the evidence, and the authorities of *Quick* and *Burns*, defence counsel submitted that in addition to a direction on the defence of not guilty by reason of insanity, the judge had to leave to the jury the question of non-insane automatism as they might conclude that the alcohol and the prescription drugs were external factors that caused automatism through their interaction with the personality disorder.[71] In quashing the verdict of guilty, the Court of Appeal held that the trial judge should have acceded to this submission and given the jury a clear direction on non-insane automatism (and so a possible acquittal if the prosecution were not able to demonstrate voluntariness). The court recorded the agreed position of counsel that 'if external factors are operative on an underlying condition which would not otherwise produce a state of automatism, then a defence of (non insane) automatism ought to be left to the jury'.[72] In other words, the fact that there is an underlying mental disorder does not mean that the only possible automatism is of the insane variety: it turns on the facts and whether external factors caused the

67 [2001] EWCA Crim 2698.
68 [2001] EWCA Crim 2698 para 12.
69 [2001] EWCA Crim 2698 paras 13 and 14.
70 [2001] EWCA Crim 2698 para 15.
71 [2001] EWCA Crim 2698 para 17.
72 [2001] EWCA Crim 2698 para 28.

automatism. This allows for the possibility of co-existing causes, and the jury must investigate the dominant cause.

12.51 What is important in this context is that the labels attached by the doctors are not governing. Accordingly, it is important to look beyond the language used by any medical witness in suggesting a legal conclusion. The corollary of this is that when providing instructions to medical experts, the legal concepts must be explained and the doctors informed that the medical concepts of insanity and automatism have to be modified to fit the legal rule.

Summary as to sane and insane automatism

12.52 In Appendix 3 to the Crown Court Benchbook 2010,[73] the judiciary has produced a summary of the issues to be considered in relation to whether there is automatism and if it is sane or insane. Some of the points listed can be combined and so the following is a summary:

1) Automatism requires a total destruction of voluntary control, not merely a reduction or impairment.
2) If it caused by a disease, it must be insane automatism; external factors causing a temporary impairment can found a defence of non-insane automatism, but it must be from factors such as concussion or anaesthesia, not self-induced intoxication.
3) The defence has an evidential burden, and the judge will decide whether the evidence goes to insanity or non-insane automatism.
4) The prosecution has to disprove automatism.
5) If the malfunction of the mind is not insanity or automatism, it is not a defence.
6) The approach to automatism caused by self-induced intoxication through alcohol or illegal drugs is governed by the approach to intoxication, namely that it cannot be a defence to offences of basic intent or recklessness, since the intoxication amounts to recklessness; but it may be raised in relation to an offence of specific intent.
7) However, in relation to action or inaction caused by legal drugs (of which an example is a failure by someone with diabetes to eat properly after insulin has been taken), the prosecution has to demonstrate recklessness in that the defendant realised the risk of criminal action.

73 Available at www.judiciary.gov.uk/publications-and-reports/judicial-college/Pre+2011/crown-court-bench-book-directing-the-jury. See also the summary at pages 318–319 of the Benchbook.

12.53 This seems to be an adequate summary, save that it does not deal with the question of mixed causes. What it reveals is the very limited scope for automatism and an even more restricted scope for it to amount to anything other than insanity and so the special verdict rather than an acquittal.

Disease of mind causing a defect of reason

12.54 While the concept of a disease of the mind is wide, a potential limitation on the scope of a ruling as to insanity is that it must be such as to have an impact on the defendant's reasoning process, namely causing a defect of reason. This is illustrated by the case of *R v Clarke*.[74] Ms Clarke was charged with shoplifting: her account was that there was no mens rea because she had simply placed goods in her bag by reason of absentmindedness. However, in support of the contention as to the lack of the formation of the necessary mental state, she adduced evidence of depression: the judge then ruled that this was something that led to the defence of insanity. In order to avoid what was then the only sentence, namely detention in hospital, Ms Clarke changed her plea to guilty. However, the Court of Appeal overturned the conviction on the basis that it was consequent upon an erroneous ruling of law. The court noted that the question addressed by the M'Naghten rules was not a momentary failure to concentrate but a loss of the 'power of reasoning' by reason of a disease of the mind.[75] In the light of the wide reading of the insanity test set out above, it is perhaps not surprising that the trial judge took the view that he did: if the defendant was not aware of what she was doing (which is the effect of her account), then it is possible to characterise that as not being aware of the nature and quality of the act. The appellate judges were aware of the result of an insanity verdict ('the disastrous consequence'[76] which she avoided by changing her plea). The options now available avoid such a result, and may make it more acceptable to describe an unconscious act such as that involved in *Clarke* as an example of insanity, albeit one that would presumably lead to an order for an absolute discharge (if the prosecution were of the view that a prosecution was necessary).

74 (1972) 56 CrAppR 225.
75 (1972) 56 CrAppR 225 p228.
76 (1972) 56 CrAppR 225 p228.

12.55 The terminology used by the Court of Appeal, namely the loss of the power of reasoning, is an approximation of the two parts of the test announced by the judges in *M'Naghten's Case*, namely that the defendant did not know 'the nature and quality of the act' or, 'if he did know it, that he did not know he was doing what was wrong'. The former has been held to refer to the physical character of the act rather than its moral or legal quality: see *R v Codere*.[77] It has been rephrased by Lord Diplock in *R v Sullivan*[78] as meaning 'he did not know what he was doing'. It is to be noted that the normal criminal trial requires the prosecution to prove the existence of a guilty mind: but if the question becomes whether the defendant did not know what he or she was doing because of a disease of the mind, the burden falls on the defence to prove this. That leaves open the possibility that neither the defence nor the prosecution meets its burden, in which case the verdict returned should be simply not guilty; equally, if the prosecution meets its burden but the defence does not meet its burden, the result will be a guilty verdict.

12.56 The second limb leading to an insanity verdict – namely that the defendant was aware of what he or she was doing but did not know that it was wrong – has given rise to an issue of what form of 'wrongness' is meant, namely contrary to the law and so legally wrong or morally wrong. The context in which this was said by the judges in *M'Naghten's Case* suggests that they meant 'wrong in law' rather than any concept of moral wrongness: in the answer to question one put by the House of Lords, the judges spoke of partial delusions and commented that someone who was unlawfully redressing a grievance based on delusions would be open to conviction and punishment 'if he knew at the time of committing such crime that he was acting contrary to law; by which expression we understand your Lordships to mean the law of the land'. Further, in the combined answer to questions two and three, in which the substantive test is set out, the judges went on to say that the question was not put to the jury in terms of the 'law of the land' in case the jury believed that it was necessary for the defendant actually to know the law (whereas the approach adopted by the criminal law is to afflict everyone with constructive knowledge of the law). An alternative formulation of the question was offered: 'If the accused was conscious that the act was one which he ought not to do, and if that act was at the same time contrary to the law of the land, he is punishable'.

77 (1916) 12 CrAppR 21.
78 [1984] AC 156.

12.57 However, given that everyone is presumed to know the law and that the insanity defence raises an issue of responsibility which can be viewed as a moral issue, there has been argument in case-law as to whether the judges meant to lay down a requirement of not knowing the moral quality of the act. This has led to different conclusions in different common law jurisdictions. In England and Wales, this question was resolved in *R v Windle*[79] by the view that legal wrongness is the question. He had killed his wife by giving her an overdose of aspirin: the evidence was that she was mentally unwell, and spoke frequently of committing suicide, and that he had absorbed her condition (which was known as folie à deux); however, it was also the evidence of the doctors called that Mr Windle knew that his action was contrary to the law. On that basis, the trial judge, Devlin J, ruled that there was no evidence of insanity; Mr Windle was convicted and sentenced to death. On appeal, it was argued that the evidence was that he was incapable of formulating a rational judgment between right and wrong and formed the view that what he was doing was right, and that this should have been left to the jury.[80] In the Court of Criminal Appeal, Lord Goddard CJ held that the trial judge had been correct. He noted:

> In the opinion of the court there is no doubt that in the M'Naghten rules 'wrong' means contrary to law and not 'wrong' according to the opinion of one man or of a number of people on the question whether a particular act might or might not be justified.[81]

12.58 The Lord Chief Justice relied on his judgment for the court in *R v Rivett*,[82] but also explained his reasoning. There were two limbs to it, namely, that: 'Courts of law can only distinguish between that which is in accordance with law and that which is contrary to law';[83] and that the special verdict was to be entered in cases where the defendant was 'insane, so as not to be responsible, according to law'.[84] This reasoning is very far from convincing: the first part rests on an assumption that moral right or wrong cannot be part of the legal process because the criminal courts are not capable of dealing with such concepts;[85]

79 [1952] 2 QB 826.
80 [1952] 2 QB 826 p828.
81 [1952] 2 QB 826 p834.
82 (1950) 34 CrAppR 87.
83 [1952] 2 QB 826 at 833.
84 [1952] 2 QB 826 at 833, referring to TLA 1883 s2(1).
85 He added: 'The law cannot embark on the question, and it would be an unfortunate thing if it were left to juries to consider whether some particular act was morally right or wrong.'

and the second part rests on the assumption that the statutory reference to responsibility must equate to questions of law only, which in turn is a corollary of the first part of the argument.

12.59 This approach has not been followed in other common law jurisdictions: the High Court of Australia declined to follow *Windle* in *R v Stapleton*;[86] and the codification of the common law in section 23 of the New Zealand Crimes Act 1961 made express reference to moral wrongness. However, *Windle* has been accepted as correct: the Court of Appeal in *R v Johnson*[87] noted that the *Stapleton* judgment was 'highly persuasive' and included 'illuminating passages indicating the difficulties and internal inconsistencies which can arise from the application of the M'Naghten Rules',[88] but that *Windle* was 'unequivocal and has, so far as we are aware, never been doubted since then in this court'.[89]

12.60 The court in *Johnson* noted that it would be sensible to review the M'Naghten rules in the light of their age, but added that it was not appropriate for the Court of Appeal to do so, and so *Windle* must be accepted. But it is worth noting the consequences: if the defendant's delusion was to the effect that something which he or she accepted was morally wrong was lawful, that would leave open the insanity verdict; but a defendant whose delusion of grandeur was to the effect that he or she was the only legitimate source of true law, but who was aware that there was a 'false' legal system in place that characterised his or her actions as unlawful, would be excluded from the verdict.

The other elements of the test

The presumption of sanity – displacing the presumption

12.61 The M'Naghten rules include as a starting point of the presumption of sanity and of responsibility for crimes.[90] The burden of establishing the defence is placed on the defendant to the standard of the

86 (1952) 86 CLR 358.

87 [2007] EWCA Crim 1978, [2007] MHLR 310.

88 [2007] EWCA Crim 1978, [2007] MHLR 310 para 21.

89 [2007] EWCA Crim 1978, [2007] MHLR 310 para 23.

90 In contrast, but equally valid as an application of a presumption, for a long time the law presumed that children aged under 14 did not know that a crime was wrong and so this had to be proved by the prosecution: this – the doli incapax rule – was abolished by Crime and Disorder Act 1998 s34 (as interpreted by the House of Lords in *R v JTB* [2009] UKHL 20, [2009] 1 AC 1310).

balance of probabilities. This standard of proof is a matter of interpretation. In reiterating the 'golden thread' of the presumption of innocence, such that the prosecution had to prove that a death was criminal rather than the defendant having to prove that it was not an accident, the House of Lords in *Woolmington v Director of Public Prosecutions*[91] made reference to the different position of insanity: Viscount Sankey noted that 'the onus is definitely and exceptionally placed upon the accused to establish such a defence'.[92]

12.62 The authority cited for this proposition was an early twentieth century authority, *R v Oliver Smith*,[93] in which the rule as to the burden of proof had been laid down and it had been indicated that any evidence of insanity in the possession of the prosecution should be provided to the defence rather than called by the prosecution. In relation to whether the judge can raise the issue, this is certainly so if the judge acts by way of clarifying that a defence argument as to the lack of voluntariness was wrong in law because it necessarily amounted to a plea of insanity: see *R v Kemp*.[94] As to whether the judge can go further and suggest that it is a matter that should be explored, the difficulty is the absence of a mechanism whereby the judge can descend into the trial arena and secure evidence. In short, if the defence does not wish to raise the issue, it will not be raised: that is, unless the prosecution can raise it.

12.63 There is a question as to whether the prosecution can raise the issue (of their own motion or as a way of responding to a judicial request). In *Bratty v Attorney-General for Northern Ireland*,[95] Lord Denning commented that *Kemp* was correct and then added that:

> The old notion that only the defence can raise a defence of insanity is now gone. The prosecution are entitled to raise it and it is their duty to do so rather than allow a dangerous person to be at large. The Trial of Lunatics Act, 1883, says that where 'it is given in evidence' that the person was insane, the jury shall return a verdict of guilty but insane. It does not say that the defence alone can give such evidence. The prosecution can give it.[96]

12.64 The context of the comments is that of automatism and a potential acquittal against which the prosecution may be arguing, but the

91 [1935] AC 462.
92 [1935] AC 462 pp475–476.
93 (1910) 6 CrAppR 19.
94 [1957] 1 QB 399.
95 [1963] AC 386.
96 [1963] AC 386 pp411–412.

comments made in the last two sentences suggest a wider coverage. It is certainly the case that the prosecution can raise arguments as to insanity if the partial defence of diminished responsibility is advanced in relation to a murder charge: see CP(I)A 1964 s6.[97] However, it might be thought that if the prosecution were to be given a right to raise insanity generally, it would have been provided for in this statute: but as it has not been, that leaves only the suggestion of Lord Denning in obiter comments in *Bratty*. It is also to be noted that the Crown Prosecution Service, in its guidance on mentally disordered offenders, simply refers to the onus being on the defendant to demonstrate the defence and does not mention the prosecution having any role in this regard.[98] The argument in favour of the prosecution having a wider role would be the need for it to operate in its 'minister of justice' role so as to ensure that the court is able to make a decision as to the true verdict reflecting the circumstances pertaining at the time of the incident in question. On the other hand, this role can be secured by the established obligation to pass any relevant evidence to the defence, particularly now that the consequences of an insanity verdict are not automatic detention, which might in the past have provided a significant disincentive to using the defence except in the most serious of cases.

12.65 The position therefore appears to be that, except in relation to the statutory right to seek to counter a claim of diminished responsibility by contending that the proper verdict is insanity, the question of insanity is a matter for the defence. Naturally, the prosecution can call evidence to counter a defence of insanity:[99] given the presumption of sanity, the prosecution will succeed if they demonstrate that the defence has not met its burden of displacing the presumption. In contrast, if the issue raised by the defence is automatism without insanity, the defence has an evidential burden and the prosecution must then demonstrate to the criminal standard that the defendant was acting in a voluntary state: see Viscount Kilmuir LC in *Bratty*, noting that:

> ... normally the presumption of mental capacity is sufficient to prove that he acted consciously and voluntarily, and the prosecution need go no further. But if, after considering evidence properly left to them by the judge, the jury are left in real doubt whether or not the accused

97 The prosecution would have to prove their contention to the normal criminal standard: see *R v Grant* [1960] Crim LR 424.

98 See www.cps.gov.uk/legal/l_to_o/mentally_disordered_offenders/index.html under 'mens rea'.

99 *R v Abramovitch* (1911) 7 CrAppR 145.

acted in a state of automatism, it seems to me that on principle they should acquit because the necessary mens rea – if indeed the actus reus – has not been proved beyond reasonable doubt.[100]

12.66 The distinction between sane and insane automatism is discussed below. The consequence of the presumption of sanity and the burden being placed on the defence in terms of compliance with basic principles is worth noting. If the basis for the claimed insanity is that the defendant does not know the nature or quality of the act he is charged with doing, the effect of the statutory requirement that it must be proved that the defendant did the act or made the omission charged means that the question of mens rea become irrelevant and thereby places a lesser burden on the prosecution. This also seems to be the case when the basis for the claimed insanity is that the defendant did not know the wrongness of his action (which at first blush suggests that there is a mens rea): in *R v Antoine*,[101] Lord Hutton noted that 'where it is established that the defendant was insane under either limb of the M'Naghten Rules ... the jury should no longer be concerned with the mental responsibility of the defendant for that offence'.[102] This undermines any distinction between the two limbs.

Insanity at the time of the act

12.67 The special verdict can only apply if the defendant was actually involved in the act or omission that forms the basis for the criminal charge. That is implicit in the M'Naghten rules. It is made express in the statutory language of TLA 1883 s2(1). If the jury is not satisfied that the defendant 'did the act or made the omission charged', the special verdict cannot be returned and the proper verdict will be a simple verdict of not guilty, as it will not have been demonstrated that the defendant was involved in the offence.

12.68 The question raised by the TLA 1883 can only be assessed if the defendant is fit to stand trial and participate in the process; if the defendant is not fit to participate, the question of following the formal fitness to stand trial process or applying to stay the proceedings on the basis of the inability of the defendant to participate will have to be considered.

12.69 In contrast to the arguments that have been accepted that the finding as to the commission of the act in the formal fitness to stand

100 [1963] AC 386 at p407.

101 [2001] 1 AC 340, [2000] MHLR 28.

102 [2001] 1 AC 340 at 374D, [2000] MHLR 28 at para 47.

trial process that it is not a criminal process because it cannot lead to a finding of guilt and punishment cannot arise, a verdict of not guilty by reason of insanity is clearly a finding made in a criminal process. This was even more clear when the verdict was one of guilty but insane, and the nature of the process has not changed as a result of the change in the terminology of the verdict.

12.70 If insanity is raised, the jury will consider whether the defendant was insane and also whether the act or omission was committed. So it is not limited to the question of the actus reus. This means that the verdict of not guilty by reason of insanity is a final determination of a criminal charge for the purposes of article 6 of the European Convention on Human Rights (ECHR) and, since the defendant could have been convicted (if the contention of insanity had not been accepted), principles of double jeopardy and the plea in bar of autrefois acquit should apply.[103]

12.71 In a further contrast to the position of those found unfit to stand trial, who may be remitted for trial in certain circumstances, those found not guilty by reason of insanity may not be remitted for trial, even though the order handed down to them may be the same: the power of remittal in paragraph 4 of Schedule 1 to the Criminal Procedure (Insanity and Unfitness to Plead) Act (CP(IUP)A) 1991 referred only to an order of admission made in relation to a finding of unfitness; and this is still the position in CP(I)A 1964 s5A(4), as inserted by section 24 of the Domestic Violence, Crime and Victims Act (DVCVA) 2004.

Insanity, mens rea and strict liability offences

12.72 As has been discussed in chapter 9 relating to fitness to stand trial, questions of mens rea cannot be raised in relation to the question of whether the act was committed. In reaching this conclusion in this context, the House of Lords in *R v Antoine*[104] adopted the reasoning of the Court of Appeal in *Attorney General's Reference No 3 of 1998*,[105] which related to insanity. The judge in the trial that led to the reference had directed an acquittal because the defendant's insanity had prevented him forming the mens rea required for the offences of aggravated burglary and affray. He relied on an authority relating to

103 See the principles set out in *Connelly v Director of Public Prosecutions* [1964] AC 1254.

104 [2001] 1 AC 340, [2000] MHLR 28.

105 [1999] 2 CrAppR 214.

the fact-finding process arising after a finding of unfitness to stand trial, *R v Egan (Michael)*,[106] in which the Court of Appeal held that dishonesty and an intention permanently to deprive, the relevant mens rea elements, had to be shown when the question arising was whether a defendant unfit to stand trial had committed the actus reus of a theft charge. In *Attorney-General's Reference No 3 of 1998*, the Court of Appeal distinguished *Egan* on the basis that it dealt with the fitness to stand trial scenario rather than insanity. But it also suggested that *Egan* was wrong. Certainly, it construed equivalent statutory language to have a different outcome. The holding was that the question under the TLA 1883 of whether the defendant 'did the act or made the omission charged' involved the prosecution proving that the defendant 'has caused a certain event or that responsibility is to be attributed to him for the existence of a certain state of affairs, which is forbidden by criminal law'.[107] This is the actus reus; it was said expressly that mens rea did not have to be proved and the defendant's state of mind was irrelevant on the statutory test (save for the question of whether he was insane).

12.73 Does this mean that issues arising from the defendant's mind are not relevant to the jury's satisfaction as to whether the act or omission was committed? Whether the 'actus' is 'reus' may turn on the perceptions of the defendant:[108] in *Antoine*, Lord Hutton noted that objective evidence of mistake or accident or self-defence required the prosecution to disprove those matters before the jury could find that the defendant did the 'act'. The Court of Appeal in *Attorney General's Reference No 3 of 1998* was also concerned with this topic, noting that there was a need not to make orders against those who do not merit being stigmatised: it gave the example of an accidental touching in an overcrowded swimming pool which might meet the actus reus of an indecent assault. This might justify an order in criminal proceedings if it was a deliberate action based on an insane perception: at the same time, the fact that a defendant had a disorder that amounted to

106 [1998] 1 CrAppR 121, [1999] 3 WLR 1204.

107 The court adopted as correct this view of the authors of Smith and Hogan, *Criminal law*, 8th edn, p28.

108 This is discussed more fully in chapter 9; examples are that what is reasonable in self-defence turns on what is perceived by the defendant, and the general principle that an honest but mistaken belief that the facts are such that an action is lawful will usually lead to an acquittal, since moral fault is assessed according to what was in the mind of the defendant. This approach was also applied to the question of secondary participation in a joint enterprise murder and the necessary knowledge of the common purpose and whether any fatal action went beyond that purpose.

insanity should not prevent him or her from being acquitted on the basis that, on an assessment of his or her state of mind, it was an accidental touching.

12.74 A question arises as to how this should be assessed if the context of insanity. In particular, given that the defendant can participate in the trial, can he or she give evidence as to perceptions at the relevant time or is the inquiry limited to objective evidence? As the question of insanity is part of a trial that is clearly criminal in nature and so has to allow the involvement of the defendant, and as it does not follow from the fact that the defendant was affected by a mental disorder that he or she cannot recall what was happening at the relevant time, a defendant must be able to give evidence. If, however, any recollection is affected by the circumstances amounting to insanity, the defendant's evidence will not support this 'objective' evidence. Similarly, it is possible that the disorder will result in a loss of recall and so the defendant cannot assist. However, this may cause a concern as to the fairness of the trial process. If the evidence of the defendant is essential, it might be argued that the effect of amnesia caused by the mental disorder is that the trial is not fair and so should not proceed. This will be a question that turns on the facts, including the evidence that can be given by other witnesses, so as to determine whether the issues arising can be assessed fairly.

12.75 There is a further possibility: if the defendant has 'partial delusions' (ie not rising to the level of insanity), he or she is to be judged according to his or her subjective perceptions in the assessment of liability. So, for example, in relation to the exculpatory effect of an honest but mistaken belief as to facts that, were they true, would mean the defendant is innocent, this should apply to an honest belief based on a delusional viewpoint if the delusion does not meet the test for insanity.

12.76 A further question is whether the insanity defence is a matter of mens rea and so involves an inquiry into whether there was a mens rea formed in circumstances of insanity (such that the intentions or foresight of the defendant are detached from reality) or whether it entails a situation in which the existence of the insanity prevents the formulation of the mens rea. In the latter scenario, mens rea issues are irrelevant. This may be important because there are many offences that do not involve a mens rea element, and so the question arises as to whether insanity can be raised.

12.77 At first sight, the language of the insanity test is bifurcated and covers two situations, one of which involves no mens rea, the other of which involves an mens rea that is excused. So, if the defendant has no perception of what he or she is doing, then mens rea will be absent (as also will be voluntariness as to conduct); but if the defendant knows what he or she is doing but does not know that it is wrong, a mens rea will be present but an additional element is also present, namely lack of knowledge of the wrongness of the conduct in light of the mental disorder.

12.78 However, it has been suggested that the special verdict is not available in relation to offences that do not have a mens rea element. Clearly, this will be of more interest in relation to summary proceedings, but it is discussed here as it is a point of principle. In *R v Horseferry Road Magistrates' Court ex p K*,[109] the Divisional Court, citing the main practitioner text, Archbold, stated that: 'Insanity ... is not a species of special defence but merely a particular situation where mens rea is lacking. Accordingly, it is available in all criminal charges where mens rea is in issue ...'. Further, in *Director of Public Prosecutions v H*,[110] the Divisional Court determined that the question of insanity was irrelevant in relation to a strict liability offence (driving with excess alcohol) and so directed a conviction on the basis that the defendant had been driving at a time when he had excess alcohol. McCowan LJ for the court stated that:

> We are quite clear ... that insanity can be a defence in the magistrates' court, but only if the offence charged is one in which mens rea is an element. Every man is assumed to be sane at the time of an alleged offence, and accordingly the burden is on the defendant to establish insanity at the time of the commission of the offence on the balance of probabilities. The defence is based on the absence of mens rea, but none is required for the offence of driving with an excess of alcohol. Hence the defence of insanity has no relevance to such a charge as it is an offence of strict liability.[111]

12.79 This is problematic. In the first place, the offences charged in *K* (affray and common assault) involved a mens rea and so the comments made were obiter, and indeed were not the focus of the question of law arising in the case; yet that is the only authority cited in *H*. In the second place, *H* was a case in which only the prosecution was represented and so the argument was perhaps limited. In the third place, the facts in *H* make the conclusion difficult to support. Mr H drove while affected by a hypomanic mood disorder; the justices accepted the evidence that the decisions of people so affected 'would

109 [1997] QB 23.
110 [1997] 1 WLR 1406.
111 [1997] 1 WLR 1406 at 1409.

probably be irrational and they all displayed a lack of appreciation of reality resulting in disinhibition in social behaviour and an impairment of judgment and moral sense'.[112] They found that Mr H knew the nature of what he was doing but did not know that it was unlawful (ie the second part of the M'Naghten test). To require a conviction in that situation, as the Divisional Court ruled, seems difficult to justify, particularly if the effect of the ruling was that insanity simply cannot be raised. That would mean that a similar conclusion would also apply if the defendant had not been aware of the nature of his actions for the purposes of the first limb of the M'Naghten rules, which could cover a situation in which there was a lack of voluntariness.

12.80 Even if it was insanity that went to the second limb, namely the knowledge of wrongness, it seems difficult to suggest that the reasons behind the insanity test, namely that mental disorder means that a person cannot be held to the same standard, should not apply: while knowledge that something is illegal or wrong is not a defence to a person who is sane, this is because the person has the ability to discover that fact and so cannot be excused for not having that knowledge, whereas insanity prevents the acquisition of that knowledge. This knowledge that something is wrong is something that is presumed in relation to adults and, since the defence of doli incapax was removed,[113] is also presumed in relation to juveniles – but is the reason children under ten are not criminally responsible. However, the point is that it is a separate question that amounts to a precursor to moral fault and criminal liability, independent of whether or not a further mens rea applies. If the view is taken that insanity means that a defendant does not have the capability of knowing moral fault and so should be treated as an infant in this regard, this is applicable to all criminal offending, including those offences without a mens rea.

12.81 Accordingly, the conclusion reached in *H* seems to run contrary to the obvious implication from the first limb of the M'Naghten rules. Lord Diplock in *R v Sullivan*[114] stated that the aim behind the M'Naghten rules was to clarify the common law position as to 'mental disorder as negativing responsibility for crimes':[115] such responsibility can be avoided both when a necessary mens rea is absent but also when a defendant is not acting voluntarily (ie insane automatism would not be possible in relation to offences that do not include

112 [1997] 1 WLR 1406 p1407.
113 See chapter 10 note 19.
114 [1984] AC 156.
115 [1984] AC 156 p170.

a mens rea). So it is suggested that *H* is erroneous, that insanity is not a defence based only on the absence of mens rea, and so can be raised in relation to strict liability offences, and certainly so if the contention is based on the first limb of the test.

12.82 Support for this contention comes from Hughes LJ in *R (Singh) v Stratford Magistrates' Court*.[116] He was dealing with a submission that the defence of insanity could not be raised in a summary trial in the magistrates' court because insanity goes to negative mens rea and the statutory process available in the summary court (namely, section 37(3) of the Mental Health Act (MHA) 1983, which is described in the next chapter) does not involve mens rea issues.[117] In dismissing this submission, Hughes LJ suggested a proper understanding of the case-law relating to mens rea questions:

> 17. What the court decided in *Attorney General's Reference No 3 of 1998* was that if (on trial on indictment) insanity is established and the question is whether the accused did the act or made the omission charged, the court is not concerned with any mental element in the offence, but only with what is conveniently called the *actus reus* . That is because if insanity be established the accused by definition has insufficient mental state for the offence.[118]

12.83 He went on to say that the proper understanding of the statutory procedures for finding the special verdict (or finding that the act was committed by a person found unfit to stand trial) was that 'it is only when insanity is once established, and one moves on to the determination whether the act or omission charged was done or made, that the state of mind of the accused is irrelevant'.[119] But *Attorney-General's Reference No 3 of 1998* and its equivalent in relation to the fitness to stand trial process, *R v Antoine*, did not mean that issues of mens rea were removed: 'On the contrary, insanity, where established by an accused, usually operates to show that he did not have the state of mind necessary for commission of the offence'.

12.84 It is submitted that this case establishes the correct understanding of the approach to insanity and the relevance of mens rea. There is clearly a two-stage process, one involving the common law test for

116 [2007] EWHC 1582 (Admin), [2007] MHLR 274.

117 [2007] EWHC 1582 (Admin), [2007] MHLR 274 para 13.

118 [2007] EWHC 1582 (Admin), [2007] MHLR 274: He added at paragraphs 18–19 that the same was the case with the question of fitness to stand trial: once the determination has been made that someone is not fit to stand trial and the court moves on to the question of whether the act was committed, mens rea questions cease to be relevant.

119 [2007] EWHC 1582 (Admin), [2007] MHLR 274 para 20.

insanity and the second involving the statutory process. At the first stage, the question is whether the defendant is within the insanity test; this may show that there is no mens rea, particularly under the second stage of the test, namely the lack of knowledge of the wrongness of the action; but may also go to undermine responsibility for the actus reus, and so can be raised even if the offence does not involve issues of mens rea. Second, there is the question of whether the statutory test for entering the special verdict is met, at which stage issues of mens rea are irrelevant. This two-stage process is clearly relevant irrespective of whether the underlying offence involves a mens rea.

Insanity and partial defences to murder

12.85 Another point arising in the context of discussions as to mens rea is the question of the relationship between insanity and the partial defences to murder, namely diminished responsibility and provocation (or its replacement, loss of control), and the separate offence of infanticide that amounts to a lesser offence to what would otherwise be a murder. The question of the offence of which the defendant was not guilty by reason of insanity – that is, whether it was murder or manslaughter or infanticide – is of real significance in relation to the disposal, since any hospital order made has to be accompanied with a restriction order if it relates to a murder charge.[120]

12.86 As has been discussed in chapter 9 relating to fitness to stand trial, diminished responsibility and provocation are classified as questions of mens rea and so cannot be raised in relation to the question of whether the act was committed.[121] The discussion there of arguments that can be put against the reasoning in the leading case of *Antoine*, which involved the question of diminished responsibility, applies also in relation to whether the verdict of not guilty by reason of insanity should allow a finding that the actus reus was of manslaughter rather than of murder. It could be suggested that it is not possible to have a finding based on diminished responsibility together with insanity, because they are on a continuum and so it cannot be possible to have both together. However, as is discussed in chapter 14, the courts have determined that the precondition for diminished responsibility – an

120 This is discussed further below; until amendments made by the DVCVA 2004, admission to hospital with a restriction order was the only disposal available if the finding related to murder.

121 This was part of the holding in *Antoine* in relation to diminished responsibility; see *R v Grant* [2001] EWCA Crim 2611, [2002] QB 1030, [2002] MHLR 41 in relation to provocation.

abnormality of mind – is not the same as the 'disease of the mind' that is behind the insanity question. This raises at least the theoretical possibility, particularly given that a defendant could have more than one form of mental disorder or disease of the mind, that someone could have diminished responsibility on the basis of one condition and a disease of the mind on the basis of another condition.

12.87 Section 52 of the Coroners and Justice Act 2009 substitutes new language for section 2(1) of the Homicide Act 1957.[122] Diminished responsibility now arises from a recognised medical condition that substantially impairs the accused's ability to understand the nature of his conduct, form a rational judgment or exercise self-control. Although these factors seem linked more to the voluntariness of conduct, and so are part of the doing of the act or the making of the omission rather than being features of the mens rea, the language of the defence still provides that the defendant is not to be convicted of murder: that means that the essential reasoning behind *Antoine*, namely that the trial could not get to consider the question of murder because it would not look into mens rea questions, still applies. However, it may also be that this new language means that diminished responsibility is now more on a continuum with the question of insanity, since a 'medical condition' that impairs responsibility for offending seems like an explanation of what amounts to a disease of the mind in the context of insanity. That would add to the suggestion made above that it may be that insanity and the new diminished responsibility test cannot operate together because they now involve overlapping issues.

12.88 In relation to provocation, there may be different points. The argument suggested in chapter 9, namely that it is not a mens rea question but a question of causation or motivation that, as with an issue such as self-defence, should be left open because it can be raised as an objective question without any need to examine the defendant's mens rea, applies equally if it arises in the circumstances of an insanity defence.

12.89 As to its replacement,[123] 'loss of control' (see sections 54–56 of the Coroners and Justice Act 2009) is made out in relation to a murder charge if there was a loss of self-control from a qualifying trigger and

122 This is in effect from 4 October 2010, by reason of Coroners and Justice Act 2009 (Commencement No 4, Transitional and Saving Provisions) Order 2010 SI No 816 para 5.

123 The relevant provisions are brought into force by the Coroners and Justice Act 2009 (Commencement No 4, Transitional and Saving Provisions) Order 2010 paras 5 and 6.

a person of the age and sex of the defendant and sharing all of the defendant's circumstances but with a 'normal degree of tolerance and self-restraint' would have lost control. The relevant qualifying triggers are a fear of serious violence from the victim or grave circumstances that caused the defendant to have a justifiable sense of being seriously wronged. While this inevitably involves looking at the state of mind of the defendant, and so the essential reasoning applied previously remains, there is also the contrary argument, namely that the test is one that can be established by objective evidence without any need to examine the mens rea of the defendant, and so should be available in determining the act of which the defendant is not guilty by reason of insanity.

12.90 A third possibility in relation to murder is the offence of infanticide under the Infanticide Act 1938 if it involves the particular elements of the actus reus, namely the killing by a woman of her own child under the age of 12 months in circumstances where her mind is disturbed. Since this can be returned as a verdict when the charge is murder and it involves a different actus reus, it is suggested that it would be open as a finding when the verdict of insanity is returned, so allowing a verdict of not guilty by reason of insanity of infanticide rather than of murder.

Evidence

12.91 The fifth question in the M'Naghten rules relates to the admissibility of expert evidence. The common law at the time was reluctant to admit expert opinion on the issue the jury had to determine.[124] In relation to insanity, this is now regulated by statute. Section 1 of the CP(IUP)A 1991 provides that '(1) A jury shall not return a special verdict ... (acquittal on ground of insanity) except on the written or oral evidence of two or more registered medical practitioners at least one of whom is duly approved'.

12.92 In *R v Borkan*,[125] it was held that similar language in relation to a finding of unfitness to stand trial in section 4(6) of the CP(I)A 1964 required that the medical evidence support a finding of unfitness. This reasoning is of persuasive value in this situation.[126] However,

124 It is now admissible in relation to the ultimate issue, the question being whether the court accepts this evidence: see *R v Stockwell* (1993) 97 CrAppR 260.

125 [2004] EWCA Crim 1642, [2004] MHLR 216.

126 The arguments against this proposition (*Borkan* being a case that did not involve argument on this point) are set out in paras 9.81–9.82.

it is clear that other evidence may also be relevant. For example, in *Attorney-General for South Australia v Brown*,[127] it was noted by the Privy Council that the conduct of the defendant at the time of a shooting was relevant.[128] Moreover, the Committee noted that its holding, which was to the effect that evidence of an irresistible impulse could not by itself be a symptom of insanity, did not mean that they were 'suggesting that legal insanity cannot be sufficiently proved without medical evidence' as the 'previous and contemporaneous acts of the accused may often be preferred to medical theory'. Rather, it held that where the defence case was based on a particular illness that required expert evidence to allow the jury to understand its consequences, medical evidence was required to explain the effect of the disorder. Since the language of the CP(I)A 1964 was introduced after *Brown*, a question arises as to whether it is in any way inconsistent with *Brown* or whether, to the contrary, it is designed to codify the effect of *Brown*.

12.93 The latter is clearly arguable: while the jury cannot speculate on the effect of a mental disorder, and so requires some expert evidence as to its operation, the facts to which it has to apply that evidence is clearly a matter for the jury. So the medical evidence on which the jury relies has to provide a proper basis for the possibility of an insanity verdict, but the factual finding as to the extent of the disorder at the relevant time remains a matter for the jury, which can reach this conclusion without medical reports that include a conclusion that the defendant was insane. In this connection, it should be noted that in *R v Roach*,[129] which is discussed below, the medical evidence on which reliance was placed spoke of 'insane automatism' and yet the appeal was successful on the basis that the judge should have given a direction on non-insane automatism as well, that being the proper understanding of the evidence given. This supports the approach outlined above: the labels attached by the doctors cannot be the deciding factor, since that is a matter of applying the law to the facts. From a practical perspective, however, it is important to ensure that experts have a proper understanding of the law and so can express a conclusion based on that.

127 [1960] AC 432.

128 [1960] AC 432 p454.

129 [2001] EWCA Crim 2698.

Partial delusions

12.94 The answers to questions one and four should not be forgotten: they indicate that if the defendant does not meet the test for insanity set out in questions two and three, and so is suffering from what are categorised as 'partial delusions', then the defendant is treated as a sane person. As noted above (see para 12.75), this in turn means that for the purposes of such issues as assessing liability in the case of a defendant who has made a mistake as to the facts, even though the mistaken perception was the result of mental disorder, that version of events may be one that has to be judged. At the same time, if the mental disorder causes disinhibition or causes a defendant to become involved in a crime that would not otherwise have occurred, it does not provide an excuse for the purposes of liability if the defendant was aware that the conduct was unlawful.

The consequence of the verdict of 'not guilty by reason of insanity'

12.95 As is described in chapter 9, section 5 of the CP(I)A 1964 as enacted provided that the consequence of a finding of not guilty by reason of insanity was admission to a psychiatric hospital as a restricted patient.[130] The propriety and proportionality of this – even though the Home Secretary could lift the restriction order and also release the detainee from hospital[131] – raised concerns. For example, it was noted in *R v Clarke*,[132] which, as discussed above, involved a shoplifting charge, that the defendant had changed her plea to one of guilty 'so as to avoid the disastrous consequences of her defence'[133] on the basis of the (wrongful) direction of the trial judge that it amounted to a claim of insanity. Mr Justice Devlin had noted in *Hill v Baxter*[134] that: 'The acquittal is now given in the illogical and disagreeable form of the verdict "Guilty but, insane," and while it seems right that in such a case some conditions should be imposed, the only restraint known to the law is indefinite detention in what used to be called a

130 In *Attorney-General's Reference (No 3 of 1998)* [1999] 2 CrAppR 214, it was noted that detention was usually in Broadmoor Hospital as a 'criminal lunatic'.

131 MHA 1959 s66; MHA 1983 s42.

132 (1972) 56 CrAppR 225.

133 (1972) 56 CrAppR 225 p228.

134 [1958] 1 QB 277.

criminal lunatic asylum',[135] which explained that it was unlikely to be raised in relation to driving offences. Indeed in *R v Windle*,[136] Lord Goddard CJ noted that it was usually only a line of defence raised in murder cases, which at the time involved the death penalty.

12.96 The CP(I)A 1964 s5 was amended by the CP(IUP)A 1991 to provide that a special verdict allowed the court to make one of four orders, namely an admission order (which had to be perfected by the Home Secretary but took effect as if it was a hospital order and to which a restriction order could be added), a guardianship order within the meaning of the MHA 1983, a supervision and treatment order, or an absolute discharge. These, the errors that might occur and other concerns and questions arising, are described in chapter 9. In particular, courts might purport to impose a hospital order; the difficulties to which this gave rise in the context of a finding of not guilty by reason of insanity are described below in relation to the limitations on appeals.

12.97 A further version of section 5 was introduced by the DVCVA 2004: it now provides that the options available on a finding of not guilty by reason of insanity are a hospital order under section 37 of the MHA 1983, which can be combined with a restriction order if the criteria under section 41 are met, or a supervision order or an absolute discharge. The option of a guardianship order has been removed. An obligation to make an admission order with a restriction order if the special verdict related to the actus reus of murder has been amended. CP(I)A 1964 s5(3) now provides that:

> (3) Where –
> (a) the offence to which the special verdict or the findings relate is an offence the sentence for which is fixed by law, and
> (b) the court have power to make a hospital order,
> the court shall make a hospital order with a restriction order (whether or not they would have power to make a restriction order apart from this subsection).

12.98 In other words, the statute still requires a restriction order in the case of a verdict or finding in relation to a murder charge but only if the court has the power to make a hospital order (which will arise only if there is supporting medical evidence and the other criteria are met).[137] The argument in favour of this mandatory combination with

135 [1958] 1 QB 277 p286.

136 [1952] 2 QB 826.

137 See para 9.180 for the contention that the criteria from the MHA 1983 are to be read across. This has meant that there is a change in access to a Tribunal: under MHA 1983 s69(2), a patient who was 'treated as subject to a hospital

a restriction order will no doubt be that Parliament may provide that this is the appropriate reaction to the involvement of the defendant in the actus reus of such a serious offence. On the other hand, given that the court has the discretion as to whether or not to make a hospital order as opposed to a supervision order if that is more suitable, it seems strange to require a restriction order rather than leaving it to the court (particularly as the addition of a restriction order might mean that a hospital order is not the most appropriate disposal).

12.99 The other powers of disposal mentioned in the revised section 5 apply equally to a finding of unfitness to stand trial but to have committed the act. The outline in chapter 9 applies also to the finding is of not guilty by reason of insanity but to have committed the act.

12.100 Although the special verdict is one of acquittal, it is treated in the same way as a conviction for various of the ancillary orders that can be made by the sentencing court or subsequently and which are designed to provide public protection. So, the 'notification and orders' provisions set out in Part 2 of the SOA 2003 apply:

a) The sex offender registration and notification provisions apply to a finding of not guilty by reason of insanity as much as to a conviction: see SOA 2003 s80.[138] Under SOA 2003 s97, the police may apply to the local magistrates' court for a notification order to be made in relation to an offender (that is, one who has not been caught by the provisions of sections 80 and following because the event occurred outside the UK); this covers a person found not guilty by reason of insanity, by reason of section 97(2) of the Act.
b) Sexual offences prevention orders to protect the public from 'serious sexual harm' from the defendant can be made by a sentencing court in relation to those found not guilty by reason of insanity of certain sexual offences and also numerous other offences which might have a sexual motive: see SOA 2003 s104(3)(a) and Schs 3 and 5. A sexual offences prevention order may also be made following an application by the police to the local magistrates' court under section 104(5), in which case it applies to a 'qualifying

order' in various situations, including by reason of an order under CP(I)A 1964 s5, was entitled to a tribunal hearing in the first six months of detention; in contrast, a hospital order patient could not apply until after six months, no doubt on the basis that there had been judicial consideration of whether hospitalisation was required at the sentencing hearing. Now that this applies in relation to an admission under the CP(I)A 1964, because the hospital order criteria apply in full, MHA 1983 s69(2) has been amended to remove the reference to the CP(IUP)A 1991: see DVCVA 2004 Sch 10 para 19.

138 A finding that a defendant not fit to stand trial but to have committed the act charged (see chapter 9) is also covered.

offender', who is defined in section 106(5)–(7) to include someone found not guilty by reason of insanity; this includes findings made before the SOA 2003 came into effect by reason of section 106(4).

c) Foreign travel orders can be made to protection children from harm from 'sex tourism' under SOA 2003 ss114–122; under section 116, a 'qualifying offender' for the purposes of these provisions includes a person found not guilty by reason of insanity.

12.101 There is also a regime of 'risk of sexual harm orders' that can be made by the magistrates' court on the application of the police in relation to a person who has engaged in sexual activity (widely-defined) in the presence of children and children need to be protected: see SOA 2003 ss123–129. This would include action of which the defendant is not guilty by reason of insanity, though the comments made in chapter 5 in relation to anti-social behaviour orders (ASBOs) and the value of making them if a person cannot comply by reason of mental disorder would apply in this context.

12.102 In addition, the provisions for making a violent offender order under section 98 and following of the Criminal Justice and Immigration Act (CJIA) 2008 provide that a 'qualifying offender' includes someone found not guilty by reason of insanity of one of the violent offences covered by the statute and sent to hospital or placed under a supervision order (see section 99(2) and (3) of the CJIA 2008).

Appeals

12.103 The Court of Appeal Criminal Division has various relevant powers arising under the Criminal Appeal Act (CAA) 1968. The first set of provisions deal with appeals against conviction. It is to be noted that CAA 1968 s5(1) applies in relation to 'an appeal against conviction' where a special verdict was returned; the heading to the section is: 'Disposal of appeal against conviction on special verdict'. This was the verdict available under the TLA 1883 until it became not guilty by reason of insanity under CP(I)A 1964 s1. Section 5 no doubt allowed an out-of-time appeal (or if a verdict is erroneously recorded as guilty but insane).[139]

139 See also the Criminal Cases Review (Insanity) Act 1999, which allows the Criminal Cases Review Commission to investigate verdicts of guilty but insane.

12.104 It is also possible that the appeal will be in relation to a conviction returned when the defendant argued that the proper verdict was not guilty by reason of insanity: the Court of Appeal has the power to substitute such a verdict (or a finding of unfitness to stand trial but that the act was committed) under CAA 1968 s6(1), provided that it has the relevant medical evidence. It may then impose such sentences as could have been imposed under CP(I)A 1964 s5 or s5A (ie hospital order, supervision order or absolute discharge; the powers of remanding the defendant for reports or treatment or the making of an interim hospital order also apply): CAA 1968 s6(2)–(7), as substituted by DVCVA 2004 s24(3).

12.105 A verdict of not guilty by reason of insanity can also be challenged under section 12 of the 1968 Act if the Court of Appeal grants leave to appeal or the trial judge certifies that an appeal is proper. The power of the Court of Appeal in such an appeal is to allow the appeal if the verdict is unsafe: CAA 1968 s13(1).

12.106 However, there is a proviso, set in CAA 1968 s13(3), that if the view of the Court of Appeal is that the verdict should have related to a different underlying charge (rather than anything relating to the finding of insanity), it may dismiss the appeal. This is a discretion; however, it is difficult to construe the provisions as allowing the Court of Appeal to substitute a verdict of not guilty of the lesser offence; this might be of some relevance in relation to questions of the appropriate disposal if the underlying offence was murder.

12.107 Under CAA 1968 s13(4), if the appeal is allowed on the basis that the finding of insanity is wrong, the Court of Appeal is required to substitute a finding of either not guilty or guilty of the offence charged or some other charge and shall sentence accordingly: but a guilty verdict can only be entered if the court views it as 'proper'. This may raise the interesting question of how the Court of Appeal is able to make any appropriate finding as to the relevant mens rea if the trial court has not investigated that issue in light of the contention described above that mens rea issues do not have to be considered. If the Court of Appeal entered a not guilty verdict, CAA 1968 s14A, as introduced by the CP(IUP)A 1991, allowed it to order admission to hospital for assessment if the acquitted person was mentally disordered. This power has been removed.[140] Any such admission will now only be possible under the civil powers contained in the MHA 1983.

140 See DVCVA 2004 s24(4).

12.108 It is also possible for the Court of Appeal to substitute a finding that the person was unfit to stand trial but committed the act, and to dispose accordingly: see CAA 1968 s14.

12.109 A gap existed in the regime under the CAA 1968 if the appeal was against the order made to dispose of the case on the basis of the special verdict. Given that the CP(I)A 1964 as it was enacted contained a mandatory disposal, it is no surprise that there would be no appeal provision in the CAA 1968 as enacted. However, when the trial court was given jurisdiction to choose the appropriate sentence in the 1991 statutory amendments, it might have been expected that there would be an amendment to the CAA 1968. However, there was not: while there was a wide definition of 'sentence' in section 50 of the CAA 1968 as 'any order made by a court when dealing with an offender', the reference to an offender was not appropriate in light of the nature of the finding, and in any event the sentence appeal provisions under section 9 of the Act required a conviction. In relation to a disposal imposed following a finding against a person found unfit to stand trial, it was at least possible to challenge it by judicial review: see *R v Mohammed Latif*.[141] However, in relation disposals following a verdict of not guilty by reason of insanity this route was not open because such a verdict followed a trial on indictment and so the jurisdiction of the judicial review court was excluded by reason of section 29 of the Senior Courts Act 1981 (which allows judicial review of the Crown Court save in relation to trials on indictment): see *R v Snaresbrook Crown Court ex p Demaar*.[142]

12.110 This gap has been filled by the addition of sections 16A and 16B of the CAA 1968 by DVCVA 2004 s25. The combined effect of these sections is that appeals can be taken against the imposition of a hospital order or a supervision order made under CP(I)A 1964 s5 (which applies to both the special verdict and when there has been a finding in relation to unfitness to stand trial). Such an appeal requires the leave of the Court of Appeal or a certificate of fitness to appeal from the trial judge. It is expressly provided that an appeal taken against an interim hospital order made under CP(I)A 1964 s5A does not prevent the trial court taking the steps it finds appropriate in relation to the

141 [2002] EWCA Crim 2115 and [2002] EWHC 1916 (Admin): this involved a challenge to the propriety of the making of an admission order rather than the making of supervision and treatment order after a finding of unfitness to stand trial but to have done the act alleged, but the Court of Appeal noted that it had no jurisdiction to consider such an appeal; it reconstituted itself as a judicial review court, and dismissed the challenge.

142 [2000] MHLR 239.

renewal of such an order or the imposition of an order on the completion of the interim order (CAA 1968 s16B(2)); the Court of Appeal may also impose an interim hospital order and pass the matter back to the trial court (CAA 1968 s16B(3)). Not surprisingly, there is no appeal against an absolute discharge.

12.111 Prosecution appeals should also be mentioned. In relation to acquittals, it is possible for the prosecution to refer a point of law involved in an acquittal on indictment to the Court of Appeal under section 36 of the Criminal Justice Act 1972. However, the verdict of not guilty by reason of insanity is a special verdict, not an acquittal (which would apply if the defendant was found not to have committed the actus reus).[143] Accordingly, the question is whether that counts as a form of acquittal: certainly, the policy behind the 1972 Act would cover such a verdict, but it would have been easy for Parliament to provide a clear indication that special verdicts are covered and it has not done so.[144] If the Court of Appeal has no jurisdiction, a question might then arise as to whether or not the prosecution could bring a challenge by way of judicial review: the issue here is the exclusion of judicial review over 'matters relating to trial on indictment' (as a result of section 29(3) of the Senior Courts Act 1981). While a trial on indictment is clearly involved, it has been held that if a judge has acted wholly outside his or her jurisdiction, the exclusion under section 29(3) does not apply. In *R v Maidstone Crown Court ex p LB Harrow*,[145] a supervision order under the CP(I)A 1964 was quashed on the basis that the judge made it after purporting to find a defendant not guilty by reason of insanity without empanelling a jury and so acting wholly outside his jurisdiction under the indictment.

12.112 In relation to sentences, the prosecution has the power under section 36 of the Criminal Justice Act (CJA) 1988 to refer an 'unduly lenient' sentence to the Court of Appeal. What amounts to a sentence and the process of sentencing is defined in CJA 1988 s35 to include whatever counts as a sentence for the purposes of the CAA 1968 except an interim hospital order: this could encompass the making of a hospital order. However, the idea of an order that has been imposed for protective purposes being 'unduly lenient' – which has

143 See, for example, *Attorney-General's Reference (No 3 of 1998)* [1999] 2 CrAppR 214.

144 In a very different context, it was held in *R v Felstead* [1914] AC 534 that the special verdict of guilty but insane was an acquittal and so the person affected could not appeal to the Court of Criminal Appeal under the Criminal Appeal Act 1907, which required a conviction.

145 [1999] MHLR 84.

connotations of not being adequately punitive – does not seem apposite to cover the making of an order under CP(I)A 1964 s5. However, as noted above, such a sentence is not made pursuant to a trial on indictment and so the prosecution would be able to take a challenge by way of judicial review.

12.113 One general point to note is that it is possible that appeals in the context of insanity will arise out of time on the basis of medical evidence coming to light after a trial process. This has been a feature in relation to appeals that were based on someone having been unfit to stand trial:[146] the same may occur in relation to an argument that someone was insane at the time of the commission of the offence, since failures accurately to identify mental disorder at the time of the trial process may be matched by failures in relation to mental health issues at the time of the incident. However, the case of *R v Shulman*[147] indicates a potential practical issue. There had been concerns about Mr Shulman's fitness to stand trial but he had not co-operated with the preparation of reports, denying that he was ill: after he was convicted and sentenced to imprisonment, his mental health difficulties became apparent and the evidence prepared indicated that he had been mentally ill at the time of the offending and at the time of the trial. The Court of Appeal admitted the evidence, but felt unable to entertain substituting a verdict of not guilty by reason of insanity, but did quash the convictions and substitute findings that he had committed the acts but had been unfit to stand trial. There were two features to the reasoning. The first was that there was no contemporaneous assessment of insanity: this may often be a feature, namely that there is better evidence relating to fitness to stand trial than of mental state at the time of the offence, simply because there is more interaction during the trial process with people who can provide relevant evidence. Second, it was noted that if the evidence was of a mental disorder that supported both insanity at the time of the offence and unfitness to stand trial, the trial court would not get to the position of considering the substantive defence of insanity.

Unfitness to plead and insanity

12.114 From the discussion above, it is clear that there is a significant overlap between unfitness to stand trial and insanity – but there are also

146 See para 9.196.

147 [2010] EWCA Crim 1034, [2010] MHLR 172.

a number of differences. The insanity defence is a matter of substantive law that is concerned with the accused person's state of mind at the time of committing the offence, while fitness to be tried is a procedural matter concerned with the accused person's state of mind at the time of his or her arraignment and trial. While the mental disorder (or impact on the mind or ability to participate from some physical cause) may apply both at the time of the offence and at the time of any trial, it is also possible that the accused may have been insane at the time of the offence but be fit to stand trial or vice versa. Which of these scenarios is likely will often turn on the nature of the disorder and questions of the time lag between the alleged offending and the trial: for example, some mental illnesses may vary significantly over time, whereas a severe learning disability is unlikely to change much over time.

12.115 The following table attempts to summarise the similarities and differences between the questions of insanity and the statutory fitness to stand trial process.

	Fitness to stand trial	**Insanity defence**
Criteria	Inability to understand charges, decide on plea, challenge jurors, instruct lawyers, follow evidence, give evidence	Defect of reason so as not to know either the nature and quality of the act or that it was wrong
Cause	Disability so as to bar trial	Disease of the mind
Relevant time	Arraignment and trial	Conduct alleged
Who can raise	Defence, prosecution or court	Defence; prosecution in response to diminished responsibility (and some dicta suggesting wider)
Timing – raising issue	Any time	During defence case (including as rebuttal)
Timing – determining issue	If raised before end of prosecution case, can be deferred until end; otherwise, determined as raised	Part of verdict

	Fitness to stand trial	Insanity defence
Burden of proof	On the party who raises it	On the party who raises it
Standard of proof	Balance of probabilities if raised by defence; beyond reasonable doubt if raised by prosecution; if raised by judge, prosecution burden unless defence take on issue	Balance of probabilities if raised by defence; beyond reasonable doubt if raised by prosecution; if can be raised by judge, prosecution burden unless defence take on issue
Requirement for medical evidence	Requires evidence from two or more registered medical practitioners at least one of who is duly approved	Requires evidence from two or more registered medical practitioners at least one of whom is duly approved
The tribunal and its role	Judge to decide if accused unfit to stand trial	Jury decision
Consequence if finding made	Jury to decide on a trial of the facts if the accused did the act or made the omission charged; if not, acquittal; if so, finding made as to that element	Jury to decide also if accused committed act: if not, acquittal; if so, special verdict of not guilty by reason of insanity
Sentencing options	1. Hospital order (with or without a restriction order) 2. Supervision order 3. Absolute discharge	1. Hospital order (with or without a restriction order) 2. Supervision order 3. Absolute discharge
Murder charge	Court must impose hospital order with restriction order if criteria for a hospital order are made out	Court must impose hospital order with restriction order if criteria for a hospital order are made out
Remission for trial	If hospital and restriction order made and trial proper	No

CHAPTER 13

Insanity in a summary trial

The availability of the defence in summary proceedings

Is the verdict applicable?

13.1 An obvious question arises as to the application of the rules set out in *M'Naghten's Case*, discussed in chapter 12, given that the answer to questions two and three refers to the direction to be given to the jury. Does that mean that they do not apply to criminal proceedings without a jury? Similarly, the statutory provisions now contained in the Trial of Lunatics Act (TLA) 1883 as to the special verdict being returned by the jury seem to suggest that it is only in relation to trials in front of a jury that special verdict can be returned. However, the opening language of section 2 of the TLA 1883 refers to a trial 'on indictment or information', which raises the question of whether the special verdict may be returned following a trial on an information laid in the magistrates' court (though that would leave open the question of how that could apply in the light of the absence of a jury).

13.2 This potential quandary was answered by the conclusion in *R v Horseferry Road Magistrates' Court ex p K*[1] that the reference to an 'information' is to the process that used to exist of laying an information in the High Court to commence a criminal prosecution (rather than the normal process of committal proceedings).[2] It was also noted that the statutory language of the special verdict was not suited to cover trials in the magistrates' court, but that the common law defence of insanity was applicable to summary proceedings. This was consistent with the indication given by the House of Lords in *R v Sullivan*[3] that the M'Naghten rules apply 'in all cases' in which it is sought 'to establish a defence on the ground of insanity'.[4] However, it was an obiter dictum.

13.3 In *K*, the magistrates' court had accepted jurisdiction with the consent of the defendant in relation to an affray and a common assault, the former being triable either way. When the matter came

1 [1997] QB 23.

2 Criminal Law Act 1967 s6(6) abolished 'any power to bring proceedings for an offence by criminal information in the High Court'; this was a process by then only available to the Attorney-General, as Administration of Justice (Miscellaneous Provisions) Act 1938 s12 abolished the process of filing informations by a private individual (via the Master of the Crown Office).

3 [1984] AC 156.

4 [1984] AC 156 Lord Diplock at p171: it must be accepted that he did not purport to be answering a question as to whether the M'Naghten rules did in fact apply in summary proceedings.

to trial, the issue was raised in the medical reports as to whether a restriction order should be made under section 41 of the Mental Health Act (MHA) 1983, which can only be made by a Crown Court;[5] while section 43 allows the magistrates' court to commit a defendant for sentence with a view to the imposition of a restriction order, this power applies only if it has convicted a defendant. The district judge sitting on the case[6] reopened the question of mode of trial and decided to commit the case for trial in the Crown Court in light of the medical reports.[7] This decision was challenged on the basis that the court could not reopen the question of mode of trial before evidence had been called;[8] the Divisional Court held that the trial had commenced with a ruling on a point of law and so mode of trial could be reopened. An argument that the question of whether a restriction order should be imposed did not justify reopening the question of mode of trial was dismissed on the basis that factors relevant to the question of the ultimate disposal were relevant to the issue of whether jurisdiction should be retained by the magistrates' court or sent to the Crown Court.

13.4 The district judge had declined to rule on the question of whether the defence of insanity could be raised in the magistrates' court. Although this was an academic question in the light of the upholding of the decision to send the case to the Crown Court, the Divisional Court heard argument on the availability of the defence of insanity in summary proceedings as it was an important point of law. The conclusion was that insanity was a common law defence applicable to all offences, or at least those involving a mens rea element;[9] the court noted that:

> It seems to us to be clearly established that the position at common law prior to 1800 was that the defence of insanity was available to all criminal prosecutions, whether brought in a magistrates' court

5 See chapter 18.

6 At that stage known as a stipendiary magistrate.

7 The affray charge could be transferred for trial; the common assault charge could be transferred as a summary offence linked to the indictable offence.

8 Magistrates' Courts Act 1980 s25(2) allows the court to move from summary trial to transfer for trial once it has begun to 'try the information'.

9 Counsel for *K* adopted the assertion in Archbold that insanity was a defence of general application that produced a situation in which mens rea was absent and so submitted that it was a defence available whenever mens rea was in issue: see [1997] QB 23 at p41. At p27, the court, citing Archbold, stated that: 'Insanity ... is not a species of special defence but merely a particular situation where mens rea is lacking. Accordingly, it is available in all criminal charges where mens rea is in issue ...'. This limitation is discussed below.

or upon indictment. In *Pleas of the Crown*, 3rd ed (1739), William Hawkins stated the position to be as follows, at pp1–2: 'Section 1. ... those who are under a natural disability of distinguishing between good and evil, as ... ideots and lunaticks ... are not punishable *by any criminal prosecution whatsoever*'. (Emphasis added.)

13.5 The court then commented that the various statutes as to the special verdict had had no impact on the common law test for insanity or its availability in summary trials, and that therefore it remained available as a defence in the magistrates' court.

13.6 The position has been put beyond doubt in *R (Singh) v Stratford Magistrates' Court*,[10] which involved a summary only offence to which the defence raised was insanity. In the Divisional Court proceedings, the prosecution contended that the defence of insanity was not available in the magistrates' court. The suggestion made[11] was that the question for the summary court was whether the act of the offence was committed (for reasons that are discussed below, relating to the process arising under section 37(3) of the Mental Health Act 1983) and as insanity negatived mens rea, the fact that the court never got to the question of mens rea meant that insanity could not be raised. The two central planks in the submission were that section 37(3) was the exclusive procedure and insanity as a defence was relevant only to issues of mens rea.

13.7 Lord Justice Hughes in the Divisional Court dealt with the submission as a matter of jurisdiction first and then as a matter of discretion. In the first place, he was of the view that there was a defence of insanity as a matter of common law that remained available in the magistrates' court and, if successful, would lead to an acquittal. He repeated the view set out in *K* that the defence of insanity was a general common law defence, noting:

> 15. Insanity was recognised as a defence long before any statutory intervention. Two early examples are *Arnold's Case* (1724) 16 St Tr 695, where the defendant shot Lord Onslow and alleged (unsuccessfully in the end) that he was mad at the time, and *Hadfield's Case* (1800) 27 St Tr 1281 where the defendant tried to assassinate King George III and was acquitted on grounds of insanity. What constituted insanity was debated until resolved by the well known decision in *M'Naghten's Case* (1843) 10 Cl & Fin 200. But insanity was thus recognised as a defence to criminal liability at common law.

10 [2007] EWHC 1582 (Admin), [2007] MHLR 274.
11 [2007] EWHC 1582 (Admin), [2007] MHLR 274 para 13.

13.8 He then commented that the various statutory provisions relating to the special verdict were relevant only to what should happen in a trial on indictment and had no impact on the test for insanity.[12] Accordingly, the starting point was that insanity could be raised in a summary trial as a 'common law defence' which '[i]f established by the accused in a case to which it is relevant ... prevents conviction'.[13]

Is the verdict limited to offences involving mens rea?

13.9 There is conflicting jurisprudence as to whether insanity can be raised as a defence in relation to offences that do not have a mens rea element. In *R v Horseferry Road Magistrates' Court ex p K*,[14] the Divisional Court, citing the main practitioner text, Archbold, stated that: 'Insanity ... is not a species of special defence but merely a particular situation where mens rea is lacking. Accordingly, it is available in all criminal charges where mens rea is in issue ...'. It is to be noted, however, that the offences charged in *K* (affray and common assault) involved a mens rea and so the comments made were obiter: they were not the focus of the question arising, which was whether a magistrate could re-open mode of trial in order to send a case to the Crown Court with a view to the making of a restriction order.

13.10 Despite these caveats, the comments in *K* formed the basis of the decision in *Director of Public Prosecutions v H*,[15] in which the Divisional Court determined that the question of insanity was irrelevant in relation to a strict liability offence (driving with excess alcohol) and so directed a conviction on the basis that the defendant had been driving at a time when he had excess alcohol. McCowan LJ for the court stated that:

> We are quite clear, therefore, that the law is as I have stated, and that insanity can be a defence in the magistrates' court, but only if the offence charged is one in which mens rea is an element. Every man is assumed to be sane at the time of an alleged offence, and accordingly the burden is on the defendant to establish insanity at the time of the commission of the offence on the balance of probabilities. The defence is based on the absence of mens rea, but none is required for the offence of driving with an excess of alcohol. Hence the defence of

12 [2007] EWHC 1582 (Admin), [2007] MHLR 274 paras 15–20.

13 [2007] EWHC 1582 (Admin), [2007] MHLR 274 para 22.

14 [1997] QB 23.

15 [1997] 1 WLR 1406.

insanity has no relevance to such a charge as it is an offence of strict liability.[16]

13.11 This suggestion that insanity cannot be raised is problematic.[17] In relation to the second limb of the M'Naghten rules, relating to knowledge of the wrongfulness of the action, this is a type of mens rea issue: but the insanity defence operates as an excuse because the defendant is not capable to knowing the illegality or wrongfulness of conduct. This is a skill that others are presumed to have once they reach the age of criminal responsibility (the presumption of doli incapax having been removed by section 34 of the Crime and Disorder Act 1998): but just as a failure of rebut doli incapax would have led to an acquittal even in relation to a matter that did not involve a mens rea, it can be considered that the first limb of the insanity test is equivalent to a finding of doli incapax and hence a reason not to convict because it demonstrates that the normal approach to responsibility does not apply.

13.12 The ruling in *H* also suggests that the first limb of the M'Naghten rules cannot be raised either: they may involve a situation in which the defendant is acting as automaton, meaning a lack of responsibility for the actus reus. Fortunately, a contrary view has been put forward in *Singh*, in which it was suggested that there were two issues in the Crown Court situation, namely, first, the question of insanity and then the special verdict based on the finding of the actus reus having been committed.[18] This suggestion arose from the fact that 'if insanity be established the accused by definition has insufficient mental state for the offence'.[19] This did not mean, however, that mens rea had no relevance to a trial if insanity was raised. Rather, 'in the procedure provided for trial on indictment, it is only when insanity is once established, and one moves on to the determination whether the act or omission charged was done or made, that the state of mind of the accused is irrelevant'.[20] This did not mean that the case-law 'removes proof of *mens rea* from a case where insanity is in issue.

16 [1997] 1 WLR 1406 at 1409.

17 This is developed in more detail in chapter 12.

18 [1997] 1 WLR 1406 para 17, citing *Attorney-General's Reference No 3 of 1998* [1999] 2 CrAppR 214.

19 [1997] 1 WLR 1406: He added at paragraphs 18–19 that the same was the case with the question of fitness to stand trial: once the determination has been made that someone is not fit to stand trial and the court moves on to the question of whether the act was committed, mens rea questions cease to be relevant.

20 [1997] 1 WLR 1406 para 20.

On the contrary, insanity, where established by an accused, usually operates to show that he did not have the state of mind necessary for commission of the offence'.[21] What the judge presumably has in mind in making this comment is the second limb of the M'Naghten rules, namely the lack of awareness of the wrongness of the conduct (which is seemingly a mens rea question). The first limb, namely where a defendant does not know the nature or quality of the act may be more suggestive of a lack of responsibility for the actus reus, is some form of automatism, rather than of a lack of mens rea.

13.13 It is submitted that this case establishes the correct understanding of the processes and the relevance of mens rea. It must first be established whether the defendant is within the insanity test (which may go to provide that there is no mens rea, particularly under the second stage of the test, namely the lack of knowledge of the wrongness of the action; but may also go to undermine responsibility for the actus reus, and so can be raised even if the offence does not involve issues of mens rea). In the Crown Court, there is then the question of whether the statutory test for entering the special verdict is met, at which stage issues of mens rea are irrelevant.

The powers of disposal and the discretion as to whether to proceed to verdict

13.14 So, it is clear that the defence of insanity applies in the summary jurisdiction. The next question that arises is whether the absence of the statutory special verdict means that the magistrates' court is compelled to acquit and release the defendant? The statutory provisions applicable to jury trials were introduced in order to clarify the power of the court to detain the defendant who was found to have been insane at the time of the offence.[22] The value of this policy might be thought to have a lesser weight in the light of the less serious nature of most summary offences. This in turn might support a view that there does not need to be a power to detain because the defendant can be left to be dealt with by the civil provisions of the MHA 1983. In support of this, see the question of diversion, where the interest in bringing a criminal prosecution might be much reduced if an acquittal on the basis of insanity is likely and the real interest in the

21 [1997] 1 WLR 1406 para 20.
22 See chapter 12.

case is securing hospital treatment that can be provided without the criminal courts.[23]

13.15 An alternative was hinted at in *K* and made express in *Singh*, namely that the court can and should make use of the power under MHA 1983 s37(3) to impose a hospital order or a guardianship order without convicting the defendant if it is satisfied 'that the accused did the act or made the omission charged'. As originally enacted, this only applied if the defendant had a mental illness or severe mental impairment, two of the categories of mental disorder under the MHA 1983: most situations of insanity would arise in the context of a mental illness. However, as a result of the changes introduced by the MHA 2007, this now applies to all forms of mental disorder and so the limited prospect of delusions without a mental illness is covered.

13.16 The court in *K*, having noted the availability of the common law defence of insanity, added that there was an apparent lacuna, specifically that nothing could be done in relation to a defendant who was acquitted;[24] however, it also noted that:

> ... section 37(3) of the Act of 1983 confers upon justices similar powers of disposal to those available in the Crown Court after a finding of 'unfitness to plead' or a verdict of not guilty by reason of insanity, as provided for by section 1 of the Act of 1964 and section 5 of and Schedule 1 to the Act of 1991.

13.17 What was raised in *Singh* was whether, when the question of insanity was an issue in the proceedings, the magistrates' court should hold a trial or could proceed without a trial under the MHA 1983. Mr Singh was charged with a summary-only offence of assaulting a police officer in the execution of his duty, contrary to section 89 of the Police Act 1996. The evidence of a consultant psychiatrist was that he had been labouring under a defect of reason from a disease of the mind so as not to know the nature and quality of his act. The district judge decided to proceed under MHA 1983 s37(3) with a view to making a hospital order or a guardianship order without a conviction, and adjourned for the preparation of the necessary second medical report. The defendant challenged this decision by judicial review; he argued that he was entitled to seek an acquittal.

13.18 Lord Justice Hughes in the Divisional Court dealt with the submission as a matter of jurisdiction first and then as a matter of discretion.

23 See chapter 5 in relation to the question of diversion and the factors relevant to that process.

24 [1997] QB 23 at p45.

Having determined that the common law defence of insanity applied in summary proceedings, the next question was the impact of the existence of the power in MHA 1983 s37(3) to make a hospital order without a conviction. There was another relevant provision, namely section 11 of the Powers of Criminal Courts (Sentencing) Act 2000, which provides:

> If, on the trial by a magistrates' court of an offence punishable on summary conviction with imprisonment, the court –
> (a) is satisfied that the accused did the act or made the omission charged, but
> (b) is of the opinion that an inquiry ought to be made in to his physical or mental condition before the method of dealing with him is determined,
>
> the court shall adjourn the case to enable a medical examination and report to be made, and shall remand him.

13.19 It was noted that this contemplated the use of MHA 1983 s37(3), given the same language as to being satisfied that the act was committed, and so the two sections were to be read together;[25] and that when this was done the two provisions together created 'a coherent scheme for dealing with most defendants in the magistrates' court who are suffering from mental illness when they appear'.[26] However, this did not support a statutory intention to abolish the common law defence of insanity: first, this would be 'so radical a change' that it would 'require express provision'.[27] Second, the provisions were concerned with mental state at the time of trial, which might involve a defendant who had recovered from whatever mental state was applicable at the time of the alleged offence, the point at which insanity was relevant, and so be excluded from the ambit of section 37(3).[28]

13.20 So the common law defence of insanity remained in place; but that did not mean that a defendant was necessarily entitled to argue for an acquittal on the basis of insanity.[29] This turned on the interplay between section 9(2) of the Magistrates' Courts Act 1980, which requires a summary court to hear the evidence in a trial, after which it 'shall convict the accused or dismiss the information'; the power to make a hospital order (or guardianship order) without a conviction in

25 [2007] EWHC 1582 (Admin), [2007] MHLR 274 para 11.

26 [2007] EWHC 1582 (Admin), [2007] MHLR 274 para 23. The reference to 'mental illness' is no doubt deliberate because MHA 1983 s37(3) was at the time only applicable if there was mental illness or severe mental impairment.

27 [2007] EWHC 1582 (Admin), [2007] MHLR 274 para 23.

28 [2007] EWHC 1582 (Admin), [2007] MHLR 274 para 23.

29 [2007] EWHC 1582 (Admin), [2007] MHLR 274 para 24.

MHA 1983 s37(3); and other common law powers to adjourn or stay trials. Lord Justice Hughes commented that the existence of section 37(3) indicated that the purpose of Magistrates' Courts Act 1980 s9(2) was to control what happened once the court had decided that there should be a trial. But there was also the power to decide not to have a trial, which could be achieved by adjourning sine die or staying proceedings as an abuse of process, but also by making use of section 37(3) if that was appropriate. He concluded that:

> Section 37(3) was enacted in the knowledge that section 9 existed. It is quite clear that it provides another case in which the court can, if it be right to do so, decline to conduct a trial. I can see no reason in section 9 for saying that an insanity case is outside the ambit of section 37(3).[30]

13.21 In fact, as MHA 1983 s37(3) was the successor to section 60(2) of the MHA 1959, and was in similar terms, it may be more correct to say that section 9 of the Magistrates' Courts Act 1980 was put in place in the knowledge that there was the power not to proceed to a conviction. The point remains that the statutory provisions co-existed in circumstances in which it could not be said that there was any suggestion that one effected the implicit repeal of the other. Accordingly, the question was how they stood together, the key to understanding which was the ambit of section 37(3). In relation to this, Hughes LJ recorded that there was only a limited difference between the parties, and in particular it was accepted for Mr Singh that the court could make an order under section 37(3) in relation to a defendant who wanted to argue that he was insane at the time of the offence and so not guilty: the dispute was whether the defendant was entitled to be acquitted (which was the contention for Mr Singh) or whether the court was entitled to act without entering a verdict of not guilty (which was the contention of the prosecution).[31]

13.22 The argument for Mr Singh was that it was possible to make an order under the MHA 1983 after a not guilty verdict because the words 'without convicting him' in section 37(3) should be interpreted as meaning 'despite acquitting him'.[32] That would allow the court to comply with the duty under Magistrates' Courts Act 1980 s9 of hearing the evidence and then convicting or dismissing the information by acquitting him (the latter course being the one that would be taken). This would avoid the problem that there is no rehabilitation

30 [2007] EWHC 1582 (Admin), [2007] MHLR 274 para 29.
31 [2007] EWHC 1582 (Admin), [2007] MHLR 274 para 27.
32 [2007] EWHC 1582 (Admin), [2007] MHLR 274 para 27.

period under the Rehabilitation of Offenders Act (ROA) 1974. It was also suggested that there was an entitlement to an acquittal to avoid breaching article 6 of the European Convention on Human Rights (ECHR) (right to a fair trial). The latter two arguments were dealt with by the court fairly briefly.

13.23 As to the ROA 1974, a 'conviction' includes – by reason of section 1(4)(b) – 'any finding (other than a finding linked with a finding of insanity) in any criminal proceedings that a person has committed an offence or done the act or made the omission charged'. This means that the ROA 1974 does not apply, but as Hughes LJ noted, it does not have to apply because the defendant has not been convicted and so does not have to reveal the finding when asked about previous convictions.[33] This is no doubt true; but it was also pointed out that the finding might appear as an antecedent in case of a further appearance in court (and so be taken into account in deciding a future sentence, including a sentence based on dangerousness). There was no particular answer given to this, save to note that neither the finding nor any disposal was criminal in nature and that it might properly be relevant to any future action taken by a criminal court.[34] The latter point is no doubt correct; but there is a somewhat more subtle question to raise, which is that various other acquittals might also be relevant – if, for example, a person is acquitted on several occasions of serious assaults because the person has made honest mistakes and has been found to have acted in self-defence when a reasonable person would not have done so, this may reveal a tendency to get into dangerous situations that might be relevant to a disposal when there is a conviction. In other words, there seems to be a differential treatment of those whose acquittal is on the grounds of insanity: this is long-established and so a challenge to it may be unlikely.

13.24 As to the final argument made, namely a right to an acquittal by reason of ECHR article 6, this was rejected with the comment that: 'If there is no breach in treating defendants charged on indictment by way of special verdict and a consequential order which often involves indefinite detention, there cannot be a breach in achieving the same result, with less draconian consequential order, by less formal machinery in the magistrates' court'.[35] This is far from convincing, however: the special verdict in the Crown Court does amount to a determination of the criminal charge and brings the criminal

33 [2007] EWHC 1582 (Admin), [2007] MHLR 274 para 30.

34 [2007] EWHC 1582 (Admin), [2007] MHLR 274 para 30.

35 [2007] EWHC 1582 (Admin), [2007] MHLR 274 para 31.

proceedings to an end (with no power of remittal for trial as applies in certain circumstances when a defendant is unfit to stand trial).[36] In other words, the power to impose any consequential order is predicated on compliance with article 6 by reaching a verdict in the criminal process. A simple finding of not guilty in the magistrates' court would equally amount to the determination of the criminal charge, whereas the making of a finding under MHA 1983 s37(3) without entering a verdict is clearly not. There is a more rational reason for the same conclusion: if the defendant meets the criteria for being placed in hospital, namely those applicable under ECHR article 5(4), it is a proportionate breach of his or her article 6 right to a speedy determination of a criminal charge for the hospital placement to be arranged.

13.25 To return to the main contention of Mr Singh, namely that the acquittal could be followed by an order under MHA 1983 s37(3), the court decided that this was not practical: it side-stepped the question of whether it would be functus officio as soon as the not guilty verdict was announced and so without power to make an order under section 37(3), and suggested that there would be real problems in making such an order, such as not having a power to require the defendant to submit to a medical examination.[37]

13.26 The final conclusion was that where a defendant raises the question of fitness to stand trial or insanity, the court should deal first with the question of whether the medical conditions for a hospital order or guardianship order are made, they being the preconditions to proceeding under MHA 1983 s37(3). Naturally, if those preconditions are not met, there is no option but to have a trial.[38] If they are met, the power to proceed under section 37(3) arises: the exercise of the discretion would turn on the interests of justice in each case, which allows consideration of the interests of the accused, for whom it may be important to demonstrate that he was legally insane at the time of the offence rather than acting with a criminal mens rea.[39] However, it was also held that the interests of the public in the making of an order under section 37(3) if the conditions for such an order are met mean that the court should make the order under section 37(3) and

36 Criminal Procedure (Insanity) Act 1964 s5A(4); see chapter 9.
37 [2007] EWHC 1582 (Admin), [2007] MHLR 274 para 36.
38 [2007] EWHC 1582 (Admin), [2007] MHLR 274 para 40. This will be subject to any arguments as to abuse of process.
39 [2007] EWHC 1582 (Admin), [2007] MHLR 274 para 34.

announce a finding of insanity rather than to enter a verdict of not guilty.[40]

13.27 Two things should be said. First, this is presented as a practical solution in the light of concerns about public safety matters. However, this effectively introduces a special verdict procedure (albeit a declaration of insanity rather than a formal verdict) in relation to a situation in which there would otherwise be an entitlement to an acquittal, which is problematic because the statutory provisions as to the special verdict are clearly limited to trials on indictment. Parliament has chosen to draw a distinction, based no doubt on the fact that summary-only offences or either-way offences that are suitable for summary trial do not raise the same public safety concerns as indictable only offences or either-way offences that merit a Crown Court trial, and this interpretation undermines this distinction.

13.28 Second, there may be a bolder argument that could have been put for Mr Singh, which is as follows. The main power to make a hospital order is in MHA 1983 s37(1) of the and turns on a conviction: section 37(3) refers back to this power with its opening clause, namely: 'Where a person is charged before a magistrates' court with any act or omission as an offence and the court would have power, on convicting him of that offence, to make an order under subsection (1)'. In such a situation, there is a power to make the order without a conviction if the court 'thinks fit'. What is not dealt with in *Singh* is whether the focus should be on the charge (the first part of the jurisdictional clause arising under section 37(3)) or the charge as it applies in the case of the particular defendant (which involves both parts of the clause and so may be preferable). If the latter, the important part of section 37(3) is the existence of the power of conviction of the defendant: since a person who was insane at the time of the offence could not be convicted, no power to make a hospital order could arise. That would limit section 37(3) to a situation in which it is not possible to make a final determination, that is when the defendant is not fit to participate in the trial.

13.29 In sum, an argument with two elements seems to require further consideration if a defendant is fit to stand trial and wishes to raise a defence of insanity at the time of the offence:

a) the impact of the right to a speedy determination of the question of guilt or innocence arising under article 6; and

40 [2007] EWHC 1582 (Admin), [2007] MHLR 274 paras 34, 38 and 39.

b) whether a hospital order or guardianship order without a conviction can be made under MHA 1983 s37(3) in the light of the fact that a conviction cannot result.

The end result of *Singh* is not inconsistent with allowing these arguments to be raised. If they are right, and the section 37(3) process is limited to situations in which the defendant is not fit to stand trial, so that a defendant who is fit to stand trial should be allowed to have a verdict in relation to insanity, this is different from the outcome in *Singh* only in limited cases, given that the trial must proceed if there is no suggestion that the defendant might need to be in hospital or placed under guardianship, and in many cases when the defendant needs to be in hospital he or she will not be fit to stand trial. The difference between the outcome in *Singh* and the alternative suggestion as to the law is that if the defendant is both fit to stand trial and in need of a hospital or guardianship placement, the Divisional Court suggested that there was a discretion to proceed under section 37(3), whereas it is suggested that arguments not adduced in the case suggest that the defendant is entitled to an acquittal in such a case. That would mean the court would have to determine whether a section 37(3) order could be made after an acquittal. But even if it could not, any need for hospitalisation or placement under guardianship could be secured via the civil provisions of the MHA 1983.

13.30 Of course, until this is argued further, the law remains as set out in *Singh*, with the discretion of the court being wider than it is suggested is proper. The court also made a sensible suggestion as to procedural matters: namely, that the potential for adjourned hearings is such that any question of insanity should, where possible, be put in front of a district judge so that continuity can be achieved.[41]

13.31 One point worth noting in this context is that the finding that the act was committed under MHA 1983 s37(3) does not permit the defendant to be committed for sentence with a view to considering the imposition of a restriction order. This power of committal arises under section 43 of the MHA 1983 but only if there has been a conviction. However, in *R v Horseferry Road Magistrates' Court ex p K*,[42] it was noted that the need to consider a restriction order might be a reason to commit for trial.

41 [2007] EWHC 1582 (Admin), [2007] MHLR 274 para 42.
42 [1997] QB 23.

CHAPTER 14

Homicide and mental disorder

continued

Introduction

14.1 In relation to a charge of murder, there are two partial defences – diminished responsibility and provocation (now known as loss of control) – which allow a defendant to be convicted of manslaughter instead. There is a third relevant area, namely the offence of infanticide, which shares some features with diminished responsibility and is a verdict that can be returned when the charge is murder, but is different in that it is also a free-standing charge (ie, the prosecution do not have to phrase the charge as murder if they accept that the elements of infanticide are present).

14.2 A verdict of manslaughter or infanticide means that the strictures imposed on judges on a conviction of murder, and in particular the mandatory sentence of life imprisonment under section 1(1) of the Murder (Abolition of Death Penalty) Act 1965, do not follow. In particular, the sentencing judge may impose a hospital disposal if the criteria for that are met: this is discussed in chapter 18. Of course, questions of diminished responsibility, provocation or infanticide relate to the state of the defendant at the time of the alleged offence, whereas the disposal relates to the state of the defendant at the time of sentencing, which may well be very different.

14.3 The partial defence of diminished responsibility is a creature of statute in England and Wales, having been introduced in the Homicide Act (HA) 1957 to provide the equivalent of what had been developed by the judges in Scotland. It has been amended significantly by section 52 of the Coroners and Justice Act 2009 with effect from 4 October 2010[1] but not retrospectively. Consequently, both the original and the amended text are discussed. Provocation was a common law defence, which was modified by the HA 1957, and has recently been amended significantly by the Coroners and Justice Act 2009 to become the 'loss of control' partial defence. Since the 2009 provisions, which came into effect on 4 October 2010[2] are not retrospective, the 1957 provisions and the case-law that developed under them may well be relevant for some time.

14.4 It may be thought strange that the consequence of diminished responsibility or provocation/loss of control is full responsibility for a different offence, namely manslaughter. It would no doubt have

1 Coroners and Justice Act 2009 (Commencement No 4, Transitional and Saving Provisions) Order 2010 SI No 816 para 5.

2 Coroners and Justice Act 2009 (Commencement No 4, Transitional and Saving Provisions) Order 2010 para 6.

been possible for the statute to have introduced a verdict reflecting that it was a murder but with a reduced responsibility. However, since manslaughter is a wide ranging offence and covers culpable homicides that do not amount to murder, the conclusion that there is guilt of manslaughter seems appropriate.

14.5 Infanticide is a statutory offence, created by the Infanticide Act 1938: it was subjected only to very minor amendment by the Coroners and Justice Act 2009.

Diminished responsibility – the Homicide Act 1957 text

Introduction to the text

14.6 Section 2 of the HA 1957 as enacted provides that:

(1) Where a person kills or is a party to the killing of another, he shall not be convicted of murder if he was suffering from such abnormality of mind (whether arising from a condition of arrested or retarded development of mind or any inherent causes or induced by disease or injury) as substantially impaired his mental responsibility for his acts and omissions in doing or being a party to the killing.

(2) On a charge of murder, it shall be for the defence to prove that the person charged is by virtue of this section not liable to be convicted of murder.

(3) A person who but for this section would be liable, whether as principal or as accessory, to be convicted of murder shall be liable instead to be convicted of manslaughter.

(4) The fact that one party to a killing is by virtue of this section not liable to be convicted of murder shall not affect the question whether the killing amounted to murder in the case of any other party to it.

14.7 The new language which has been substituted by the Coroners and Justice Act 2009 (which is discussed in more detail below) involves the following: there has to be an 'abnormality of mental functioning' arising from a recognised medical condition that explains or contributes significantly to the conduct; and it has to substantially impair the ability of the defendant to understand the nature of his or her conduct, form a rational judgment or exercise self-control.

Diminished responsibility in the Scottish common law

14.8 The concept of diminished responsibility is borrowed from the common law of Scotland.[3] Its interesting history is set out in the case of *Scarsbrook (or Galbraith) v HM Advocate* by a five-judge High Court of Justiciary.[4] At paragraph 41, the court described the concept in the following terms:

> ... responsibility and diminished responsibility are legal, rather than medical or psychological, concepts. In our law diminished responsibility applies in cases where, because the accused's ability to determine and control his actings is impaired as a result of some mental abnormality, his responsibility for any killing can properly be regarded as correspondingly reduced. The accused should, accordingly, be convicted of culpable homicide rather than of murder. Since this conclusion as to his reduced level of responsibility is a legal conclusion, it is not the function of the witnesses, lay, psychological, medical or psychiatric, to say whether an accused's responsibility can properly be regarded as diminished. Rather, they give evidence as to the accused's mental state. It is then for the judge to decide whether, at its highest, this evidence discloses a basis upon which the law could regard the accused's responsibility as being diminished. If the judge decides that the evidence could not meet that test, then the defence must be withdrawn from the jury's consideration. If, on the other hand, the judge decides that, at its highest, the evidence could justify the conclusion in law that the accused's responsibility was diminished, then the judge must direct the jury that, depending on whether or not they accept that evidence, they can return a verdict of culpable homicide. It will then be for the jury to consider the evidence and, depending on their view of it, to decide whether, if convicting, to convict the accused of murder or of culpable homicide.

14.9 The court's account of the development of the concept can be summarised as follows. It had been mentioned in a charge to a jury in 1867 and a comparative book authored in the USA but drawing on Germanic criminal codes;[5] it had then been referred to in subsequent reports of judgments from 1909 onwards, though the terminology

3 However, it has now been replaced by a statutory test, introduced by Part 7 of the Criminal Justice and Licensing (Scotland) Act 2010, section 168 of which introduces sections 51A and 51B to the Criminal Procedure (Scotland) Act 1995 to define 'insanity' and 'diminished responsibility'. There are also provisions relating to fitness to stand trial.

4 [2001] ScotHC 45, 2001 SCCR 551.

5 [2001] ScotHC 45, 2001 SCCR 551 paras 23 and 24, referring to *HM Advocate v Dingwall* (1867) 5 Irv 466 (per Lord Dea) and Francis Wharton's *Treatise on mental unsoundness embracing a general view of psychological law*, described as 'an American work purchased by the Advocates Library'.

had varied;[6] from 1946 onwards the phrase 'diminished responsibility' took root.[7] What became accepted as the elements of the test were set out in the 1923 case of *Savage*,[8] and summarised in *Scarsbrook* at paragraph 29 as follows:

> Lord Alness ... gave four criteria. The first is 'aberration or weakness of mind' ... The second criterion ... is 'some form of mental unsoundness' ... The third is 'a state of mind bordering on, though not amounting to, insanity' ... The last of the criteria is 'a mind so affected that responsibility is diminished from full responsibility to partial responsibility'...

14.10 The High Court of Justiciary in *Scarsbrook* was keen to point out that this was merely an example of practical guidance given to the jury to assist them to answer the legal question relating to the different levels of responsibility that mark out murder and culpable homicide. This was summarised as follows:

> [42] ... the law recognises a class of states of mind in respect of which an accused's responsibility is diminished. In other words, if the accused's state of mind was of that kind when he killed the deceased, then the law recognises that he was not fully responsible for his act and, for that reason, holds that he should be convicted of the less serious crime of culpable homicide. In his first three criteria in *Savage* Lord Alness gave examples of states of mind which the law had recognised as being members of this general class of states of mind where the law would hold that a person's responsibility was diminished. The fourth, tautologous, criterion was really an unsatisfactory attempt to define this general class – and was, as such, different in kind from the first three criteria.

14.11 The court then noted that '[t]he critical question for the law of diminished responsibility is to see where the limits of the general class lie'. It declined to give a definitive answer, but noted two established propositions: first, that voluntarily-induced conditions from alcohol,

6 [2001] ScotHC 45, 2001 SCCR 551 para 25, referring to *HM Advocate v Edmonstone* 1909 2 SLT 223 (headnote referring to diminished responsibility as a summary of the judge directing the jury that the law required that the mind of the defendant be affected to such an extent that responsibility was reduced from full to partial responsibility); *HM Advocate v Savage* 1923 JC 49 ('partial responsibility'); in *Muir* v *HM Advocate* 1933 JC 46 ('lessened responsibility', 'partial insanity'); *Kirkwood* v *HM Advocate* 1939 JC 36 (plea of 'diminished responsibility', though the judge preferred 'impaired responsibility'); *HM Advocate* v *Braithwaite* 1945 JC 55 ('this defence of diminished responsibility'); *Russell v HM Advocate* 1946 JC 48 ('reduced responsibility').

7 It was used in *Carraher v HM Advocate* 1946 JC 108, at trial and on appeal; and in *Caldwell v HM Advocate* 1946 SLT.

8 *HM Advocate v Savage* 1923 JC 49.

drugs or glue would not found the partial defence; and that a psychopathic personality disorder was also excluded.

14.12 The Scottish judicial creation of diminished responsibility has the following elements:

a) it leads to a conviction of culpable homicide (the equivalent to manslaughter in English terminology) rather than murder;
b) as it is a legal concept, the judge determines whether there is evidence on the basis of which such a conviction would be proper, namely the existence of 'an abnormality of mind which substantially impaired the ability of the accused, as compared with a normal person, to determine or control his acts';[9] this could take the form of a different perception from a normal person or a different ability to form a rational judgment as to whether a particular act is right or wrong or should be performed (or a combination of these features);
c) the abnormality must be recognised by the medical profession, though it might be congenital, derive from an organic condition, a psychotic illness or the effect of trauma;
d) the abnormality must have had substantial effects in relation to the act of killing, such as would be the case if the state of mind bordered on insanity, though a state on that borderline is an example of what is sufficient to meet the test rather than a prerequisite;
e) for policy reasons, self-induced intoxication excludes the possibility of the defence, as does a psychopathic personality disorder;
f) if there is evidence to be left to the jury, the question for them – with the appropriate direction depending on the facts – is that 'they must be satisfied that, by reason of the abnormality of mind in question, the ability of the accused, as compared with a normal person, to determine or control his actings was substantially impaired' in order to return a verdict other than guilty of murder.

Comparison between the Scottish jurisprudence and the Homicide Act 1957

14.13 The HA 1957 imported into English law the test developed by the Scottish judiciary; as such, it marks the failure of the English common law judges to develop such a test. The elements of the substantive test in the statute are that there has to be 'an abnormality of mind'. This abnormality can arise from various causes: 'a condition

9 [2001] ScotHC 45, 2001 SCCR 551 para 54(2).

of arrested or retarded development of mind or any inherent causes or induced by disease or injury'; this is an approximation of what had been developed in Scotland. In addition, the abnormality has to substantially impair responsibility. There is a procedural point, namely that the burden of proof is on the defence, which means that it is on the balance of probabilities. These are all matters that were part of the Scottish jurisprudence.

Comparison with insanity

14.14 Given the reference in the Scottish case-law to the borderline of insanity being an example of what would lead to a conclusion of diminished responsibility, and the obvious similarity between the removal of responsibility through the insanity test and the reduction of responsibility through the diminished responsibility concept, it is worth comparing the elements of the two concepts to determine the commonality and to contrast the differences.

14.15 The substantive test for diminished responsibility requires a particular mental state (which must arise from certain causes, albeit widely drawn) and consequences from that state. Similarly, insanity involves a two-fold test:[10] the presence of a disease of the mind, and that it has the result that the actor does not know what he or she is doing or that it is wrong. In the case of insanity, the person has no criminal responsibility if the test is made out: but there may be consequences, including detention on the basis of his or her mental health. In the case of diminished responsibility, the outcome is that the defendant remains criminally responsible, but for a lesser offence than the murder with which he or she has been charged: this also has consequences as to the outcome since the mandatory sentence of life imprisonment for murder no longer applies; a hospital disposal will often also be the outcome.[11]

14.16 There are therefore parallels in the structure of the two tests and their outcome. The difference is as between no criminal responsibility and responsibility for a lesser offence: at first sight, the partial defence of diminished responsibility provides an additional grade between no responsibility (insanity) and full responsibility (guilt) in relation to the offence of murder by reducing the conviction to one of

10 See chapter 12 for a more detailed discussion.

11 However, as is developed in chapter 18, there is significant case-law to the effect that this is not a required sentence.

manslaughter, providing additional flexibility in relation to sentence to reflect the reduced responsibility.

14.17 However, there are also significant differences between the two tests. The question of diminished responsibility arises only on a charge of murder,[12] which means that in relation to every other offence, it is insanity or nothing in terms of responsibility. Although it might well be sensible to allow courts to make findings of diminished responsibility in relation to all offences, it is to be noted that significant differences between a murder charge and other offences make the need for a diminished responsibility finding more acute in such a case. First, mental health problems that do not amount to insanity might persuade a prosecutor not to proceed in relation to other charges;[13] second, such problems may persuade a judge to impose a disposal that reflects the reduced responsibility of such a defendant. In contrast, when a death has been caused by a deliberate act that might amount to murder, the use of prosecutorial discretion not to prosecute is less likely because the public interest in favour of prosecution will be stronger; and the absence of any sentencing discretion if the conviction is for murder means that a sentence other than a mandatory life sentence can only be imposed if there is a partial defence that reduces the conviction to manslaughter, in relation to which sentencing is a matter for judicial discretion.

'Abnormality of mind'

'Abnormality of mind' and 'disease of mind'

14.18 One question relevant to whether the step from diminished responsibility to insanity in the limited context of a murder charge is seamless is whether an 'abnormality of mind' means the same as a 'disease of the mind' under the insanity test. This turns on whether the language of the M'Naghten test, as developed in the middle of the nineteenth century by the judiciary, conveys something different from the statutory language introduced in the middle of the twentieth century, which language was developed by the Scottish judiciary.

14.19 As has been developed in more detail in chapter 12, a 'disease of the mind' rests on the juridical construct of the mind rather than the brain and whether there has been a defect of reason that relieves the

12 In *Campbell* [1997] Crim LR 495, Sedley J sitting in the Crown Court ruled that it could not be raised in relation to an attempted murder; this should also cover murder-related offences such as conspiracy to murder.

13 See chapter 5 for discussion of diversion from prosecution.

defendant from responsibility. In *R v Kemp*,[14] Devlin J ruled that a physical condition not accompanied by a permanent degeneration of the brain that caused a man to carry out an attack without any volition on his part could only give rise to a claim of insanity. His rationale was that:

> The law is not concerned with the brain but with the mind, in the sense that 'mind' is ordinarily used, the mental faculties of reason, memory and understanding.[15]

14.20 The need for a disease of the mind is meant to exclude situations where the lack of the ability to realise the nature or quality of the act or its wrongfulness arises from 'brutish stupidity without rational power'.[16] As has been noted, the Scottish judiciary excluded from a finding of diminished responsibility those with a psychopathic personality disorder, which is a personality disorder that is understood as an inability to avoid abnormally aggressive or seriously irresponsible conduct.[17]

14.21 In both situations, the concern was with the ability to act in a manner that justified the attribution of criminal responsibility (subject to an exception for psychopathic personalities): insanity excluded it completely and diminished responsibility did so partially. Despite this context and the easy explanation that diminished responsibility was designed to provide a response to the situation where someone approached insanity but did not quite meet the test, the picture that has developed is slightly more complex.

14.22 Initially, the English judiciary seemed unwilling to give an explanation of what the statutory language in HA 1957 s2 meant. In *R v Spriggs*,[18] the Court of Criminal Appeal upheld the approach of the trial judge of providing the jury with a copy of the statutory language and telling them that it was their job to apply it. Lord Goddard CJ indicated:[19]

14 [1957] 1 QB 399.

15 [1957] 1 QB 399 p407.

16 [1957] 1 QB 399 p408.

17 See Mental Health Act (MHA) 1983 s1 (as enacted and before its amendment by the MHA 2007) in England and Wales; the equivalent Scottish legislation, the Mental Health (Scotland) Act 1984 did not have a separate definition of psychopathic disorder, but did refer in section 17 to mental disorder 'manifested only by abnormally aggressive or seriously irresponsible conduct', which had a requirement that there be treatment available.

18 [1958] 1 QB 270.

19 [1958] 1 QB 270 p274.

> ... we cannot see that a judge dealing with this matter can do more than to call the attention of the jury to the exact terms of the section which Parliament has enacted and leave them to say whether upon the evidence they are satisfied that the case comes within the section or not. When Parliament has defined a particular state of things, as they have defined here what is to amount to diminished responsibility, it is not for judges to re-define or to attempt to define the definition.

14.23 He noted that it was a novel concept that had been borrowed from Scottish law, which 'recognizes that a man may be not quite mad but a border-line case, and that is the sort of thing which amounts to diminished responsibility'.[20] The contentions of counsel for Mr Spriggs that the judge should direct the jury as to the differences between the intellect and the mind and explain to them that an abnormality of mind could relate to disturbed will and emotions were dismissed as 'metaphysical distinctions' which the judge did not have to explain.[21]

14.24 Fortunately, it was soon held that a judge could try to give further explanations to illustrate the concept to the jury: *R v Walden*.[22] In this case, the judge had given the jury an explanation of what was meant by insanity and had indicated that diminished responsibility amounted to bordering between insanity and sanity. The Court of Criminal Appeal determined that this was not a misdirection, but merely a helpful illustration to the jury of what they might consider.

14.25 Soon, however, a Court of Criminal Appeal consisting of the judges who had given the judgment in *Walden* and the ruling in *Kemp* and the new Lord Chief Justice had to consider the test in the HA 1957 in the following circumstances. The appellant in *R v Byrne*[23] was described as a 'sexual psychopath', which Lord Parker CJ explained in the following terms:[24]

> The nature of the abnormality of mind of a sexual psychopath, according to the medical evidence, is that he suffers from violent perverted sexual desires which he finds it difficult or impossible to control. Save when under the influence of his perverted sexual desires he may be normal. All three doctors were of opinion that the killing was done under the influence of his perverted sexual desires, and although all

20 [1958] 1 QB 270 p276.

21 [1958] 1 QB 270 p277, commenting on submissions recorded at pages 272 and 273 to which the prosecution was not even called upon to reply. As is noted above, the Scottish judiciary had sought to explain to juries what factors could indicate diminished responsibility.

22 [1959] 1 WLR 1008.

23 [1960] 2 QB 396.

24 [1960] 2 QB 396 at 400.

> three were of opinion that he was not insane in the technical sense of insanity laid down in the M'Naughten Rules it was their view that his sexual psychopathy could properly be described as partial insanity.

14.26 Mr Byrne had been convicted of murder, the trial judge having told the jury that HA 1957 s2 'is not there to give protection where there is nothing else than what is vicious and depraved' and directed that the partial defence was not available if the jury found that Mr Byrne was normal in all respects but for his impulse or urge to have sex which he found 'very difficult or perhaps impossible' to avoid.[25]

14.27 Having explained Mr Byrne's condition, Lord Parker CJ then commented that:[26]

> 'Abnormality of mind,' which has to be contrasted with the time-honoured expression in the M'Naughten Rules 'defect of reason,' means a state of mind so different from that of ordinary human beings that the reasonable man would term it abnormal. It appears to us to be wide enough to cover the mind's activities in all its aspects, not only the perception of physical acts and matters, and the ability to form a rational judgment as to whether an act is right or wrong, but also the ability to exercise will power to control physical acts in accordance with that rational judgment. The expression 'mental responsibility for his acts' points to a consideration of the extent to which the accused's mind is answerable for his physical acts which must include a consideration of the extent of his ability to exercise will power to control his physical acts.

14.28 This in turn meant that the trial judge had misdirected the jury because he had indicated that difficulty or even inability to control impulses would not be an abnormality of mind, whereas the true construction was that such a situation was within the section. There are two parts to the chain of reasoning in *Byrne*. First, there is a contrast between 'abnormality of mind' in the diminished responsibility test and 'defect of reason' in the insanity test: but the 'defect of reason' is the consequence of the 'disease of the mind' and it is the latter that should be compared with the phrase 'abnormality of mind'.

14.29 The second part of the reasoning is that the consequence of the 'abnormality of mind', namely the reduction in mental responsibility, is used to explain what must be meant by 'abnormality of mind'. This is more satisfactory, and indeed was key to the explanation in *Kemp* as to what was meant by the language of the insanity test. So, Devlin J in *Kemp* noted that the disease of the mind test was designed to deal

25 [1960] 2 QB 396 at 401.
26 [1960] 2 QB 396 at 403.

with the legally relevant question of whether the person was able to exercise a choice and so could be held responsible for their actions; similarly, the ability to exercise will-power is part of the reasoning in *Byrne*, which feeds into the question of the level of responsibility that should be ascribed. But one part of the finding in *Kemp* was the need to avoid exculpating brutish stupidity and a failure to control a reasoning process because that skill had never been learned. There was no imperative to reach such a conclusion when the effect was reduced responsibility rather than no responsibility: and so that supported a different understanding of what was an abnormality of the mind as opposed to a disease of the brain. However, the court did say that the judge could properly say that the statutory language equated to what was in popular language thought to be on the borderline of insanity, but it was made plain that this was not in the legal sense of the insanity test as set out in *M'Naghten*.[27]

14.30 Following this decision, it became accepted that it was in fact necessary to give the jury assistance on what was meant by diminished responsibility, rather than simply giving them the statutory language as had been suggested in *Spriggs*: see *R v Terry*[28] and *R v Gomez*.[29] However, in *R v Turnbull*[30] the Court of Appeal refused leave to appeal in the following circumstances. Mr Turnbull had a psychopathic personality disorder, which was an abnormality of mind arising from inherent causes. The only real issue was whether the judge had given an adequate direction on the question of whether there had been a substantial impairment of responsibility (which is discussed below). The particular difficulty was that, in addition to the effect of the psychopathic personality disorder, there was intoxication. Having held that the trial judge's direction had properly drawn a distinction between a killing prompted by intoxication and one caused by the psychopathic disorder, the court added that:

> ... for the future it ought to be accepted that the only summing up required under section 2 of the Act of 1957 is to direct the jury that they must look for the three elements of the defence to which I have referred. They should be told that if the three elements of the defence are shown to be present on the balance of probabilities, then the defence of diminished responsibility is made out.[31]

27 [1960] 2 QB 396 at 404.
28 [1961] 2 QB 314.
29 (1964) 48 CrAppR 310.
30 (1977) 65 CrAppR 242.
31 (1977) 65 CrAppR 242 pp244–245.

14.31 The three elements referred to are the need for an abnormality of mind; the need for it to have arisen from an appropriate cause; and the need for a substantial impairment of responsibility. Since these are all mentioned in the statute, this suggests that there is little to do beyond setting out the relevant language. However, the cases of *Terry* and *Gomez* were not cited to the court, and its comments are obiter in the light of the conclusion that there was no error with the direction that was given on the only issue raised in the case, which was the final element of the test. Given the broad interpretation adopted in *Byrne*, it seems clearly essential to give the jury some guidance on what is meant. Indeed, in *R v Sanderson*,[32] the Court of Appeal commented that:

> Cases of diminished responsibility can become difficult and confusing for a jury, and it is important that the judge in directing the jury should tailor his directions to suit the facts of the particular case. We think it will rarely be helpful to the jury to read to them [HA 1957] section 2(1) in its entirety.

14.32 The language the Court of Appeal used in explaining the test of diminished responsibility in *Byrne* has introduced the idea that an irresistible impulse is a partial defence, albeit only to murder. However, a question arises as to the extent to which this can be differentiated from automatism. The general concept of voluntariness underlies the criminal law, and the contention that someone was acting as an automaton – ie not responsible for their actions, as they are not willed – requires a total loss of control. If this loss of control is caused by a disease of the mind, it amounts to a contention of insanity. If a disease of the mind is not acting, the finding is not guilty by reason of the prosecution failure to prove voluntariness. The language in *Byrne* suggests that there is something that is less than a total loss of control but is nevertheless irresistible.

14.33 Aside from the question of what is meant in theory by this distinction, there is the practical difference of how it can be proved. At one point in *Byrne*, Lord Parker CJ makes reference to the difficulty of being able to prove whether the situation is that a person did not control as opposed to could not control their action. The latter should be a situation of involuntariness leading to an acquittal or an insanity verdict. The Lord Chief Justice commented that the distinction was not capable of proof as: 'There is no scientific measurement of the

32 (1994) 98 CrAppR 325 at 334.

degree of difficulty which an abnormal person finds in controlling his impulses'.[33]

14.34 The state of knowledge may have improved, but the problem remains. For example, in *Khan v R*,[34] Aikens LJ stated:[35]

> Scientific understanding of how the mind works and the extent to which states of mind and physical responses to them have physical or chemical causes have undoubtedly advanced considerably since Lord Parker made those statements. But we venture to suggest that, even today, it is impossible to provide any accurate scientific measurement of the extent to which a particular person who is suffering from an 'abnormality of mind' resulting from one of the causes set out in the parentheses in [HA 1957] section 2(1) could understand or control his physical impulses on a particular occasion. In other words, there is no simple scientific test of whether a defendant's 'mental responsibility for his acts and omissions in doing or being a party to the killing' is 'substantially impaired'.

14.35 The effect of this is, as Lord Parker CJ noted, that the jury has to approach the matter as best they can:

> These problems which in the present state of medical knowledge are scientifically insoluble, the jury can only approach in a broad, common sense way.[36]

14.36 The case of *Byrne* has been endorsed on many subsequent occasions, so it is not in doubt that it sets out the law in relation to the question of what counts as an abnormality of mind. This level of contrast between diminished responsibility and insanity was made clear by the Privy Council when it considered the statutory provisions introduced into the Bahamas by the Bahamas (Special Defences) Act 1959, which were in similar terms, namely an 'abnormality of mind ... as substantially impaired his responsibility'. In *Rose v R*,[37] the trial judge had concluded that the language of the statute was designed to give the jury an option on the border between insanity and responsibility: the evidence in the case had revealed a difference of medical opinion, one doctor had found delusions caused by a head injury; the other doctor expressed the view that there was no serious mental illness. The trial judge had read out the M'Naghten rules in full and had then instructed the jury that they did not apply but that they were

33 (1977) 65 CrAppR 242 p404.
34 [2009] EWCA Crim 1569.
35 [2009] EWCA Crim 1569 at para 18.
36 [1960] 2 QB 396 at 404.
37 [1961] AC 496.

relevant because they allowed the jury to understand what was meant by the 'borderline of insanity' test that was conveyed by the diminished responsibility language. The Privy Council held, as would be held by the High Court of Justiciary in Scotland in *Scarsbrook* (noted above), that this was a serious misdirection because the test framed in terms of proximity to insanity was merely an example rather than the test in law (and in any event involved the word 'insanity' used in a popular rather than legal manner): the test for diminished responsibility involved asking the much wider question framed in *Byrne*.

14.37 Another example of this can be found in the case of *R v Seers*,[38] in which the judge had dealt with a case of a man with a depressive illness by directing the jury in terms of the need for a borderline of insanity or for partial insanity: the Court of Appeal quashed a conviction for murder on the basis that in relation to some mental states that could well found a plea of diminished responsibility, instructing the jury by reference to borderline insanity was apt to mislead.

14.38 In summary, an 'abnormality of mind' does not require a mental illness or have to meet a medical definition. Rather, it is a legal term and relates to a state of mind, covering all the workings of the mind in relation to the question of criminal responsibility, such as the forming of understanding or judgment and the ability to control behaviour. There is, however, a limitation in the cause of the abnormality, namely the question of the origin of the disorder, which is covered in the next section.

Aetiology

14.39 Certain other propositions have been established. One relates to the question of the aetiology of the abnormality of mind. As was noted in the case of *Turnbull*, referred to above, the partial defence requires an abnormality of mind but also that it arises from one of the causes set out in the statute, namely:

i) a condition of arrested or retarded development of mind,
ii) any inherent causes or
iii) induced by disease or injury.

In *Gomez*, the Court of Criminal Appeal noted that this meant it would be an error for a trial judge to indicate that the statute required that 'a man [be] born with some abnormality'.[39]

38 (1984) 79 CrAppR 261.

39 On the facts, the court doubted that the judge meant that only some abnormality existing at birth could count; but it clarified that this would be wrong: (1964) 48 CrAppR 310 at 314. Confusingly, however, the court noted

14.40 In relation to the specific categories of aetiology, it has been noted, first, that they are exclusive; second, that certain conditions fall within one of them; and third, that because of the inclusion of this language as to the origin of the abnormality of mind, it is implicit that the section requires expert evidence if the defendant is to demonstrate that the defence exists. A fourth proposition in this context is that the defence must provide a proper basis for the expert opinion evidence.

Exclusive categories of aetiology

14.41 Taking these points in turn, first, that the potential causes for the abnormality as listed in the statute are exclusive. In *R v Dix*,[40] which is discussed further below, it had been part of the submission for Mr Dix that the parenthetical phrase in the statute – '(whether arising from a condition of arrested or retarded development of mind or any inherent causes or induced by disease or injury)' – was exclusive of the causes of the abnormality of mind and very broad. This was part of the submission that it was a matter that could be proved without expert evidence being called:[41] this would presumably be on the basis that a non-expert could give evidence that the defendant appeared somehow different or had suffered a head injury or had changed after an illness. The Court of Appeal commented that as a matter of logic, the argument that the jury could make their own decision without expert evidence 'is inseparable from the proposition that the part of HA 1957 s2(1) in parenthesis is descriptive of all forms of abnormality of the mind so that no proof is required that an accused's asserted abnormality of mind falls within the categories described within the brackets'. The argument was rejected on the basis that *Byrne* had determined the need for proof that the condition of mind arose from one of the specified causes. While this is hardly a ringing endorsement of the view that the parenthetical list is an exclusive list, this does appear to be the logic of the list, in light of the absence of language – such as 'or any other cause' – as might allow other possible origins of the abnormality to be determined by case-law.

that the judge might just have been meaning to say that 'by some abnormality was meant some inherent cause, some inherent congenital weakness': since an abnormality caused by injury can count, it cannot be right to suggest that the test is limited to congenital weaknesses, and so it should be understood that the court was meaning only to refer to the inherent causes part of the test.

40 (1982) 74 CrAppR 306.

41 (1982) 74 CrAppR 306 at 310. This is discussed below.

14.42 In any event, it is a settled proposition. So the Court of Appeal in *R v Sanderson*[42] noted that: 'It is now well established by authority that for abnormality of the mind to come within the subsection it must be caused by one of the matters listed in the subsection'.

Certain conditions fall within one of the categories of causes

14.43 As to what is covered by these different causes – 'a condition of arrested or retarded development of mind or any inherent causes or induced by disease or injury' – it is to be noted that shortly after the HA 1957 was passed, the MHA 1959 was enacted. It contained in section 4 a definition of 'mental disorder' stating that it meant 'mental illness, arrested or incomplete development of mind, psychopathic disorder and any other disorder or disability of mind'. The Act also contained definitions of 'severe subnormality', which along with mental illness and psychopathic disorder was a basis for admission for treatment under section 26 of that Act, and of psychopathic disorder. A 'subnormality' was a 'state of arrested of incomplete development of mind ... which included subnormality of intelligence'; a 'severe subnormality' was a version of that the rendered the person incapable of living an independent life or preventing serious exploitation. Psychopathy was defined as involving abnormally aggressive or seriously irresponsible conduct, but only if the conduct reflected a 'persistent disorder or disability of mind'; it was expressed that it did not have to include a subnormal intelligence. Of course, these definitions cannot be carried across to the HA 1957, but they give an indication of what was understood by the language used at the time.

14.44 So the phrase 'an arrested or retarded development of mind' might be thought to cover situations of learning disabilities; it might also be thought to cover a personality disorder of the sort that involves a failure to develop the normal response in society, of which a psychopathic personality disorder might be an example.[43] But there have also been suggestions that psychopathy is to be treated as being an 'inherent cause': so in *R v Turnbull*,[44] which involved a combination of psychopathy and intoxication, the agreed position at the trial and on appeal was that the former was an abnormality of mind due to inherent causes.

42 (1994) 98 CrAppR 325 at 334.

43 See chapter 1 for a more detailed discussion on what is meant by the terms used in mental health law, which do not necessarily overlap with medical understanding.

44 (1977) 65 CrAppR 242.

14.45 Guidance on what is covered by the reference to 'inherent cause' and 'induced by disease' was given in *Sanderson*.[45] In this case, the appellant had been convicted of murder after a trial in which there was a difference of expert opinion as to whether a paranoid condition was a psychosis arising from internal causes (albeit exacerbated by drug use) or from drug abuse alone. The jury had sent a note in which it asked for assistance on what was meant by 'induced by disease or injury' and whether a paranoid psychosis could be included whether or not it was induced by drugs. The judge had directed the jury that there was no evidence as to whether or not a paranoid psychosis had arisen or could arise from disease and so he was unable to answer the question: in fact, he went further and stated that 'nobody speaks of paranoid psychosis arising from disease or injury'. But the scenario in front of the jury was that one expert said that the abnormality of mind arose from an illness and the other said it arose just from drug abuse, so the judge failed to assist the jury properly and in fact misstated the evidence. The Court of Appeal concluded that the conviction was unsafe because of the potential confusion in the minds of the jury in light of the direction; it suggested that the probable meaning of 'induced by disease or injury' was 'organic or physical injury or disease of the body including the brain' because the statute did not use the language of the insanity test, namely disease of the mind, but included as permissible causes of an abnormality of mind 'any inherent cause'. The submission made had the consequence that the statutory language relating to disease or injury would cover both functional and organic mental illnesses, whereas the conclusion following from the court's interpretation was that 'any inherent cause' would cover a functional mental illness, whereas 'induced by disease or injury' would cover organic mental illnesses.

14.46 Three points should be made: first, it does not seem that it should be necessary to prove which of the statutory phrases covers the particular circumstance; all that is necessary is that the abnormality of mind has one of the causes. The second point is that psychiatry is not the most exact of sciences, and so it may be that there is difficulty in identifying with any level of confidence what the particular cause is. Third, it is also possible that a particular defendant may have an abnormality of mind arising from a combination of causes, which may not all be of the same category.

14.47 Consequently, while there may be no harm in a trial judge following the guidance in *Sanderson* to the effect that the judge should

45 (1994) 98 CrAppR 325 at 334.

direct the jury on which of the potential causes of the abnormality had been raised,[46] it may be that the judge and the parties should err on the side of caution in being overly inclusive rather than too restrictive in trying to pigeon-hole the cause in any trials that have to apply the diminished responsibility standard rather than the new test, which is discussed below.

Requirement for expert evidence

14.48 The case of *R v Dix*[47] provides suitable authority for the proposition that expert evidence is necessary. On the facts, the defendant made full admissions to the police about killing the victim, a friend; he indicated it was at her request, as she was the victim of domestic abuse. No medical evidence was adduced, it being contended that it was not necessary to demonstrate the origin of the abnormality of mind. The judge ruled that there was nothing to go to the jury, and so Mr Dix changed his plea to guilty of murder. The Court of Appeal dismissed an appeal, Shaw LJ commenting that *Byrne* stood for the proposition that the defendant had to prove both that there was an abnormality of mind and that it arose from one of the specified conditions; and that 'what emerges from Lord Parker's statement is that scientific evidence of a medical kind is essential to establish' the aetiology (and also that it amounted to a substantial impairment of responsibility).[48]

14.49 It is true that there is a description in *Byrne* of the elements of diminished responsibility in which it is stated that 'the accused must show' that there was an abnormality 'and ... that such abnormality ... arose from a condition of arrested or retarded development of mind or any inherent causes, or was induced by disease or injury'.[49] However, it was not part of the decision in *Byrne* that this required supporting medical evidence. Indeed, there are two clear arguments against this proposition: first, the court in *Byrne* was clear to make the point that the statutory test was one that left the decision to the jury, having outlined that it was a broad question.[50] More importantly, the statutory language is in contrast to that arising in relation to the ques-

46 (1994) 98 CrAppR 325 at 334. The comment on the facts was that there was no suggestion of an 'arrested or retarded development of mind' or of 'injury' and so the judge should have limited his directions to 'arising from any inherent cause' 'induced by disease'.

47 (1982) 74 CrAppR 306.

48 (1982) 74 CrAppR 306 at 311.

49 [1960] 2 QB 396 at 403.

50 [1960] 2 QB 396 at 403.

tion of insanity where it has been provided by statute that the defence can only meet its burden of proof on the basis of medical evidence:[51] this clearly allows an argument that, this model not having been followed, the statute does not place the burden on the defendant by way of medical evidence.

14.50 At best, what was said in *Byrne* was that, in contrast to the question of whether there was an abnormality of mind:

> The aetiology of the abnormality of mind (namely, whether it arose from a condition of arrested or retarded development of mind or any inherent causes, or was induced by disease or injury) does, however, seem to be a matter to be determined on expert evidence.[52]

14.51 But this is a somewhat tentative comment and not part of the ratio, which was in the context of whether the judge had been correct to say that a sexual psychopath could not claim diminished responsibility. Accordingly, one can see the basis for the argument in *Dix* that since it is a matter for the jury to determine whether there is an abnormality of mind – which is defined as a state of mind that differs from the normal – jurors should be able to make their own judgment of that essentially factual question: while medical evidence might well assist (and it is fair to say that the Court in *Byrne* proceeded on the basis that medical evidence invariably would be called) it is a different matter to saying that the burden of proof *cannot* be met without medical evidence. It was also noted that it was the reverse of the proposition that the jury could reject evidence on which both the defence and prosecution agreed led to a conclusion of diminished responsibility (though, of course, in that situation one would usually expect that there would not be a trial).

14.52 However, the defence argument was rejected and *Dix* establishes the proposition that medical evidence is, as was said in the case, a 'practical necessity' in light of the burden of proof on the defence.[53] The court gave no indication of when it might be possible to conclude that there was an abnormality of mind without expert evidence: that is left open. The Court of Appeal in *Dix* was prepared to certify as a point of law of general public importance – the precursor for an appeal to the House of Lords[54] – whether there was always a need for expert evidence; but the matter did not proceed to the House of Lords.

51 See chapter 12.

52 [1960] 2 QB 396 at 403.

53 (1982) 74 CrAppR 306 at 312. See paras 14.80–14.83 below for discussion of this.

54 See Criminal Appeal Act 1968 s33.

Defence's obligation to provide proper evidence

14.53 This leads into the fourth proposition, namely that the defence has an obligation to provide proper evidence. This can be seen to cover two separate questions: one is expert evidence on the question; the other is factual evidence on the basis of which the expert view can be verified. The latter point raises a number of issues and is discussed in a separate section below.[55] In relation to the question of the existence of material on the basis of which a jury can properly conclude that there was a disability of mind, expert evidence will be important and essential to allow a conclusion as to the aetiology. However, whether there is an abnormality of mind remains a question of fact for the jury, in relation to which they can use their own views of matters such as what the accused had said or done in order to assess whether they accept that the test is met. So, Lord Parker CJ said in *Byrne*:[56]

> Whether the accused was at the time of the killing suffering from any 'abnormality of mind' in the broad sense which we have indicated above is a question for the jury. On this question medical evidence is no doubt of importance, but the jury are entitled to take into consideration all the evidence, including the acts or statements of the accused and his demeanour. They are not bound to accept the medical evidence if there is other material before them which, in their good judgment, conflicts with it and outweighs it. The aetiology of the abnormality of mind (namely, whether it arose from a condition of arrested or retarded development of mind or any inherent causes, or was induced by disease or injury) does, however, seem to be a matter to be determined on expert evidence.

Intoxication

14.54 The need for proof that the abnormality of mind arises from certain permitted causes does mean that intoxication cannot found the partial defence, since that is what might be termed an external cause of a temporary abnormality. (It may be necessary for the prosecution to prove that there was a drunken intent, but that is necessarily proved before there is consideration of whether there is diminished responsibility.) However, there may be a significant role in practice for questions of intoxication. First, intoxication might trigger what amounts to a psychotic state (ie a recognisable psychiatric illness) or long-term alcoholism or drug abuse might cause physical consequences that

55 See paras 14.76–14.79 below.

56 [1960] 2 QB 396 at p403.

amount to an injury or disease; and second, there might be an interplay between intoxication and an abnormality of mind.

14.55 The impact of simple intoxication was considered in *R v Fenton*,[57] involving a defendant who killed four people in a short period of time. The doctors giving evidence agreed there was psychopathy; he was also affected by a reactive depression and, at the time of the killings, had been intoxicated. The jurors had indicated their view that the homicides would not have occurred if Mr Fenton had not been intoxicated. The judge had directed the jury to convict of murder if the effect of the factors other than intoxication would not substantially impair the responsibility of the defendant. This approach was upheld by the Court of Appeal, which rejected the argument that psychopathy meant that the defendant was unable to resist becoming intoxicated (such that the intoxication had to be viewed as part of the abnormality of mind). Lord Widgery CJ indicated that:[58]

> We recognise that cases may arise hereafter where the accused proves such a craving for drink or drugs as to produce in itself an abnormality of mind; but that is not proved in this case. The appellant did not give evidence and we do not see how self-induced intoxication can of itself produce an abnormality of mind due to inherent causes.

14.56 In short, the jury has to disentangle the effect of intoxication and the effect of the abnormality of mind. *Fenton* was endorsed in *R v Gittens*:[59] in this case, the judge had directed the jury to consider the substantial cause of the killing, the defendant having a personality disorder but also having had alcohol. The direction was based on comments made in *R v Turnbull*,[60] in which the Court of Appeal had decided that it had not been a misdirection for a judge to ask the jury to consider whether a psychopathic personality disorder or intoxication had been the main factor in a killing. Lord Widgery CJ set out the jury direction, which included the indication that the jury should ask, 'Do we think it more probable than not that at that time Turnbull's responsibility was substantially impaired by the fact that he suffers from a psychopathic disorder?' and ended with the question 'What is the substantial cause of his stabbing this man in this horrible and savage way?' The Chief Justice commented: 'That is exactly the right test'.[61] Unfortunately, he did not differentiate between the

57 (1975) 61 CrAppR 261.
58 (1975) 61 CrAppR 261 at 263–264.
59 [1984] QB 698.
60 (1977) 65 CrAppR 242.
61 (1977) 65 CrAppR 242 at 246.

first question, which is one that asks the jury to put aside the evidence of intoxication and concentrate on the abnormality of mind, and the second question, which asks the jury to choose between two alternative causes.

14.57 In *Gittens*, Lord Lane CJ accepted that the latter question was not the one properly to pose to the jury, and reiterated the point from *Fenton* that:[62]

> The jury should be directed to disregard what, in their view, the effect of the alcohol or drugs upon the defendant was, since abnormality of mind induced by alcohol or drugs is not (generally speaking) due to inherent causes and is not therefore within the section. Then the jury should consider whether the combined effect of the other matters which do fall within the section amounted to such abnormality of mind as substantially impaired the defendant's mental responsibility.[63]

Alcoholism

14.58 While simple intoxication is not enough, abuse of alcohol (or drugs or solvents and so on) can give rise to a defence under HA 1957 s2 if it causes damage to the brain or there is an irresistible craving that has the impact that consumption is involuntary. The latter point is implicit in the comment from *Fenton* quoted above, which raised the prospect of a successful defence if a defendant had 'such a craving for drink or drugs as to produce in itself an abnormality of mind'. It was made more clear in *R v Tandy*.[64] This involved a woman who was an alcoholic and who had, on the occasion in question, when she strangled her child, drunk a much stronger liquor than she usually consumed: she was convicted of murder after the judge directed the jury that if her first drink on the day of the killing had been a matter of choice, she could not succeed on diminished responsibility. The dispute in the case had involved three areas: the first was whether the killing reflected grossly impaired judgment and emotional responses as a result of alcoholism or was the result of intoxication; the second

62 [1984] QB 698 at 703.

63 See also *Sanderson* (1994) 98 CrAppR 325, discussed above, which involved a defendant who killed in circumstances involving paranoia: one expert indicated that he was of the view that there was an underlying disorder exacerbated by drug-abuse over years; but another felt that it was a transient side-effect of taking drugs. The Court of Appeal held that the judge had been correct to direct the jury that if they preferred the evidence of the doctor that Mr Sanderson's paranoia had been caused by drug abuse and there was no underlying psychotic illness, he could not demonstrate diminished responsibility. See page 334. (The conviction was quashed on the basis of an incorrect direction as to aetiology.)

64 [1989] 1 WLR 350.

was whether the intoxication on the day in question was something that had been involuntary, which turned on the level of the craving; and the third was whether the killing would have occurred but for the intoxication.

14.59 The Court of Appeal noted the elements of the defence that Ms Tandy had to prove, namely an abnormality of mind, that it was induced by the disease from which she suffered (alcoholism), and that it substantially impaired her responsibility. Watkins LJ noted[65] that the second element would not be established:

> ... unless the evidence showed that the abnormality of mind at the time of the killing was due to the fact that she was a chronic alcoholic. If the alcoholism had reached the level at which her brain had been injured by the repeated insult from intoxicants so that there was gross impairment of her judgment and emotional responses, then the defence of diminished responsibility was available to her, provided that she satisfied the jury that the third element of the defence existed. Further, if the appellant were able to establish that the alcoholism had reached the level where although the brain had not been damaged to the extent just stated, the appellant's drinking had become involuntary, that is to say she was no longer able to resist the impulse to drink, then the defence of diminished responsibility would be available to her, subject to her establishing the first and third elements, because if her drinking was involuntary, then her abnormality of mind at the time of the act of strangulation was induced by her condition of alcoholism.

14.60 He then contrasted this to a failure to resist an impulse to drink: if that was the circumstance in which she became intoxicated, leading to an impaired judgment, she could not claim diminished responsibility. The appeal in *Tandy* was dismissed on the basis that the evidence was of the latter position. This approach was endorsed by the Court of Appeal in *R v Dietschmann*,[66] Rose LJ stating that:

> 13. The general rule that drink does not give rise to an abnormality of mind due to inherent causes was authoritatively established in *R v Fenton* ... and confirmed in *R v Gittens* ... In line with those authorities, *R v Tandy* ... established that drink is only capable of giving rise to a defence under s2 if it either causes damage to the brain or produces an irresistible craving so that consumption is involuntary.

14.61 It is to be noted that this does not require brain damage: an abnormality of mind will occur when there is a craving for alcohol such that it is involuntary.

65 [1989] 1 WLR 350 at 356.

66 [2001] EWCA Crim 2052.

Abnormality of mind combined with intoxication

14.62 If there is both an abnormality of mind and intoxication, how does the defendant demonstrate the effect of the non-intoxicant features of his or her condition as at the time of the killing. When *Dietschmann* was appealed to the House of Lords, it was this issue that was the focus. Lord Hutton, speaking for the House, suggested an appropriate direction to a jury:[67]

> Assuming that the defence have established that the defendant was suffering from mental abnormality as described in section 2, the important question is: did that abnormality substantially impair his mental responsibility for his acts in doing the killing? You know that before he carried out the killing the defendant had had a lot to drink. Drink cannot be taken into account as something which contributed to his mental abnormality and to any impairment of mental responsibility arising from that abnormality. But you may take the view that both the defendant's mental abnormality and drink played a part in impairing his mental responsibility for the killing and that he might not have killed if he had not taken drink. If you take that view, then the question for you to decide is this: has the defendant satisfied you that, despite the drink, his mental abnormality substantially impaired his mental responsibility for his fatal acts, or has he failed to satisfy you of that? If he has satisfied you of that, you will find him not guilty of murder but you may find him guilty of manslaughter. If he has not satisfied you of that, the defence of diminished responsibility is not available to him.

14.63 The circumstances in that case were that the appellant had punched and kicked a man, causing death; he had been drunk at the time. The evidence from two psychiatrists called at the trial was that he was suffering from an abnormality of mind, namely a depressed grief reaction to the death of a close relative. But they disagreed on the impact of alcohol: one thought that there was also an alcohol dependency syndrome at the time of the killing, and that intoxication acted to disinhibit, without which he would have exercised self-control and not become involved in the attack. The other did not think that alcohol was a factor: he was of the opinion that Mr Dietschmann had been in a transient psychotic state at the time of the incident and would probably have killed even if he had been sober.

14.64 The reason the matter proceeded to the House of Lords was that an answer was needed to the question of whether the impact of intoxication was that the defendant could only meet his burden of proof in relation to diminished responsibility if he showed that the

67 [2003] UKHL 10, [2003] 1 AC 1209, [2003] MHLR 333 at para 41.

homicide would have occurred even if he had not taken any alcohol (and that it would have been in the context of his responsibility being diminished by the underlying abnormality of mind). The trial judge had directed the jury along these lines, and the Court of Appeal had upheld this approach.

14.65 This direction had been given because it had become accepted that the effect of *Gittens* was that the defendant had to show (on the balance of probabilities) that the killing would have occurred in the absence of intoxication. The rationale for this was that in the absence of that being proved, there was no adequate causal link with the abnormality of mind. This had been the approach adopted in *R v Atkinson*[68] and in *R v Egan*,[69] and it was the basis for the direction of the trial judge in Mr Dietschmann's case and for the Court of Appeal upholding the direction. However, the House of Lords held that these cases had misstated the effect of *Gittens*, and that all that was required was that the jury put the evidence of intoxication on one side, not that they also find that there would probably have been a killing without intoxication. Lord Hutton indicated[70] that the correct approach was that the statute:

> ... does not require the abnormality of mind to be the sole cause of the defendant's acts in doing the killing. In my opinion, even if the defendant would not have killed if he had not taken drink, the causative effect of the drink does not necessarily prevent an abnormality of mind suffered by the defendant from substantially impairing his mental responsibility for his fatal acts.

14.66 The consequence of this is that the jury are required to convict of manslaughter if the defendant demonstrates that, notwithstanding the intoxication, the abnormality of mind was still such that his responsibility was diminished.[71]

14.67 An obvious question then arises as to how this fits with the approach noted above – and which was not up for argument in front of the House of Lords in *Dietschmann* – that those whose illness is

68 [1985] Crim LR 314.

69 (1992) 95 CrAppR 278.

70 [2003] UKHL 10, [2003] 1 AC 1209, [2003] MHLR 333 at para 18.

71 In relation to Mr Dietschmann, as the jury had not been asked to address whether the depressed grief reaction to the death of a close relative provided diminished responsibility, the case was remitted for consideration of whether that question could be addressed without a retrial. The Court of Appeal decided that there should be a retrial: [2003] EWCA Crim 1257. He was convicted of murder at the retrial and subsequently had a minimum term of 14 years fixed on his life sentence: see [2006] EWHC 418 (QB).

alcoholism have to demonstrate that they had not voluntarily taken alcohol at the time of the killing. The outcome of the ruling in *Dietschmann* is that it is entirely possible that there could be a disinhibiting effect from alcohol but that an abnormality of mind represented by an underlying disorder or disease, such as a personality disorder, was also a concurrent cause and which led to a diminished responsibility for the killing. But if the underlying cause of the abnormality is alcoholism or a craving for alcohol, what is the effect of the comment of Watkins LJ in *Tandy* that an impulse to drink that led to the impairment of judgment and emotional response precluded a finding of diminished responsibility – in other words, that a defendant whose disease was alcoholism had to demonstrate that a decision to drink in a situation where a death occurred was one compelled by the disease rather than being a matter of choice.

14.68 In *R v Wood*,[72] the defendant had an alcohol dependency syndrome, and the trial judge directed the jury that a killing which occurred after drink – which was in response to an unwanted sexual advance – could only be treated as a case of diminished responsibility if the defendant also proved that his drinking was involuntary: 'A man's act is involuntary if, and only if, he could not have acted otherwise. Giving in to a craving is not an involuntary act, even if it is very difficult to do otherwise'.[73] The judge added: 'An alcoholic not suffering from severe withdrawal symptoms, who tops up his overnight level or who later chooses to accept a drink after he's reached his normal quota, is not drinking involuntarily'. This was held to be a misdirection, the Court of Appeal concluding that there had been an overly prescriptive misunderstanding of the proper approach, as *Tandy* had been diluted by *Dietschmann*. Sir Igor Judge P noted the following steps for the jury to consider.[74] First, they had to determine whether there was an abnormality of the mind: this might be more likely to be the conclusion if there was brain damage, but that was not necessary. If the defendant overcame that hurdle, the next question was to consider the effect of alcohol consumed as a result of the illness and exclude the effect of any alcohol consumed voluntarily. This being the proper question, the problem identified with what the trial judge had said was that it implied that there might have been an element of choice in the defendant's consumption of alcohol even though there was a craving: if it was a craving, it could properly be

72 [2008] EWCA Crim 1305, [2008] 2 CrAppR 34.

73 [2008] EWCA Crim 1305, [2008] 2 CrAppR 34 para 18.

74 [2008] EWCA Crim 1305, [2008] 2 CrAppR 34 para 41.

considered to be the result of the abnormality of mind and so to be taken into account.[75]

14.69 In *R v Stewart*,[76] the Court of Appeal revisited this ruling and decided it was not sufficient. In particular, Lord Judge CJ, as he had become, commented[77] that the jury could not properly be asked to separate out each drink taken and decide whether it was the result of the alcoholism or choice. The suggestion was that the question for the jury was to consider 'the nature and extent of the syndrome and whether, looking at the matter broadly, his consumption of alcohol before the killing is fairly to be regarded as the involuntary result of an irresistible craving for or compulsion to drink'.[78]

14.70 It is to be noted that various mental disorders may be linked to drug or alcohol abuse, or that a defendant with a mental disorder may also have alcoholic traits. It seems appropriate that this broad approach to whether alcohol was the result of the disorder or voluntary should be adopted when there is such co-morbidity.

Substantial impairment of responsibility

14.71 The final part of the test for diminished responsibility is the need for a substantial impairment of responsibility. This requires a causal connection between the abnormality of mind and the killing, since otherwise there is no ground for saying that responsibility is impaired.

14.72 Although the statutory test does not refer to the legal responsibility for the killing, but instead uses the word 'mental responsibility', it seems clear that this is a question of whether legal responsibility ought to be ascribed. As such, it is essentially a mixed legal and factual question for assessment by the jury. That in turn means that medical expert evidence is in no sense binding because the jury may differ from the doctor or doctors on that issue: indeed, given that it is not a clinical question, doctors might find that it is not a matter on which they feel comfortable giving evidence, and it may be that there could be no complaint if there was no medical evidence on this part of the test. The approach to medical evidence was part of the discussion of the test in *Byrne*, Lord Parker CJ commenting that substantial impairment:[79]

75 [2008] EWCA Crim 1305, [2008] 2 CrAppR 34 para 42.
76 [2009] EWCA Crim 593, [2009] 2 CrAppR 500.
77 [2009] EWCA Crim 593, [2009] 2 CrAppR 500 para 28.
78 [2009] EWCA Crim 593, [2009] 2 CrAppR 500 para 31.
79 [1960] 2 QB 396 at 403–404.

> ... is a question of degree and essentially one for the jury. Medical evidence is, of course, relevant, but the question involves a decision not merely as to whether there was some impairment of the mental responsibility of the accused for his acts but whether such impairment can properly be called 'substantial,' a matter upon which juries may quite legitimately differ from doctors.

14.73 This does not prevent a judge from withdrawing a charge of murder from the jury at the end of the prosecution case, so leaving only the question of manslaughter. In accordance with the normal principles that arise from *R v Galbraith*,[80] the judge may withdraw a charge from the jury if there is no reasonable prospect of a jury returning a conviction that would be safe. In *R v Khan*,[81] the Court of Appeal accepted that this might apply in a case of diminished responsibility, even if the prosecution challenged it. Lord Justice Aikens, having noted that this prospect was theoretically possible, commented that it would rarely be proper if the prosecution actively challenged the defence.[82] On the facts, the defence argument was that the case should be withdrawn because the only expert evidence supported a finding of substantial impairment, but the judge's ruling that there remained a question for the jury to determine on the facts was upheld. The reason for this approach was explained at paragraph 18: Aikens LJ commented that the features that were relevant were the comprehension of the defendant as to the physical acts involved in the killing and the degree of control over it. He noted that: 'Scientific understanding of how the mind works and the extent to which states of mind and physical responses to them have physical or chemical causes have undoubtedly advanced' in recent decades, but that the position remained that 'it is impossible to provide any accurate scientific measurement' of the person's understanding of or control over his or her actions. That meant that 'there is no simple scientific test of whether a defendant's "mental responsibility for his acts and omissions in doing or being a party to the killing" is "substantially impaired"'.

14.74 Should guidance be given to the jury on what is meant by 'substantial'? The Court of Appeal in *R v Lloyd*[83] upheld a direction that the jury should follow its common sense in interpreting the word,

80 [1981] 1 WLR 1039, (1981) 73 CrAppR 124.
81 [2009] EWCA Crim 1569, [2010] 1 CrAppR 74.
82 [2009] EWCA Crim 1569, [2010] 1 CrAppR 74 para 42.
83 [1967] 1 QB 175.

but assisting them by saying that it was somewhere between total and trivial or minimal.

14.75 As noted above, one of the complicating factors may be the interaction between the disinhibiting effect of alcohol or some other intoxicant and the relevant abnormality of mind. In *Stewart*, the Court of Appeal, having clarified the approach that should be taken in terms of splitting the impact of voluntary and involuntary consumption of alcohol, gave guidance on the question of how the judge could assist the jury on the question of whether there was a substantial impairment of responsibility. Lord Judge CJ noted that:

> The jury ... may properly be invited to reflect on the difference between a failure by the defendant to resist his impulses to behave as he actually did, and an inability consequent on it to resist them.[84]

He then noted that the relevant features that would inform this judgment were likely to be:

> (a) the extent and seriousness of the defendant's dependency, if any, on alcohol (b) the extent to which his ability to control his drinking or to choose whether to drink or not, was reduced, (c) whether he was capable of abstinence from alcohol, and if so, (d) for how long, and (e) whether he was choosing for some particular reason, such as a birthday celebration, to decide to get drunk, or to drink even more than usual.[85]

He also added that features such as the pattern of drinking in the days before the killing and the decision-making on other day-to-day matters would also be relevant.

Evidence from the defendant

14.76 It has already been commented above that expert evidence will be essential to demonstrate an abnormality of the mind and its cause; this is even though the question remains for the jury and it can reject an expert view, at least as to whether there is an abnormality of mind.[86] Of course, there might also be situations in which there is a difference of expert opinion which the jury will have to determine.

14.77 In addition, the expert opinion will have to have a basis in fact. While some of the expert view may come from an assessment of the defendant and so be direct evidence, and there may be circumstantial

84 [2009] EWCA Crim 593, [2009] 2 CrAppR 500 at para 33.

85 [2009] EWCA Crim 593, [2009] 2 CrAppR 500 at para 34.

86 See *Byrne* [1960] 2 QB 396 at p403. In relation to aetiology, the jury may reject the view that the defendant has met the burden of proving that.

evidence as to what was done and said at the time of the killing from which the causation between the abnormality and the act can be verified, in other circumstances it may be that information from the defendant is important. This may give rise to two issues. First, if the expert has taken into account what the defendant said in the course of an examination as to his or her understanding of what was happening at the time of the events in question, that is hearsay if the expert takes it into account as an indication of the truth of what was happening. However, the parties may agree that it is admissible nevertheless (under the Criminal Justice Act 2003 s114(1)(c)); alternatively, it may be admissible in the interests of justice (section 114(1)(d)), particularly if account has to be taken of whether the defendant is in a fit state to give evidence in court.

14.78 The second issue is that, since the question remains one for the jury, is there an obligation for the defendant to give evidence or call other factual evidence? It seems that there is at least an obligation to lay a foundation. In *R v Ahmed Din*,[87] the prosecution had been content to accept that the medical evidence of a delusional motivation for killing supported diminished responsibility and so had cross-examined only to the extent that they removed the possibility of a verdict based on insanity. However, the trial judge had intervened to ask questions as to the accuracy of the underlying diagnosis that Mr Din had been delusional, and so left it to the jury to determine whether they were satisfied that there was an abnormality of mind. This turned on whether his belief that his wife was having an affair was delusional or something in relation to which there was a reasonable ground for the belief: the wife had not been called to give evidence to the effect that there was no basis for Mr Din's belief. The Court of Criminal Appeal upheld the murder conviction, and noted that it was necessary for the prosecution to probe the facts on the basis of which there was a claimed abnormality of mind, the burden of establishing that being on the defence. This in turn means that the defence has to lay an appropriate evidential foundation.

14.79 However, this defence duty does not necessarily require the defendant to give evidence. In *R v Bathurst*,[88] the Court of Appeal quashed a conviction of murder and substituted a conviction of manslaughter on the basis that the trial judge had made adverse comments on the failure of the defendant to give evidence. The Court of Appeal noted that it would rarely be proper for such adverse comments to be made.

87 [1962] 1 WLR 680.
88 [1968] 2 QB 99.

On the particular facts, in the absence of any suggestion that the defendant was seeking to fabricate an abnormality of mind, it was not proper for the judge to have commented.[89] That particular point may now be subject to the fact that adverse inferences may be drawn if a defendant does not give evidence: see section 35 of the Criminal Justice and Public Order Act 1994. However, as is noted in chapter 11, this is subject to whether or not there is a medical reason for a defendant not to give evidence. This may cover most situations;[90] and if the facts are as in *Bathurst*, the propriety of an adverse inference direction might be questioned.

Burden of proof on the defendant

14.80 The language of HA 1957 s2(2) indicates that 'it shall be for the defence to prove that the person charged is by virtue of this section not liable to be convicted of murder'. In early case-law, it was established that this required proof on the balance of probabilities: see *R v Dunbar*.[91] In this regard, diminished responsibility is different from provocation, which has to be disproved by the prosecution if raised on the evidence. The effect of the burden of proof being on the defendant is that it seems to be a matter of the choice for the defendant as to whether to invite the jury to consider the issue.[92]

14.81 There are various cases that suggest a reverse onus of proof on a defendant breaches the presumption of innocence, and it is certainly the case that the interpretive obligation under section 3 of the Human Rights Act 1998 has been used to lead to the language of reverse burdens being interpreted as placing an evidential burden on the defendant when it would be disproportionate to interpret the

89 There were differences of view as between experts, which had been explored during the trial, but they were based on their different opinions of what the facts revealed rather than whether the defendant had lied to them.

90 There might be cases where a defendant has recovered and so is fit to give evidence: so, in *R v Bradshaw* (1986) 82 CrAppR 79, a defendant could properly give evidence, and it could rightly be concluded that there was an inadequate foundation for the defence if the doctor's assessment was based solely on the defendant's account.

91 [1958]1 QB 1.

92 See *R v Kooken* (1982) 74 CrAppR 30, in which the Court of Appeal held that a judge had been right not to raise diminished responsibility against the wishes of the defendant, and doubted that the judge had a power to raise the issue; and *R v Campbell* (1987) 84 CrAppR 255, in which the Court of Appeal determined that the burden of proof was on the defence and the statute allowed the matter to the defence to decide whether to raise the issue.

language as imposing an evidential burden only: see *R v Lambert*[93] and various cases following that decision.

14.82 As to whether *Dunbar* still stands in the light of *Lambert*, it is to be noted that the Court of Appeal hearing in *Lambert* was joined with the appeals of Ali and Jordan, which related to diminished responsibility.[94] The court found against them on the practical basis that it would be difficult for the prosecution to prove the negative, namely that diminished responsibility was absent, particularly as they could not secure a medical report if the defendant was unwilling to co-operate.[95] It was also noted that the option of raising diminished responsibility was a matter to the advantage of the defendant if he or she sought to raise it. This leads to the argument that since the question of diminished responsibility only arises if the prosecution has proved that there was what would otherwise be a murder (actus reus and murder), it is proportionate for the defendant to prove that grounds for reducing the conviction to a lesser offence.

14.83 Having said that, the essential rationale for the position adopted in *Lambert* is that a conviction for a more serious offence should not rest on the failure of the defendant to prove that he or she is only guilty of a lesser offence. That also applies in relation to a conviction for manslaughter as opposed to murder. It is worth noting that petitions to appeal by Messrs Ali and Jordan were dismissed when the House of Lords accepted the case of *Lambert* for hearing[96] (though this might be on the basis that the Appeal Committee felt that they raised no additional issues).

The role of the prosecution

14.84 The fact that it is a defence means that the charge brought has to be murder: in other words, the prosecution cannot charge manslaughter on the basis of diminished responsibility. They can, however, accept that such a plea is a satisfactory resolution of the charge brought: indeed, if there is no realistic prospect of conviction for murder, it would be contrary to the Code for Crown Prosecutors to insist on a trial. Note, however, the comment in *Ahmed Din*, mentioned above, suggesting a prosecution duty to probe the evidence: this must, of

93 [2002] 2 AC 69.
94 [2002] QB 1112.
95 [2002] QB 1112 para 19.
96 [2002] QB 1112 p1127.

course, be subject to the assessment made by the prosecution of the need to do that.

14.85 There may be instances in which the prosecution may take a more active position. If the defence contention is of insanity, it is open to the prosecution to argue that the true situation is one of diminished responsibility: and if the contention of the defence is of diminished responsibility, the prosecution can adduce evidence of insanity. The power in both these situations arises from section 6 of the Criminal Procedure (Insanity) Act 1964, which states:

> **6. Evidence by prosecution of insanity or diminished responsibility**
> Where on a trial for murder the accused contends –
> (a) that at the time of the alleged offence he was insane so as not to be responsible according to law for his actions; or
> (b) that at that time he was suffering from such abnormality of mind as is specified in subsection (1) of section 2 of the Homicide Act 1957 (diminished responsibility),
>
> the court shall allow the prosecution to adduce or elicit evidence tending to prove the other of those contentions, and may give directions as to the stage of the proceedings at which the prosecution may adduce such evidence.

14.86 This language supports the view that it cannot be a matter for the prosecution to bring a charge of manslaughter on the grounds of diminished responsibility, given that permission to adduce such evidence to rebut a contention of insanity would not be necessary if it was open to them to bring a charge of manslaughter in such a circumstance. Naturally, this does not prevent the prosecution indicating that they have evidence supporting a defence of diminished responsibility and indicating that they would not seek to counter such a plea being entered.

14.87 It is long established that the prosecution have a duty to tender to the defence any evidence of a medical nature that might be relevant: see *R v Casey*, which related to evidence of insanity but would apply equally to anything that might go to a lesser charge.

14.88 There was a long-standing tradition of medical reports being obtained in relation to all murder charges. The validity of this, which often involved the prosecution making the arrangements on behalf of the court, for whom the report was prepared, was challenged in *R v Reid*.[97] There were complexities arising from the fact that the report might count as a document that had to be revealed by the prosecution to co-defendants in accordance with the Criminal Procedure and

97 [2001] EWCA Crim 1806, [2002] 1 CrAppR 234.

Investigations Act 1996. The court ruled that the practice should stop because the prosecution should not act as the agent of the court and there was no statutory basis for the practice.

14.89 However, if a defendant charged with murder is released on bail, there remains extant the requirement in section 3(6A) of the Bail Act 1976 (inserted into the Act in 1982) that the court must impose a condition as to examination by two psychiatrists, unless it considers that there is satisfactory evidence of his mental condition.

Diminished responsibility and provocation

14.90 It is possible that a defendant will raise alternative defences, perhaps denying murder on the basis that there was no mens rea, but also arguing that either provocation or diminished responsibility was available. It is established that the jury should consider issues in the order lack of mens rea, provocation and diminished responsibility because of the different burdens of proof. If the prosecution does not prove mens rea, there should be an acquittal; if mens rea is proved but it arose in a situation of provocation, the defence has an evidential burden and the prosecution have to show that provocation does not apply; but, as noted above, the burden of proving diminished responsibility lies on the defence.

14.91 Another question that might arise in this context is whether the jury should be asked the basis for a verdict of manslaughter. This might be relevant to the sentence to be imposed. While it seems that it is permissible to ask the jury the basis for the conviction, the Court of Appeal in *R v Cawthorne*[98] suggested that this was a problematic course of action and that the better approach was for the judge to form a view as to the appropriate basis for the conviction and any sentence. On the one hand, there may be difficulties if different jurors had different reasons for concluding that the proper verdict was manslaughter. However, the jury has the responsibility of assessing the proper verdict, including the basis for it; and it may be that clear directions in advance will allow the jury to assess properly the basis for the verdict.

Sentencing

14.92 The maximum sentence for manslaughter is life imprisonment. Chapter 17 contains an account of the features relevant to the discretion of the court in sentencing when life imprisonment is available.

98 [1996] 2 CrAppR(S) 445.

Appeals

14.93 There are a number of issues of law that might arise in the course of a trial involving diminished responsibility that justify an appeal if the conviction is of murder. In addition to the normal process of criminal appeals, the involvement of mental disorder may allow further evidence to develop (as a particular mental disorder may take time to manifest itself or a defendant may provide instructions that do not allow diminished responsibility to be raised). See chapter 21 as to the issues arising in appeals out of time.

The new test for diminished responsibility

14.94 Section 52 of the Coroners and Justice Act 2009 has replaced the test for diminished responsibility.[99] The new language is:

(1) A person ('D') who kills or is a party to the killing of another is not to be convicted of murder if D was suffering from an abnormality of mental functioning which –
- (a) arose from a recognised medical condition,
- (b) substantially impaired D's ability to do one or more of the things mentioned in subsection (1A), and
- (c) provides an explanation for D's acts and omissions in doing or being a party to the killing.

(1A) Those things are –
- (a) to understand the nature of D's conduct;
- (b) to form a rational judgment;
- (c) to exercise self-control.

(1B) For the purposes of subsection (1)(c), an abnormality of mental functioning provides an explanation for D's conduct if it causes, or is a significant contributory factor in causing, D to carry out that conduct.

99 This is in effect from 4 October 2010, by reason of the Coroners and Justice Act 2009 (Commencement No 4, Transitional and Saving Provisions) Order 2010 para 5. The Act is the outcome of a process starting with a review of the law of homicide (see *Hansard* HC Debates vol 425 cols 1579–1580, 28 October 2004,), which led to the Law Commission report of November 2006, *Murder, manslaughter and infanticide* (available at www.justice.gov.uk/lawcommission/docs/lc304_Murder_Manslaughter_and_Infanticide_Report.pdf), a July 2008 consultation paper, *Murder, manslaughter and infanticide: proposals for reform of the law* (available at http://webarchive.nationalarchives.gov.uk/+/http://www.justice.gov.uk/publications/cp1908.htm), and then the legislation. There is also a corresponding change to section 6 of the Criminal Procedure (Insanity) Act 1964, the power of the prosecution to call evidence of insanity or diminished responsibility, so that references to abnormality of mind become abnormality of mental functioning.

14.95 In short, diminished responsibility now requires a recognised medical condition, which in turn means that medical evidence will be essential; it changes the reference to the 'mind' to mental functioning. The substantial impairment test remains, but instead of referring to responsibility, the test requires substantial impairment of the ability to understand the nature of conduct, form a rational judgment or exercise self-control: these factors, and in particular the latter feature, stress the voluntariness of conduct. In addition, the causation test is clarified to require a significant contribution to the cause, which is roughly what developed under the case-law relating to intoxication and an abnormality of mind.

14.96 The Explanatory Notes published with the Act[100] indicate that Parliament believes that it has provided a 'modernised definition'.[101] This is not helpful in answering the important question of whether Parliament believes that it has changed the law. One possibility from the new language is that it may be more on a continuum with the question of insanity, since a 'medical condition' that impairs responsibility for offending seems like an explanation of what amounts to a disease of the mind in the context of insanity.

Infanticide

14.97 A further specific partial defence to consider is infanticide. This can be viewed as a form of diminished responsibility in a situation that would otherwise be murder. If the charge is murder but the facts also amount to infanticide, that verdict can be returned. However, the elements are not exactly the same as diminished responsibility. It can also be viewed as an entirely separate form of homicide, and because it is a separate offence, the prosecution can bring a charge phrased as infanticide (unlike in relation to a situation of manslaughter on the grounds of diminished responsibility, which must be charged as murder).

14.98 Section 1(1) of the Infanticide Act 1938 provided initially that:

> (1) Where any woman by any wilful act or omission causes the death of her child being a child under the age of twelve months, but at the time of the act or omission the balance of her mind was disturbed

100 Available at www.legislation.gov.uk/ukpga/2009/25/resources.

101 Coroners and Justice Act 2009 Explanatory Notes para 327. See also chapter 16 of the supplement to the Crown Court Benchbook for the views of the Judicial College: available at www.judiciary.gov/publications-and-reports/judicial-college/2011.

> by reason of her not having fully recovered from the effect of giving birth to the child or by reason of the effect of lactation consequent upon the birth of the child, then, notwithstanding that the circumstances were such that but for this Act the offence would have amounted to murder, she shall be guilty of ... infanticide, and may for such offence be dealt with and punished as if she had been guilty of the offence of manslaughter of the child.

14.99 This was supplemented by section 1(2), which provided that a conviction for infanticide could be returned on a charge of murder. Subsection (3) also provides that verdicts of manslaughter and not guilty by reason of insanity remain possible.

14.100 The elements of infanticide involve the special actus reus circumstance that the victim must be the infant child of the defendant. It is also provided that there must be a disturbance to the balance of the mind by reason of the effects of childbirth or lactation. The statutory language does not require an element of causation between the balance of the mind being disturbed and the killing: just that they co-exist. However, the existence of a causal link will be relevant to sentence. The absence of any causal link suggests that the disturbed mind criterion is an element of the factual situation that must exist in the course of which the defendant formed the relevant mens rea, and so properly considered to be part of the actus reus. This in turn would mean that a defendant charged with murder who was unfit to stand trial in circumstances where she would be able to argue for a conviction for infanticide should be able to argue that she committed the actus reus of the latter rather than of murder. The same should apply if the defendant argued insanity and the question was what actus reus had been committed.

14.101 As to what is clearly a mens rea element, namely wilfulness, this is normally taken to cover intention or recklessness: see *Sheppard.*[102] An argument against this is that the language of the section refers to the verdict being returned instead of murder, which requires intention, such that wilfulness must be taken to amount to the mens rea applicable to murder.

14.102 The limited circumstances of the charge[103] mean that diminished responsibility may still have a significant role. For example, if the victim child is over 12 months or is not the child of the defendant,

102 [1981] AC 394.

103 Much more limited than, for example, in New Zealand, where infanticide covers the killing of children under the age of ten (Crimes Act 1961 s178); note, however, that New Zealand does not have a general defence of diminished responsibility.

but she is affected by the same disturbance of the mind, diminished responsibility must be used; however, while the mental state is likely to amount to an abnormality of mind (or mental functioning, under the new statutory language) the need for a causative link in relation to diminished responsibility is an additional hurdle.

14.103 The particular benefit of a conviction for infanticide is that there is an established pattern of leniency in sentencing, even though the maximum sentence is life imprisonment. In *R v Sainsbury*,[104] in quashing a sentence of detention and substituting a probation order, the Court of Appeal noted that statistics from the decade previous to the case indicated that of the 59 cases of infanticide, 52 led to probation orders and seven to hospital disposals (only one of which involved a restriction order).[105]

14.104 Section 57 of the Coroners and Justice Act 2009 has introduced a slight amendment to the language of both Infanticide Act 1938 s1(1) and (2) to provide that if the circumstances would otherwise be murder or manslaughter, the verdict can be infanticide. The effect of this is that a verdict of infanticide can also be returned when the offence would otherwise be unlawful act manslaughter.

Provocation and loss of control

Introduction

14.105 As has been described above, the partial defence to murder of diminished responsibility had to be introduced to English law by Parliament, as the judges of the English common law, unlike the Scottish judges, had not developed the concept. In contrast, the partial defence of provocation was introduced by the common law so as to reduce murder to manslaughter if the killing occurred in a situation where a defendant lost control for reasons that were within parameters that were found understandable.

14.106 It was modified by the HA 1957, and has recently been amended significantly by the Coroners and Justice Act 2009 to become the 'loss

104 (1989) 11 CrAppR(S) 533.

105 It appears that some custodial sentences have been passed subsequently, though they remain rare: see Appendix D of *Murder, manslaughter and infanticide*, Law Com No 304 (2006), the study which led to the reforms to diminished responsibility, provocation and infanticide. The appendix, 'Infanticide and related diminished responsibility manslaughters: an empirical study' by RD MacKay, found three custodial sentences.

of control' partial defence. Since the 2009 provisions, which came into effect on 4 October 2010,[106] are not retrospective, the 1957 provisions and the case-law that developed under them may well be relevant for some time.

14.107 Provocation does not apply to any offence other than murder, though it covers liability as a principal or as a secondary party.[107] It has been held expressly not to apply to attempted murder: see *R v Bruzas*.[108] It is unlikely to apply to a conspiracy to murder: a loss of control, which is the essence of the defence, is inconsistent with the formation of an agreement that is central to a conspiracy;[109] and there is a discretion in relation to sentencing for a conspiracy charge, unlike for a substantive charge of murder, which is a central reason for having a partial defence. In this regard, conspiracy to murder is similar to attempted murder and the same approach is likely.

14.108 What is regarded as the classic common law definition of provocation is that of Devlin J in the case of *R v Duffy*,[110] in which he noted that:

> Provocation is some act, or series of acts, done by the dead man to the accused which would cause in any reasonable person, and actually causes in the accused, a sudden and temporary loss of self control, rendering the accused so subject to passion as to make him or her for the moment not master of his mind.

14.109 In HA 1957 s3, this definition was modified and restated in the following terms:

> Where on a charge of murder there is evidence on which a jury can find that the person charged was provoked (whether by things done or by things said or by both together) to lose his self control, the question whether the provocation was enough to make a reasonable man do as he did shall be left to be determined by the jury; and in determining that question the jury shall take into account everything both done and said according to the effect which, in their opinion, it would have on a reasonable man.

106 Coroners and Justice Act 2009 (Commencement No 4, Transitional and Saving Provisions) Order 2010 para 6.

107 *R v Marks* [1998] Crim LR 676.

108 [1972] Crim LR 367. The law of attempt was subsequently codified in the Criminal Attempts Act 1981, which contains no reference to provocation being available.

109 There are arguments the other way: an agreement and hence a conspiracy can be formed quickly, and so it is not necessarily inconsistent with the idea of loss of control. Similarly, the lesser stigma of having the offence recorded as manslaughter would also be relevant.

110 [1949] 1 All ER 932n.

14.110 The Coroners and Justice Act 2009 includes the following elements:

i) By section 56, the common law defence of provocation is abolished.
ii) By section 54, a new defence of 'loss of control' in introduced, which applies if there is a loss of self-control that causes the defendant's acts or omissions in the killing, there was a qualifying trigger for the loss of self-control, and 'a person of D's sex and age, with a normal degree of tolerance and self-restraint and in the circumstances of D, might have reacted in the same or in a similar way to D'.
iii) Section 54(3) indicates that 'the circumstances of D' means those circumstances that 'bear on D's general capacity for tolerance or self-restraint'.
iv) Section 55 sets out what is a legitimate 'qualifying trigger', which can arise from a fear of serious violence by the victim or something said or done that was extremely grave and caused a justifiable sense of being seriously wronged.

14.111 In these settings, a question arises as to the relationship between mental disorder and the loss of self-control, and whether a defendant who has a mental disorder is to be judged in a manner that allows the effect of the mental disorder in relation to the power of self-control to be taken into account.

Provocation – the Homicide Act 1957

The modification of the common law test

14.112 It is to be noted that the language of section 3 of the HA 1957 is somewhat wider than the common law test as set out in *Duffy*. The statute makes it clear that words alone or in combination with other conduct may provide a basis for the defence, whereas the common law test required some acts. In addition, the common law summary suggested that the provoking conduct had to come from the victim: that is not the case with the statutory language, and so the words or conduct on which the defendant relies may come from a third person and need not come from the victim. Nor, it should be noted, is it necessary for the conduct or words in question to be aimed at the defendant: the question arising is the impact on the defendant. As an example of this, see *R v Doughty*,[111] in which the provoking conduct was a baby crying, which was clearly not directed at the defendant.

111 (1986) 83 CrAppR 319.

14.113 The common law test of what amounted to provocation remained in place: see, for example, *R v Whitfield*,[112] which applied the subjective and objective parts of *Duffy*. In *R v Ahluwalia*,[113] Lord Taylor CJ noted the following modified version of the *Duffy* test that took into account the changes introduced by the HA 1957:[114]

> 'Provocation is some act, or series of acts done (or words spoken) ... which would cause in any reasonable person and actually causes in the accused, a sudden and temporary loss of self-control, rendering the accused so subject to passion as to make him or her for the moment not master of his or her mind'. The bracketed words are added and seven words removed in accordance with the Homicide Act 1957. Otherwise that definition has stood ever since.

14.114 Lord Taylor CJ endorsed the following summary of the changes caused by the statute:

> (i) It made it clear that 'things said' alone may be sufficient provocation, if the jury should be of the opinion that they would have provoked a reasonable man ... (ii) It took away the power of the judge to withdraw the defence from the jury on the ground that there was no evidence on which the jury could find that a reasonable man would have been provoked to do as the defendant did ... (iii) It took away the power of the judge to dictate to the jury what were the characteristics of the reasonable man ...[115]

14.115 The substantive questions arising under the provocation test are, first, whether there was a sudden loss of self-control; second, whether this was caused by provoking conduct; and third, whether the reasonable person would have lost his or her self-control.

The roles of judge and jury

14.116 The statutory test in HA 1957 s3 suggests that two distinct questions arise: the first is whether there is evidence of provocation such as to be left to the jury (which is a question for the judge to determine); the second is then the substantive question of provocation, which is

112 (1976) 63 CrAppR 39.

113 (1993) 96 CrAppR 133.

114 (1993) 96 CrAppR 133 p137.

115 At pages 137–138, quoting from page 337 of the sixth edition of Smith and Hogan, *Criminal law*. See also *Director of Public Prosecutions v Camplin* [1978] AC 705, discussed below, in which Lord Diplock noted at page 716 that the statute was designed to mitigate some of the harshness of the common law, such as the holding in *Bedder v Director of Public Prosecutions* [1954] 1 WLR 1119 that a physical ailment to which a taunt had been directed could not be taken into account.

for the jury. It has been determined that questions of the onus and standard of proof in relation to provocation are as with self-defence, namely once there is evidence of provocation, the prosecution has to disprove its existence to the criminal standard: see *R v McPherson*.[116]

14.117 The question of whether there is evidence fit to be left to the jury means that there is a duty upon the judge to raise and leave the question to the jury even if it has not been raised by the defendant (in contrast, for example, to the law relating to diminished responsibility, which involves a burden on the defence and so is not a matter that a judge can develop independently). However, the judge is not required to leave the question of provocation if there is only speculative evidence of any provocative conduct or words. This applies even if there is evidence of loss of self-control: so in *R v Acott*,[117] the House of Lords held that the trial judge had been right not to leave provocation to the jury in the absence of evidence that there was provoking conduct or words, despite the prosecution having cross-examined the defendant on the basis that Mr Acott's victim, his mother, must have caused him to lose his self-control and attack her. The context of this was a defence that the victim had died as a result of falling rather than as the result of an attack, and so the prosecution was seeking to undermine the defence of not being involved in the death.

Mental disorder and the need for a sudden loss of control

14.118 Evidence of mental disorder may be relevant to the substantive questions arising. For example, there may be an argument as to whether a sudden loss of control was the result of mental disorder or as a response to provocative conduct.

14.119 It has also been argued that mental disorder should be taken into account in determining whether there was a loss of control that can be described as 'sudden'. It is to be noted that the purpose of

116 (1957) 41 CrAppR 213.

117 [1997] 1 WLR 306, [1997] 2 CrAppR 94. See also *R v Coutts* [2006] UKHL 39 (HL), [2006] 1 WLR 2154, [2007] 1 CrAppR 60: in this case, the prosecution alleged a deliberate killing and the defence had been that it was an accident during consensual asphyxial sex; as such, prosecution counsel had submitted that the judge should not leave to the jury the possibility of a verdict of manslaughter, and defence counsel had agreed that it should not be left to the jury. On appeal to the House of Lords, it was determined that this was a material irregularity because the judge should leave to the jury any obvious and viable alternative verdict, irrespective of the wishes of the parties. The interests of society in allowing the jury to reach a proper verdict are more important than allowing the parties to control what is left to the jury, which may be for tactical reasons.

requiring a sudden loss of control is to make sure that the defendant had acted in a way that meant that he or she was responding to the provocative conduct in a way that reflected a loss of control as opposed to a planned attack for reasons such as revenge or punishment. It is clearly arguable that the requirement of suddenness is an evidential matter, designed to ensure that there is actually a loss of control; the case-law supports this.

14.120 A challenge to the requirement for suddenness was tried in relation to a woman who had been in an abusive relationship that had led to a diagnosis of 'battered woman syndrome', which may be considered to be a psychological disorder or vulnerability: in *R v Ahluwalia*,[118] it was argued that the syndrome meant that a response from provocation offered to a battered woman might well involve a 'slow-burn' rather than an immediate response. Lord Taylor CJ accepted this, noting:[119]

> ... the subjective element in the defence of provocation would not as a matter of law be negatived simply because of the delayed reaction in such cases, provided that there was at the time of the killing a 'sudden and temporary loss of self-control' caused by the alleged provocation. However, the longer the delay and the stronger the evidence of deliberation on the part of the defendant, the more likely it will be that the prosecution will negative provocation.[120]

14.121 In other words, as long as when the loss of control came, it came upon the defendant suddenly, it was possible that there could be a period of delay. Applying that to the facts, the Court of Appeal held that the judge had been entitled to direct the jury that a 'sudden and temporary loss of control' was required because the direction did not require an immediate loss of control following the last provocative act or statement. Of course, it might be helpful if a trial judge were to explain the potential relevance of the interplay between a disorder and a delayed reaction. What might apply to battered woman syndrome might apply to other forms of mental disorder: for example, a defendant who reflects continually on provocation because of an obsessive element of a personality disorder may lose control suddenly after a delayed period.

118 (1993) 96 CrAppR 133.

119 (1993) 96 CrAppR 133 p139.

120 See also *R v Thornton (No 2)* [1996] 1 WLR 1174, [1996] 2 CrAppR 108.

Mental disorder and the gravity of the provocation

14.122 There is a second way in which conditions such as battered woman syndrome or mental disorder might be relevant, that is in assessing the seriousness of the provocative conduct. The effect of provocative language or conduct might be viewed as more serious by someone who has battered woman syndrome because of her knowledge that it is likely to be a precursor to a more worrying course of conduct. In other words, what is unlikely to be viewed as provocative to many people may be viewed in a more sensitive fashion by someone with a disorder, so making it more likely that there was a loss of control from provocative conduct or language. The gravity of the provocation is viewed from the perspective of the defendant, and so is effectively entirely subjective.

14.123 This approach was endorsed by the House of Lords in *R v Morhall*:[121] the issue in this case was whether the judge had given an adequate direction on the relevance of the fact that the defendant was addicted to glue-sniffing. The provocative taunting of him related to his addiction, and the trial judge had limited his direction to the jury to indicating that the addiction was something that should be taken into account. The Court of Appeal had ruled that the judge had if anything been generous because any discreditable conduct was irrelevant as it was repugnant to the concept of the reasonable man.

14.124 The House of Lords disagreed: Lord Goff held that the Court of Appeal's reasoning 'flows from a misunderstanding of the function of the so-called "reasonable person test" in this context'. The purpose was 'to introduce, as a matter of policy, a standard of self-control which has to be complied with if provocation is to be established in law'.[122] Accordingly, characteristics, or indeed any past discreditable conduct, could affect the gravity of the provocation. Applying that to mental disorder, a taunt directed at a past and transient episode of illness is something that might affect the gravity of the provocation and so provide the starting point for the assessment of whether it did cause the defendant to lose self-control (the subjective test, discussed above) and whether that would be the reaction of the reasonable person.

121 [1996] AC 90.
122 [1996] AC 90 pp97–98.

Mental disorder and the reasonable person

14.125 The final element of the test is the reasonable person: not only does the provocation have to cause the defendant to lose self-control, it must be that this would have been the effect on a reasonable person. However, it has been determined that the reasonable person is in fact a hybrid having some of the defendant's characteristics and some objective characteristics. The precise mix has been the subject of significant judicial disagreement and has engaged the House of Lords or Privy Council on several occasions.

14.126 The starting point for a discussion of the more recent developments is that in *Director of Public Prosecutions v Camplin,*[123] it was noted that the jury had to assess the characteristics of the defendant both in relation to how they affected the seriousness of the provocation but also from the point of view of whether it was reasonable to respond to it, subject to the caveat that ordinary self-control would be expected. The specific question arising in the case was whether the reaction of a 15-year-old was to be judged against what was to be expected of an adult or a juvenile. Lord Diplock set the test as follows:

> The judge ... should ... explain ... that the reasonable man ... is a person having the power of self-control to be expected of an ordinary person of the sex and age of the accused, but in other respects sharing such of the accused's characteristics as they think would affect the gravity of the provocation to him; and that the question is not merely whether such a person would in like circumstances be provoked to lose his self-control but also would react to the provocation as the accused did.[124]

14.127 The reason for this approach was that the public policy element adopted by the judges who had developed the partial defence at common law was that there should be no excuse allowed for someone who was exceptionally pugnacious or excitable, and so society was entitled to accept that a defendant should be 'possessed of such powers of self-control as everyone is entitled to expect that his fellow citizens will exercise in society'.[125] The test propounded allowed differences reflecting age and gender, which on the facts meant that Mr Camplin was to be judged as a 15-year-old boy, because the question was the level of self-control to be expected of a male of that age.

123 [1978] AC 705. Also reported at (1978) 67 CrAppR 14.
124 [1978] AC 705 at p718.
125 [1978] AC 705 p717.

14.128 It has also been suggested that this means that characteristics that are in the form of a mental disorder are to be taken into account. So, in *R v Newell*,[126] the Court of Appeal endorsed the view suggested in a New Zealand authority that '"characteristics" ... is wide enough to apply not only to physical qualities but also to mental qualities'.[127] However, the Court in *Newell* then held that chronic alcoholism was not relevant on the facts because there was no connection between the provocative words and conduct and the alcoholism. This, however, seems to be a matter relevant to the gravity of the provocation not whether the test of self-control was affected.

14.129 Applying the approach of a psychological facet being a relevant characteristic, in *Ahluwalia* the Court of Appeal noted that the trial judge had not had the benefit of evidence that might have allowed him to determine that battered woman syndrome amounted to a characteristic (though he had properly directed the jury that they could take into account the history of violence in the relationship).[128] But in the subsequent case of *R v Thornton (No 2)*,[129] it was noted that a personality disorder in conjunction with battered woman syndrome amounted to a characteristic that the jury could take into account in assessing how the notional reasonable person would react.

14.130 However, there was a Privy Council decision to the contrary. In *Luc Thiet Thuan v R*,[130] the issue was the application of the law to a man who had brain damage that reduced his ability to exercise self-control. The relevant Ordinance in Hong Kong was in the same terms as section 3 of the HA 1957. A majority of the Privy Council held that the proper test in relation to the ability to exercise self-control was objective and so did not allow account to be taken of the brain damage. This necessarily cast doubt on *Ahluwalia* and *Thornton*. Lord

126 (1980) 71 CrAppR 331.

127 (1980) 71 CrAppR 331 p339: the court in *Newell* was citing from the case of *R v McGregor* [1962] NZLR 1069, which was construing the statutory codification of provocation in New Zealand, which involved an objective test of a person 'having the power of self-control of an ordinary person, but otherwise having the characteristics of the offender': Crimes Act 1961 s169; the defence there has now been repealed in its entirety by the Crimes (Provocation Repeal) Amendment Act 2009.

128 The appeal on the basis of provocation failed, but succeeded on an argument of diminished responsibility, namely evidence of a major depressive episode that had not been used in the trial: the murder conviction was quashed and a retrial was ordered.

129 [1996] 1 WLR 1174, [1996] 2 CrAppR 108. See also *R v Dryden* [1995] 4 All ER 987, in which it was held that held that an obsessive character was relevant.

130 [1996] 3 WLR 45, [1997] AC 131.

Steyn dissented, suggesting that while irascibility and pugnacity were irrelevant to the objective test, other characteristics were to be taken into account.

14.131 The House of Lords then considered the question of what amounted to a characteristic in *R v Smith (Morgan)*,[131] in which the issue was the relevance of a mental disorder, namely a severe depression, that on the evidence reduced his power of self-control. By a majority of three to two, the House determined that all characteristics were to be taken into account and the defendant was to be judged according to whether it was reasonable for him or her to have lost self-control: in other words, the test for the law was whether the defendant had met the standard to be expected of him or her. However, a nine-member bench of the Privy Council was convened to consider the equivalent test in article 4 of the Homicide (Jersey) Law 1986 in the case of *Attorney-General for Jersey v Holley*.[132] The context was whether alcoholism was a characteristic to be taken into account, and by a majority of six to three, it was decided to follow *Luc Thiet Thuan v R* rather than *R v Smith (Morgan)*: it has been decided by a five-judge Court of Appeal that *Holley* rather than *Smith* now sets the law in England and Wales: see *R v James, R v Karimi*.[133]

14.132 The essence of the reasoning in *Holley* was that, as a matter of statutory construction, the legislature had endorsed an objective standard for whether loss of self-control was excusable, and so it was not permissible for the judiciary to undermine this standard. This in turn meant that while the gravity of the provocation could be assessed by reference to the characteristics of the defendant, it was the necessary to apply an objective standard, even though that might be a standard that a defendant could not meet on account of his or her characteristics. Having said it was necessary to have an objective test, the Privy Council did endorse the view in *Camplin* that it was possible to take into account the age and sex of the defendant. Lord Nicholls for the majority said that this was 'not an exception to this uniform approach'.[134] Rather it was an application of it because '[t]he powers of self-control possessed by *ordinary* people vary according to their age and, more doubtfully, their sex'. The conclusion was that alcoholism was not to be taken into account at the stage of determining whether the loss of self-control was objectively justifiable.

131 [2001] 1 AC 146.

132 [2005] UKPC 23, [2005] 2 AC 580.

133 [2006] EWCA Crim 14, [2006] 2 WLR 887.

134 [2005] UKPC 23, [2005] 2 AC 580 at para 13.

14.133 The situation in *Ahluwalia* and *Thornton* was expressly taken into account. In the majority decision, Lord Nicholls commented that if there was evidence of battered woman syndrome, or indeed of post-natal depression or a personality disorder:

> ... the evidence of the woman's condition may be relevant on two issues: whether she lost her self-control, and the gravity of the provocation for her. The jury will then decide whether in their opinion, having regard to the actual provocation and their view of its gravity for the defendant, a woman of her age having ordinary power of self-control might have done what the defendant did.[135]

14.134 In summary, battered woman syndrome might reduce a defendant's capacity to maintain her self-control: but the reasonable woman in her situation is expected to retain an objectively-expected capacity for self-control. However, the fact that the defendant was a long-term victim of abuse such that ongoing abuse or provocative language increased the gravity of the provocation to her is something that is to be taken into account in assessing the seriousness of the situation in relation to which reasonable self-control is required.

14.135 This line of reasoning would be equally applicable to any other form of psychological or mental disorder. Accordingly, mental disorder can be relevant to the question of whether there was a loss of self-control and also to the assessment of the gravity of the provocation – but the defendant is then judged according to the standards of a non-mentally disordered person of the same age and gender.

14.136 This in turn will mean that it is particularly important in a criminal trial involving a defendant with a mental disorder or vulnerability that full consideration is given to the question of the alternative defence of diminished responsibility. The availability of this alternative was part of the reasoning of the Privy Council as to why it was appropriate to restrain the ambit of provocation. This is even though, as has been noted above, the burden of proof is different, as the defendant has to prove the existence of diminished responsibility.

14.137 Of course, often the two lines of defence may be run at the same time (and the defence may also suggest a further alternative, namely that the mens rea was not formed, which may then lead to a manslaughter conviction on the basis of an unlawful and dangerous act if the defendant had the mens rea for the relevant unlawful act). As is discussed above, another question that might arise in this context is whether the jury should be asked to outline the basis for their verdict if they return a conviction of manslaughter: see para 14.91 above.

135 [2005] UKPC 23, [2005] 2 AC 580 at para 25.

Loss of control – the Coroners and Justice Act 2009

14.138 Section 56 of the Coroners and Justice Act 2009 abolishes the common law defence of provocation and introduces the loss of self-control defence (which reduces the offence to manslaughter: section 54(7)). Under section 54(1), this involves a) a loss of control from b) a qualifying trigger which c) is judged against an objective test. The prosecution have to disprove the loss of self-control if there is sufficient evidence that could allow a jury properly directed reasonably to conclude that the defence might apply (sections 54(5) and (6)).

14.139 The relevant 'qualifying triggers' for the defendant's loss of self-control are those set out in section 55 of the Act, and can be either a fear of violence from the victim, a justifiable sense of being seriously wronged by anything said or done, or a combination. These triggers have various elements and restrictions. In relation to the defendant's fear of serious violence from the victim:

i) this can be against the defendant or another identified person; as such, it excludes a situation involving a fear that the victim will use violence against people generally;
ii) this is a subjective test, there being no reference to any need for reasonable grounds for the belief;
iii) section 55(6)(a) excludes anything incited by the defendant as an excuse for violence.

14.140 If the trigger is the justifiable sense of being seriously wronged:

i) this is expressed as being from things done or said; but
ii) they have to reveal 'extremely grave' circumstances;
iii) anything that the defendant incited as an excuse for violence is excluded;
iv) further, section 55(6) provides that it cannot be sexual infidelity (and so this cannot be a qualifying trigger);[136]
v) the Explanatory Notes to the statute[137] suggest that the question of whether the sense of being seriously wronged is 'justifiable' is an objective one, namely that it is not whether the defendant has that belief but whether an objective person would think so;[138]
vi) this leaves open the question of whether the extreme gravity is judged from a subjective or objective perspective;

136 See *R v Clinton* [2012] EWCA Crim 2 for a restrictive reading of what is excluded as 'sexual infidelity'.

137 Available at www.legislation.gov.uk/ukpga/2009/25/resources.

138 Coroners and Justice Act 2009 Explanatory Notes para 346.

vii) finally, in contrast to the threat of serious violence trigger, the thing done or said does not have to be by the victim of the homicide, since language to that effect is missing; this creates the unusual situation that a loss of control in one context has to be directed only to the person who caused the loss of control to be within the defence but can be directed to anyone else if it is the other context; this is particularly problematic if the loss of control was caused by a combination of triggers.

14.141 As to the objective test, this is phrased in section 54(3) as requiring that 'a person of D's sex and age, with a normal degree of tolerance and self-restraint and in the circumstances of D, might have reacted in the same or in a similar way to D' (D being defined in the section as meaning the defendant). Section 54(3) indicates that 'the circumstances of D' means those circumstances that 'bear on D's general capacity for tolerance or self-restraint'. The Explanatory Notes indicate that the effect of this is that:

> ... a defendant's history of abuse at the hands of the victim could be taken into account in deciding whether an ordinary person might have acted as the defendant did, whereas the defendant's generally short temper could not. Consequently, when applying the test in subsection (1)(c) the jury will consider whether a person of the defendant's sex and age with an ordinary level of tolerance and self-restraint and in the defendant's specific circumstances ... might have acted as the defendant did.[139]

14.142 This suggests that the aim is to reinstate the position in *Ahluwalia* and *Thornton* and so reverse *Holley*. Consistently with this, it is made clear that the loss of control does not have to be sudden: see section 54(2); accordingly, the 'slow burn' loss of control is clearly not a problem, though it will remain the case that the prosecution will be able to suggest as a matter of evidence that any delay indicates that there was either not a loss of control or that there was no causation. Despite these extensions of the objective test, the qualifying triggers are clearly much narrower than those applicable under the previous regime.

139 Coroners and Justice Act 2009 Explanatory Notes para 338.

CHAPTER 15

Other substantive issues

Mens rea and mistake of fact

15.1 Aside from the questions of insanity and the partial defences to murder already described, there are various other instances where issues of mental disorder may have an impact on questions of substantive law. There will also be evidential questions, in particular in relation to whether a mens rea was formed. A person with a mental disorder must be shown to form the mens rea just as anyone else, and this will involve taking into account his or her particular circumstances. The existence of a mental disorder may be relevant to this. If, for example, the mens rea is recklessness, and so the question is whether there was an appreciation of a risk and a determination to run it when it was unreasonable to do so, the appreciation of the risk is a subjective matter: see *R v G*.[1] If a defendant was less likely to appreciate the risk because of a mental impairment or disorder of some sort, then that is an evidential matter that the prosecution has to overcome. Lord Bingham explained his conclusion by noting that:

> ... it is not clearly blameworthy to do something involving a risk of injury to another if (for reasons other than self-induced intoxication ...) one genuinely does not perceive the risk. Such a person may fairly be accused of stupidity or lack of imagination, but neither of those failings should expose him to conviction of serious crime or the risk of punishment.[2]

15.2 The same approach will apply in relation to any state of mind that is subjective. Similarly, there is the question of whether a defendant should be judged on the basis of his or her mistaken view of the facts. It is clear that there are some situations in which an honestly held but mistaken view of the facts will lead to an acquittal on the basis that the defendant should be judged according to his or her view of the facts. This will be the case even if that view is not held on reasonable grounds: the reasonableness of the belief is an evidential matter that goes to the question of whether the view of the facts is honestly held.

15.3 A centrally important case in relation to mistake of fact is *R v Morgan*.[3] In short, the House of Lords held that rape, as its elements were defined at the time, involved an actus reus of intercourse without consent and a mens rea of an intention to have non-consensual intercourse (or at least intercourse without caring whether there was

1 [2003] UKHL 50, [2004] 1 AC 1034.
2 [2003] UKHL 50, [2004] 1 AC 1034 para 32.
3 [1976] AC 182.

consent). This in turn meant that an honestly held but mistaken belief that a women was consenting to sexual intercourse provided a defence to the charge (though it is worth noting that on the facts, which involved a violent gang rape, the House determined that there was no prospect that the jury would have accepted an honest belief in consent).

15.4 The issue returned to the House of Lords in the case of *B v Director of Public Prosecutions*:[4] this was in relation to the offence of inciting gross indecency, contrary to section 1(1) of the Indecency with Children Act 1960. This states that:

> Any person who commits an act of gross indecency with or towards a child under the age of 14, or who incites a child under that age to such an act with him or another, shall be liable on conviction on indictment to imprisonment for a term not exceeding two years, or on summary conviction to imprisonment for a term not exceeding six months, to a fine not exceeding [the prescribed sum], or to both.

15.5 The House of Lords determined that a mens rea was to be implied: this was in accordance with the presumption that applies to a statutory offence that does not specify a mens rea unless the presumption in favour of a mens rea was displaced. This in turn meant that a genuine belief that a child was over 14 meant that the defendant was to be acquitted. Lord Nicholls noted that while the common law had previously supported as a general proposition that an honest mistake had to be on reasonable grounds,[5] the modern trend was to focus on the honesty of the belief, leaving reasonableness as a question of evidence. He commented that:

> Considered as a matter of principle, the honest belief approach must be preferable. By definition the mental element in a crime is concerned with a subjective state of mind, such as intent or belief. To the extent that an overriding objective limit ('on reasonable grounds') is introduced, the subjective element is displaced. To that extent a person who lacks the necessary intent or belief may nevertheless commit the offence. When that occurs the defendant's 'fault' lies exclusively in falling short of an objective standard. His crime lies in his negligence. A statute may so provide expressly or by necessary implication. But this can have no place in a common law principle, of general application, which is concerned with the need for a mental element as an essential ingredient of a criminal offence.[6]

4 [2000] 2 AC 428.

5 Citing *R v Tolson* (1889) 23 QBD 168.

6 [2000] 2 AC 428 at 462.

15.6 Lord Steyn phrased the point in the following way:

> There has been a general shift from objectivism to subjectivism in this branch of the law. It is now settled as a matter of general principle that mistake, whether reasonable or not, is a defence where it prevents the defendant from having the mens rea which the law requires for the crime with which he is charged.[7]

15.7 This will, of course, mean that an honest belief in an innocent state of affairs that has its origin in or is assisted by mental disorder may lead to an acquittal. In this regard, as has been noted in the discussion on insanity, if the defendant's views are altered by partial delusions, he or she is to be judged according to normal principles, which will include the mistake as to fact principles.

15.8 Aside from these matters, which go to the question of whether the prosecution are able to prove the necessary mens rea of offences other than those of strict liability, there are also positive defences that might allow account to be taken of mental disorder: these are self-defence and duress.

Self-defence

15.9 Section 3(1) of the Criminal Law Act 1967 makes it lawful to use 'such force as is reasonable in the circumstances' to prevent crime or carry out a lawful arrest. If evidence of self-defence is raised, the prosecution has to prove that it is absent.[8] Although the reasonableness of the force used is an objective matter,[9] the starting point is subjective factors in the mind of the defendant: this is because the circumstances on the basis of which reasonableness is to be judged are subjectively defined. In summarising the law, Lord Morris in *Palmer v R*[10] stated that:

> If there has been an attack so that defence is reasonably necessary, it will be recognised that a person defending himself cannot weigh to a nicety the exact measure of his defensive action. If the jury thought that in a moment of unexpected anguish a person attacked had only done what he honestly and instinctively thought necessary, that would be the most potent evidence that only reasonable defensive action had been taken.[11]

7 [2000] 2 AC 428 at 477–478.

8 See, for example, *R v Lobell* [1957] 1 QB 547.

9 See also Criminal Justice and Immigration Act (CJIA) 2008 s76.

10 [1971] AC 814 at 832. See now CJIA 2008 s76(7).

11 [1971] 1 All ER 1077.

15.10 This can be seen as an application of the 'honest but mistaken' belief idea described above. Case-law confirms this. In *R v Gladstone Williams*,[12] a man assaulted a youth in the belief that he was entitled to detain him as he had just committed a mugging: the Court of Appeal held that he was entitled to be acquitted on the basis of his honestly held view. This was endorsed by the Privy Council in *Beckford v R*,[13] which involved a murder conviction returned against a police officer who had shot a man in the belief that it was necessary for self-defence. The test for self-defence is, therefore, that a person may use such force as is reasonable in the circumstances as he or she honestly believes them to be.

15.11 One more recent authority should be mentioned in case it is thought to have cast some doubt on the interplay between the honesty of the belief and mental disorder. In *R v Martin*,[14] a defendant shot and killed a burglar: on appeal from his conviction for murder, there was fresh medical evidence available that suggested that Mr Martin would have a perception of greater danger than was accurate. Lord Woolf CJ for the Court of Appeal stated:

> 67. We would accept that the jury are entitled to take into account in relation to self-defence the physical characteristics of the defendant. However, we would not agree that it is appropriate, except in exceptional circumstances which would make the evidence especially probative, in deciding whether excessive force has been used to take into account whether the defendant is suffering from some psychiatric condition.

15.12 The context of this comment was a discussion as to whether the fresh medical evidence would have been admissible in relation to the question of self-defence. At the outset of the judgment, the court had cited *Beckford* and summarised the law as involving the defendant being judged on the basis of any honest but mistaken belief as to the facts. Since the Court of Appeal gives no indication that it does not accept the law as set out in *Beckford*, the comment made should be understood as limited to the question of the admissibility of the evidence. This seems clear from the context: the court had noted the general limitation that expert evidence was not admissible on matters on which the jury did not require assistance,[15] that Mr Martin had been

12 (1984) 78 CrAppR 276.
13 [1988] AC 130.
14 [2001] EWCA Crim 2245, [2003] QB 1, [2002] 1 CrAppR 27.
15 [2001] EWCA Crim 2245, [2003] QB 1, [2002] 1 CrAppR 27 para 63.

able to give an account of the situation that he believed he was in[16] and that it was improper for an expert to give an opinion on whether this was an honestly-held view, that being the question for the jury.[17] There had been significant evidence before the jury that Mr Martin was both eccentric and terrified. The final conclusion on the point was that:

> 71. ... if the medical issues had been deployed at the trial, far from assisting the jury it would have tended to confuse them and would have distracted them from their task.

15.13 In summary, therefore, a mental disorder may well be relevant to the assessment of the situation which the defendant perceives: it may support an honest belief even if that seems to be unlikely from an objective standpoint. It is against that honestly perceived situation that the reasonableness of the force used is to be judged. But the normal rules as to the admissibility of expert evidence will apply: since any unusual perception of a defendant as a result of mental disorder may well be a matter which is outside the expertise of the jury, it is a matter on which expert evidence is admissible, though *Martin* suggests that this will have to be assessed against whether the perception of the defendant is properly before the jury without any need for expert assistance.

Duress

15.14 Duress is a defence that provides an excuse from criminal liability as opposed to a justification, such as arises when self-defence is raised: both lead to an acquittal in criminal proceedings, but a justified action is lawful whereas excused action is not, which will have more of an impact if civil action is taken arising out of the harm caused. Duress has two forms: duress by threats and duress of circumstances. Duress involves involves a constrained choice between a rock and a hard place, and so differs from automatism, which involves an absence of choice. When the defence are able to produce valid evidence of duress, the prosecution is required to prove beyond a reasonable doubt that the defendant was not acting under duress: see *Director of Public Prosecutions for Northern Ireland v Lynch*.[18] However, it has

16 [2001] EWCA Crim 2245, [2003] QB 1, [2002] 1 CrAppR 27 para 68.
17 [2001] EWCA Crim 2245, [2003] QB 1, [2002] 1 CrAppR 27 paras 69 and 70.
18 [1975] AC 653.

limits in the sense that it cannot be raised in relation to murder or attempted murder: see, respectively, *R v Howe*[19] and *R v Gotts*.[20]

Duress by threats

15.15 In *R v Hasan*,[21] the defendant said he became involved in an aggravated burglary after being threatened by an associate with a reputation for violence. Lord Bingham summarised the identified requirements of the defence:[22]

a) it is not applicable to murder or attempted murder (or, possibly, some forms of treason);
b) a threat of death or serious injury is required;
c) the harm would befall the defendant, a family member or someone close or for whom the defendant was responsible;
d) the defence is largely objective, in contrast to the largely subjective perceptions relevant to other defences;
e) a causative link between the threat and the offence is required;
f) no evasive course is available that the defendant could reasonably be expected to take.

15.16 The main issue in the case was an additional limitation on the defence, namely that it could not be used if the threats came from someone within a criminal grouping and were to be expected. The question posed was whether the test should be that the defendant subjectively foresaw those threats or objectively ought to have foreseen them. The House of Lords applied an objective test as a matter of policy, namely the importance of discouraging criminal association,[23] which meant that Mr Hasan could not rely on the defence. This in turn would mean that a mental disorder that undermines the ability of the defendant to perceive the likelihood of threats is not relevant; were it relevant, the argument would no doubt be that this would encourage gangs to recruit from those with a mental impairment or some disorder that made them more trusting.

15.17 There are three other parts of the test where there could be arguments about the extent to which subjective matters might be relevant. One is the nature of the threat of death or serious injury: does there have to be an honest belief or honest and reasonable belief that the

19 [1987] AC 417.
20 [1992] 2 AC 412.
21 [2005] 2 AC 467, [2005] UKHL 22.
22 [2005] 2 AC 467, [2005] UKHL 22 para 21.
23 [2005] 2 AC 467, [2005] UKHL 22 paras 38 and 39.

threat exists and will be carried out? A second is the robustness of the defendant in being able to resist the threats: is the test a reasonable person standard, or a hybrid person with reasonable steadfastness judged in the light of the nature of the defendant? A third is linked to the requirement that there be no reasonably available evasive course of action: is that to be objectively assessed or is it a question that involves looking at the perceptions of the defendant as to what else might be feasible and asking whether one of those steps was reasonably to be expected instead of committing the crime charged?

15.18 In relation to the first part, Lord Bingham in *Hasan* held that there was a need for both a subjective belief and that it be on reasonable grounds. He stated:[24]

> It is of course essential that the defendant should genuinely, ie actually, believe in the efficacy of the threat by which he claims to have been compelled. But there is no warrant for relaxing the requirement that the belief must be reasonable as well as genuine.

15.19 As to the second part, that is the standard of resistance to be expected, Lord Bingham endorsed the trial judge's direction that the test involved looking at what 'a reasonable person of a defendant's age and background' would have done, but did not address it further. This issue had been discussed in other cases prior to *Hasan* and the reference to the defendant's 'background' is the key element that might allow mental disorder to be relevant. In *R v Graham*,[25] Lord Lane CJ had referred to a 'sober person of reasonable firmness, sharing the characteristics of the defendant' as being the standard.[26] It is to be noted that the Chief Justice made this comment in the context of suggesting that consistency in criminal defences was required and that provocation, self-defence and mistake of fact relied on objective standards. As has been discussed above, this is no longer an accurate statement in relation to mistake and self-defence, as subjective elements are important. While his point about the need for consistency in criminal defences remains true, which would suggest that there should be a move towards introducting subjective standards, that would be contrary to the holding in *Hasan*, which emphasised the need for objectivity.

15.20 However, other cases have developed the issue of characteristics of a defendant that should be taken into account in assessing whether the response to the threat was justified. These were summarised in

24 [2005] 2 AC 467, [2005] UKHL 22 at para 23.

25 [1982] 1 WLR 294.

26 [1982] 1 WLR 294 at p300 for the full passage.

R v Bowen,[27] which involved a defendant of low intelligence who had repeatedly obtained goods on credit by deception because, on his account, he was required to do so by two men who threatened to fire-bomb his family. Attempting to synthesise the principles to be obtained from the authorities on the relevant characteristics, Stuart-Smith LJ set out the following:[28]

> (1) The mere fact that the accused is more pliable, vulnerable, timid or susceptible to threats than a normal person are not characteristics with which it is legitimate to invest the reasonable/ordinary person for the purpose of considering the objective test.
> (2) The defendant may be in a category of persons who the jury may think less able to resist pressure than people not within that category. Obvious examples are age, where a young person may well not be so robust as a mature one; possibly sex, though many women would doubtless consider they had as much moral courage to resist pressure as men; pregnancy, where there is added fear for the unborn child; serious physical disability, which may inhibit self protection; recognised mental illness or psychiatric condition, such as post traumatic stress disorder leading to learned helplessness.
> (3) Characteristics which may be relevant in considering provocation, because they relate to the nature of the provocation, itself will not necessarily be relevant in cases of duress. Thus homosexuality may be relevant to provocation if the provocative words or conduct are related to this characteristic; it cannot be relevant in duress, since there is no reason to think that homosexuals are less robust in resisting threats of the kind that are relevant in duress cases.
> (4) Characteristics due to self-induced abuse, such as alcohol, drugs or glue-sniffing, cannot be relevant.
> (5) Psychiatric evidence may be admissible to show that the accused is suffering from some mental illness, mental impairment or recognised psychiatric condition provided persons generally suffering from such condition may be more susceptible to pressure and threats and thus to assist the jury in deciding whether a reasonable person suffering from such a condition might have been impelled to act as the defendant did. It is not admissible simply to show that in the doctor's opinion an accused, who is not suffering from such illness or condition, is especially timid, suggestible or vulnerable to pressure and threats. Nor is medical opinion admissible to bolster or support the credibility of the accused.

15.21 The court also commented on the need for defence counsel to make sure that any submission that the defendant had a relevant

27 [1997] 1 WLR 372, [1996] 2 CrAppR 157.
28 [1997] 1 WLR 372 at 379.

characteristic was raised with the judge so that there could be a ruling on the point.

15.22 The parts of this summary that may allow questions of mental disorder to be relevant are: a psychiatric condition may make someone less able to resist pressure, but it will depend on the nature of the disorder; and expert evidence will be admissible in relation to the typical effect of the particular disorder; however, characteristics that are due to self-induced abuse of substances cannot be relevant. As to the first two elements, the limitations noted in *R v Martin*, discussed above, must be borne in mind: namely that the courts seem to have a reluctance to allow expert evidence on the ultimate question in front of the jury. This means that it is important to build a foundation for the evidence by emphasising that the point on which expert evidence is given is beyond the likely understanding of the jury.

15.23 As to the limitation from self-induced abuse, the fourth point from the summary, a question that arises is whether it can be said to apply in relation to a mental disorder that has an independent existence even though it might have been induced by substance abuse. In other words, is the restriction meant to apply just to the addiction and its possible impact on the ability to resist, or would it apply to all the consequences that might flow from the substance abuse, including separate mental disorders? While it is no doubt understandable that the transitory effects of alcohol or drug abuse will not be taken into account, the origin of a more permanent mental disorder may be considered something that is more a factor of the setting in which the incident occurred than a feature directly relevant to the fairness of imposing liability.

15.24 The application of the principles in *Bowen* led to the conclusion that his suggestibility was not relevant; and that his low IQ was not something that made him less able to withstand pressure, though the court noted that his condition was something that was 'short of mental impairment or mental defectiveness'. However, it does not appear that there was evidence in the case beyond the fact that Mr Bowen was suggestible as a general matter. The argument from counsel was limited to one to the effect that his low IQ meant that he could not respond to the situation sensibly by seeking help from the police, which seems to go more to the final potentially relevant feature, which is discussed below.

15.25 The question of what was meant by 'mental impairment or mental defectiveness' came back to the Court of Appeal in the case of *R v Antar*.[29] This involved a defendant with an IQ of 51 and who was

29 [2004] EWCA Crim 2708.

abnormally suggestible, who was charged in relation to a street robbery and alleged that he was acting under duress from one of his two co-accused. The Court of Appeal referred to *Bowen* and also to case-law dealing with the question of knowledge of lack of consent in a sexual context[30] and the exclusion of a confession because a mentally vulnerable individual with a low IQ was not provided an appropriate adult in interview,[31] and suggested that at least in principle expert evidence was admissible to the effect that Mr Antar had a very low IQ, was cognitively impaired, had a moderate learning disability and was significantly suggestible.[32] It held that the judge erred in not allowing the evidence to be heard by the jury on the question of duress. It had been ruled inadmissible because the judge formed the view, based on the voir dire and the evidence in the trial prior to the voir dire, that Mr Antar was not as impaired as the psychologist opined and that his condition did not amount to a mental impairment of the sort suggested by the court in *Bowen*.

15.26 Of course, what remains unclear is precisely how Mr Antar's mental impairment would have affected his ability to resist the compulsion to which he was subjected. The transcript of the judgment does not indicate whether the expert evidence met the requirement of showing that the condition identified meant that the defendant was more susceptible to pressure (and indeed the extracts that are quoted seem to go more to features relevant to the admissibility of the interview). In sum, it remains unclear as to how far mental disorder or other characteristics that may reduce the ability to withstand pressure are relevant, particularly as *Hasan* emphasised the importance of an objective test.

15.27 The final potential area of relevance is the extent to which someone might have been less able to recognise alternative courses of action because of mental disorder. As noted, this was the argument advanced in *Bowen* but rejected on the basis that a low IQ did not indicate a lower ability to withstand pressure. The court did not specifically address the point made by counsel, and so it may be thought that it might still be a relevant argument to raise: it would, however, have to be justified as an exception to the objective nature of the defence.

30 *R v Masih* [1986] Crim LR 395.

31 *R v Silcott* (1991) *Times* 9 December: see chapter 4.

32 [2004] EWCA Crim 2708 at para 41. The expert changed her view on the learning disability aspect in the course of a voir dire to suggest that it was mild not moderate: this did not make a difference, the Court of Appeal held.

Duress of circumstances

15.28 Duress of circumstances is a separate type of duress, arising out of a situation other than one involving threats of violence. Rather, it involves a person being driven to commit a crime because he or she finds that there is no alternative. An example of the successful use of the defence (at least in the sense that it was ruled that it should have been left to the jury) is *R v Martin*.[33] The facts involved a charge of disqualified driving: the judge had ruled that duress of circumstances was not an available defence in relation to an absolute offence, and the appeal was to the effect that this was an error of law. Simon Brown J, giving the judgment of the Court of Appeal, held that the judge had erred in law and that the conviction based on a guilty plea was unsafe. This scenario in which it had been proposed to raise duress of circumstances was that Mr Martin's wife threatened to commit suicide (and acted in a fashion that revealed that she was distraught) unless Mr Martin drove her son to work to avoid him being late and losing his job.

15.29 Building on the case of *R v Conway*,[34] the judge summarised the law as follows:[35]

> First, English law does, in extreme circumstances, recognise a defence of necessity. Most commonly this defence arises as duress, that is pressure upon the accused's will from the wrongful threats or violence of another. Equally, however, it can arise from other objective dangers threatening the accused or others. Arising thus it is conveniently called 'duress of circumstances'. Secondly, the defence is available only if, from an objective standpoint, the accused can be said to be acting reasonably and proportionately in order to avoid a threat of death or serious injury. Thirdly, assuming the defence to be open to the accused on his account of the facts, the issue should be left to the jury, who should be directed to determine these two questions: first, was the accused, or may he have been, impelled to act as he did because as a result of what he reasonably believed to be the situation he had good cause to fear that otherwise death or serious physical injury would result? Second, if so, may a sober person of reasonable firmness, sharing the characteristics of the accused, have responded to that situation by acting as the accused acted? If the answer to both those questions was yes, then the jury would acquit: the defence of necessity would have been established.

33 (1989) 88 CrAppR 343.

34 (1988) 88 CrAppR 159.

35 (1989) 88 CrAppR 343 at 345–346.

15.30 It will be seen that, as with duress by threats, the same arguments can be put as to the potential relevance of mental disorder if it might have an impact on such matters as the level of resistance to be expected and the availability of alternative courses of action. There is no reason to suspect that they would have any greater prospect of success, however.

PART V

Mental disorder and sentencing

CHAPTER 16

General matters

Introduction

16.1 There has been significant development of the statutory framework relating to sentencing. Whereas statutes until recent decades would do no more than set out the sentencing powers open to the court and maximum sentences applicable to each offence, the legislature has now produced both significant guidance as to what magistrates and judges should do in the exercise of their sentencing powers and also established mechanisms for a more systemic provision of guidance than that provided through the Court of Appeal and its occasional guideline sentences. Accordingly, there are now statutory purposes of sentencing,[1] statutory guidance as to setting of tariffs in murder cases,[2] and a Sentencing Council that provides guidance that has to be taken into account.[3]

16.2 In addition, there have been developments in relation to the sentencing options available. Aside from amendments made to long-established sentences and orders, including those arising under the Mental Health Act (MHA) 1983, namely hospital orders and guardianship orders, the criminal courts have been equipped with new sentences and consequent orders based on the idea that action should be taken to pre-empt dangerous recidivists, both in the form of detention on the grounds of a finding of dangerousness (extended sentences, automatic life sentences and then a regime of dangerous offender sentencing provisions in the CJA 2003) and also in the form of orders aimed at the ongoing control over people who have committed offences which are designed to prevent further offending.

16.3 The interplay of this structure with questions of mental disorder involves issues of principle as well as practicalities. At the level of principle are questions of the value of the various elements of theory behind the sentencing framework when applied to those with mental disorder, given the need to secure justice within that framework; there are also the practical questions of the extent to which the sentencing

1 Criminal Justice Act (CJA) 2003 s142, discussed below.

2 Introduced by CJA 2003 s269 after it was decided that the requirements of article 6 of the European Convention on Human Rights (ECHR) (right to a fair trial) meant that a judge rather than the Home Secretary had to fix the tariff period for a mandatory life sentence prisoner (see *R (Anderson) v Home Secretary* [2002] UKHL 46, [2003] 1 AC 837).

3 Coroners and Justice Act 2009 s118, replacing the Sentencing Advisory Panel and the Sentencing Guidelines Council: the latter was introduced by CJA 2003 s167; CJA 2003 s169 continued the existence of the Sentencing Advisory Panel, which was established by Crime and Disorder Act (CDA) 1998 s81. CJA 2003 s172 requires that regard be had to this guidance.

options provided are suitable for those who are mentally disordered in terms of their ability to comply and to secure whatever outcomes for which the sentences are designed.

16.4 One point worth noting is the question of responsibility that is central to criminal law. As is illustrated by the defence of insanity, the substantive criminal law draws a clear line between a limited set of circumstances in which mental disorder provides that a mentally disordered person is not responsible for his or her criminal actions; there is a further limited gradation of responsibility in relation to murder by the partial defences of diminished responsibility and provocation or loss of control. However, these limitations of the substantive criminal law are not the whole picture, as the criminal justice system has flexibility at two additional stages to allow account to be taken of a reduced level of responsibility. The first is at the decision as to whether to commence or continue a prosecution, where questions of mental disorder are relevant: see chapter 5 and the questions of diversion from the criminal justice system. One of the features that may be taken into account at that stage is the likely penalty.

16.5 This reflects the second area of flexibility, namely that at the sentencing stage, the court may decide to dispose of the case in a non-punitive manner. In particular, there are specific powers of disposal under the MHA 1983 that allow the criminal courts to impose orders that are similar in effect to the civil powers that exist to detain people on account of their mental disorder. This reinforces the option of diversion, since the value of criminal proceedings in those circumstances may be open to question (or at least the value in the light of the costs of the criminal process). If neither diversion nor a non-punitive sentence is appropriate, perhaps because of the nature of the offence, the sentencing process may nevertheless allow an outcome that reflects a lower level of culpability, whether by mitigation of the punitive sentence imposed or by the creation of a disposal that focuses more on rehabilitation of the mental disorder.

16.6 It is also to be noted that the growth of sentencing options based on dangerousness and preventing future offending gives rise to the question of whether mental disorder may be a ground for imposing a more severe sentence because the presence of mental disorder may raise the risk posed by the defendant.

16.7 It is also necessary to provide a reminder that assumptions may be unfair: just as assumptions that mental disorder is to be equated with danger are inappropriate – rather the question should be whether the evidence demonstrates of a particular mentally-disordered individual that there is danger arising from that disorder – so it should not be assumed that the presence of mental disorder equates to a reason for a reduction in culpability. In short, it may be that on the facts of a case, the presence of mental disorder has no bearing on the level of culpability for an offence.

16.8 This chapter will examine some of the more general questions as to the sentencing framework and its interplay with questions of mental disorder. Subsequent chapters will examine hospital disposals and custodial and community sentences.

16.9 A final introductory point is that a development of recent years in other common law jurisdictions has been the creation of specialist mental health courts to whom offenders with mental health difficulties are sent. This was recommended for England and Wales by the Bradley Report of April 2009,[4] and was then trialled at magistrates' courts in Brighton and Stratford, East London with apparent success, but not taken further.[5]

The purposes of sentencing

Youth justice

16.10 The legislature has provided guidance in relation to the youth justice system: so section 44 of the Children and Young Persons Act 1933 requires that regard be had to the welfare of children before a court. Section 37 of the Crime and Disorder Act 1998 sets as the youth justice system's principal aim the prevention of offending by children and young people; and any person or body who has functions in that system – including, for example, the Youth Offending Teams established by the Act but also the police and Crown Prosecution Service – must have regard to the aim.

Adult offenders

16.11 The CJA 2003 added a legislative statement of purpose for sentencing in relation to adult offenders (ie those 18 or over at the time of

4 *Lord Bradley's review of people with mental health problems or learning disabilities in the criminal justice system*, April 2009, available at www.dh.gov.uk/en/Publicationsandstatistics/Publications/PublicationsPolicyAndGuidance/DH_098694.

5 See *Mental Health Court pilot: feasibility of an impact evaluation*, Ministry of Justice Research Summary 7/10, and *Process evaluation of the Mental Health Court pilot*, Ministry of Justice Research Series 18/10, both September 2010 and both available at www.justice.gov.uk/publications/research-and-analysis/moj/2010/mhc-process-feasibility-evaluation.

conviction).[6] The CJA 2003 s142(1) requires any court dealing with an offender to have regard to five purposes of sentencing, namely:

(a) the punishment of offenders,
(b) the reduction of crime (including its reduction by deterrence),
(c) the reform and rehabilitation of offenders,
(d) the protection of the public, and
(e) the making of reparation by offenders to persons affected by their offences.[7]

Disapplication of sentencing purposes

16.12 However, CJA 2003 s142(2) disapplies section 142(1) if a sentence is made under the MHA 1983 involving detention in hospital: section 142(2)(d) lists hospital orders (including interim hospital orders) and also the hospital direction sentence under MHA 1983 s45A (which involves an underlying prison sentence). Strangely enough, this means that the statutory purposes *do apply* before the imposition of a guardianship order under the MHA 1983 or any form of community order involving conditions of treatment for mental disorder. These various substantive sentencing options are discussed below. So when the conditions for a hospital order are made out, the judge has to determine whether it is appropriate to impose a hospital disposal or follow the statutory purposes of sentencing to determine the proper sentence other than a hospital disposal.[8]

16.13 This leads to a puzzle. In relation to a hospital placement, it is no doubt sensible to allow a court to impose as a sentence something that gives priority to the treatment needs of the defendant even if that does not satisfy the purposes of sentencing – for example, it may be that a defendant has a mental disorder that has no link whatsoever to the crime committed, such that treatment cannot meet any of the needs of sentencing, but that a court finds a hospital order to be the most suitable disposal. But if a person with a severe mental health condition can properly be treated outside a hospital setting, the purposes of sentencing apply and such a result can only be achieved with regard had to those purposes. This should be possible if the mental

6 CJA 2003 s142(2)(a).

7 CJIA 2008 s9 adds CJA 2003 s142A, purposes of sentencing of those under 18; it also excludes sentences of detention in hospital (including a hospital direction under MHA 1983 s45A, even though such an order cannot be made in relation to a person of that age).

8 See chapter 18 for the guidance on how to exercise the discretion to impose a hospital disposal.

disorder is causally-linked to the offending, such that dealing with the disorder will reduce the prospect of recidivism and so provide protection to the public and secure the rehabilitation of the offender more effectively than a sentence that turns more on punitive aims. It may be more difficult if the offending is not linked to the disorder: however, it may be possible for a sentencer to conclude that, having had regard to the purposes of sentencing, it is nevertheless appropriate to give priority to treatment needs. But it is strange that it has to be justified as a matter of principle when detention in a hospital does not.

16.14 A second puzzle arises from the inclusion of a hospital direction under MHA 1983 s45A as a situation in which the sentencing principles are disapplied. As is noted in more detail in chapter 18, this sentence involves an underlying prison sentence which is served in hospital for so long as the criteria for hospitalisation are made out, but otherwise involves a sentence of imprisonment. Does this mean that the sentence of imprisonment is imposed for reasons other than the purposes of sentencing, including punishment and protection? Given that these are the obvious reasons for the underlying sentence of imprisonment in a section 45A order, the question prompted is why the purposes of sentencing were disapplied?

16.15 The statutory purposes of sentencing are also disapplied if the offender falls within various mandated sentencing options, including the mandatory life sentence for murder.[9] As originally drafted, the dangerous offender sentencing provisions of sections 225 and following of the CJA 2003 were also exempted, suggesting that they were to take priority over any sentence that would be felt appropriate by application of the purposes of sentencing: this was perhaps unusual, because those purposes allow for public protection and also for the reduction of crime (which can be secured by incapacitation). However, as part of the reforms of these sentences introduced by the Criminal Justice and Immigration Act (CJIA) 2008, this has been modified, and so the purposes of sentencing are only disapplied if the offender is felt to require imprisonment or detention for life under section 225(2) or 226(2): see CJIA 2008 Sch 22 para 64, under minor and consequential amendments. This in turn means that if the offender qualifies for a dangerous offender disposal of a lesser magnitude, namely imprisonment or detention for public protection

9 And also, by reason of CJA 2003 s142(2)(c), the mandatory minimum custodial sentences for firearms, burglary and drugs offences: see Firearms Act 1968 s51A(2) and Powers of Criminal Courts (Sentencing) Act (PCC(S)A) 2000 ss110 and 111.

or an extended sentence, the sentence has to be justified by following the purposes of sentencing. The interplay between these sentences and the use of a hospital order is discussed in chapter 18.

Interplay between sentencing purposes and mental disorder

16.16 While the purposes of sentencing are disapplied if a hospital order is imposed, the language of CJA 2003 s142(2) is not the whole story. It will be seen in chapter 18 that the question of whether to impose a hospital order is a matter of discretion, requiring a finding that medical criteria for the order are met and that it is the most suitable disposal. Case-law has suggested that a defendant who retains responsibility despite having a mental disorder may qualify for a punitive sentence on the basis that the hospital order is not the most suitable disposal in that situation. It is suggested that this discretion cannot be exercised in such as way as to always apply a punitive sentence when partial responsibility is retained, since that would have the effect of nullifying the existence of section 142(2). This proposition is developed further in chapter 18.

16.17 However, there is clearly an element of discretion as between a hospital order or a sentence that is designed to reflect the purpose of sentencing. Accordingly, the question of the applicability of the sentencing purposes to an offender who is mentally disordered might arise. There are two different scenarios to consider: one is the relevance of mental disorder at the time of the offence (which goes to the question of the responsibility for the offending); the other is the relevance of mental disorder at the time of the sentencing (which may go to the question of the practicability of securing the purposes of sentencing in light of the mental disorder of the defendant).

16.18 While the presence of a mental disorder may reduce responsibility for a crime, it may not: it will depend entirely on the circumstances. In some situations, the question of punishment will be inapposite because of the presence of mental disorder. For example, in *Phillip and John v R*[10] the Privy Council considered the effect of the two-prong test for insanity in section 21 of the St Lucia Criminal Code, which has a codification of the M'Naghten rules[11] as the first prong but has a further test that the act was done 'under the influence of a delusion of such a nature as to render him ... an unfit subject for

10 [2007] UKPC 31, [2009] MHLR 352.

11 See chapter 12 above.

punishment of any kind in respect of such act'. The Privy Council confirmed that this further prong was an alternative and wider test than that set out in the common law rules, designed to deal with a situation in which a delusion as to the presence of an outside influence caused a defendant to commit acts he knew to be forbidden. The aim of the test was to deal with a situation in which the threat of punishment would have no deterrent effect, and the object of retribution would be repugnant to the conscience of the ordinary citizen, such that criminal sanctions would be inappropriate and pointless.[12]

16.19 If mental disorder takes away responsibility because it was operating at the time of the crime, the state of the defendant at the time of sentence is irrelevant, since if there is no responsibility at the time of the crime, there is nothing that merits punishment. But in English law there is a clear line between having no responsibility and having some responsibility, even if reduced. So, in *R v Drew*,[13] the House of Lords confronted the question of the propriety of imposing a life sentence on someone who was convicted of a second serious offence but who also met the criteria for the imposition of a hospital order. As to whether punishment was proper in relation to a mentally disordered offender, Lord Bingham noted that the life sentence was partly punitive in purpose and effect and that the minimum term specified under a life sentence was designed to meet the needs of retribution. He then commented:

> It may also be accepted as wrong in principle to punish those who are unfit to be tried or who, although fit to be tried, are not responsible for their conduct because of insanity ... But the appellant did not claim to be unfit to plead and advanced no defence of insanity. Instead, he pleaded guilty to an offence of which an essential ingredient was an intention to cause grievous bodily harm to another. The Recorder of Cardiff did not regard the appellant as other than criminally culpable. Had he done so he would not have specified a minimum term based on a notional sentence of 8 years. The appellant's mental illness could properly be relied on as mitigating the criminality of his conduct but not as absolving him from all responsibility for it. Mr Davies laid stress on the stigma attaching to a sentence of life imprisonment, which he criticised as unfair in the case of a mentally-disordered defendant such as the appellant. It is of course true that conviction of serious violent crime carries a stigma. But the appellant will have

12 [2007] UKPC 31, [2009] MHLR 352: see Lord Carswell at paragraph 24 of the judgment of the Board.

13 [2003] UKHL 25, [2003] 1 WLR 1213, [2003] MHLR 282. Discussed further below in chapter 18.

been stigmatised less by the sentence passed upon him than by his voluntary admission of guilt.[14]

16.20 In short, unless mental disorder is such as to remove responsibility, punishment may be appropriate. While there is no general scheme for ascribing something less than a conviction on the grounds of diminished responsibility, which applies only in relation to murder, it is possible to mitigate the level of criminality at the stage of sentencing. In addition to the question of whether mental disorder should reduce the seriousness of the offence, which is discussed below, it will also be relevant to ask whether a particular sentence will impact more upon an offender with a mental disorder such as to make it impractical, more harsh, or otherwise undesirable. This question may also apply even if there is no question of a reduced level of responsibility in relation to the crime: a person who was responsible at the time of the offence may not have the capacity to benefit from or otherwise respond to the purposes of the given sentence.

16.21 An analogy may be drawn with fitness to stand trial: someone who committed the actus reus but was unfit to participate in the trial process can be dealt with by way of a limited range of disposals only, none of which have any punitive purpose (and this will be so even though the person might have been fully responsible at the time of the criminal act). Similarly, it is possible that a person who was fit to stand trial and was found guilty or entered a plea of guilty might become unfit between conviction and sentence. Although the statutory process for determining fitness to stand trial does not have a provision that deals with the question of what is to happen in that scenario, namely unfitness to stand trial at the sentencing stage, the general common law requirement that a person be able to participate in the trial will include the sentencing process.[15]

16.22 In such a situation, a court may have the option of adjourning further, including making use of section 36 of the MHA 1983 or suitable bail conditions as to treatment designed to secure fitness for further participation. Article 6 of the ECHR (right to a fair trial) guarantees both the right to participate and the right to a determination within a reasonable time. At some stage, the latter will outweigh the former, and it is suggested that when that stage arrives, the court will have only the option to make an order that is justified under ECHR

14 [2003] UKHL 25, [2003] 1 WLR 1213, [2003] MHLR 282 para 16.

15 For example, the tariff-setting process was held to be covered by ECHR article 6: *Anderson v Secretary of State for the Home Department* [2002] UKHL 46, [2003] 1 AC 837.

article 5.1(e) if it involves detention. A sentence that has to be justified by reason of article 5.1(a) must be imposed following a process that complies with article 6, which is not possible if the defendant cannot participate, but there is no such requirement if article 5.1(e) applies. If the order does not involve detention, the appropriate provision of the Convention is article 8: again, if the order ceases to have a punitive purpose, it is suggested that it will be possible to step outside the provisions of article 6, and a community-based disposal will be a proportionate response within the meaning of article 8.2.

16.23 It is also possible that a defendant being sentenced who has mental health difficulties will meet the tests for fitness to stand trial and participate, but only just. In such a case, it will be appropriate to analyse the extent to which the purposes behind a particular sentence are likely to be secured in the light of the mental disorder. Hence the requirement set out in CJA 2003 s157 (and discussed in chapter 17) that the effect of a custodial sentence on a person's mental disorder be considered. This reflects the fact that there are often features of an individual, whether a form of disability or something else, that make the impact of a sentence proportionately more harsh, such that a lower quantum of sentence has a similar effect. This requires an investigation of the ability of a prison setting to deal with the needs of the defendant and the ability of the defendant to deal with a custodial setting. As such, the approach set out under CJA 2003 s142 has to be supplemented by this additional, welfare-based consideration in the case of a mentally-disordered offender.

16.24 This power to move outside the purposes of sentencing and the additional need to have regard to the consequences of custody on a mental disorder may also introduce the question of the prohibition on a public body from causing a consequence that would amount to a breach of articles 3 and 8 of the ECHR. The application of these principles is considered further in chapters 17 and 19.

Hierarchy of sentences and seriousness of offending

Hierarchy of sentences

16.25 The general scheme for sentencing has a hierarchy, involving absolute and conditional discharges at the bottom of the scale, followed by fines, community sentences and then custodial sentences. The existence of this hierarchy is made most clear in relation to community and custodial sentences: the former cannot be imposed unless the offending to be dealt with is serious enough to warrant such a sentence[16] or if a defendant aged over 16 has carried on committing offences despite three or more previous fines since the age of 16 and it would be in the interests of justice to make a community order instead of a further fine.[17] A custodial sentence is not within the discretion of the sentencing court unless neither a fine nor a community sentence is adequate to deal with the seriousness of the offending.[18]

Assessing the seriousness of an offence

16.26 The central question as to the placement of the offender on the hierarchy is the seriousness of the offence or of the 'combination of the offence and one or more offences associated with it'.[19] An 'associated offence' is defined in section 161 of the PCC(S)A 2000 as an offence of which the defendant is convicted or sentenced on the same occasion or which he or she admits and asks to be taken into consideration for the purpose of sentencing. There are two components of seriousness in relation any case: one will be the assessment of the facts, and the other will be the guidance given in various sources as to what is meant by the concept of seriousness.

Facts

16.27 If there was a trial, the judge will decide the relevant facts on the basis of the evidence called. If there has been a guilty plea, the defendant should indicate if the prosecution's basis for the charge is not accepted. If the prosecution does not accept the defence basis for the plea, the process of a *Newton* hearing has to be followed to determine the proper basis for sentencing if the difference between the parties is material.[20] Naturally, a contested basis of plea is part of a trial and so the defendant must meet the fitness to plead or participate tests. A defendant who is fit will be expected to give evidence as to why his or her account is to be accepted, failing which an adverse inference may be drawn; however, any difficulty in giving evidence on account of mental disorder may be relevant (by analogy with the provisions

16 CJA 2003 s148(1).
17 CJA 2003 s151.
18 CJA 2003 s152(2).
19 CJA 2003 ss148(1) and 152(2).
20 See *R v Newton* (1982) 77 CrAppR 13.

as to the drawing of adverse inferences during a trial, described in chapter 11).

16.28 The process of setting out a basis for plea has become formalised in recent years, leading now to the Plea and Sentence Document – see part IV.45 of the Consolidated Practice Direction.[21] In the magistrates' court, rule 37.10(5) of the Criminal Procedure Rules 2011[22] requires the defence to give a written basis for plea and the court can then determine how to proceed.

Factors relevant to seriousness

16.29 Statutory guidance on how seriousness is assessed is set out in CJA 2003 ss143–146. The elements of this, and the relevance of issues of mental disorder, are:

a) '[C]ulpability in committing the offence and any harm which the offence caused, was intended to cause or might foreseeably have caused': section 143(1). Mental disorder might have an impact on the question of what harm was intended or foreseen or could have been foreseen by the defendant.
b) Previous convictions[23] aggravate the current offence if that is reasonable in light of the nature of each of the previous offences and the time that has elapsed: section 143(2). Again, if any of the previous offending was affected by mental disorder, that might be a ground for displacing this presumption of aggravation; this might be particularly so if the previous offence was dealt with by way of a disposal that reflected the treatment needs of the defendant rather than representing a punitive response.
c) The commission of an offence on bail has to be treated as an aggravating factor: section 143(3). However, it may be that the effect of mental disorder in any further offending, particularly if it has gone unrecognised and/or untreated, will mean that this obligatory aggravation is not given any real weight.
d) A guilty plea must be taken into account, as well as the stage of the proceedings at which it was indicated and the circumstances of the indication: section 144. Guidance on this was given by the Sentencing Guidelines Council[24] in the guideline 'Reduction in

21 www.justice.gov.uk/courts/procedure-rules/criminal/pd_consolidated.

22 SI 2011 No 1709.

23 Previous convictions in the UK count in this situation, by reason of CJA 2003 s143(4); section 143(5) provides that convictions outside the UK may be treated as an aggravating factor.

24 See note 3 above and para 16.31 below.

sentence for a guilty plea', as revised in 2007. Mental disorder may be relevant. For example, an indication of a guilty plea at the earliest reasonable opportunity is needed in order to obtain the maximum discount. But complications arising from a defendant's mental disorder – such as whether he or she is fit to participate – might mean that it took longer for an assessment to be made of whether a guilty plea was proper, with the result that a guilty plea entered relatively late in the process might still be regarded as being entered at the first reasonable opportunity.[25]

e) There are statutory aggravating factors. So a motivation for offending that rests on various prejudiced attitudes (racial, religious, based on disability or sexual orientation) must be treated as aggravating the offence: see sections 145 and 146. Again, it is possible that a mental disorder is the cause of any such prejudice – for example, a delusional system may include features that lead a defendant to exhibit aggravating prejudices; if so, it is open to argument that it should not be treated as a significant aggravation, given the diminished control exercised by the defendant. It can be suggested that the aggravation felt by the victim should reasonably be reduced by the knowledge that mental disorder was involved; and it is certainly the case that the moral culpability of the defendant, which is what sentencing is supposed to reflect, is reduced if mental disorder was the reason for such aggravating behaviour.

16.30 Also relevant to assessing the seriousness of the offence will be guidance given by the Court of Appeal in various cases, which may relate either to elements of the sentencing framework or to the approach to be taken to a particular type of offence. In relation to the test of seriousness, the Court of Appeal in *R v Howells*[26] set out various features to be taken into account. Mental disorder may be relevant to some of these. For example, if the case is at the borderline of custody, the nature and extent of the intention of the defendant may be relevant, since deliberate and premeditated crime is more serious: and the

25 The obligation of an advocate to assess complications arising from mental disorder should not be held against the defendant; however, it would be proper to indicate at an early stage that this is the issue in the case in order to allow it to be managed properly. See chapter 6: questions such as fitness to stand trial are raised on the plea and case management hearing form for the Crown Court, and alerting the court to an issue that might require case management is an obligation that arises out of the duty to seek to assist the court to meet the overriding objective under the Criminal Procedure Rules.

26 [1999] 1 WLR 307, [1999] 1 CrAppR 98.

focus on the conduct or motive of the defendant may mean that an intention formed in the context of a mental disorder is less serious. It was also expressed that 'mental or physical disability' could be taken into account.

16.31 Guidelines are also issued by the Sentencing Guidelines Council, which have to be taken into account under CJA 2003 s172, or its replacement, the Sentencing Council, which have to be followed unless it would be contrary to the interests of justice by reason of section 125 of the Coroners and Justice Act 2009.[27] There are also established principles of sentencing such as the totality of the sentence (when there is more than one offence and some consecutive sentences are in question),[28] and parity between co-defendants.

Mitigation

16.32 Once the assessment of the seriousness of the offence has been made, the next question will be the mitigation that is relevant to the particular defendant. The statutory basis for this is section 166 of the CJA 2003, which provides a general power to mitigate a sentence by taking into account relevant features (section 166(1)).

16.33 In the December 2004 Guideline on 'Overarching principles: seriousness', the Sentencing Guidelines Council noted that the question of culpability will be reduced by various factors, including 'mental illness or disability'.[29] This is a narrower phrase than 'mental disorder' as used in the MHA 1983, which covers any disorder or disability of mind. It is possible that the language used in the Guideline is an oversight and the Council meant to cover all forms of mental disorder. It is also possible that there was a conscious decision to seek to exclude personality disorders, which do not amount to a mental illness or a learning disability (which is perhaps prima facie what is conveyed by the language used).

16.34 There are two reasons to suggest that the different language was a matter of oversight rather than choice. First, the recently updated guidance relating to assault, now in the form of a Definitive Guideline from the Sentencing Council, lists 'mental disorder or learning disability' as a factor indicating lower culpability and also as providing

27 The Sentencing Advisory Panel and the Sentencing Guidelines Council were established (or continued) under CJA 2003 ss167 and 169. They were replaced by the Sentencing Council by Coroners and Justice Act 2009 s118. All guidelines are available at www.sentencingcouncil.org.uk/index.htm.

28 See CJA 2003 s166(3).

29 Guidance para 1.24.

mitigation: this follows the updated language of the MHA 1983, which has the general definition of mental disorder and then additional provisions if the mental disorder is in the form of a learning disability.[30]

16.35 Second, the language used in the older guidance was not apt to exclude personality disorder for two reasons. If the aim was to cover only a learning but not a personality disorder, the phrase used in the unamended MHA 1983 was 'mental impairment' (which became learning disability when revisions were made by the MHA 2007). And so 'mental disability' – which was only used in the catch-all part of the definition, namely 'any other disorder or disability of mind' – could well include a personality disorder. Whatever is the reason behind the language used in the Guidelines, the new language used in the more recent guidelines is preferable, as it fits better with the statutory language in the MHA 1983.

16.36 The effect of mitigation that arises from mental disorder may be that a community sentence may be imposed in place of a custodial sentence on the basis of the seriousness of the offending being taken back below the level that requires a custodial sentence, even though the offence by itself might prima facie require such a sentence: see CJA 2003 s166(2).[31]

Saving language

16.37 There is also a specific saving provision for mentally disordered offenders in CJA 2003 s166(5), which indicates that nothing in the provisions as to community and custodial sentences mentioned above, or in relation to the fixing of fines in section 164,

> ... is to be taken –
> (a) as requiring a court to pass a custodial sentence, or any particular custodial sentence, on a mentally disordered offender, or
> (b) as restricting any power (whether under the Mental Health Act 1983 (c 20) or otherwise) which enables a court to deal with such an offender in the manner it considers to be most appropriate in all the circumstances.

30 Similarly, new definitive guidance on burglary uses the phrase 'mental disorder or learning disability'.

31 See also CJA 2003 s149(1), which provides that: 'In determining the restrictions on liberty to be imposed by a community order or youth community order in respect of an offence, the court may have regard to any period for which the offender has been remanded in custody in connection with the offence or any other offence the charge for which was founded on the same facts or evidence'.

16.38 Subsection 166(6) provides that the definition of 'mentally disordered' is that used in the MHA 1983.[32]

Summary

16.39 The seriousness of the offence involves looking at the nature of the offence and the circumstances in which it was committed; personal mitigation is then taken into account, and the hierarchy of sentencing is applied. Matters of mental disorder can be relevant in relation to assessing the seriousness of the offence and can also be relevant as mitigation. In addition, the sentencing court has the power to determine whether or not to impose a disposal that is designed specifically to deal with questions of mental disorder rather than to try to place the offender appropriately within the hierarchy. However, this option contains an element of circularity if a Mental Health Act disposal is considered, because such has to be the 'most suitable' disposal (the language of MHA 1983 s37(2)(b)): and this might be conditioned by questions of whether there is culpability that makes a punitive response appropriate.[33]

The application of the finding of seriousness to the hierarchy

16.40 A discharge is a suitable order for a low level of seriousness. The statutory provision, section 12 of the PCC(S)A 2000, refers to it being 'inexpedient to inflict punishment' in the light of the circumstances, including 'the nature of the offence and the character of the offender'. Although the reference to the character of the offender is often taken to cover factors such as the absence of previous convictions, the wider question is that of the expediency of punishment in all the circumstances. Accordingly, if the particular facts involve an offender whose actions were largely caused by mental disorder, though not to the extent that they met the legal test for insanity, it may be that his or her culpability is particularly low and that punishment is not an appropriate response to guilt, even if the nature of the offence would

32 This adds to the lack of fit between the Guideline as to the seriousness of offending. Although it was issued at the time when the MHA 1983 still referred to the different categories of mental disorder, the statutory language in CJA 2003 s166 (and its predecessor, PCC(S)A 2000 s158) was to the all-inclusive concept of mental disorder.

33 The interplay between the idea of punitiveness and the appropriateness of the disposal under the MHA 1983 is considered in detail in chapter 18, which considers hospital orders.

usually call for a sentence higher up the hierarchy. This might also be a suitable conclusion if action has been taken under the civil provisions of the MHA 1983 or if an outpatient treatment package has been arranged under community care provisions, on the basis that recreating a similar response as a sentence would be superfluous.

16.41 A discharge can be absolute, in which case that is the end of the matter; or it can be conditional for a period of up to three years, the effect of which is that the matter will be at an end provided that no further offence is committed within the period set: if that is breached, the offender can be sentenced for the offence that led to the conditional discharge as well as the further offence (see PCC(S)A 2000 s13).

16.42 The legislative provisions relating to fines are now contained in CJA 2003 ss162–165. The court must inquire into the financial circumstances of the individual, and take them and the seriousness of the offence into account: section 164. Depending entirely on the consequences of the mental disorder, it may be that a defendant with mental disorder has problems in obtaining funds or in managing to make arrangements as to payment.

16.43 The questions arising in relation to the imposition of a community order or a custodial sentence require a more detailed analysis, which are set out in the following chapters. Disposals under the MHA 1983 are also dealt with separately – they are not meant to be punitive, and so their placement on the hierarchy raises a conceptual difficulty: it has to be answered, however, in the context of the Court of Appeal not being able to substitute a more serious sentence unless the trial court imposed an unduly lenient one.

Ancillary and preventive orders

16.44 A significant and growing range of ancillary orders can be made as well, and there may be a role for mental disorder in determining whether to make these. Some orders are also open if the defendant has not been convicted but found to have committed the actus reus.[34] In addition, there are now various orders that can be made of a preventive nature, some of which are ancillary to a conviction and others of which are civil orders made by the civil courts or sometimes by the magistrates' court under its civil jurisdiction.

34 See chapters 9 and 10; the same may follow a finding of not guilty by reason of insanity, decribed in chapter 12.

Costs

16.45 One order that will often be considered is that of the payment of the costs of being prosecuted. This arises under section 18 of the Prosecution of Offences Act 1985 in relation to someone who has been convicted; the payment of a 'just and reasonable' amount may be ordered. Mental disorder may be relevant in two ways: it may be a consequence of mental disorder that a defendant is of a lower income and so less able to meet a costs order; and if the mental disorder has been implicated in the criminal conduct, but not to the extent as to amount to insanity, there is an argument that the reduced responsibility, which will be a mitigating feature in relation to sentence, should provide a level of mitigation in relation to a costs order as well.

Compensation, confiscation and restitution

16.46 Another common financial order is compensation for any personal injury, loss or damage suffered by the victim of a crime. The relevant legislation is PCC(S)A 2000 ss130–133, which among other things makes the compensation order something that can be made in place of a sentence (other than a mandatory sentence). The means of the defendant are relevant, as with relation to costs: see section 130(11). This has led to jurisprudence to the effect that an order should be payable within a reasonable time.[35]

16.47 The order can be made if it is appropriate to do so, and this is often taken to exclude any situations of complexity, since the compensation order, being an ancillary order, should be a simple matter[36] (and any dispute by the defendant as to the amount to be awarded has to be determined on evidence):[37] the view taken is that any complexities can be left to the civil courts. Having said that, it is to be noted that a court must give reasons for not making a compensation order, which suggests that orders are presumptively to be made. There is perhaps an argument that mental disorder and its impact on civil litigation, including questions of the capacity of a person with mental disorder to conduct litigation in the absence of a litigation friend, is such that

35 See, for example, *R v Bagga* (1989) 11 CrAppR(S) 497.

36 See, for example, *R v Donovan* (1981) 3 CrAppR(S) 192: a compensation order for loss of use of a car that had been taken without consent from a car hire company was not appropriate as there was an argument about the proper quantum.

37 See *R v Horsham Justices, ex p Richards* (1985) 82 CrAppR 254.

a compensation order may often not amount to a simple order that is the aim behind the regime.[38]

16.48 The proceeds of criminal activity may be confiscated under the Proceeds of Crime Act 2002. Orders can be made after conviction, and there is also in Part V of the Act a civil regime as to the recovery of the proceeds of 'unlawful conduct'; this may allow action against a defendant found unfit to stand trial but to have committed the actus reus. The details of these powers are beyond the scope of this text: but there does not seem to be any particular feature arising from mental disorder that should impact on the assessment of the criminal lifestyle and means of the defendant to pay, the central features of the statute. However, the process of confiscation is one that has to follow requirements of fairness: so it may be that matters such as the obligation of the defendant to supply information as part of the criminal confiscation process, failing which inferences can be drawn, may have to take account of any excuse based on mental disorder.

16.49 Items used for crime may be forfeited under PCC(S)A 2000 ss143–145. The main power depends on a conviction and so cannot be used in relation to a finding of having committed the act in the unfitness to stand trial process: the same is so in relation to orders to restore stolen goods to their owner under PCC(S)A 2000 s148. It is to be noted that the power to order the forfeiture of drugs and items used for drug trafficking, which arises under section 27 of the Misuse of Drugs Act 1971, also rests on a conviction: so it cannot be used if the person is unfit to stand trial but to have committed the actus reus. The same is so of a forfeiture of a firearm under section 52 of the Firearms Act 1968 after a conviction under that Act, or of an offensive weapon after a conviction under section 1 of the Prevention of Crime Act 1953, crossbows under section 6 of the Crossbows Act 1987, counterfeit currency or equipment for using it under section 24 of the Forgery and Counterfeiting Act 1981, or written material that is covered by the racial hatred parts of the Public Order Act 1986 under section 25 of the Act.

16.50 Another method for forfeiture arises under the Obscene Publications Act 1959: this provides for the seizure and destruction of obscene publications being sold commercially without a conviction (though there is also a duty to make an order for forfeiture is there is a conviction under the Obscene Publications Act 1964). The process under the Obscene Publications Act 1959 no doubt engages rights to

38 See also the powers to make reparation orders under PCC(S)A 2000 ss73–75 in relation to defendants under 18.

property under the ECHR, and common law rights to a fair process, which may require that consideration be taken of mental disorder if that is a reason why, for example, the operator of the premises cannot make proper representations against forfeiture.[39]

Disqualifications

16.51 Some ancillary orders are designed to prevent further offending. Disqualification from driving is an example (though, of course, that can be seen as being part of a punishment in many situations).[40] Aside from the various situations in which disqualification is required under the Road Traffic Offenders Act 1988 for various road traffic offences[41] and for receiving too many penalty points, there is a general power to disqualify after conviction for any offence: see PCC(S)A 2000 s146. If the car is used for an offence, the power to disqualify arises under section 147. These all require a conviction. There may be scenarios in which mental disorder is implicated in poor driving so as to make it sensible to consider a protective disqualification: but this requires a conviction and the general point about not making assumptions that mental disorder leads to poor driving should be made. However, in this regard it is to be noted that many mental disorders are classed as medical conditions that have to be reported to the DVLA (Driver and Vehicle Licensing Agency) as they potentially impact on driving ability.[42]

16.52 There are also provisions relating to the disqualification of people from working with children after conviction of an offence with a child victim: see Part II of the Criminal Justice and Court Services Act (CJCSA) 2000. Also covered in this situation was a charge of an offence and a hospital or guardianship order being made in respect of the act or omission: so it covered findings of not guilty by reason of insanity or orders made in relation to those unfit to stand trial: see CJCSA 2000 ss28 and 29.[43] This was supplemented by the Vetting

39 See also Children and Young Persons (Harmful Publications) Act 1955 s3.

40 See also disqualification from being a director under the Company Directors Disqualification Act 1986.

41 Note that Road Traffic Offenders Act 1988 s34 also allows disqualification for offences involving taking motor vehicles (whether theft or taking without consent or being carried) or going equipped to do so.

42 For a guide to this see Directgov at www.direct.gov.uk/en/DisabledPeople/MotoringAndTransport/Yourvehicleandlicence/DG_10029770. Many physical conditions are covered by this requirement.

43 They refer to a 'relevant order' which in CJCSA 2000 s30 is defined as a hospital or guardianship order.

and Barring Scheme under the Safeguarding Vulnerable Groups Act 2006, which created the Independent Barring Board, now renamed the Independent Safeguarding Authority by the Policing and Crime Act 2009, but subject to a review by the current government.

Other preventive orders

Introduction

16.53 Another range of orders are designed to prevent the circumstances in which offending might occur (which is of course part of the rationale behind disqualifications). So the Licensed Premises (Exclusion of Certain Persons) Act 1980 allows orders to be made to bar people convicted of offences of violence in a public house or other licensed premises from entering such premises. Along similar lines, those who are convicted of disorder at or connected with football matches may be made subject to orders excluding them from organised matches if such an action would help to prevent further violence: this is in accordance with the Football Spectators Act 1989, as amended.

16.54 This approach has been extended in two ways: a wider range of situations is covered, and there have been developments allowing an order to be made without a conviction. This latter development may mean that orders might be made in relation to someone who was not convicted for reasons relating to mental disorder.

Harassment

16.55 The starting point for this expansion was the Protection from Harassment Act 1997. This created an offence of harassment (see sections 1 and 2) and an aggravated offence of putting a person in fear of violence (section 4). It also allowed the civil courts to grant an injunction to prevent harassment; the criminal courts could also grant an injunction, called a restraining order, in the event of a conviction under sections 2 or 4. Breach of a restraining order is a separate criminal offence, as is the breach of a civil injunction: the latter criminal offence was supplemental to the normal process of contempt for breach of an injunction. The Domestic Violence, Crime and Victims Act 2004 has extended the restraining order regime by removing the reference to sections 2 and 4 of the 1997 Act: this means that the order can be made after a conviction for any offence.

Sexual offending orders

16.56 A range of protective orders has also been introduced in relation to sexual offending. This started with the notification requirements imposed on sex offenders under the Sex Offenders Act 1997, which were supplemented by civil sex offender orders under section 2 of the CDA 1998 and restraining orders added as section 5A of the 1997 Act by the CJCSA 2000. The relevant regime is now contained in Part II of the Sexual Offences Act (SOA) 2003, which contains notification requirements and allows the making of sexual offences protection orders, foreign travel orders or risk of sexual harm orders.

16.57 The notification provisions involve anyone who is convicted of a sexual offence, or found not guilty by reason of insanity or to have committed the act after being found not fit to stand trial, or who accepts a caution in relation to such an offence, to be placed on the register of sex offenders. A restriction order means that there is a life-long requirement to be on the register; a hospital order without restriction carries with it a seven-year registration requirement. In addition, anyone who is not caught by requirement to register because any relevant offence was outside the UK can be included by order of the magistrates' court on an application by the police: see SOA 2003 ss97–103. This includes anyone who was subject to the equivalent of a finding of not guilty by reason of insanity or that he or she was unfit to be tried but committed the actus reus, or accepted a caution. Failing to meet the requirements of the notification regime is a criminal offence.

16.58 The sexual offences protection order regime, under SOA 2003 ss104–113, is based on the need to offer protection against serious sexual harm (which means physical or psychological harm caused by sexual offending: see section 106); the court can impose such conditions as are necessary to deal with the risk. Such an order can be made on conviction for a listed offence or on a finding of not guilty by reason of insanity in relation to such an offence or a finding of the commission of the actus reus by a defendant unfit to stand trial. It is also possible for such an order to be made on an application by the police if a person has a relevant conviction or finding (or its equivalent outside the UK) and subsequently has acted in a way that gives reasonable grounds to suggest that an order is necessary. An order will last for at least five years and may be indefinite. Breach of it is a criminal offence.

16.59 The foreign travel order regime, under SOA 2003 ss114–122, is designed to protect against those who travel abroad to commit sexual offences involving children. It is similar in relation to its criteria and processes as a civil sexual offences protection order, and so covers those who were found not guilty by insanity or to have committed the actus reus after being unfit to stand trial of a relevant qualifying offence.

16.60 Risk of sexual harm orders, under SOA 2003 ss123–129, are also designed to protect children, and relate to sexual conduct that involves or occurs in the vicinity of a child: they require conduct, not conviction for conduct, and so will include activity that could not lead to a conviction for reasons of mental disorder.

Anti-social behaviour

16.61 The most well-known order that does not require a conviction is the anti-social behaviour order (ASBO), introduced by Part I of the CDA 1998 and gradually extended since. This allows magistrates to make orders prohibiting further anti-social conduct on an application by the police, a local authority or a social landlord. Breach of the order is a criminal offence. The main test on the merits is that making the order is necessary to prevent further anti-social conduct: this may intersect with questions of mental disorder in two ways. First, it may be that there are other steps that can be taken, whether under the MHA 1983 or community care legislation, to provide treatment that dealt with any anti-social conduct. Second, as noted in para 5.37, it may be that an order could not have any efficacy because a particular mental disorder meant that a recipient could not abide by the order; in such a case, it might be open to argument as to whether such an order is necessary because of its lack of any potential efficacy. CDA 1998 s1C allows ASBOs to be made on conviction.

16.62 The banning of people from licensed premises has been extended by Part I of the Violent Crime Reduction Act 2006, which allows drinking banning orders to be made to prevent disorderly conduct caused by alcohol; it may include prohibitions on entering off-licence premises. This may be seen as a particular type of ASBO: it is a civil order, but breach of it is a criminal offence. It is gradually being extended to the criminal courts as an order that can be made on conviction as well.

16.63 The football banning order regime has also been extended to cover civil orders as well: Football Spectators Act 1989 s14B has been added to allow an order to be made on a complaint by the police.

Expansion into other areas

16.64 As for expanding the regime of orders designed to prevent further offending into different areas, an example is the making of travel restriction orders on those convicted of various drug trafficking offences if the sentence imposed was four years or more: see Criminal Justice and Police Act 2001 s33. Travelling abroad when banned from doing so is a criminal offence.

16.65 Another example is that financial reporting orders may be made under section 76 of the Serious Organised Crime and Police Act 2005 following a conviction of an offence involving theft, fraud or money laundering if there is a 'sufficiently high' risk of a further offence: the order requires that the person provide an account of their financial activities to a person specified by the court.

16.66 Another example is the serious crime prevention order under section 19 of the Serious Crime Act 2007 following conviction: this requires reasonable grounds to believe that the public would be protected by the order disrupting involvement in further serious crime, the terms being whatever the court directs to achieve that aim. In addition, the High Court can make such an order under section 1 of the Act if the person has been 'involved in' serious crime. This does not necessarily require a conviction, as section 2 defines involvement as including facilitating the commission of an offence: this could include someone found not guilty by reason of insanity or someone unfit to stand trial but to have committed the actus reus if that conduct facilitated the commission of an offence by another. Also covered is conduct 'likely to facilitate the commission by himself or another person of a serious offence ... (whether or not such an offence was committed)': it is open to argument that this covers a situation in the person was not guilty by reason of insanity and/or committed the actus reus without anyone else being facilitated.

16.67 Another relatively new order is the violent offender order, which arises under Part 7 of the Criminal Justice and Immigration Act 2008. This is a civil order sought by the police against someone who poses a current risk of 'serious violent harm'; it can be made by a magistrates' court if the relevant criteria are made out, for a period of from two to five years. The person against whom the order is made must have received a custodial sentence of at least 12 months or a hospital order after conviction of or being found not guilty by reason of insanity of a homicide offence or causing grievous bodily harm; it also covers someone found to be under a disability and to have committed the actus reus of such an offence.[44] In addition to the previous court process, there must be subsequent behaviour that gives a reasonable ground to believe that the order is necessary.[45] The necessity is of protecting the public from the risk of serious violent harm (whether physical or psychological) from a further specified offence. This requirement, in section 98, raises the question of whether it can apply if the person remains under a disability such that conviction of a further offence is not possible because any verdict would be of not guilty by reason of insanity or could only cover the actus reus on a finding of unfitness to stand trial.

Deportation

16.68 Another possible ancillary order is deportation if the person convicted is not a British citizen. Section 32 of the UK Borders Act 2007 requires the courts to make a deportation order if a sentence of imprisonment is made (of any length in relation to certain offences and of 12 months or more in relation to any other offence).[46] Section 33 provides various grounds not to deport, which include the fact that an order is in place under the MHA 1983; it is also possible to avoid deportation if that would breach rights under the ECHR, which might be made out if an offender has mental health problems that cannot adequately be dealt with in the country to which they would be deported. In *R (Razgar) v Home Secretary*,[47] the House of Lords noted that foreseeable adverse consequences to the mental health of someone subject to deportation could give rise to arguments under both ECHR article 8 and, in a more extreme situation, article 3.

Rehabilitation of offenders

16.69 The Rehabilitation of Offenders Act 1974 makes provision for those given sentences of less than 30 months to allow that conviction to be spent for the purposes of disclosure in a time frame set by section 5 of the Act. (There are exceptions: in more sensitive matters, disclosure is still required.) There is specific provision for hospital orders:

44 See CJIA 2008 s99.

45 CJIA 2008 s100.

46 Recommendations for deportation may be made under Immigration Act 1971 s3(6) if the automatic provisions do not apply.

47 [2004] UKHL 27, [2004] 2 AC 368, [2004] MHLR 218.

under section 5(7), the rehabilitation period is five years from the date of conviction or two years from the date of release, whichever is the later. A guardianship order seems to be caught by section 5(8), as 'any other penalty': it is spent as soon as it has been lifted.

CHAPTER 17

Mental disorder and custodial sentences

continued

17.116 Tariff setting

The structure of a life sentence • The release provisions • The judicialisation of tariff-setting • The current statutory provisions for murder • The regime for discretionary lifers • Public protection sentences • Case-law

Introduction

17.1 The hierarchy of sentences described in chapter 16 means that a custodial sentence is permissible only if the offence meets a level of seriousness that requires a custodial response and any mitigation that is available to the offender does not take it below that threshold. This is subject to caveats that a mandatory life sentence is the only possible response to a conviction for murder and that there are various mandatory custodial sentences for certain repeat offending (subject to such a sentence being unjust) and for various firearms and weapons charges (subject to exceptional circumstances).[1] There are also dangerous offender provisions under which public protection becomes prominent: these can include indeterminate sentences, discretionary life imprisonment or imprisonment for public protection, but also determinate sentences with an extra element of supervision in the community. Even when public protection is key, the seriousness of the offending is relevant: this is because indeterminate sentences require both the need for public protection and a level of seriousness.

17.2 This chapter describes the relevance of mental disorder when a custodial sentence is being considered. This involves a number of questions:

i) whether mental disorder may reduce the seriousness of the offence or supplement the mitigation of the offender;
ii) whether the availability of non-punitive orders under the Mental Health Act (MHA) 1983 allows a court to impose an order that reflects features other than the seriousness of the offence; and
iii) special procedural requirements that have to be followed when a defendant is mentally disordered (which assist to ensure that the substantive issues are canvassed).

The last chapter outlined the first question, and this chapter considers it again, and also deals with the third question. The interplay between custodial sentences and hospital disposals is considered in chapter 18 on hospital orders, since one of the criteria for a hospital order is that is the most suitable disposal: this may be affected by the question of whether a punitive sentence should be imposed. In that context, it is also to be noted that serving prisoners can be transferred to hospital if necessary, as described in chapter 20: this is the only route into hospital for someone convicted of murder.

1 See paras 17.49–17.50 below.

17.3 The Powers of Criminal Courts (Sentencing) Act (PCC(S)A) 2000 was designed to consolidate provisions relating to sentencing, and it had a code relating to custodial sentencing in Part V of the Act; chapter 1 of that Part had various general provisions, including general restrictions on discretionary custodial sentencing (in section 79), general criteria going to the length of these sentences (section 80), and various procedural requirement, namely pre-sentence reports (section 81), medical reports for mental disordered offenders (section 82) and provisions relevant to unrepresented defendants (section 83). However, the aim to provide a consolidation statute was short-lived, as most, but not all, of these provisions have been replaced by provisions in the Criminal Justice Act (CJA) 2003. In addition, many of the provisions relating to hospital disposals are in the MHA 1983.

Procedural requirements

17.4 The procedural framework relating to the imposition of a custodial sentence involves the following:

i) there are restrictions on the imposition of custodial sentences on defendants who are not legally represented (section 83 of the PCC(S)A 2000);
ii) pre-sentence and medical reports are required (now governed by CJA 2003 ss156–158).

Unrepresented defendants

17.5 The PCC(S)A 2000 s83 provides that a sentence of imprisonment shall not be imposed on an unrepresented defendant who has not previously been sentenced to imprisonment in the UK, unless the reason for the lack of representation is that the person's resources took them outside the criteria for public funding, or he or she had public funding but lost it on account of conduct. A breach of this provision renders the sentence unlawful:[2] however, it may be that the

2 See, by analogy, *In re McC* [1985] AC 528, in which it was determined that a failure to alert a juvenile defendant to the availability of legal aid before a custodial sentence was imposed meant that there was a breach of a condition precedent to the jurisdiction to impose the sentence (and so the justices could be sued for acting in excess of jurisdiction). The relevant provision was article 15(1) of the Treatment of Offenders (Northern Ireland) Order 1976 SI No 226 (NI4), which provides: 'A magistrates' court on summary conviction or a court of assize or county court on conviction on indictment shall not pass a sentence

appeal court, so long as it complies with the procedural requirement, can pass the same sentence on the merits, and thereby substitute an equivalent but lawful sentence.[3]

17.6 This statutory prohibition covers a limited range of circumstances. However, it does not follow that a court will be right to impose a custodial sentence on an unrepresented defendant who has a previous custodial sentence or who is unrepresented because he or she cannot show that the public funding test is met for reasons of finance or who lost funding for reasons of misconduct. For example, if the failure of a defendant to pay for a lawyer is not a free choice because of mental disorder, the need to ensure a fair trial may require that a lawyer be appointed even if the defendant does not take the necessary steps or has lost legal representation as a result of misconduct. This is supported by the European Court of Human Rights's (ECtHR's) decision in *Megyeri v Germany*,[4] although the factual context was very different. Mr Megyeri was detained as a result of criminal proceedings in which he was found to have committed the acts but to not be responsible in light of a schizophrenic psychosis at the time; he had been represented during the trial, but not during proceedings to review his detention. He had not asked for a lawyer and so it could be said that his autonomous choice not to have a lawyer had been respected. The question arising was whether the absence of a legal representative during reviews of detention breached article 5(4) of the European Convention on Human Rights (ECHR), the habeas corpus provision. The ECtHR noted that:

> The judicial proceedings referred to in Article 5(4) need not always be attended by the same guarantees as those required under Article 6(1) for civil or criminal litigation. None the less, it is essential that the person concerned should have access to a court and the opportunity to be heard either in person or, where necessary, through some form

of imprisonment, borstal training or detention in a young offenders centre on a person who is not legally represented in that court and has not been previously sentenced to that punishment by a court in any part of the United Kingdom, unless either – (*a*) he applied for legal aid and the application was refused on the ground that it did not appear his means were such that he required assistance; or (*b*) having been informed of his right to apply for legal aid and had the opportunity to do so, he refused or failed to apply.'

3 *R v Howden* [2007] 1 CrAppR(S) 31: a four-year sentence for causing grievous bodily harm was quashed for breach of PCC(S)A 2000 s83, but as the sentence was not wrong in principle or manifestly excessive the Court of Appeal determined that its power under section 11 of the Criminal Appeal Act 1968 to sentence the appellant 'differently' included imposing the same substantive sentence but after following a lawful procedure.

4 (1993) 15 EHRR 584.

of representation. Special procedural safeguards may prove called for in order to protect the interests of persons who, on account of their mental disabilities, are not fully capable of acting for themselves ...[5]

17.7 The final sentence can no doubt be carried across to article 6, which governs a criminal trial: indeed, it may be argued that it should be carried across to article 6 in an a fortiori sense, given that article 6 expressly refers to the need for fairness, whereas it becomes part of article 5(4) only as an implied component of a judicial process being followed. On the facts of *Megyeri*, it was held that reviews should entail legal representation for the detainee in the absence of special circumstances: 'The importance of what is at stake for him – personal liberty – taken together with the very nature of his affliction – diminished mental capacity – compel this conclusion'.[6] A custodial sentence is no doubt of equal importance.

17.8 In this connection, it is worth noting that Part III.30.3 of the Consolidated Criminal Practice Direction[7] notes that: 'All possible steps should be taken to assist a vulnerable defendant to understand and participate in those proceedings. The ordinary trial process should, so far as necessary, be adapted to meet those ends'. This is consistent with the approach suggested in *Megyeri*. Accordingly, the discretion given under PCC(S)A 2000 s83 should be read so as to comply with the requirements of *Megyeri* and the Practice Direction. This may entail the appointment of someone to operate as an advocate to the court if a defendant refuses assistance but is unable to self-represent for reasons of mental disorder.

17.9 It is worth commenting that, while section 83 does not cover a hospital order, it has also been established in case-law that the defendant should be legally represented before such an order is imposed unless there are exceptional circumstances: *R v Blackwood*.[8]

Pre-sentence reports

Need for a pre-sentence report

17.10 The use of pre-sentence reports is regulated by CJA 2003 ss156 and 158. The context is the substantive requirement that a custodial sentence

5 (1993) 15 EHRR 584 para 22.
6 (1993) 15 EHRR 584 para 23.
7 www.justice.gov.uk/courts/procedure-rules/criminal/pd_consolidated.
8 (1974) 59 CrAppR 170 at 171–172. The court noted that this was particularly so if a restriction order was in prospect, but it did not limit its concern to such a situation.

cannot be imposed unless neither a fine nor a community sentence is adequate, and that a community sentence cannot be imposed unless the offence is serious enough to justify it: see sections 152 and 148 respectively.[9] Section 156 provides that the formulation of these conclusions, together with the further opinion as to what is a commensurate term in the light of the seriousness of the offending, must not be made without consideration of a pre-sentence report unless the court forms the view that such a report is not necessary: section 156(3) and (4).[10] It is to be noted that section 156(6) provides that a failure to obtain a pre-sentence report does not mean that any custodial or community sentence passed is invalid; however the appeal court must obtain a pre-sentence report unless it considers that one was not necessary at the time of the sentence or that it is not necessary at the time of the appeal (as set out in section 156(7)). In relation to offenders aged under 18, the requirement for a pre-sentence report is more strict: section 156(5) and (8) provide that the sentencing court or appeal court cannot form the view that a pre-sentence report is not necessary unless there has been a previous such report that has been considered.

17.11 A pre-sentence report is defined in CJA 2003 s158, which includes reference to it containing 'information as to such matters, presented in such manner, as may be prescribed by rules made by the Secretary of State': section 158(1)(a). Pursuant to this, guidance has been given, most recently in Probation Instruction 5/2011.[11]

Types of pre-sentence report

17.12 There are three types of pre-sentence report: oral, fast delivery and standard delivery. The oral or fast delivery reports are the ones on which increasing reliance is supposed to be placed because of the growing emphasis on speed in the criminal justice system. The policy is to use a standard report only when it is not possible to provide sufficient information by use of the fast delivery report. However, paragraph 5.3 of PI 5/2011 notes that there are various complex cases in which a standard pre-sentence report should be used, and includes in this category situations involving significant mental health issues. This may require liaison between various agencies to formulate appropriate recommendations and provide relevant information to

9 These provisions are discussed further at para 17.47 and in chapter 19.

10 PCC(S)A 2000 s81 was in similar terms.

11 Available at www.justice.gov.uk/guidance/prison-probation-and-rehabilitation/probation-instructions/index.htm.

the court as to matters such as the impact of a particular sentence on the vulnerabilities of a particular defendant. It follows from this that the pre-sentence report can be a good starting point for the compilation of relevant information for decision-making as to whether there are specific treatment arrangements that can be put in place for a defendant's needs.

Content of a pre-sentence report relating to a mentally disordered defendant

17.13 The second edition of the Probation Bench Handbook[12] noted at pages 47–48 that, in relation to a mentally disordered offender, the pre-sentence report should address various issues, namely:

Culpability:
- How does the mental disorder bear upon the offender's personal responsibility for his/her conduct?

Risk:
- Does the disorder make further offending more likely?
- Does the disorder increase any risk to self or others?
- What can be done to minimise any risk identified?

Feasibility:
- Does the disorder make it unlikely that the offender would be able to comply with the Requirements of a Community Order?
- What would be the implications of a custodial sentence?

Supervision:
- What work would be undertaken in the course of a Community Order?
- Is the offender able to participate in an accredited programme?
- Would the psychiatric services be involved?
- How would liaison with mental health services take place under the Care Programme Approach?
- Can the order be supervised to National Standards?

17.14 This summarises the various issues that might be relevant in the sentencing of a mentally disordered offender: whether there is an impact on culpability, risk posed and the impact or practicability of the sentence, arising from the disorder.

Risk assessment

17.15 It is also worth noting that a common feature of pre-sentence reports is the use of a form of risk assessment, the Offender Assessment

12 This was a 2007 publication of the National Probation Service, and is gradually being replaced as the new probation trusts publish more local guidance.

System (OASys).[13] This is designed to provide a view on the likelihood of further offending and of the risks arising from such offending, and how to manage them. In the Probation Bench Handbook, this was described as the 'cornerstone of probation's work with offenders'.[14]

17.16 It involves questions in relation to 12 aspects of the defendant's life, the answers to which are assigned a numerical score. The total allows the offender to be placed on a scale relating to the risk of further offending. The areas are: 1) offending information, 2) analysis of offences, 3) accommodation, 4) education, training and employability, 5) financial management and income, 6) relationships, 7) lifestyle and associates, 8) drug misuse, 9) alcohol misuse, 10) emotional well-being, 11) thinking and behaviour and 12) attitudes. Also assessed is the risk of serious harm to others, which is one of four categories, defined as follows:

- Low: current evidence does not indicate likelihood of causing serious harm.
- Medium: there are identifiable indicators of risk of serious harm. Potential to cause harm but unlikely to do so unless there is a change of circumstances.
- High: identifiable indicators of risk of serious harm. Potential event could happen at any time and impact would be serious.
- Very high: imminent risk of serious harm. Potential event is more likely than not to happen imminently. The impact would be serious.

17.17 This is not the place in which to set out a full account of the potential arguments as to the reliability or otherwise of the OASys tool. The Court of Appeal has endorsed a singularly disinterested approach: in *R v Boswell*,[15] a challenge to a sentence of imprisonment for public protection included a challenge to the OASys conclusion as to risk, but Dyson LJ commented that: 'Those tools are no doubt the product ... of a good deal of research and provide a satisfactory basis for reaching conclusions of the kind that were reached in this case'.[16] Indeed, the Court of Appeal in *R v S and others*[17] suggested that:

13 For more information on this, see paragraph 4.90 and following of Creighton and Arnott, *Prisoners: law and practice*, LAG, 2009. See also Prison Service Order (PSO) 2205, *Offender assessment and sentence management*, available at www.justice.gov.uk/guidance/prison-probation-and-rehabilitation/psipso/psos.htm.

14 Probation Bench Handbook appendix 1.

15 [2007] EWCA Crim 1587.

16 [2007] EWCA Crim 1587 para 12.

17 [2005] EWCA Crim 3616, [2006] 2 Prison LR 119.

> It is only likely to be in very rare cases that it will be incumbent on a judge to permit the author of a pre-sentence report to be cross-examined in relation to assessment of seriousness. It is, of course, open to counsel to make submissions about the contents of a report in relation to a defendants' history of criminal offending and all other material matters.[18]

17.18 Three short points should be made. First, there are various statements in the Probation Bench Handbook to the effect that the tools are based on research as to their effectiveness; but it is also noted that:

> The OASys Data Evaluation and Analysis Team (ODEAT) conducts research on the reliability and validity of OASys assessments. This includes analysis to determine how strongly each section is associated with further offending and how well OASys predicts future re-offending, of a violent and non-violent nature.[19]

This comment is open to a range of interpretations, from noting that it reflects a sensible desire to provide a continued validation of the tool, to an indication that the tool is a work in progress whose reliability has not been adequately demonstrated for the purpose for which it is used, namely to allow a sentencer to say with confidence that a criminal sanction responding to risk should be imposed.

17.19 Second, it is worth noting how risk assessment tools such as OASys work and the inherent limitations on what they are able to do in relation to the individual defendant. There are a significant number of tools designed to predict recidivism on an actuarial model, namely the idea that certain features in a person's past are linked with further offending and so can provide a guide as to the risk of reoffending. In his text, *Treating violence*, Tony Maden notes:

> The principle underlying standardized risk assessment is simple. It began in the Canadian prison system, where administrators collected information about a large number of offenders, then collated it with reoffending data. Using simple statistics, it was possible to construct statements of probability ... The life insurance industry uses the same method and it is for that reason it is known as actuarial risk assessment.[20]

17.20 Some tools measure only unchanging factors (typically called static factors), such as age of first offending and number of convictions. Other tools may combine these static factors with dynamic factors,

18 [2005] EWCA Crim 3616, [2006] 2 Prison LR 119 para 100.

19 Probation Bench Handbook p53.

20 Tony Maden, *Treating violence*, Oxford University Press, 2007, p79.

namely ones that are amenable to change over time. However, there are disputes within the area as to whether assessing static measures only provides a more accurate prediction than tools that incorporate dynamic factors. Maden gives a hint of the dispute (and of his position in it):

> While enthusiasts argue that actuarial methods should supplant clinical estimation of risk, a more balanced review concludes that the proper place of such instruments is as an adjunct to good clinical practice.[21]

17.21 This dispute has also been recognised judicially, albeit outside the UK: in *Director of Public Prosecutions v Moolarvie*, Blaxell J of the Western Australia Supreme Court noted that:[22]

> It is ... clear from a number of published articles in reputable international journals ... that these tools are at an early stage of development and involve an area of behavioural science which is the subject of some controversy.

17.22 This dispute links back the first point made above, namely that there is ongoing research as to the reliability of the particular tools. Also to be noted is the inherent limitation of what can be produced by an actuarial tool: it is not and cannot be an assessment of the individual. Just as an actuary working within the life insurance industry cannot predict the death of an individual, but can say only what will happen on average to a group of people with the identified characteristics, so it is for the actuarial tools and their ability to predict future crime: so a score on a tool that reveals a 30 per cent risk of committing a further sexual offence within the next ten years means that 30 per cent of people sharing the defendant's characteristics will commit a further offence in that time period. The tool cannot go further and say whether the defendant is in the part of the group who will or the group who will not commit a further offence.

17.23 The third brief point to note is that there is a contrast between the deferential acceptance of the tools in court proceedings in England and Wales, as outlined above, and the approach to such evidence in

21 Maden p97. (The citations to the 'enthusiasts' and those who are 'more balanced' are omitted.) Still, both are better than those who merely rely on their professional judgment, and provide 'unstructured clinical assessments', whom Maden describes as 'men in three-piece suits and half-moon glasses; unlikely gurus, perhaps, but they have the same reliance on charismatic authority. They are right because of who they are, and the classic response to challenge is: "And who are you?"' (pp63–64).

22 [2008] WASC 37 at para 41: Supreme Court of Western Australia, judgments available at http://decisions.justice.wa.gov.au/supreme/supdcsn.nsf.

other jurisdictions. An Australian judgment has already been cited. Another example is *R v Peta*,[23] in which the New Zealand Court of Appeal – in the context of what is called an extended supervision order, which allows post-sentence supervision of child sex offenders – expressed its surprise as to the limited numbers of challenges to the risk assessment evidence called by the Crown in the form of contrary evidence called by the defendant;[24] it then proceeded to deal at length with the value of the tools and the need to explain them properly to the court.

Medical reports

The duty to obtain a medical report

17.24 The provisions relating to pre-sentence reports are applicable to all offenders: in relation to mentally disordered offenders, there are specific duties to obtain medical reports and, before passing a custodial sentence, to consider the effects of custody on that person's mental condition and the treatment which may be available for it. CJA 2003 s157 provides that:

> (1) Subject to subsection (2), in any case where the offender is or appears to be mentally disordered, the court must obtain and consider a medical report before passing a custodial sentence other than one fixed by law.[25]

17.25 So, the triggers for the obligation under CJA 2003 s157 are that there is a prospect of a custodial sentence and the offender 'is or appears to be mentally disordered' (with a cross-reference to the definition of mental disorder in the MHA 1983 in subsection (5)). Subsection (2) disapplies the obligation if the circumstances of a case mean that it is unnecessary to obtain a report. Given that the purposes for which a report is obtained include questions of the effect of custody on a defendant's mental disorder and the treatment for it, it may only be a limited set of situations in which consideration of a report will not be necessary. One example will be when the defendant has spent as much time in custody on remand as will have to be served under the sentence and so will be released immediately. Even if the court already has a significant amount of information about the defendant's mental disorder, for example because the trial has been

23 [2007] 2 NZLR 627.

24 [2007] 2 NZLR 627 para 13.

25 Its predecessor, PCC(S)A 2000 s82, was in similar terms.

concerned with issues arising from mental disorder, it may be open to question whether the evidence deals with the issues that arise at the time of sentence or needs to be updated: for example, a finding against a defendant in a trial may be a significant factor that causes a psychiatrist to revise the opinion earlier expressed, and some mental disorders may change significantly in a short period of time.

17.26 The final clause of CJA 2003 s157(1) means that it is also not necessary to obtain a medical report when the sentence is fixed by law, namely mandatory life imprisonment for murder (or detention for life for a younger offender). This is language that appeared in predecessor provisions: see, for example, section 4(1) of the CJA 1991. It is suggested that the language ought to be reconsidered and that judges be reminded of their discretion to obtain a medical report even if there is no duty to do so. This is because, while the sentence is fixed by law in the sense that it must be one of life imprisonment, it is two parts, with the outer-envelope of custody for life being one but with a tariff or minimum term that has to be served before the detainee can be considered for release on licence. This tariff will reflect the same sorts of factors as affect the length of a determinate sentence and so there is no reason why different considerations should apply because the defendant has a mental disorder.[26]

17.27 There was a further exception to the duty to obtain a medical report in the immediate predecessor section, PCC(S)A 2000 s82: it was not necessary in relation to an automatic life sentence. However, it was a practical necessity. This was because the sentence could be avoided if there were exceptional circumstances: and to avoid breaching the prohibition on arbitrary detention in ECHR article 5, it was held in *R v Offen and others*[27] that this test was made out if the defendant did not pose a significant risk to the public. Evidence to this effect might well come from a psychiatric or psychology report that addressed the factors viewed by those professions as relevant to issues of risk. So, in the case of Mr Offen, the Court of Appeal overturned an automatic life sentence and substituted a sentence of three years' imprisonment partly on the basis of psychiatric evidence to the effect that the risk to the public was not of serious harm. In the case of a co-appellant, Mr Okwuegbunam, the Court of Appeal upheld the automatic life sentence on the basis that in the absence of expert evidence (which it noted could come in the form of a medical report or a pre-sentence

26 See discussion at paras 17.116–17.137.

27 [2000] EWCA Crim 96, [2001] 1 WLR 253, [2001] Prison LR 283.

report), the fact that he had committed two serious offences placed him within the rationale of the automatic life sentence provisions.

17.28 So psychiatric evidence could be key to demonstrating that there were exceptional circumstances. The dangerous offender provisions of the CJA 2003 now apply in this situation:[28] these are in many respects wider than the automatic life sentence, but also allow the making of a hospital order.[29] The central feature in the assessment of a dangerous offender is the risk to the public: the specific question is whether there is a significant risk to members of the public of serious harm occasioned by the commission of further offences of the sort specified in the legislation.[30] The statute does not require psychiatric evidence to support such a finding, but a defendant may wish to call such expert evidence if it supports a view that the risk he or she poses does not meet the statutory test. What is at stake justifies such a course of action.

17.29 Any failure to obtain a medical report when the duty arises, including an erroneous conclusion that it is not necessary, does not invalidate the sentence. However, an appeal court must remedy the error by obtaining a report: see CJA 2003 s157(4). It is also provided in section 157(7) that the duty arising under section 156 is not displaced by the provisions relating to a medical report: in other words, the requirement to obtain a medical report does not affect the requirement to obtain a pre-sentence report.

Form and content of medical report

17.30 The medical report can be written or oral. It has to be provided by a doctor approved for the purposes of MHA 1983 s12: see CJA 2003 s157(6). As has already been described in chapter 7, it is possible for a medical report to be obtained as a result of a remand to hospital under MHA 1983 s35. This little used power has the advantage of allowing an assessment to be made following observation in a hospital setting and with the scrutiny of a clinical team: this might better ensure that a reliable assessment is made of the mental disorder. It is no doubt preferable to an assessment in a prison setting if that is the only alternative; however, it is only permissible if it is not practicable

28 See paras 17.96–17.115.

29 This was not so if the defendant met the criteria for an automatic life sentence: see paras 17.88–17.95.

30 This was initially presumed from the commission of a second offence: CJA 2003 s229(3) as enacted, with a proviso that the assumption could be displaced if it was unreasonable.

to obtain a report on bail, which test might apply if the defendant cannot properly be admitted to bail.

17.31 The Probation Service's Bench Handbook contains several relevant suggestions: first as to the nature of the author of the report and his or her geographic location. It is noted that while a General Practitioner might be approved for the purposes of section 12: 'The court will best be served if the report is provided by a general or forensic psychiatrist'.[31] It is also noted that: 'Best results will generally be obtained from commissioning reports from the offender's catchment area services. This allows resources to be matched to proposals and ensures delivery of the service is the responsibility of the reporting doctor'.[32] An identified problem is that reports prepared out of the relevant catchment area often mean that 'difficulties ... arise in attempting to realise the proposal'.

17.32 The Handbook also comments on the value of the court being clear as to what it is looking for in a report:

> It is always helpful if the court specifies what is required in any psychiatric report, for example the existence of a mental disorder, the relationship between the disorder and offending behaviour, any risk the offender poses to self or others and opinion on what disposals would both address the offender's disorder and reduce offending. If a custodial sentence is being considered it would help if the court specifically asked the psychiatrist to address the impact of a custodial sentence on the disorder and any available treatments.[33]

17.33 The Handbook adds that if the court is contemplating a public protection sentence, it is also helpful if the court seeks an opinion as to the test to be applied under that legislation, namely the risk to members of the public of serious harm by the commission by the offender of further specified offences.

17.34 In separate guidance given in the Code of Practice issued by the Secretary of State for Health under section 118 of the MHA 1983, it is noted at paragraph 33.16 that:

> A medical report for the court should set out:
> - the material on which the report is based;
> - how that material relates to the opinion given;
> - where relevant, how the opinion may relate to any other trial issue;
> - factors relating to the presence of mental disorder that may affect the risk that the patient poses to themselves or to others, including the risk of re-offending; and

31 See Probation Bench Handbook p46.

32 Probation Bench Handbook p47.

33 Probation Bench Handbook p47.

- if admission to hospital is recommended, what, if any, special treatment or security is recommended and whether the doctor represents an organisation that is able to provide what is required.

The report should not speculate about guilt or innocence.[34]

17.35 The Code also notes the existence of CJA 2003 s157 and suggests that:

> It may, therefore, be appropriate to include recommendations on the disposal of the case. In making recommendations for disposal, the doctor should consider the longer-term, as well as immediate, consequences. Factors to be taken into account include:
> - whether the court may wish to make a hospital order subject to special restrictions;
> - whether, for restricted patients, the order should designate admission to a named unit within the hospital;
> - whether, in the event of the court concluding that a prison sentence is appropriate, the offender should initially be admitted to hospital by way of a hospital direction under section 45A; and
> - whether a community order with a mental health treatment requirement may be appropriate.[35]

17.36 These specific sentencing options are considered in chapters 18 and 19; they may arise as alternatives to custody. Another specific question that must be addressed in any medical report is the effect of custody if a defendant has a mental disorder. This is discussed below.

17.37 A practical question that may arise is as to the funding of the preparation of reports. The Probation Service's Bench Handbook notes that:

> Funding is available for psychiatric reports in the Magistrates' Courts (but not in the Crown Court) and for remands on bail, the Probation Service will act as commissioning agents for the psychiatric report on behalf of the court. For those in custody, including cases in the Crown Court, the prison will be responsible for arranging the report. The [National Health Service] NHS is now responsible for health care centres in prisons, and arrangements will be in place to assess and report on offenders remanded in custody. The court must send a clear instruction to the prison that a report has been ordered.[36]

34 There is equivalent guidance in Code of Practice for Wales paras 32.12 and 32.13.

35 Code of Practice para 33.18. Welsh Code of Practice para 32.15 is in similar terms.

36 Probation Bench Handbook p47.

The duty to consider the effects of custody

17.38 Turning then to the question that the court must answer for which a medical report is required, and hence a matter that must be addressed in a medical report, CJA 2003 s157(3) provides that:

> Before passing a custodial sentence other than one fixed by law on an offender who is or appears to be mentally disordered, a court shall consider –
> (a) any information before it which relates to his mental condition (whether given in a medical report, a pre-sentence report or otherwise); and
> (b) the likely effect of such a sentence on that condition and on any treatment which may be available for it.

17.39 The reference in section 157(3)(a) to 'any information' means that it may be possible to make use of material that is not contained in a medical report specifically sought for court purposes. For example, it may be that the defendant has been involved with various services and so material is available from them (though perhaps subject to issues around whether that information is protected by confidentiality to the extent that it should not be revealed, even to a court, unless a specific direction is given). Not to be underestimated in this situation is the potential for information from social workers and carers, who may have important insights into the operation of a defendant's disorder.

17.40 To consider the effect of a custodial sentence on a defendant's mental disorder and the treatment for it requires an investigation of the ability of a prison setting to deal with the needs of the defendant and the ability of the defendant to deal with a custodial setting. This inevitably entails that the approach that is set out under the heading of the purposes of sentencing by reason of CJA 2003 s142, discussed in chapter 16, must be supplemented by this additional, welfare-based consideration in the case of a mentally-disordered offender.

17.41 In this context, it is to be noted that powers exist to transfer a prisoner to a psychiatric hospital if he or she develops a mental disorder: see MHA 1983 s47, discussed in chapter 20. It is suggested that there is a difference between a situation in which a prisoner develops a mental disorder during the course of a prison sentence and one in which the disorder develops or deteriorates because of the prison sentence. If the latter is a foreseeable consequence of a sentence, there must be a question-mark over whether the sentence is compliant with article 3 of the ECHR, namely the absolute prohibition on anything that is inhuman or degrading.

17.42 In *Price v UK*,[37] the ECtHR considered the case of a woman with significant physical disabilities and problems with her kidney who was given a seven-day sentence for contempt of court in civil proceedings. She was held in a police station and then a prison, but the facilities were not able to cope with her needs. In particular, she had to sleep one night in her wheel-chair, which meant that she became particularly cold, had had to be assisted on and off the toilet by male prison officers, and had required catheterisation because of problems with urine retention. The court held that this amounted to degrading treatment, the particular concerns being that the sentence was harsh and also that no efforts were made to find out whether the detention facilities would be able to cope with Ms Price's needs. In a concurring opinion joined by Judge Costa, Judge Bratza, the UK's permanent judge on the court, expressed his view that the fault lay with the judge, who passed sentence without investigating whether custodial facilities would be adequate.

17.43 Although this is a different factual scenario, the implication is that a court has to be cognizant of the impact of a sentence and if the consequence is foreseeable suffering of a nature that causes significant problems in light of a person's disability, that can amount to a breach of article 3. A prison setting will only lead to a breach of this article if there is a level of suffering that goes beyond that to be expected in a legitimate form of punishment. See, for example, *Lorse v Netherlands*,[38] in which a breach of article 3 was found in the light of the evidence of the impact of a high secure regime, and in particular repeated strip-searching, namely that it caused identifiable mental health difficulties for an inmate; the prison authorities were aware of this but continued the regime of regular strip-searches. The court commented[39] that part of the factual matrix was that the strip-searches had never provided any evidence of any matters that revealed security concerns. The prison authorities would no doubt suggest that this lack of evidence revealed the success of the regime: but the approach taken by the court suggests that positive evidence of success is required. That does mean, naturally, that there may be situations in which action taken for security reasons might be justified despite the fact that it also caused mental health problems, albeit that the test was not met on the facts.[40]

37 [2001] Prison LR 359, (2002) 34 EHRR 1285.

38 [2003] Prison LR 407, (2003) 37 EHRR 105.

39 [2003] Prison LR 407, (2003) 37 EHRR 105 para 73.

40 See also *Drew v UK* App No 35679/03, [2006] MHLR 203. He had been sentenced to an automatic life sentence rather than to hospital, even though

17.44 As has been noted in chapter 16, the purposes of sentencing in CJA 2003 s142 are disapplied if a hospital order is made. It is suggested that this power to move outside the purposes of sentencing should be combined with the need to have regard to the consequences of custody on a mental disorder and the prohibition on a public body from causing a consequence that would amount to a breach of ECHR article 3. The consequence is that care must be taken to justify any sentence other than a hospital order if there is evidence that a deterioration in a mental disorder is the likely consequence of a custodial sentence. This does not mean that a custodial sentence will not be possible. For example, it may be that a mental disorder that is likely to respond quickly to treatment will allow release in a short time: if a lengthy custodial sentence is proper (for example, because there was no connection between the mental disorder and the offence), then the court may be able to justify a custodial sentence. But it will have to make sure that arrangements are in place to secure appropriate treatment. This may mean investigation as to whether a transfer under MHA 1983 s47 can be put in place or whether an order under section 45A of the Act can be made (see chapters 20 and 18 respectively).

17.45 This requirement to take into account the effect of a custodial sentence does not apply if the custodial sentence is a mandatory life sentence for murder. However, the exclusion of the duty does not prevent it arising as a proper exercise of discretion. So, as noted above, the sentence imposed is a two-part sentence, the life sentence being the mandatory outer envelope but with the important tariff element for the purposes of punishment. If the consequence of a defendant having a mental disorder that will be affected adversely by time in prison custody is that there is an additional degree of hardship, there is no reason why this should not be taken into account in the setting of the tariff. This is a matter of mitigation of the punitive tariff or minimum term. Equally, it may be appropriate for the court to make inquiries as to the potential for the defendant being transferred speedily to hospital under MHA 1983 s47 (the section 45A route not being available in relation to murder).

he needed to be in hospital; his condition deteriorated during a period of eight days that he was in a prison medical wing before being transferred to hospital under MHA 1983 s47 where effective treatment was again commenced. It was held that this did not reach the threshold of severity necessary for a finding of a breach of article 3: however, less speedy action might have been problematic. It was also noted by the court that there had been no complaint made in relation to article 5, but hinted that there should have been such a complaint because of the need to have a proper relationship between the place of detention and the needs of the defendant.

Determinate sentences and the impact of mental disorder

17.46 Sentences with a definitive end-date are determinate sentences. There are three types of determinate sentence:

i) imprisonment (or detention, depending on the age of the offender) imposed on the basis of the seriousness of the offence,
ii) extended sentences imposed on the basis of the dangerousness of the offender and
iii) suspended sentences.[41]

The criteria that justify these different sentences, and the potential impact of mental disorder, are as follows.

Imprisonment on ground of seriousness

17.47 A custodial sentence may eventuate if an assessment of the seriousness of the offence and any aggravating and mitigating factors that apply[42] leads to the conclusion that an offence or its combination with an associated offence 'was so serious that neither a fine alone nor a community sentence can be justified' (CJA 2003 s152).[43] Mental disorder may affect the assessment of the seriousness of the offence and also provide mitigating features for the offender: however, two things should be noted if mental disorder is present and means that a disposal under the MHA 1983 may be appropriate. In the first place, the statutory framework provides that the purposes of sentencing set out in CJA 2003 s142 are disapplied when an order is made under the MHA 1983 that involves detention in hospital (see section 142(2)(d)). In addition, the process of assessing the seriousness of the offence and fixing a sentence that matches that seriousness does not restrict the power to impose a disposal under the MHA 1983 if that is the most appropriate outcome (see section 166(5)).

17.48 As is discussed in more detail in chapter 18, MHA 1983 s37(2)(b) in turn provides that a hospital order does not have to be imposed if it is not felt to be the most suitable disposal even though the medical criteria are made out. The element of circularity between the propositions that a punitive sentence can be avoided to allow a disposal under

41 Others are on the statute books, namely the custody plus and intermittent custody sentences of the CJA 2003, but these have not been brought into effect.

42 See chapter 16 for a discussion of the assessment of seriousness.

43 An alternative scenario is that the defendant declines to cooperate with a condition in a community sentence: see CJA 2003 s152(3).

the MHA 1983 when the latter is a discretionary matter and may turn on whether punitive needs are given precedence may present some difficulties. Clearly, there will be circumstances in which a mentally-disordered offender will be subject to a custodial sentence.

17.49 As to the length of the sentence, CJA 2003 s153 provides that the sentence imposed must be for 'the shortest term ... that in the opinion of the court is commensurate with the seriousness of the offence' and any associated offences. That is subject to a caveat that Parliament has taken to intervening in this calculated by introducing mandatory minimum terms. This commenced with the Crime (Sentences) Act (C(S)A) 1997.[44] By sections 3 and 4 of the Act, mandatory minimum terms of seven years' imprisonment and three years' imprisonment for a third drug trafficking offence involving class A drugs and a third domestic burglary respectively were introduced. In each case, the sentence could be avoided if it would be unjust. It was not necessary to make a finding that mental disorder meant that the sentence was unjust, because section 37(1A) was added to the MHA 1983[45] to make it clear that a hospital order could be made in these situations (in contrast, at that time, to the language applicable to the automatic life sentence, described below).

17.50 These mandatory minima became sections 110 and 111 of the PCC(S)A 2000, and the language of MHA 1983 s37(1A) was amended accordingly.[46] Subsequently, CJA 2003 s287 added section 51A to the Firearms Act 1968 to introduce a minimum term of five years' imprisonment for an adult or young adult and three years' detention for a youth convicted of certain serious firearms offences unless there are exceptional circumstances; CJA 2003 Sch 32 para 38 amended MHA 1983 s37(1A) to make clear that hospital order could be made nevertheless. Finally, section 29 of the Violent Crime Reduction Act 2006 introduced the offence of using someone to mind a dangerous weapon (including firearms and some offensive weapons and knives), and section 29(4) and (6) introduced minimum sentences of five years' detention or imprisonment for an adult offender and three years' detention for a youth, again subject to an exceptional circumstances finding. MHA 1983 s37(1A) was again amended to provide that a hospital order could be imposed.[47]

44 Its rationale was set out in the March 1996 government white paper, *Protecting the public: the government's strategy on crime in England and Wales* (Cm 3190).

45 C(S)A 1997 Sch 4 para 12.

46 PCC(S)A 2000 Sch 9 para 90.

47 Violent Crime Reduction Act 2006 Sch 1 para 2.

17.51 Those sentenced to a custodial sentence are released at the half-way point and are subject to supervision in the community until the end of the sentence, and also the prospect of recall to prison if the Secretary of State is not happy with the risk presented: see CJA 2003 ss254–256A.

Extended sentences

17.52 The purposes of sentencing include both backward-looking punitive concerns and also forward-looking rehabilitative and protective concerns. Reliance on the seriousness of offending emphasises the punitive, which may also have a limiting effect if the offence is not as serious as it might have been, perhaps as a matter of luck. However, the need to impose a length of sentence that is proportionate to the seriousness of the offence gives way to a longer sentence if the needs of public protection become more prominent.

17.53 There have been several iterations of this approach in determinate sentences, which can be seen as a middle-way between a standard custodial sentence and the indeterminate sentencing option described below. In the CJA 1991, section 1(2) allowed the imposition of a custodial sentence on the basis not just of seriousness but also on the basis of only such a sentence being adequate to protect the public from serious harm from the assailant in a sexual or violent offence. If the latter applied, the length of the sentence need not be 'commensurate to the seriousness' (the limitation for custody based on the seriousness of the offence in section 2(2)(a)) but should be for 'such longer term ... as ... is necessary to protect the public from serious harm from the offender': section 2(2)(b). This became PCC(S)A 2000 s80(2)(b).

17.54 There was an additional option available to the sentencing court in the case of a sexual offence. Under section 44 of the CJA 1991, the court could direct that the period on licence after release be extended (with the possibility of an administrative recall to prison). The standard licence period under the CJA 1991 went to the three-quarter point of the sentence; but it ran to the end of the sentence if an order was made under section 44. This was modified by the Crime and Disorder Act (CDA) 1998, section 58 of which introduced a new form of sentence, the extended sentence, for violent or sexual offences: this consisted of a custodial term plus an extension period during which the offender would be on a licence that was supplemental to that arising by reason of the custodial terms; the basis for such an arrangement was that the standard period on licence would not be adequate to protect the public from further offending or securing the offender's rehabilitation. This became PCC(S)A 2000 s85.

17.55 Then came the CJA 2003. The longer than commensurate sentence was removed, but new dangerous offender provisions in CJA 2003 ss224–236[48] were brought into effect in April 2005.[49] They had significant provisions requiring indeterminate sentences, which are described below, and a substantially amended extended sentence. It remained a sentence involving a period in custody and then an additional period of supervision in the community. However, there was limited discretion involved. In short, the dangerous offender provisions turn on, first, a list of 'specified offences', over 150 sexual or violent offences carrying imprisonment of at least two years; those that carry a maximum sentence of ten years or more are 'serious offences'.[50] The second element is an assessment of dangerousness, namely whether there is a significant risk to members of the public of serious harm occasioned by the commission of further specified offences. By 'serious harm' is meant 'death or serious personal injury, whether physical or psychological': section 224(3).

17.56 The process of determining whether this test is made out involved taking into account the nature and circumstances of the offence, and any pattern of behaviour or information about the offender: CJA 2003 s229(2). If the offender was aged 18 or over and had committed a second specified offence, the court was required to assume that the dangerousness test was met unless that would be unreasonable in the light of the nature and circumstances of each of the offences involved and any pattern of offending, and any information about the offender. This was optional in the case of those under 18. As is described below, a finding of dangerous combined with the commission of a serious offence led to a mandatory indeterminate sentence for those aged 18 or over; if combined with a specified offence, it led to a mandatory extended sentence. For those aged under 18, the extended sentence was required in two situations: first, in relation to a specified offence that was not serious but combined with a finding of dangerousness. However, if the offence was a serious offence, the indeterminate sentence would only follow if the extended sentence would not be adequate to protect the public from the risk identified: section 226(3).

48 CJA 2003 Part 12 Chapter 5.

49 Criminal Justice Act 2003 (Commencement No 8 and Transitional and Saving Provisions) Order 2005 SI No 950.

50 CJA 2003 Sch 15 lists the relevant offences.

17.57 The extended sentence under the CJA 2003 as enacted involved a custodial term commensurate with the seriousness of the offence (set in accordance with the requirements of CJA 2003 s153(2), but of at least 12 months) plus an 'extension period' necessary to provide protection from the offender's dangerousness by way of the supervision in the community on licence. The licence period could be of up to five years for a violent offence or eight years for a sexual offence (CJA 2003 ss227(4) or 228(4)). However, the aggregate sentence – ie custodial term plus extension period – could not exceed the statutory maximum for the offence (sections 227(5) and 228(5)). The release of those subject to an extended sentence was not the automatic release at the half-way point of a determinate term imposed for the purposes of punishment. Release from the custodial part of the sentence would follow only if the Parole Board was satisfied that the risk posed was low enough to make release safe. If released on licence during the custodial part of the sentence, that was on licence. During the entire licence period, whether following release ordered by the Parole Board or at the end of the custodial element of the sentence, the offender could be recalled to prison on the basis of risk: the regime for this was set in CJA 2003 ss254–256A.

17.58 In practice, the dangerous offender sentencing provisions caused significant problems, in particular because of the large number of people given an indeterminate sentence for a relatively minor index offence: such prisoners were not realistically able to secure release on tariff expiry because the tariffs were short and they were unable to secure access to offending behaviour courses in this period and so could not show that the risk they posed had been released. This is described further in relation to indeterminate sentences. The response to the problems identified was that sections 13–18 of the Criminal Justice and Immigration Act (CJIA) 2008 introduced significant changes:

i) the presumption as to the existence of dangerousness if a defendant was convicted of a second specified offence was removed;
ii) the duty to impose an indeterminate sentence for a serious specified offence by an adult combined with a finding of dangerousness became a matter of discretion; moreover, the discretion could be exercised only if the offender had a previous conviction for one of 22 more serious specified offences (listed in CJIA 2008 Sch 4 and added as Schedule 15A to the CJA 2003) or the tariff set to reflect the seriousness of the index offence and associated offending was at least two years (before any credit for time in custody).

In relation to a defendant under 18, the latter condition applies irrespective of the nature of any previous offending;

iii) this restriction on the indeterminate sentence was accompanied by a widened ambit for extended sentence for adults: it can be imposed for serious specified offences as well as others (as it always did in relation to those aged under 18 if there is no need for an indeterminate sentence);

iv) however, the use of the extended sentence also became discretionary, that discretion turning on whether there is a previous conviction for one of the grave offences in CJA 2003 Sch 15A or the custodial part of the sentence is at least four years;[51]

v) in addition, the length of the extension period is now a matter for the discretion of the court, without the limitations of the previous section 227(4); and

vi) if imposed, there is automatic release on licence at the half-way point of the custodial part of the extended sentence.

17.59 In considering the interplay between the dangerous offender sentences and mental disorder, it was to be noted that CJA 2003 s302 and Sch 32 para 8 amended MHA 1983 s37 in the following significant ways:

i) the language relating to the automatic life sentence regime taking precedence over the making of a hospital order was removed; and

ii) MHA 1983 s37(1A) was amended, making it plain that nothing in those dangerous offender sentencing provisions or any other minimum term provisions prevented the making of a hospital order.

In short, even when the dangerous offender provisions were almost mandatory in their operation, a hospital disposal could be made: indeed, the preservation of the hospital order option was effectively the only discretionary power that was available on the finding of dangerousness to avoid the imposition of some form of custodial sentence with a protective element to it.

51 These preconditions are the same as those applicable to an indeterminate sentence, since a four-year custodial sentence will lead to a two-year tariff, since a tariff involves halving the notional determinate term: this is because parole eligibility in relation to a determinate term arises at the half-way point of the sentence, but only at the end of a tariff period, and so the tariff set has to be halved to have the same effect.

Suspended sentences

17.60 The suspended sentence regime has also been changed significantly in recent years. Traditionally, a suspended sentence operated as a method of holding a threat over a defendant designed to deter further offending during the period for which the sentence was suspended. Then, section 5 of the CJA 1991 changed the governing provision (in section 22 of the Powers of Criminal Courts Act 1973) to indicate that a suspended sentence could only be imposed if the custodial threshold was passed but there were exceptional circumstances that allowed that to happen. This became section 118 of the PCC(S)A 2000. Mental disorder could give rise to exceptional circumstances under this test. For example, in *R v Bainton*,[52] an assistant at a post office stole some £221,000 at the instigation of her husband, who threatened to force her into prostitution if she did not carry out the thefts. The expert evidence was that the result of physical and sexual abuse by her husband over a long period, which caused her to attempt suicide, was that she had battered woman syndrome, described as a form of post-traumatic stress disorder. The Court of Appeal held that these features, including the element of coercion, justified suspending for two years the sentence of two years' imprisonment that had been imposed by the judge.

17.61 In addition, a court passing a suspended sentence could add a fine or a compensation order (section 118(5)) or make a suspended sentence supervision order placing the detainee under the supervision of a probation officer as well (section 122).

17.62 Under the CJA 2003, the new regime for suspended sentences, contained in sections 189 and following, is substantially different: there is no need for exceptional circumstances and the court may add various conditions that are similar to those applicable to a community sentence (and described in chapter 19). The custodial period can be of 28 to 51 weeks according to the statute and the supervision period of between six months and two years; however, in the commencement order, transitional provisions allow it to be 14 days to 12 months.[53] The custodial period may be activated if the offender commits a further offence or breaches a supervision condition. These conditions, set out in section 190, include such matters as a mental health treatment requirement, or requirements relating to drug rehabilitation or alcohol treatment. Accordingly, questions of mental

52 [2005] EWCA Crim 3572, [2006] MHLR 183.

53 Criminal Justice Act 2003 (Sentencing) (Transitory Provisions) Order 2005 SI No 643.

disorder may lead a court to consider the making of a suspended sentence. Under section 191, reviews of the operation of the order may be carried out by the court.

17.63 Accordingly, a suspended sentence is now one where there is a threat of custody hanging over the defendant if certain requirements are not met or a further offence is committed.

Interplay with mental disorder – summary and examples

Summary of current statutory regime

17.64 The current regime for custodial sentences means that the framework allows a judge to impose a hospital order in place of a custodial sentence whether or not the basis for the latter is the seriousness of the offending or the needs of public protection. This is discussed further in chapter 18 in relation to the imposition of a hospital order because such an order is a matter of discretion, and questions of culpability may be relevant to this.

17.65 If the offender does not qualify for a disposal under the MHA 1983, or it is decided that a custodial sentence should be imposed, mental disorder may be relevant in assessing whether the seriousness of the offence means that the custodial threshold is passed. This may occur because it may take the seriousness back below that level by making the offence less serious if it occurred in the context of mental disorder: if there was a direct or indirect link between the offending and the disorder, it can be seen as less serious. In addition, and irrespective of any link between the disorder and the offence, the existence of mental disorder may provide personal mitigation that reduces the final conclusion on seriousness. Even if the custodial threshold is still passed, mental disorder may mean that the length of the sentence should be reduced to reflect either the role of mental disorder in the offending or the additional impact that a sentence will have in light of mental disorder.

17.66 One entirely pragmatic point should be noted as well, which is that if the defendant has spent time in detention in hospital prior to sentence, perhaps being assessed for a possible hospital order that is not then imposed, the time spent in detention under the MHA 1983 should be taken into account in setting the length of any custodial sentence: see CJA 2003 ss240 and 242, the latter section including detention under MHA 1983 ss35, 36, 38 and 48 as being time in custody for which credit should be given under CJA 2003 s240. There should be nothing to prevent a judge taking into account any time placed under the civil provisions after arrest: but see *R v Belford*,[54] in which it was held that it was not a factor that had to be taken into account because the civil detention would have occurred in any event. However, it would be strange if detention for the same purpose under section 36 should count but an alternative approach using section 3 detention should not.

17.67 The Court of Appeal often makes the point that sentencing turns largely on the facts; that may also apply to interventions by the Court of Appeal, which is supposed to intervene in relation to a sentence when it is wrong in principle or manifestly excessive. However, it is apparent that the Court of Appeal has often taken the view that it is able to intervene even if the sentence imposed by the court below is not open to criticism: many examples of this exist, which demonstrate that the Court of Appeal may be seen as providing a supplemental and second consideration of the discretion that exists in relation to sentencing. These examples are important because even though the question of sentence may be one that turns on the facts, there is the countervailing consideration that like cases should be treated alike and so the willingness of the Court of Appeal to intervene creates a legitimate expectation of similar treatment. What may be seen as a sub-group of instances of the Court of Appeal intervening even though there was no error in the approach of the sentencing judge, there are many instances where updated evidence has allowed a different sentence to be imposed. This latter point is considered in two contexts: first, the normal process of an appeal, which is discussed here; the second context is appeals out of time, which may involve separate questions and which are discussed in chapter 21.

Examples of the Court of Appeal correcting sentencing judges

17.68 An example of the Court of Appeal taking a different view from a trial judge is *R v Sippings*,[55] which involved a conviction for voyeurism by a man with mental health issues. The voyeurism had a number of aggravating features, in that it had continued over a number of years and the victim was a teenage girl, who had been photographed in her bedroom: some of the photos were taken when she was still a child and so charges of taking indecent photographs of a child were also involved. The judge imposed an extended sentence under PCC(S)A 2000 s85 which consisted of nine months' imprisonment and an

54 [2000] MHLR 198.
55 [2008] EWCA Crim 46, [2008] MHLR 90.

extension period of three years. The medical evidence available to the judge noted that Mr Sippings had been treated as an in-patient for severe anxiety and agoraphobia, and that a custodial sentence would have an adverse impact on his mental state; updated evidence for the Court of Appeal outlined his anxiety in prison and indicated that he was not coping well. The appeal court took the view that the medical reports revealed a sad, lonely man with mental health difficulties who was in need of continuing psychiatric help. It set aside the custodial sentence as not being necessary and substituted a community rehabilitation order with requirements to attend sex offender work, receive mental health treatment and not communicate with the victim. This could be characterised as the Court of Appeal determining that the judge had erred in principle because he had not taken proper account of the reasoning behind the offending, which the medical evidence showed was mental disorder and so not something that passed the custodial threshold.

17.69 Another example of the Court of Appeal reaching a different conclusion from the sentencing judge that could be seen as in reality a different exercise of discretion is *R v Shane Lewis*.[56] Here, the offender had several recent convictions for offensive weapons or bladed instruments: as a result of these, he was subject to a suspended sentence with supervision and mental health requirements. When he came to be sentenced for a further offensive weapon charge, which the expert evidence characterised as a cry for help in the context of defaulting on treatment and taking steps to seek to be arrested, the judge noted that his only choices were a hospital order or a custodial sentence: as the former was not available on the facts, he held that the latter was inevitable and so he imposed a custodial sentence and activated the suspended sentence. The Court of Appeal determined that the proper sentence was a community sentence with conditions to protect the public. While this could be characterised as an instance of the judge making an error of law if he felt that custody was the only response once a suspended sentence had been passed, judicial comments on sentencing are not statutes and so should be read sensibly, and so the sentencing remarks could properly be seen as the judge indicating that his view of further offending after a suspended sentence realistically meant that custody was the proper sentence.[57]

56 [2010] EWCA Crim 133, [2010] MHLR 70.

57 Equally, in *R v Briscoe* [2010] EWCA Crim 373, [2010] MHLR 92, there was a relatively minor breach of a non-molestation order after a significant period of compliance with it, by a patient who was mentally ill and generally compliant with treatment and support. The judge sentenced him to six months'

17.70 See also *R v Mukendi*,[58] in which the Court of Appeal quashed a suspended sentence of 30 weeks for theft of a car, and replaced it with a community order with similar requirements, including a mental health requirement, relying on the fact that Mr Mukendi had spent three months on remand, which equated to a six-month custodial sentence, but which would not count in the future if the suspended sentence was activated. The Court of Appeal found that the custodial length was difficult to justify in that context.

17.71 The Court of Appeal may also intervene in situations in which the sentence is wrong in principle because the sentencing court has created a legitimate expectation that a particular sentence would be imposed but then imposes a more serious one. An example of this in a mental health context is *R v Chapman*.[59] This was a challenge to a sentence of detention imposed for a significant sexual assault by a young offender with various developmental disorders who had been under the influence of alcohol at the time. The judge had on various occasions allowed steps to be taken to refer Mr Chapman to specialist facilities, including various adjournments necessitated while practical steps were being taken: Mr Chapman co-operated and was in treatment by the time of being sentenced. The judge had indicated that a custodial sentence was required because a hospital order could not be imposed as Mr Chapman did not need in-patient treatment. The Court of Appeal held that the sentence both breached a legitimate expectation that a sentence would be imposed that allowed the treatment regime to continue, as it had been time-consuming to set it up, and that it was manifestly excessive. The reasons for the latter conclusion were based on Mr Chapman's age, previous good character, early plea and his co-operation with and response to the assessments carried out. The Court of Appeal determined that the proper sentence was a community order requirements of supervision and mental health treatment for two years, and also an order not to contact the victim.

imprisonment less time on remand, which equated to three months: the Court of Appeal overturned this, holding that the custodial threshold was not passed in the light of the time spent in custody. It imposed a community sentence, including with a mental health requirement, concurrent with one to which he was already subject. Again, offending in the context of an existing supervision order may seem to be a proper basis for concluding that the custodial threshold is met, even for a less serious offence: so this can be seen as an example of the Court of Appeal simply taking a different view without necessarily finding a standard basis for intervention.

58 [2010] EWCA Crim 280, [2010] MHLR 90.

59 [2010] EWCA Crim 565, [2010] MHLR 102.

17.72 These are examples of the Court of Appeal substituting a different kind of sentence. What may be more common is for the court to find that the relevant threshold was passed but that the judge had overstated the level of seriousness and so erred in the quantum of sentence. A recent example of this is *R v Orchard*,[60] which involved sexual offending by one patient in a psychiatric unit against another patient; a sentence of two years' imprisonment was reduced to 18 months to reflect both that the judge had placed the offence too high on the scale and had not given adequate account of Mr Orchard's mental disorder.

17.73 A judge may also err by imposing too light a sentence, which the prosecution may appeal on grounds of undue leniency. It has been determined that the existence of a mental disorder may be a reason for the Court of Appeal not to increase a custodial sentence even though it was unduly lenient. This happened in *R v Khan, Khan and Khan*,[61] in which a woman convicted of people smuggling and sentenced to three years' imprisonment was found to have been sentenced unduly leniently. The proper sentence, held the Court of Appeal, was five years' imprisonment: in relation to Mrs Khan's co-defendants, the sentence was increased from three to four years (with a discount to reflect the double jeopardy element of allowing a prosecution appeal) but not in her case, even though her mental disorder (a fluctuating depression) was held not to be sufficient to justify a hospital order.

Examples of the Court of Appeal exercising its discretion

17.74 There are a number of instances also where mental health problems have caused the Court of Appeal to determine that a sentence should be amended even though there was nothing wrong with it. For example, in *R v Ball*,[62] a sentence of four months' imprisonment, suspended for two years, with a mental health treatment requirement and a two-year supervision requirement was replaced with a community order with a two-year supervision requirement and a mental health treatment requirement. The offence was of causing danger to road users by removing road closed signs, the circumstances being a depressed off-duty police officer who had taken anti-depressant and sleeping tablets beyond the recommended dose and had consumed alcohol. The Court of Appeal commented that the sentence imposed was not wrong in principle, but it nevertheless quashed it as an act of mercy.

60 [2010] EWCA Crim 1538, [2010] MHLR 212.
61 [2010] EWCA Crim 2880, [2011] MHLR 14
62 [2007] EWCA Crim 3099, [2008] MHLR 48.

17.75 Another example of this is *R v Airey*:[63] the offence here was aggravated arson, the victims being Ms Airey's parents, who had returned home to discover the fire and extinguished it (such that, perhaps fortuitously little damage was done). She had problems with alcohol abuse and depression and the offence occurred after she had mixed alcohol and tablets. The medical reports available for the sentencing judge concluded that there was a significant risk of self-harm and of further similar reoffending; it was also noted that there were shortages of provision for the relevant treatment she required. The judge rejected a recommended community order and imposed a prison sentence of three years and nine months, which he had reduced in the light of Ms Airey's mental health problems. The Court of Appeal indicated that the sentence was right in principle – but it pointed to a number of features that put the offence towards the bottom-end of the scale of seriousness, noted that she had been in custody for over ten months and that this had meant that her children might end up homeless, and that her psychiatric condition could be treated in the community, and quashed the prison sentence. The sentence substituted was a community order with several conditions, including an alcohol treatment requirement and an order not to approach her parent's house. Again, the Court of Appeal suggested that it was exercising a discretion in this regard rather than correcting an error by the judge.

Examples of the Court of Appeal responding to updated medical evidence

17.76 Cases such as *Sippings*, described above, show the value of updated medical or other evidence. Similarly in *R v Peltier*,[64] a defendant who had committed three street robberies had a custodial sentence of 54 months set aside: the Court of Appeal commented that the time he had already spent in custody, nine months,[65] together with the progress he had made in relation to accepting the need for treatment for mental disorder and avoiding cannabis, meant that a three-year community order with supervision for its entire time and mental health treatment for 18 months could offer better protection to the public. The Court of Appeal also added a curfew order for three months, which could be seen as partly punitive but also of assistance

63 [2009] EWCA Crim 2106, [2009] MHLR 398.

64 [2008] EWCA Crim 3210, [2009] MHLR 130.

65 A feature also in *Airey*, discussed above.

in preventing Mr Peltier from mixing with friends who might encourage him to return to drug abuse and undermine his treatment.

17.77 Another example of the importance of updated medical evidence is *R v Singleton,*[66] in which an offence of aggravated arson led to a sentence of five years' imprisonment on the basis that Mr Singleton committed the offence while withdrawing from alcohol abuse. Although he had a diagnosis of schizophrenia, it was thought that this was under control at the time: subsequent medical evidence, that was available for the Court of Appeal, indicated that there had probably been a relapse in Mr Singleton's medical condition, in part because he had not been taking his medication reliably. The appeal led to the quashing of the prison sentence and the use of a community order with a mental health treatment requirement, the evidence being that he could be managed in the community. It was no doubt significant that the offending seemed on the further evidence to be linked to the disorder not the alcohol abuse.

17.78 In some situations, however, the Court of Appeal may take a pragmatic view of what should happen. A recent example of this is *R v Morris.*[67] This involved an indecent exposure situation, though it was not clear whether there was a sexual element to the offence or a drunken urination; when arrested, he was found to have a knife, which led to a charge of possession of a bladed instrument. The judge imposed 26 weeks' imprisonment for outraging public decency offence, which he felt involved a sexual element, and 12 weeks' consecutive for the knife. By the time the appeal was ready to be heard, based on the judge having no proper basis for finding a sexual aggravation, Mr Morris was transferred to hospital under MHA 1983 ss47/49 (on which see chapter 20), and the prognosis was that he was likely to be in hospital for some time. The Court of Appeal reduced the custodial sentence in the light of the lack of a proper basis for the judge's factual conclusion, but did not impose a hospital order, even though it noted that would probably have been the judge's conclusion had the full medical picture been known, because the section 47 order had the same effect and would lead to him remaining in hospital on release from the custodial sentence.

66 [2008] EWCA Crim 468, [2008] MHLR 104.

67 [2009] EWCA Crim 2211, [2009] MHLR 323.

Example of the Court of Appeal finding that mental disorder is of limited relevance

17.79 There may also be instances in which there is only limited mitigation from mental disorder: for example, in *R v Whitnall*,[68] a mentally-ill man caused death by dangerous driving, which occurred when he was manic and in a psychotic state, which had been triggered by cannabis abuse. Although the sentencing judge indicated that mental illness was a mitigating factor, the sentence imposed was six years' imprisonment, which reflects a high sentence for the offence.[69] The Court of Appeal suggested that as Mr Whitnall was not insane, he knew what he was doing and that it was wrong, and that the fact that he had made an appointment to see a community drug team indicated that he had insight into his problems; it held that the sentence was justified. However, it can be suggested that this is an example of the court taking a very black and white view that is inconsistent with other cases, to Mr Whitnall's bad luck.

Indeterminate sentences and mental disorder

17.80 There are three types of indeterminate sentence:

i) the mandatory life sentence for murder,
ii) the discretionary life sentence for various offences and
iii) the imprisonment (or detention) for public protection sentence introduced by the CJA 2003 (which replaced the automatic life sentence provision introduced by the CDA 1998).

17.81 A common feature of life sentences is that they have two parts to them: there is the life sentence and there is a minimum term that has to be served before consideration can be given to release (which will be on licence and so subject to the possibility of recall). This section will describe first the circumstances in which the different indeterminate sentences may be applied; it will then consider the process of the setting of the tariff period.

68 [2006] EWCA Crim 2292, [2006] MHLR 318.

69 *R v Richardson and others* [2006] EWCA Crim 3186 provides guidelines for sentencing for this offence, and indicates that seven years and above should be reserved for the most serious examples.

Circumstances in which the different indeterminate sentences may be applied

Mandatory life imprisonment for murder

17.82 If a defendant is convicted of murder, the only sentence is a mandatory life sentence.[70] This means that the maximum period of detention is the life of the offender. Other options, including that of imposing a hospital order, are not open, even if the defendant meets the criteria for such a sentence. It will only be possible if the conviction is not for murder: for example, if his or her state at the time of the offence was such that the partial defence of diminished responsibility is open on the facts or a verdict of not guilty by reason of insanity is returned. (There is also the possibility that the defendant is not fit to stand trial and so there is a finding relating to the actus reus only, which may lead to a hospital disposal.) For a defendant convicted of murder who needs to be in hospital, the only route is transfer under MHA 1983 s47; not even the possibility of the court securing this by making use of a hospital direction under section 45A is available.

17.83 This is increasingly difficult to justify because the trend of jurisprudence relating to life sentences has been to equate those imposed for murder and for other offences. So it is now the case that the tariff-setting process is judicialised in relation to all life sentences; and that post-tariff detention or release is controlled by the Parole Board. Historically, the Home Secretary made the decisions on tariffs and release; then, from the CJA 1991, the fixing of the tariff and the release of discretionary lifers was given to the trial judge and the Parole Board respectively; and following from jurisprudence in the European Court of Human Rights, as from the CJA 2003, the judiciary fixes the tariff of a mandatory lifer and the Parole Board determines release. Despite these important mechanics of the life sentence being equated, however, the mandatory outer envelope of the sentence remains fixed at life for a murder conviction.

17.84 As noted, a homicide committed in a situation of diminished responsibility leads to a verdict of guilty of manslaughter and a sentencing discretion. It is possible that a defendant did not allow this partial defence to be run, such that any conviction had to be for

70 Murder (Abolition of Death Penalty) Act 1965 s1. If the offender was under 18 when he or she committed the murder, the sentence is detention at Her Majesty's pleasure (see PCC(S)A 2000 s90); if aged over 18 but under 21 at the date of conviction, the sentence is custody for life (PCC(S)A 2000 s93). So life imprisonment follows if the offender was 18 or over at the time of the offence and 21 or over at the time of conviction.

murder and there was no possibility of anything other than a life sentence. There has in the past existed a mechanism for dealing with mandatory lifers who should have argued diminished responsibility, been convicted of manslaughter and dealt with by way of a hospital order and restriction order: this was the grant of 'technical lifer' status. This is discussed in chapter 21, since the method of dealing with this situation is now to commence an appeal out of time.

Discretionary life sentence

17.85 The discretionary life sentence has existed for many years in relation to offences for which Parliament has fixed the maximum sentence at life imprisonment. It is now incorporated into the dangerous offender provisions noted below, as a result of which it has changed in scope. Originally, it was to be used if an offender committed a serious example of an offence carrying a maximum sentence of life and the evidence was that he or she presented a risk of further serious offending over a time-scale that could not adequately be assessed by the court, such that a determinate sentence could not protect the public.[71]

17.86 Mental disorder associated with ongoing crime alone was not sufficient in the absence of an offence of sufficient gravity. So in *R v Simmonds*,[72] the Court of Appeal quashed a life sentence imposed for an arson by a man found to have a psychopathic disorder that did not meet the criteria for a hospital order: his ongoing risk arose from his disorder, but there were no recommendations for a hospital order after his suitability had been tested through an interim hospital order. The Court of Appeal held that the index offence did not justify a long-enough determinate sentence to make a life sentence proper and substituted a determinate sentence of six years' imprisonment. Naturally, there would also be questions as to why a hospital disposal could not be used: this is discussed in the next chapter, though it is worth commenting that the case of *Simmonds* occurred before the changes to the criteria for a hospital order, which may have made such a disposal more likely because of the removal of the treatability requirements.

71 See *R v Chapman* [2000] 1 CrAppR 77. This built on *R v Hodgson* (1968) 52 CrAppR 113 and *Attorney-General's Ref No 32 of 1996 (Whittaker)* [1997] 1 CrAppR(S) 261.

72 [2001] EWCA Crim 167, [2001] MHLR 54.

Background to the current regime

17.87 The legislature sought for a decade or so to reduce significantly the discretion that existed in relation to those who were assessed as dangerous. There were two steps to this, the first being the automatic life sentence regime, which covered a relatively small number of offences but also took away the power to impose a hospital disposal. The second was the initial dangerous offender sentencing regime of the Criminal Justice Act 2003, which was broader but gave discretion to make use of a hospital order disposal.

Background to the current regime – automatic life sentences

17.88 Under section 2 of the C(S)A 1997, the automatic life sentence regime was introduced: although the statute heading described the sentence as a mandatory life sentence for a second serious offence, it was known as an automatic life sentence to differentiate it from a mandatory sentence for murder. Section 2 required a life sentence for the second conviction for one of a list of several serious offences (all of which carried discretionary life imprisonment)[73] unless there were exceptional circumstances: in effect the discretionary life sentence became a mandatory sentence unless these exceptional reasons could be found.

17.89 In contrast to the language applicable to the various mandatory minimum determinate terms for certain offences, described above, C(S)A 1997 Sch 4 added language to MHA 1983 s37 to the effect that an automatic life sentence was to be treated in the same way as a mandatory life sentence for murder: the power to impose a hospital order was disapplied. When the PCC(S)A 2000 was passed as a consolidation statute, C(S)A 1997 s2 became section 109 of the PCC(S)A 2000. PCC(S)A 2000 Sch 9 para 90 made the necessary amendments to the MHA 1983 to maintain the position excluding a hospital order if the criteria for an automatic life sentence were made out.

73 The offences for England and Wales were set out in C(S)A 1997 s2(5), and were: attempted murder, conspiracy to murder or incitement to murder, soliciting murder (Offences Against the Person Act 1861 s4), manslaughter, wounding causing grievous bodily harm with intent (Offences Against the Person Act 1861 s18), rape or attempted rape, intercourse with a girl under 13 (Sexual Offences Act 1956 s5), possessing a firearm with intent to injure, using a firearm to resist arrest, or carrying a firearm with criminal intent (Firearms Act 1968 ss16, 17 and 18); and robbery using a firearm or imitation firearm within the meaning of that Act. Equivalent offences for Scotland and Northern Ireland were set out in section 2(6) and (7).

17.90 There were human rights based legal challenges both the provisions as a whole and also to the interaction between the statutory provisions and the hospital order regime. The more general challenge was in *R v Offen*,[74] the argument being that there was a risk of disproportionate detention that would be inhuman and degrading and so contrary to article 3 of the ECHR or arbitrary and so contrary to article 5. The Court of Appeal held that the legislation allowing an automatic life sentence to be avoided on a finding of exceptional circumstances should be construed so as to avoid these potential problems (by way of the interpretive obligation in section 3 of the Human Rights Act 1998, namely to follow any possible interpretation that avoided a breach of the ECHR provisions). This required a purposive interpretation rather than one that relied on the ordinary meaning of language: the latter would give a limited set of circumstances in which a life sentence could be avoided for the commission of a second serious offence. The statutory purpose was identified as the establishment of a norm that those who commit two serious offences are a danger to the public and so should receive a life sentence. This meant that a person would be an exception to the norm if all the relevant circumstances revealed that he or she did not pose an unacceptable risk to the public. Account could be taken of factors such as the time between offences, any different nature of the offences, and also expert evidence (risk assessments from psychiatrists having been used in some of the cases that were argued together on this appeal).

17.91 It was possible that mental disorder might be a relevant factor in this assessment. So, in *R v Newnham*,[75] after concluding that the fact that a defendant was suffering from acute mental illness at the time of the offence was not by itself an exceptional circumstance, it was noted that it might be relevant to risk and so a factor allowing the conclusion that the defendant was not dangerous. On the facts, the attempted armed robbery was carried out with no real competence and no aggression, and so the involvement of mental illness in combination with these features allowed a conclusion that there were exceptional circumstances.

17.92 The question of whether meeting the criteria for a hospital order amounted to exceptional circumstances was also considered in *R v Drew*.[76] The defendant admitted a second serious offence, was found to meet the criteria for the imposition of a hospital order, but

74 [2001] 1 WLR 253, [2000] Prison LR 283.

75 [2000] 2 CrAppR(S) 407.

76 [2003] UKHL 25, [2003] 1 WLR 1213, [2003] MHLR 282.

sentenced to life imprisonment because the judge found that this did not amount to exceptional circumstances. The challenge to this relied on human rights arguments, namely that it amounted to inhuman or degrading punishment to impose a prison sentence on someone who qualified for a hospital order and so breached article 3 of the ECHR. The House of Lords endorsed the view of the Court of Appeal in *R v Offen* that an offender could avoid an automatic life sentence on the grounds of exceptional circumstances if he or she did not constitute a significant risk to the public. This meant that the statutory regime was not in breach of article 3 as the sentence would reflect the need to protect the public and reflect the culpability of the offender; nor would it breach article 5, since the sentence in that situation would not be arbitrary.[77] It was also concluded that a life sentence had advantages in relation to the aim of protecting the public because detention was not limited to matters of risk arising from the medical condition of the defendant, as was the case if detention was under the MHA 1983.

17.93 As to the propriety of imposing punishment when a defendant was mentally disordered, the House of Lords held that while it would be wrong in principle to punish those who were unfit to be tried or were not responsible for their conduct because of insanity, that was not the case in front of it: Mr Drew had admitted a serious offence (causing grievous bodily harm with intent), and the effect of his mental illness was to mitigate rather than absolve him of responsibility. This in turn meant that a sentence of imprisonment could be imposed even where the conditions for the imposition of a hospital order were met (which, it noted, was a matter of discretion not duty).[78] There was a further argument based on the lack of access to medical treatment: but it was held that this failed on the facts because Mr Drew had been transferred to hospital under MHA 1983 s47, and was not shown to have suffered appreciably in the time between admission to prison and transfer to hospital.

17.94 An application was then made to the ECtHR, though only raising article 3: *Drew v UK*.[79] The court found that the distress caused by the deterioration in Mr Drew's condition during the eight days he was

77 It is to be noted that the argument of the appellant was limited to article 3: see paragraph 5 of the opinion of Lord Bingham for the House; article 5 had been relied on as a supplemental argument in the Court of Appeal, where it was dismissed – [2001] EWCA Crim 2861, [2002] MHLR 65.

78 See [2003] UKHL 25, [2003] 1 WLR 1213, [2003] MHLR 282 paras 16 and 17 of the opinion.

79 App No 35679/03, [2006] MHLR 203.

held in a prison medical wing before being transferred to hospital where effective medication was again commenced did not reach the threshold of severity necessary for a finding of a breach of article 3; as such, the complaint was found inadmissible. However, the court gave a hint at what did not appear to have been argued when it commented at paragraph 40:

> The applicant was a convicted offender and has raised no complaint about his place of detention under Article 5§1 (cf *Aerts v Belgium* (1998) 29 EHRR 50 para 46). The Court nonetheless considers it a matter of some concern that the applicant was required by law to be sent immediately to prison, contrary to the opinions of the two psychiatrists who gave evidence at the disposal hearing and to the wishes of the sentencing judge, all of whom expressed the view that a hospital order with a restriction would have been more appropriate.

17.95 The importance of the reference to *Aerts* is that the ECtHR in that case found that there was a breach of article 5(1) when a defendant sentenced to an order of detention in hospital was held for too long in a prison as a place of safety pending the hospital bed becoming available: the principle established was that the place of detention must match the purposes of detention. It is only a short step from that to determine that a defendant must be placed in a detention setting that meets his or her needs: this would mean that if the judge felt that exercise of his or her sentencing powers led to a conclusion that a place in hospital should be ordered, that option should be open. This would be particularly so if the offence was one attributable to mental disorder, which was the situation in *Aerts*. The ECtHR was perhaps hinting in *Drew* that article 5 would have been a more fruitful line of complaint. It seems that the hint was taken when the automatic life sentence provisions were replaced.

Background to the current regime – the initial dangerous offender provisions

The dangerous offender sentencing provisions as enacted

17.96 The PCC(S)A 2000 s109 was repealed when the dangerous offender provisions of CJA 2003 ss224–236[80] were brought into effect in April 2005.[81] At the same time, CJS 2003 s302 and Sch 32 para 8 amended MHA 1983 s37 in the following significant ways:

80 CJA 2003 Part 12 Chapter 5.

81 Criminal Justice Act 2003 (Commencement No 8 and Transitional and Saving Provisions) Order 2005 SI No 950.

i) the language relating to the automatic life sentence regime taking precedence over the making of a hospital order was omitted: it was not replaced by language making the hospital order subservient to the new (and extended) regime for the disposal of dangerous offenders that replaced the automatic life sentence regime; and
ii) MHA 1983 s37(1A) was amended, making it plain that nothing in those dangerous offender sentencing provisions or any other minimum term provisions prevented the making of a hospital order.

17.97 The dangerous offender provisions rested initially on a list of 'specified offences', over 150 sexual or violent offences which carried imprisonment of at least two years; those with a maximum sentence of ten years or more are 'serious offences'. CJA 2003 Sch 15 lists the relevant offences. As originally enacted, there were two main elements to the regime for those convicted of a specified offence: first, the court had to carry out an assessment of dangerousness. Then; if there was a finding of dangerousness, the court had to impose either an indeterminate sentence if the offence was a serious specified offence committed by an adult and otherwise an extended sentence. For those under 18, an extended sentence was possible for a serious offence also. In relation to adults, the preservation of the hospital order option was effectively the only discretionary power that was available on the finding of dangerousness to avoid the imposition of some form of custodial sentence with a protective element to it.

17.98 Dangerousness is made out if there is a significant risk to members of the public of serious harm occasioned by the commission of further specified offences. The definition of 'serious harm' in CJA 2003 s224(3) is 'death or serious personal injury, whether physical or psychological'. The process of determining whether this test is made out is set out in section 229 and initially was as follows:

i) If it was a first specified offence, or the offender was under 18 (even if the offender had committed more than one specified offence), the court had to take account of the nature and circumstances of the offence, and could take into account any pattern of behaviour or information about the offender: section 229(2).
ii) If it was second conviction and the offender was aged 18 or over, the court was required to assume that the dangerousness test was met unless that would be unreasonable in the light of the nature and circumstances of each of the offences involved and any pattern of offending, and any information about the offender. This was similar to the automatic sentence provisions introduced

in the C(S)A 1997 (though in different language, and, it is to be noted, the presumption arose from the commission of a second specified offence, not a second serious such offence, and so it was much broader in scope than the C(S)A 1997); the first part of the test, however, involved just one offence and an assessment of dangerousness.

17.99 There are two types of indeterminate sentence for adults, and two equivalents for those under 18, which are available to deal with a finding of dangerousness after the commission of a serious specified offence. The first is the discretionary life sentence or detention for life for those under 18; the other is the new sentence of imprisonment for public protection or detention for public protection for those under 18. See CJA 2003 ss225 and 226. The discretionary life sentence would be used if the criteria for such a sentence were met in light of the 'seriousness of the offence, or of the offence and one or more offences associated with it';[82] otherwise, an adult had to receive 'imprisonment for public protection'. In the case of those under 18, an indeterminate sentence could be avoided if an extended sentence would be adequate to protect the public from the risk identified: section 226(3). (The extended sentence provisions are described above: see paras 17.52–17.59.)

Guidance on the dangerous offender provisions as enacted

17.100 The new regime for dangerous offenders was subject to significant guidance in several cases. One question arising was the choice between indeterminate terms, namely the life sentence or the new public protection sentence. In *R v Kehoe*[83] the Court of Appeal noted that the effect of the availability of a public protection sentence was that a life sentence was not necessary to protect the public if a sentence of imprisonment for public protection could be imposed. That in turn meant that a life sentence should be reserved for cases where the culpability of the offender was particularly high or the offence was particularly grave, and so made it more limited than it had been before.

17.101 On the assessment of dangerousness and the test on the merits for such a finding, the starting point is *R v Lang*.[84] Guidance was given as to three elements of the test of dangerousness, namely what sort of risk is significant, what sort of harm is serious, and who is to be

82 The assessment of the seriousness of the offence is discussed in chapter 16.

83 [2008] EWCA Crim 819, [2009] Prison LR 353.

84 [2005] EWCA Crim 2864, [2006] 1 WLR 2509, [2006] 2 Prison LR 98.

protected. The Court of Appeal noted that a significant risk requires more than a mere possibility of its occurrence: the court adopted the Oxford Dictionary definition of 'noteworthy, of considerable amount or importance'. It also noted that the definition of serious harm, and its inclusion of psychological harm, was well-known and case-law arising from the CJA 1991 would continue to apply, including, for example, that serious psychological injury could arise from sexual assaults that involved minor physical harm.[85] The group to be protected – 'members of the public' – could include specific members of the public, and particular groups (including prison officers and staff in psychiatric hospitals); it was also noted that the term was wider than a descriptor such as 'others', which would exclude the offender, and so the court implied that a sentence could be imposed to protect against self-harming behaviour.

17.102 The court commented on the application of the test to the nature of the likely offending. If the foreseen further offending was both specified and serious, that would usually meet the risk of serious harm test, but not necessarily: the example given was that robbery could accommodate various factual scenarios, not all of which would involve serious harm. If the foreseen offence was not serious, the court commented that this would rarely meet the test, even if it was likely that there would be frequent such offending.

17.103 The court also noted that the presumption of dangerousness arising from the second specified offence in the case of an adult was a rebuttable presumption and that it could be displaced if there was not a significant risk of serious offending: this is consistent with the approach described above in the *Offen* judgment, namely that a court could find it unreasonable to make the assumption set out in the statute in the absence of a positive finding as to the necessary risk. As Rose LJ put it for the court, 'the language of the statute indicates that judges are expected, albeit starting from the assumption, to exercise their ability to reach a reasonable conclusion in the light of the information before them'.

17.104 The court also formulated guidance as to the procedure to be followed. Not surprisingly, it noted that the assessment of the risk of further offending involved taking account of all relevant features, such as the nature and circumstances of the index offence and any past criminality (details of which had to be provided to the court, though features such as the sentence imposed would be relevant), and whether it revealed a pattern of offending; relevant socio-economic

85 [2005] EWCA Crim 2864, [2006] 1 WLR 2509, [2006] 2 Prison LR 98 para 11.

factors should be assessed, including accommodation, employability, education, associates, relationships and drug or alcohol abuse. The pre-sentence report would usually be the source of information about these matters. Also relevant would be matters such as the offender's thinking process, attitude towards offending and supervision, and his or her emotional state. Such information might be in a pre-sentence report, but might be found also in medical reports. However, the court suggested that medical reports might only be necessary for a proper risk assessment in a small number of cases, namely those where mental abnormality was suggested.

17.105 This differential approach to pre-sentence and medical reports is no doubt consistent with the statutory language as to procedures to be followed: CJA 2003 s156 requires a pre-sentence report before a custodial sentence is imposed, but not if the court concludes that such a step is unnecessary; in contrast, a medical report is only necessary, pursuant to CJA 2003 s157, if the defendant appears to be mentally disordered and then the report is aimed at the question of the impact of the sentence on the treatment available rather than on questions of dangerousness. However, there is clearly a discretion as to the obtaining of medical reports, and the suggestion in *Lang* as to this being limited merits two comments. First, in the light of what is at stake, it is hardly disproportionate to request that medical reports be provided in all cases (at least unless there is a good reason). Second, the assessment of dangerousness, or risk assessment in general, is a matter on which forensic psychiatrists and forensic psychologists specialise, and in relation to which there has been a significant amount of research in recent years. It is worth noting that in some other jurisdictions that have similar preventive detention regimes, medical reports are essential before preventive detention is imposed. For example, the New Zealand sentence of preventive detention, which rests on a finding of a 'significant and ongoing risk to the safety' of the community cannot be imposed without medical reports;[86] and Australian statutes such as the Dangerous Prisoners (Sexual Offenders) Act 2003 in Queensland or the Crimes (Serious Sex Offenders) Act 2006 in New South Wales have similar requirements.[87] While the CJA 2003 is different in that Parliament has not made medical reports an express requirement, the important point

86 Sentencing Act 2002 (New Zealand) ss87 and 88.

87 Section 8 of the Queensland statute (Dangerous Prisoners (Sexual Offenders) Act 2003) requires a judge to order psychiatric examinations if satisfied that there are 'reasonable grounds for believing the prisoner is a serious danger to the community' unless a preventive order is made; the NSW statute, which

to note is that the purpose of considering medical reports is to obtain full information on a question on which appropriate expertise can be brought to bear; and the fact that this purpose has led to express requirements as to medical reports in some jurisdictions but not in England and Wales does not undermine the importance of making sure that judges are adequately informed.

17.106 The CJA 2003 does not require medical reports from the fields of forensic psychiatry or forensic psychology that are usually associated with expertise in risk assessment. However, the probation service (and the prisons) have a standard tool, the OASys.[88] The Court of Appeal has been reluctant to extend to endorse what may seem to be obvious rights in relation to a criminal justice system based on adversarial cross-examination. In *R v Boswell*,[89] a challenge to a decision to impose imprisonment for public protection failed. One ground of challenge was to the OASys conclusion as to risk: Dyson LJ set a singularly non-interventionist approach when he commented: 'Those tools are no doubt the product ... of a good deal of research and provide a satisfactory basis for reaching conclusions of the kind that were reached in this case'.[90]

17.107 Indeed, in an earlier case, *R v S and others*[91] the Court of Appeal commented that, in relation to a challenge to a risk assessment in a pre-sentence report:

> It is only likely to be in very rare cases that it will be incumbent on a judge to permit the author of a pre-sentence report to be cross-examined in relation to assessment of seriousness. It is, of course, open to counsel to make submissions about the contents of a report in relation to a defendants' history of criminal offending and all other material matters.[92]

17.108 The Court of Appeal in *Lang* also provided a reminder of the fact that the sentencing judge had to make the final decision, commenting of expert reports that: 'The sentencer will be guided, but not bound by, the assessment of risk in such reports'. However, the need for fairness

relates to post-sentence supervision, requires a medical report to accompany the application (section 6).

88 For more information on this, see paragraph 4.90 and following of Creighton and Arnott, *Prisoners: law and practice*, LAG, 2009; see also Prison Service Order (PSO) 2205, *Offender assessment and sentence management*, available at www.justice.gov.uk/offenders/psos.

89 [2007] EWCA Crim 1587.

90 [2007] EWCA Crim 1587 at para 12.

91 [2005] EWCA Crim 3616, [2006] 2 Prison LR 119.

92 [2005] EWCA Crim 3616, [2006] 2 Prison LR 119 at para 100.

was reiterated: 'A sentencer who contemplates differing from the assessment in such a report should give both counsel the opportunity of addressing the point'. It was also commented that reasons for decisions should usually be given,[93] so as to identify the information taken into account. Also specifically noted was the option of making use of a disposal under the MHA 1983 if the relevant criteria were met.

17.109 *Lang* was supplemented in further cases, including some that there were more risk-averse than the tenor of *Lang*. For example, in *R v Johnson*,[94] the Court of Appeal noted that the absence of previous convictions did not preclude a finding of dangerousness, that previous convictions for non-specified offences could be relevant and significant, for example if they showed a pattern of escalating seriousness, and that the absence of harm in the index offence might be a matter of luck and could not prevent a finding of risk of causing serious harm in the future. This clearly undermined any suggestion that might be raised after *Lang* that minor offending in the index offence or the past made it unlikely that a finding of dangerousness would be made. One additional comment from *Johnson* is of particular importance for mentally disordered offenders. Sir Igor Judge P noted that features such as:

> ... inadequacy, suggestibility, or vulnerability ... may serve to mitigate the offender's culpability. In the final analysis however they may also serve to produce or reinforce the conclusion that the offender is dangerous. In one of the instant cases it was suggested that the sentence was wrong because an inadequate offender had suffered what was described as an 'aberrant moment'. But, as experience shows, aberrant moments may be productive of catastrophe. The sentencer is right to be alert to such risks of aberrant moments in the future, and their consequences.[95]

17.110 Unfortunately, the court did not go on to emphasise the importance of a disposal by way of hospital order (though on the facts none of the defendants whose cases were being considered were suitable for a hospital order).

93 As was required in general in relation to sentencing decision by reason of CJA 2003 s174(1)(a).

94 [2006] EWCA Crim 2486, [2007] 1 WLR 585, [2006] 2 Prison LR 159.

95 [2006] EWCA Crim 2486, [2007] 1 WLR 585, [2006] 2 Prison LR 159 at para 10(iv).

The current regime

The problems caused by the dangerous offender provisions as enacted

17.111 In practice, the dangerous offender sentencing provisions caused significant problems, in particular because large numbers of people were given indeterminate sentences with a short tariff to reflect the relatively minor nature of the index offending. The problem was that such people might be released on licence fairly speedily, but this could only be done if the Parole Board were satisfied that they could be released without undue risk to the public (ie the obverse of the test for the imposition of the sentence). The Board could not make such a finding in practice unless the prisoner had undertaken appropriate courses and interventions designed to reduce the risk to an acceptable level.[96]

17.112 However, this was not happening. The extent of the problem was made plain in *R (Walker and James) v Secretary of State for Justice*,[97] in which it was held by the Court of Appeal that the failure to provide adequate resources to allow those made subject to such sentences to undertake offending-behaviour work to demonstrate that their risk had been reduced by the time their cases were considered by the Parole Board was irrational. This conclusion was not appealed when the case proceeded to the House of Lords (on a question relating to ECHR article 5).[98]

Amendment to the dangerous offender sentencing provisions

17.113 Amendments were made to the regime by sections 13–18 of the CJIA 2008 as from 14 July 2008 by reason of the Criminal Justice and Immigration Act 2008 (Commencement No 2 and Transitional and Saving Provisions) Order 2008.[99] In short:

a) The presumption as to the existence of dangerousness if a defendant was convicted of a second specified offence was removed.
b) The duty to impose at least imprisonment for public protection for a serious specified offence by an adult on the finding of dangerousness became a matter of discretion and one that arose only if the offender had a previous conviction for one of 22 more

96 Tariff setting and release is described below.

97 [2008] EWCA Civ 30, [2008] 1 WLR 1977, [2008] Prison LR 63.

98 *R (James, Lee and Wells) v Secretary of State for Justice* [2009] UKHL 22, [2009] 2 WLR 1149, [2009] Prison LR 371.

99 SI 2008 No 1586. For guidance from the Court of Appeal on the amended regime, see *R v C and others* [2008] EWCA Crim 2790, [2009] Prison LR 353.

serious specified offences (including inchoate or party liability for those offences) listed in CJIA 2008 Sch 4 (and added as Schedule 15A to the CJA 2003) or the tariff set to reflect the seriousness of the index offence and associated offending was at least two years (before any credit for time in custody). In relation to a defendant under 18, the latter condition applies irrespective of the nature of any previous offending.

c) The ambit of the extended sentence for adults was widened: it now covers serious specified offences as well (as it always did in relation to those aged under 18 if there is no need for an indeterminate sentence) and is discretionary, that discretion turning on whether there is a previous conviction for one of the grave offences in Schedule 15A or the custodial part of the sentence is at least four years.[100] In addition, the length of the extension period is now a matter for the discretion of the court, without the limitations of the previous section 227(4).

d) The extension of the scope of the extended sentence in turn means that an indeterminate sentence is only necessary if an extended sentence would not achieve appropriate public protection.

The dangerous offender provisions and mental disorder

17.114 The current legislative regime involves a mandatory life sentence for murder and two forms of discretionary indeterminate sentence if an offender commits a serious specified offence and is assessed to be dangerous. In relation to murder, if mental disorder does not amount to diminished responsibility or contribute to a loss of control defence so as to reduce the conviction to murder, it is of no relevance to the imposition of the life sentence. However, it may be relevant to the setting of the tariff, described below. In relation to discretionary life sentences, mental disorder may be relevant in two ways. In the first place, it may be a feature that supports the necessary finding of dangerousness as to the future. But, second, it may be a reason that allows the court to avoid a custodial sentence because the statutory regime now provides that a hospital order may be made. However, it is to be noted that the criteria for the imposition of a hospital order involve a finding that it is the most suitable disposal: as such, there

100 These preconditions are the same as those applicable to an indeterminate sentence, since a four-year custodial sentence will lead to a two-year tariff, since a tariff involves halving the notional determinate term: this is because parole eligibility in relation to a determinate term arises at the half-way point of the sentence, but only at the end of a tariff period, and so the tariff set has to be halved to have the same effect.

is a matter of judgment. The relevance of custodial alternatives to the hospital order is discussed in the next chapter.

17.115 There may be a pragmatic reason to impose a custodial sentence, namely a refusal by the defendant to co-operate with the necessary investigation and report-writing that might lead to a hospital disposal. A recent example of this is *R v Maynard*.[101] This involved a patient of long-standing, who killed another patient, was convicted of murder at trial but had a conviction for manslaughter on the grounds of diminished responsibility put in place by the Court of Appeal on the basis of further evidence. The Court of Appeal adjourned the case: although the medical evidence before the court had dealt with the need for a hospital disposal, no bed had been identified and so a hospital order could not be put in place. But Mr Maynard refused to co-operate with any assessment, his belief being that he would be released earlier if made subject to a prison sentence. The Court of Appeal indicated that there was no practical alternative but to impose a sentence for public protection purposes, as the evidence demonstrated dangerousness: this was shown by the fact that the doctors had recommended a restriction order accompany any hospital order. It considered that this should be a life sentence because the offence was grave, the victim had been vulnerable and the killing had been planned and then efforts had been made to conceal the weapon used.

Tariff setting

The structure of a life sentence

17.116 A life sentence is in two parts. There is an outer envelope, namely the life of the defendant. There is then a mechanism for determining how much of that is served in custody. An initial period must be served for the purposes of punishment and deterrence (namely the more usual components of a sentence); thereafter, unless the crime was very exceptional and required a whole life tariff, the defendant will remain in custody for preventive purposes if necessary. This may be for the remainder of his or her life. If released, he or she will be on licence for the remainder of his or her life, which brings with it the possibility of recall to prison for further preventive detention until a further decision is made as to release. A sentence of imprisonment or detention for public protection is an indeterminate sentence and so has the same structure: there is one difference, namely that if the

101 [2010] EWCA Crim 2854, [2011] MHLR 93.

detainee is released on licence, it is possible for the licence to be cancelled after ten years (and so it is possible that the outer envelope will not be the life of the defendant).

The release provisions

17.117 The release provisions are found in section 28 of the C(S)A 1997. Release depends on the Parole Board finding that the risk posed by the prisoner no longer requires detention. The test is in section 28(6): a direction for release can be made only if the Board 'is satisfied that it is no longer necessary for the protection of the public that the prisoner should be confined'. However, the Board will not consider the case unless the prisoner makes an application, and that possibility does not arise until after the prisoner has served the minimum term set.

The judicialisation of tariff-setting

17.118 In the past, the Home Secretary was the one who fixed the tariff and determined release, though taking advice from the Parole Board. Gradually, the whole process has been judicialised. The CJA 1991 allowed sentencing judges to fix tariffs in discretionary lifer cases and the Board to release. Eventually, the CJA 2003 extended this to mandatory lifers: during the intervening period, it had been suggested that the mandatory life sentence was different in that it marked punishment for the offence and so questions such as setting of tariffs and release were matters of the administration of the sentence rather than anything that attracted ECHR articles 5 and 6. However, caselaw developed in the ECtHR and the domestic courts considering the ECHR: the revised conclusions were that article 6 required that a judge fix the tariff and that article 5(4) required that a judicial body consider whether any grounds for preventive detention continued to apply in relation to all life sentences, including those for murder.

17.119 The key domestic decision was that of the House of Lords in *R (Anderson) v Secretary of State*[102] to the effect that ECHR article 6 meant that the regime whereby the minimum term for a mandatory sentence was fixed by the Home Secretary and the judicial input was the making of recommendations by the trial judge and the Lord Chief Justice[103] was incompatible with the need to have sentencing

102 [2002] 2 UKHL 46, [2003] 1 AC 837, [2003] Prison LR 36.

103 See Practice Direction (Criminal Proceedings: Consolidation) [2002] 1 WLR 2870 para 49.

decisions made by the judiciary. This was the corollary of the ECtHR's finding in *Stafford v UK*[104] that release had to be determined by a body such as a Parole Board to comply with article 5(4), reversing earlier conclusions to the effect that the mandatory life sentence meant that the offender had no further rights under article 5 because of the nature of the sentence and so any release, being purely discretionary, could be left to the Executive.

17.120 In *Anderson*, Lord Bingham noted that *Stafford* relied on the development of practice in England and Wales – setting punitive tariffs and then releasing on the basis of a risk assessment – that meant that life sentence for murder could not be regarded as entirely punitive, such that fixing the tariff was a sentencing exercise. The situation was that: 'The tariff, which reflects the individual circumstances of the offence and the offender, represents the element of punishment'.[105] In endorsing this in *Anderson*, Lord Bingham accepted that 'the fixing of a convicted murderer's tariff, whether it be for the remainder of his days or for a relatively short time only, involves an assessment of the quantum of punishment he should undergo'.[106] The regime as to release then in place, in C(S)A 1997 s29, leaving the final decision to the Home Secretary after a recommendation by the Board, was found incompatible with the ECHR.

The current statutory provisions for murder

17.121 The government quickly remedied the problem identified in *Anderson*. As from 18 December 2003, anyone convicted of murder has the tariff set by the trial judge. However, the Secretary of State persuaded Parliament to include significant elements of guidance for the judiciary. So, CJA 2003 s269 requires the trial judge to specify a minimum term unless the seriousness of the offence prevents it (because a whole life tariff is appropriate). In setting the terms, the judge is required to take into account the categorisation of the seriousness of the murder, which is contained in Schedule 21 to the Act. This sets out three categories: normal seriousness, particularly high (eg two or more victims) and exceptionally high (eg two or more victims and sadistic conduct); it also sets out aggravating and mitigating features. The starting point for the three bands is 15 years, 30 years and whole life, with the final decision turning on the aggravating and

104 (2002) 35 EHRR 32, [2002] Prison LR 181.
105 (2002) 35 EHRR 32, [2002] Prison LR 181 para 79.
106 [2002] 2 UKHL 46, [2003] 1 AC 837, [2003] Prison LR 36 para 24.

mitigating features. These starting points apply to adults; there is a lesser scale for those under 18.

17.122 Mental disorder is specifically listed in paragraph 11(c) to the Schedule as a potential mitigating factor. It refers to 'the fact that the offender suffered from any mental disorder or mental disability which (although not falling within section 2(1) of the Homicide Act 1957 (c.11)) lowered his degree of culpability'.[107] Also potentially relevant is paragraph 11(d), which refers to matters that amount to provocation (but again not in the sense that allows the formal reduction to a verdict of manslaughter): since this may include an over-reaction caused by a mental disorder, the presence of a mental disorder might be relevant.

17.123 These provisions mean that even though it is not necessary to obtain a medical report when the sentence is fixed by law (see CJA 2003 s157, discussed above), there may be an essential reason to do so if there is an indication that mental disorder may have had some role, because that has to be reflected in the tariff set. Accordingly, it may be a practical necessity to obtain a report.

17.124 In addition to the provisions relating to sentences after the Act came into effect, it was also provided that all existing mandatory lifers could apply to the High Court for a judicial determination of the tariff (replacing the one that had been fixed or setting it for the first time if the Home Secretary had not yet done so). This was slightly more complex because it was accepted that the guidance in Schedule 21 reflected an increase in the likely tariff, and so it could not fall foul of the prohibition on retrospective increases in sentence set out in ECHR article 7. This was achieved by indicating that the tariff could not be increased if fixed and could not exceed the tariff that would likely have been fixed if that had not yet been done.

The regime for discretionary lifers

17.125 For discretionary lifers, the process of the judge setting the minimum term had commenced with the CJA 1991, and the relevant provision became section 82A of the PCC(S)A 2000. The process to be followed is that the judge identifies the term that would have been imposed if a determinate sentence had been possible (the notional determinate term) and then halves that, so as to allow access to the Parole Board at the same time as would have been allowed if a determinate term had been imposed. This was because under section 35 of the CJA 1991, a prisoner serving four years or more could seek parole after one

107 See chapter 14 above.

half of his or her sentence.[108] This reduction reflects the fact that the specified period is a 'real time' sentence which will have to be served in full, unlike determinate custodial sentences where the offender serves half to two-thirds of their sentence.

Public protection sentences

17.126 The sentences of imprisonment and detention for public protection are indeterminate sentences (CJA 2003 ss225(4) and 226(4)). Section 82A of the 2000 Act was applied, subject to an amendment to insert section 82A(4A) to provide that a whole life tariff could not be passed. The reason for this was that the court should impose a discretionary life sentence rather than a public protection sentence in such a situation. The CJA 2003 s230 and Sch 18 made provisions as to release: in effect, the release regime applicable to life sentence prisoners set out in C(S)A 1997 s28 applied as the definition of 'life sentence' in C(S)A 1997 s34 was extended to cover the public protection sentences. The only real difference between a life sentence and a public protection sentence is that the former never expires whereas the latter might be brought to an end if the prisoner has been released and after ten years on licence is judged not to require ongoing supervision: C(S)A 1997 s31(A), inserted by CJA 2003 Sch 18 para 2. The test is whether the Parole Board 'is satisfied that it is no longer necessary for the protection of the public that the licence should remain in force'.

Case-law

17.127 The relevance of mental disorder to the setting of the tariff has been considered in a number of recent cases, including the use of whole life tariffs. One high-profile such case is *R v Coonan (formerly Sutcliffe)*,[109] which related to the multiple murderer dubbed 'the Yorkshire Ripper'. He was convicted of 13 counts of murder committed between 1975 and 1980, after the judge refused to accept pleas of guilty to manslaughter on the basis of diminished responsibility and the jury rejected the partial defence, which was supported by three psychiatric opinions and said to arise from command hallucinations to kill from a 'divine mission' he was given. He also admitted seven

108 It was suggested that the judge could fix a period up to two-thirds of the notional determinate term: *R v M (discretionary life sentence) R v L* [1999] 1 WLR 485 (CA). This was never satisfactory, since it was supposed to be a matter of additional public protection, which was the function of the Board. In practice, the half-way point was invariably used.

109 [2011] EWCA Crim 5, [2011] MHLR 55.

counts of attempted murder. A whole life tariff was set, which the Court of Appeal held was proper. The point argued on appeal was limited to the effect of mental disorder, since it was accepted that the crimes were of the sort that justified a whole life tariff unless mental disorder provided a mitigating feature. There was again supporting medical evidence, since Mr Coonan had been detained in the psychiatric hospital system with an established diagnosis of paranoid schizophrenia since shortly after his trial. His treating psychiatrist provided a report to support the view that this mental disorder was the key to the offending.

17.128 The Court of Appeal, however, decided that the tariff had to be set on the basis that the jury had rejected his account of an illness-based motivation for his offending and so it was not proper for this to be accepted for the purpose of setting the tariff. The court accepted that the rejection by the jury of diminished responsibility did not necessarily mean that there was *not* a mental disorder that reduced culpability: in the light of the number of instances where, as has been noted above, the acceptance of the partial defence has led judges in sentencing to conclude that a defendant retained substantial responsibility, this concession of the vice versa is only fair. However, the court commented that the account at trial on which the rejected expert evidence had depended came from Mr Coonan and the view of his current responsible clinician that his culpability was reduced also depended on that. In addition, the court went through a forensic analysis of a number of reasons why his account had probably been rejected by the jury and stated that it was made no more credible by its repetition in subsequent years. That left the point that the offences in themselves made clear that Mr Coonan was somehow abnormal, but the seriousness of the offending justified the whole life tariff.

17.129 Of course, the significant elephant in the room in the analysis of the Court of Appeal is that Mr Coonan had been detained in the psychiatric system since shortly after his conviction and sentence, with an established diagnosis of paranoid schizophrenia. It is worth noting what this involves: a transfer to hospital and ongoing detention there rests on the Secretary of State being satisfied on expert evidence that there is a mental disorder that requires detention, which has to be reviewed by the judiciary in the form of the Mental Health Review Tribunal and now the First-tier Tribunal.[110] The conclusion of the Court of Appeal implies that the jury saw through attempts to hoodwink them at the trial, and nothing has changed: and so if many

110 See chapter 20 for the account of the process under MHA 1983 s47.

years of psychiatric assessment and treatment on the basis of the diagnosed mental disorder do not amount to a change on which the court can act, that implies that all those involved in ensuring that Mr Coonan remains in a hospital setting have been fooled.

17.130 It is also worth noting that an analysis of the features on which the Court of Appeal rely in concluding that the jury had been right to reject the account of diminished responsibility given at trial reveals that there are various features that do not support the court's view. To give an example, it is noted that Mr Coonan's account in police interview did not explain his 'divine mission': but no basis is given for assuming that a person with paranoid schizophrenia would explain his or her reasoning to the police after arrest, or why it is more likely that a person with mental illness would be consistent in his or her account compared to a person without such an illness. Similarly, the court comments that he had lied to the police; but no basis is given for saying that those who have paranoid schizophrenia do not lie. A further point of the court is to note that there was a conscious decision to move the location of the killings because of police activity in the area of his initial killings: again, what is it that prevents a person with paranoid schizophrenia from realising that he has to avoid the police to continue with his mission? In short, it seems that the Court of Appeal has concluded that the account of paranoid schizophrenia is not credible by applying judicial 'common sense' in an area which is beyond judicial expertise.

17.131 A whole life term was also imposed in the case of *R v Hardy*,[111] who admitted three murders of women who worked as prostitutes, two of whom were dismembered for the purposes of disposal of the bodies. The trial judge had found in a contested facts hearing that two of women had been deliberately killed in the course of sadistic sexual conduct. The medical evidence was that Mr Hardy had a personality disorder, and so had an abnormality of mind: however, the defence did not proceed with a claim of diminished responsibility. Accordingly, the judge proceeded on the basis that he was fully responsible – though he noted that there had subsequently been a finding that he suffered from a schizo-affective disorder of a sort that justified his detention in hospital, which had been upheld by a tribunal, this was not a feature he took into account. Indeed, it is not clear that the judge took into account the accepted personality disorder as a mitigating feature, merely commenting that matters such

111 [2010] EWHC 1064 (QB), [2010] MHLR 324.

as accepting responsibility, pleading guilty and having a personality disorder counted for little in light of the gravity of the offending.[112]

17.132 In contrast, a whole life tariff was set aside and the length of the fixed tariff was reduced on account of mental disorder in *R v Leigers.*[113] This involved a killing by a man who had a past conviction for a diminished responsibility manslaughter; the index offence occurred while he was subject to ongoing supervision, but the jury rejected an argument that his responsibility was diminished and he was convicted of murder. The Court of Appeal found that the judge was wrong to impose a whole life tariff on the basis of the risk posed by Mr Leigers, that being the function of the life sentence: and it held that the appropriate tariff in accordance with the provisions of the CJA 2003 was to be reduced by five years in the light of the mental disorder (from 30 years to 25 years), since it was a mitigating feature even though it did not meet the test for diminished responsibility.[114]

17.133 There have been other instances in which mental disorder has been a mitigating factor in relation to murder convictions:

- In *R v Horton,*[115] a murder occurred in the context of a depressive illness, though it was not such as to diminish his responsibility: the tariff was reduced by two years to 12 years to reflect the mental disorder.
- In *R v Rajesh Kumar Dass,*[116] the judge fixing the tariff on a man who killed three members of his family was also satisfied that there was mitigation arising from mental disorder that had not allowed a conclusion that there was diminished responsibility. On the facts, the tariff was fixed at 15 years.
- In *R v Carpenter,*[117] a tariff was reduced in relation to a woman who instigated a very brutal contract killing and who had a personality disorder arising from childhood abuse, was of impaired intelligence, had suffered a brain injury and was depressed at the time.
- Similarly, in *R v H (Attorney-General's Reference No 126 of 2006),*[118] in raising a tariff on the basis that it was unduly lenient, the Court

112 [2010] EWHC 1064 (QB), [2010] MHLR 324 para 12.

113 [2005] EWCA Crim 802, [2006] MHLR 301.

114 The court then set a tariff of 22 years less time spent on remand because the date of the offence meant that it was necessary to fix the tariff at the level that would have been set before the CJA 2003 came into effect if that was lower.

115 [2006] EWHC 3035 (QB), [2007] MHLR 35.

116 [2006] EWHC 3254 (QB), [2007] MHLR 37.

117 [2006] EWHC 3122 (QB), [2007] MHLR 32.

118 [2007] EWCA Crim 53, [2007] MHLR 64.

of Appeal confirmed that a juvenile defendant convicted of murder who had an adjustment disorder was able to use the disorder to justify a reduced tariff.

17.134 Accordingly, *Coonan* and *Hardy* may involve unusual and extreme instances in which a whole life tariff reflected the particular gravity of the offending; there is certainly a clear line of authority making clear that mental disorder that does not meet the test for diminished responsibility may nevertheless provide mitigation that reduces the level of the tariff.

17.135 It has also been found to be a mitigating feature in relation to manslaughter if a life sentence is imposed. *R v Bryan*[119] involved a defendant who had a diagnosis of schizophrenia, who had a diminished responsibility manslaughter conviction from 1994. His further offences were two further diminished responsibility manslaughters, one of an acquaintance in 2004, who was killed and dismembered by Mr Bryan when he was on leave, and a patient in the hospital to which he had been sent on remand for the first killing. The latter killing was said by Mr Bryan to have had a partly sexual motivation. The trial judge imposed an automatic life sentence (the killings having occurred before the dangerous offender provisions of the CJA 2003 came into effect to replace the automatic life sentence) and fixed a whole life tariff, finding that sadistic and sexual overtones in the killings made them more serious. The tariff was quashed by the Court of Appeal on the basis that, while Mr Bryan's risk meant that he was likely to remain in detention for the rest of his life, the reduction of his culpability by reason of mental disorder was such that the proper tariff was 15 years. The Court of Appeal found that the medical evidence suggested that the mental disorder was the key motivating factor in the offending, and that the aggravating sadism and sexual overtones were in fact symptomatic of the illness.[120]

17.136 The same approach will apply in relation to other offending that may lead to a discretionary life sentence. See, as an instance of this, *R v Jan*,[121] in which the Court of Appeal held that it was appropriate to impose a tariff on a man with mental health problems who had engaged in a sustained campaign leading to serious offences of aggravated arson, so setting aside a judge's failure to impose a tariff;

119 [2006] EWCA Crim 379, [2006] MHLR 197.

120 The existence of the automatic life sentence also prevented discussion in that case of whether it would have been better to make use of a hospital disposal.

121 [2007] EWCA Crim 3223, [2008] MHLR 52.

however the court did not engage in any discussion of whether and how his mental disorder was relevant.

17.137 As has been noted above, the fixing of the tariff controls the minimum period a defendant will have to serve before the possibility of applying for parole release arises: the relevance of mental disorder to treatment in prison is discussed in chapter 20.

CHAPTER 18

Disposals under the Mental Health Act 1983

continued

Introduction

18.1 In chapter 16, the general approach to sentencing was outlined, including the centrality of seriousness and the growth of public protection; and the role of mental disorder was noted. Chapter 17 was concerned with the use of custodial prison sentences. This chapter considers the powers of detention that are available as sentences under the Mental Health Act (MHA) 1983. Under section 37 of the MHA 1983, the powers available to both the Crown Court and the magistrates' court on conviction are the hospital order and the guardianship order;[1] an interim hospital order may be made under section 38. The Crown Court has supplemental powers, namely that of combining the hospital order with a restriction order for purposes of public protection under section 41, which produces a different regime for the management of the patient while in hospital and a different process for discharge, and also that of combining the hospital order with a prison sentence in the form of a hospital and limitation direction under section 45A.

18.2 The significant development in the statutory framework relating to sentencing has included Parliament setting out the purposes of sentencing – in relation to adults, these are: punishment, crime reduction (including by deterrence), reform and rehabilitation, protection of the public and reparation.[2] The existence of mental disorder in a defendant does not mean that the purposes of sentencing cannot apply: it will depend on the circumstances.[3] Equally, it may be possible to secure some of these purposes by way of a hospital order: for example, it may provide for the reduction of crime and the protection of the public by containment, reform and rehabilitation; it may be an order that a defendant does not wish for and so provide deterrence; it may be argued that from the perspective of the defendant, the loss of liberty is something that can be viewed as punitive. While reparation is not a purpose that can be secured by a hospital order, that is hardly served by a prison service either; and there is no prohibition on combining a hospital order with an order to make reparation.

18.3 However, there is no requirement to justify a hospital order by reference to the statutory purposes of punishment, because they do not apply if an order involving detention is made under the MHA

1 The guardianship provisions are considered in chapter 19, along with other non-custodial sentences that have a special mental health component.

2 Criminal Justice Act 2003 s142(1).

3 See chapter 16.

1983.[4] The legislative framework permits the use of a hospital order disposal in all situations where custody might result, save only in relation to the mandatory life sentence for murder. Thus, the mandatory minimum sentences for various offences are subject to an exception allowing a hospital order to be imposed; and the dangerous offender provisions may also be avoided if a hospital order is the better sentence.

18.4 However, because a hospital order is only imposed if it is the most suitable disposal, there is still room for interplay between the question of whether a response in accordance with the purposes of sentencing is the more appropriate sentence.

18.5 This chapter discusses the prerequisites for the imposition of a hospital order and also the questions of judgment and discretion that are involved. It will also consider the issues that arise in relation to the use of the restriction order and the hospital and limitation direction, and outline in more detail the issues that arise in the exercise of judgment as to whether a hospital disposal or one that accords more with the statutory purposes of sentencing should be imposed.

18.6 Statistics indicate that for the past five or so years, around 900 hospital orders are made each year, and more than half of those are combined with restriction orders. Much lower use is made of the interim hospital order, but hardly any use is made of the hospital direction: in 2010–11, which is after the criteria for this order have been extended (as is described below), only one order was made.[5]

Obtaining relevant information

18.7 Part III of the MHA 1983 provides various powers for the criminal courts to obtain information on defendants who have mental health problems. The pre-trial and pre-sentence powers to remand a prisoner for a medical report or for treatment, under MHA 1983 ss35 and 36, have been discussed in chapter 7 above. Also to be noted is

4 MHA 1983 s142(2)(d). See chapter 16 for the discussion of the strange consequences of this.

5 See the National Health Service (NHS) Statistics of October 2011, *Inpatients formally detained in hospitals under the Mental Health Act 1983 and patients subject to supervised community treatment, Annual figures, England 2010/11*, available at www.ic.nhs.uk/statistics-and-data-collections/mental-health/mental-health-act/inpatients-formally-detained-in-hospitals-under-the-mental-health-act-1983-and-patients-subject-to-supervised-community-treatment-annual-figures-england-2010-11.

that section 157(1) of the Criminal Justice Act (CJA) 2003 requires a court to obtain a medical report before passing a custodial sentence if 'the offender is or appears to be mentally disordered'.[6] The report under this section, which can be an oral report, must be provided by a psychiatrist (ie someone approved under section 12 of the MHA 1983 as having expertise in psychiatry),[7] and should provide information of the sort that the court has to take into account under CJA 2003 s157(3), namely the condition and the likely effect of a custodial sentence on the condition and the treatment for it.[8] It is possible that such a report might be more useful if obtained following an assessment in a hospital setting, in which case use can be made of the power under MHA 1983 s35. It is also possible for a defendant to be placed on bail with a condition of co-operation with a medical report:[9] this will be more appropriate if the court has in mind some form of community-based disposal.

18.8 The question of how a court will deal with a defendant's mental disorder will invariably involve two questions: one is what the mental disorder is, and the other will be how can it be dealt with. While it is to be expected that report writers will be able to deal with both questions, there may be a gap in information as to what is available if the report writer is not attached to a suitable provider of treatment, and also how it is to be funded. In case of difficulty about securing the relevant information, MHA 1983 s39 allows the court to order the relevant health service bodies to provide information as to the facilities that are available for the purposes of a hospital order or interim hospital order. This covers both local facilities and those out of the area: the obligation to provide information to the court is limited only by the test of whether the body involved can reasonably obtain the information the court requires. MHA 1983 s39(1B) was added by the MHA 2007 to make it clear that if the defendant is under 18, the

6 This does not arise in relation to a sentence fixed by law, and the court can disapply the requirement if it forms the view that it is unnecessary: CJA 2003 s157(2).

7 CJA 2003 s157(6).

8 Information might also be provided in the pre-sentence report, which has to be provided under CJA 2003 s156: it may be that the information in this report – which could include second-hand information provided following discussion with mental health professionals – might be sufficient to allow the court to form the view that there is no need to obtain a full psychiatric report.

9 Bail Act (BA) 1976 s3(6)(d).

information to be provided includes that relating to facilities suited for that age group.[10]

18.9 The Code of Practice issued under section 118 of the MHA 1983 includes further details on the content of the obligation arising. Part 33 of the English Code notes that primary care trusts should have a specific person who is given the task of responding to requests for information from courts; in part 32 of the Welsh Code, the responsibility is placed on local health boards and the Welsh Ministers as well. Specifically noted in both Codes is the obligation to ensure that prompt assessment is provided so that the trial process can be completed speedily and the most suitable disposal found for the defendant.[11]

18.10 The Codes also provide useful guidance on what should be contained in medical report.[12] So, paragraph 33.8 of the English Code suggests that a doctor asked to give evidence as to a possible admission under Part III of the MHA 1983 is not being asked for a general report but for advice on diversion from prison (through a hospital order or a community order with a mental health treatment requirement, which is discussed in chapter 19). Paragraph 32.4 of the Welsh Code is to similar effect, and goes on in paragraphs 32.12 and 32.15–32.17 to suggest that a report should contain:

i) the data on which it is based;[13]
ii) an explanation of the relationship between the data and the opinion;
iii) an indication of how the opinion is relevant to the issue raised, whether a trial issue or a factor relevant to sentencing, including risk to self and risk of re-offending; if the report is pre-trial, it may

10 See also MHA 1983 s131A, added by MHA 2007 s31, to make arrangements for those under 18: specifically, the managers of hospitals are under a duty to ensure that the environment of a patient under 18 'is suitable having regard to his age (subject to his needs)'. These are known as Child and Adolescent Mental Health Services (CAMHS).

11 English Code para 33.6; Welsh Code para 32.20.

12 See also the discussion of the Probation Bench Handbook in chapter 17 at paras 17.13–17.14.

13 English Code paras 33.9 and 33.11 and Welsh Code para 32.5 note that doctors should obtain documents such as pre-sentence reports, Inmate Medical Records, previous psychiatric reports, and witness statements and information about the offence charged; independent sources of information should be secured (which could come from GP records, previous engagement in psychiatric treatment and patterns of behaviour). It is noted that any gaps in the material available should be recorded in the report.

be appropriate to suggest a further opinion should be obtained after conviction;

iv) if admission to hospital is suggested, there should be an indication of any special treatment or security issues and how they are to be addressed; this may include recommendations that a restriction order be used in conjunction with a hospital order, or that a hospital and limitation direction be made, or that the court consider its power to specify that the hospital order should lead to admission to a particular unit (all of which issues are discussed further in this chapter).[14]

18.11 It should also be noted that the provisions of Part 33 of the Criminal Procedure Rules 2011[15] relating to the duties of expert witnesses and the contents of what should be contained in an expert report also apply. Rule 33.3 is the most important, requiring an expert report to include a statement of truth and a statement that the expert is aware of their duty to assist the court, and to set out the following:

- details of qualifications, experience and accreditation;
- details of any literature or other information relied on;
- a statement of the facts given to the expert 'which are material to the opinions expressed in the report, or upon which those opinions are based'; any facts within the knowledge of the expert must be stated;
- indicate who carried out any examination used for the report, and set out their qualifications, experience and accreditation, and whether the expert was involved in supervising;
- summarise the findings and conclusions, including any qualification on the opinion or any relevant range of opinion, and give reasons.

18.12 Both Codes of Practice also note that doctors should not speculate about guilt or innocence: this suggestion should be recognised as having exceptions in that medical opinions are necessary or permissible in relation to questions of whether a defendant is not guilty by

14 English Code paras 33.15 and 33.18–33.23 are similar. Welsh Code para 32.6 and English Code para 33.10 note that doctors who recommend admission to hospital should have access to a bed or should refer the case to a clinician who does have such access. If this recommendation is made in relation to a person under 18, it is noted that someone with the appropriate specialist knowledge should be involved. Paragraphs 32.7 and 33.12 of the two Codes also note the importance of involving the multidisciplinary team before recommending admission to hospital.

15 SI 2011 No 1709.

reason of insanity or committed a homicide when their responsibility was diminished. While it remains the case that the question of the proper verdict remains one for the jury, who do not have to accept the views expressed by medical experts, opinions on those questions are appropriate.

18.13 It is also worth noting that a doctor preparing a report for court may meet different ethical obligations when compared to the writing of a report in a purely health setting. So paragraphs 33.9 of the English Code and 32.5 of the Welsh Code note that doctors should 'identify themselves to the person being assessed, explain who has requested the report and make clear the limits of confidentiality in relation to the report'. It is also noted that it should be explained that information in reports, including the medical opinion expressed, might also be taken into account if the court decides that a punitive sentence is to be imposed.

18.14 In relation to the potential for a guardianship application, MHA 1983 s39A requires a local authority social services department to provide information about the availabilities and operation of guardianship powers; and how the guardian's powers would be exercised. The Codes of Practice note the need for local authorities to have a named person to respond to requests from the courts about mental health services provided in the community, including under guardianship: see paragraph 32.22 in the Welsh Code and paragraph 33.7 in the English Code. The Codes are wider than the statute.

Interim hospital order

18.15 One of the possibilities noted in paragraph 33.13 of the English Code of Practice and paragraph 32.8 of the Welsh Code is that if a doctor cannot give a confident opinion at the time of sentencing that a hospital order is appropriate, consideration should be given to recommending an interim hospital order. This is a relatively rarely-used power: in the year 2010–11, NHS statistics record 150 admissions under MHA 1983 ss38, 44 and 46, rather than the latter being a now repealed power is unlikely to have counted for much and section 44 being an admission pursuant to a committal by the magistrates to allow the Crown Court to consider a restriction order (which is discussed below).[16]

16 See the National Health Service (NHS) Statistics of October 2011, available at www.ic.nhs.uk/statistics-and-data-collections/mental-health/mental-health-

Criteria

18.16 In relation to those who have been convicted, whether in the Crown Court or in the magistrates' court, and irrespective of age (and so covering adults and children), an interim hospital order can be made under MHA 1983 s38, but only with a view to the making of a hospital order under section 37 of the Act. Also necessary is medical evidence (which can be written or oral) from two doctors, one of whom must be approved under section 12 of the Act as a psychiatrist,[17] that satisfies the court that the offender has a mental disorder and 'there is reason to suppose that the mental disorder from which the offender is suffering is such that it may be appropriate for a hospital order to be made in his case'.[18] There are no specific time limits on the age of the medical evidence, but as has been held in relation to the making of a hospital order (see para 18.47), the statutory test is such that there must be up-to-date medical evidence.

18.17 Evidence that a bed is available is a precondition to the making of an interim hospital order. The time limit for one being available is 28 days.[19] The defendant can be placed in a 'place of safety' in the interim: this will invariably be a prison or other place of detention, but could be a hospital other than that named as the hospital for the interim hospital order.[20] There must also be a link between the hospital where the defendant will be placed on the interim hospital order and the medical evidence given as to the criteria for the making of an order, since one of those giving evidence must be a doctor at the relevant hospital.[21]

18.18 An interim hospital order can also be made if the Crown Court process involves a finding of unfitness to plead but that the defendant committed the actus reus or the special verdict of not guilty by reason

act/inpatients-formally-detained-in-hospitals-under-the-mental-health-act-1983-and-patients-subject-to-supervised-community-treatment-annual-figures-england-2010-11.

17 MHA 1983 s54(1).

18 MHA 1983 s38(1)(b).

19 MHA 1983 s38(4). This is rather than seven days applicable under sections 35 or 36. The information can come from the hospital managers or the responsible clinician (RC), ie the approved clinician who will have the overall responsibility for the treatment. See the discussion at paras 18.48–18.49 below: in relation to a hospital order, the period is mandatory and so placement outside the period is unlawful; the same analysis will apply in relation to a section 38 order.

20 See MHA 1983 s55(1) for the definition of what counts as a place of safety; and Children and Young Persons Act 1933 s107(1) in relation to a child.

21 MHA 1983 s38(3).

of insanity is returned: see section 5A(2) of the Criminal Procedure (Insanity) Act 1964, as amended by section 24 of the Domestic Violence, Crime and Victims Act 2004. But an interim hospital order cannot be made if the magistrates' court makes a finding that the defendant committed the act without going on to convict (as discussed in relation to fitness to participate and findings of insanity in summary proceedings, chapters 10 and 13 above).[22] This may reflect a view that the nature of the offending over which summary jurisdiction is retained is such that it would be disproportionate to engage in making an interim order (particularly as it may last for up to 12 months, as is described below). On the other hand, given that the aim of a hospital order is to ensure that a defendant obtains suitable treatment, and so is not punitive, and the interim hospital order is designed to assess whether a hospital order is needed and can be put into practice, this may be an unfortunate gap in the legislative scheme.

18.19 However, it is a gap that can be filled with some creative use of other provisions. In the first place, under section 11 of the Powers of Criminal Courts (Sentencing) Act (PCC(S)A) 2000, the magistrates' court has a duty to adjourn for a medical report if, in relation to an imprisonable offence, it finds that the act was done (or omission made) and also that an inquiry ought to be made into the medical condition of the defendant before dealing with the case further. This can be on bail for up to four weeks or in custody for up to three weeks. A remand on bail can be made conditional on co-operation with the preparation of a medical report or reports (BA 1976 s3(6)(d)); this can be read together with MHA 1983 s35 if the preparation of a report on bail is not practicable, though there is the additional requirement for a section 35 order that a doctor has provided a report to the effect that there is reason to suspect mental disorder. A further alternative approach is to grant bail if arrangements have been made to detain the patient under the civil powers of the MHA 1983: the preparation of a medical report can be achieved in that setting.[23]

22 For a case in which this was done in error, see *Bartram v Southend Magistrates' Court* [2004] EWHC 2691 (Admin), [2004] MHLR 319.

23 See chapter 6 for more on the question of the use of bail; note also the discussion in chapter 7 of the possible limitations imposed by section 35 in relation to matters such as the granting of leave of absence and of the power to transfer, which may mean that the option of a release on bail to allow the civil powers to be used is the better option.

Length and renewal

18.20 The length of an interim hospital order may be up to 12 weeks in the first instance, and it may be extended to a maximum of one year, though the renewals cannot be for longer than 28 days at a time.[24] Naturally, this will only occur if the court cannot decide whether or not to make a hospital order. Time spent in custody under MHA 1983 s38 should be taken into account in reducing any custodial sentence imposed if a full hospital order is not imposed: this follows from CJA 2003 ss240 and 242. The former requires the court imposing a sentence to reduce it by the period for which the offender has been remanded in custody; the latter includes detention under section 38 as within the definition of a remand in custody.

18.21 The medical evidence for a renewal must come from the responsible clinician, that is, the approved clinician in charge of the patient's case, and often known as the RC.[25] An 'approved clinician' (AC) is a person certified (by the Secretary of State for England or the Welsh Ministers for Wales) to act in that role.[26] Under MHA 1983 s12(2A) of the Act, such a clinician 'shall be treated as also approved' as having the necessary special experience in the diagnosis and treatment of mental disorder if he or she is a medical doctor. Note that it is also possible to be an AC and RC without being also a medical doctor. This was designed to ensure that psychologists could take charge of cases: the rationale for this was that, particularly in relation to offenders whose mental disorder is personality disorder, the treatment options might be more a matter of psychological treatments than pharmaceutical. This in turn means that while the initial loss of liberty under an interim hospital order requires evidence from two doctors, one of whom must be a psychiatrist, the further detention, which can be for a longer period in total, might be based on evidence from clinicians who are not doctors. It is possible that this will be challenged on grounds of non-compliance with the European

24 MHA 1983 s38(5).

25 MHA 1983 s55(1).

26 MHA 1983 s145. Directions as to the process for becoming an approved clinician are in the Mental Health Act 1983 Approved Clinician (General) Directions 2008 (available at www.dh.gov.uk/en/Publicationsandstatistics/Legislation/Directionsfromthesecretaryofstate/DH_086548). The task is carried out by primary care trusts on the direction of strategic health authorities and the relevant clinicians have to undertake an approved training course. Separate but equivalent directions exist for Wales and can be found at www.wales.nhs.uk/sites3/page.cfm?orgid=816&pid=33956 (as secondary legislation under the MHA 1983).

Convention on Human Rights (ECHR). The argument is that the European Court of Human Rights (ECtHR) has indicated that 'objective medical expertise' is necessary to ground the lawfulness of detention: see *Winterwerp v Netherlands*.[27] The question arising is whether this procedural prerequisite can be met by a psychologist: given the training and expertise of psychologists and the acceptance by Parliament that they can be in charge of treatment, it seems unlikely that a court would reject evidence on the basis that the clinician is not medically qualified. But the fact that the initial detention requires a medical doctor to support it creates the room for argument. There are, however, other ECHR arguments, discussed below under the effect of an interim order.

18.22 The renewal can be made without the presence of the defendant in court, provided that he or she is legally represented.[28] In the absence of statutory criteria for the exercise of this discretion, it must be exercised in a judicial manner. In light of the importance of the rights to liberty and to participate in criminal proceedings, it is likely that this power can be exercised lawfully only if the defendant cannot attend court for reasons of the severity of his or her condition or voluntarily waives the right to attend; in other words, it should not be exercised on the basis of administrative convenience. In support of this view, see by analogy *R (Kenneally) v Snaresbrook Crown Court*,[29] in which it was held that the power to make a hospital order under MHA 1983 s51 without the defendant being at court on the basis that it was 'impractical or inappropriate' to bring the detainee before the court should be interpreted restrictively as it involved deprivation of liberty, such that it could only be 'inappropriate' to bring someone before a court if a high degree of disability was present. Having said that, there are two points that mean that the analogy is not complete: in the first place, section 51 has the specific statutory language relating to it being 'impractical or inappropriate', which is not present in section 38; further, the renewal of the section 38 order is for a maximum of four weeks, whereas the making of a hospital order under section 51 is for at least six months. Despite the incomplete analogy, the question of inappropriateness involves a wide discretion, and loss of liberty for four weeks together with the fact that, as noted below, it may involve treatment without consent is a significant matter. It will be different if the defendant gives a capacitated consent not to be

27 (1979) 2 EHRR 387 at para 39.

28 MHA 1983 s38(6).

29 [2001] EWHC Admin 968, [2002] MHLR 53.

present, since the defendant is able to waive any rights if he or she so chooses.

18.23 There is no express language in MHA 1983 s38 that equates to the provisions of sections 35(8) and 36(7) that allow a defendant to adduce his or her own evidence to seek to terminate an interim hospital order.[30] However, given that liberty is in issue, it is not tenable that a defendant is not able to call evidence to seek to end an interim hospital order or to argue against its renewal: as such, the presence of the express language in the remand powers makes it plain that defendants may call evidence in those situations but does not exclude that right in the situation of the interim hospital order. In addition, as is described below, it is possible to appeal against the imposition of an interim order.

Purpose

18.24 The aim of an interim hospital order is to allow confirmation as to whether or not the criteria for a hospital order are present, namely that the defendant has a mental disorder of a nature or degree that requires detention in hospital for treatment and that appropriate treatment is available. These are all discussed in detail below.

18.25 Before the MHA 2007 amended the criteria for detention under a hospital order, such an order was possible only if the defendant had one (or more) of four categories of mental disorder and the court had to make a finding as to the category as well as the severity of the condition. Since a medical report might well be made in a prison setting (given the limited use of MHA 1983 s35 or s36, noted in chapter 7) the difficulty of forming a view as to diagnosis and as to the seriousness of the condition in the context of the pressures of writing a report for court proceedings could be problematic. In addition, two of the categories of mental disorder – mental impairment and psychopathic personality disorder – could only be the basis for detention if the defendant was treatable: it was the treatability of psychopathic personality disorder that was perhaps the most contentious, since the treatment process might depend on the co-operation of the patient. As such a patient who turned out not to be treatable could not be detained,[31] it was sensible to test the prospect of treatability.

30 See chapter 7.

31 'Psychopathic disorder' was defined in MHA 1983 s1 as originally enacted as a disorder that resulted in abnormally aggressive or seriously irresponsible conduct; the need for treatability was part of the admission criteria, but was originally interpreted as not being part of the discharge criteria (because it was

18.26 As has been discussed in chapter 2, the four categories have been removed and replaced by the single concept of mental disorder (though with additional requirements for longer-term detention if the disorder is in the form of a learning disability). While the treatability requirement has been removed in relation to psychopathic disorder or mental impairment, there is still the question of the nature or degree of the disorder and the new question, introduced by the MHA 2007, of whether appropriate treatment is available in the setting in which the defendant will be placed. An additional question that might make an interim order sensible is the need to consider whether the additional safeguards of a restriction order – on which see below – are appropriate on the facts.

18.27 One potential limitation on the power of making an interim hospital order was noted by the Court of Appeal in *R v Galfetti*,[32] albeit in passing: May LJ noted at paragraph 7 that: 'It was common ground before this court that the purpose of an interim hospital order is to assess whether it would be appropriate to make a hospital order for an offender suffering from mental illness'. He then added that it was not the purpose of such an order 'to hold the position until a place in an appropriate hospital is available for an offender for whom a hospital order is known to be appropriate'.

18.28 This latter comment appears unnecessarily restrictive. The particular problem in *Galfetti* was the lack of a suitable bed to allow the judge to make a hospital order: there had been repeated adjournments, during which time the defendant had been in custody because a transfer to hospital under MHA 1983 s48 had come to an end when a Mental Health Review Tribunal concluded that he did not need to be in hospital. Despite this, the evidence to the court still supported the making of a hospital order. Had the factual situation been that Mr Galfetti was subject to an interim hospital order, that the assessment purpose had been completed in the sense that it had been decided that he met the criteria for a hospital order but no suitable placement had been found – which might relate to the need to place a defendant in a specialist hospital or in a particular level of security, or to secure appropriate funding for a placement – and the question arose as to whether an interim order could be renewed, the dictum from May LJ would suggest that it could not.

---

not expressed to be part of the criteria applicable to section 72): see *R v Canons Park Mental Health Review Tribunal ex p A* [1995] QB 60; in *Reid v Secretary of State* [1999] 2 AC 512, the House of Lords held that detention would not be appropriate if the disorder was not treatable.

32 [2002] EWCA Crim 1916, [2002] MHLR 418.

18.29 The unsatisfactory nature of this conclusion is made apparent by considering what would happen to such a defendant: given the conclusion that the defendant required to be detained, release on bail would not be suitable; so a remand into custody (or the imposition of a custodial sentence) would be the only realistic option. This would mean the placement in prison of someone who needed to be in a hospital setting. Fortunately, the comments of May LJ were obiter, because the factual situation before the court did not involve an interim order. It is difficult to understand why the renewal of an interim order is not 'warranted' – the relevant language[33] – by the need to await a suitable bed. When the test for renewal is added to the criteria for the imposition of an interim order, namely evidence of mental disorder and reason to believe that a hospital order may be appropriate, the statutory power to make an interim hospital order arising 'before making a hospital order',[34] the relevant preconditions seem to be met when the problem preventing the making of a hospital order is that a placement suitable to be specified for the purposes of section 37 has not yet been found.

Effect

Detention in hospital

18.30 The legal effect of an MHA 1983 s38 order is set out in section 40(3): a constable or any person directed by the court may convey the defendant from court to hospital within the time period specified in the court order (which has to be within 28 days, by virtue of section 38(4)). If the bed is not immediately available, directions may be given for the conveyance and detention of the defendant in a place of safety, which will often be a prison.[35]

18.31 If the hospital cannot admit the patient within the period specified, what should happen? There is a question as to whether such a problem should ever arise, because section 40(3) provides that the hospital managers 'shall admit ... and thereafter detain him': this language provides the authority for detention and also suggests that they do not have an option to refuse. This makes sense in that the interim order can only be made if the hospital indicates to the court

33 MHA 1983 s38(5)(b).

34 MHA 1983 s38(1).

35 It may also be a police station or a hospital that can offer a temporary place: see MHA 1983 s55(1). See chapter 3 for a discussion of the place of safety provisions and the policy against the use of police stations.

that arrangements have been made. But the practical realities are that a hospital may find that it has offered a bed but then the space disappears because of an emergency situation; or that the condition of the defendant has deteriorated (whether in the place of safety, or after admission) so as to make it no longer appropriate for the hospital to offer a place. The only option in that case is to return the matter to court immediately. Since the making of an interim hospital order is a sentence, it can be varied within 56 days by the same judge of the Crown Court (under PCC(S)A 2000 s155) or by the magistrates' court (under Magistrates' Courts Act 1980 s142, which allows a variation in the interests of justice). Even though the sentence would remain the same, ie an interim hospital order, and only the mechanics would change, namely the place to which the defendant was sent pursuant to the order, it is to be hoped that this would be construed as within the power to vary a sentence.

Detention in a place of safety

18.32 If a place of safety is used, the directions for detention there will provide the necessary authority for conveyance and detention and further conveyance to the hospital once the bed is available: the authority as to conveyance is 'to the hospital specified' and so can be from the place of safety or directly from the court.[36] The statutory language does not have any express provision for transfers between places of safety: this is in contrast to the language of MHA 1983 ss135 and 136, which were amended by the MHA 2007 to allow transfers between places of safety in short-term police detention.[37] It might be suggested that a court could include in its directions under section 38(4) as to the use of a place of safety a provision to allow transfer to any other suitable location as the needs of the defendant might require; however, this is not consistent with the statutory language that requires the court to give directions relating to 'a place of safety' rather that referring to 'a place or places of safety'.

18.33 However, it is arguable that a transfer between places of safety is possible. If the place of safety is a prison, a transfer to a suitable

36 Care must be taken to ensure that anyone who carries out the conveying of the defendant is a constable or has a specific authorisation from the court, failing which there may be a claim for false imprisonment on the basis that there is detention without authority; note that the need for bad faith or negligence in MHA 1983 s139 may be satisfied by a lack of authority: *R (TTM (by his litigation friend TM)) v Hackney LBC and East London NHS Foundation Trust* [2011] EWCA Civ 4.

37 MHA 1983 ss135(3A) and (3B) and 136(3) and (4).

hospital may be ordered under MHA 1983 s48, which covers 'persons detained in a prison or remand centre, not being persons serving a sentence of imprisonment'. If the place of safety is a hospital, the statutory language as to transfer is as follows. Section 19(3) of the Act provides that a patient detained under the civil provisions may be transferred between hospitals operated by the same management structure; and section 19(1) allows transfers between hospitals operated by different bodies.[38] Schedule 1 to the Act applies section 19 to patients detained under the criminal provisions, subject to an amendment that is not material: again, this would seem to authorise transfers between different hospitals operated as a place of safety. However, these provisions can only apply during the period during which detention is authorised pending admission to the hospital to be used for the interim hospital order, and if it becomes apparent that the admission to that hospital is not possible then the purpose of the place of safety direction has ceased and the matter should be returned to the court for an appropriate further order to be made.

Absconding patients

18.34 The MHA 1983 s 38(7) allows the arrest of a patient who absconds from a hospital or during conveyance. The patient can be returned to court, which may set aside the order and use some other power. Section 38(7) does not, it should be noted, apply to abscondees from places of safety: however, section 137 provides that anyone who is in a place of safety is in legal custody and section 138 provides a power for such a patient to be 'retaken' by the person who had custody of the defendant, by a constable or by an approved mental health professional.[39]

ECHR and detention

18.35 The detention of a patient in hospital takes away his or her right to liberty. In ECHR terms, the right to liberty in article 5(1) is accompanied by a right to a review of the lawfulness of detention in article 5(4). As an interim hospital order follows a conviction, its lawfulness arises under article 5(1)(a). But as it is on the basis of mental

38 See also Mental Health (Hospital, Guardianship and Treatment) (England) Regulations 2008 SI No 1184 regs 7, 10 and 11 for more detailed regulation; and regulation 23 of the equivalent regulations for Wales, SI 2008 No 2439.

39 See the discussion in chapter 3 about powers of arrest in relation to places of safety.

disorder, it is also covered by article 5(1)(e). While it is possible for detention to be lawful by reason of more than one provision, the fact that the court order is made only if there is a basis to suspect mental disorder will mean that article 5(1)(e) will be the focus. The requirements for this are summarised in chapter 1: in short, it is necessary that there be expert evidence that shows that there is a mental disorder that warrants detention on an ongoing basis.

18.36 The criteria for an MHA 1983 s38 order to be made should satisfy article 5(1)(e) at the outset: there is a need for expert evidence as to mental disorder and the reason to suppose that a hospital order might be imposed implies that there will be good evidence of a current nature or degree that warrants detention, which will justify it for at least a short term for assessment. Whether the criteria continue to be met if and when the order is renewed will turn on the reason for the renewal. If, for example, it has not been determined whether or not the nature or degree of the disorder warrants detention, the fact that the civil provisions limit detention for this purpose to 28 days[40] may be argued by analogy. The criminal context might justify some additional time if there are concerns about public safety: but they may also arise in a civil context. While the initial period under section 38 is 12 weeks, which is three times longer than the maximum in a civil setting, this does not mean that it should be the norm. However, if the reason for a renewal is a matter that does not cast doubt on whether there is a mental disorder that justifies detention, such as trying to find a suitable bed, then article 5(1)(e) will be met.[41]

18.37 As to ECHR article 5(4), this is usually achieved by the Mental Health Tribunal deciding whether or not a patient should be released. However, patients under an interim hospital order do not have any right of access to a tribunal: patients under an interim hospital order are not mentioned in the list of those able to apply to a tribunal, set out in MHA 1983 s66 (for civil patients) and section 69 (for criminal patients). But they do have access to the criminal court and can argue against the renewal of detention or seek its termination. A mechanism involving a review by a tribunal is not necessary if a court assesses whether to renew detention in hospital, whether under a further interim order or by imposing a hospital order, in a way that considers the lawfulness of detention. In such a situation, the court is involved in a process that satisfies both article 5(1) and

40 See chapter 2 and the discussion of MHA 1983 s2.

41 See, however, the procedural argument noted at para 18.21 above if the evidence for the renewal comes from someone who is not a psychiatrist.

(4).[42] However, the importance of a patient being able to apply to a court to challenge the lawfulness of detention will not necessarily be met by periodic renewals.[43] This potential problem will be resolved by the Crown Court allowing patients detained under interim orders to make applications to bring forward any date set for a further consideration of the case on the grounds that the criteria are not made out.

Treatment under an interim order

18.38 As to the separate fundamental right to autonomy, which is reflected in ECHR article 8 and engaged in relation to questions of treatment, the MHA 1983 introduced a separate regime for the imposition of treatment without consent, set out in Part IV of the 1983 Act. This is described in chapter 2. Patients detained under section 38 are covered by this regime.[44] It provides as follows:

i) under MHA 1983 s63, treatment[45] by or under the direction of the clinician in charge of the patient can be given without the consent of the patient, but
ii) medication cannot be given for more than three months without consent or the approval of a second doctor (by reason of section 58),
iii) electro-convulsive therapy requires consent or, if the patient cannot consent, approval by a second doctor (by reason of section 58A), and
iv) particularly invasive treatments – psychosurgery and the use of hormone implants to reduce the male sex drive – require consent and a second medical opinion and support from two non-medical

42 It is suggested that if the clinical team in the hospital setting forms the view that the requirements for detention in hospital are no longer met, they should make arrangements with the court for the matter to be returned there so as to avoid a breach of ECHR article 5(1)(e).

43 See *Rakevich v Russia* [2004] MHLR 37, *Gorshkov v Ukraine* [2006] MHLR 32, and *Kucheruk v Ukraine* [2008] MHLR 1; in *R (Rayner) v Secretary of State for Justice* [2008] MHLR 115, the Court of Appeal accepted that there was a trend of construing article 5(4) so as to require a patient to be able to make an application, rather than relying on some other process (in the context, the duty of the Secretary of State to make a reference) – but it noted that the ability of a patient to apply to a court for an order as to the making of a reference was sufficient.

44 The patient meets the requirement of being 'liable to detention'.

45 'Medical treatment' is widely defined in MHA 1983 s145 to include nursing, psychological treatments and rehabilitative work.

reviewers (see section 57 and the Mental Health (Hospital, Guardianship and Treatment (England) Regulations 2008).[46]

These exceptions are all in turn subject to the emergency treatment provisions of section 62, which allows urgent treatment that is immediately necessary to save the patient's life, prevent a serious deterioration of the patient's condition, alleviate serious suffering or prevent violent or dangerous behaviour.

Differences from hospital order patients

18.39 It is worth noting that MHA 1983 s56(3) expressly exempts from the definition of 'liable to be detained' a patient who is detained in a place of safety under sections 37 or 45A of the Act: there is no similar language in relation to a person detained in a place of safety pending admission to a hospital under section 38, though such a person would be within the definition of 'patient' under section 145 of the Act, namely a person suffering or appearing to suffer from mental disorder and is arguably liable to be detained in the light of the making of the court order. Since the place of safety under section 38 may well be a prison or some other place where treatment without consent is not appropriate, there is no good reason why the place of safety detention pending admission under section 38 should not be treated in the same way as a section 37 place of safety.[47]

18.40 There are two other differences as between patients detained under section 38 and those who have been subject to a final sentence: the RC has power under MHA 1983 s17 to grant leave of absence to a hospital order patient, and transfers between hospitals may be effected through section 19. However, section 40(3) requires detention of an interim hospital order patient in accordance with the terms of section 38. In the *Reference Guide to the Mental Health Act 1983*,[48] issued by Department of Health, it is said at paragraph 3.20 that leave of absence is permissible for a patient detained under sections 35

46 SI 2008 No 1184. Psychosurgery is listed as a particularly invasive treatment in MHA 1983 s57; the hormone treatment is added by the Regulations, made under section 57(1)(b); other treatments can be added by the Code of Practice issued under section 118. The equivalent regulation for Wales is contained in SI 2008 No 2439, made by the National Assembly for Wales.

47 See paragraph 7.15 of the *Reference Guide to the Mental Health Act 1983*, mentioned below, which suggests that 'in principle' the consent to treatment provisions apply to those under a place of safety.

48 September 2008, available at www.dh.gov.uk/en/Publicationsandstatistics/Publications/PublicationsPolicyAndGuidance/DH_088162.

or 36 if the remanding court so permits. However, paragraph 7.14, which relates to interim hospital orders, does not state that there is a similar power, but instead that leave is not permitted. Since leave may be a necessary part of the assessment or treatment process (for example how a patient copes with leave may be important in terms of assessing the disorder or as part of the treatment regime, which includes rehabilitation), it is just as important as in relation to a section 35 or 36 patient. Moreover, the language as to detention is similar. Accordingly, there is no obvious reason why the court should not have the same power to authorise the granting of leave of absence for a person detained under an interim hospital order, and a request should be made at the time of remand.

18.41 Paragraph 3.20 of the Reference Guide also states that transfer between hospitals for those under sections 35 or 36 requires a new remand to the different hospital: paragraph 7.14 notes the absence of a power of transfer in relation to interim hospital order patients. This is consistent with the power being to remand to 'a hospital' rather than to 'such hospital or hospitals as may be specified' (or similar language). This may be of reduced importance in the era of hospital trusts that manage several units, since transfer between different units managed by the same trust is an administrative matter that does not involve the use of section 19 powers.

Appeals

18.42 Section 50(1) of the Criminal Appeal Act 1968 includes an interim hospital order within the definition of what amounts to a sentence for the purposes of appeals to the Court of Appeal from the Crown Court; for the purpose of appeals from the magistrates' court to the Crown Court, section 108 of the Magistrates' Courts Act 1980 provides that a 'sentence' includes 'any order made on conviction', which is wide enough to include an interim hospital order. A renewal of an interim order should also be covered, given that it has the same effect. It may be argued that the existence of this right of appeal is the explanation for the absence of the express language as to the right to seek to set aside an interim hospital order in the same way as is permitted in relation to the remand powers under MHA 1983 ss35 and 36: but it seems cumbersome to have to take an appeal, and so it is suggested that this argument is less strong than that set out at para 18.23 above.

Hospital order

Introduction

18.43 The power to make a hospital order following conviction arises under MHA 1983 s37(1), which applies in both the Crown Court and the magistrates' court if the offence is one that carries imprisonment.[49] In the Crown Court, this order can be combined with a restriction order, which is dealt with below; the magistrates may commit for sentence to the Crown Court if they form the view that a restriction order might be appropriate. There are no age restrictions on the making of a hospital order: ie, it applies to adults and to children.[50]

18.44 The effect of the making of a hospital order is discussed in full below. However, since an understanding of what happens may be relevant to the exercise of discretion as to whether one should be made, the effect is worth noting at the outset. In brief:

i) a hospital order patient has the status of a patient detained under a civil detention for treatment order, including the powers that exist to transfer between hospitals, grant leave, and place on a community treatment order (though the latter does not apply if a restriction order is in place, and the exercise of the transfer and leave powers in relation to a restricted patient require the consent of the Secretary of State for Justice);

ii) the patient must be released if the criteria for detention no longer apply, as decided by a tribunal or the hospital managers or the RC, the person in charge of treatment[51] (though in the case of a restricted patient, the Secretary of State must agree to a release by the hospital managers or RC); there is no right of access to a tribunal in the first six months;

iii) detention may be renewed if the criteria for detention continue to apply (but if a restriction order is made, there is no need for renewal, and so detention continues until it is found that the criteria for detention no longer apply);

iv) the patient is subject to the provisions regulating treatment without consent.

49 The relationship between the hospital order and mandatory and quasi-mandatory sentences of imprisonment (both those for murder and the dangerous offender and minimum term provisions) is considered separately below.

50 This is in contrast to a guardianship order, discussed below, which is only available for a person aged 16 or over.

51 MHA 1983 s55(1) contains the definition; the term appears in various parts of the Act.

18.45 The important question of the discretion as to whether to impose a hospital order turns on whether it is the most suitable disposal, which will usually turn on the question of whether a custodial sentence should be imposed. This interplay is considered separately: but it is an exercise of judgment that can arise only if the various preconditions for making a hospital order are met, which are discussed first.

Procedural requirements

18.46 The procedural requirements are similar to those applicable to the making of an interim hospital order. So there must be medical evidence (which can be written or oral) from two doctors, one of whom must be approved under section 12 of the Act as a psychiatrist,[52] that satisfies the court as to the medical components of the test for detention. Although one of the changes introduced by the MHA 2007 was that the person in charge of treatment, previously called the responsible medical officer (or RMO) and now called the responsible clinician (or RC), no longer has to be doctor,[53] for the purposes of evidence relating to the imposition of a hospital order, there is still a requirement that evidence from doctors be provided to the court.

18.47 Under MHA 1983 s12(1), medical recommendations used to support applications to detain under sections 2 and 3 of the Act shall be made no more than five days apart and section 6(1) provides that the application authorises detention only so long as it starts within 14 days of the date of the last medical examination. There are no equivalent statutory requirements in relation to the making of a hospital order. However, in *R v Preston*,[54] the Court of Appeal confirmed that reports based on recent assessments were required so that a view could be formed of whether the defendant's condition at the time of sentence met the requirements of the statute. The reports available in relation to Mr Preston included one that was based on a recent assessment; but the other, although written recently, was from a doctor who had not actually seen him for 30 months. A hospital order made by the sentencing judge was quashed because the absence of two up-to-date

52 MHA 1983 s37(2)(a) sets the requirement for two opinions from registered medical practitioners; section 54(1) sets the requirement that one must be section 12 approved.

53 This is particularly designed to allow psychologists to be in charge of treatment, though it could also extend to nurses, occupational therapists, or social workers.

54 [2003] EWCA Crim 2086, [2004] MHLR 277.

assessments meant that the sentencing court could not be satisfied that the criteria for a hospital order were made out.

18.48 In addition, MHA 1983 s37(4) requires evidence that a bed is available within 28 days 'beginning with the date of the making of' the hospital order (ie, that date is day one of the 28-day period).[55] Section 40(1) provides that a hospital order gives authority to convey the patient to the hospital specified in the order 'within a period of 28 days' and for the hospital managers to admit and detain him or her. If the bed is not immediately available, the defendant can be held in a 'place of safety' in the interim: this will invariably be a prison or other place of detention, but could be a hospital other than that named as the hospital for the hospital order.[56] The possible lacuna in the statutory provisions as to the absence of any transfer between places of safety, and the suggested routes to achieve flexibility in this regard discussed above in relation to the interim hospital provisions, apply equally in the case of a hospital order.

18.49 In the event that the bed that has been offered has to be withdrawn, MHA 1983 s37(5) allows the Secretary of State to specify a different hospital as the hospital to which the hospital order authorises detention. This provides an alternative method to bringing the case back to court for the sentence to be varied under PCC(S)A 2000 s155 or Magistrates' Courts Act 1980 s142, discussed above in relation to interim hospital orders. It was determined in *R (DB) v Nottinghamshire Healthcare NHS Trust*[57] that if the placement in a hospital occurred outside the 28-day period, it was not lawful; the defendant, it was noted, would be entitled to walk out of any place of safety once the period had expired. The Court of Appeal suggested that courts should include a direction that if the defendant had not been admitted to hospital within 21 days, the matter should be returned to court.

18.50 In relation to the hospital involved, it is to be noted that if the hospital order is combined with a restriction order (on which see below), section 47 of the Crime (Sentences) Act (C(S)A) 1997 allows the court to specify a hospital unit in which the patient should be held, at least initially. This power is explicable by the fact that a single hospital structure may consist of many different areas, perhaps on different sites, with different levels of security: so if a court wishes to indicate

55 MHA 1983 s38(4). It can come from the hospital managers or the AC who will have the overall responsibility for the treatment of the defendant.

56 See MHA 1983 s55(1) for the definition of what counts as a place of safety; and Children and Young Persons Act 1933 s107(1) in relation to a child.

57 [2008] EWCA Civ 1354, [2008] MHLR 376.

that the hospital order should take effect by limiting the patient to a unit with a particular level of security, that can be done by making an order under the C(S)A 1997. The intersection of the administrative power in MHA 1983 s37(5) to change the relevant hospital with the judicial power to specify a particular unit at a particular hospital is untested. There is a comment in paragraph 33.20 of the English Code of Practice that the consent of the Secretary of State is required for any transfer from a named Unit, though it is not clear that can apply prior to admission to that Unit. Since the issue will necessarily arise within the time period for a Crown Court to vary a sentence, the sensible thing might be to have the matter returned to court if the unit specified cannot accept the patient.

18.51 One pragmatic point to note is that a defendant who does not wish to be subject to a hospital order (and it is sometimes the view of a defendant that a prison sentence will lead to earlier release or offer less stigma than a hospital placement) may frustrate the possibility by refusing to co-operate with the necessary investigation and report-writing: as an example, see *R v Maynard*.[58]

18.52 Two other procedural matters are worth mentioning. First, it has been noted by the Court of Appeal that it is 'most desirable' that a defendant be legally represented 'except in the rarest cases' when a hospital order is in prospect: *R v Blackwood*.[59] Second, if the person is represented and is already subject to an interim hospital order, it is possible for a hospital order to be made without the defendant being present: see MHA 1983 s38(2). In connection with this, it has been noted above that an interim order can be renewed without the defendant being present, and it has been suggested that this should only be possible (subject to a capacitated consent to be absent) for good reasons, not just administrative convenience. The same argument will apply in relation to the imposition of a section 37 order on an a fortiori basis, given that it may lead to a significant period of detention.[60]

58 [2010] EWCA Crim 2854, [2011] MHLR 93.

59 (1974) 59 CrAppR 170 at 171–172. The Court noted that this was particularly so if a restriction order was in prospect, but it did not limit its concern to such a situation.

60 As was the case in *R (Kenneally) v Snaresbrook Crown Court* [2001] EWHC Admin 968, [2002] MHLR 53, which involved a hospital order being made under MHA 1983 s51: as is discussed in relation to the interim hospital order, there is the difference that there is specific language in section 51 that is missing in section 38.

The criteria for making a hospital order

Summary

18.53 The criteria as to the merits for the making of an order are set out in MHA 1983 s37(2). The court must be satisfied of the following matters:

a) that the offender is suffering from mental disorder;
b) that it is of a nature or degree making it appropriate for him or her to be detained in hospital for medical treatment;
c) that appropriate treatment is available for him or her; and
d) that a hospital order is the most suitable disposal in the light of 'all the circumstances including the nature of the offence and the character and antecedents of the offender, and to the other available methods of dealing with him'.

18.54 The first three matters, which are listed in section 37(2)(a), turn on the medical evidence that must be adduced; the fourth, which is set by section 37(2)(b), does not and so is a matter of judgment for the court, though it will no doubt be informed by medical evidence.

The medical criteria

Introduction

18.55 The medical criteria in MHA 1983 s37 involve a number of questions, namely what is meant by mental disorder, what counts as medical treatment, what nature or degree makes detention in hospital for that treatment appropriate, and what is appropriate treatment? These questions are also to be asked in relation to the imposition of a civil order, discussed in chapter 2. There are two differences to note in terms of structure, however. The civil test involves questions of the appropriateness and necessity of treatment; under section 37, there is an appropriateness test but no necessity test, and the appropriateness test is phrased differently. In relation to detention for treatment in hospital under MHA 1983 s3, the appropriateness and detention tests are in separate phrases: the mental disorder has to be 'of a nature or degree which makes it appropriate for him to receive medical treatment in a hospital' and it has to be shown that the treatment 'cannot be provided unless he is detained'; the latter question is part of the supplemental test that treatment must also be necessary for the protection of the patient or others. In relation to section 37, there is one test, namely, the mental disorder must be 'of a nature or degree which makes it appropriate for him to be detained in hospital for medical treatment'.

18.56 The difference is explained by the context, of which there are two features. In the first place, a civil detention order cannot be used if a patient is willing to be a voluntary patient (hence the phrase 'cannot be provided unless he is detained'); but the different dynamic in a criminal setting would make it wrong to prevent a defendant accessing treatment that he or she was willing to accept. In the second place, the difference between civil and criminal patients in this regard is not necessarily so great: a civil patient might accept treatment and then change his or her mind, but can then be detained if he or she tries to leave against medical advice (under MHA 1983 s5, which allows short-term detention until a longer-term order can be put in place); the criminal hospital order contains this element of compulsion in the first place.

18.57 Two further points should be made. First, the section 37 test incorporates an additional question of whether the order is appropriate: it is suggested that if the additional civil detention tests are met (for example, that detention in a hospital is necessary for the protection of the patient or the public), then the appropriateness test is going to be met unless the circumstances are very unusual. Second, a hospital order lasts for six months and is then renewed under section 20(4)(c), which applies also to civil patients and includes the test that 'it is necessary for the health or safety of the patient or for the protection of other persons that he should receive such treatment and it cannot be provided unless he is detained under this section'.[61] This reflects the fact that the patient passes into the civil mental health system and if the patient remains willing to receive treatment such as is necessary for the protection of himself or herself or others, that achieves any ongoing purpose of the criminal justice system.

18.58 Accordingly, the medical criteria in the civil and criminal parts of the statute are the same in substance, with the differences in the language explained by the different value to be attached to voluntariness in light of the context. The detailed discussion in chapters 1 and 2 of the medical criteria is applicable to section 37. The following points are the most important.

61 The renewal provisions do not apply if the patient is a restricted patient, but the tribunal test under MHA 1983 ss72 and 73 is similarly worded and so indirectly applies.

The definition of 'mental disorder'

18.59 The definition of 'mental disorder' in MHA 1983 s1 is that it means 'any disorder or disability of the mind'; prior to the MHA 2007, it was necessary to find that the mental disorder amounted to mental illness, mental impairment, severe mental impairment or psychopathic disorder. This old categorisation has been removed, though if the mental disorder amounts to a 'learning disability' ('a state of arrested or incomplete development of the mind which includes a significant impairment of intelligence and social functioning') it must also be 'associated with abnormally aggressive or seriously irresponsible conduct' to be covered by section 37.[62] Dependence on drugs or alcohol is excluded (though any distinct mental disorder that results from such addiction will be outside this exclusion and so included): this is narrower than the previous exclusions, which also covered immoral conduct and sexual deviancy.

18.60 In relation to learning disability, it is to be noted that:

- the definition requires an impairment of *both* intelligence and social functioning, so both must be assessed: see *R v McDonagh*;[63]
- 'seriously irresponsible' conduct has been given a restrictive meaning, at least in a civil context: see *Re F*;[64]
- conduct can be 'associated with' a disorder without causation: see the discussion in the High Court in *R (P) v Mental Health Review Tribunal and Rampton Hospital*;[65] and in the Court of Appeal in *P* and also in *Lewis v Gibson*,[66] it was noted that the absence of recent conduct that was abnormally aggressive or seriously irresponsible could mean that the disorder no longer persisted but could also mean that it persisted but had not recently manifested itself.

18.61 The MHA 2007 amended the coverage of the MHA 1983 so that all forms of personality disorder are covered (not just those that amount to psychopathic disorder) and removed the exclusion based on 'sexual deviancy', which means that recognised mental disorders such as paedophilia are clearly covered and so may be suitable for a mental health disposal. It is also important to note that a personality disorder is a widely-defined concept: see the World Health Organization

62 See MHA 1983 s1(2A), (2B) and (4) as amended by the MHA 2007.

63 [2008] NICA 6, [2008] MHLR 219. (Court of Appeal in Northern Ireland.)

64 *F (a child) (care order: sexual abuse)* [2000] 1 FLR 192, *Re TF (a child: guardianship)* [1999] MHLR 175.

65 [2001] EWHC Admin 876, [2002] MHLR 250 at para 26.

66 Respectively, [2002] EWCA Civ 697, [2002] MHLR 253 at paras 23–25; and [2005] EWCA Civ 587, [2005] MHLR 309 at para 31.

(WHO) classification document, ICD-10, which defines it as a 'deeply ingrained and enduring behaviour patterns, manifesting as inflexible responses to a broad range of personal and social situations'.[67] Again, it is important to note that these disorders are now clearly covered by the MHA 1983, which has been extended by Parliament to allow them to be within the remit of the hospital system.

Medical treatment

18.62 What counts as medical treatment is widely defined by MHA 1983 s145(1); it 'includes nursing, psychological intervention and specialist mental health habilitation, rehabilitation and care'. By section 145(4), which was added by the MHA 2007,[68] it has to have as its purpose 'to alleviate, or prevent a worsening of, the disorder or one or more of its symptoms or manifestations'. Prior to the MHA 2007, it was necessary to find that if there was mental impairment or psychopathic disorder, the disorder was treatable, which meant that treatment 'was likely to alleviate or prevent a deterioration of his condition' or its symptoms or manifestations: now the treatment has to have that purpose, which it may have without any prospect of success.[69] However, the 'appropriate treatment' test discussed below may mean that if nothing can be shown to work, there will be no appropriate treatment and so detention will not be proper on that basis.

Nature or degree

18.63 This is a disjunctive test: see *R v Mental Health Review Tribunal ex p Smith*.[70] This may mean that a chronic and relapsing condition which is currently not of a degree that warrants detention for that reason may nevertheless be of a nature that does justify detention, for example because the apparent recovery is somewhat fragile. It may also be that expert evidence is necessary as to whether an example of a degree of disorder is a single incident or an instance of something that is likely to recur, such that the nature of the disorder might justify ongoing intervention.

Appropriateness of detention

18.64 The appropriateness of detention is linked to the nature or degree of the disorder and involves investigation of whether a treatment

67 See the introductory comments to paragraphs F60–69 of ICD-10.

68 Introduced by MHA 2007 s7(2).

69 The test applies to all forms of disorder.

70 4 August 1998, (1999) 47 BMLR 104, [1999] COD 148.

programme is appropriately provided in hospital. This does not necessarily involve full-time in-patient treatment because it has been recognised that the granting of leave (under MHA 1983 s17) is part of the rehabilitation process and can amount to treatment. The key phrase in relation to whether a patient can be treated without consent, for example, is whether he or she is liable to be detained (see section 56), which covers someone who is on leave. It has been established that someone is properly subject to the provisions of the statute, and so the consent to treatment provisions despite spending the majority of his or her time out of hospital: this is discussed in detail in chapter 2, the point being that a patient does not have to need full-time in-patient treatment to meet the requirements for a hospital order. The consequence of this is that a patient who seems relatively well but who might well deteriorate in a prison setting may meet the statutory test for a hospital order and so meet the criteria for admission.

18.65 In this context, it should also be noted that the MHA 2007 also introduced the regime of community treatment orders (CTOs), designed to make it easier for patients to be maintained in the community with the prospect of recall to hospital if necessary. This is available for patients placed under hospital orders (though not if a restriction order is also in place). So it may be that a hospital order involves a limited period in hospital before a community-based regime with the prospect of recall to hospital if necessary is put in place.

The 'appropriate treatment' criterion

18.66 Added to the MHA 1983 by MHA 2007 s4 is a requirement that detention for treatment under section 37 (and also under section 3 or the renewal provisions of section 20)[71] only occur if appropriate treatment is available. This is so even if detention for treatment is appropriate. What is appropriate treatment is defined in MHA 1983 s3(4)[72] as 'medical treatment which is appropriate in his case, taking into account the nature and degree of the mental disorder and all other circumstances of his case'.[73] The test, it is to be noted, is not

71 It also appears in MHA 1983 s36, the Crown Court remand for treatment; the additional Crown Court powers under sections 45A and 51(6), discussed below; the Secretary of State's powers of transfer under sections 47 and 48; and the tribunal powers of discharge in section 72. Some of these changes are effected by MHA 2007 s4, some by s5.

72 Added by MHA 2007 s4(3).

73 This is also the test that is applied by the doctor who assesses the ongoing need for medication that continues beyond three months: see MHA 1983 ss58 and 64(3).

limited to treatment that is clinically appropriate. Guidance on the operation of the MHA 1983 in the Code of Practice issued under MHA 1983 s118 by the Secretary of State and the Welsh Ministers[74] provides that account should be taken of both the nature and degree of the disorder and all the circumstances of the patient 'including cultural, ethnic and religious considerations'.[75]

18.67 It is also clear that the test allows consideration of the proportionality of the treatment and of being placed in a hospital setting, including perhaps such matters as the prospects of success in treatment, the likely side-effects and so on: so paragraph 6.11 of the English Code of Practice and paragraph 4.10 of the Welsh Code suggest that account be taken of, among other things:

> ... the location of the available treatment; the implications of the treatment for the patient's family and social relationships, including their role as a parent; its implications for the patient's education or work; and the consequences for the patient, and other people, if the patient does not receive the treatment available. (For mentally disordered offenders about to be sentenced for an offence, the consequence will sometimes be a prison sentence.)[76]

18.68 The attitude of the defendant towards the treatment might also be relevant. The English Code of Practice notes that a clinically suitable treatment that will only be provided on the basis of engagement 'can potentially remain appropriate and available'.[77] If it can 'potentially' be appropriate treatment, it may also not meet the test. In particular, paragraph 6.17 of the English Code and paragraph 4.16 of the Welsh Code note that: 'Simply detaining someone – even in a hospital – does not constitute medical treatment'. This may be a particular issue in relation to those with a personality disorder that requires treatment of a psychological nature that depends on the co-operation

74 The Code does not set law, but the guidance in it carries great weight and should be followed – certainly by mental health professionals – unless there is good reason not to, and so it can amount to a form of soft law for the purposes of assessing the accessibility and foreseeability of the law for the purposes of phrases such as 'in accordance with the law' in the ECHR: see *R (Munjaz) v Mersey Care NHS Trust* [2005] UKHL 58, [2006] 2 AC 148, [2005] MHLR 276. It cannot amount to guidance on the law that is binding on the courts.

75 English Code para 6.8; Welsh Code para 4.7. See also the following paragraphs in each Code as to what can be taken into account. This is discussed fully in chapter 2.

76 Of course, it may also be that the consequence will be a community sentence with a condition of treatment and the knowledge that the civil provisions of the MHA 1983 will be available as a back-up.

77 Code of Practice para 6.19; Welsh Code para 4.17.

of the defendant. Case-law in relation to tribunal decisions has indicated that lack of co-operation that is unlikely to change may mean that a patient should not be in hospital: so in *MD v Nottinghamshire Health Care NHS Trust*,[78] it was accepted that mere containment was not the function of the hospital system (and there would be no appropriate treatment); and in *DL-H v Devon Partnership NHS Trust and Secretary of State for Justice*,[79] it was noted that it is necessary to give an individualised assessment of the treatment available for a personality-disordered patient and the patient's willingness to engage or resistance to engagement.

18.69 As has been noted at para 18.62 above, the question of whether a personality disorder was treatable had supposedly been removed from the statute: but the appropriate treatment test may have preserved it. This may also support the use of an interim hospital order to assess the availability of treatment that is appropriate. However, caution should be exercised before concluding that treatment in not appropriate because of non-co-operation. Chapter 35 of the English Code of Practice gives further guidance on questions of particular relevance to people with a personality disorder. It notes that, while there must be a clinical judgment made about the individual circumstances of the patient, there are various relevant themes. In the first place, it is noted that there is generally a need for 'relatively intense and long term, structured and coherent' treatment approaches (paragraph 35.10), in which patients may not engage for some time for lack of motivation (paragraph 35.11).[80] It is also noted that even if the patient is not engaged in such a programme, he or she may require other treatments, including nursing and specialist care, to manage the risks posed, which may count as appropriate medical treatment (paragraph 35.11).

18.70 Of course, it remains important to secure engagement as: 'Sustainable long-term change is more likely to be achieved with the voluntary engagement of the patient' (paragraph 35.10). But it may be difficult to suggest that an attitude of non-co-operation shown at the outset of what may be a long-term treatment process – which is likely

78 [2010] UKUT 59 (AAC), [2010] MHLR 93.

79 [2010] UKUT 102 (AAC), [2010] MHLR 162.

80 It is noted that the usual treatment process is psycho-social (Code of Practice para 35.12), reflecting the fact that personality disorders are formed as a result of psychological deficits caused by problems in a person's social development. In other words, the problem took a long time to develop, so it will take a long time to deal with.

to be what will be in front of a court – means that appropriate treatment is not available.

18.71 In addition to the breadth of what can be considered under the appropriate treatment test, it is to be noted that the court does not have to determine what treatment package would secure the best outcome for the patient. This is the point made at paragraph 6.12 of the Code of Practice:[81]

> Treatment need not be *the most appropriate* medical treatment that could ideally be made available. Nor does it need to address *every* aspect of the person's disorder. But the treatment available at any time must be *an appropriate response to the patient's condition and situation*. (Emphasis added.)

18.72 In other words, something that amounts to a suitable response will meet the test even if there might be arguments that there is a better package of treatment. This may link back to questions of diagnosis, since different treatments may be more suitable for different conditions: but the question for the court will be limited to whether what is proposed is appropriate for whatever the condition is.

18.73 There is also a temporal limitation on the concern of the court, which has to consider the current position of the patient, not what is likely to happen in the future. This is stated at paragraph 6.20 of the English Code of Practice:[82]

> People called on to make a judgment about whether the appropriate medical treatment test is met do not have to be satisfied that appropriate treatment will be available for the whole course of the patient's detention ... What is appropriate may change over time, as the patient's condition changes or clinicians obtain a greater understanding of the patient's case. But they must satisfy themselves that appropriate medical treatment is available for the time being, given the patient's condition and circumstances as they are currently understood.

18.74 This is because the ongoing treatment of the patient is subject to reviews, and the bodies conducting those reviews will consider the appropriate treatment test at that time. However, it is to be remembered that the availability of treatment that is appropriate means its actual not theoretical availability[83] – this may be important if the patient requires specialist intervention which is available only in certain hospitals.

81 Welsh Code para 4.11.

82 Welsh Code para 4.18.

83 Code of Practice para 6.13 provides that: 'Medical treatment must actually be available to the patient. It is not sufficient that appropriate treatment could theoretically be provided'. See Welsh Code para 4.12.

Disputes about the medical criteria

18.75 Expert witnesses will not always agree as to the medical criteria. For example, in *Peter Kiernan v Harrow Crown Court,*[84] the Divisional Court dealt with a challenge to a decision by the Crown Court on a committal for sentence. Four psychiatrists gave oral evidence, two to the effect that there was a mental illness requiring hospital treatment, and two suggesting that there were no signs of mental illness (who had the support of a further opinion in a written report). The Divisional Court quashed the hospital order made by the Crown Court judge because his reasons for preferring the first two doctors were inadequate and the evidence against a finding of mental illness was stronger.

18.76 There may also be disputes about other medical criteria. So in *R v Reid,*[85] a defendant who admitted rape and attempted kidnapping had been admitted to psychiatric hospitals on several occasions with a psychotic illness, and he had been transferred from prison to hospital while on remand. But there was a disagreement between experts as to whether there was schizophrenia exacerbated by cannabis abuse (a chronic condition) or a series of drug-induced psychoses that would not recur if the defendant did not abuse drugs. The judge accepted the latter contention and did not impose a hospital order, an assessment which the Court of Appeal held was open to him.

Combination with other sentences

18.77 The MHA 1983 s37(8) provides that a sentence of imprisonment cannot be passed at the same time as a hospital order is made,[86] nor can a community order be made, and it also excludes two youth sentencing options, referral orders and orders binding over parents or guardians. This means that other orders can be made, including the ancillary orders described in chapter 16. However, the Court of Appeal has emphasised the need to take a practical approach. For example, in *R v Taher Ahmed Chowdhury,*[87] it was noted that an anti-social

84 [2003] EWCA Crim 1052, [2005] MHLR 1. The matter was commenced as an appeal to the Court of Appeal; however, because of limitations in the jurisdiction of the Court of Appeal in relation to committals for sentence (section 10 of the Criminal Appeal Act 1968 at that time not covering a hospital order), the court reconstituted itself as a judicial review court.

85 [2005] EWCA Crim 392, [2006] MHLR 180.

86 But see MHA 1983 s45A, discussed below, which amounts to a hospital order combined with a prison sentence.

87 [2011] EWCA Crim 936, [2011] MHLR 157.

behaviour order (ASBO) was not excluded, though it was not used on the facts as that would be artificial. See also *R v Helen Patsalosavvis (aka Costi)*,[88] in which the Court of Appeal rejected the use of an ASBO on the basis that it would not be of practical assistance; there was no suggestion that it could not be imposed.

18.78 Section 37(8) is in terms limited to the sentencing options for one offence. In *R v Rogerson*,[89] the question was whether it was appropriate to pass a custodial sentence and a hospital order on the same occasion in relation to different offences. The appellant had admitted various motoring offences and was committed for sentence in the Crown Court, where he also admitted a further offence of manslaughter. This led to a hospital order together with a restriction order, but the judge then dealt with the motoring offences by way of a custodial sentence of 21 months. The Court of Appeal noted that the sentence was technically lawful but wholly impractical and so inappropriate: the custodial sentence was quashed, allowing the hospital order to commence its operation.

The restriction order

Introduction

18.79 When a hospital order is made under MHA 1983 s37, reasons to be concerned about the danger posed by the defendant may lead to the making by the Crown Court of a further order under section 41 of the Act, namely a restriction order. Section 41(1) provides:

> (1) Where a hospital order is made in respect of an offender by the Crown Court, and it appears to the court, having regard to the nature of the offence, the antecedents of the offender and the risk of his committing further offences if set at large, that it is necessary for the protection of the public from serious harm so to do, the court may, subject to the provisions of this section, further order that the offender shall be subject to the special restrictions set out in this section ...

18.80 The restriction order regime was introduced by the MHA 1959, section 65 of which allowed such an order when 'having regard to the nature of the offence, the antecedents of the offender and the risk of his committing further offences if set at large', the order was 'necessary for the protection of the public'. The MHA 1983 has changed the

88 [2010] EWCA Crim 1383, [2010] MHLR 191.
89 [2004] EWCA Crim 2099, [2006] MHLR 175.

test to one of being 'necessary for the protection of the public from serious harm'; the features to be taken into account are similar.

18.81 The effects of such an order are set out in section 41(3), namely the hospital order does not need to be renewed under section 20 of the Act (and so it continues until it is discharged), a separate release mechanism is in place (under which the Mental Health Tribunal or the Secretary of State for Justice may release the defendant on conditions and with the prospect of recall to hospital if concerns about risk emerge),[90] and questions of transfer between hospital and the granting of leave require the permission of the Secretary of State for Justice. The use of a restriction order allows the court to secure a regime that entails a more significant focus on public protection (and invariably involves a higher level of security and a longer stay in hospital).

18.82 Under the MHA 1959 and the MHA 1983 as enacted, the restriction order could be for a specified period or without limit of time. The latter type of order was highly recommended in case-law, and the power to make a time limited restriction order was removed by section 40 of the MHA 2007.

18.83 The statutory language indicates that there are a number of procedural prerequisites, including the level of the court and the calling of oral evidence. There are also a significant number of substantive issues arising: the features that can be taken into account, whether the medical evidence must support the making of a restriction order, what is the test of necessity (is it affected by other steps that can be taken, over what time period is if judged), and what is meant by serious harm to the public.

18.84 As with the question of whether to impose a hospital order, there is a level of circularity as there is a discretion not to apply the purposes of sentencing if a hospital order is available, but also a discretion not to impose a hospital order, which has been interpreted to mean that culpability by someone who qualifies for a hospital order can be reflected by not imposing a hospital order and instead following the purposes of sentencing. This is discussed separately below,

90 The CTO regime introduced by the MHA 2007 does not apply in the case of a restricted patient: MHA 1983 s41(3)(aa). This is because it mirrors the conditional discharge regime and so its application would allow a conditional discharge that side-stepped the normal process for imposing a conditional discharge. However, there does not seem any obvious reason why the statute could not have provided for a CTO with the consent of the Secretary of State and the power of recall to be exercised by the Secretary of State as well: this is similar to what happens in relation to the granting of leave, and the CTO is meant to work as a form of long-term leave.

as is the option of combining imprisonment with a hospital direction under MHA 1983 s45A,[91] which incorporates a prison sentence in the background together with a direction that the sentence be served in hospital for so long as that is appropriate.

Procedural prerequisites for a restriction order

Crown Court order and committal by magistrates' court

18.85 A restriction order must accompany a hospital order, and so the criteria for the hospital order must be made out. In addition, it can only be made by the Crown Court. If magistrates believe that one may be proper, the defendant may be committed to the Crown Court under MHA 1983 s43, though only if the defendant is at least 14 (and so it applies to the youth court as well). In the extreme situation in which a younger child might be suitable for a restriction order, the trial proceedings must be in the Crown Court. It only applies if there has been a conviction: so it does not arise if the magistrates have made a finding under section 37(3) without a conviction, on which see chapters 10 and 13. In such situations, the trial process must have occurred in the Crown Court.

18.86 On such a committal, the magistrates may also place the defendant in hospital, under MHA 1983 s44, if satisfied that there is a bed available: they may also make directions for the defendant to be held in a place of safety pending a hospital bed becoming available, though the 28-day time limit on such a placement is removed by section 44(3).

18.87 Section 44 contains no express reference to the need for the court to act upon medical evidence: however, the power can only be exercised if there is a committal under section 43, which in turn can occur only if the magistrates' court would have been in a position to make a hospital order following a conviction, and so the prerequisites of section 37, including the medical evidence, must be present. Section 43 also provides, in subsections (2) and following, that the Crown Court may investigate further by way of remands under sections 35 or 36 or the making of an interim hospital order under section 38 of the Act, and that it is not bound to make a hospital order or to add a restriction order.

91 Introduced by C(S)A 1997 s46 in relation to psychopathic disorder; extended to all forms of disorder by the MHA 2007.

Oral evidence

18.88 A further statutory procedural prerequisite is that there must be oral evidence from one of the doctors whose reports support the making of a hospital order: section 41(2). As is discussed below, this does not necessarily mean that the doctor giving evidence supports the making of a restriction order.

Legal representation

18.89 Case-law has produced a further procedural prerequisite, which is the need for the defendant to be represented: given that the effect of a restriction order can be compared to a life sentence in many respects in that it is possible for the detention to be for an indeterminate period of time and also possible that any release from detention will be on the basis of a liability to be recalled to hospital (since discharge can be conditional and so subject to recall), this is an understandable requirement for fairness to be secured. So, in *R v Blackwood*,[92] the Court of Appeal expressed the view that the defendant should be represented by counsel, both when a hospital order was in contemplation but also and particularly so when a restriction order was in prospect.

Provisional views of the judge

18.90 In *R v Goode*,[93] a question arising was whether there was a problem if a judge expressed a view at the outset of the sentencing hearing that on the basis of the material already known to her – including the written reports that did not favour a restriction order[94] – that such an order was nevertheless appropriate. The Court of Appeal dismissed the claim that the judge should not hear the matter on the basis of apparent bias, namely that she had formulated a concluded view, because it was nothing more than a provisional view that was open to change before the final decision was reached (and indeed it would have been open to criticism to form a provisional view and not alert the parties so that they could deal with it).[95]

92 (1974) 59 CrAppR 170 at 171–172.

93 [2002] EWCA Crim 1698, [2002] MHLR 337.

94 See the discussion below as to the ability of the judge to disagree with the recommendation of the doctors.

95 [2002] EWCA Crim 1698, [2002] MHLR 337 paras 46 and 47.

Power to specify hospital unit

18.91 One of the requirements for a hospital order is that a bed must be available in a hospital. As has been noted in chapter 1, there are different levels of security in the hospital system, and the management of a particular hospital may cover several sites. If a restriction order is made and the court wishes to ensure that the defendant is placed in a part of a particular hospital that has a specific level of security, section 47 of the C(S)A 1997 allows the court to specify a hospital unit in which the patient should be held, at least initially. This power depends on the existence of a separate unit, but section 47(3) defines this simply as some part of the hospital that is treated as a separate unit, which means that it may be satisfied by something as simple as being a ward that has a different level of security. However, it is to be noted that this can only control the initial admission of the patient, since he or she will then be open to being transferred in accordance with the provisions of the MHA 1983.

The test on the merits for a restriction order

18.92 The grounds for the making of a restriction order are set out in MHA 1983 s41(1). The language in this provision was changed from that applicable under the MHA 1959. Now, if the Crown Court has made a hospital order, it may add a restriction order, namely 'that the offender shall be subject to the special restrictions' listed in section 41(3), if that is necessary to protect the public from serious harm. The factors relevant are 'the nature of the offence, the antecedents of the offender and the risk of his committing further offences if set at large'.

18.93 Section 41(1) opens with the phrase: 'When a hospital order is made'. But, in light of the fact that the discretion in section 37(2)(b) – ie the finding that it is the most suitable disposal – may turn on whether a restriction order is to be added, the decision making process should not be linear but instead should consider the situation as a whole, namely reading sections 37 and 41 together.

18.94 Two points are worth making as to the statutory language: first, the aim of the restriction order is the protection of the public, and so this is the concern that must arise, rather than self-harm. Second, the test to be applied is one of necessity rather than a lesser standard such as desirability. The proper understanding of this language has given rise to a significant body of case-law, not all of which is easy to reconcile.

The guidance in *Birch*

18.95 The starting point for a discussion of the jurisprudence is the Court of Appeal decision in *R v Birch*.[96] This involved a successful appeal against the imposition of a restriction order. The offence was a killing in the context of a relationship that had deteriorated. The parties had separated; Ms Birch persuaded her husband to come to her flat, arranged for a friend to leave and lock the door, and she then shot him with a shotgun she had obtained and stabbed him five times with a knife. The prosecution account was that it was a planned and premeditated killing and she was charged with murder, but the defence account, while accepting that Ms Birch's conduct was culpable, suggested that the killing was not as culpable as the prosecution contended. A plea of guilty to manslaughter on the basis of diminished responsibility was accepted by the prosecution and the trial judge. This relied on medical evidence as to depression. Ms Birch had a background of self-harming behaviour and alcohol abuse, and had returned to over-use of alcohol in the time leading up to the killing, was jealous of her husband and his new partner, and developed a depressive illness. There was evidence that she intended to kill herself as well as her husband.

18.96 The authors of the medical reports supported a hospital order on the basis of the risk of self-harm, but suggested that a restriction order was not necessary because there was no danger to the public. One doctor gave oral evidence and repeated his view that there was no need for a restriction order: any risk to the public would only occur if there was a similar relationship with similar problems that coincided with a similar mental state. The judge, however, imposed a restriction order, reasoning that the offence was a serious offence of violence with a degree of premeditation and it was not possible to rule out the risk of further offences of violence.

18.97 Lord Justice Mustill noted that if a judge had decided that the criteria for a hospital order were made out, he or she had then to determine whether the criteria for a restriction order were made out. If so, there was a choice as to whether to impose such an order, the alternative being a prison sentence, which might be a difficult decision for a judge:

> He is required to choose between an order without restrictions, which may enable the author of a serious act of violence to be at liberty only a matter of months after he appears in court, and a restriction

96 (1990) 90 CrAppR 78.

> order which may lead the offender to be detained for a long time: longer in some cases than the period which he would serve if sent to prison ...[97]

18.98 So the practical effects of the orders, including the possibility of release, could be taken into account. It was held that a prison sentence might be imposed on a defendant whose disorder merited treatment in hospital both if no place in a hospital could be found and where there was an element of culpability which merited punishment, such as where there was no connection between disorder and offending or disorder merely reduced rather than displaced responsibility.[98]

18.99 In reaching these decisions, the judge did not require medical support for a restriction order. This was a matter of statutory interpretation. This had been held to be the position in relation to the restriction order under section 65 of the MHA 1959. In *R v Royse*,[99] the Court of Appeal had held that: 'The section puts the responsibility squarely on the shoulders of the judge to make a section 65 order if, in his opinion, it is necessary for the protection of the public so to do, whether or not the doctors advise such an order should be made'[100] and so rejected a contention that the order was inappropriate without medical support.[101] The Court of Appeal in *Birch* upheld this approach in the following terms:

> Did the judge in the Crown Court have jurisdiction to make an order under section 41, where those doctors who expressed an opinion on the matter were unanimous that the appellant was not dangerous? It is in our judgment quite clear that the answer is 'Yes.' There is a contrast between the language of section 37(2) and 41(1) and (2). Before a hospital order can be made, the court must be satisfied of the stated conditions 'on the written or oral evidence of two practitioners.' But where a restriction order is in question, section 41(2) requires no more than that the court shall hear the oral evidence of one of the

97 (1990) 90 CrAppR 78 p87. The authority cited for this proposition was *R v Haynes* (1981) 3 CrAppR(S) 330, which had considered the question previously arising, namely whether the restriction order should be limited in time or unlimited and had rejected the view that any restriction order should be limited by reference to the likely length of any custodial sentence that would be put in place had a hospital order not been imposed.

98 (1990) 90 CrAppR 78 pp88–89.

99 (1981) 3 CrAppR(S) 58.

100 (1981) 3 CrAppR(S) 58 p60.

101 Having stated the principle, the Court of Appeal then quashed the restriction order, finding that it was not justified on the facts in the light of further medical evidence as to the progress being made by Ms Royse (who had been convicted of manslaughter on the grounds of diminished responsibility). See chapter 21 for a discussion of the role of updated medical evidence on appeal.

medical practitioners. It need not follow the course which he recommends. Section 41(1) makes the assessment of the risk, in the light of the factors there identified, one for the court.

18.100 As for the criteria for a restriction order, the Court of Appeal noted the differences between section 41 and its predecessor, section 65 of the MHA 1959. The latter relied on:

a) the nature of the offence,
b) the antecedents of the offender and
c) the risk of his committing further offences if at large.

The first two criteria remained the same in the MHA 1983, and Mustill LJ noted that there was a reference only to antecedents, rather than character and antecedents, the language used in section 37(2)(b) in relation to a hospital order. The third criterion, however, had changed from the risk of further offences and was now the risk of serious harm from further offences. This meant that previous cases where relatively minor offending had led to restriction orders would no longer apply. As Mustill LJ noted:

> ... the word 'serious' qualifies 'harm' rather than 'risk.' Thus the court is required to assess not the seriousness of the risk that the defendant will re-offend, but the risk that if he does so the public will suffer serious harm. The harm in question need not, in our view, be limited to personal injury. Nor need it relate to the public in general, for it would in our judgment suffice if a category of persons, or even a single person, were adjudged to be at risk: although the category of person so protected would no doubt exclude the offender himself. Nevertheless the potential harm must be serious, and a high possibility of a recurrence of minor offences will no longer be sufficient.[102]

18.101 So anti-social recidivism cannot lead to a restriction order. However, the test is not limited to personal injury, nor need it relate to the public in general (so, for example, risk to a carer or family member would suffice). Equally, a relatively minor offence cannot preclude a restriction order being made if the court forms the view that the risk in the future meets the test: the nature of the offence and the past offending of the defendant are relevant, but they feed into the question of whether protection from serious harm necessitates a restriction order. This point was made by Mustill LJ in the following terms:

> ... there is nothing in the Act which requires a causal connection between the offender's mental state and what the professionals call the 'index offence'. It is sufficient for section 41 that the defendant is a convicted offender, and that the conditions of section 41 are satisfied

102 (1981) 3 CrAppR(S) 58 pp87–88.

> ... It would however be a mistake to equate the seriousness of the offence with the probability that a restriction order will be made. This is only one of the factors which section 41(1) requires to be taken into account. A minor offence by a man who proves to be mentally disordered and dangerous may properly leave him subject to a restriction.[103]

18.102 Just as the absence of any link between the offending and the mental disorder of the defendant does not preclude the imposition of a hospital order (though it may be relevant to the discretion as to whether a hospital order is the most suitable disposal, which is discussed below), so the lack of a connection between the mental disorder and the index offence does not preclude a restriction order. The decision as to the restriction order turns on the existence of the danger to the public from further offending, not the commission of an offence which by itself reveals a danger to the public. In other words, while it must be necessary for there to have been an offence carrying a prison sentence – that being the precondition for the imposition of a hospital order – the Court of Appeal in *Birch* suggests that there is no need for any connection between the offence and the finding of dangerousness as to the future. So that finding may arise from other information, including the psychiatric evidence, without any reliance on the index offence.

18.103 However, there is a statutory construction argument to put against this. The language of section 41 requires that the court have regard to 'to the nature of the offence, the antecedents of the offender *and* the risk of his committing further offences if set at large' (emphasis added). It could easily have been phrased as referring to the nature of the offence, antecedents *or* the risk of further offences, which would have made clear that if any of the features alone justified the conclusion as to future risk, that would be enough. On the phrasing as used, it is open to argument that the court is required to have regard to all features and that the risk should arise from all the factors taken into account, namely on a cumulative basis.

18.104 This interpretation would not preclude a restriction order following from a less serious offence: for example, it may be that the index offence, although itself minor, was an obvious indicator of an escalating scenario. However, it would be less likely that the court could conclude that a restriction order was needed if the offence and the offender's previous convictions did not themselves raise concern. The point to make in support of this interpretation is that predicting

103 (1981) 3 CrAppR(S) 58 p88.

the future is difficult, and so it should only be permissible to make an order based on future risk if the past conduct and index offence offer good support for the existence of that risk.

18.105 Although this argument does not fit well with the comments in *Birch*, it is fair to point out that it is not addressed in the judgment. Naturally, unless there is a decision to the contrary, the law is that a restriction order can follow a less serious offence, even if that does not by itself point to a risk of escalation, if there is a basis for forming the view as to future risk.

18.106 What of the vice versa situation, namely a serious offence but limited evidence of a risk in the future? If the question is future risk, it might be thought that a restriction order does not flow – even presumptively – from a serious offence. In *Birch*, having indicated that a relatively minor offence may lead to a restriction order, Mustill LJ commented that: 'In theory the converse is also true'.[104] But he then cautioned that 'the Court will need to be very sure of its ground in such a case'. So, commenting on the facts in front of the court, it was noted that: 'This was a very serious offence and a low risk of repetition would justify a restriction order'.[105] However, the court then determined that there was not such a risk and quashed the restriction order.

18.107 It is important to note the reasoning that was rejected by the court. The prognosis for Mrs Birch was positive, such that her release was likely to occur relatively soon. Mustill LJ commented that it was 'attractive ... reasoning' to suggest that a restriction order should be imposed in the light of the prognosis for Ms Birch's recovery, in the light of the 'evident disproportion between the premeditated taking of life, and a period of confinement unlikely (judging by what we were told) greatly to exceed two or three years'.[106] In other words, when viewed through punitive spectacles, the limited period of detention was not appropriate. But this approach was 'not what the Act contemplates' and so was not followed. In short, an approach based on the idea that hospitalisation is designed to satisfy the aims of punishment is not appropriate when the court is contemplating how to exercise the judgments that arise under the MHA 1983, including whether to add a restriction order.[107]

104 (1981) 3 CrAppR(S) 58 p88.
105 (1981) 3 CrAppR(S) 58 p90.
106 (1981) 3 CrAppR(S) 58 p90.
107 (1981) 3 CrAppR(S) 58: Mustill LJ noted that it seemed to be a 'crime of illness not wickedness' (at page 90), and so the level of culpability requiring a punitive response was somewhat limited.

18.108 In summary, the following points arise from *Birch*, though some may be subject to counter argument:

i) The question relevant to whether to make a restriction order is the risk of serious harm to the public or any member of the public.
ii) This may arise even if the index offence is not a serious offence; conversely, it does not automatically follow in the case of a serious offence if the court is satisfied that, even though a hospital order is proper, there is no real evidence as to risk.
iii) The judge may make a restriction order even if the doctors giving evidence do not support it, though it might well be that the judge had no proper basis to disagree with doctors who have been in a better position to assess and formulate a view as to the risk posed by the defendant and were of the opinion that there were inadequate grounds to impose a restriction order.
iv) The use of disposals under the Mental Health Act, including the use of a restriction order, are discretionary; a prison sentence remains an alternative, particularly if there are questions of culpability to address.

18.109 These points have been revisited by the Court of Appeal in a number of cases.

Risk of serious harm to the public, and the necessity of guarding against it

Serious harm to the public

18.110 In relation to what amounts to 'serious harm', all that had been said in *Birch* was that: 'The harm in question need not, in our view, be limited to personal injury'.[108] Of course, in the context, there had been a homicide and the concern was a similar offence, which would clearly amount to serious harm. It was more of an issue in *R v Cox*,[109] the context being an affray from the brandishing of a penknife with a four-inch blade and threatening people with it, though the defendant's account was that he had used the knife to scare off the two victims rather than to threaten them; there was also a charge of criminal damage to a booklet in a police station. Mr Cox was already subject to a hospital order, and had a lengthy history of both offending and of psychiatric treatment. Although the medical evidence supported just

108 (1990) 90 CrAppR 78 at p88.
109 [1999] MHLR 30.

a further hospital order, the court imposed a restriction order as well on the basis that:

i) it was desirable to have some form of independent control of release; and
ii) the second hospital order within a short period of time and this time for a serious offence indicated that a restriction order was needed.[110]

The Court of Appeal dismissed an appeal against the restriction order.[111] The argument on appeal focussed on the failure of the sentencing judge to refer to the statutory criteria and the fact that the affray had not produced any actual bodily harm. The court concluded that it had been open to the judge to find the affray to be a 'nasty case' and stated that 'it is difficult, in our judgment, to say that should he offend again there was no risk of anyone suffering serious harm',[112] which was rephrased in concluding comments as 'there is a considerable risk that he will reoffend again, and in our judgment there is a real, rather than a fanciful or remote, risk that if he does so the public would suffer serious harm'.[113]

18.111 The court commented on what was meant by 'serious harm', though in passing. It noted that the term was not defined in the MHA 1983, but had been defined in section 31(3) of the Criminal Justice Act (CJA) 1991 as 'death or serious injury, whether physical or psychological'.[114] This was for the purposes of assessing whether a 'longer than commensurate' sentence should be imposed under CJA 1991 s2(2) in relation to violent and sexual offences: it had to be 'necessary to protect the public from serious harm from the offender'. When sentencing provisions were consolidated into the PCC(S)A 2000, the 'longer than commensurate' sentence provisions were placed in section 80(2)(b) of the Act and the definition in section 161(4) was that references to 'protecting the public from serious harm from him shall be construed as a reference to protecting members of the public from death or serious personal injury, whether physical or psychological, occasioned by further such offences committed by him'. The

110 [1999] MHLR 30 para 19. The first hospital order related to a conviction for dishonest use of electricity: paragraph 9.

111 The appeal was supported by additional evidence as to improvements in Mr Cox's insight to his illness and hence compliance with treatment: the Court of Appeal did not comment on the further evidence.

112 [1999] MHLR 30 para 25.

113 [1999] MHLR 30 para 34.

114 [1999] MHLR 30 para 24.

sentencing regime was replaced by the dangerous offender provisions of sections 224–236 of the CJA 2003; in this statute, the definition of 'serious harm' in section 224(3) is 'death or serious personal injury, whether physical or psychological'.

18.112 These variations in the definition of 'serious harm' are semantic: accordingly, the approach adopted in *Cox* should continue to apply. These sentencing provisions and restriction orders share a public protection aim which means that it is appropriate to carry the definition across. An indication of the approach to be adopted, using the CJA 2003, was given in *R v Lang*,[115] in which the Court of Appeal noted that:

> 11. Serious harm is defined in section 224(3) as meaning 'death or serious personal injury, whether physical or psychological'. It is a concept familiar since the Criminal Justice Act 1991 section 2(2)(b) and previous decisions of this Court will continue to be relevant to its assessment. For example, as was said in *R v Bowler* 15 CrAppR(S) 78, sexual assaults which are relatively minor physically may lead to serious psychological injury; and downloading indecent images of children may cause serious psychological injury to a child arising not only from what the child has been forced to do but also from the knowledge that others will see what they were doing (see *R v Collard* [2004] Crim LR 757).

18.113 In *Narey v HM Customs and Excise*,[116] it was held that the importation of 3.8kg of cocaine involved the potential for serious harm to the public.[117] This suggests that it is not necessary for the serious harm to be inflicted directly by the defendant: it is sufficient if the offence is of a sort that feeds into unwise, self-harming behaviour by others, even others who may be exercising autonomous choices.

Less serious offence leading to restriction order

18.114 The focus on the future means that a restriction order is possible following a less serious offence. This was upheld in *R v Kamara*:[118] the index offence was an assault occasioning actual bodily harm from a punch, and, although the defendant had various previous convictions, none of them had involved serious harm. The Court of Appeal noted that it was open to the judge to conclude that there was the risk of future assaults being more serious, such that there was a necessity

115 [2006] 1 WLR 2509. [2006] 2 Prison LR 98.

116 [2005] EWHC 784 (Admin), [2005] MHLR 194.

117 [2005] EWHC 784 (Admin), [2005] MHLR 194 para 19.

118 [2000] MHLR 9.

to protect against the risk of serious harm. (On the facts, this was supported by one doctor who gave evidence, though not by another.)

18.115 Similarly, the Divisional Court hearing a challenge to a restriction order imposed following a finding made under the Criminal Procedure (Insanity and Unfitness to Plead) Act 1991 (discussed in chapter 9) in *Jones v Isleworth Crown Court*[119] held that it had been open to the judge to view the conduct of the defendant as escalating in seriousness. On the facts, this was not just the conduct as reflected in the charges before the court, which were of burglary, but the information that his mental health problems included hallucinations with commands to harm others and complications from drug abuse and had involved incidents of aggression while in hospital awaiting trial.

18.116 It is not necessary for there to be a suggestion of an escalation in conduct. In *R v Golding*,[120] the index offence was a domestic burglary, and the evidence was that his chronic mental health disorder was complicated by drug abuse, a habit which he fed by burglary: as such, the Court of Appeal held that it was inherently likely that his further offending might involve confrontations with householders and so was inherently risky. Similarly, in *R v Steele*,[121] the Court of Appeal upheld a restriction order imposed in relation to index offences of a very minor nature (theft of a pair of police gloves from outside a public house, shoplifting of food, possession of cannabis and failure to surrender): the context was of disengagement from treatment and substance abuse leading to public order offending and aggressive incidents in hospital, albeit that none had led to any harm to anyone, more serious offending in the past and a period of time spent in high secure hospital conditions following a riot in prison. The Court of Appeal held that it had been open to the sentencing judge to conclude that the criteria for a restriction order were met in the context.

18.117 There are some contrasting decisions. The Court of Appeal in *R v Steward*,[122] which involved what was charged as an assault occasioning actual bodily harm (though involving breaking a tooth and loosening another tooth of the victim during a scuffle following an attempted theft of a bag), set aside a restriction order on a defendant who had long-standing mental health problems, and previous convictions, including for arson, assault and possessing an offensive weapon. It accepted that there was a risk of further offending and that there was

119 [2005] EWHC 662 (Admin), [2005] MHLR 93.

120 [2006] EWCA Crim 1965, [2006] MHLR 272.

121 [2010] EWCA Crim 605, [2010] MHLR 107.

122 [2008] EWCA Crim 1255, [2008] MHLR 148.

a risk of some harm, but held that there was insufficient evidence of a risk of serious harm.[123] It went so far as to comment that: 'It must surely be rare indeed that a Hospital Order with a restriction can be triggered by such an offence as this'.[124] This is perhaps going too far, since evidence of matters other than the particular offence is relevant.

18.118 Similarly, in *R v Hurst*,[125] which involved a 'road-rage' assault, the Court of Appeal quashed a restriction order in circumstances in which there was a high risk of reoffending but the judge had not explained why he felt that there was a risk of serious harm being involved and the Court of Appeal could not see such a risk.[126]

More serious offence not leading to a restriction order

18.119 Along similar lines to the question of whether a less serious offence may be a precursor to more violent incidents is the question of whether the defendant's actions, while serious, are an isolated incident. This was, in effect, the conclusion in *Birch*, though the court commented that the sentencing judge would have to be sure of his or her ground: see para 18.106 above. This clearly allows a conclusion that further serious offending is unlikely even though there has been a serious offence.

18.120 Naturally, this will turn on the facts. If the judge does not impose a restriction order, that will require a prosecution appeal on the grounds of undue leniency. If the judge is not persuaded against a restriction order following a serious offence, the Court of Appeal will usually assess whether the judge reached a conclusion open to him or her, provided that relevant factors were taken into account and the proper approach in law was identified. So in *R v Goode*,[127] the offence was a serious attack by a father on his son that represented the first instance of offending during a long psychiatric history (of some 25

123 See also *R v Haile* [2009] EWCA Crim 1996, [2009] MHLR 300, in which the defendant admitted a sexual assault and an attempted robbery, and asked that two further attempted robberies be taken into consideration: the judge imposed a restriction order against the advice of the doctors on the basis of the violence in the offending; the Court of Appeal overturned this on the basis that more was needed than citing the violence in the offending of the defendant to disagree with the doctors, such as an escalating pattern of violence. The sentencing judge had seen such a pattern, but the Court of Appeal disagreed.

124 [2005] EWHC 784 (Admin), [2005] MHLR 194 para 8.

125 [2007] EWCA Crim 3436, [2007] MHLR 43.

126 [2007] EWCA Crim 3436, [2007] MHLR 43 paras 31 and 32.

127 [2002] EWCA Crim 1698, [2002] MHLR 337.

years): the Court of Appeal held that it had been open to the judge to conclude that the test for a restriction order was made out. Similarly, in *R v Rosso,*[128] in which a defendant had been convicted of causing grievous bodily harm with intent, arising from a struggle with police officers who were assisting the execution of a warrant under MHA 1983 s135 to allow Mr Rosso to be assessed under the civil provisions, during which an officer was injured with a knife, the Court of Appeal dismissed a challenge to the imposition of a restriction order that was based on the fact that there had been no previous violence during a long history of mental disorder. It found that the index offence and the mental instability it demonstrated justified a restriction order despite the fact that there had been no previous violence and it occurred during the tense circumstances of the execution of a warrant.[129]

18.121 However, a contrasting case is *Narey v HM Customs and Excise,*[130] the drug-importation case mentioned above. The judge had not made a finding as to the risk of further offending but commented that the defendant appeared to be unpredictable.[131] The Divisional Court, having accepted that the offence was one of the sort that might cause serious harm, concluded that the restriction order was not justified because there was insufficient evidence to support a finding of the risk of further offending. In other words, the risk of harm from further offending is one thing, but this involves looking at what the offending might be as well as how likely it is that it might occur. This is consistent with the approach in *Birch,* where the restriction order was set aside on the basis that there was no real risk of a repeat of the offence.

The public

18.122 The question of what was meant by the public or any member of the public was raised in *R v Jones.*[132] A mother was convicted of child cruelty on the basis of leaving her young daughter in some woods; she was alone for 30 hours before being found after Ms Jones gave some clues. The daughter was already in care, but had been having contact with her mother. The judge imposed a prison sentence of five years, but on appeal the Court of Appeal followed the recommendations of

128 [2003] EWCA Crim 3242, [2003] MHLR 404.
129 [2003] EWCA Crim 3242, [2003] MHLR 404 para 26.
130 [2005] EWHC 784 (Admin), [2005] MHLR 194.
131 [2005] EWHC 784 (Admin), [2005] MHLR 194 paras 19 and 20.
132 [2000] MHLR 12.

the medical experts that a hospital order was more suitable. It considered whether a restriction order should be used in the light of the risks that Ms Jones would have another child. The court held that no person was at risk and so a restriction order was not required:[133] the context of this was the court's recitation of counsel's submissions that 'the public' did not include unborn children and that the law provided other methods for protecting such children (including applications under the Children Act 1989).

Necessity of the restriction order

18.123 So there are two points arising from *Jones*. The first, which is likely to be of relevance only in unusual circumstances, is that the concern must be current persons, not unborn children. The second, which is of much wider importance, is that the test of whether a restriction order is necessary must allow for consideration of whether other mechanisms mean that a restriction order, even if desirable or sensible, cannot be described as necessary. The need to approach this question in a practical fashion may provide an explanation for a decision that otherwise is difficult to understand, *R v Chowdhury*.[134] He had committed a serious attack after disengaging from treatment prematurely when he took a trip to Bangladesh as part of his rehabilitation from an episode of mental illness. The Court of Appeal quashed a restriction order made against the medical opinions on the basis that the real concern in the case, namely of Mr Chowdhury disengaging if he travelled abroad, was met by an undertaking he gave to allow his psychiatrist to have control with his passport. The important practical point arising from this is that if the main concern for the court is to ensure that a defendant continues with a regime of treatment, which may turn on whether or not the defendant accepts the need for treatment (often referred to as insight into being ill), then the test of necessity may not be met.

Time-scale

18.124 Another question that might arise is the time-scale involved in assessing the risk of serious harm or the necessity of the protective mechanism of the restriction order. This is because the effect of the restriction order is not only that there are additional controls on the progress that the patient makes towards release but there is (or at

133 [2000] MHLR 12 para 48.
134 [2011] EWCA Crim 936, [2011] MHLR 157.

least has been)[135] a different regime as to release: namely it can be 'conditional', meaning that there is a power of recall, and subject to conditions, a common one of which would be the taking of medication in the community. A restriction order will continue for the rest of the life of the defendant unless either a tribunal grants an absolute discharge under MHA 1983 s73 or the Secretary of State for Justice either grants an absolute discharge or lifts the restriction order under section 42 of the Act.[136] If the restriction order is not lifted, the patient remains subject to the prospect of administrative recall to hospital on the warrant of the Secretary of State, which has some similarities to being on a life licence under an indeterminate sentence of imprisonment.

18.125 The question of whether the different regime on release can be taken into account at sentencing was raised in *R v Kamara*,[137] in which the treating psychiatrist sought a restriction order in order to secure compliance with treatment after release (which he envisaged would be after a matter of months). The particular concern for the doctor was that Mr Kamara had a history of defaulting on medication and then committing further offences. The second doctor who supported a hospital order had formulated a lesser view of risk and indicated that securing compliance with medication was not appropriate by itself. As already noted above, the Court of Appeal accepted that there was a risk of serious harm from further offending: it also accepted that it could be (and on the facts was) appropriate to use a restriction order in relation to a patient who would only need short-term hospital treatment in order to provide for conditions on his release to assist to reduce the risk he posed.

18.126 It is worth noting that there is a clear argument against this. The context of the risk assessment carried out by the sentencing court is to determine whether the 'special restrictions' should be applied: those special restrictions are set out in section 41(3), and at the time of the *Kamara* judgment were that the hospital order does not expire and so does not need to be renewed (which implies a degree of longevity to the order), during which time the various management powers (including transfer and leave, which may often be matters relevant to rehabilitation processes) have to be exercised with the consent of the Secretary of State. The point to be noted is that the different release

135 See the discussion of the impact of the CTO regime below.

136 If the restriction order is lifted, the patient will stay in hospital under the hospital order.

137 [2000] MHLR 9.

provisions relevant to restricted patients are not mentioned as features relevant to the restriction order. The only reference to a 'special restriction' relating to release is that the power of discharge exercised by the RC or hospital managers requires the consent of the Secretary of State (and would lead to a discharge under section 23 of the Act not under section 42, the conditional discharge power of the Secretary of State).

18.127 Since *Kamara* was decided, the list of special restrictions has been supplemented by the amendment introduced by the MHA 2007. This introduced the CTO regime for civil patients and added section 41(3)(aa) to include as a special restriction the fact that this regime is not available for restricted patients. Since this involves release from hospital subject to an ongoing obligation to take medication, it strengthens the argument that the focus of the sentencing court should be the regime to which the patient will be subject during detention and before release, and not the regime that will be possible after release.

18.128 It is difficult to ascertain whether this was argued in *Kamara*: the contention of counsel was summarised as being one of it not being open to a doctor to ask for a restriction order when it was known that release would be suitable after a few months;[138] this is a respectable argument in the sense that if one reviews the 'special restrictions', they are consistent with a longer-term detention. However, it is a slightly more focussed argument that is needed to test the conclusion reached in *Kamara* that it is possible to have a restriction order in order to secure a release with a conditional discharge including a condition as to the taking of medication.[139]

138 Paragraph 19. This might be suggested by the approach of the Court of Appeal in *Birch*, in which it was noted that a hospital order alone 'may enable the author of a serious act of violence to be at liberty only a matter of months after he appears in court', in contrast to a restriction order 'which may lead the offender to be detained for a long time: longer in some cases than the period which he would serve if sent to prison': (1990) 90 CrAppR 78 at 87.

139 See also *R v Kearney* [2002] EWCA Crim 2772, [2003] MHLR 183: the judge had imposed a restriction order against the weight of the medical evidence on the basis that it would be of assistance to the defendant and to the public for him to be recalled to hospital in case of any repeat behaviour of the sort involved in the index offence (an assault on community mental health workers trying to persuade him to come to hospital when his mental health deteriorated after a bereavement); the Court of Appeal noted that the judge had not addressed the statutory test, and they took the view that it was not made out. However, the Court of Appeal did not expressly deal with the issue of whether the judge had been wrong to look to the question of control after release from hospital.

18.129 There are several additional points to note in this regard. First, any decision as to conditions will be taken at the time of release, and so the assessment by the trial court of what might or might not happen is somewhat speculative.

18.130 Second, there need not be a condition relating to the taking of medication. The effect of a conditional discharge is that the patient is subject to recall (and release is therefore conditional), not that it is a release on the basis of ongoing compliance with certain conditions. It is possible to have a conditional discharge without any conditions; this is particularly clear if the conditional discharge is made by a tribunal under section 73, which notes, in section 73(3)(b), that the patient has to comply with 'such conditions (if any)' as may be imposed. The language of section 42(3), relating to a conditional discharge by the Secretary of State is less clear, since it refers to a release 'absolutely or subject to conditions': but there is no requirement that any condition be one relating to the taking of medication.

18.131 Moreover, there is no enforcement mechanism relating to conditions. The power of recall to hospital, which exists under section 42(3), is one that depends on the existence of a deteriorated mental state such as to warrant placement in hospital, not merely the breach of any condition[140] (though such a breach may provide evidence that there had been a deterioration in a mental state). So not only will a criminal court passing the restriction order be speculating as to whether any release will include a condition that medication be accepted, but there can be no direct enforcement of that condition.

18.132 The reason why no enforcement is possible is that once a restricted patient has been released, the provisions of the MHA 1983 allowing treatment without consent no longer apply. As a result, it has been held that a condition that purports to require a patient to accept medication must refer to the fact that it is always subject to the patient's right to give or withhold consent: see *R (SH) v Mental Health Review Tribunal*.[141] Accordingly, a court passing a restriction order on the basis that it will secure ongoing acceptance of medication by someone who has a chronic condition that deteriorates without medication must note that this regime will be subject to the views of and cooperation by the patient.

18.133 All that being said, it is no doubt proper to say that the vast majority of conditional discharges will involve a condition that the patient

140 Otherwise there may be a breach of ECHR article 5(1): see *Kay v UK* (1998) 40 BMLR 20.

141 [2007] EWHC 884 (Admin), [2007] MHLR 234.

continue to co-operate with any requirements of the supervising psychiatrist, including as to the taking of medication; and it is also no doubt true that the existence of the prospect of recall will play a role in the technique of managing the patient in the community so as to ensure co-operation with ongoing medication. This supports the line of reasoning in *Kamara*. However, the test remains the necessity of the order. So, in *R v Acharya*,[142] the basis for the restriction order was the need to ensure compliance with medication: it was quashed by the Court of Appeal as not being justified on the evidence (and the court held that the sentencing judge had erred in not taking account of the disadvantages of the restriction order for the treatment programme). While the question of whether it was legitimate to use the restriction order for this purpose was not addressed, the necessity test that is the prerequisite for the order being made in the first place suggests that the willingness of a patient to accept treatment is a strong feature against the necessity of a restriction order if the central concern is the ongoing taking of medication.

18.134 It is also suggested that this line of reasoning, namely the importance of securing compliance after release, has to be revisited now that the CTO regime has been introduced by the MHA 2007. As noted above, this is available in relation to those not subject to a restriction order. The effect of the CTO, which is summarised in chapter 2, is that the patient is subject to ongoing obligations as to medication and is subject to recall to hospital because the underlying detention under MHA 1983 s3 (which is the result of a section 37 order) is suspended. In short, this is a regime that reflects what happens under a conditional discharge but is only available in relation to a non-restricted patient. To return to the point made in *Jones*: alternative protective mechanisms may mean that the restriction order is not required: and if the focus is on long-term management and cooperation with treatment, the availability of the CTO may provide an answer to this concern and so undermine the necessity of a restriction order.[143]

Rehabilitation and discretion

18.135 One final point to note is that there may be arguments on the particular facts to the effect that the restriction order is counter-productive to rehabilitation and so may not secure the purpose of protecting the public. This links to the question of the responsibilities of the medical

142 [2005] EWCA Crim 772, [2005] MHLR 28.

143 The existence of the CTO regime was noted in the case of *Chowdhury*, noted above.

professionals involved. The restriction order regime means that the views of the clinical team as to release and transfer are subject to a dual key: but there is an entirely separate matter of whether the medical professionals are less able to carry out their task of achieving progress for their patients in the form of moves to less secure hospitals, obtaining leave of absence or discharge if they are subject to the restriction order regime. As to the first point, in *R v Cox*[144] one of the comments made by the sentencing judge as to why the restriction order was proper was the need to ensure that release was subject to some form of independent control (through the Ministry of Justice or the tribunal). This does not seem to have been challenged in the case, but could be characterised as reasoning that the treating team is not to be trusted to make decisions as to release (as they can in relation to a non-restricted patient). This is inconsistent with an approach of respecting professional judgments as to patients, particularly on questions of prognosis and ongoing assessment, which are not matters over which the courts have expertise. However, the entire basis for the restriction order is subjecting the defendant to the regime of having a control on leave, transfer and release that is independent of the treating team (ie a dual key approach). The less pejorative way of looking at this is that, irrespective of the abilities of the clinical team, the risks involved are such that a review is necessary before a patient is transferred or released, whether on leave or through discharge from hospital.

18.136 But the separate issue is that the restriction order may have a negative impact on the treatment and rehabilitation of the patient and hence the prospect of the patient being ready for transfer, leave or discharge. This may arise in many ways: for example, the need to secure the agreement of the Secretary of State for Justice for therapeutic steps such as the granting of leave to visit the community may put a strain on the relationship between the clinical team and the patient and slow down rehabilitative functions. This is because the RC will not be able to provide some obvious incentives to cooperation with treatment, such as additional leave, without persuading the Secretary of State. In an extreme situation, it may be arguable that this will increase the risk posed by the patient, including to staff.

18.137 This is relevant for a court because there is a discretion as to the imposition of a restriction order even if the criteria are made out. In *Birch*, there was a discussion of this discretion in the context of the possibility that a defendant who qualified for a hospital order with a

144 [1999] MHLR 30 at para 19.

restriction order might nevertheless be sent to prison. Confirmation that the discretion also extends to the possibility of problems with the treatment programme came in *R v Mahmood*.[145] The offending in this case was a robbery with a meat cleaver by a young woman with learning difficulties and drug abuse problems: the psychiatrists, who did not believe that a restriction order was necessary, noted that the treatment programme included seeking to teach appropriate behaviour to Ms Mahmood by using various techniques, including the granting of leave from hospital, which was hindered by the restriction order regime. On this basis, the Court of Appeal quashed the restriction order imposed by the sentencing judge, Garland J for the court noting that 'since the very experienced psychiatrist having her care takes the view that section 41 is a hindrance rather than a help, we take the view that it would be appropriate to allow the appeal to the extent of quashing the section 41 order'. The reasoning, it has to be accepted, does not deal with the mechanics of why the factual conclusion meant that there should not be a restriction order, but there was no criticism of the trial judge's finding that the criteria were made out, and so the judgment makes sense as one that goes to the discretion to impose a restriction order.

18.138 Similarly, in *R v Acharya*,[146] the Court of Appeal quashed a restriction order that had been imposed against the views of the medical witnesses, citing the need to balance the concerns raised so as to justify an order (which on the facts related to compliance with medication) against the disadvantages to the flexibility of the treatment programme and reintegration of the offender into the community caused by such an order.[147] Again, the reasoning as to this is not clear, because the court's concluding paragraph was that the restriction order was not justified rather than that it should not be imposed as a matter of discretion:[148] however, the balancing act adopted, which, as it is not mentioned in the statutory criteria, can only be relevant as a matter of the discretion as to the imposition of a restriction order.

145 [2002] MHLR 416.

146 [2005] EWCA Crim 772, [2005] MHLR 28.

147 [2005] EWCA Crim 772, [2005] MHLR 28 para 15.

148 [2005] EWCA Crim 772, [2005] MHLR 28 para 16. This was also the case in *R v Hurst* [2007] EWCA Crim 3436, [2007] MHLR 43 at para 33. The Court of Appeal in *R v Osker* [2010] EWCA Crim 955, [2010] MHLR 115 also noted the views expressed by the medical witnesses of the value of flexibility in treatment that was possible without a restriction order, but also expressed their view that the criteria for the order were not made out.

18.139 The difficulty of securing reintegration into society, which is an important pathway for treatment,[149] also arose in *R v Helen Patsalosavvis (aka Costi)*,[150] where the Court of Appeal considered a case of a restriction order that was both positively disadvantageous in terms of treatment and rehabilitation and of questionable value in terms of preventing re-offending and so did not secure its purpose. She had made several hoax calls as to the presence of bombs at Heathrow Airport: the restriction order imposed did not deal with the problem of further similar offending because it did not make it more difficult for her to make phone calls, and it was suggested in the medical evidence for the Court of Appeal that the longer term detention might make worse the maladaptive behaviour that characterised her personality disorder. The court set aside the restriction order as not being helpful.[151]

The role of medical evidence and expert opinion

The approach in principle

18.140 An important question that has arisen in many cases is the relationship between the view of the doctors as to the need for a restriction order and the decision of the judge. As already noted, the Court of Appeal in *Birch*[152] was clear that as a matter of statutory interpretation, medical support for a restriction order was not a jurisdictional prerequisite to its imposition. The court followed a holding to this effect in relation to the restriction order under section 65 of the MHA 1959: *R v Royse.*[153] In that case, having noted that the decision was one for the judge, and so rejecting a contention that the order was inappropriate without medical support, the court then quashed the restriction order, finding that it was not justified on the facts in the light of further medical evidence as to the progress being made by Ms Royse (who had been convicted of manslaughter on the grounds of diminished responsibility).[154] The same happened in *Birch*.

149 [2005] EWCA Crim 772, [2005] MHLR 28 para 14.

150 [2010] EWCA Crim 1383, [2010] MHLR 191.

151 Again, the reasoning is not clear as to whether the criteria for a restriction order were not made out or whether the court was exercising its discretion.

152 See above at para 18.99.

153 (1981) 3 CrAppR(S) 58.

154 See chapter 21 for a discussion of the role of updated medical evidence on appeal.

18.141 Two questions illustrate the potential concerns as to the extent of this principle:

i) What is the judicial skill that allows disagreement with the doctors?
ii) Are there any practical problems?

The first is exemplified by the factual situations in both *Birch* and *Royse*. It can be rephrased as a question of the ability of the criminal courts to formulate a view as to risk that does not rely on medical evidence. In some situations, it may be based entirely on the prognosis for the mental disorder. In that scenario, diagnosis and the assessment of what is likely to happen in the future arising from the medical condition of the defendant are both matters beyond the skill-set of a judge in the absence of expert support. However, there is the difference in language between sections 37 and 41, on which the court relied in *Birch*, namely that the statute allows reliance to be placed on matters other than the medical opinion expressed, including the offence and the previous convictions. This in turn means that the prediction need not be based only on the medical expert evidence. But it is likely that the medical opinion will take those features into account, that being a skill in particular of forensically-trained psychiatrists. In addition, it may be that the offence and antecedents of the defendant do not indicate risk, and so the need for a restriction order can only arise from the prognosis of the disorder: if that is so, then the statement of principle in *Birch* has to be limited accordingly.

18.142 This reflects what happened in the case (and in *Royse*). The Court of Appeal relied on the views of the doctors, who did not feel that the risk posed by Ms Birch was sufficient to warrant a restriction order. As Mustill LJ put it, in the light of the fact that the homicide, clearly a very serious matter, had occurred in the context of a relationship breakdown and alcohol abuse – features which are hardly uncommon – the question for the court was whether there was even a low risk of repetition:

> What is the likelihood that a relapse, combined with slipping back to alcohol and tranquillisers, will put another person in peril? It seems to us that we have nothing to go on except the evidence of the doctors, which has struck us as responsible, and which is not patently unsound. We have no basis for a personal judgment which we could prefer to theirs. They have studied the appellant, we have not. Dr Holton has seen her repeatedly and has had an opportunity to judge the improvement in her condition. We have not.[155]

155 (1990) 90 CrAppR 78 at p90.

18.143 This was a sensible reminder that the judicial skill-set does not extend to making judgments about the prognosis for a defendant. Another practical point also noted in the judgment was that the judge might often have nothing on which to rely aside from the medical evidence, given that the defendant might often have no antecedents and might have pleaded guilty, giving the judge no opportunity to form a judgment by observing the defendant in the course of a trial.[156] In any event, there must be a question as to whether the opportunity to observe a defendant during a trial is a sensible basis on which to counter an expert medical view as to the risks of the future. As has been discussed in relation to the question of fitness to stand trial, the real evidence of the judge's assessment of what is actually happening in the court room may have some relevance when compared with an expert assessment made in advance. But it is more difficult to argue that the approach of the defendant to the unusual situation of a trial reflects on his or her future risk.

18.144 The extent to which the judge is free to impose a restriction order when the doctors do not support it is also a matter of practicalities. There is the possibility that the hospital authorities will not be willing to accept a defendant under a restriction order. This is a key question because a statutory precondition for the making of a hospital order is that there is a bed available for the patient,[157] and if that bed is not available to a patient under a restriction order, then the hospital order cannot proceed. It is suggested that it behoves a court to inquire as to whether the offer of a bed to a defendant based on medical reports supporting a hospital order only remains on offer if a restriction order is added.

18.145 This is consistent with the principle accepted in various settings that a court cannot compel a doctor to act contrary to his or her view of what is medically proper. To give an example: if a tribunal wishes to release a patient from hospital on a conditional discharge with a condition of out-patient treatment by a psychiatrist and all potential supervising psychiatrists are unwilling to accept the role because they take the view that the patient's condition is such that he ought to remain an in-patient, the tribunal is not able to compel a doctor to offer supervision (and must decide whether the patient is to remain in detention or should be released without such a condition). In this

156 (1990) 90 CrAppR 78 p87.

157 See para 18.48 above.

context, see the case of *R (IH) v Secretary of State for the Home Department*[158] and its ECtHR corollary in *Kolanis v UK.*[159]

18.146 This approach, namely of paying particular heed to the views of the relevant mental health professionals, was followed by the Court of Appeal in a case arising under the MHA 1959, in which the restriction order regime was first developed, namely *R v Blackwood*[160]: commenting on the provisions of section 60(3) of the MHA 1959, which have become section 37(4), namely the requirement that a court must be satisfied that arrangements have been made to admit the defendant to a hospital, Browne J stated:

> It seems to us ... that it is most desirable that in every case where section 60 and section 65 orders are being considered, either the doctor from the hospital concerned should give oral evidence or, if that is not possible, the doctor who is going to give the evidence should be fully informed about the views of the doctor who is going to be in charge of the case at the hospital. This should make sure that there is no misunderstanding between the doctors and the Court about whether or not the case is suitable for a section 65 order and also that there is no misunderstanding about whether the hospital is willing to accept the patient if a section 65 order is made.[161]

The application of these principles

18.147 The fact that the decision is one for the sentencing judge to make has been stated on numerous occasions, but with a variety of emphases. At one extreme, there are dicta suggesting that the matter is entirely one for the sentencing judge. For example, in *R v Cox,*[162] one of the points argued was that the judge had given inadequate weight to the views of the doctors that a restriction order was not required. This was dismissed with the comment that the making of a restriction order was 'simply and solely a question for the judge'.[163]

18.148 A case following a different approach was *R v Reynolds:*[164] the sentencing judge had imposed a restriction order against the views of the doctors in a case involving three assaults, one of them being an unlawful wounding (from a knife) and two being assaults occasioning actual bodily harm (from hitting someone with a brick and

158 [2004] 2 AC 253, [2004] MHLR 51.

159 (2006) 42 EHRR 206, [2005] MHLR 238.

160 (1974) 59 CrAppR 170.

161 (1974) 59 CrAppR 170 p173.

162 [1999] MHLR 30.

163 [1999] MHLR 30 para 33.

164 [2000] MHLR 188.

biting a police officer), which had occurred while the defendant was unwell. The judge's reasoning for imposing a restriction order was his concern that there was not a suitable plan in place to educate Mr Reynolds about his long-standing cannabis use, such that there was a risk of him returning to using cannabis outside hospital and so exacerbating his medical condition. The judge indicated that he was relying on his experience as a criminal law judge.[165] However, the medical evidence was to the effect that it was a generalisation that cannabis use exacerbated some psychoses; and it was also noted that the doctors were aware of the issue and were formulating a plan as to what to do.[166] The Court of Appeal quashed the restriction order. Two comments by His Honour Judge Fawcus, giving the judgment of the court, are worth noting. The first was that the requirement in section 41(2) that oral evidence had to be heard indicated that 'on hearing the evidence there must be at least some basis upon which the doctor is able to say, and to persuade the court, that a restriction order is appropriate'.[167] This goes too far if it meant to convey that the doctor has to persuade the court as to the need to impose a restriction order. However, a second comment qualifies this statement:

> We are far from saying that in appropriate circumstances it might not be appropriate for a judge to be unhappy to the extent of not being prepared to accept the oral evidence that he had before him. However, having read the transcript of [the evidence] called in this case, we feel that ... that the judge was really relying on his own experience in court, ... but unsupported by evidence in this particular case from the doctors which could have justified him in imposing that order.[168]

18.149 This is wholly consistent with the proper understanding of the *Birch* judgment, namely that the judge has the final decision as to how to interpret the factual situation,[169] but there has to be an evidential basis for any decision that disagrees with the expert evidence called if that is against the imposition of a restriction order. See also *R v*

165 [2000] MHLR 188 para 12.
166 [2000] MHLR 188 para 19.
167 [2000] MHLR 188 para 18.
168 [2000] MHLR 188 para 20.
169 An example of this may arise from the fact that the doctors might not in fact directly address the statutory language, such that their conclusions have to be interpreted by the judge: see, for example, *R v Chalk* [2002] EWCA Crim 2435, [2002] MHLR 430, in which the Court of Appeal noted at paragraph 34 that it was important that doctors addressed the section 41 criteria. *In R v Anderson* [2009] EWCA Crim 405, [2009] MHLR 162, a doctor used language consistent with the section 41 test but did not actually address it: the Court of Appeal upheld the judge's finding that the criteria were made out on the basis of the evidence called.

Acharya,[170] in which the Court of Appeal noted that 'the final responsibility for the making of a restriction order fairly and squarely on the shoulders of the trial judge', but stressed that it had to take into account the features of the restricted patient regime that the doctors had pointed out were disadvantageous.[171] The issue was summarised by King J in *R v Hurst*[172] as follows:

> The section places responsibility for making a restriction order on the judge if, in his opinion, it is necessary for the stated purpose. The fact that all the medical witnesses advise against such an order does not mean that it is wrong in principle. However, there must be evidence on which to base such an order.[173]

18.150 The Court of Appeal seems to adopt a slightly different approach if the basis for the disagreement between the judge and the doctors is on the risk of further offending. The process of risk assessment in the statute turns on not just the medical condition of the defendant but also criminogenic features such as previous offending and the circumstances of the current offence. An example of this is *R v Goode*,[174] in which the offence was a serious attack by repeated stabbing of his son by a father who was in a delusional state at the time. He had no previous convictions, had been compliant with his treatment, and the doctors expressed the view that a restriction order was not needed; but the judge disagreed. An appeal failed: the issue was not whether there was a risk of serious harm from any further offending (which seemed obvious in the light of the index offence),[175] but whether the risk of any further offending was real. The doctors, noting that the defendant had only had three breakdowns in his mental state in 25 years, and that those involved in his care would be more alert to the signs of problems, were of the view that there was a very low risk of further offending.[176] The Court of Appeal held that the judge had been within her powers to disagree with the level of confidence expressed by the doctors as to the low risk of further offending in the light of the circumstances of the index offence, which had taken all involved by surprise.[177]

170 [2005] EWCA Crim 772, [2005] MHLR 28.
171 [2005] EWCA Crim 772, [2005] MHLR 28 para 15.
172 [2007] EWCA Crim 3436, [2007] MHLR 43.
173 [2007] EWCA Crim 3436, [2007] MHLR 43 para 8.
174 [2002] EWCA Crim 1698, [2002] MHLR 337.
175 [2002] EWCA Crim 1698, [2002] MHLR 337 para 37.
176 [2002] EWCA Crim 1698, [2002] MHLR 337 paras 17–23.
177 [2002] EWCA Crim 1698, [2002] MHLR 337 paras 41–42.

18.151 It may be said that this did not involve the judge expressing a view about a matter exclusively within the domain of the mental health professionals, because it was an opinion about the risk of further offending.[178] It will be recalled that *Birch* involved a serious offence and the Court of Appeal was able to conclude that there was a low likelihood of recurrence and so no need for a restriction order. The difference in *Goode* was the nature of the offence meant that there was less of a basis to be satisfied that the risk would not recur: it was not linked to an unusual set of circumstances. Having said that, since doctors will be expected to take into account such matters as the nature of the offending, there must be a proper evidential basis for any disagreement with the doctors even if it relates to a question that is not entirely a matter for medical expertise. So in *R v Osker*,[179] the offence was a public nuisance from a threat to commit suicide in a public setting; the defendant had previously threatened to cause a gas explosion in her flat, and this was central to the judge's view that a restriction order was necessary. The Court of Appeal, in quashing the restriction order, noted the importance of the judge asking the expert witnesses their view of the features on which the judge proposed to reach a different conclusion: on the facts, the psychiatrist who gave oral evidence had taken the earlier incident into account in formulating his risk assessment, but had not been asked about it by the sentencing judge.

18.152 Of course, there is the alternative situation of medical evidence in support of a restriction order, which the judge accepts but should not have done. This was the situation in *R v Cooper*,[180] in which there was medical evidence from doctors called by the prosecution that supported a restriction order, though a third report did not: the reports from the prosecution did not address the criteria for a restriction order whereas the third did and concluded that they were not met. The offence involved the sexual touching of a young girl and the theft of her underwear. The judge adopted the view of one of the doctors called by the prosecution, which was to the effect that such offending tended to escalate: the Court of Appeal quashed the restriction order, noting that the offending behaviour of Mr Cooper and a generalised comment about the tendency of sex offending involving children to

178 Another example of this is *R v Griffith* [2002] EWCA Crim 1838, [2002] MHLR 427.

179 [2010] EWCA Crim 955, [2010] MHLR 115.

180 [2009] EWCA Crim 2646, [2009] MHLR 350.

escalate – even if the judge was able to back that up with his own experience in the criminal courts – was not sufficient.[181]

18.153 One final point to note in this context is that in many of the successful appeals against the imposition of a restriction order, the medical evidence that is available to the appellate court has been different from that available to the sentencing court; the impact of this is considered further in chapter 21 relating to appeals.

Hospital orders and custodial sentences

Introduction

18.154 As has been described in chapter 17, there are custodial sentences based on the seriousness of the offending and others based on the need to secure the protection of the public. Aside from the mandatory life sentence, however, these sentences need not be imposed if a hospital order is the better option. However, if a court has formed the view that the offender has a mental disorder, that detention in hospital for medical treatment is appropriate, and that appropriate treatment is available, the final question arising under section 37(2) of the MHA 1983 is whether the hospital order is the 'most suitable method of disposing of the case' in the light of 'all the circumstances including the nature of the offence and the character and antecedents of the offender, and to the other available methods of dealing with him'. Those other methods may include a custodial sentence, whether based on seriousness or public protection. There is a risk of circularity here, and so this section examines the question of the judgment that has to be exercised.

The factors relevant to the discretion in the Mental Health Act 1983

Disagreeing with the medical experts

18.155 The final part of the test for a hospital order clearly engages an exercise of a judicial discretion by the sentencing court, which will be informed by medical evidence; it allows the court to find that another sentence is preferable despite support for a hospital order in the medical evidence. It is also possible that a judge could decide that an order is the most suitable disposal despite a contrary view from the

181 [2009] EWCA Crim 2646, [2009] MHLR 350 paras 14–16.

doctors giving evidence: however, there is not the same latitude to disagree with medical evidence against a hospital order, because it is also necessary that a bed be available: so medical witnesses who stick to their view despite a conversation in court with a judge who takes a contrary position cannot be forced to make a bed available.[182]

Character and antecedents

18.156 Reference to the 'character and antecedents' of the offender in a criminal sentencing context may suggest that an offender with numerous previous convictions may be more likely to receive a punitive sentence even though he or she has a mental disorder. However, the language of punishment does not fit easily with the fact that the purposes of sentencing set out in section 142(1) of the CJA 2003 – which include punishment, deterrence and public protection – are disapplied if a sentence is made under the MHA 1983 involving detention in hospital.[183] This is equally as circular as the language of MHA 1983 s37. One part of the statutory regime suggests that punitive aims are a reason for not making a hospital order, whereas the other means that the suitability of the defendant for a hospital order means that the punitive purpose behind sentencing is disapplied. It will be suggested that there has been insufficient attention paid to the chronology of these two statutory sections.

Guidance from the Court of Appeal

18.157 The lack of clarity in the statutory language as to when a hospital order is suitable has not been resolved by consistent guidance from the Court of Appeal as to the use of the hospital order as opposed to other sentencing options when the medical criteria are met. The senior judiciary would no doubt respond that sentencing is an art that turns on the particular facts and circumstances: but it is equally true that the absence of any consistent guidance might mean that exactly the same facts as presented to different judges result in very different sentences, which turns the disposal of the case into a question of the luck of getting one judge or constitution of court. This is contrary to the principle of law having an appropriate degree of objectivity and predictability.

182 See by analogy *R (Buckowicki) v Northamptonshire County Council* [2007] EWHC 310 (Admin), [2007] MHLR 121: the criminal courts cannot compel a local authority to accept a section 37 guardianship order if the authority thinks it is not appropriate.

183 CJA 2003 s142(2).

18.158 The need for the hospital order to be the most suitable disposal originates in the MHA 1959.[184] Considering this language in *R v Morris*,[185] Lord Parker CJ had commented that:

> although the discretion there laid down is very wide indeed, the basic principle must be that in the ordinary case where punishment as such is not intended, and where the sole object of the sentence is that a man should receive mental treatment and be at large as soon as he can safely be discharged, a proper exercise of the discretion demands that steps should be taken to ...

impose a hospital order rather than rely on a transfer by the Secretary of State.[186]

18.159 But what if securing treatment is not the sole object of the sentence? Lord Parker continued:

> Of course there may be cases where, although there is a substantial impairment of responsibility, the prisoner is shown on the particular facts of the case nevertheless to have some responsibility for the act he has done, for which he must be punished, and in such a case, although as the court reads the sentence imposed by the judge this was not such a case, it would be proper to give imprisonment allowing the Secretary of State to exercise his powers ... in order that any necessary mental treatment should be given.

This comment was obiter because the question strictly in front of the Court of Criminal Appeal in *Morris* was whether the judge had been wrong to impose a sentence of imprisonment because he was not satisfied that the level of security at the hospital that had a place for the defendant was adequate. Nevertheless, it suggests that there is a distinction between a sentence based on punishment and a disposal aimed at securing treatment, and that the former rather than the latter is appropriate when responsibility remains. But this is too narrow: unless a defendant is not guilty by reason of insanity, he or she will have some responsibility. Hence, applying this approach might mean that very few hospital orders would be imposed.

18.160 In another example of similar vintage, *R v Gunnell*,[187] it was confirmed that a sentence of imprisonment was appropriate to secure public protection against a defendant convicted of multiple serious sexual offences (four rapes and two attempted rapes) even though he met the criteria for a hospital order to treat his psychopathic mental

184 MHA 1959 s60, the predecessor to MHA 1983 s37: the relevant language is the same.

185 [1961] 2 QB 237.

186 [1961] 2 QB 237 p243.

187 (1966) 50 CrAppR 242.

disorder. It does seem, however, that the Court of Criminal Appeal, which was hearing an appeal without the benefit of any legal representation, was concerned about the risks of escape from even a secure hospital and the fact that Mr Gunnell was being allowed leave from such a hospital: the Lord Chief Justice commented that public safety was served by a prison sentence rather than relying on 'a doctor and patient relationship under which it might be considered safe for him to be free, whereas from the public angle he remains a menace'.[188] The situation, in other words, was that the needs of treatment could be met by a transfer to hospital from prison on the direction of the Secretary of State, but the needs of public protection should be met by the use of a prison sentence. It is to be noted that there has been both a significant change in the level of security in hospitals since the time of this case, and also much subsequent case-law involving comments as to the levels of security in those hospitals.

18.161 There have also been contrary cases. In *R v Howell*,[189] Lord Lane CJ criticised a trial judge for sentencing a man convicted of two rapes to imprisonment rather than to hospital. Mr Howell had a mental illness as well as a serious personality disorder, and the trial judge's concern about public safety was such that he was not prepared to countenance release by a Mental Health Review Tribunal without the additional safeguard of that merely leading to a transfer back to prison and release only through the process applicable to prisoners. The Court of Appeal imposed a hospital order with a restriction order, commenting that where such a disposal was recommended and a secure bed was available, that was the course to take: the decision of the trial judge was viewed as understandable but not proper. No cases are cited in the judgment in *Howell*, and no reason is given as to why the approach of the trial judge was wrong in principle.

18.162 *Howell* was followed in *R v Mbatha*,[190] which involved serious and serial sexual offending of the sort present in *Gunnell*, the defendant having a manic depressive psychosis for which he did not reliably take treatment. The Court of Appeal, presided over by the Lord Chief Justice, overturned a sentence of imprisonment and put in place a hospital order with a restriction order, even though the trial judge had found that there was a significant element of criminality in that the defendant was fully aware of his actions and so was blameworthy. It is possible that the court was influenced by additional

188 (1966) 50 CrAppR 242 p246.
189 (1985) 7 CrAppR(S) 360.
190 (1985) 7 CrAppR(S) 373.

medical evidence suggesting that there was more of a link between the offending and the illness than the trial judge had found, but that is not made clear in the judgment.

18.163 With that background, in *R v Birch*[191] Mustill LJ noted that the use of a hospital order was a humane option compared to a custodial sentence, and that its purpose was to ensure the provision of necessary treatment 'in the hope and expectation of course that the result will be to avoid the commission by the offender of further criminal acts'.[192] This presupposes a connection between the offending behaviour of the defendant and the untreated or inadequately treated mental disorder: the corollary would be that if there was no such link, then a hospital order would not be the most suitable disposal.

18.164 The court in *Birch* suggested that a sentencing judge confronted by a defendant with a mental disorder should adopt the following approach. The first step was to consider 'whether a period of compulsory detention is apposite'.[193] However, the context of this comment was the making of a choice between treatment in detention and treatment under a probation order, and so it does not assist on the question of the appropriateness or otherwise of a punitive form of detention: rather, it turns on whether the treatment that is necessary is such that it has to be provided in a custodial setting. The second and third steps were to consider whether the conditions for a hospital order were made out and, if so, whether a restriction order should be imposed. After discussing the principles relevant to the latter, the court noted that there was always a discretion as to whether to impose a hospital order and/or a restriction order even if the relevant criteria were met. It added[194] that the exercise of choice in this context could properly take into account the practical effects of the orders, including the possibility of release: the court specifically mentioned that one of the effects of the MHA 1983 was that restricted patients might be released by the Mental Health Review Tribunal or the Home Secretary, whereas the MHA 1959 left the decision to the Home Secretary alone, which might mean that the patient was released earlier than would have happened previously. In the light of these factors, the court suggested that a sentencing court might have to impose a prison sentence on a defendant whose disorder merited treatment in

191 (1990) 90 CrAppR 78.
192 (1990) 90 CrAppR 78 p85.
193 (1990) 90 CrAppR 78 p87.
194 (1990) 90 CrAppR 78 pp88–89.

hospital in two scenarios, one where no place in a hospital could be found, and second:

> Where the sentencer considers that notwithstanding the offender's mental disorder there was an element of culpability in the offence which merits punishment. This may happen where there is no connection between the mental disorder and the offence, or where the defendant's responsibility for the offence is 'diminished' but not wholly extinguished.[195]

18.165 However, in rejecting an argument that a restriction order was appropriate in order to secure a longer period of detention in hospital,[196] the court commented that this approach was 'not what the Act contemplates'. This comment was in the context of whether or not to impose a restriction order, but is of wider value because it suggests that punitive thinking is not an appropriate part of the reasoning process when dealing with an offender with a mental disorder. This is consistent with the provisions of CJA 2003 s142(2), which disapply the principles of punishment when a disposal under the MHA 1983 is appropriate, and so in turn consistent with the view that the court is entitled to take a different approach in dealing with an offender who happens to be mentally disordered. Having said that, it is fair to comment that *Birch* involved an offence that was causally linked to the illness,[197] which leaves open the question of whether a crime not causally linked with the mental disorder might have been treated differently.

18.166 The comments in *Birch* are consistent with the earlier case-law in suggesting that culpability in offending may mean that punishment is merited: that would provide an explanation for *Mbatha* as turning on the different approach that is appropriate if there is a link between the offending and the disorder. However, the Court in *Birch* felt that *Mbatha* stood for the proposition that 'even where there is culpability' a dangerous offender who meets the criteria for a hospital order with a restriction order should be dealt with in that fashion.[198] This

195 (1990) 90 CrAppR 78 p89.

196 The prognosis for Mrs Birch was that it was likely that she would be fit for release relatively soon. Mustill LJ commented that while it was 'attractive ... reasoning' to suggest that a restriction order should be imposed in light of the prognosis, in the light of the 'evident disproportion between the premeditated taking of life, and a period of confinement unlikely (judging by what we were told) greatly to exceed two or three years': page 90.

197 Mustill LJ noting that it seemed to be a 'crime of illness not wickedness': (1990) 90 CrAppR 78 p90.

198 (1990) 90 CrAppR 78 p89.

raises a separate line of reasoning, which is also raised by *Gunnell* and *Howell*, namely that of public protection. Even if mental disorder is not directly linked to offending, it may have an indirect link: for example, it may mean that an offender does not have a stable foundation in his or her life and so criminal activity is more likely. That could mean that treating a mental disorder is a sensible method of securing public protection.

18.167 Case-law subsequent to *Birch* has not assisted to provide any real clarity as to the role of culpability in the discretion in play in MHA 1983 s37. There have been cases that have emphasised that there is no need for a connection between mental disorder and offending. In *R v Paul Lee Smith*,[199] the possibility of a hospital order had been rejected by the trial judge because there was no connection between Mr Smith's mental disorder and his offence of rape, but the Court of Appeal found that this was an error. The medical evidence before the trial judge supported the making of an interim hospital order under MHA 1983 s38: one of psychiatrists had indicated that this was necessary, inter alia, because the clinicians wanted to formulate a better understanding of the link between the mental disorder involved and the offence,[200] which would no doubt have implications for the treatment programme. But the trial judge's view was that there was no evidence of such a connection and so a custodial sentence was inevitable, which he imposed. The Court of Appeal substituted a hospital order with a restriction order (the defendant having been transferred from prison to hospital and medical reports of the sort that would have followed an interim hospital order having been provided). Commenting on the trial judge's approach, Keene LJ noted in his judgment for the court that:

> 9. We are bound to say that we consider that the learned judge placed undue emphasis on the absence of any causal link between mental illness and the offence. On the authorities, the better view seems to be that such a link is not a precondition to the making of a hospital order under section 37 of the Mental Health Act 1983: see *R v McBride* [1972] Crim LR 322 and *R v Hatt* [1962] Crim LR 647. Indeed, such is the wording of that section that it seems that a hospital order may be made even though the mental disorder suffered by the defendant has developed since the date of the offence.[201]

199 [2001] EWCA Crim 743, [2001] MHLR 46.
200 [2001] EWCA Crim 743, [2001] MHLR 46 para 5.
201 [2001] EWCA Crim 743, [2001] MHLR 46 at para 9.

18.168 It is true that there is no language in section 37 suggesting any need for a connection between the offending and the mental disorder, though that could be a factor relevant to the discretion in play. The Court of Appeal in *Smith* gives little explanation as to why it exercised that discretion in favour of making a hospital order (rather than leaving the situation as it was, namely of a prison sentence but with treatment in an appropriate setting by use of the transfer powers that exist under the MHA 1983). It moves from a description of the clear evidence of illness that can be ameliorated by treatment to a conclusion that a hospital order was therefore appropriate without any explanation of why it was the most suitable method.[202] The trial judge in *Smith* may have been in error to the extent that he apparently excluded the possibility of a hospital order before the further investigation of whether there was a link between the disorder and the offending: but his line of reasoning that the absence of a link was a proper basis for imposing a prison sentence was supported by the authorities, including *Birch*, which is not referred to in *Smith*.

18.169 There are numerous instances of the Court of Appeal substituting a hospital order for a custodial sentence without explaining the basis for finding that such a disposal is the most suitable:[203] naturally, given the attraction of pragmatic sentencing, it is to be expected that there will be decisions where common humanity leads to a result that could no doubt be rationalised if more thought was applied and the various hoops set in the law were gone through.

18.170 However, there are also cases more consistent with the approach set out in the earlier cases. In *R v Nafei*,[204] a serious drugs importation was carried out by a man who was found to be mentally unwell at the time of arrest by customs officers and who had a long-standing mental illness. The sentencing judge had reports recommending a hospital order; but he relied on the lack of any causal link between the mental disorder and the offending (such that medical treatment would not reduce the risk of reoffending), and the sentencing policy towards drug smuggling and its emphasis on custodial sentences to

202 [2001] EWCA Crim 743, [2001] MHLR 46 paras 11–13; it was recorded at paragraph 14 that the prosecution agreed that a hospital order was appropriate.

203 Other examples of hospital orders being made by the Court of Appeal without any explanation, and sometimes without any reference to the need to find it to be the most suitable disposal, include *R v Melbourne* [2000] MHLR 2; *R v Budgen* [2001] EWCA Crim 1708, [2001] MHLR 138; *R v Gunning* [2002] EWCA Crim 634, [2002] MHLR 139; *R v Doonan* [2005] EWCA Crim 1182, [2005] MHLR 210.

204 [2004] EWCA Crim 3238, [2006] MHLR 176.

provide deterrence, given that vulnerable people were often recruited to act as couriers, to justify a sentence of imprisonment.[205] The Court of Appeal upheld the approach of the judge and the sentence of 12 years' imprisonment. It noted that:

i) the lack of a connection between the offence and the mental condition did not preclude the making of a hospital order, but was a significant feature in the exercise of the discretion that existed under the statute; and
ii) regard had to be had to the nature of the offence, since some offences – drug importation being an obvious example – attracted deterrent sentences in relation to which the personal circumstances of the offender counted for little.

Davis J, for the court, noted that 'in circumstances such as the present, we at present find it difficult to envisage a case where the discretion to make a hospital order will be likely to be exercised'.[206]

18.171 The court went further, noting that even if the drug importation was linked to mental disorder, it did not follow that a hospital order would ordinarily be appropriate: that would depend on the circumstances of the case, bearing in mind the policy considerations affecting sentencing for such offences and the need to retain effective deterrence. The court seemed particularly concerned at the risk of people being released after a relatively short period of time.[207] This is an appropriate line of reasoning if the purposes of sentencing set in CJA 2003 s142(1) apply, but they do not if a hospital order is to be imposed (see section 142(2)). There is the danger that if the sentencing court exercises its discretion as to whether or not to impose a hospital disposal by looking at the punitive needs behind sentencing, this will nullify the existence of section 142(2) and the disapplication of these aims if the criteria for a hospital order are made out.

18.172 Another constitution of the Court of Appeal went further still in the case of *R v Khelifi*,[208] which involved a multi-handed bank fraud. Mr Khelifi, who had numerous previous convictions for matters of dishonesty, admitted his part and was sentenced to five years' imprisonment, which was at the top of the range imposed. An interim

205 It was reduced in length as his vulnerability was relevant to his recruitment and he would face difficulties in custody in the light of his mental illness.

206 [2004] EWCA Crim 3238, [2006] MHLR 176 para 14.

207 [2004] EWCA Crim 3238, [2006] MHLR 176 para 15. In a much less serious case involving a small-scale supplier of drugs, a hospital order was imposed by the Court of Appeal in *R v Doonan* [2005] EWCA Crim 1182, [2005] MHLR 210.

208 [2006] EWCA Crim 770, [2006] MHLR 257.

hospital order under MHA 1983 s38 had been made, at the end of which a hospital order under section 37 was recommended. But the trial judge indicated that justice would not be done by the imposition of a hospital order. As was perhaps to be expected, Mr Khelifi was admitted to the prison hospital wing, and subsequently transferred to hospital under MHA 1983 s47, the evidence being that treatment he needed was not available in the prison setting. Dismissing the appeal against the prison sentence, the Court of Appeal held that there was no presumption in favour of a hospital order being made if the defendant's condition met the criteria for such an order: rather, the defendant's psychiatric condition was an important but not overriding factor in the way the sentencing judge exercised his or her discretion. On the facts, it agreed with the trial judge that the seriousness of the offending justified a prison sentence, and the prospect of Mr Khelifi responding to treatment and being released would not have been right. The court was content that his medical needs could be met by the powers of the Secretary of State to transfer a serving prisoner to hospital.

18.173 The court does not cite any authority for its proposition that there is no presumption in favour of a hospital order if the criteria are met: indeed, the only authority mentioned in the judgment is *Nafei*; an attempt by counsel to limit the reach of that case to drug-related offending because of the accepted view that personal circumstances cannot be taken into account there was rejected. Rather, it was said that: 'The need to assess the personal circumstances of the offender in the light of the seriousness of the offence is a feature of all sentencing and it will not only be in cases of drug crime that it may be necessary to sentence ill patients to a prison term'.[209] This is an understandable statement in the light of the language of MHA 1983 s37(2)(b) taken alone: but as has been noted in relation to *Nafei*, Parliament has disapplied the statutory purposes of sentencing when a hospital order is open.

18.174 See also *R v Khan, Khan and Khan*,[210] in which a woman convicted of people smuggling met the criteria for a hospital order but was found also by the trial judge to have exaggerated her symptoms: he imposed a custodial sentence to reflect the gravity of the offending and her central role in it. By the time of the appeal hearing, she had spent time in the prison hospital wing but was about to be moved to the main prison. The Court of Appeal held, citing *Khelifi*, that a

209 [2006] EWCA Crim 770, [2006] MHLR 257 para 11.
210 [2010] EWCA Crim 2880, [2011] MHLR 14.

hospital order was not inevitable: it commented that the appropriate sentence was the one that reflected the seriousness of the offending, in relation to which the welfare of the offender was one consideration only. It upheld the prison sentence, though in relation to an application that was made to increase the sentence as unduly lenient, it held that Mrs Khan's mental state – which fluctuated – was a reason not to increase the sentence even though it was unduly lenient.

18.175 It is worth noting in relation to this case that the factual scenario was one in which it can be suggested that there was some concern as to whether the defendant was as ill as the medical reports to the trial judge suggested, given that she was well enough to be placed on the main location in the prison: the Court of Appeal does not refer to having updated medical evidence beyond reciting her move to normal location.

18.176 In the context of this case-law, it is difficult to synthesise a summary. Accordingly, this is a tentative attempt:

i) The MHA 1983 s37 indicates that a hospital order is a discretionary disposal if it is the most suitable in the circumstances.
ii) Since this discretion only arises if the medical criteria are met, the fact that the medical criteria are met cannot control the exercise of discretion that then arises.
iii) On the language of section 37, there is no need for a causal link between the offending and the imposition of a hospital order. While the existence of a causal link cannot condition the exercise of the discretion, it can be a factor and should be an important factor because that will allow action to be taken to secure treatment that might reduce the risk of further crime.
iv) However, the language of section 37 cannot be taken in isolation, and in particular proper account has to be taken of CJA 2003 s142, which sets out the normal punitive and protective purposes of punishment but disapplies these if the criteria for a hospital order are made out.
v) This language was enacted in the context of case-law construing section 37 alone developing the proposition that culpability could be a basis for imposing a punitive sentence rather than a hospital order disposal.
vi) Given that a hospital order is not excluded if there was no link between the offence and the disorder, and given that culpability cannot be the sole criterion, as that would rob section 142(2) of any role, it is suggested that the most natural meaning of the discretions in sections 37 and 142 respectively is that the starting

point is that a hospital order should follow if the medical criteria are met, even if there is culpability, since otherwise section 142(2) will be nullified.

The various compulsory or quasi-compulsory sentences

18.177 It is suggested that the synthesis given in the preceding paragraph is supported by the relationship between the hospital order and the various compulsory and quasi-compulsory orders, which are described in chapter 17. In short, Parliament has expressly provided that hospital orders can be made even when otherwise a compulsory minimum term would follow. In addition, it allowed a hospital disposal in place of the dangerous offender provisions during the short period of time that they were compulsory rather than, as they have become, discretionary. This was a change from the position under the automatic life sentence regime, which prevented a hospital order. The fact that this changed, together with the current situation that only in the case of a mandatory life sentence for murder does a court not have the power to impose a hospital order, suggests that there is parliamentary support for the use of a hospital disposal. There is a further supportive element, namely the extended coverage of the MHA 1983 as a result of the MHA 2007, such that the definition of mental disorder now covers all forms of personality disorder and there are no exclusions for conditions such as paedophilia: see chapter 2 for a full description of this.

Mandatory minima

18.178 In relation to mandatory minimum terms, C(S)A 1997 ss3 and 4 required seven years' imprisonment and three years' imprisonment for a third drug trafficking offence involving class A drugs and a third domestic burglary respectively, unless it would be unjust. However, section 37(1A) was added to the MHA 1983[211] to make it clear that a hospital order could be made in these situations (in contrast, at that time, to the language applicable to the automatic life sentence, described below). These became sections 110 and 111 of the PCC(S)A 2000, and the language of section 37(1A) was amended accordingly.[212] Subsequently, CJA 2003 s287 added section 51A to the Firearms Act 1968 to introduce a minimum term of five years' imprisonment for an adult or young adult and three years' detention for a youth

211 C(S)A 1997 Sch 4 para 12.
212 PCC(S)A 2000 Sch 9 para 90.

convicted of certain serious firearms offences unless there are exceptional circumstances; CJA 2003 Sch 32 para 38 amended MHA 1983 s37(1A) to make clear that hospital order could be made nevertheless. Finally, section 29 of the Violent Crime Reduction Act 2006 introduced the offence of using someone to mind a dangerous weapon (including firearms and some offensive weapons and knives), and sections 29(4) and (6) introduced minimum sentences of five years' detention or imprisonment for an adult offender and three years' detention for a youth, again subject to an exceptional circumstances finding. MHA 1983 s37(1A) was again amended to provide that a hospital order could be imposed.[213]

Dangerous offender sentencing

18.179 Under C(S)A 1997 s2, the automatic life sentence regime was introduced: a life sentence was required for the second conviction for one of a list of several serious offences (all of which carried discretionary life imprisonment)[214] unless there were exceptional circumstances. In effect the discretionary life sentence became a mandatory sentence unless these exceptional reasons could be found. C(S)A 1997 Sch 4 added language to MHA 1983 s37 to the effect that an automatic life sentence was to be treated in the same way as a mandatory life sentence for murder in disapplying the power to impose a hospital order. When the PCC(S)A 2000 was passed as a consolidation statute, C(S)A 1997 s2 became section 109 of the PCC(S)A 2000. PCC(S)A 2000 Sch 9 para 90 made the necessary amendments to the MHA 1983 to maintain the position excluding a hospital order if the criteria for an automatic life sentence were made out.

18.180 The Court of Appeal ruled that exceptional circumstances would be made out if the offender could show that he or she was not dangerous: *R v Offen*.[215] This followed a purposive interpretation, namely that the purpose behind the legislation was to establish a norm that a

213 Violent Crime Reduction Act 2006 Sch 1 para 2.

214 The offences for England and Wales were set out in C(S)A 1997 s2(5), and were: attempted murder, conspiracy to murder or incitement to murder, soliciting murder (Offences Against the Person Act 1861 s4), manslaughter, wounding causing grievous bodily harm with intent (Offences Against the Person Act 1861 s18), rape or attempted rape, intercourse with a girl under 13 (Sexual Offences Act 1956 s5), possessing a firearm with intent to injure, using a firearm to resist arrest, or carrying a firearm with criminal intent (Firearms Act 1968 sections 16, 17 and 18); and robbery using a firearm or imitation firearm within the meaning of that Act. Equivalent offences for Scotland and Northern Ireland were set out in section 2(6) and (7).

215 [2001] 1 WLR 253, [2000] Prison LR 283.

second conviction revealed a danger to the public that required a life sentence, which meant that a person would be an exception to the norm if all the relevant circumstances revealed that there was not an unacceptable risk. This would not arise from mental disorder alone; nor did the fact that a person required treatment amount to exceptional circumstances. This was established by the House of Lords in *R v Drew*.[216] It is appropriate to point out that the House, in noting why the use of a life sentence would not necessarily be arbitrary, pointed out that a life sentence had advantages in terms of protecting the public because detention was not limited to matters of risk arising from the medical condition of the defendant, as was the case if detention was under the Mental Health Act.

18.181 The House of Lords also considered the propriety of imposing punishment when a defendant was mentally disordered. It held that while it would be wrong in principle to punish those who were unfit to be tried or were not responsible for their conduct because of insanity, that was not the case in front of it: Mr Drew had admitted a serious offence (causing grievous bodily harm with intent), and the effect of his mental illness was to mitigate rather than absolve him of responsibility. This in turn meant that a sentence of imprisonment could be imposed even where the conditions for the imposition of a hospital order were met (which, it was noted, gave a discretion to impose a hospital order not a duty).[217]

18.182 The ECtHR was asked only to consider ECHR article 3: *Drew v UK*.[218] The court that the distress caused by the deterioration in Mr Drew's condition during the eight days he was held in a prison medical wing before being transferred to hospital under MHA 1983 s47, where effective medication was again commenced, did not reach the threshold of severity necessary to breach article 3. But it did raise a point under article 5, commenting that although no complaint had been made, it was 'a matter of some concern that the applicant was required by law to be sent immediately to prison, contrary to the opinions of the two psychiatrists who gave evidence at the disposal hearing and to the wishes of the sentencing judge, all of whom

216 [2003] UKHL 25, [2003] 1 WLR 1213, [2003] MHLR 282.

217 See [2003] UKHL 25, [2003] 1 WLR 1213, [2003] MHLR 282 paras 16 and 17 of the opinion. There was a further argument based on the lack of access to medical treatment; but it was held that this failed on the facts because Mr Drew had been transferred to hospital under MHA 1983 s47, and was not shown to have suffered appreciably in the time between admission to prison and transfer to hospital.

218 App No 35679/03, [2006] MHLR 203.

expressed the view that a hospital order with a restriction would have been more appropriate'.

18.183 The PCC(S)A 2000 s109 was repealed when the new dangerous offender provisions of CJA 2003 ss224–236[219] were brought into effect in April 2005.[220] These are outlined in chapter 17. Importantly for present purposes, CJA 2003 s302 and Sch 32 para 8 amended MHA 1983 s37 in the following significant ways:

i) the language relating to the automatic life sentence regime taking precedence over the making of a hospital order was omitted: it was not replaced by language making the hospital order subservient to the new (and extended) regime for the disposal of dangerous offenders; and
ii) section 37(1A) was amended, making it plain that the nothing in the dangerous offender sentencing provisions or any other minimum term provisions prevented the making of a hospital order.

18.184 In the guidance of the Court of Appeal as to these dangerous offender provisions, one of the reminders noted in the case of *R v Lang*[221] was that the option of making use of a disposal under the MHA 1983 if the relevant criteria were met remained available. In the subsequent case that emphasised more the importance of responding to risk, *R v Johnson*,[222] the Court of Appeal also noted that mental disorder might support a finding of dangerousness. Sir Igor Judge P noted at paragraph 10(iv) of the judgment that 'inadequacy, suggestibility, or vulnerability ... may serve to mitigate the offender's culpability. In the final analysis however they may also serve to produce or reinforce the conclusion that the offender is dangerous'. Unfortunately, the court did not go on to emphasise the importance of a disposal by way of hospital order (though on the facts none of the defendants whose cases were being considered were suitable for a hospital order).

Dangerous offender sentencing and restriction orders – overlap

18.185 It can be seen that the dangerous offender provisions have a number of similarities to the restriction order regime – but there are also differences. First, in both situations, the question is the risk of serious harm to the public; in relation to the dangerous offender sentencing

219 CJA 2003 Part 12 Chapter 5.

220 Criminal Justice Act 2003 (Commencement No 8 and Transitional and Saving Provisions) Order 2005 SI No 950.

221 [2005] EWCA Crim 2864, [2006] 1 WLR 2509, [2006] 2 Prison LR 98.

222 [2006] EWCA Crim 2486, [2007] 1 WLR 585, [2006] 2 Prison LR 159.

provisions, this is in relation to further specified offences, whereas in relation to a restriction order there is no such limitation. However, it would be unusual for the serious harm in the latter situation to arise from a circumstance that was not also a violent or dangerous offence.

18.186 Second, in neither situation is it necessary for the index offence to be serious for the finding of dangerousness to follow: however, the indeterminate sentence under the dangerous offender provisions can only follow from an index offence that is a serious specified offence, whereas the only requirement in relation to an indeterminate hospital order and restriction order is that the offence be imprisonable (and so this is much broader). In both situations, a serious offence by itself does not necessary lead to an indeterminate sentence if there is no finding of dangerousness.

18.187 Third, in both cases, the judge has to make the decision, and is not bound to follow any expert reports; but in relation to the dangerous offender provisions, it is perhaps less likely that there will be expert evidence, no doubt based on the idea that the expertise of judges extends to assessments of the risk of future offending.

18.188 There was a significant difference in that the dangerous offender provisions as enacted involved a limited discretion: that, however, was remedied when the significant amendments were made to the regime by sections 13–18 of the Criminal Justice and Immigration Act 2008. But even in its initial form, there was a significant discretion if the offender met the criteria for a hospital order because the latter could take priority.

18.189 So, the legislative regime currently in place is that a court is not required to pass a custodial sentence under the dangerous offender provisions: a short-lived requirement to do so was expressly removed, and this was done after concern was raised about the propriety of placing someone who needed to be in hospital in a prison setting. However, it remains the case that there is a discretion as to the imposition of a hospital order as well, turning on it being the most suitable disposal. Just as there is a lack of clarity in the case-law relating to the use of a hospital order as opposed to a punitive sentence of imprisonment, so there is contrasting case-law in relation to the use of a dangerousness-based preventive sentence of imprisonment.

Dangerous offender sentencing and restriction orders – case-law

18.190 There have been a number of cases relating to the question of whether a custodial sentence with preventive purposes – initially the discretionary life sentence and then the dangerous offender provisions as well – can or should be used instead of a hospital order with a restriction order. This first proposition seems to be that if the dangerousness of the offender is one that arises from mental disorder, a hospital disposal should follow. So in *R v Howell*,[223] Lord Lane CJ commented that: 'In circumstances such as these, where medical opinions are unanimous and a bed in a secure hospital is available, we think that a hospital order under s37 of the Act should be made together with a restriction order without limit of time under s41'.[224] The 'circumstances such as these' were that Mr Howell had been convicted of two rapes, had numerous previous convictions and had both a mental illness and a serious personality disorder. As such he was thought to be 'extremely dangerous'. The trial judge – whose reasoning was said to be understandable – had such concerns about public safety that he was not prepared to countenance release by a Mental Health Review Tribunal without the additional safeguard of that merely leading to a transfer back to prison and release only through the process applicable to prisoners. The Court of Appeal disagreed with this approach. Shortly thereafter, the Court of Appeal reached a similar conclusion in *R v Mbatha*.[225]

18.191 These cases endorse the view that public safety concerns can properly be dealt with by way of a disposal under the MHA 1983, which has public safety tests for ongoing detention, and there is a clear hint from the Court of Appeal to the effect that such a disposal should be the normal course. This view was endorsed by the House of Lords in *R v Drew*.[226] The main issue was the lawfulness of the requirement then existing to impose an automatic life sentence even in the case of an offender who qualified for a hospital disposal. This was held to be permitted, as long as there was a mechanism to secure transfer to hospital for treatment. In particular, it was said that the effective duty to impose an indeterminate sentence of imprisonment had an objective justification to it, which Lord Bingham summarised as follows:

> (1) Defendants sentenced to determinate sentences of imprisonment must be released after serving a specified proportion of their sentences and are subject to recall for a limited period only. If on release they are still dangerous, they are a source of risk to the public.

223 (1985) 7 CrAppR(S) 360.

224 (1985) 7 CrAppR(S) 360 p361.

225 (1985) 7 CrAppR(S) 373.

226 [2003] UKHL 25, [2003] 1 WLR 1213, [2003] MHLR 282.

(2) Defendants made subject to hospital orders, whether restricted or not, are entitled to release when the medical conditions justifying their original admission cease to be met: *R v London South and South West Region Mental Health Review Tribunal ex p Moyle* [1999] MHLR 195, [2000] Lloyd's LR Med 143; *R (Von Brandenburg) v East London and The City Mental Health NHS Trust* [2002] QB 235, [2001] MHLR 36, paragraph 18. Further, they are liable to recall only on medical grounds. They may be a source of danger to the public even though these medical conditions are not met. While it is possible to argue, as Mr Davies did, about the magnitude of this risk, it cannot be said not to exist.

(3) A defendant sentenced to life imprisonment under section 109 is not deprived of all his rights. He may appeal against imposition of the sentence. He may appeal against the minimum term specified by the judge. He is eligible for release on the expiry of that term and is entitled to be released if he is no longer a source of danger to the public. But the decision whether it is safe to release him will be taken by the Parole Board, as an independent body acting judicially, which will not be confined to the medical considerations of which, alone, a Mental Health Review Tribunal may take account, and he is liable to recall indefinitely if he appears to present a danger to the public, the grounds of recall, again, being broader than in the case of a restricted patient. In short, an automatic life sentence affords a measure of control not available under the other available orders.[227]

18.192 This may at first sight seem to differ from the suggestions in *Howell* and *Mbatha*, given the emphasis on risk arising from factors other than mental disorder. This, however, is a matter of the context of the comments. The question arising in *Drew* was whether the legislation in question was incompatible with the requirements of the Human Rights Act 1998 and the relevant provisions of the ECHR on the basis that they could not be operated in a manner that was compatible with human rights standards. It is in this context that the House of Lords drew attention to the potential scenarios in which it might be appropriate to make use of a prison disposal, so providing an objective justification for the legislation. In any event, the legislative context is now different in two regards: the legislation now provides a discretion and so the question that arises is how should the discretion be exercised (not whether it was legitimate for Parliament to require a prison sentence). In addition, the basis for detention under the MHA 1983 has been amended, and so the judgment of the sentencing court has to be exercised in the new framework. As has been noted in chapter 2, the extension of the definition of what amounts

227 [2003] UKHL 25, [2003] 1 WLR 1213, [2003] MHLR 282 para 21.

to a mental disorder and the removal of requirements such as that a psychopathic personality disorder must be treatable[228] means that there may be a greater prospect that someone whose dangerousness is based on repeat offending will be classified as suffering from a personality disorder that amounts to a mental disorder for the purposes of the MHA 1983.[229]

18.193 Accordingly, the argument that succeeded on the limited question in issue in *Drew* as to the validity of a prison sentence does not provide any significant assistance to justify the use of a custodial sentence as an exercise of the discretion that is now in play. It is also important to recognise that the House of Lords expressly endorsed the line of authority started by *Howell* and *Mbatha*, rejecting an argument put forward that they were in error. Lord Bingham noted:

> 22. In the course of his argument for the Home Secretary, Mr Perry gently suggested that Court of Appeal decisions generally encouraging the making of hospital orders where the relevant medical criteria were met might, in the absence of adversarial argument, have given less than adequate weight to the differing conditions governing the release and recall of restricted patients as opposed to life sentence prisoners. He instanced authorities such as *R v Howell* (1985) 7 CrAppR(S) 360; *R v Mbatha* (1985) 7 CrAppR(S) 373; *R v Mitchell* [1997] 1 CrAppR(S) 90; *R v Hutchinson* [1997] 2 CrAppR(S) 60. There may be some force in this criticism, and we would accept that these differing conditions are a matter to which sentencing judges and appellate courts should try to give appropriate weight. The difficulties caused to prison managements by the presence and behaviour of those who are subject to serious mental disorder are, however, notorious, and we would need to be persuaded that any significant change in the prevailing practice was desirable.

18.194 In short, the practice established by these cases was not in error, though it was proper that courts should be alert to the difficulties

228 Note, however, the argument as to whether the need for 'appropriate treatment' may introduce some argument as to efficacy: see chapter 2 at paras 2.86–2.87.

229 It is worth noting in this connection that the first Act of the Scottish Parliament was the Mental Health (Public Safety and Appeals) Scotland Act 1999, which amended the Mental Health (Scotland) Act 1984 so as to require an appeal against ongoing detention in hospital to be refused if a restricted patient was 'suffering from a mental disorder the effect of which is such that it is necessary, in order to protect the public from serious harm, that the patient continue to be detained in a hospital, whether for medical treatment or not'. This was upheld by the Privy Council in *A v Scottish Ministers* [2001] MHLR 192, 2001 SLT 1331, and then by the ECtHR in *Reid v UK* (2003) 37 EHRR 211, [2003] MHLR 226.

caused by the situation in which someone might have to be released from hospital because their ongoing risk was not a matter that justified detention on mental health grounds. The comments of Lord Bingham were obiter, as they were not directly necessary for the decision in *Drew*. However, they were found helpful when the issue of the choice between hospital and prison disposals for public protection against someone who qualified for a hospital order with a restriction order was confronted by the Court of Appeal in *R v IA*.[230] The defendant committed several serious sexual assaults on young boys, including rape, and was also convicted of having offensive weapons. An interim hospital order had been made, reports at the end of which confirmed that IA was mentally disordered, having mental impairment, and recommended a hospital order with a restriction order. The judge, however, noting that it was not possible to say when or whether it would ever be safe to release IA, whom he regarded as posing a grave danger, imposed an indeterminate sentence of custody for life (as he was aged 18).[231]

18.195 On appeal, the sentence was set aside and a hospital order together with a restriction order was imposed. The reasoning of the Court of Appeal is instructive in the light of the public safety concerns behind the judge's sentencing decision. Lord Justice Mance, delivering the judgment, first noted that the choice of a hospital order depended on whether it was the 'most suitable' disposal.[232] This involved weighing the relative advantages and disadvantages of the two possible sentences, namely an indeterminate prison sentence or a hospital order with a restriction order without limit of time:

> 41. ... On the one hand, this was very serious offending, with serious impact on the victims and their families and in respect of which the appellant cannot be fully excused of all responsibility. On the other, he is someone with diverse and unusual problems, who the doctors unanimously advise would benefit by treatment in a psychiatric hospital. On the one hand, as the history to date shows, a custodial sentence (especially for life) affords the most clear-cut security to the public. On the other hand, it does not by itself guarantee that the appellant will receive the assistance that may enable his problems to be overcome, and (as this case shows) a sentencing judge's hope and expectation that there may be a transfer under section 47 to a hospital for treatment may, for one reason or another, not be realised.

230 [2005] EWCA Crim 2077, [2005] MHLR 336.

231 The offences occurred before the dangerous sentencing provisions under the CJA 2003 came into effect.

232 [2005] EWCA Crim 2077, [2005] MHLR 336 paras 40 and 41; see also the discussion above starting at para 18.154.

18.196 In relation to the public safety question, Mance LJ noted that *Drew* required judges to recognise the differences between an indeterminate hospital disposal and an indeterminate prison sentence. However, he added: 'This does not mean assuming that the latter regime, which has the advantage of guaranteeing hospital treatment, will in any particular case necessarily afford significantly less protection to the public than the former'.[233]

18.197 On the facts, while the judge had been right to bear in mind that the risks posed by IA did not necessarily arise only from mental disorder and so would not inevitably be covered by the grounds for detention under the MHA 1983, this had to be weighed against other factors that were relevant to the exercise of the discretion in play, namely his psychiatric problems, the benefit he was likely to receive from treatment in hospital ('which alone offers any prospect of rehabilitation and ultimately release into the community'). That meant that in relation to questions of public safety, the fact was that placement in a suitable treatment environment could be achieved by way of a hospital order more surely than by hoping that there would be a transfer by the Secretary of State, which was inevitably a situation of significant uncertainty.[234] The conclusion of the Court of Appeal was that:

> ... on the evidence before us, the regime of a hospital order with restriction is designed and able to offer very great protection, if necessary indefinite, for the public in respect of the risks posed by this appellant. Further, the evidence suggests that the real risks are, in the case of this particular appellant, associated with conditions in respect of which medical treatment would be appropriate. In these circumstances, we have come to the conclusion that the right order, particularly in circumstances where the judge's own hope and expectation have not been fulfilled and it remains uncertain whether or when they ever would be, is a hospital order with restriction.[235]

18.198 A similar issue confronted the Court of Appeal in *R v Simpson*,[236] which related to a life sentence imposed on public safety grounds shortly after *IA* had been decided. The offence was an attempted murder, but linked to a delusional disorder; although there were reports

233 [2005] EWCA Crim 2077, [2005] MHLR 336 para 37.

234 [2005] EWCA Crim 2077, [2005] MHLR 336 paras 42 and 43. It was noted that the court had called for information from the Secretary of State about the prospects of IA being transferred to hospital under MHA 1983 s47 but had not received anything. He had not been transferred since the life sentence had been imposed.

235 [2005] EWCA Crim 2077, [2005] MHLR 336 para 43.

236 [2007] EWCA Crim 2666, [2007] MHLR 320.

recommending a hospital order with a restriction order, which was to involve a placement in a medium secure hospital setting, the judge imposed a life sentence after considering the dangerous offender provisions of the CJA 2003. The judge's rationale was the better protection offered by a custodial sentence, apparently in particular in relation to risks of escape.[237] However, noted the Court of Appeal, no explanation was given as to why the obviously important need of public protection was better achieved by imprisonment in light of the physical security arrangements at the hospital, the checks kept on patients, and the monitoring of their mental state, which was more likely to detect any of the delusions such as caused Mr Simpson's offending, and the ability of the regime under a hospital order to secure a rehabilitation into the community if that became possible.[238] In short, as had happened in *IA*, any additional physical security of a prison setting had to be weighed against the benefits of a hospital disposal, and when that was done, the fact that a criteria for discharge under the MHA 1983 were limited to risks that were linked to medical conditions did not lead to a conclusion that less protection to the public would result. The sentence of life imprisonment was quashed and a hospital order with a restriction order imposed, the criteria for which were made out.

18.199 This approach has also been endorsed in a number of appeals out of time (the special factors relevant to which are considered in chapter 21). For example, in *R v David Hempston*,[239] the question was whether the correct sentence was life imprisonment or a hospital order with a restriction order in relation to a series of offences including rape: the additional feature was that the life sentence had been imposed in 1978, had been the subject of an unsuccessful appeal, and was then referred back to the Court of Appeal by the Criminal Cases Review Commission on the basis that Mr Hempston had been detained in hospital since 1982. The Court of Appeal sitting in 2006 imposed the hospital disposal: it noted that Mr Hempston was not without responsibility for his offending, but that a hospital disposal was the proper outcome. *Drew* and *IA* were put forward in argument for Mr Hempston, though it has to be accepted that the Court of Appeal's final reasoning as to its conclusion was less than clear.[240]

237 [2007] EWCA Crim 2666, [2007] MHLR 320 para 17.

238 See [2007] EWCA Crim 2666, [2007] MHLR 320 para 28 in particular for the evidence of the benefits of placing Mr Simpson in a hospital setting.

239 [2006] EWCA Crim 2869, [2011] MHLR 99.

240 See also *R v O* [2011] EWCA Crim 376, [2011] MHLR 106, to similar effect.

18.200 One practical point which arises from cases such as *IA* and *Simpson* is that any impression that a sentencing judge might have that hospital security is poor might need to be countered by evidence. This should describe both the physical arrangements in place but also the relational security arising from the checks that staff can carry out. A further practical point is that the element of judicial discretion involved in deciding the appropriate sentence includes the need to assess the benefit to be obtained from a hospital placement as opposed to a prison placement, which might deal with any public safety concerns. Expert witnesses can no doubt be asked to comment on these features. Since a prison sentence does not preclude treatment in a hospital setting by way of a transfer to hospital, the expert evidence may sensibly extend to explaining the benefits of a hospital placement without having to await or rely on action by the Secretary of State (which was one of the features of *IA*).

18.201 Another supporting case is *R v David William Beatty*,[241] which involved someone given a life sentence because of doubts about his treatability, but who was subsequently given 'technical lifer' status on the basis that the updated medical evidence showed that he would have received a hospital order if the material had been in front of the judge. This meant that he was treated as if a hospital order had been made, a process that has now been stopped: the reasons for this are discussed in chapter 21. The Court of Appeal substituted hospital and restriction orders, commenting that it was proper to do so rather than impose a prison sentence when the criteria for a hospital order were made out, and also that it would be difficult to image circumstances in which the court would not substitute a hospital order with a restriction order when a life sentence prisoner had been granted 'technical lifer' status; and that in the circumstances which such a status might in the past have been granted, it was important to allow the Court of Appeal to intervene.[242]

18.202 Despite these cases, there have been others supporting the use of a prison sentence on someone who meets the criteria for a hospital

241 [2006] EWCA Crim 2359, [2006] MHLR 333.

242 *Beatty* was endorsed in *R v Hughes* [2010] EWCA Crim 1026, [2010] MHLR 188: David Clarke J for the court, including Lord Judge CJ, noted at paragraph 20 that the comments of Scott Baker LJ pointed to a powerful principle, and he set out at paragraph 19 the advantages of a hospital disposal, as advanced by a psychiatrist giving evidence to the court: 'It will provide continuity of care by forensic psychiatrists in a secure hospital for as long as is necessary, until his discharge becomes possible through decreasing levels of security, or by satisfying the First Tier Tribunal (as it now is), which applies rigorous standards to the assessment of future risk'.

disposal. This happened in *R v Dass*,[243] in which the Court of Appeal accepted that a 1998 murder conviction relating to the killing of three family members was unsafe in the light of fresh evidence that undermined the prosecution account at the trial, which had been supported by medical evidence, that Mr Dass had been feigning signs of mental illness. This version had evidently been accepted by the jury in preference to the defence account, which was also supported by evidence, that Mr Dass was mentally ill to the extent that his responsibility was diminished and so the proper verdict was manslaughter.[244] A few months after his conviction, Mr Dass had been transferred to a high secure hospital and had remained in the hospital system since that time. The Court of Appeal accepted that the new evidence supported a finding of diminished responsibility and so rendered the convictions unsafe: as the prosecution did not seek to retry the issue, the court substituted convictions for manslaughter. Moving then to sentence, the suggestion on behalf of Mr Dass was that he should be maintained in hospital, where he had been for some considerable time, by way of a hospital order with a restriction order. This was supported by unanimous medical evidence as to the existence of a mental disorder of a nature or degree making hospital treatment appropriate. However, one doctor giving evidence on the appeal for the prosecution doubted that a hospital order disposal was proper as it did not offer the same protection to the public in light of the focus on whether there was a risk arising from a recurrence of mental illness as opposed to the more general question of the risk of re-offending for whatever reason.

18.203 The Court of Appeal decided that a life sentence was the most appropriate disposal for Mr Dass because of the questions it had as to whether the hospital order system provided equal protection to the public, the inability of the psychiatrists to say that Mr Dass would no longer present a threat to society if his symptoms subsided (ie, whether there were risks that did not arise from his mental illness) and the consequent complexities of assessing the risk that he might pose in the future, and its view that there was an element of culpability because the illness was put forward as having a disinhibiting effect rather than being the sole cause of his offending (as, for example, had it been an illness involving command hallucinations).[245] The court

243 [2009] EWCA Crim 1208, [2009] MHLR 288.

244 An alternative possibility does exist, namely that the jury accepted that Mr Dass was mentally ill but found that it did not meet the statutory test of substantially diminishing his responsibility.

245 [2009] EWCA Crim 1208, [2009] MHLR 288 paras 47–49.

was also concerned about the placement of Mr Dass in a low secure unit that did not involve supervision by a forensic psychiatrist.

18.204 It may be that *Dass* involved an unusual set of circumstances in which the doctors were unable to identify whether the cause of danger arose from mental disorder or also from other sources, despite him having been in hospital for some time. However, it is also worth analysing the reasoning of the Court of Appeal. In the first place, it expressed that it had its doubts about whether there was any general rule that that a hospital order would be imposed if the medical criteria were made out and noted that there was clearly a jurisdiction to impose a prison sentence.[246] The latter comment is clearly correct, but the starting point is questionable in the light of the dicta in *Howell*, *Mbatha* and *Drew*, which endorse a general rule to that effect. The importance of this as the starting point is the need to find good reasons not to impose a hospital order rather than vice versa: the court in *Dass* adopted the contrary approach, concluding as it did that it was not persuaded that a hospital order was the most suitable disposal and so a prison sentence should follow.[247]

18.205 Another concern is that the court makes no mention of the features that favour a hospital order. Rather, it refers to Mr Dass's degree of culpability on the basis that his illness at most disinhibited him, and its concerns about his placement in a low secure hospital without a forensic psychiatrist in light of the danger he posed and his ability to be manipulative.[248] As to the first of these points, the emphasis on Mr Dass's culpability is somewhat discordant with the conclusion reached on the appeal against conviction that his responsibility was substantially diminished. In short, if responsibility has to be substantially diminished to become manslaughter rather than murder, it must be an unusual situation in which the responsibility that remains (ie that cannot be attributed to the mental disorder) can also be significant.

18.206 It is worth noting that two of the three psychiatrists who gave evidence to the Court of Appeal supported the making of a hospital order, and the basis on which the third did not was his view that a hospital disposal alone was inappropriate without clear evidence of a link between the mental disorder and the killing. He did, however, support the view that Mr Dass needed to be in hospital, but as a transferred prisoner. This view that a hospital order requires a link

246 [2009] EWCA Crim 1208, [2009] MHLR 288 para 47.
247 [2009] EWCA Crim 1208, [2009] MHLR 288 para 49.
248 [2009] EWCA Crim 1208, [2009] MHLR 288 para 49.

between the disorder and the offence does not represent the law,[249] and the factual basis for the view was rejected by the court with its substitution of the diminished responsibility verdict.

18.207 As to the placement of Mr Dass in a low secure unit and without supervision by a forensic psychiatrist, the Court of Appeal was reflecting concerns raised in evidence by a forensic psychiatrist.[250] It is no doubt generally the case that those with training and experience as forensic psychiatrists are best placed to deal with patients who have been involved in incidents of violence. However, that doctor still supported Mr Dass being placed in a hospital. More importantly, the context of this placement must be recognised: Mr Dass had been moved to a high secure hospital from prison (where forensic psychiatrists would have been in control of his case) and spent six years there before being transferred to the low secure hospital, where he remained; during this time, he was a restricted patient (as a serving prisoner transferred under MHA 1983 s47 with a restriction direction under section 49) and so any transfer would have involved the agreement of the Secretary of State: that would depend on satisfaction as to the safety of such a move.[251] In this context, the limited evidential basis against the imposition of a hospital order stands out.

18.208 Having outlined why *Dass* should be easy to distinguish and involves reasoning that is questionable in a number of respects, it does provide a reminder that a prison sentence is a possible outcome in relation to a diminished responsibility manslaughter or any other serious offence. The same occurred in *R v Welsh*,[252] though again there are significant questions as to the reasoning adopted. The Court of Appeal dismissed an appeal against the imposition of life imprisonment with a minimum term of 12 years on a man who stabbed his victim but whose responsibility was substantially diminished so as to reduce the offence to manslaughter on account of his paranoid schizophrenia at the time. Medical reports from both the prosecution and the defence recommended a hospital order and restriction order disposal under MHA 1983 ss37 and 41; and Mr Welsh had been in hospital prior to his guilty plea, having not been fit to stand trial until after treatment. Moreover, after the sentence and before the appeal,

249 See paras 18.159–18.176 above.

250 [2009] EWCA Crim 1208, [2009] MHLR 288 para 35.

251 It is also worth noting that the second doctor who favoured the making of a hospital order was content that the current placement was suitable: [2009] EWCA Crim 1208, [2009] MHLR 288 para 35.

252 [2011] EWCA Crim 73, [2011] MHLR 71.

he had had to be transferred to hospital under section 47 of the Act because he did not take medication in prison and had deteriorated.

18.209 The Court of Appeal held that the life sentence was proper because:

i) Mr Welsh retained substantial responsibility for the offence because he had a propensity for violence which predated his schizophrenia (as he had a number of convictions from prior to diagnosis) and had deliberately taken a knife to the party at which the killing occurred; and
ii) public confidence in the need to protect the public and reflect the gravity of the offence was not satisfied by the test for release under the MHA 1983 but was satisfied by the test for release from a life sentence under C(S)A 1997 s28, which allowed account to be taken of danger that did not arise from mental disorder.[253]

18.210 On one level, it may be that this is similar to *Dass* in that there was a basis for a view that the defendant posed a danger arising from features other than mental disorder and so risks from factors other than mental disorder should be relevant to release (which would mean having the Parole Board as the decision-maker). However, it was not explained how Mr Welsh's pre-diagnosis violence raised an ongoing concern that could be separated from concerns linked to his illness. The chronology was that he had convictions for offences of violence up to 1999, when he would have been around 30, and was diagnosed with schizophrenia in 2002: that would raise questions of whether he had grown out of any juvenile and young adult behavioural problems, and also whether this older offending was the result of as yet undiagnosed schizophrenia. As to the taking of the homicide weapon to the party, there is no indication as to why that was not causally linked to the disorder. Indeed, the court noted[254] that apparently rational behaviour after the crime, in concealing the weapon and disappearing for some ten days, could not give a clue as to how responsible he was for the killing: it is not explained why the taking of the knife was any different.

18.211 As to the proposition that the life sentence regime offers superior protection of the public, Moses LJ for the court cited *R v Drew*:[255] however, as already noted, the question for the House of Lords there was whether a legislative regime could be justified or was necessarily

253 [2011] EWCA Crim 73, [2011] MHLR 71 para 17.
254 [2011] EWCA Crim 73, [2011] MHLR 71 para 11.
255 [2003] UKHL 25, [2003] 1 WLR 1213, [2003] MHLR 282, discussed above.

incompatible with the ECHR, which raises very different considerations from those that arise when the question is whether to impose a hospital order on a patient whose condition so clearly requires it. Given that schizophrenia is a chronic condition, that Mr Welsh had been unfit to stand trial for some time, and that he did not have the capacity to consent to treatment when unwell and so might not receive treatment in prison,[256] the two likely scenarios that would follow the decision to uphold the life sentence were that he would be treated, returned to prison to deteriorate and be returned to hospital, which must raise concerns under article 3 of the ECHR; or that he would simply be held in hospital as a transferred patient, such that a hospital order would be the honest sentence.

18.212 Even more worrying is the use of reasoning that relies on public confidence: given that Mr Welsh's responsibility was substantially diminished because of the involvement of mental illness and the forensic hospital system is designed to protect the public, it would be hoped that public confidence – which should be taken to be the confidence of the properly informed public – should be satisfied that the hospital system is as able than the prison system to offer protection from dangerous patients. In any event, as was made plain in cases such as *IA*, the benefits to the patient of being in a hospital setting and the benefits to the public of securing treatment have also to be considered. That was clearly relevant on the facts, given that mental disorder that played a significant role in the offending.

18.213 In summary, there will no doubt be situations in which a defendant convicted of a serious offence such as manslaughter on the basis of diminished responsibility will not receive a hospital order. But they will be usual. For example, if there was a short-term disorder that diminished his or her responsibility at the time of the crime but is not ongoing. While there is no doubt a discretion as the use of a hospital disposal, which turns on whether it is the most suitable disposal, it is suggested that it will invariably meet the test of being the most suitable disposal. It will be unusual for the danger posed by the defendant to arise from factors that do not relate to his or her mental disorder, which the hospital system is best placed to treat and can do

256 [2003] UKHL 25, [2003] 1 WLR 1213, [2003] MHLR 282 para 8. There might be arguments as to treatment without consent in his or her best interests under the Mental Capacity Act 2005 if capacity is lacking, since sections 5 and 6 of that Act allow treatment without consent and necessary and proportionate restraint.

so in the relevant degree of security.[257] Any restrictive approach taken to a hospital order, relying on features such as the responsibility of the defendant, is problematic for a number of reasons: first, there will always be some responsibility if the verdict is not the special verdict of not guilty by reason of insanity, but a hospital disposal is not limited to that situation; second, the dangerous offender provisions do not exclude the use of a hospital order; third, the statutory purposes of sentencing in CJA 2003 s142 do not apply if there is a hospital disposal (or, indeed, an indeterminate dangerous offender sentence).[258] These features, together with the problems that might arise under ECHR articles 3 and 5 of sending to prison someone who clearly needs to be detained for medical treatment, support the primacy of using a hospital disposal when the criteria are made out rather than a dangerousness-based custodial sentence. There is one caveat that must be addressed, however: that is the existence of another relatively new sentence, namely the hospital direction, which is described next, and allows a combination of a prison sentence and a transfer to hospital.

Hospital direction

Background

18.214 In the context of the judgment as to whether to impose a hospital disposal rather than a prison sentence, it is worth noting that there is another sentencing option available under the MHA 1983 that allows the court to combine a prison sentence and a transfer to hospital. This hybrid order exists under MHA 1983 s45A, which was added by C(S)A 1997 s46.

18.215 The background to this hybrid sentence is important to understand its purpose. In the government white paper *Protecting the public: the government's strategy on crime in England and Wales,*[259] what was described as the proposed 'central change' was an order for 'certain

257 In this regard, as has been noted, a court that has any concerns about the level of security is able to make a direction under C(S)A 1997 s47 to specify the hospital unit in which the patient should be held, at least initially. See para 18.91 above.

258 They do apply in relation to an extended sentence, which is a form of imprisonment: but it is now a discretionary sentence and does not prevent the use of a hospital order.

259 Cmd 3190 March 1996. The relevant discussion is in chapter 8, which for some reason dealt with sex offenders and mentally disordered offenders.

mentally disordered offenders for whom the present form of hospital order is unsatisfactory, particularly those who are considered to bear a significant degree of responsibility for their offences'[260] such that a fixed period in detention might be required 'because the offender is found to bear some significant responsibility for the offence notwithstanding his disorder, or because the link between the offending behaviour and the mental disorder is not clear at the time of sentencing'.[261] The hybrid disposal was a method to enable 'the requirements of sentencing in such cases to be met' by allowing a person sent to hospital to be remitted to prison 'if he recovered or was found to be untreatable during the fixed period set by the court',[262] so as to 'enable the courts to deal with some of the most difficult cases in a way which took proper account of the offender's need for treatment; the demands of justice; and the proper right of other people to be protected from harm'.[263]

18.216 Raising the 'requirements of sentencing' in the context of sending someone to hospital is a recipe for confusion: the purpose of the court in this situation is to divert him or her away from the criminal justice system. This is why the purposes of sentencing, as set out in the CJA 2003, subsequent to the introduction of section 45A, are disapplied when a person is sentenced to a hospital order disposal or a section 45A sentence.[264]

18.217 At the time the hybrid order was introduced, the reference to a defendant being found untreatable and requiring to be released on that ground raised the scenario of someone with psychopathic disorder. That could be a problem only in a very small number of cases. It would mean that a person had been found to meet the requirements for detention (including an assessment of treatability), perhaps after an interim hospital order, but that the doctors making the assessment had got it wrong. This in turn would be an unusual situation, since it would require that the treatment programme in hospital did not stop someone's condition getting worse: preventing a deterioration in a condition, including the symptoms and conse-

260 *Protecting the public: the government's strategy on crime in England and Wales* para 8.12.

261 *Protecting the public: the government's strategy on crime in England and Wales* para 8.13.

262 *Protecting the public: the government's strategy on crime in England and Wales* para 8.13.

263 *Protecting the public: the government's strategy on crime in England and Wales* para 8.12.

264 See chapter 16 at paras 16.12–16.15.

quences, amounted to treatability. And any such conclusion as to failure should only be reached after a lengthy period of trying, including possibly a period of the disorder getting worse before it got better in the long term.[265] So this ought to entail a significant time in detention in any event. In short, it is possible that the perception of a problem was somewhat unrealistic. It is perhaps more likely that there were a number of situations in which clinicians would conclude, perhaps understandably, that the management difficulties caused by some patients whose problems required very long-term intervention was not something for which overstretched health service budgets should be used when other patients also had needs to be met.

Initial provision and limitations

18.218 However, there was one valid reason to have the section 45A sentence initially, which was that the C(S)A 1997 also introduced the automatic life sentence provision that required a prison sentence even if a person met the criteria for a hospital order: this at least allowed the person given a custodial sentence because Parliament had deemed it necessary to prevent the use of a hospital order alone to be sent to hospital. However, section 45A as originally inserted into the MHA 1983 applied only to those who suffered from a psychopathic disorder.[266] The criteria were that the court had considered making a hospital order but had rejected it in favour of imprisonment (unless there was no such discretion available, as was the case with the automatic life sentence provisions),[267] but the offender had a mental disorder of a nature or degree making detention in hospital for treatment appropriate and was treatable. The order made, a 'hospital direction', took effect as a direction to place the prisoner in hospital (and so required evidence such as was required in the case of a hospital order that there was a bed available within 28 days); and it was to be combined with a 'limitation direction', namely that the patient be treated as if subject to a restriction order under MHA

265 See chapter 2 at paras 2.44–2.45.

266 See chapter 1. This limitation to psychopathic disorder was recorded in the white paper, at para 8.13, as being a recommendation from a 'Department of Health and Home Office Working Group on Psychopathic Disorder', though it was noted that the government was deciding whether to allow the order to cover all types of mental disorder.

267 In other words, it was possible to combine an automatic life sentence with a hospital direction; however, it was not possible to use it in connection with the mandatory life sentence for murder.

1983 s41 while in hospital. The power to specify a particular unit in a hospital under C(S)A 1997 s47, discussed at para 18.91 above, also applies when a section 45A order is made.

18.219 There were two specific and fairly obviously problematic limitations with this initial provision, the first one of which still remains. The hospital direction can be combined only with a sentence of imprisonment and so cannot be used in relation to someone whose age means that a custodial sentence will be one of detention rather than imprisonment, that is someone under the age of 21 at the time of the conviction.[268] That the reference in MHA 1983 s45A to imprisonment was meant to be the technically correct meaning of the word rather than a reference to any custodial sentence was confirmed in *R v Burridge*,[269] in which a 20-year old was sentenced to detention for public protection under the dangerous offender provisions of the CJA 2003 and made subject to a hospital and limitation direction. The Court of Appeal quashed the section 45A order, though it is to be noted that counsel did not suggest any argument to the contrary. This meant that the mental disorder from which the defendant suffered was relevant only as a mitigation of the minimum term under the indeterminate sentence.

18.220 The absence of any power to secure immediate hospital treatment for someone who is given a sentence of detention appears to have no good reason, particularly as the detainee will serve a sentence of detention in prison once he or she becomes 21. This produces an argument in favour of a non-technical interpretation of the word imprisonment, so as to include any custodial sentence. In support of this, it might be suggested that if the word in the legislation had been 'detention', it is unlikely to have been construed so as to mean only the sentence imposed on those under 21. However, the counter-argument is that the legislature could easily have used a term that was apt to include all forms of custodial sentence.

18.221 The second problem was the limitation of the regime to those diagnosed with a psychopathic disorder, which was criticised by the courts. In *Drew*, the House of Lords concluded that there was no breach of the ECHR in requiring an automatic life sentence on a man who met the criteria for a hospital order and needed treatment for mental illness, but added that the whole dispute could have been avoided if section 45A covered all forms of mental disorder. Lord Bingham said:

268 See PCC(S)A 2000 s89.

269 [2009] EWCA Crim 1693, [2009] MHLR 297.

> Had it been open to the Recorder to make an order under section 45A (which it was not, because the appellant was not suffering from psychopathic disorder) it seems likely that he would have done so. This would have avoided the ill effects which the appellant undoubtedly suffered as a result of his confinement in prison. We hope that further thought may be given to exercise of the power conferred by section 45A(10).[270]

18.222 The statutory power referred to was that allowing the Secretary of State to extend the coverage of the hospital direction to other forms of mental disorder. This view as to the need to extend the order was endorsed by the Court of Appeal in *R v IA*[271] and in *R v Staines*,[272] which is discussed below. While it might be suggested that it would be far too easy for a court to make a finding that someone mentally ill retained a level of responsibility that justified some punitive response as well, the problem identified in *Drew* was a real one in that the defendant was out of a therapeutic setting for several days. Moreover, the purpose of the hybrid order might well be satisfied much more easily in relation to mental illness: for example, there might well be situations in which a psychotic illness that was diagnosed as schizophrenia turned out to be a more short-lived drug-induced and not chronic state, leading to a much more speedy release than might otherwise have been expected. If the defendant retained responsibility for his or her crime, that might be felt inappropriate. However, no amendment was made until it became necessary as a result of the changes introduced by the MHA 2007. Before turning to that, there was some case-law on the initial position.

Guidance on the initial provision

18.223 The use of the sentence as it applied to those with psychopathic disorder was considered by the Court of Appeal in *R v Staines*. Ms Staines suffered significant abuse in her young life. In 2000, she killed a man in gruesome and bizarre circumstances. A plea of guilty to manslaughter on the basis of diminished responsibility was accepted

270 [2003] UKHL 25, [2003] 1 WLR 1213, [2003] MHLR 282 at para 21. Lord Bingham had noted at paragraph 13 that the limitation to psychopathic disorder was 'perhaps surprising, given that in Scotland section 59A of the Criminal Procedure (Scotland) Act 1995, inserted by section 6(1) of the Crime and Punishment (Scotland) Act 1997, provides for a disposal by means of a sentence of imprisonment and an allied hospital order in any appropriate case, whatever the nature of the mental disorder'.

271 [2005] EWCA Crim 2077, [2005] MHLR 336 at para 47.

272 [2006] EWCA Crim 15, [2006] MHLR 184.

by the prosecution and the judge. The evidence was that she had a personality disorder amounting to psychopathic disorder within the MHA 1983, and that it was treatable; there was also a tentative view that she might have a mental illness as well. One doctor suggested that the preferable sentence was a life sentence combined with a hospital direction under section 45A, in case Ms Staines refused to co-operate with treatment and so had to be released from hospital as being untreatable; the other doctor supported a hospital order with a restriction order because she might seek to avoid confronting her problems, and so would undermine treatment, if there was an option of being transferred to prison. The judge preferred the former view.

18.224 After some three-and-a-half years, Ms Staines sought to appeal the sentence on the grounds that she had demonstrated that she was indeed treatable, and there was much stronger evidence that she had been mentally ill as well: indeed, a Mental Health Review Tribunal had reclassified her so that she was detained under both psychopathic disorder and mental illness. By the time of the hearing of the appeal, some five years had passed. The Court of Appeal accepted that the up-to-date evidence suggested that there was both mental illness and personality disorder at the time of the offence: but it noted that it was not clear whether the mental illness played any, or any significant, role in the homicide, that its presence would not reduce her culpability for the killing when compared to having a personality disorder alone, and the existence of mental illness as well as a psychopathic disorder did not make it inappropriate to use a prison sentence together with a hospital direction to secure additional protection to the public. It was also noted on the facts that there was no realistic prospect that Ms Staines would be placed in prison either in the foreseeable future or when she was fit to be released from hospital: the court expressed the view that should would remain in hospital pending the consideration of her case by the Parole Board, and any uncertainty as to that did not mean that the sentence as imposed was incorrect.

18.225 A number of comments can be made about this. In the first place, the Court of Appeal deals with the diminished responsibility finding by noting that Ms Staines retained substantial responsibility: as has been noted above in relation to the option of the hospital order and restriction order for a diminished responsibility manslaughter, a finding of diminished responsibility requires a substantial impairment of responsibility, which does not leave much room for the motif that the defendant was in control in a manner that retained significant responsibility. Second, the court approached the question by asking whether it was appropriate for the sentencing court to have acted as it did, rather than considering what was appropriate on the up-to-date evidence, which the Court of Appeal has done in many cases: see chapters 17 and 21 in particular. In particular, the court did not explain why it did not act on the current evidence that undermined the fears behind the reasoning of the judge. It is also difficult to understand why the now well-established mental illness did not make a difference, or why it was necessary for the Parole Board to be involved if Ms Staines would not be put into a prison setting.

Amendment by the Mental Health Act 2007

18.226 The current criteria for the use of this hybrid order consequent on the amendments introduced by the MHA 2007 are that written or oral evidence from two doctors indicates that the offender is suffering from mental disorder (of any sort, not limited to psychopathic disorder), that it is of a nature or degree which makes it appropriate for him to be detained in a hospital for medical treatment, and that appropriate medical treatment is available; it remains necessary that the court has rejected the option of a hospital order in favour of imprisonment. Accordingly, the offender is a prisoner who is transferred to hospital as a patient at the outset but will go to prison if he or she ceases to meet the criteria for detention in hospital and there is still time to serve on the sentence (though if the criteria for detention in hospital continue to be met, the patient will remain in hospital even if the sentence of prison has expired).

18.227 Two comments are worth making about the retention and indeed expansion of the hospital direction. First, the significant problem caused by having an automatic life sentence that had to be imposed even if the defendant needed to be in hospital, which was the concern identified in *Drew* as the basis for suggesting that the criteria be expanded, was removed when the automatic life sentence provisions were replaced by the CJA 2003, as the dangerous offender sentencing provisions did not exclude the use of a hospital order disposal. As such, one of the justifications for the hybrid order had been removed; and, specifically, the judicial call to extend the scope of the hybrid order to cover mental illness as well was in the context of judges otherwise being forced to order the detention of mentally ill people in a prison.

18.228 Second, a concern behind the hybrid order was the prospect of having to release those with severe personality disorders if they turned out not to meet the treatability test. Even though this was something that would happen only rarely, it was a concern that was removed by the MHA 2007, as has been described in chapter 2.

18.229 The third basis for the hybrid order was the need to ensure a certain period of detention in order to meet the purposes of sentencing; but as has been described, this has the potential to cause confusion and is undermined by the fact that the aim behind hospital orders is to divert a person away from the punitive system.

18.230 Despite all these matters, the hybrid order has been maintained and extended. However, it is suggested that the statutory purpose should be kept in mind: the aim was to ensure a period of detention and hence public protection if a person sent to hospital for treatment turned out not to be fit for treatment and so would have to be released while untreated and hence still dangerous.

18.231 However, the Court of Appeal has not emphasised this approach: rather, it has essentially followed the same line as in *Staines* in relation to an offender who was clearly affected by mental illness when offending. In *R v Benjamin Alan Cooper*,[273] there was a homicide of a former partner and an attempt to kill a step-father. Both crimes were driven by delusions triggered by drug abuse, as he believed that his former partner was plotting to kill him and that his step-father was involved in a financial conspiracy against him, and so a plea of manslaughter on the basis of diminished responsibility was entered for the homicide; there was also a guilty plea to the attempted murder. The judge imposed imprisonment for public protection and added a hospital direction: the reasoning was that although neither offence would have occurred but for the mental disorder, the attack on Mr Cooper's step-father occurred when he had some self-control and was based on the delusion as to financial matters, and he had some responsibility because of the role of drug abuse in triggering the illness.

18.232 The Court of Appeal dismissed the appeal, noting that the hospital direction provisions had been extended to mental illness-based offending and Mr Cooper was within the purpose of the sentence because he retained responsibility. In relation to evidence that Mr Cooper might be at risk of a relapse if transferred to prison, the court emphasised the importance of public protection against someone who might relapse, rather than the potential problem from the perspective of ECHR article 3 of subjecting someone to action that might cause their disorder to deteriorate, and expressed confidence that he would remain in hospital until the Parole Board considered his case. All the comments made above about the suitability of a hospital order and restriction order in relation to an offender with mental disorder

273 [2010] EWCA Crim 2335, [2010] MHLR 240.

are equally applicable to this reasoning, as are the comments about *Staines*.

Hybrid order and life sentence

18.233 One particular issue that has arisen in the context of hospital and limitation directions accompanying life imprisonment is the setting of a tariff, that is the minimum term to be served for the purposes of punishment (on which see chapter 17). A reminder that this should reflect the punitive aspect of sentencing rather than the protective aspect was provided in *R v McMillan*.[274] This involved a conviction for manslaughter on the grounds of diminished responsibility on the basis of a plea accepted by the prosecution; the automatic life sentence provisions then in effect were applied, coupled with a hospital and limitation direction pursuant to MHA 1983 s45A. The judge made an order under PCC(S)A 2000 s82A(2) that the minimum term provisions should not apply because she could not contemplate any release in the light of the evidence of the risk of further offending: that would mean that Mr McMilan's case would never be considered by the Parole Board, which decides on the release of life sentence prisoners (in other words, he would necessarily serve the rest of his life in detention).

18.234 The Court of Appeal held that the judge had made an error of law and set a minimum term of nine years: the question of the tariff, it noted, turned on the seriousness of the offence, with questions of risk dealt with through the envelope of the indeterminate sentence and the fact that no release would in fact occur until both the punitive tem had been served and the risk posed was suitably reduced. It was noted by the court that evidence from the psychiatrists at the hospital where Mr McMilan was detained noted the importance of a fixed minimum term as a method to assist the development of a treatment plan, which would also provide a time-scale to assist him to engage in treatment. For another example of a similar judicial error and its correction by the Court of Appeal, see *R v Daniel Richard House*,[275] which involved attempted murder and attempted rape committed by a man with a mental illness and a personality disorder that might not have been treatable. He had been transferred to prison after his mental illness had responded to treatment, and again the evidence was that the whole life tariff meant that he was given a low priority in terms of

274 [2005] EWCA Crim 222, [2005] MHLR 90.
275 [2007] EWCA Crim 2559, [2007] MHLR 318.

access to rehabilitative treatment, since those who might be able to make a meaningful application for release are given higher priority. The Court of Appeal confirmed that the failure to specify a tariff is a proper exercise of judicial discretion only in the very exceptional case when the seriousness of the offence justifies life-long detention.

The effects of a hospital order or direction

Introduction

18.235 By reason of MHA 1983 s40(1), a hospital order provides authority for a constable (meaning someone holding that office), an approved mental health professional or whoever is acting under the direction of the court to convey the person to hospital: this is subject to any place of safety provisions made by the court if the hospital bed is not available immediately. By necessary and express corollary, it also provides authority for the managers of the relevant hospital to detain the patient. In terms of the regulation of what happens after admission, section 40(4) is the key provision:

> (4) A patient who is admitted to a hospital in pursuance of a hospital order ... shall, subject to the provisions of this subsection, be treated for the purposes of the provisions of this Act mentioned in Part I of Schedule 1 to this Act as if he had been so admitted or placed on the date of the order in pursuance of an application for admission for treatment ..., duly made under Part II of this Act, but subject to any modifications of those provisions specified in that Part of that Schedule.

18.236 The 'application for admission for treatment' is the application under section 3 of the Act. MHA 1983 Sch 1 provides the details of the application to the hospital order patient of the provision of Part II of the Act, that which governs civil patients. The Schedule is in two parts, the first applying to non-restricted patients and the second to restricted patients.

18.237 These provisions do not apply, at least not expressly, when a hospital direction is made. The effect of this is set out on section 45B of the Act: there is authority to convey and detain in the same way as in relation to a hospital order (section 45B(1)), and the provisions relating to transfer directions and restriction directions, in sections 47 and 49 respectively, are applied. These are described in chapter 20, relating to the transfer of serving prisoners to hospital: but they essentially provide that the transferee is treated as though a hospital order and restriction order had been made (sections 47(3) and 49(2)), and so the provisions of Schedule 1 are thereby relevant. In addition, section 45B(3) requires the RC to provide annual reports to the Secretary of State, which mirrors section 49(3).

Hospital order without restrictions

18.238 In *Birch*[276] the effect of a hospital order was summarised in the following terms at pages 84–85 of the report:

> Once the offender is admitted to hospital pursuant to a hospital order or transfer order without restriction on discharge, his position is almost exactly the same as if he were a civil patient. In effect he passes out of the penal system and into the hospital regime. ... There are certain differences between the positions of the offender and of the civil patient, relating to early access to the Review Tribunal and to discharge by the patient's nearest relative, but these are of comparatively modest importance. In general the offender is dealt with in a manner which appears, and is intended to be, humane by comparison with a custodial sentence. A hospital order is not a punishment. Questions of retribution and deterrence, whether personal or general, are immaterial. The offender who has become a patient is not kept on any kind of leash by the Court, as he is when he consents to a probation order with a condition of inpatient treatment. The sole purpose of the order is to ensure that the offender receives the medical care and attention which he needs in the hope and expectation of course that the result will be to avoid the commission by the offender of further criminal acts.

18.239 In brief, the most important features are as follows:

i) A hospital order patient has the status of a patient detained under the a civil detention for treatment order, including the powers that exist to transfer between hospitals, grant leave, and place on a community treatment order (though the latter does not apply if a restriction order is in place, and the exercise of the transfer and leave powers in relation to a restricted patient require the consent of the Secretary of State for Justice).

ii) The patient must be released if the criteria for detention no longer apply, as decided by a tribunal or the hospital managers or the RC, the person in charge of treatment[277] (though in the case of a restricted patient, the Secretary of State must agree to a release

276 (1990) 90 CrAppR 78.

277 MHA 1983 s55(1) contains the definition; the term appears in various parts of the Act.

by the hospital managers or RC). There is no right of access to a tribunal in the first six months.

iii) Detention may be renewed if the criteria for detention continue to apply (but if a restriction order is made, there is no need for renewal, and so detention continues until it is found that the criteria for detention no longer apply).

iv) The patient is subject to the provisions regulating treatment without consent.

18.240 In relation to non-restricted patients, some of the provisions of MHA 1983 Part II apply without modification and others apply with modifications as set out in the Schedule. Taking these various provisions as they are listed in the civil part of the statute:

- Section 17 (leave): this applies without modification (see Schedule 1 Part 1 para 1).
- Sections 17A–17G (CTO): some of this applies without modification (paragraph 1) but other parts are modified (paragraphs 2, 2A and 2B), but only to reflect that the basis for detention is the hospital order not the application for admission; in terms of substance, the CTO regime applies without modification.
- Section 18 (absconding): applies with modifications (paragraphs 2 and 4), but these are only to remove limitations relevant only to civil detention other than under section 3, and so in terms of substance this applies without modification.
- Section 19 (transfer between hospitals or between guardianship and hospital): applies with modifications (paragraphs 2 and 5), but only to reflect that the basis for detention is the hospital order not the application for admission; in terms of substance, this applies without modification.
- Section 19A (regulations as to community patients): applies with a modification (paragraphs 2 and 5A), but again only to reflect the fact that the hospital order is the basis for detention.
- Section 20 (duration of order and renewal provisions): applies with a substantive modification (paragraphs 2 and 6), which is that the six-month time limit starts to run from the date the hospital order is made not the date of admission to hospital; while the date of admission and the date of the order might be the same, it might differ if a bed is not immediately available and the place of safety provisions are used; what is worth noting in this connection is that the test for renewal is the same for a hospital order or civil patient, and so even though the criteria for the application of

a hospital order is slightly different, it becomes the same test for detention after the initial period.

- Section 20A (duration of CTO and renewal): applies without modification (paragraph 1).
- Section 20B (effect of expiry of CTO): applies with a modification to reflect that the initial order was a hospital order (paragraphs 2 and 6A).
- Sections 21, 21A and 21B (provisions as to patients absent without leave, and the different steps that have to be taken if they are taken into custody within 28 days or after longer than 28 days): apply without modification (paragraph 1).
- Section 22 (effect of imprisonment on civil admissions): applies with a modification to note that the basis for admission is the hospital order (paragraphs 2 and 7).
- Section 23 (power of RC, hospital managers and nearest relative to discharge): applies with a substantive modification, namely that the nearest relative cannot discharge (paragraphs 2 and 8). This does mean that the patient can be discharged as soon as the RC or hospital managers believe that the criteria for detention no longer apply; this can occur during the first six months of the order (which is the minimum period before an application can be made to a tribunal).
- Section 24 (powers to visit and examine patients): applies without modification (though subparagraphs (1) and (2) are not relevant because they relate to the excluded power of the nearest relative to discharge under section 23).
- Section 25 (barring process of the nearest relative discharge): irrelevant in the light of the modification of section 23.
- Section 26–28 (identification of the nearest relative): apply without modification (paragraph 1); although the nearest relative does not have a power under section 23, he or she may have other roles to play, and so is still relevant.
- Sections 29 and 30 (replacement of nearest relative in relation to admission under section 3, discharge under section 23, and applications to the tribunal in such a situation, and discharge of such a replacement): at first sight, not relevant because it relates to section 23, but there may be a gap in the legislation to the extent that the involvement of the nearest relative at all arises by virtue of Part II and the powers of application to a tribunal. The potential gap is that the power to change the nearest relative includes situations where this isn't one or the person is unsuitable, for

example because of a poor relationship with the patient, and that should apply to a hospital order patient as well; the strange thing is that section 31 does apply.

- Section 31 (county court rules): applies without modification (paragraph 1), though the county court is involved in the section 29 process, which does not seem to apply according to the Schedule but, as noted, possibly should with relevant modifications.
- Section 32 (regulation making power, including as to forms and record-keeping): applies without modification (paragraph 1).
- Section 33 (provisions as to wards of court, including restrictions on Part II applications without court permission): does not apply.
- Section 34 (interpretation): applies without modification (paragraph 1).

18.241 In addition, the powers relating to applications to the relevant tribunal in Part V of the Act are covered by the Schedule. The main power for civil applications is in section 66: this applies with modifications that remove the reference to applications being possible when things that cannot happen to hospital order patients apply: paragraphs 2 and 9 of the first part of the Schedule. This means that applications to the tribunal can be made when CTOs are made or revoked, there is a transfer from guardianship to hospital, the hospital order is renewed, or a patient who absconded is recaptured and detained in hospital. The general power of the Secretary of State to refer a case to a tribunal, which arises under section 67, applies without modification (paragraph 1). The duty of the hospital managers to refer the case to a tribunal if the patient does not apply for a tribunal is made applicable with a substantive modification (paragraphs 2 and 10): in relation to civil patients, there is a duty to make a referral after six months and thereafter at intervals of three years (or one year in relation to a patient under 18); in relation to hospital order patients, only the latter duty arises, unless the patient has been transferred from guardianship to hospital, in which case the six-month duty of referral arises.

18.242 However, there are additional provisions as to applications to tribunals that apply only to patients detained under Part III. These are contained in section 69. In particular, the nearest relative may exercise the power of application to a tribunal of a hospital order patient. (There are also provisions allowing patients transferred from prison to hospital to make immediate applications to a tribunal.)

18.243 One further point to note is that any previous hospital order (or guardianship order) ceases to have effect,[278] so that the latest made is the one that governs; see section 40(5). The importance of this is that any right that a patient may have to apply to a tribunal will end because the rights to apply under the new order, which do not arise until six months have passed, will take precedence.

18.244 In terms of the test before the tribunal, this is set out in section 72: the same test applies to a patient detained under section 3 or section 37, which is whether the test for admission under section 3 continues to apply. If it does not, the tribunal must discharge. By the time a section 37 patient is before a tribunal, the detention will have been renewed under section 20, at which point the same test is applied to a civil patient and a criminal patient.

Hospital order with restrictions

18.245 The summary of the effect of a restriction order in *Birch* is in the following terms, at page 85 of the report: after noting that there is a 'marked contrast' with the hospital order, and that '[a] restriction order has no existence independently of the hospital order to which it relates', the Court of Appeal commented:

> Nevertheless, it fundamentally affects the circumstances in which the patient is detained. No longer is the offender regarded simply as a patient whose interests are paramount. No longer is the control of him handed over unconditionally to the hospital authorities. Instead the interests of public safety are regarded by transferring the responsibility for discharge from the responsible medical officer and the hospital to the Secretary of State alone (before September 30, 1983) and now to the Secretary of State and the Mental Health Review Tribunal. A patient who has been subject to a restriction order is likely to be detained for much longer in hospital than one who is not, and will have fewer opportunities for leave of absence.

18.246 The starting point of the applicable regime is MHA 1983 s41(3), which defines the special restrictions. They are that:

i) any provisions as to the length of detention or the need to renew the order do not apply: this removes the effect of section 20;
ii) the community treatment order regime does not apply;
iii) the provisions relating to applications to tribunals under sections 66 and 69 do not apply;

278 There is saving language in case the new order is quashed on appeal.

iv) leave under section 17, transfer under section 19 and release under section 23 requires the consent of the Secretary of State; and the granting of leave includes the power of the Secretary of State to recall the patient from leave.

18.247 These provisions lead to some further modifications of Part II of the Act as a result of Part II of Schedule 1 to the Act: paragraphs 2 together with 3, 5 and 7 make the relevant changes. In addition, the parts of section 18 that allow a hospital order or civil admission order to lapse if a patient is absent without leave for six months are omitted by reason of paragraph 4; and the provision that a prison sentence of longer than six months brings an admission to an end is also disapplied by paragraph 6. These latter provisions are explicable by the fact that the restricted hospital order is effectively a life-long order unless it is lifted by a positive decision that it is not necessary to continue it.

18.248 Section 70 is the section that contains the power to apply to a tribunal. It provides a right to apply after six months from the relevant hospital order, direction or transfer and then after a further six months there is an annual power to apply. In addition, under section 71, the Secretary of State may make a reference to the tribunal at any stage. The tribunal will apply the test under section 73. In essence, if the criteria for detention are not made out, there must be a discharge; but that will be a conditional discharge unless the patient shows that it should be absolute – the latter means that the patient is no longer subject to a restriction order. A conditional discharge means that the patient may be recalled, that power belonging the Secretary of State and exercisable under section 42. In addition, conditions may be placed on the discharge of the patient, such as residence in a hostel, supervision, and the taking of medication; if these have to be arranged, the discharge will be a deferred conditional discharge. Recall may occur if the mental condition of the patient deteriorates: this may occur even if there is compliance with conditions, and breach of conditions is not by itself enough unless it is an indicator that the mental state of the patient may justify detention.

Hospital direction and limitation direction

18.249 The effect of an order under MHA 1983 s45A is as though a transfer direction with a restriction direction had been given under sections 47 and 49 of the Act, as described in chapter 20. This in effect reproduces the regime applicable to a restricted patient, but with the difference that the powers of release under section 23 are likely to lead to a transfer to prison. This can occur under section 50 of the

Act, based either on the need for treatment having ended or the conclusion being reached that no effective treatment can be given: this may be because the patient is unwilling to co-operate. In addition, the case may be heard by a tribunal, which will sit under section 74 of the Act. This allows it to consider the criteria under section 73 applicable to a restricted patient, but with the difference that it may recommend that the patient remain in hospital if not granted release from the underlying custodial sentence: this covers the situation of a patient who will deteriorate if sent to a prison setting. If the patient may be released if the Parole Board so decides, it is also possible for the patient to remain in hospital pending that decision: this may be a pragmatic decision, if for example he or she has been detained in hospital for some time and so is not known to the prison service, such that the compilation of reports for the Board will be problematic.

Appeals

18.250 Decisions made to impose a hospital order, restriction order or hospital direction are all sentencing decisions and so subject to appeal to the Court of Appeal. A decision by the magistrates to impose a hospital order is also a sentence that can be appealed to the Crown Court. One gap has been identified: in *R v Galfetti*,[279] it was noted that a decision to adjourn pending the availability of a hospital bed is not appealable. However, any failure to take into account the effect of the additional time spent in custody would be open to appeal if that was wrong in principle.

18.251 Naturally, there may also be appeals on the basis that a hospital order should have been imposed, perhaps with a restriction order, instead of a custodial sentence. It has been determined in *R v Bennett*[280] that a hospital order and restriction order is not more severe than a prison sentence: this is relevant because a restriction on the Court of Appeal is that it cannot impose a higher sentence than that appealed. However, it may be that a limitation direction, which supplements a custodial sentence, is more severe, at least unless the underlying prison sentence is reduced.

18.252 Separate consideration is given in chapter 21 to the issues that arise in relation to appeals made out of time, which have arisen on many occasions in situations of offenders with mental disorder issues.

279 [2002] EWCA Crim 1916, [2002] MHLR 418.
280 [1968] 1 WLR 988, (1968) 52 CrAppR 514.

CHAPTER 19

Mental disorder and community sentences

Introduction

19.1 The two disposals that are available to deal with a defendant who has mental health difficulties but who does not need to be placed under a hospital order are the guardianship order that arises under section 37 of the Mental Health Act (MHA) 1983 and also the community order under the Criminal Justice Act (CJA) 2003, to which can be added various requirements including ones relating to mental health treatment or treatment for other matters, such as drugs or alcohol misuse, that might be implicated in mental disorder problems. It may also be possible to take a practical course such as granting a conditional discharge if arrangements have been made under community care powers (described in chapter 2).

19.2 It is to be noted that the statutory purposes of sentencing, as set out in section 142 of the CJA 2003,[1] apply to a guardianship or community order, and so these sentences must be justified after taking into account those purposes. In addition, the assessment of seriousness of offending applies in relation to a community order: CJA 2003 s148 indicates that the offending must be serious enough to warrant a community order. Regard must also be had to any time spent in custody pre-sentence when determining the restrictions on liberty imposed: CJA 2003 s149. As an exception to the seriousness requirement, however, section 151 allows a community order if that would be in the interests of justice in the light of previous sentences meaning that a fine is not appropriate.

19.3 The CJA 2003 s166 includes a general saving for mitigation and also indicates that there is no restriction on the use of a Mental Health Act disposal, which will include a guardianship order. It is perhaps strange that section 142 applies to a guardianship order, given the general saving provision in section 166 in relation to custodial and community orders.

19.4 A court considering either of the above community sentences must order and consider a pre-sentence report: CJA 2003 s156(3).

Guardianship

19.5 In Part II of the MHA 1983, guardianship may be put in place under section 7 by the patient's nearest relative or an approved mental health professional,[2] supported by two medical recommendations to

1 Discussed in chapter 16.

2 See chapter 1 for an explanation of these terms.

the effect that the patient has a mental disorder of a nature or degree that warrants the use of guardianship and that it is necessary for the welfare of the patient or the protection of others. Section 37 of the Act allows a court to impose such an order after a conviction or, in the case of the magistrates, after a finding that the person committed the actus reus of the offence charged: see the discussion of this in the context of unfitness to stand trial or insanity in chapters 10 and 13.

19.6 The preconditions are that, on the basis of two medical reports, the nature or degree of the mental disorder warrants guardianship and that the order is the most suitable disposal. The factors relevant to this are, as with a hospital order, the circumstances pertaining, which includes the nature of the offence and the character and antecedents of the offender, and the alternatives.

19.7 The absence of the necessity test is explicable, as it is in relation to the use of a hospital order, by the fact that such a test might exclude someone who was willing to accept the order. In both the civil and criminal setting, the person must be at least 16.

19.8 The powers available to the guardian are to control the residence of the person subject to guardianship, to require that access be given to a medical practitioner and also to require that the subject attend a nominated place for medical treatment, occupation, training or education (see MHA 1983 s8). The effect of a section 37 guardianship order is the same as a civil order: see MHA 1983 s40(2); this is subject to some modifications by reason of Schedule 1 to the Act. This means, among other things, that the patient may be transferred to section 3 detention if necessary (section 19), the order lasts for six months and then has to be renewed under section 20 for a further six months and then for a year at a time, and the patient may seek discharge from the local authority, the clinician designated as the responsible clinician for the case or a tribunal (sections 23, 34 and 66). The nearest relative of a patient may discharge a civil guardianship order but not a criminal one: this is the effect of MHA 1983 Sch 1 Part II para 8.

19.9 Since the use of guardianship is minimal, it may be that the usual providers of reports to courts are less familiar with what is available. MHA 1983 s39A allows a court to request information as to whether a guardian is available and how the powers will be exercised. This may be important because a guardianship order cannot be made unless the person named as the guardian is willing to act: MHA 1983 s37(6). This has been determined to mean that the guardian, which may be a local authority, can take a view that the order is not appropriate. In

R (Buckowicki) v Northamptonshire County Council,[3] the local authority declined to accept a patient under guardianship after admitting a charge of affray, taking the view that alcohol-induced behaviour by the patient meant that he posed risks that could not be dealt with by a guardianship order. A judicial review challenge to this position failed, the High Court finding that the judicial view that guardianship was the most suitable order was subservient to the willingness of the guardian to act, which was a matter of professional judgment and judicially-reviewable only on the standard grounds on the merits, namely whether it was rational. The judge in the criminal court made a community order instead.

19.10 There has been one case in which use of the guardianship order was encouraged. In *Bartram v Southend Magistrates' Court*,[4] the defendant was found to have committed the actus reus of causing unnecessary suffering to an animal, but when the matter came back to court for sentence, the criteria for a hospital order were not made out: the recommendation was that what was then called a community rehabilitation order be put in place. The district judge decided that as section 37 no longer applied, a trial was necessary. The Divisional Court quashed this decision and directed that the magistrates consider making use of a guardianship order if the criteria for a hospital order were still not made out. While it was no doubt correct for the court to say that the magistrate was wrong for not exploring the possibility of a guardianship order, it may be that the judges did not have in mind the practical position that such orders are rarely made and so local authority guardianship teams may not be particularly well-engaged in the criminal justice process.

The community order

Background

19.11 The consolidation of sentencing powers in the Powers of Criminal Courts (Sentencing) Act (PCC(S)A) 2000 included a range of community orders, listed in section 33(1) of the Act, to which could be added specific requirements. Perhaps the most important one in the context of a mentally disordered offender was the community rehabilitation order which arose under section 41 if placing a person over 16

3 [2007] EWHC 310 (Admin), [2007] MHLR 121.
4 [2004] EWHC 2691 (Admin), [2004] MHLR 319.

under supervision was desirable to secure rehabilitation and protect the public from further offending. The order could last for between six months and three years. An additional requirement that the supervisee receive treatment for mental disorder could be imposed if the court was able to conclude that there was a disorder that required treatment, was susceptible to treatment, and practical arrangements had been made which could be as an in-patient; this also required the agreement of the supervisee to co-operate. The court also had to be satisfied that a hospital or guardianship order were not needed: this might be a fine line to draw if the treatment involved being an in-patient. These additional requirements were set out in Schedule 2 to the Act; paragraph 5 dealt with the treatment requirement. As a matter of procedure, it was necessary to have evidence from a section 12 approved psychiatrist as to the medical condition and the fact that an MHA 1983 s37 order was not necessary.

19.12 For an offender under 18, PCC(S)A 2000 s63 provided for a supervision order to which could be attached a medical treatment requirement.

The current regime

19.13 The CJA 2003 amended the structure applicable to those over 16 in that there is now a single sentence, the community order, to which various requirements can be added, which are listed in section 177 and include residence, remaining away from a specified place, mental health treatment, drug rehabilitation or alcohol treatment, and supervision. These requirements, it should be noted, can also be added to a suspended sentence. Youth community orders are also in place, and in this regard the CJA 2003 preserves the supervision order under PCC(S)A 2000 s63, to which requirements can be added.

19.14 The court must ensure that the requirements added to a community order are both compatible with each other and suitable for the offender. So CJA 2003 s148(2)(a) notes that any requirement or requirements in a community order 'must be such as, in the opinion of the court, is, or taken together are, the most suitable for the offender' and section 177(6) indicates that the use of two or more requirements means that the court 'must consider whether, in the circumstances of the case, the requirements are compatible with each other'.

19.15 The CJA 2003 ss196–223 give further details about the various requirements that can be imposed. The mental health treatment requirement is set out in sections 207 and 208, and matches what was in the PCC(S)A 2000 in large regard. The treatment can be under a doctor or psychologist[5] or both 'with a view to the improvement of the offender's mental condition' (CJA 2003 s207(1)). In the context of the Mental Health Act, it has been held that the reference to treatment of a condition includes treatment of the symptoms or consequences of a condition, even if the underlying condition is unaffected:[6] for example, the ability to manage the consequences of a personality disorder would count, even if the personality disorder remained unaffected. Whether that applies in this situation depends on whether the reference to the improvement of the person's 'mental condition' includes the symptoms or consequences. It should be noted that there is a separate requirement in section 207(3) that there must be medical evidence that the condition 'is such as requires and is susceptible to treatment': this is language that suggests a need for success to be expected. There is nothing that indicates that progress in terms of symptoms and consequences would not meet the tests; and, using the example of a personality disorder, if progress in terms of managing symptoms means that there is a reduced prospect of further criminal behaviour, that meets the purpose of the sentence.

19.16 The place of treatment can be as an in-patient or out-patient, and in a National Health service (NHS) or private hospital or care home (CJA 2003 s207(2)). The only limitation is that it cannot be in a high secure setting. As described at the outset of this book, there are locked facilities that offer low or medium secure provision: these are included under this definition, though it might be questionable as to whether a person should be in locked accommodation on a voluntary basis, which is important because of the interplay between a community order and a hospital order. This arises because subsection (3) prevents a mental health treatment requirement unless the medical evidence[7] before the court demonstrates the need for treatment and treatability (as noted above) but also that the condition '(a)(ii) is not such as to warrant the making of a hospital order or guardianship order'.

19.17 The court must also be satisfied that the practical arrangements are in place, including the consent of the defendant. The kind of treatment is 'as may be specified in the relevant order', but CJA 2003 s207(2) goes on to draw a distinction as to the 'nature' of the treatment, which is not to be specified. In other words, the court does not

5 Who must be chartered by the British Psychological Society: CJA 2003 s207(6).

6 See the discussion in chapter 2 at para 2.44.

7 Which must come from a psychiatrist approved under MHA 1983 s12: see CJA 2003 s207(5), which reads in MHA 1983 s54.

have to be concerned to specify the details of the treatment regime. But what of the fact that courts cannot be expected to predict the course of treatment, and that modifications to the kind or location of treatment may be necessary for progress or to counter problems that might arise in the course of treatment? This is covered by section 208, which makes provision for treatment at another place if the doctor or psychologist in charge believes that treatment 'can be better or more conveniently given' elsewhere. The patient must consent. Under section 208(2), the place of treatment may include residence at a place that could not have been specified in the original order: this will include a place that does not amount to a hospital or care home. At first sight, it may include a high secure setting; however, such a placement is only available for a detained patient: see chapter 1.

19.18 Also of potential value in a case involving mental disorder are the requirements as to drug or alcohol treatment: a number of patients in the criminal justice system with mental disorder may also have a problem with alcohol or drug abuse. Equally, there are other conditions such as generally being under supervision that might be of value on the facts.

Examples of use

19.19 The hierarchy of sentencing severity indicates that a community order is just one step below custody. Given that a court may take into account matters such as personal mitigating circumstances and also time spent in custody prior to trial, it is clear that a community sentence may be a suitable response to offending which is serious enough prima facie to require a custodial sentence. Reference may be made to the examples given in chapter 17 of the Court of Appeal replacing custodial sentences with community orders in light of such features as time spent on remand and the value of ongoing supervision and treatment in offering public protection via rehabilitation.

19.20 This can include homicides, including manslaughters and infanticides, and matters such as serious robberies. So in *Attorney-General's Reference No 83 of 2001 (Fidler)*,[8] the court declined to find unduly lenient a community rehabilitation order with treatment requirements on someone who had robbed an off-licence with a chrome object. Mr Fidler had schizophrenia complicated by substance abuse, and had admitted the offending. For the court, Judge LJ noted that: 'Where sentencing judges are satisfied that occasion requires it, they have to

8 [2001] EWCA Crim 2443, [2002] MHLR 266, [2002] 1 CrAppR(S) 139.

balance the demands of justice with what are sometimes described as the calls of mercy'.[9] He added that it was proper for a court to take 'a constructive course to seek to achieve the rehabilitation of the offender ... [which] ... would be likely to provide both the offender and the community as a whole with the best possible long-term solution to the problems which the offender otherwise presented'.[10] In relation to a killing, it has been found to be an appropriate sentence for manslaughter based on diminished responsibility arising out of depressions and post-traumatic disorders such as battered woman syndrome: see, for example, *R v Higgins*,[11] *R v Gardner*,[12] and *R v Fell*.[13]

Breach

19.21 There are provisions for what should happen if an offender breaches a community order. This is in contrast to a guardianship order. The details are provided in Schedule 8 to the CJA 2003, which is given effect by section 179. Paragraph 5 of the Schedule requires the relevant probation officer supervising the order to issue a warning if he or she considers that there has been a failure to comply with a community order without reasonable excuse: details have to be provided. A further breach within 12 months will lead to the matter being brought before the magistrates' court or the Crown Court and, if the breach is proved, more onerous conditions may be added to the community order or the offender may be resentenced, at which point the extent of compliance with the order will be taken into account.

19.22 Special provision is made in paragraph 11 of the Schedule relating to medical treatment requirements (and also drug and alcohol treatment requirements). The court may not find a failure to comply 'on the ground only that he had refused to undergo any surgical, electrical or other treatment if, in the opinion of the court, his refusal was reasonable having regard to all the circumstances'. It is not clear what this adds to the general test on the question of whether there was a breach.

9 [2001] EWCA Crim 2443, [2002] MHLR 266, [2002] 1 CrAppR(S) 139 para 26.

10 [2001] EWCA Crim 2443, [2002] MHLR 266, [2002] 1 CrAppR(S) 139 para 27. It was noted at paragraph 28 that he was making progress in treatment.

11 [1996] 1 CrAppR(S) 271.

12 (1993) 14 CrAppR(S) 364.

13 [2000] 2 CrAppR 464.

PART VI

Post-sentence matters

CHAPTER 20

Mental disorder during the sentence

Introduction

20.1 This chapter considers the course of the sentence for an offender with mental disorder. There are three typical areas:

a) what happens to someone given a disposal under the Mental Health Act (MHA) 1983;
b) the arrangements for those who receive a custodial sentence but need to be placed in a psychiatric hospital for treatment, which may be something that is recognised by the sentencing court; but a serving prisoner may develop a mental disorder during his or her sentence;
c) the arrangements made when a prisoner has difficulties engaging with the normal process of sentence planning and management of prisoners, failures in relation to which may have an adverse effect on the circumstances in which the prisoner lives or release.

Disposals under the Mental Health Act 1983

Hospital order – treatment and progress

20.2 A patient sentenced or made subject to a hospital order, with or without a restriction order, will be released from hospital when the criteria for detention no longer apply. This is required by article 5(1) and (4) of the European Convention on Human Rights (ECHR). Although there is no express right to treatment under the MHA 1983 that will assist progress to release, that can be found by implication: first, detention is for treatment, which must have the purpose of improving the condition of the patient (MHA 1983 s145(4)); detention brings with it the application of the treatment without consent provisions of Part IV of the MHA 1983; and detention is only lawful if appropriate treatment is available, and this test may be difficult to meet if no progress is being made. These issues are discussed further in chapter 2.

20.3 The question of whether a patient has made progress such that release is possible (or, rather, whether detention remains necessary) is assessed administratively and judicially.

Administrative release

20.4 The administrative process arises under MHA 1983 s23, which allows the responsible clinician (RC) or the hospital managers to discharge the patient.[1] The statute is phrased as a general discretion, but the Code of Practice issued under section 118 of the MHA 1983 indicates that the reverse of the criteria for detention should guide the discretion: see paragraphs 31.14 and following of the English Code, and paragraphs 27.14 and following of the Welsh Code. This can occur at any time after admission: there is no minimum term that has to be 'served' (which is the language of punishment, which is not the purpose of a hospital disposal).

20.5 The RC and managers can discharge a restricted patient as well, but this requires the consent of the Secretary of State: it is one of the special restrictions arising under MHA 1983 s41. In such a situation, the Secretary of State would also consider the power under section 42 of the Act to determine whether the discharge should be conditional or absolute. This mirrors the powers of the tribunal, described below.

20.6 In addition, there is the prospect of a discharge from hospital on the community treatment order (CTO) regime in MHA 1983 ss17A–17G, which suspends the operation of the detention order for so long as the CTO exists, but allows the patient to be subject to treatment in the community: this is outlined in chapter 2. The CTO regime is not available in the case of a restricted patient – this is perhaps because the effect of a CTO is somewhat similar to a conditional discharge. However, it would have been possible to make a CTO subject to the consent of the Secretary of State, as is the case with section 17 leave. Both types of patient are eligible for release from hospital under section 17 leave, which can be for extended periods: the detention order remains in force in such a situation and recall from leave may be ordered by the RC or, in relation to a restricted patient, by the Secretary of State (see MHA 1983 ss17 and 41).

Rights to apply to a tribunal

20.7 As a non-restricted patient is treated as though he or she has passed into the civil system, the powers of the tribunal are as with a civil patient – but one significant difference is that the power of application arises only after six months. The provisions as to applications to a tribunal are unnecessarily convoluted. The starting point is that MHA 1983 s40(4) indicates that a patient under a hospital order is

1 In relation to a civil patient, the nearest relative can also discharge the patient, but this is one of the differences for a hospital order patient. See the discussion in chapter 18 as to the effect of a hospital order.

treated as if detained under a section 3 admission for treatment, but subject to modifications as set out in MHA 1983 Sch 1 Part 1. One such modification is that section 66, which gives civil patients various rights to apply to a tribunal on the happening of various events, applies to a hospital order patient with modifications set out in Schedule 1 Part I para 9. This removes the parts of section 66 that apply to civil patients arising by reason of admission and also to the nearest relative of the patient if he or she is displaced under section 29 or barred from exercising the discharge power under section 23; none of these are relevant to hospital order patients. In addition, some parts of section 66(1) have been revoked as a result of changes introduced by the MHA 2007.[2]

20.8 What is left in MHA 1983 s66 for a hospital order patient is subsections 66(1)(ca) and (cb), which relate to the making and revoking of a community treatment order, (e), which relates to a transfer from guardianship to hospital, (f), which relates to the renewal of the hospital order, (fza), which relates to the renewal of a community treatment order, and (fa) and (faa), which relate to the decisions to maintain treatment or community treatment orders in relation to patients who have been absent without leave for more than 28 days. Subsection (2) of section 66, which contains the time limits during which the applications may be made to a tribunal, is also amended by removing the parts that relate to those provisions of subsection (1) that are removed.

20.9 The most important right is that arising on the renewal of the order under MHA 1983 s20, which will happen after six months. At first sight, there is a right to apply to a tribunal if the patient is transferred from detention under a hospital order to placement under a community treatment order: but it is then necessary to look to section 69, subsections (3)–(5) of which provide that if this happens within the first six months of the hospital order, there is no right to apply to the tribunal until after the period of six months has expired. Section 69 then also provides that the nearest relatives of both hospital order and guardianship order patients have the right to apply to a tribunal if the patient does not exercise that right. It would be much easier if section 66 did not apply to hospital order patients and section 69

2 Notably, MHA 1983 s66(1)(d) allowed an application where the classification of mental disorder under which the patient was detained was changed; this covered a hospital order patient, who was detained under one of the four classifications and so could apply to a tribunal if the basis for detention was altered. When the classifications were removed, the right to apply to a tribunal was also removed – see MHA 2007 s55 and Sch 11.

listed the circumstances in which rights to apply under that section arose and whether they could be exercised by both patients and nearest relatives.

20.10 If a restriction order is in place, one of the special restrictions applied by reason of MHA 1983 s41(3)(b) is that no application can be made under sections 66 and 69(1). In addition, section 41(3)(aa) provides that restricted patients cannot be subject to the community treatment order provisions. Accordingly, Part II of Schedule 1, which is relevant to restricted patients, does not apply any parts of section 66 to those patients. Instead, section 70 provides that a restricted patient may apply in the period of six to 12 months after the hospital order, hospital direction or transfer direction is given, and in every 12-month period thereafter.

The test for the tribunal

20.11 Once the matter is in front of a tribunal, the regime differs according to whether the patient is restricted or not. In relation to a non-restricted patient, arising under MHA 1983 s72, there is a duty to discharge if the criteria for detention are not made out; in addition, there is a general discretion to discharge, though it may be difficult to imagine when it could be proper to use it if the criteria for detention are made out. In addition, recommendations can be made for the use of a CTO, leave or transfer, though the tribunal has no power to secure the use of those powers: it may reconvene if the recommendation is not followed, but is limited to the use of its power of discharge.

20.12 For a restricted patient, the tribunal considers the matter under MHA 1983 s73: this requires it to discharge if the criteria for detention are not met, and creates the presumption that the discharge will be conditional. This means that the patient is subject to recall if his or her mental state deteriorates, and also allows the tribunal to add conditions. Conditions are not required, but are usually added, and will typically be matters such as cooperation with supervision, residence and acceptance of ongoing treatment.

The role of victims

20.13 One development of recent years has been the involvement of victims in questions of release. Under sections 35 and following of the Domestic Violence, Crime and Victims Act 2004, the making of a hospital order with a restriction order or a hospital and limitation direction after a conviction, a finding of not guilty by reason of insanity or a finding that the actus reus was committed in relation to a violent or sexual offence gave the victim an entitlement to make representations about any conditions that should be imposed on discharge and to receive information about those conditions. The process is that the local probation board contacts the victim or victims to ascertain his, her or their views and then acts as the conduit. The decision-maker – whether administrative or judicial – is required to take the representations into account.

20.14 By MHA 2007 s48 and Sch 6, the coverage of these provisions was expanded so that it now applies when a hospital order is made without a restriction order, and also so that it covers the making of representations if the person is to be released on a CTO.[3]

20.15 As to the propriety of this, it is to be noted that the same conduct might have led to diversion into the civil mental health system; and if the criminal justice system is involved and the decision is reached that a hospital order is appropriate, the aim of the sentencing court is to pass the patient into the civil system. These features suggest that the criminal justice concept of victim involvement should not be applied. On the other hand, if harm has been caused, there is a victim irrespective of what happens to the assailant: it is this latter view that has won through.

MAPPA

20.16 A further regime to note in relation to sexual or violent offenders is the Multi-Agency Public Protection Arrangements (MAPPA) system established by section 67 of the Criminal Justice and Court Services Act (CJCSA) 2000. This has covered hospital and guardianship orders from the outset, and also findings of not guilty by reason of insanity or that he or she committed the actus reus after being found unfit to stand trial: CJCSA 2000 s68.[4] It has been re-enacted in an expanded

3 There are two apparent gaps: the statutory language does not cover the situation of a person made subject to a hospital order without a conviction by the magistrates' court (under MHA 1983 s37(3)) or by the Crown Court when it is not practicable for them to be brought to court (under MHA 1983 s51).

4 The making of an order by the magistrates under MHA 1983 s37(3) does not seem to be covered by the interpretation provisions, which are phrased so as to cover the formal process in the Crown Court (since there is no special verdict in the summary process nor the finding that the defendant is 'under a disability'); nor would an order made under section 51 by the Crown Court, since there is no relevant finding.

form through sections 325–327B of the Criminal Justice Act (CJA) 2003.[5]

20.17 The statute, however, merely provides the bare bones of a system of risk assessment and management that covers a significant number of people. In the most recent annual report from the Ministry of Justice,[6] it was noted that there are 51,500 offenders covered. The annual reports from individual police and probation areas give details of what is done by the MAPPA system locally. Suffice to say, the regime of co-operation established involves National Health Service (NHS) bodies, local authorities and also housing providers. Consequently, the carrying out of MAPPA assessments may be key to the making of practical arrangements for release.

Guardianship orders

20.18 In the case of those who receive a guardianship order, the discharge possibilities are as with those under a hospital order: administrative release under MHA 1983 s23 by the responsible clinician or the local social services authority, or under section 72 by the tribunal. The test for the latter is whether it is shown that the patient is not mentally disordered or that the disorder is not of a nature or degree to warrant guardianship: the burden of proof is on the patient, no doubt on the basis of an argument that the patient is not detained: there is a significant counter argument in that guardianship will often include conditions as to residence that may be enforced by arrest, the practical effect of which may be the sort of close supervision that may pass from being a restriction on freedom of movement to detention.

Transfer from prison to hospital

Introduction

20.19 As has been noted in Part V, a person who needs to be in hospital may be sentenced to imprisonment notwithstanding that need. This will occur if the mandatory life sentence for murder is imposed; it may occur in other situations if the judge decides that the hospital order is not the most appropriate disposal in the light of the culpability of

5 The same gaps identified in note 3 remain apparent.

6 *Annual statistics on Multi-agency public protection arrangements (MAPPA) eligible offenders*, October 2011, available at www.justice.gov.uk/publications/statistics-and-data/prisons-and-probation/mappa.htm.

the offender. It may also be that a person sent to prison by the courts when mentally well develops a disorder while in prison, whether as a recurrence of an existing episodic illness or as a new development in his or her health.

20.20 Just as the Secretary of State for Justice (who took over this role from the Home Secretary when the Ministry of Justice was created) has powers to transfer a remand prisoner to a psychiatric hospital (see MHA 1983 s48, as discussed in chapter 8), so there are powers to transfer a serving prisoner to hospital. The main power is that arising under MHA 1983 s47, the 'transfer direction'. In addition, section 22(2) of the Prison Act 1952 indicates that a prisoner in custody may be taken to a hospital for 'investigation, observation or treatment' if the Secretary of State is satisfied of the need for 'medical investigation or observation or medical or surgical treatment of any description'. This seems to cover mental disorder and psychiatric treatment: however, such a transfer would not be on the same terms as those that apply under the MHA 1983.[7]

Prisoners covered by the transfer direction

20.21 The MHA 1983 s47 applies to those serving sentences of imprisonment, which is defined in subsection (5) so as to include:

a) 'any sentence or order for detention made by a court in criminal proceedings', but not an order made following a finding of insanity or unfitness to stand trial (which cannot lead to detention in prison save for a temporary holding under the place of safety provisions);
b) detention for failing to enter into recognisances to keep the peace (which can lead to an order for committal to custody under section 115(3) of the Magistrates' Courts Act 1980); and
c) committal to serve a sentence on default of payment of a sum adjudged to be paid on conviction.

All other detainees should be covered by MHA 1983 s48. There is also language relating to armed forces personnel serving sentences of service detention under the Armed Forces Act 2006, who are excluded from the operation of section 47.

7 In particular as to treatment, there might be an argument that if the transferee was without capacity, treatment could be given under Mental Capacity Act 2005 ss5 and 6.

Criteria for transfer

Clinical matters

20.22 Medical evidence must satisfy the Secretary of State that the prisoner is mentally disordered, that the disorder is of nature or degree to make detention in hospital for medical treatment appropriate, and that appropriate medical treatment is available. In contrast to a transfer under MHA 1983 s48, there is no requirement that there be an 'urgent need' for treatment.

20.23 The nature or degree, appropriateness and appropriate treatment criteria are the same as those set out in relation to MHA 1983 ss3 and 37, and so reference should be made to chapters 2 and 18 above. In essence:

- A 'mental disorder' is any disorder or disability of mind, though if it is a learning disability it is also necessary that it be associated with abnormally aggressive or seriously irresponsible conduct. The only exclusion from the definition of mental disorder is addiction to alcohol or drugs. The new definition is deliberately wider.
- 'Medical treatment' is widely defined, extends to nursing and psychological intervention, can cover dealing with the symptoms or consequences of the disorder without necessarily affecting the underlying disorder, and, while it need not have any guarantee of being effective, must at least have the purpose of assisting.
- The nature of a disorder refers to its current severity, and the nature of a disorder is its duration and prognosis, and particularly its tendency to relapse. Detention can be justified on the basis of nature even if the current degree is not severe.
- The appropriateness of detention turns on the question of whether the treatment should be provided at a hospital; in a civil context, this may raise questions of whether the treatment can be provided as an out-patient or as an informal patient, but in relation to serving prisoners the alternative is treatment in a prison context.
- The appropriate treatment criterion means that there must be treatment that is appropriate in light of both clinical and non-clinical factors.

20.24 It is noted in the English Code of Practice issued under section 118 of the MHA 1983, at paragraphs 33.31 and 33.32, that arrangements ought to be made by prison health care staff and NHS commissioners to ensure that any needs for in-patient treatment are identified and acted upon within the same time-frame as would apply to the admission of a patient from the community; and even if there is consent to treatment in the prison, an assessment should be made of whether the environment contributes to the disorder.[8] These latter factors are also relevant to the question of expediency.

Expediency

20.25 In addition to the essentially clinical questions that govern transfer, the Secretary of State has to be 'of the opinion having regard to the public interest and all the circumstances that it is expedient' to order the transfer.

20.26 It is well-established that prisons contain a disproportionate number of people with mental disorders, and that the prison setting is often far from therapeutic, which may produce risks of self-harming behaviour, including suicide.[9] The question then arising is whether there is a duty to find transfer expedient; put another way, are there situations in which the medical criteria are met but it is not expedient to effect a transfer?

20.27 In the relevant policy statement, *Good Practice Procedure Guide: The transfer and remission of adult prisoners under s47 and s48 of the Mental Health Act*,[10] it is noted at paragraph 3.25 that: 'The Secretary of State does not have to agree to transfer'. It is then noted that the test is 'whether it is expedient and in the public interest': this inaccurately paraphrases the statutory test by introducing a suggestion that transfer has to be both expedient and in the public interest. The statute refers to the transfer being expedient in light of the public interest and all the relevant circumstances.

20.28 The Good Practice Procedure Guide also indicates at paragraph 3.26 the factors that are considered relevant, which are:

8 Paragraphs 32.23–32.25 of the Welsh Code are to similar effect.

9 For a general account, see Marshall, Simpson and Andrews, *Healthcare in prisons*, available at www.hcna.bham.ac.uk/documents/11_HCNA3_D3.pdf. See also the Bradley Report, *Lord Bradley's review of people with mental health problems or learning disabilities in the criminal justice system*, Department of Health, April 2009 (available at www.dh.gov.uk/en/Publicationsandstatistics/Publications/PublicationsPolicyAndGuidance/DH_098694), which at pages 105–106 noted that there had been significant delays in securing the transfer of mentally ill prisoners to hospital, arising from a lack of appropriate beds and lack of speed in the making of assessments, and suggested that there be a 14-day target for such a transfer.

10 Department of Health, April 2011, available at www.dh.gov.uk/en/Publicationsandstatistics/Publications/PublicationsPolicyAndGuidance/DH_125767.

- any risks associated with the prisoner (escape risk, nature and history of offending, notoriety, victim issues), and the public protection implications;
- whether public confidence could be undermined by allowing the transfer;
- the court's intention at the time of sentencing to imprisonment
- the effect of any pending appeal;
- whether appropriate treatment can be provided in prison;
- the length of time the prisoner still has to serve, behaviour and current security category;
- medical opinion, past and presenting symptoms and level of clinical risk (eg actively suicidal, assaultive).

20.29 It is difficult to understand the relevance of some of these features. Taking them in order:

- The issue of risk is clearly relevant. But that ought to go more to the question of the level of security of the hospital placement rather than whether there is a transfer: as discussed in relation to whether to use a hospital disposal or a prison disposal, the hospital system has the appropriate tools for public protection.
- The next factor, public confidence, is more problematic – but if it is taken to be properly informed public confidence, which takes into account relevant features such as the rights of the patient to proper treatment and the ability of the hospital to secure public protection, then it should not cause problems.
- The third factor noted, the intention of the sentencing court, will often be wholly irrelevant: in the first place, the Secretary of State may be responding to a changed condition; second, the court will have sentenced in the knowledge that a transfer could take place; third, any court intention to deprive a prisoner of the treatment he or she needs would be irrational and corrected on appeal.
- It is also difficult to see what effect a pending appeal can have on whether someone who needs treatment should have it. In any event, the Court of Appeal would be able to take into account the move to hospital.
- The question of whether appropriate treatment can be provided in prison would obviously be relevant – but if that is the position, it may be less likely that detention in hospital is appropriate. The approach to this factor should no doubt take as a starting point that paragraph 33.2 of the Code of Practice states that those in prison have the same rights to assessment and treatment as anyone else: that must reflect on whether there is a significant better quality of treatment is available in hospital.

- The relevance of the time remaining in prison is considered below.
- As to the medical matters, these may be relevant to the first factor and they are relevant to the medical criteria for transfer: if the Secretary of State is not of the view that these criteria are met, the question of transfer does not arise.

20.30 As to whether it is correct to say that there is no obligation to effect a transfer, this was considered in *R (D) v Home Secretary and National Assembly for Wales*.[11] The question arising was whether the failure to secure the transfer of a young offender in a timely fashion breached ECHR article 8 (right to respect for private and family life). Stanley Burnton J noted that the section should be construed 'with an appreciation both of the benefits of an appropriate transfer and of the consequences of a transfer for the liberty of the person concerned',[12] which meant that there could be a duty to secure a transfer: the Secretary of State had accepted that this could be the case in some circumstances, and the question was what those circumstances were.[13] The judge's conclusion was that:

> ... once the prison service have reasonable grounds to believe that a prisoner requires treatment in a mental hospital in which he may be detained, the Home Secretary is under a duty expeditiously to take reasonable steps to obtain appropriate medical advice, and if that advice confirms the need for transfer to a hospital, to take reasonable steps within a reasonable time to effect that transfer.[14]

20.31 As to whether article 8 was breached, it was noted that: 'Inappropriate retention of a prisoner in a prison or [young offenders institution] may infringe his rights under Article 8' and indeed might breach article 3 (prohibition of torture and inhuman or degrading treatment or punishment) if it was sufficiently serious. If the latter situation pertained, there would be 'an absolute duty to prevent or bring to an end his inhumane treatment'.[15] On the facts, there was no breach of articles 8 or 3, though that was largely on causation grounds in that while additional things could have been done it was not shown

11 [2004] EWHC 2857 (Admin).

12 [2004] EWHC 2857 (Admin) at para 20.

13 [2004] EWHC 2857 (Admin) at paras 27 and following.

14 [2004] EWHC 2857 (Admin) at para 33.

15 [2004] EWHC 2857 (Admin) at para 33. For an example of a finding of such a breach, see *Dybeku v Albania* [2009] MHLR 1, which involved a prisoner whose mental disorder deteriorated in prison: this led to no change to his regime save for short admissions to the prison hospital.

that they would have achieved a speedier resolution to the problems caused by keeping D in custody. In particular, suitable placements were lacking, and the medical reports provided were inconsistent.

Procedural requirements

20.32 The procedural requirements for a transfer under MHA 1983 s47 are similar to those arising under section 48, namely there must be two medical reports (section 47(1)), and at least one of them must come from psychiatrist approved for the purposes of section 12 of the Act (section 54(1)). There is no statutory requirement that the reports be in writing; they must, however, deal with the criteria on the merits outlined above. Accordingly, in *R (F) v Secretary of State for Justice*,[16] the Court of Appeal upheld the conclusion of the trial judge[17] that a warrant should not have been issued when one of the medical reports had not addressed the issue of the treatability of F's psychopathic disorder (which was a requirement at the time, being before the MHA 2007 came into effect).[18]

20.33 However, there is an arguably contrasting case. In *R (SP) v Secretary of State for Justice*,[19] the defect in the recommendations was that an old form had been used by one of the doctors: this meant that there was only one expert statement as to the availability of appropriate treatment in hospital, which was by then a requirement for admission following the changes introduced by the MHA 2007. The Court of Appeal determined that the relevant test was whether the decision-maker at the Ministry of Justice was able to be satisfied that the test for transfer was made out, and this could include implication. In particular, it could be implied that there was appropriate treatment: that arose on the facts from the recommendation that SP, who was diagnosed as having a severe personality disorder, should be transferred to a unit that specialised in patients with such a condition.

20.34 Can these cases stand together? The need for appropriate treatment is just as much part of the current test of detention as treatability was part of the former test: so they are both fundamental. Moreover,

16 [2008] EWCA Civ 1457, [2008] MHLR 370.

17 [2008] EWHC 2912 (Admin), [2008] MHLR 361.

18 The judge had declined to grant relief on the basis that subsequent evidence of treatability had been supplied: the Court of Appeal overturned this conclusion on the basis that the detention was unlawful and the discretion as to the granting of a remedy in judicial review proceedings was not a proper basis for declining to recognise the lack of lawfulness of the detention.

19 [2010] EWCA Civ 1590, [2011] MHLR 65.

in both situations, an individual assessment was or is required – just as the treatability of a particular patient had to be assessed, rather than treatability in general of a group of patients, so the availability of appropriate treatment is a matter that turns on the condition and circumstances of the particular patient.[20] Accordingly, even though the Court of Appeal in *SP* is no doubt correct that a sensible reading of a document is proper, it remains problematic to suggest that an assessment of appropriate treatment being available can be implied rather than being expressly assessed and reasoned.

20.35 The importance of adequate reasoning is also worth noting. It is a requirement in many public law situations, including in relation to the reports used in a section 47 transfer. In *R (DK) v Secretary of State*,[21] a transfer that took place just before a prisoner was due to be released from prison was quashed on the basis that the doctors had not given reasons to support the treatability requirement that then applied (the diagnosis being of a psychopathic personality disorder and the transfer occurring before the MHA 2007 amended the relevant definitions).

20.36 It is to be noted that there is no express provision as to the date of the medical reports, in contrast to the position applicable to civil detention: see the 14-day provision governing the maximum time gap between the medical assessment and the admission set in MHA 1983 s11(5). In *R v Home Secretary ex p Gilkes*,[22] Dyson J suggested that specific time limits were unnecessary but that there was a need for reports that were 'reliable', and this could not be assumed in the case of an old report from the fact that it coincided with a more recent report.[23] The question of reliability would turn on the circumstances, including on the facts that the disorder in question was known to be unstable: that meant that a report from the end of October could not reasonably be relied on for action taken in early December. This approach might allow reliance on an older report if the mental disorder was more stable, but in practice it is to be expected that up-to-date reports will be the norm.

20.37 Also worth noting is that, although the reference in MHA 1983 s47(1) to the transfer being effected by warrant suggests that a written document is required, the Good Practice Procedure Guide indicates

20 It is not simply a clinical matter – rather, as noted in chapter 2, it has to involve an assessment of questions of proportionality arising from non-clinical factors as well.

21 [2010] EWHC 82 (Admin), [2010] MHLR 64.

22 [1999] EWHC 47 (Admin), [1999] MHLR 6.

23 [1999] EWHC 47 (Admin), [1999] MHLR 6 para 15.

at paragraph 4.36 that an oral authority can be given by the relevant officials of the Secretary of State, provided that the prison governor also agrees.

20.38 A final procedural requirement is that there must be a bed available in the hospital specified in the direction and the transfer must take place within 14 days beginning on the date the relevant warrant of transfer is made: MHA 1983 s47(2). The statutory language does not indicate that the consent of the relevant hospital is required, nor is there express power to override a refusal by a hospital to accept a patient (which might, for example, be based on clinical views that the patient is not suited to a particular hospital). It seems unlikely that a clinical team would be compelled to accept a patient against the wishes of the team.

Effect of transfer

20.39 The MHA 1983 s47(3) provides that: 'A transfer direction with respect to any person shall have the same effect as a hospital order made in his case'. This is described in chapter 18: so detention in hospital is lawful, and treatment is governed by the consent to treatment provisions of Part IV of the 1983 Act. Another important effect is that the patient will remain in detention even if he or she has reached the date on which release from prison would have followed. This is because the hospital order is renewable until such time as the criteria for detention cease to apply. The patient is referred to as a 'notional' section 37 patient.

20.40 The fact that a transfer may extend detention has led to concern about the use of the transfer power just before a determinate sentence would have come to an end. This was challenged in *Gilkes*, but it was held that it had not been a problem on the facts. However, comments by the Court of Appeal in *R (F) v Secretary of State for Justice*[24] suggest that transfers at the end of the sentence should occur only in exceptional cases. Hence the reference noted above in the list of factors that will be taken into account to the time the prisoner has left to serve: part of the context is that a released prisoner may be detained under the civil provisions, but this will at least involve a decision by an independent approved mental health professional and might well involve medical recommendations by doctors who do not have any involvement with the criminal process, and so it will not create the same impression that it amounts to an extension of the sentence of the court.

24 [2008] EWCA Civ 1457, [2008] MHLR 370 at para 31.

Restriction direction

20.41 The MHA 1983 s49 is also relevant. This provides a power to add to the transfer direction a restriction direction, which places the patient in the same position as if a restriction order had been made under section 41 of the Act. As such, the consent of the Secretary of State is required for matters such as leave or transfer. In addition, the patient can be returned to prison if the need to be in hospital ceases. The making of a restriction direction also means that section 47 of the Crime (Sentences) Act 1997 applies, and so the Secretary of State may specify a hospital unit in which the patient is to be detained.

20.42 It is a matter of discretion as to whether to impose a restriction direction – this is in contrast to a remand prisoner, whose transfer has to be accompanied by a restriction direction.[25] However, the policy has been to impose a restriction direction unless the patient was a matter of days away from release (which, as noted below, brings the restriction direction to an end) and is assessed not to pose a risk to the public. A challenge to this approach was made in *R (T) v Home Secretary*:[26] the argument was that treating the patient as a restricted patient was only proper if there was a need for public protection, such that the criteria relevant to the imposition of a restriction order under MHA 1983 s41 should apply. This contention was rejected on the basis that section 49 did not refer to public protection at all; and that the policy appropriately allowed the retention of the power to remit the patient to prison.[27]

20.43 Any restriction direction ceases to have effect on the date the patient passes his or her release date: see MHA 1983 s50(2) and (3). This involves disregarding any power of release exercisable by the Parole Board: in *R (RD and PM, and EM and others) v Secretary of State for Work and Pensions*,[28] it was confirmed that this excludes life sentence prisoners. In relation to determinate sentences, this will arise as of the date of entitlement to release. The lifting of the restriction direction means that the transfer direction remains in place and the patient becomes a notional section 37 patient, though the effects

25 See chapter 8.

26 [2003] EWHC 538, [2003] MHLR 239.

27 [2003] EWHC 538, [2003] MHLR 239 para 35. The Good Practice Procedure Guide referred to above does not give any indication that there is a policy on the use of the restriction direction or what it might be: it simply refers to the power to remit to prison and to specify a hospital unit.

28 [2010] EWCA Civ 18, [2010] MHLR 72. The main issue in the case was the interpretation of welfare benefits regulations, which did not use similar language and were held to have effect as of tariff expiry.

of the restriction direction and any ongoing involvement from the Secretary of State cease.

Bringing the transfer to an end

20.44 If the transfer direction is made without a restriction direction, the patient becomes simply a hospital order patient; this also happens if a restriction direction is made but comes to an end. Release is as for a hospital order patient. The patient is able to apply to a tribunal to be discharged: the right to apply arises on transfer, by reason of MHA 1983 s69(2). In addition, the RC and hospital managers have powers of discharge under section 23.

20.45 If a restriction direction is made, the patient can be returned to prison while the restriction direction remains in force. The relevant statutory provision is MHA 1983 s50, which allows the return of the patient to prison if the RC indicates that treatment is no longer required or 'no effective treatment ... can be given'. So any decision by the RC or managers under section 23 would lead to remittal under section 50. The relevant criteria are not precisely the same: the section 50 test may be wider. If section 23 is taken to incorporate the reverse of the test for detention, it being satisfied would mean that the section 50 test was met because treatment in a hospital would no longer be required. However, the lack of effective treatment test might be met even if the nature of the disorder was such that treatment was required and appropriate treatment was available: the latter might not be effective for the particular patient, for example because of a lack of co-operation.

20.46 The restriction direction patient may also apply to a tribunal: MHA 1983 s70 provides that such a right to apply arises once in the period between six and 12 months after the making of the transfer direction. However, there is a complexity in the statutory language, since the restriction direction is parasitic on the transfer direction, and such patients have the right to make an application immediately by section 69(2). The special restrictions under section 41(3)(b) exclude any right arising under sections 66 or 69(1), which seems not to exclude the right under section 69(2).

20.47 Once the matter is before a tribunal, it will consider the case under section 74, which allows it to reach a conclusion as to whether the criteria for detention are made out but also to recommend that the patient stay in hospital if not discharged. This latter provision deals with a situation in which the patient is likely to deteriorate if returned to prison and so require to be transferred back to hospital.

But the tribunal does not have an express mandate to consider the effective treatment test that arises under section 50.

20.48 Paragraphs 33.33 of the Code of Practice for England, and 32.33 of the Welsh Code, note the importance of making sure that there is proper continuity of care: a return should not occur without a planning meeting under the Care Programme Approach (CPA) process, often known as a section 117 meeting, to which prison staff should be invited.[29]

20.49 The decision to remit is a public law decision and so open to challenge on judicial review grounds, including human rights arguments. In *R (IR) v Dr Shetty and Home Secretary*,[30] the contention was that IR was of 'unsound mind' and so could only be detained in hospital by reason of ECHR article 5(1)(e), and that a court had to make the decision by reason of article 5(4). It was also contended that article 3 would also be breached by reason of the past experience of his mental disorder deteriorating in prison, leading to self-harm and his transfer to hospital. Munby J rejected the arguments on the basis that the precursor question to the applicability of article 5 was whether there was unsoundness of mind such as to require hospital detention: in that regard, the Home Secretary was entitled to accept the medical evidence, particularly as it came from the treating clinician, that there was no need to be in hospital. As to article 3, it was determined that the mere fact that prison might produce a relapse was not enough: the question was whether the relapse would amount to a breach of article 3, and that was not demonstrated on the evidence.[31]

Use

20.50 The most recent statistics indicate that around 500 serving prisoners per year are transferred to hospital, the vast majority with a restriction direction: this has been so for the last three years, increased from 400 per year in 2006–07 and 2007–08.[32] This increase may reflect the

29 See chapter 2 for an outline of the CPA process.

30 [2003] EWHC 3022 (Admin), [2004] MHLR 111.

31 See also *R (D) v Secretary of State for Justice* [2009] EWHC 473 (Admin), [2009] MHLR 133: an injunction to prevent the return of a prisoner under section 50 was discharged as the evidence indicated that the test for return was met and that the prison would be able to cope with the consequences of the disorder, including self-harm.

32 See the NHS Statistics of October 2011, *Inpatients formally detained in hospitals under the Mental Health Act 1983 and patients subject to supervised community treatment, Annual figures, England 2010/11*, available at www.ic.nhs.uk/statistics-and-data-collections/mental-health/mental-health-act/inpatients-

growth of the prison population. Around a third go into independent hospitals.

Technical lifers

20.51 One particular group of prisoners transferred under MHA 1983 s47 are the 'technical lifers'. This is a status formerly given by the Secretary of State to people sent to prison under a life sentence who should have been sent to hospital under a hospital order. At paragraph 15.47 of Prison Service Order (PSO) 4700,[33] the circumstances in which such a status could be granted were listed as including when the life sentence was imposed because no suitable bed was available; or the medical reports before the court were inaccurate or none were presented; another situation could be where the defendant to a murder charge declined to allow a diminished responsibility verdict to be allowed. The effect of the status, which was only granted after consultation with the Lord Chief Justice and the trial judge (if available), was that the patient was treated as though in hospital as a restricted patient and so would be released without reference to the Parole Board.[34] Rather, the recommendation of the tribunal under MHA 1983 s74 would be the only judicial involvement. In *R (IR) v Dr Shetty and Home Secretary (No 2)*,[35] it was argued that the granting of this status was a sentencing decision and so had to be taken by a court in order to comply with ECHR article 6 (right to a fair trial). Although this challenge was rejected on the basis that the status was a matter linked to the administration of a sentence and so article 6 did not apply, it would no doubt be apparent that it was inconsistent with the general principle of the separation of powers for a judicial decision to be converted into a different form of sentence by administrative action.

20.52 In addition, in *Benjamin and Wilson v UK*,[36] the European Court of Human Rights (ECtHR) had determined that the fact that the release mechanism involved the tribunal making a recommendation rather than directing release meant that there was a breach of article 5(4), because it requires that a court be able to direct release. Those

formally-detained-in-hospitals-under-the-mental-health-act-1983-and-patients-subject-to-supervised-community-treatment-annual-figures-england-2010-11.

33 PSOs are available at www.justice.gov.uk/guidance/prison-probation-and-rehabilitation/psipso/psos.htm.

34 PSO 4700 para 15.49.

35 [2003] EWHC 3152 (Admin), [2004] MHLR 130.

36 App No 28212/95, [2003] MHLR 124.

bringing the challenges to the technical lifer status perhaps did not realise that the effect was likely to be the restoration of the judicialisation of sentences and release by abolishing the granting of technical lifer status. This happened as from April 2005, the government citing *Benjamin and Wilson* in the Parliamentary Answer in which the policy change was announced.[37] A challenge to the change of policy was dismissed in *R (Donaldson and Barker) v Home Secretary*.[38]

20.53 The effect of the change of policy was that release of people in hospital became a matter for the Parole Board, that ongoing supervision would be through the criminal justice agencies and that any prospect of recall would involve the person going to prison before being transferred to prison. Accordingly, the benefits of technical lifer status – release, supervision and recall being though mental-health services – required the life sentence to be replaced by a hospital order (which would be with a restriction order, since the patient would almost inevitably meet the risk to the public test). For those who might have qualified for the status, it became necessary for any inappropriate life sentence to be corrected by the Court of Appeal. In *R v David William Beatty*,[39] the Court of Appeal confirmed that someone granted 'technical lifer' status would invariably be able to have his or her life sentence corrected to hospital and restriction orders by the Court of Appeal. See chapter 21 for further discussion of appeals, including those outside normal time limits.

20.54 For those still in hospital with technical lifer status, two practical points should be noted. First, their release will still be governed by MHA 1983 s74; second, it may be appropriate to have their status regularised by judicial action, namely through the Court of Appeal (via an appeal out of time or a second appeal through the Criminal Cases Review Commission).

Mental disorder and the treatment of prisoners

20.55 As has been described in chapter 17, there are custodial sentences that are designed to punish but also sentences that are designed to secure public protection. Of the latter, the most serious offences lead to an indeterminate sentence, which will consist of a minimum term to be served for purposes of punishment and thereafter detention

37 Baroness Scotland, *Hansard* HL Debates vol 668 col 39WS, 24 January 2005.

38 [2006] EWHC 1107 (Admin), [2006] MHLR 100.

39 [2006] EWCA Crim 2359, [2006] MHLR 333.

until the Parole Board is satisfied that the risk posed by the prisoner has been reduced sufficiently to allow release. The expansion of indeterminate sentences for public protection in the CJA 2003 was held by the Court of Appeal in *R (Walker and James) v Secretary of State for Justice*[40] to bring with it a duty to provide adequate resources to allow offending-behaviour work to be done. This is because such work is necessary to allow prisoners to demonstrate that their risk had been reduced when they appear in front of the Parole Board.[41] In addition, there is a general concern to reduce the risk posed by all prisoners, even those who are released automatically from determinate sentences. Even those prisoners may benefit from early release on a risk-assessed basis, pursuant to the Home Detention Curfew provisions currently contained in section 246 of the CJA 2003.

20.56 The Prison Act 1952 creates the structure for the management of prisons, supplements by formal Rules issued as statutory instruments. More detailed policy statements are issued, known as PSOs[42] and Prison Service Instructions (PSIs).[43] The policy relating to prisoners who have disabilities, PSO 2855, is designed to ensure that actions comply with the requirements of the Disability Discrimination Act 1995 as updated (which is being supplemented and replaced by the Equality Act 2010). The essential requirements of this legislation are that the needs of disabled prisoners be taken into account by modifying relevant arrangements so that they can apply to prisoners with disabilities. This is the principle of 'reasonable accommodation', essentially that changes that can be made without disproportionate cost should be made. This basic standard is set out in paragraph 1.10 of the order, which notes that: 'The Prison Service ensures that all prisoners are able, with reasonable adjustment, to participate equally in all aspects of prison life without discrimination'.

20.57 Chapter 8 gives further detail on what amounts to 'reasonable adjustments'. Examples of relevant factors are set out in paragraph 8.1 (and further examples are given in the chapter and in annexes C and D):

40 [2008] EWCA Civ 30, [2008] 1 WLR 1977, [2008] Prison LR 63.

41 This conclusion was not appealed when the case proceeded to the House of Lords (on a question relating to ECHR article 5): *R (James, Lee and Wells) v Secretary of State for Justice* [2009] UKHL 22, [2009] 2 WLR 1149, [2009] Prison LR 371.

42 PSOs are available at www.justice.gov.uk/guidance/prison-probation-and-rehabilitation/psipso/psos.htm.

43 PSIs are available at www.justice.gov.uk/guidance/prison-probation-and-rehabilitation/psipso/psis/index.htm.

> ... whether taking particular steps would be effective in overcoming the difficulty that disabled people face in getting access; the extent to which it is practicable for the service provider to take the step; financial and other costs of making the adjustments; the amount of disruption caused by taking the steps; money already spent on making adjustments; the availability of financial or other assistance.

20.58 Various parts of PSO 2855 give information on how this is to be secured in several parts of prison life. In relation to programmes designed to tackle offending behaviour and so reduce the risk posed by a prisoner, paragraph 6.36 notes that: 'It is vital that prisoners with disabilities can access any offending programmes as identified in their sentence plan, with adjustments made as necessary, eg relocation of a course if inaccessible'. This is supplemented by PSI 31/2008, which relates to the allocation to different prisons of prisoners with disabilities and emphasises that prisoners should be allowed access to prisons at which their sentence planning requirements can be met.

20.59 The importance of all this was emphasised in *R (Gill) v Secretary of State for Justice*,[44] in which it was held that the offending behaviour courses made available to a prisoner with a learning disability had not met the requirements of the policies as to reasonable accommodation. In essence, existing programmes had not been adjusted or other relevant changes made so as to ensure that Mr Gill had access on equal terms to other prisoners, even though that could have been done without disproportionate effort or expense.

44 [2010] EWHC 364 (Admin), [2010] MHLR 135.

CHAPTER 21

Appeals

Appeal routes

Introduction

21.1 Most substantive matters that have been discussed in this text have an appeal route. Those available in relations to verdicts, findings and sentences are summarised below. A separate issue is the process for appeals outside the normal time limits: this may arise more frequently in the context of mental disorder because the presence of mental disorder or a reliable picture of how serious it was at the time of the offence, trial or sentence may only be recognised after a significant period of assessment.

Conviction appeals from the Crown Court

21.2 From a Crown Court trial on indictment, appeals go to the Court of Appeal and are governed by the Criminal Appeal Act (CAA) 1968. Sections 1–8 relate to appeals against conviction, the test for the Court of Appeal being whether the conviction is 'unsafe' (section 2): this may arise if, for example, a conviction of murder was returned following an erroneous direction as to diminished responsibility or as to insanity, or if the defendant should have been found unfit to stand trial. Leave to appeal from the Court of Appeal or the trial judge is required (section 1). The court may substitute a conviction for a lesser offence if 'on the finding of the jury it appears to the Court of Appeal that the jury must have been satisfied of facts which proved him guilty of the other offence' (section 3) or it may order a retrial 'if the interests of justice so require' (section 7) or enter a verdict of acquittal. Questions of mental disorder may be relevant to this 'interests of justice' test: for example, if a defendant has developed a mental disorder, the features relevant to diversion from the criminal justice system may apply with the additional consideration that the defendant will have spent some time serving whatever sentence was imposed.

21.3 If the Court of Appeal finds that the proper verdict should have been not guilty by reason of insanity, that verdict can be substituted: section 6. Appropriate medical evidence is required, and the Court of Appeal can then sentence as if the Criminal Procedure (Insanity and Unfitness to Plead) Act (CP(IUP)A) 1991 applied.[1] Section 6 also allows the Court of Appeal to intervene if it finds on the evidence that

1 If an interim hospital order is made, the further consideration of the case will be remitted to the Crown Court: CAA 1968 s6(5).

the defendant was in fact unfit to stand trial but committed the actus reus and so should not have been convicted but instead dealt with on that basis.[2]

Appeals in insanity and unfitness to stand trial findings

21.4 In the case of a finding of not guilty by reason of insanity in the Crown Court, there is a separate right of appeal (given that the verdict is not a conviction), arising under CAA 1968 ss12–14.[3] The test again is whether the verdict is unsafe: the court can substitute a conviction if that would be 'proper', and acquittal or a finding that the defendant was unfit but committed the offence.

21.5 Sections 15 and 16 provide for appeals against findings of unfitness to plead (which, it is worth recalling, might be raised by the prosecution and judge and argued against by the defence) and/or a finding that the act or omission was committed (which the defendant may deny even if he or she accepts the finding of unfitness), the test for the Court of Appeal being the safety of the finding. If it is not safe, a verdict of acquittal is required (so there is no possibility of a retrial): see section 16(4).[4]

Sentence appeals from the Crown Court

Jurisdiction

21.6 The CAA 1968 s9 gives the Court of Appeal jurisdiction to consider appeals against sentence, defined in CAA 1968 s50 as 'any order made by a court when dealing with an offender', and expressly including a hospital order, an interim hospital order or a hospital direction; the statute does not mention a guardianship order, but that is within the general language. However, orders made on a finding of unfitness to stand trial but to have committed the actus reus were outside the statute because section 9 refers to a sentence after conviction and section 50 refers to the 'offender', which would not be cover someone whose

2 See chapters 9 and 12 for further details as to these.

3 See also CAA 1968 s5, relating to appeals against conviction when the verdict was guilty but insane: see chapter 12 for a further discussion of these powers.

4 In *R v Norman* [2008] EWCA Crim 1810, [2008] MHLR 206, the Court of Appeal suggested that this gap be filled in order to secure the public interest. See also *R v MB* [2010] EWCA Crim 1684, [2011] MHLR 163.

mens rea had not been assessed.[5] Also excluded was an order made following a finding of not guilty by reason of insanity.[6] CAA 1968 ss16A and 16B were added by the Domestic Violence, Crime and Victims Act 2004 to allow the Court of Appeal to consider appeals against a hospital order or a supervision order made in those situations (but not an absolute discharge).

21.7 The CAA 1968 s10 provides for appeals on a committal from the magistrates' court for sentence. In both situations, leave to appeal is required from the Court of Appeal or the sentencing judge.

Not increasing severity

21.8 There is no statutory test for appeals against sentence: rather, CAA 1968 s11(3) allows the Court of Appeal to 'pass such sentence or make such order as they think appropriate' if the view is that the offender should be sentenced 'differently'. The only limits are that the court below must have had the power to impose the relevant sentence or order and the result must be that 'taking the case as a whole, the appellant is not more severely dealt with'. Similarly, if the Court of Appeal quashes a conviction and substitutes a conviction for a different offence, it may then impose a sentence for that offence but not one of greater severity: see section 3(2). Section 4(3) contains a similar provision if the Court of Appeal allows an appeal in relation to part of an indictment.[7]

21.9 A question that arises in this context is whether a hospital order is more severe than a prison sentence. Both involve detention, the hospital order being renewable (or if combined with a restriction order being indeterminate) and perhaps involving a longer period in detention. But the hospital order is not a punitive sentence and so it does not lend itself readily to questions of severity. In *R v Bennett*,[8] which involved a conviction for indecent assault, the Court of Appeal emphasised the remedial nature of the hospital order in holding that

5 Judicial review was available – see *R v Mohammed Latif* [2002] EWCA Crim 2115 and [2002] EWHC 1916 Admin, [2003] MHLR 305: the process was outside the court's jurisdiction relating to trial on indictment and so the prohibition on judicial review in Senior Courts Act 1981 s29 did not apply.

6 Nor was judicial review available as the verdict followed a trial on indictment: see *R v Snaresbrook Crown Court ex p Demaar* [2000] MHLR 239.

7 There is no such limitation if the court overturns a finding of not guilty by reason of insanity and imposes a conviction instead; it may then impose any sentence 'authorised by law': CAA 1968 s5(2).

8 [1968] 1 WLR 988, (1968) 52 CrAppR 514. This considered statutory language prior to the CAA 1968 that was to the same effect.

it was possible to impose such an order together with a restriction order in place of a sentence of three years' imprisonment. The prison sentence had been imposed because the medical evidence before the sentencing court was not sufficient to justify a hospital order, though Mr Bennett was subsequently transferred to hospital by the Secretary of State. Widgery LJ stated:

> In our judgment, a hospital order, which is a remedial order designed to treat and cure the appellant, cannot be regarded as more severe than a sentence of imprisonment, even though in certain events the hospital order may involve the detention of the appellant for a longer period of time.[9]

21.10 A significant number of questions still remain, however. For example, would the same approach apply in relation to a short sentence (say a sentence of less than six months, the initial length of a hospital order)?[10] Or would it be more severe to impose a hospital order in place of a suspended sentence with a treatment requirement? Or a community order with a treatment requirement? And would it make a difference if the treatment requirement was as an out-patient or an in-patient?

21.11 In a similar vein, there might be a question as to whether the replacement of a sentence of imprisonment with a hospital and limitation direction is impermissible, since that involves both an underlying prison sentence but detention in hospital for so long as the defendant meets the criteria for placement in hospital (which might be for the entirety of the sentence). Given that the hospital element is protective rather than punitive, and a prisoner can be transferred to hospital and held beyond the end-date of the prison sentence in any event, it may be argued that such a sentence is not more severe. In connection with this, see *R v Hendy*:[11] the main issue in this case was whether an old murder conviction should be quashed because of a misdirection as to the true impact of mental disorder and intoxication combined when the partial defence of diminished responsibility was raised.[12] The Court of Appeal having confirmed that the

9 [1968] 1 WLR 988 at page 991, (1968) 52 CrAppR 514 at 518.

10 As noted in chapter 18, it is possible for the responsible clinician (RC) or the hospital managers to release a patient from a hospital order within the first six months, though the patient has no right to apply to a tribunal in that period.

11 [2006] EWCA Crim 819, [2006] MHLR 244.

12 See the discussion of this in chapter 14: the conviction occurred before the House of Lords in *R v Dietschmann* [2003] UKHL 10, [2003] 1 AC 1209, [2003] MHLR 333 clarified the correct approach, and so the judge's direction had been incorrect.

misdirection meant that the conviction was unsafe, the questions arose as to whether there should be a retrial and what the proper sentence would be if it substituted a manslaughter conviction. In relation to the latter, the prosecution conceded that a life sentence with a hospital and limitation direction would breach the prohibition on increasing the severity of the sentence arising under CAA 1968 ss3 and 4.[13] The court also noted that such a sentence was probably not available on a retrial and that it would be an abuse of the process of the Court of Appeal to direct a retrial solely to allow such a sentence to be imposed,[14] and so it dealt with the case by putting in place hospital and restriction orders.

21.12 While there is no reasoned argument in the case, it is adequate authority for the proposition that a combination of a punitive sentence with the protective element of an order under MHA 1983 s45A is a more severe sentence than the punitive sentence alone.

Principles applicable to the Court of Appeal's intervention

21.13 As noted, CAA 1968 s11 allows the Court of Appeal to sentence a defendant differently and not more severely. This appears to give risk to a general discretion tempered only by the fact that the sentence cannot be increased. There are conflicting principles in play in the Court of Appeal's review. One is the problem of a situation in which the same facts lead to hugely different sentences because of the contrasting views of individual judges: this undermines the requirement of legality, namely the need for outcomes that are predictable and not dependent on the assignment of a particular judge, which can be seen as akin to the flip of a coin. To deal with this, the Court of Appeal should be keen to intervene to reduce disparities: this is consistent with the approach being developed in recent years of more guidelines for sentencing judges, all of which are designed to produce greater consistency.

21.14 On the other hand, there is a general approach to appeals that the decision of a lower court judge will be assessed on the basis of whether it was open to the judge; this is somewhat similar to the approach taken in judicial review proceedings, and reflects the fact that the decision as to sentencing is given to the judge and the Court of Appeal has a corrective function rather than an original sentencing one.

21.15 The Court of Appeal seems to favour the latter approach, even though CAA 1968 s11(3) does not contain any such limitation on the

13 [2006] EWCA Crim 819, [2006] MHLR 244 para 53.

14 [2006] EWCA Crim 819, [2006] MHLR 244 para 52.

powers of the Court of Appeal but suggests that there is a general power to take a different view, and even though an obvious purpose of providing for a Court of Appeal review is to provide for better consistency as between judges. The usual approach adopted by the court is whether a sentence was wrong in principle or manifestly excessive: this is consistent with allowing a significant amount of discretion to individual judges. The court will also intervene if a sentence is unlawful because it is outside the relevant statutory powers or if there has been a breach of an expectation created that a lesser sentence would be imposed.

21.16 In addition, as has been noted in chapter 17, the court has been willing to intervene on the basis of fresh evidence of the impact of mental disorder and the suitability of a defendant for a custodial sentence: this shows that section 11(3) can be used to correct a situation when the sentencing judge was effectively misled by the gaps in the evidence of mental disorder.

Prosecution appeals

21.17 An acquittal may lead to the referral of any point of law involved to the Court of Appeal under section 36 of the Criminal Justice Act (CJA) 1972: this is not properly an appeal in that the verdict of the trial court remains. The need for an acquittal means that it cannot apply in relation to a special verdict of not guilty by reason of insanity, which is not an acquittal; it could apply to a decision made within the unfitness to stand trial process if a verdict of not guilty results, and so would not cover a finding that the defendant committed the actus reus.

21.18 An appeal against a terminating ruling relating to an offence included in the indictment arises under CJA 2003 s58, though only if the prosecution agree that the defendant should be acquitted if the appeal is not successful. This means it will only be used in relation to a decision that effectively brings a prosecution to an end: this also means that it is unlikely to be used by the prosecution in relation to matters such as rulings on whether a defendant can properly argue that he or she is under a disability, seek the special verdict of not guilty by reason of insanity or a partial defence such as diminished responsibility.

21.19 In relation to sentences, the prosecution power is that under section 36 of the CJA 1988 to refer an 'unduly lenient' sentence to the Court of Appeal; what amounts to a sentence is as under section 50 of the CAA 1968, save that an interim hospital order is excluded (see

CJA 1988 s35(6)). Accordingly, this could encompass the making of a hospital order instead of the use of a custodial sentence. It might also be argued that the failure to impose a restriction order together with a hospital order is covered: however, since the purpose of a restriction order is protective, it may be difficult to see how it features within the concept of being 'unduly lenient' and its connotations of not being adequately punitive.

Interlocutory appeals

21.20 Interlocutory appeals also arise, at the behest of either prosecution or defence, in relation to rulings made in complex, lengthy or serious cases. This was originally limited to serious fraud cases: see section 7 and following of the CJA 1987. The more general use of such a power is a feature of section 29 and following of the Criminal Procedure and Investigations Act (CPIA) 1996. Questions of law that involve matters relevant to mental disorder may arise in this context: as an example, see the discussion of *R v B, W, S, H and W*[15] and *R v MB*[16] in chapter 9. This related to the question of whether there should be a single trial of defendants who were fit to stand trial and two who were unfit to stand trial, including the main defendant, in relation to sexual abuse allegations. The judge's ruling that the main defendant should be tried separately was appealed to the Court of Appeal under CPIA 1996 s35 in the first case; the findings against the main defendant after the Court of Appeal overturned this ruling were set aside by the court in the second case.

Appeals from the magistrates' court

21.21 Appeals from the magistrates' court go the Crown Court. Section 108 of the Magistrates' Courts Act 1980 provides a general right to appeal conviction or sentence: this will include the making of a hospital order, but not the situation in which the magistrates have made an order under section 37(3) of the Mental Health Act (MHA) 1983 without convicting a defendant. However, MHA 1983 s45 provides that the same right of appeal arises as if a conviction had been entered.

21.22 Both prosecution and defence may also appeal decisions of magistrates by way of the case stated appeal to the High Court: this arises under Magistrates' Courts Act 1980 s111 and allows the High Court

15 [2008] EWCA Crim 1997, [2008] MHLR 320.
16 [2010] EWCA Crim 1684, [2011] MHLR 163.

to rule on whether the magistrates' court was correct in any questions of law that arose before it. This was the method used to allow the question of the correct approach to fitness to stand trial in the youth court in *Crown Prosecution Service v P*:[17] see the discussion in chapter 10. In addition, there is the right to seek judicial review, which is often used interchangeably (and may be a more obvious remedy if the magistrates decline to state a case): this was used in *R (P) v Barking Magistrates' Court*,[18] which raised similar issues. Part 64 of the Criminal Procedure Rules 2011[19] sets out the procedure to be followed.

21.23 The Crown Court's jurisdiction on appeal from the magistrates' court is also subject to a further case stated appeal and also judicial review: see sections 28 and 29 of the Senior Courts Act 1981.

Correcting a sentence

21.24 An additional feature to be noted is that sentences can be amended by the sentencing court. This power arises in the magistrates' court under Magistrates' Courts Act 1980 s142 (which has no time limit), and in relation to the Crown Court it arises under section 155 of the Powers of Criminal Courts (Sentencing) Act (PCC(S)A) 2000 (and can be exercised for 56 days). Under the predecessor to PCC(S)A 2000 s155, section 11 of the Courts Act 1971, it was determined that this could be used to change a short sentence of imprisonment to a hospital order with a restriction order in light of the development of clear signs of mental illness in prison: see *R v Sodhi*.[20]

Appeals out of time

Time limits for appeals

21.25 Under rule 63(2) of the Criminal Procedure Rules 2011, there are 21 days for service of the notice of appeal in relation to an appeal to the Crown Court from the magistrates; but it may be reduced or extended by the Crown Court under rule 63(9). The time limit for

17 [2007] EWHC 946 (Admin), [2007] MHLR 262.

18 [2002] EWHC 734 (Admin), [2002] MHLR 304. It has also been adopted as a possible solution if a defendant in a summary trial might also be acquitted on the ground of insanity at the time of the trial: see *R (Singh) v Stratford Magistrates' Court* [2007] EWHC 1582 (Admin), [2007] MHLR 274.

19 SI 2011 No 1709.

20 (1978) 66 CrAppR 260.

appealing to the Court of Appeal are contained in the CAA 1968, section 18 of which sets a 28-day limit for notice of an application for leave to appeal, but allows the court to extend or curtail the time; rules 65(3) and (4) of the Criminal Procedure Rules 2011 make further provision for this. If leave to appeal is refused, there is a 14-day time limit for renewing the application: rule 65(5).

21.26 These relatively short time limits reflect the importance of finality in criminal proceedings. However, the inclusion of provisions allowing for time limits to be extended makes the point that there may be good reasons for a failure to meet a time limit or that the value of finality is of lesser weight than the importance of correcting a finding made. The Court of Appeal is able to grant leave to appeal significantly out of time. For example, in *R v Erskine; R v Williams*,[21] discussed below, extensions of time of 20 and eight years were granted.

21.27 A further possibility is that there will be an appeal that is unsuccessful but then additional evidence comes to light that suggests a need for the matter to be reconsidered. The provisions relevant to this scenario are contained in the CAA 1995, which established the Criminal Cases Review Commission.[22] It has the power to refer summary convictions and sentences to the Crown Court (see CAA 1995 s11), and to refer to the Court of Appeal convictions and sentences on indictment and also verdicts of not guilty by reason of insanity and findings of unfitness to stand trial but to have committed the actus reus (see section 9). The effect of the reference is as if an appeal has been lodged.

Fresh evidence on appeals

Statutory provision

21.28 In the Crown Court, an appeal is a hearing de novo and so relies on the evidence that is called by the parties then. If the appeal is in the Court of Appeal, it operates as a review court: but it has the facility to consider evidence that was not adduced in the trial court. The relevant statutory provision is CAA 1968 s23, which provides that:

> (1) For the purposes of an appeal, or an application for leave to appeal, under this Part of this Act the Court of Appeal may, if they think it necessary or expedient in the interests of justice –
>
> ...

21 [2009] EWCA Crim 1425, [2009] MHLR 215, [2009] 2 CrAppR 29.

22 This replaced a more limited power of the Home Secretary to refer cases back to the court.

(c) receive any evidence which was not adduced in the proceedings from which the appeal lies.

(2) The Court of Appeal shall, in considering whether to receive any evidence, have regard in particular to –

(a) whether the evidence appears to the court to be capable of belief;

(b) whether it appeals to the court that the evidence may afford any ground for allowing the appeal;

(c) whether the evidence would have been admissible in the proceedings from which the appeal lies on an issue which is subject to the appeal;

(d) whether there is a reasonable explanation for the failure to adduce the evidence in those proceedings.

21.29 The test on the merits, therefore, is the 'interests of justice', which is clearly a wide discretion; and the features set out in subsection (2) are examples of features that may be relevant.

Guidance on CAA 1968 s23

21.30 In *R v Erskine; R v Williams*,[23] the Court of Appeal sought to give guidance on the approach to the use of CAA 1968 s23 in the context of two out of time appeals against murder convictions; both defendants sought to raise arguments that diminished responsibility manslaughter was the correct conviction.[24] Mr Erskine had killed seven elderly people and tried to kill another, but he denied the offending and so the jury did not consider the potential of a diminished responsibility verdict, even though there was clear evidence of mental disorder. He was convicted of murder, sentenced to life imprisonment, soon transferred to hospital, and some time later admitted his offending: it seemed that his earlier position had been based on a delusional belief that conviction of murder would lead to execution. The up-to-date medical evidence supported the view that his responsibility for the killings had been diminished. Mr Williams had admitted a murder and was sentenced to life imprisonment: he

23 [2009] EWCA Crim 1425, [2009] MHLR 215, [2009] 2 CrAppR 29. The guidance it gave was in similar terms to that given the previous year in *R v Diamond* [2008] EWCA Crim 923, [2008] MHLR 124, at paras 21 and following, which in turn referenced the guidance given in *R v Neaven* [2006] EWCA Crim 955: to be true to its principles, the Court in *Erskine and Williams* should perhaps simply have indicated that these previous cases set out the principles to be followed.

24 [2009] EWCA Crim 1425, [2009] MHLR 215, [2009] 2 CrAppR 29 at paras 41 and following, the court analysed various previous cases: it did so in the context of its concern that cases were fact-specific and so should be cited only if they established rather than reproduced a principle.

had declined to co-operate with pre-trial investigations to confirm whether a head injury he had suffered had caused an organic personality disorder, though subsequently he had been transferred to hospital and further investigations confirmed the full extent of his brain injury and a diagnosis of bipolar disorder was also made. There was a difference of view among the medical experts as to whether there had been diminished responsibility at the time of the offending.

The need to raise contradictory defences and the difficulty of tactical decisions

21.31 In terms of the approach to adopt, the Court of Appeal noted that the starting point was that all relevant issues should be in front of the trial court, including contradictory defences of non-involvement and involvement with diminished responsibility;[25] denial of involvement to see whether it was successful, but then raising an alternative defence on appeal, was not permitted, and so a good reason for such a scenario being presented to the Court of Appeal had to be identified. This would mean, for example, that a deliberate decision not to raise a line of defence now relied on might fall flat.

21.32 An example of this scenario is provided by *R v Diamond*:[26] the appellant had refused to co-operate with medical reports to support a diminished responsibility plea and gave clear instructions to deny involvement in the offence, but was convicted of murder. He also declined to allow diminished responsibility to be raised on appeal. Some years later, he accepted the true picture; supporting medical evidence of diminished responsibility was put forward and a reference made by the Criminal Cases Review Commission. But the Court of Appeal would not hear the evidence on the basis that there was a tactical decision taken, albeit by someone who was not 'normal' in the light of mental disorder: it was suggested that intervention would be proper if the decision was materially affected by the mental condition, but in the absence of such evidence there would be no reasonable excuse for evidence having not been adduced at trial.

21.33 The evidence in the case was that Mr Diamond was known to have a psychopathic personality disorder at the time of the trial; paranoid schizophrenia was subsequently diagnosed, though there were disputes about its presence or role at the time of the offending. What is missing in the discussion by the Court in *Diamond* is an analysis of the extent to which the clearly established personality disorder might

25 [2009] EWCA Crim 1425, [2009] MHLR 215, [2009] 2 CrAppR 29 para 82.
26 [2008] EWCA Crim 923, [2008] MHLR 124.

have caused him to adopt an unrealistic approach to the tactical decisions or at least have contributed to that decision so as to mean that what was classified as a tactical choice was in reality one conditioned by the mental disorder from which he suffered.

21.34 As was noted in *R v Criminal Cases Review Commission ex p Pearson*:[27] 'The overriding discretion conferred on the Court enables it to ensure that, in the last resort, defendants are sentenced for the crimes they have committed and not for psychological failings to which they may be subject'. Accordingly, a decision not to allow a certain line of defence that was influenced by mental disorder might well provide a ground for allowing it to be raised on appeal. This does not seem to have featured in *Diamond*, since the court did not even get to the question of considering the further evidence: it may be that there were significant differences of view between the experts such that the court would have concluded that on the merits it did not support a finding that the conviction was unsafe: that would be preferable to not even considering the question.

21.35 An example of the Court of Appeal going further is *R v Moyle*.[28] It was considering a murder conviction. First, it was unable to accept evidence available on the appeal, which was four years after the trial, that the appellant had been unfit to stand trial: the problem was the contemporaneous evidence supporting fitness to stand trial arising from the fact that the trial team and judge had felt able to proceed. But it commented that there was strong evidence supporting both diminished responsibility for the killing and also that the decision not to advance the partial defence was affected by the disorder and so compromised the instructions given, which in turn meant that it was in the interests of justice to allow it to be advanced on appeal. The fresh evidence was admitted, the murder conviction was quashed and a conviction for manslaughter was substituted, and the appropriate sentence was found to be a hospital order combined with a restriction order.

The difficulty of raising fitness to stand trial

21.36 Echoing the first part of *Moyle*, the court in *Erskine* also warned against raising arguments as to fitness to stand trial in out of time appeals on the basis that the issue was one that contemporaneous assessments by the trial advocates (together with any judicial

27 [2000] 1 CrAppR 141 at p164.
28 [2008] EWCA Crim 3059, [2009] MHLR 91.

oversight) were difficult to overturn.[29] It is suggested that this should not be taken too far: lawyers and judges are not experts on assessing whether someone has a mental disorder that means that fitness to stand trial is compromised; if evidence of that was missed but it later becomes apparent that it was missed, the Court of Appeal has the jurisdiction to remedy this defect.

21.37 This has happened. For example, in *R v Johnson*,[30] a 1976 conviction for murder was set aside in 2002 on the basis that an assessment at the time of the trial that Mr Johnson was not mentally ill was shown to be wrong. However, the fresh expert evidence did rely in part on contemporaneous records and the fact that he had been diagnosed as having paranoid schizophrenia a relatively short time after the trial. This, however, should be seen more as a matter going to the credibility of the evidence rather than as a separate precondition to the intervention of the court.

The analysis required

21.38 Clearly, it is important in this context to ensure that any supportive contemporary evidence is brought to the attention of the court. Indeed, the need for supportive contemporary evidence would also be important in relation to whether a substantive defence would be successful, given the difficulty of assessing this, often long after the trial.[31] The court in *Erskine and Williams* suggested that the following approach should be adopted:

> 92. The court will normally expect the parties to provide a detailed analysis of the facts to assist it in the application of the statutory test, including an analysis of the following:
>
> (i) The psychiatric and/or psychological evidence or other information in relation to the appellant's mental state which was available at the time of trial.

29 [2009] EWCA Crim 1425, [2009] MHLR 215, [2009] 2 CrAppR 29 paras 84 and following.

30 [2002] EWCA Crim 1900, [2002] MHLR 308.

31 See, for example, *R v Shulman* [2010] EWCA Crim 1034, [2010] MHLR 172. This defendant had not co-operated with the preparation of reports for the trial, and the relevant medical evidence was raised on appeal. The Court of Appeal declined to enter a verdict of not guilty by reason of insanity, but did substitute findings of unfitness to stand trial but to have committed the acts because: i) there was no contemporaneous evidence to support insanity at the time of the offence, but there was support for unfitness to stand trial; and ii) if the evidence supported both insanity and unfitness, the latter would be raised first and if successfully so the court would not investigate the former.

(ii) The evidence which has become available since the trial, and an explanation why it was not available at trial.

(iii) The circumstances in which the appellant sought to raise on the appeal (a) the evidence available at the time of the trial and (b) evidence that has become available since the trial.

(iv) The reason why such evidence or information as was available at the time of the trial was not adduced or relied on at trial. This will ordinarily include details of the advice given, the reasons for the appellant's decision at trial and ... any relevant evidence of the mental condition in the period leading up to and at the time of the trial and its impact on his decision making capacity.

(v) The impact of the fresh evidence on the issues argued at trial and whether and the extent to which it involves a re-arguing of issues considered at trial.

(vi) The extent to which the opinions of the experts are agreed and where they are not.

21.39 Reference should also be made to rule 68(7) of the Criminal Procedure Rules 2011, which sets out the rules as to the modification of the other parts of the Rules relating to the reception of evidence.

21.40 On the facts, Mr Erskine had the benefit of contemporaneous evidence supporting diminished responsibility and it was clear that his instructions had been flawed because of his mental disorder (albeit that he had been fit to stand trial). The further evidence was admitted and his convictions for murder were quashed, being replaced by convictions of manslaughter on the grounds of diminished responsibility. (The attempted murder conviction remained). This allowed the Court of Appeal to consider a hospital order disposal, which it was persuaded was the most suitable disposal, together with a restriction order. But Mr Williams was assessed as having made a clear choice to admit murder and the fresh evidence did not demonstrate that the decision was impaired: his appeal was therefore dismissed. A contrasting example is *R v Murray*,[32] which involved a January 2004 guilty plea to murder, even though there was evidence of diminished responsibility and that would have been accepted by the prosecution, leading to a manslaughter conviction: in July 2008, the Court of Appeal accepted the updated evidence that the decision to plead guilty was affected by mental abnormality that meant she had been unfit to stand trial.[33]

32 [2008] EWCA Crim 1792, [2008] MHLR 191.

33 See also *R v Grant* [2008] EWCA Crim 1870, [2008] MHLR 203, which relied on medical evidence obtained shortly after a trial. In *R v Walton (aka Wright)* [2010] EWCA Crim 2255, [2010] MHLR 335, the defendant was serving a custodial sentence for various offences but was then found not fit to stand trial in relation to another matter; the evidence meant that he would have been

Citation of authority and hearing evidence on commission

21.41 Two final points to note about the guidance in *Erskine* are, first, that the Court of Appeal took the opportunity to suggest that most previous appellate decisions turned on their facts and so should not be cited: only those that establish principles are important.[34] Second, the court also provided a useful reminder that when fresh evidence is to be adduced, CAA 1968 s23(4) allows it to be called before one member of the court rather than the full court, and this may be a convenient approach to adopt, depending on a range of factors, such as the relevance of credibility, the nature, length and complexity of the evidence, the scope of the dispute, its importance in the appeal, and the availability of the experts.[35] It was also noted that the regulation of expert evidence in Part 33 of the Criminal Procedure Rules 2011 would apply, and so the court should be invited to issue appropriate case management directions.

Personality disorders and young offenders

21.42 One final point in this context is that mental disorder in the form of a personality disorder is something that may be particularly difficult to diagnose in relation to young offenders. This was part of the holding in *R v Hendy*,[36] which has already been mentioned above. In addition to finding that the verdict of murder rather than diminished responsibility manslaughter was unsafe because of a misdirection relating to the vexed question of intoxication and mental disorder and their combined effect on responsibility, the Court of Appeal found that the verdict was unsafe because the updated medical evidence was that Mr Hendy had had a personality disorder at the time of the offence. He was 16 at the time of the fatal assault, which was in 1992: when he was transferred to hospital in 1993, it was on the basis that he had

similarly affected at the time of the other offences, and so findings that he was unfit but committed the acts were substituted. In *R v Shulman* [2010] EWCA Crim 1034, [2010] MHLR 172, there had been concerns about Mr Shulman's fitness to stand trial but he had not co-operated with the preparation of reports, denying that he was ill: after he was convicted and sentenced to imprisonment, his mental health difficulties became apparent and the evidence prepared indicated that he had been unfit to stand trial. The Court of Appeal quashed the convictions and substituted findings that he had committed the acts.

34 [2009] EWCA Crim 1425, [2009] MHLR 215, [2009] 2 CrAppR 29 paras 63 and following.

35 [2009] EWCA Crim 1425, [2009] MHLR 215, [2009] 2 CrAppR 29 paras 6 and following.

36 [2006] EWCA Crim 819, [2006] MHLR 244.

a psychopathic personality disorder. The Court of Appeal allowed the introduction of evidence that Mr Hendy had been so disordered at the time of the offence and commented at paragraph 48 of its judgment that:

> ... We were impressed by the evidence given orally by Professor Taylor relating to the difficulty of diagnosing a personality disorder in a young man under the age of 18. We note that the respondent neither called nor sought to place before this court any written evidence putting in issue the evidence given by Professor Taylor. We are acutely conscious of the fact that Professor Taylor's evidence is based on a retrospective assessment of the appellant. However, ... the retrospective evidence is given by a doctor who treated the appellant for a number of years post-trial. In the circumstances, it seems to us that it is in the interests of justice that we should receive it.[37]

Fresh evidence and the safety of convictions

21.43 If fresh evidence is accepted, the test as to whether it renders the conviction unsafe – the key question – involves the application of the approach established by the House of Lords in *R v Pendleton*.[38] Lord Bingham noted at paragraphs 18 and 19 that the appellate court had to bear in mind that juries were the decision-makers but that the jury did not give reasons for decisions: this meant that the court had to evaluate whether the fresh evidence might reasonably have affected the decision of the jury. If so, it would effectively follow that the conviction was unsafe.

21.44 It is to be noted that a conviction may also be unsafe if there has been a guilty plea: see *Murray*, mentioned above.

Updated evidence and sentencing

21.45 It seems clearly established that updated evidence that suggests the sentencing judge would have imposed a hospital disposal will allow the Court of Appeal to do just that, even though the judge's sentence

37 The court specifically distinguished *R v Andrews* [2003] EWCA Crim 2750, in which it had been noted that retrospective medical evidence was to be viewed with scepticism. There was also evidence in Mr Hendy's case by Professor Taylor to the effect that there was a depressive mental illness as well: it is not clear from the reasoning of the court whether this was also accepted, since the only comment in the relevant passage at paragraph 48 relates to the personality disorder issue.

38 [2001] UKHL 66, [2002] 1 WLR 72. See also its application by the Privy Council in *Dial and another v Trinidad and Tobago* [2005] 1 WLR 1660.

was proper in the light of the information then available to him or her (and so not wrong in principle or manifestly excessive). This is what happened in *R v De Silva*:[39] the appellant had been sentenced to life imprisonment for arson, and the information before the trial judge was to the effect that he was mentally ill but that this had not been the cause of his offending; none of the doctors recommended a hospital order. Almost three years later, he was admitted to hospital and a reassessment of his illness led to the conclusion that it was linked to the offending, at least in the sense that it disinhibited him. The Court of Appeal noted that the situation in front of it was one in which the judge had not had all the relevant information (obviously because the medical evidence had been to a different effect at that time). As such, it felt able to distinguish the case of *R v Castro*[40] and to put a hospital order and restriction order in place. The situation in *Castro* was that a man sentenced to five years' imprisonment for drug importation was transferred to hospital after a serious incident of self-harm;[41] an appeal out of time was commenced but dismissed for two reasons. The first was the point already made in chapter 18 that it might be appropriate to deal with some offences such as drug importation by putting public protection to the fore and so favouring a custodial sentence. The second was that there was no proper evidence that the mental disorder had any role in the offending, and certainly that there had been no evidence to that effect before the sentencing judge. Lord Lane CJ stated:

> This Court will very seldom, in cases of this sort, where mental illness is concerned, interfere with a sentence of imprisonment which was properly imposed in the light of the evidence which was available to the sentencing judge.[42]

21.46 It seems that what is meant by 'cases of this sort' are ones in which mental disorder appears after sentence and is not linked to the offending, as the court then noted the powers of transfer under MHA 1983 s47 to deal with a situation in which 'mental illness supervenes after the imprisonment has started'[43] before adding that:

39 (1994) 15 CrAppR(S) 296.

40 (1985) 81 CrAppR 212, (1985) 7 CrAppR(S) 68.

41 He was returned to prison because of a shortage of beds in the relevant hospital; it was noted that this did not affect the fact that he still needed to be in hospital.

42 (1985) 81 CrAppR 212 at 215, (1985) 7 CrAppR(S) 68 at 71.

43 This leaves open the question of what the response should be if the mental disorder develops between conviction and sentence: see the discussion in chapter 18 as to the relevance of mental disorder at the time of sentence even if not linked to the offending.

> Where evidence becomes available after the sentence to show that the mental illness was present in the defendant before the offence was actually committed, then it may be correct and desirable for this Court to intervene ...

21.47 This is what was done in *De Silva*. A more recent example is *R v David Hempston*:[44] in this case, life sentences were imposed for rape and related offences in 1978, the sentencing judge not having had evidence to support making a hospital order (though in part because he declined to adjourn to obtain further evidence). The Court of Appeal upheld the sentence, but the matter was returned to the court almost three decades later on a reference by the Criminal Cases Review Commission. The current medical evidence was to the effect that there was probably a mental illness at the time of the offending. The Court of Appeal considering the reference agreed to impose a hospital order with a restriction order,[45] commenting that:

> ... the real question is whether, on the psychiatric evidence now available and in the light of what has happened with the appellant since 1978, the court in 1978 would and should have made a Hospital Order with a Restriction Order. In the light of the new evidence, it is agreed that that is a question for this Court to consider on the totality of the evidence and that we are not concerned with the now academic question of whether the judge, 28 years ago, was manifestly wrong on material that he had.[46]

21.48 This suggests that the Court of Appeal adopt some sort of hybrid approach to cases involving mental disorder that by the time of the appeal makes a hospital disposal correct. There has to be look back to what the sentencing judge did, but not an assessment of whether his or her decision was correct on the normal approach of being manifestly excessive or wrong in principle: rather, the Court of Appeal makes a fresh decision on the basis of the current evidence.[47] Naturally, this entails that the criteria for a hospital order are met at the time the Court of Appeal acts.

21.49 However, there have also been suggestions that the Court of Appeal may properly intervene when the evidence is of a mental disorder that has developed subsequently to the sentencing decision.

44 [2006] EWCA Crim 2869, [2011] MHLR 99.

45 See chapter 18 at para 18.199 for a comment on the lack of clarity of the reasoning of the Court of Appeal on the question of why the hospital disposal was the most suitable on the evidence.

46 [2006] EWCA Crim 2869, [2011] MHLR 99 para 13.

47 For another example, see *R v O* [2011] EWCA Crim 376, [2011] MHLR 106.

This is a potential interpretation of comments in *R v Wang*.[48] The defendant was sentenced to life imprisonment on the basis of the danger she posed; she was mentally ill, but it was assessed as being of a low grade. Evidence available to the Court of Appeal, which heard the matter more than two years after sentence, was to the effect that there was probably a much more serious mental disorder at the time of the incident and sentence. By that time, Ms Wang had been transferred to hospital under MHA 1983 s47, to which a restriction direction had been added. The Court of Appeal imposed a hospital order with a restriction order, but not on the basis that the judge would have done so if the full picture had been presented. Indeed, the court made no finding as to the impact of the disorder on the offending. Giving the judgment of the court, Hodge J noted the powers of the Court of Appeal were prescribed by section 11 of the CAA 1968, which meant that it could do what the Crown Court could do but not act more severely. He added at paragraph 18 that on the facts: 'It is clear to us that the appellant's mental health has deteriorated significantly since trial. The judge, rightly in our view, passed a life sentence'. However, the court felt that it was right to sentence Ms Wang 'differently', that being the test in the CAA 1968, because of the picture now presented.

21.50 While there is no engagement with any of the authorities, it is suggested that the Court of Appeal in *Wang* has done the right thing and gone back to the statutory basis for sentence appeals and asked itself the correct question: this is a step on from the position in *De Silva* and *Hempston*, which engaged with the question of whether the trial judge would have acted differently had the true picture been known. Rather, the Court of Appeal is concerned with what is the correct sentence on the basis of the evidence in front of it, and if that is a different sentence from that imposed, it can intervene.

21.51 One final point to note in this context is that the Court of Appeal is not deprived of jurisdiction to consider an appeal if the matter has been before it already on a reference on the basis of undue leniency (as described above), even though the respondent can counter-appeal and seek a reduction in sentence in that situation. Rather, the fact that the matter has been before the court in that situation is a matter relevant to the question of whether to allow any extension of time. This was determined in *R v James Francis Hughes (jurisdiction)*,[49] in which the Court of Appeal considered its jurisdiction to hear an

48 [2005] EWCA Crim 3238, [2006] MHLR 109.

49 [2009] EWCA Crim 841, [2010] MHLR 183.

appeal by someone whose determinate sentence for aggravated arson had been increased to life imprisonment on a reference determined in 2003;[50] the basis for the appeal was that Mr Hughes had been transferred to hospital in 2005 and diagnosed as having paranoid schizophrenia and a personality disorder and the evidence was that he had been so disordered at the time of the offences. A differently-constituted Court of Appeal subsequently quashed the life sentence and found that a hospital order with a restriction order was a more suitable disposal.[51]

Evidence of progress and restriction orders

21.52 One other aspect of fresh evidence to note is that of progress made by a defendant in hospital and the assistance that gives in the determination of whether a restriction order should have been made. Since a restriction order is a matter of risk assessment, which is simply an effort to predict future human behaviour, the experience of what happens in practice is invariably more reliable. So, for example, if a restriction order is based on the argument that the patient is not likely to gain insight and so is less likely to improve because he or she will not take medication voluntarily, but the patient then demonstrates significant progress in understanding his or her illness, the question might arise as to whether the restriction order is necessary. The further question is whether that progress is a basis for the Court of Appeal to intervene: in other words, is hindsight a reason to overturn the sentence imposed.

21.53 One of the things that is apparent from the case-law discussed in chapter 18 as to the relationship between the views of the doctors as to the need for a restriction order and the decision of the judge is that the Court of Appeal has often been able to intervene to overturn a restriction order that the doctors had not supported when progress by the patient has indicated that the doctor was correct about the risks. So, in *R v Royse*,[52] the Court of Appeal, having held that a judge could impose a restriction order against the views of the doctors, quashed the restriction order made on the basis that it was not justified in the light of further medical evidence as to the progress being made by Ms Royse (who had been convicted of manslaughter on the grounds of diminished responsibility). This was also the approach adopted

50 [2003] EWCA Crim 683.

51 [2010] EWCA Crim 1026, [2010] MHLR 188.

52 (1981) 3 CrAppR(S) 58.

by the Court of Appeal in the leading case of *R v Birch*,[53] which also involved a manslaughter conviction.

21.54 There have been various other examples of this approach:

i) In *R v Reynolds*[54] the Court of Appeal found that the judge had erred in his approach to the evidence called before him, but supplemented that by noting that up-to-date evidence demonstrated that concerns expressed by the sentencing judge had been shown to be less strong than the judge had considered. (The particular concern of the judge was Mr Reynold's approach to cannabis use: the evidence adduced before the Court of Appeal revealed positive progress was being made in encouraging abstinence and an understanding of the importance of avoiding cannabis.)[55]

ii) Another example is *R v Steward*,[56] in which the Court of Appeal quashed a restriction order: it was clearly not happy as to the criteria being made out on the basis of the evidence before the sentencing judge, but added that updated medical evidence made it clear that the restriction order was not necessary.

iii) In *R v Hurst*,[57] the Court of Appeal allowed further medical evidence against the use of a restriction order, but it is apparent that it would have quashed the order without this further material.[58]

21.55 The further material adduced before the Court of Appeal need not necessarily deal with progress made by the defendant in a hospital setting. So, in *R v Osker*,[59] the sentencing judge had relied on an earlier incident in the defendant's antecedents to justify the restriction

53 (1990) 90 CrAppR 78.

54 [2000] MHLR 188.

55 [2000] MHLR 188 paras 21–23. See also *R v Mahmood* [2002] MHLR 416, in which a doctor who had not favoured a restriction order at the sentencing stage gave a more detailed account of why it was not needed, and indeed was a hindrance to treatment, in a report to the Court of Appeal: it quashed the restriction order.

56 [2008] EWCA Crim 1255, [2008] MHLR 148.

57 [2007] EWCA Crim 3436, [2007] MHLR 43.

58 See [2007] EWCA Crim 3436, [2007] MHLR 43 para 33. For another example, see *R v Ristic* [2002] EWCA Crim 165, [2002] MHLR 129, in which the Court of Appeal concluded (though without setting out its reasoning as opposed to stating its conclusion) that a restriction order was probably not appropriate at the time of sentence and was not appropriate in the light of updated medical evidence. In *R v Acharya* [2005] EWCA Crim 772, [2005] MHLR 28 further medical evidence supporting the view of the psychiatrist that a restriction order was not needed was admitted and taken into account in the decision to quash a restriction order.

59 [2010] EWCA Crim 955, [2010] MHLR 115.

order. The psychiatrist who gave evidence to the sentencing judge was able to explain to the Court of Appeal that the incident had been known about by him and taken into account in his risk assessment.[60] Another psychiatrist provided to the Court of Appeal a more detailed account of this earlier incident and an explanation of why it did not merit a restriction order.[61]

21.56 Naturally, further medical evidence may support the making of a restriction order. For example, in *R v Golding*,[62] a restriction order had been imposed on the basis of the risk that an offender with mental health and drug abuse problems would continue to pay for his drug habit by further burglaries in which he might confront a householder: the RC, who supported the restriction order, gave evidence to the Court of Appeal that included reference to an altercation in which Mr Golding had been involved in the hospital and an instance of him abusing drugs when on leave. However, the Court of Appeal did not specifically refer to this evidence as supporting the dismissal of the appeal.[63]

21.57 This case-law clearly favours the admission of further medical evidence to assist the Court of Appeal to determine whether a person should be sentenced differently. However, there have been dicta to the effect that further medical evidence does not assist, since the question for the Court of Appeal is whether the sentence was wrong in law or principle in the light of the information available to the judge. So in *R v Griffith*,[64] the Court of Appeal dealt with a ground of challenge to a restriction order that further evidence showed it was not necessary by commenting that such a submission was for the Mental Health Review Tribunal.[65] This seems to posit an erroneous assumption that the tribunal can change a patient's status from restricted to non-restricted, which it cannot: under MHA 1983 s73, the tribunal may discharge and lift the restriction order (by an absolute discharge) or discharge and leave the restriction order in place (by a conditional discharge), but has no power to allow ongoing detention as a non-restricted patient by lifting the restriction order. Under

60 [2010] EWCA Crim 955, [2010] MHLR 115 para 12.

61 [2010] EWCA Crim 955, [2010] MHLR 115 paras 14 and 16.

62 [2006] EWCA Crim 1965, [2006] MHLR 272.

63 There have been other examples of this, namely further medical evidence being admitted but not commented on in dismissing an appeal against a restriction order: *R v Cox* [1999] MHLR 30, *R v Goode* [2002] EWCA Crim 1698, [2002] MHLR 337.

64 [2002] EWCA Crim 1838, [2002] MHLR 427.

65 [2002] EWCA Crim 1838, [2002] MHLR 427 para 17.

MHA 1983 s42, the Secretary of State may lift a restriction order and so change the basis of the detention of the patient. The only judicial method to change the patient's status is by way of an appeal to the Court of Appeal.

21.58 There is a further point of principle in favour of the approach adopted by the Court of Appeal in most cases. It is able to make interim hospital orders (since CAA 1968 s11(3) allows the Court of Appeal to make an order the Crown Court could make)[66] and is able to call for information under MHA 1983 s39.[67] So it is plainly within the jurisdiction of the Court of Appeal to hear further evidence. Even though it may be necessary also to meet the interests of justice test in CAA 1968 s23, the case-law suggests that difficulties have not yet arisen in practice in this regard.

Technical lifers

21.59 As has been described in chapter 20, there is a group of life sentence prisoners transferred to hospital under MHA 1983 s47 who are called 'technical lifers'. This reflects an acceptance that the proper disposal was a hospital order (with a restriction order) rather than the life sentence that was imposed. This could reflect the lack of a suitable bed at the time of sentencing, or that the medical reports before the court were inaccurate (or none were presented), or that the defendant to a murder charge declined to allow a diminished responsibility contention to be put forward.[68] Even though the status would only be granted after consultation with the Lord Chief Justice and the trial judge (if available), it was not a judicial decision, though it subverted a judicial decision. The main problem was the effect of the status: release from a life sentence is a matter for a judicial body, the Parole Board. However, a technical lifer's case was determined by a tribunal, which applied a similar risk-based test, albeit one that concentrated on mental health related risks only, but which could only recommend release because the status of the patient was formally that of a transferred prisoner: the relevant provision, MHA 1983 s74, involves the Secretary of State having the final decision. In *Benjamin and Wilson v UK*,[69] the European Court of Human Rights found that

66 See *R v Cooper* [2001] EWCA Crim 57, [2001] MHLR 2.

67 As was done in *R v Jones* [2000] MHLR 12 para 28.

68 See Prison Service Order 4700 para 15.47, available at www.justice.gov.uk/guidance/prison-probation-and-rehabilitation/psipso/psos.htm.

69 App No 28212/95, [2003] MHLR 124.

this breached article 5(4) of the European Convention on Human Rights (ECHR), which requires that a court be able to direct release.

21.60 In principle, it is clearly correct that sentences and release should be wholly judicialised in order to comply with ECHR articles 6 and 5(4): however, the effect of the challenges to the use of technical lifer status was that the many practical advantages of the system were likely to be lost. In particular, the patient could only be released if the Parole Board said so (not the tribunal that considered the case of those in hospital); moreover, the supervision on release would be the responsibility of the criminal justice agencies, and any recall would have to be to prison. This was indeed what happened as from April 2005, the government announcing in January 2005 citing *Benjamin and Wilson* in the Parliamentary Answer in which the policy change was announced.[70] As a result, if a life sentence prisoner should be released and supervised through the mental health system, any necessary amendment to a sentence will have to be made by the Court of Appeal. In *R v David William Beatty*,[71] the Court of Appeal confirmed that someone granted 'technical lifer' status would invariably be able to have his or her life sentence corrected to hospital and restriction orders by the Court of Appeal.

70 Baroness Scotland, *Hansard* HL Debates vol 668 col 39WS, 24 January 2005. A challenge to the change of policy was dismissed in *R (Donaldson and Barker) v Home Secretary* [2006] EWHC 1107 (Admin), [2006] MHLR 100.

71 [2006] EWCA Crim 2359, [2006] MHLR 333.

Index